The Companion Website for *International Business*
Students' side, featuring . . .

Practice Quiz – Detailed Results Page

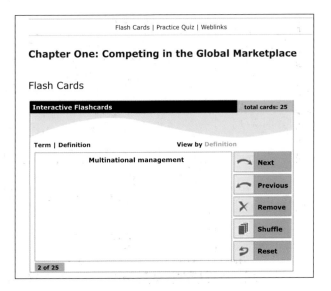

Flash Cards: Key Term

Flash Cards: Definition

INTERNATIONAL BUSINESS

STRATEGY AND THE MULTINATIONAL COMPANY

INTERNATIONAL BUSINESS

STRATEGY AND THE MULTINATIONAL COMPANY

JOHN B. CULLEN

Professor in the Department of Management,
Washington State University

AND

K. PRAVEEN PARBOTEEAH

Associate Professor in the College of Business,
University of Wisconsin, Whitewater

Publisher: John Szilagyi
Development Editors: Elizabeth Renner and Felisa Salvago-Keyes
Production Editor: Alf Symons
Marketing Manager: David Wilfinger
Text Design: Karl Hunt at Keystroke, Alf Symons and Alex Lazarou
Copy-editor: Liz Jones
Proofreader: Alison Elks and Sally Critchlow
Indexer: Jackie Butterley
Graphics: Integra and Chartwell
Cover Design: Christian Munoz
Composition: Karl Hunt at Keystroke
Companion Website Designer: Aptara

First published 2010
by Routledge
270 Madison Ave, New York, NY 10016

Simultaneously published in the UK
by Routledge
2 Park Square, Milton Park, Abingdon, Oxon OX14 4RN

Routledge is an imprint of the Taylor & Francis Group, an informa business

© 2010 Taylor & Francis

Typeset in Sabon by Keystroke, 28 High Street, Tettenhall, Wolverhampton
Printed and bound in India by Replika Press Pvt Ltd

Library of Congress Cataloging-in-Publication Data
Cullen, John B. (John Brooks), 1948-
    International business : strategy and the multinational company / John B. Cullen, K. Praveen Parboteeah.
        p. cm.
    1. International business enterprises—Management. I. Parboteeah, Praveen. II. Title.
    HD62.4.C847 2009
    658.4'012—dc22   2008049344

ISBN 10: 0–415–80057–9 (hbk)
ISBN 10: 0–203–87941–4 (ebk)

ISBN 13: 978–0–415–80057–0 (hbk)
ISBN 13: 978–0–203–87941–2 (ebk)

To
Jean and Jaye
and
Kyong, Alisha, and Davin

Brief Contents

Detailed Contents

Part One
Introduction to International Business

Part Two
The Global Context of Multinational Competitive Strategy

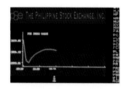

Part Three
The Institutional and Cultural Context of Multinational Competitive Strategy

Part Four
Multinational Operational and Functional Strategies

Part Five
Ethical Management in the International Context

Feature Topics

IB STRATEGIC INSIGHT

Examples from real companies that highlight how the content is used in strategy formulation or implementations

IB ETHICAL CHALLENGE

Examples from the popular press that show ethical issues relevant to the chapter content.

IB SMALL BUSINESS INSIGHT

A strategic insight example based on small businesses or entrepreneurs.

COUNTRY FOCUS

Examples that show you the unique characteristics of a region or country that are relevant to the chapter topics.

IB SUSTAINABILITY PRACTICES

Examples of what multinationals are doing to make their activities more environmentally responsible.

Chapter Introductory and Concluding Material

Preview IB Strategic Insight

Brief case to add realistic context to chapter material and serve as early referent to the strategic implications of the material.

Concluding Case Study with Case Discussion Points

Similar to Preview IB Strategic Insight.

International Business Skill Builder

Experiential exercise relevant to chapter content.

Key Concepts

Discussion Questions

Preface

The globalization of markets and companies, the impact of the possible recession, the emergence of the BRIC (Brazil, Russia, India, and China) economic bloc and the pressures for companies to become more environmentally sustainable define international business today. No companies are immune to such environmental forces. To cope adequately with this complex global environment, international managers need to be able to develop and implement successful strategies. *International Business: Strategy and the Multinational Company* is designed to provide students with the latest insights into the complexity of managing multinationals and domestic operations across borders. The text uses a strategic perspective as the dominant theme to explore international business and its implications for the multinational company (MNC). This text is the first international business text that uses this critical emphasis on strategic decision making as the cornerstone of its approach.

Pedagogical Approach

International Business: Strategy and the Multinational Company provides a thorough review and analysis of international business using several learning tools:

Strategy as the Theme   All chapters have been written using strategy as a unifying theme that is highlighted for the learner through the relevance of the material. This theme provides the students with the ability to see how the various functional areas of international business contribute to the overall strategy of the MNC.

Application-based   All chapters give the learner three opportunities to apply the knowledge gained from reading the chapter—an International Business Skill Builder, Chapter Internet Activity, and an end-of-chapter Case Study. These exercises provide deeper insights into the challenges faced by international business managers.

Current   The text contains the latest international business information and examples. It is the first to address the issue of sustainability practices in the international business area.

Economical   The book is priced worldwide at a price nearly half that of many other international business texts.

Key Features

Chapter Case Studies, Internet Activities, and International Business Skill Builders End-of-chapter projects include cases and activities, which give the learner the opportunity to apply text material to real-life international business problems.

Extensive Examples Throughout the text, many examples enhance the text material by showing actual international management situations. These examples are illustrated in six different formats:

- *Preview IB Strategic Insights* show you how real MNCs handle issues to be discussed in the chapter.
- *IB Strategic Insights* give information on the strategic implications for international businesses that relate to the current discussion in the text.
- *IB Small Business Insights* highlight chapter material of particular relevance to small businesses.
- *Country/Regional Foci* are discussions that show you the unique characteristics of the region or country that are relevant to the chapter topics.
- *IB Ethical Challenges* are examples of situations faced by multinational managers in dealing with issues being discussed in the chapter.
- *IB Sustainability Practices* show you what multinationals are doing to implement such sustainable practices.

Learning Aids The companion website (**www.cullenib.com**) also contains an extensive selection of Internet links to resources and information that are updated regularly.

Current Data All chapters have been updated to include the latest research, examples, and statistics in multinational management, creating the most accurate and current presentation possible.

Contents

The book is divided into five major sections. Each section contains chapters that provide information on essential topics of international business. The intent is to give you an overview of the complex and exciting world of international business.

The first section provides an introduction to the field of international business, including background on globalization and how MNCs compete strategically. It is important that you first understand the strategic choices open to MNCs. With that understanding, you will have a better appreciation of the information provided in later chapters that provides essential material for understanding international business.

Part Two of your text is intended to provide you with an understanding of the global context in which MNCs compete. Chapter 1, in Part One, touched on the issue of how growing international trade and investment combined with global economic integration is changing the competitive landscape for MNCs. Two additional chapters will show you how money moves across borders to make international transactions possible. One chapter overviews the basics of foreign exchange. There you learn what affects the varying values of currencies from different countries and how international managers manage cross-border money transactions. A second chapter discusses how MNCs, in today's global financial systems, get capital from bond and stock markets outside of their own countries.

Part Three looks inside the countries where MNCs do business. Here you will learn how MNCs adjust their strategies and operations to the local context. One chapter looks at how culture influences the conduct of international business. The other chapter focuses on social institutions such as the legal and political systems. It also considers the effects of religion on an MNC's operations and strategies when doing business in countries or areas of the world with particular religious institutions.

Part Four of your text brings you inside the MNC to look at the functional and operational strategies that support the broader multinational strategies that you learned about in Chapter 2. This is the largest part of the book because there are many issues that an MNC must consider in conducting its international businesses. One chapter shows how MNCs actually set up operations in different countries through techniques such as joint ventures or licensing. The second chapter in this part looks at how companies adjust their marketing and supply-chain management strategies to support operations in varied countries. The third and fourth chapters show how MNCs develop specialized accounting systems and manage their financial systems to conduct cross-border activities successfully.

Because running an MNC is an organizational challenge, Part Four contains a chapter devoted to organizational structures for international operations. Similarly, because of the complexities of dealing with managers and workers located anywhere in the world, a full chapter is also dedicated to international human resource management. Part Four concludes with a chapter on e-commerce for the MNC. This chapter focuses on the unique challenges of running an international operation via the Internet.

Part Five, the final part of your text, contains only one chapter, "Managing Ethical and Social Responsibility in an MNC." However, the challenges of managing ethical issues in varied cultural and institutional contexts cannot be overestimated. While you will not learn how to be ethical by reading this chapter, you will be introduced to the basics of ethical reasoning and some of the issues you need to consider when faced with ethically challenging decisions.

Support Materials

International Business offers a website for both students and instructors at **www.cullenib.com**. This site contains supplements to the text that give students and instructors many options for learning and teaching the text content.

For Instructors

Web support is available with the following features:

Instructor's Manual   Chapter-by-chapter outlines with teaching tips, web and in-class excercises, and video resources.

Test Bank   A full test bank for each chapter, with multiple choice and true/false questions, available as Word documents or in a format compatible with uploading to Blackboard or WebCT.

PowerPoint® Slide Presentations   Instructors can access more than 40 slides per chapter illustrating the main points of each text.

Weblinks   Useful links are provided as instructional resources, including all the links in the Instructor's Manual.

For Students

Web support is available with the following features:

Practice Quizes   Self-tests for each chapter provide students instant feedback on their answers.

Flashcards   Interactive flashcards allow students to test their knowledge of the book's key concepts.

Weblinks   All the book's informational links are provided to give students easy access to online resources.

Acknowledgments

Numerous individuals helped make this book possible. Most of all, we must thank our families for giving us the time and quiet to accomplish this task:

- Jean Johnson, Professor of Marketing at Washington State University, John's wife, read and commented on all chapters. Her suggestions improved both the content and the writing, and resulted in a better product. She also authored Chapter 10 on international marketing.
- Kyong Pyun, Praveen's wife, was very helpful during this project. She allowed uninterrupted blocks of time to finish the project. She also worked on the instructor's manual, completing the teaching outline, presentations and other support material. Alisha, Praveen's daughter, was also very patient as she endured Daddy's focus on the project. Davin, Praveen's three-year-old son, was also very helpful as he checked progress very regularly.

This text would not be possible without the support of a professional editorial team. In particular, our thanks go to Routledge editor John Szilagyi, who encouraged us to write a text on international business and weathered with us the challenges of this formidable task. Developmental editor Elizabeth Renner worked us on track for a very tight writing schedule. Our thanks also go to several other professionals who contributed to this project, including Charles A. Rarick, who contributed to the cases in the book.

We also appreciate the effors of individuals involved in marketing and production.

The authors would like to thank the many reviewers from a wide array of colleges and universities who provided valuable feedback in crafting the manuscript.

John B. Cullen
K. Praveen Parboteeah

About the Authors

John B. Cullen is Professor of Management at Washington State University, where he teaches courses on international management, business ethics, organizational theory, and strategic management. He received his PhD from Columbia University.

In addition to numerous presentations at Asian and European universities, Professor Cullen has been a visiting professor at l'Université Catholique de Lille in France and, as a Fulbright Scholar, at Waseda and Keio Universities in Japan.

Professor Cullen is the author or co-author of five books, including *International Management: Strategy and the Multinational Company*, and over 60 journal publications. His research has appeared in journals such as *Administrative Science Quarterly*, *Journal of International Business Studies*, *Academy of Management Journal*, *Organization Science*, *Decision Sciences*, *American Journal of Sociology*, *Journal of Management*, *Organizational Studies*, *Management International Review*, *Journal of Vocational Behavior*, *Journal of Business Ethics*, *Organizational Dynamics*, and the *Journal of World Business*.

Professor Cullen's major research interests include the effects of social institutions and national culture on ethical outcomes and work values, the management of entrepreneurial firms in changing environments, trust, and commitment in international strategic alliances, ethical climates in multinational organizations, and the dynamics of organizational structure.

Professor Cullen has consulted with both private and public organizations in the US and elsewhere in the areas of international management, organizational design, and ethics management.

K. Praveen Parboteeah is an Associate Professor of International Management in the Department of Management, University of Wisconsin–Whitewater. He received his PhD from Washington State University, and holds an MBA from California State University–Chico and a BSc (Honors) in Management Studies from the University of Mauritius.

Parboteeah regularly teaches international management, business ethics, and strategic management at both undergraduate and graduate levels. He has received numerous teaching awards and is included in multiple editions of *Who's Who Among America's Teachers* and is a University of Wisconsin–Whitewater Master Teacher and Teaching Scholar.

Parboteeah's research interests include international management, ethics, and technology and innovation management. He has published over 25 articles in leading journals such as the *Academy of Management Journal*, *Organization Science*, *Decision Sciences*, *Journal of Business Ethics*, *Journal of International Business Studies*, and *Management International Review*. He has received numerous awards for his research, including the Western Academy of Management Ascendant Scholar award and the 2007–8 University of Wisconsin–Whitewater Research Award.

Parboteeah has been involved in many aspects of international business education at the University of Wisconsin–Whitewater. He chaired the International Committee in the college of business and economics and is the exchange faculty coordinator for the exchange programs in France, namely ESC Rouen and the Burgundy School of Business in Dijon. He was part of the team that received grants from the US Department of Agriculture to further agricultural exchanges between the US markets and emerging markets such as China and India. For these efforts, the emerging markets program was awarded the Small Business/Export Assistance Governor's Award in 2005. He also lectures regularly at the WHU–Otto Beisheim School of Management in Germany and at the Lok Jack Graduate School of Business in Trinidad.

Of Indian ancestry, Parboteeah grew up on the African island of Mauritius and speaks Creole, French, and English. He currently lives in Whitewater with his South Korean wife Kyong, daughter Alisha and son Davin.

INTERNATIONAL BUSINESS

Introduction to

Introduction to International Business

part one

1 Competing in the Global Marketplace

After reading this chapter you should be able to:

- Define international business.

- Understand the nature of an MNC.

- Understand the key forces that drive globalization and the current global economy.

- Know the basic types of economies that make up the world's competitive landscape.

- Appreciate the role that low-cost countries and rapidly emerging economies play in today's world.

- Appreciate the importance of sustainability in the new global environment.

As the Preview IB Strategic Insight shows, savvy managers all over the world keep an eye open for international business opportunities. Often, in today's competitive world, the only opportunity to grow a business and its profitability is when a company leaves its home country. However, with these opportunities come the challenges of running a multinational operation. For the Shoprite case you can see the challenges faced by management when employees come from different cultures, when local laws and political institutions have different requirements for companies, and when foreign currencies must be managed in different economic environments. These are just a small sample of the many topics to consider in international business. To help you understand and meet the challenges of international business, the objective of this text is to show you how companies such as Shoprite succeed in the global marketplace and how they cope with the many complexities of running an international operation.

Whether a business is large or small or located in whatever continent, the pressures to think global continue to grow. Consider just a few examples: if you look at the clothes

South Africa's Shoprite: The Next Walmart?

PREVIEW IB
STRATEGIC INSIGHT

Already operating with over 700 stores in 16 countries such as Mauritius and Madagascar, Shoprite (www.shoprite.co.za), the South African Walmart wannabe, recently entered India with the largest superstore in this vast country. Only given the opportunity to go international in 1994 after the fall of apartheid, Shoprite now gets over half its revenue outside of South Africa. Shoprite is now the largest retailer in Africa.

Because Shoprite operates mostly in poorer developing nations, its target customers are low- to middle-income customers. Most multinational retailers ignore this niche. However, with profits rising over 16 percent last year and a $1.2 billion market capitalization, the model seems successful.

In spite of its success, Shoprite also faces many challenges in running its multinational operations. African currencies are highly volatile, making the costs of supplies and the value of sales unpredictable. When the South African rand soared to over 100 percent against the dollar in just three years, the costs of supplies sourced from home in South Africa soared as well. Now 60 percent of suppliers in Madagascar are local. In addition, strict local laws such as those in Egypt can also force local sourcing.

Shoprite, the South African Walmart wannabe

With over 63,000 employees speaking many different languages and complex differences in local laws regarding health, employment, taxes, etc., organizational challenges are constant. Like many multinationals, Shoprite uses technology to help manage these complex operations. A satellite system tracks shipping and sales, and suppliers and local stores are linked with an ecommerce system (http://www.shoprite.co.za/pages/127416071/Careers/Support--Operations.asp).

Source: Based on *The Economist*, 2005, "Africa's Walmart heads east," www.economist.com, January 13; www. shoprite.co.za/

you wear, the cars you drive, or the computers that sit on your desk, or keep track of your money in the bank, all have some components produced or sold by companies engaged in international business. Why? The major reason is the unrelenting pressures of globalization.

Globalization is the worldwide trend of the economies of the world becoming borderless and interlinked—companies are no longer limited by their domestic boundaries and may conduct any business activity anywhere in the world. Globalization means that companies are more likely to compete anywhere. Many companies now sell anywhere, source their raw materials or conduct research and development (R&D) anywhere, and produce anywhere.

Trade barriers are falling, and world trade among countries in goods and services is growing faster than domestic production. Money is flowing more freely across national borders as companies seek the best rates for financing anywhere in the world, and investors look for the best returns anywhere in the world. The Internet crosses national boundaries with the click of a mouse, allowing even the smallest of businesses to go global immediately. Consequently, companies can no longer afford the luxury of assuming that success in their home market equates to long-term profitability—or even survival.

Globalization is perhaps the major reason why you should study international business. In today's Internet-connected world, you may have little choice. With companies increasingly looking at global rather than domestic markets, managers must become international in outlook and strategies. Your suppliers, your research and development, your manufacturing facilities, your strategic alliance partners, and your customers increasingly come from beyond your national borders. Foreign competition and doing business in foreign markets are daily facts of life for today's managers. Successful managers must become international in outlook. These are executives with the ability and motivation to meet and beat the challenges of international business. The study of international business helps prepare you to deal with this evolving global economy and to develop the skills necessary to succeed in business in a globalizing world.

To provide you with a basic background in international business, this book introduces you to the latest information on how managers respond to the challenges of globalization and conduct competitive international operations. You will see how businesses both large and small deal with the complexities of national differences in cultural, economic, legal, ethical, religious, and political systems. You will learn how multinational managers use their understanding of these national differences to formulate strategies that maximize their companies' success in globalizing industries. You will also learn how multinational managers implement international strategies with supporting marketing, financial, organizational, and human resource management systems.

To help you better understand the real world of international business, you will find several types of real business examples in this and the following chapters. **Preview IB Strategic Insights** show you how real **multinational companies** handle issues to be discussed in the chapter. **IB Strategic Insights** give information on the strategic implications for international businesses that relate to the current discussion in the text. **IB Small Business Insights** highlight chapter material of particular relevance to small businesses. **Country/Regional Focuses** are discussions that show you the unique characteristics of the region or country that are relevant to the chapter topics. **IB Ethical Challenges** are examples of

globalization
the worldwide trend of economic integration across borders allowing businesses to expand beyond their domestic boundaries

multinational company (MNC)
any company that engages in business functions beyond its domestic borders

situations faced by multinational managers in dealing with issues being discussed in the chapter. Finally, as you will learn later in this chapter, most multinationals are also implementing measures to make their activities more environmentally responsible. The book also contains **IB Sustainability Practices**, showing you what multinationals are doing to implement such sustainable practices.

The Nature of International Business

A company engages in **international business** when it conducts any business functions beyond its domestic borders. What kinds of business activities might make a company international? The most apparent activity, of course, is international sales. When a company produces in its own country and sells in another, it engages in the simplest level of international activity. However, as you will see in much more detail later in the book, crossing national borders opens up more international options than simply selling internationally.

international business
when a company conducts any business functions beyond its domestic borders

In this text, we refer to any company engaging in international business as a multinational company or MNC. This is a broad definition, which includes all types of companies, large and small, that engage in international business. Most multinational companies, however, are also multinational corporations—the companies are publicly owned through stocks. Most often, when you see references to MNCs in the popular business press, the reference is to multinational corporations. The largest multinationals are all public corporations. Exhibit 1.1 lists the top MNCs in the world. Smaller MNCs are often privately owned, but many of their business activities may be conducted outside their own country. Smaller, non-public MNCs are also becoming increasingly important as it becomes more common for smaller organizations to compete globally. Some entrepreneurs create businesses that go international from the start.

To introduce some of the international options, consider the following hypothetical company that produces PCs. As a domestic-only company it can manufacture the chips and other electronic components, build the cases, assemble the components and sell the computers, all in its home country. However, the firm might not be able to compete successfully using this approach. The local market may be stagnant, with competitive pricing and lower profit margins. Even in a growing market, competitors like Dell Computer might source high-quality, low-cost components from anywhere in the world. Competitors might also find lower production costs in low-cost countries, allowing them to offer lower prices. What can this company do?

As an MNC, the firm might sell PCs to overseas buyers in countries with less competition and higher prices. Several other international activities might increase its competitive strength. For example, this company might locate any of the steps in obtaining components or completing production in other countries. It might buy the highest-quality chips from Taiwan, use the lowest-cost assemblers in Vietnam, and sell primarily in Europe and the US. For any of these steps, the company might outsource the activity to local companies in another country or own its own factories within another country. As you will see in later chapters, MNCs must develop strategies and systems to accomplish all or some of these international business tasks.

Next, we will consider the forces that drive the new economic reality facing the next generation of international managers and MNCs.

Exhibit 1.1 **Top 10 Companies in the World Based on Profitability, Growth, and Revenues**

Most Profitable	Profits ($ millions)	Country	Fastest Growing	% Change Revenues	Country	Most Revenues	Revenues ($ millions)	Country
Exxon Mobil	40,610	US	Tata Steel	353.2	India	Wal-Mart	378,799	US
Royal Dutch Shell	31,331	UK/ Netherlands	Freeport-McMoRan Copper & Gold	208.7	US	Exxon Mobil	372,824	US
General Electric	22,208	US	Intesa Sanpaolo	132.3	Italy	Royal Dutch Shell	355,782	UK/Netherlands
BP	20,845	UK	KFW Bankengruppe	111.3	Luxembourg	BP	291,438	UK
Gazprom	19,269	Russia	Enterprise GP Holdings	90.9	US	Toyota	230,201	Japan
HSBC Holdings	19,133	UK	AT&T	88.6	US	Chevron	210,783	US
Chevron	18,688	US	ArcelorMittal	78.7	US	ING Group	201,516	Netherlands
Petronas	18,118	Russia	CVS Caremark	74.2	US	Total	187,280	France
Total	18,042	France	Mapfre Group	73.4	Spain	General Motors	182,347	US
J.P. Morgan Chase & Co.	15,365	US	Iberdrola	73	Spain	ConocoPhillips	178,558	US

Source: Adapted from data in http://money.cnn.com/magazines/fortune/global500/2008/full_list/

Globalization: A Dynamic Context for International Business

Globalization is not a simple uniform evolutionary process. Not all economies of the world benefit equally or participate equally. In the recent past, financial crises, terrorism, wars, SARS, increased border security, and a worldwide economic stagnation have limited, or in some cases even reversed, some of the aspects of globalization. You will see below, in the context of the discussion of the major drivers of globalization, some of the effects produced by political, economic, and sociocultural upheavals. Consider Exhibit 1.2, which shows the history of globalization's major events. Look at this video for further information on globalization: www.stwr.org/globalization/commanding-heights-the-battle-for-the-world-economy.html.

The financial crisis of 2008 demonstrated just how interconnected the global economy has become in the last few decades. When failures and bad debt in the home mortgage industry forced some US banks and other financial institutions out of business, the US stock market declined quickly and precipitously. Almost immediately, financial institutions around the world followed the US market. Look at this video for an overview of the crises: www.pbs.org/newshour/video/module.html?mod=0&pkg=8102008&seg=1, and the Country/Regional Focus below, which shows the impact of the financial crisis on India.

Before discussing the key globalization trends that affect international business, it is useful to look at some commonly used classifications of the world's countries. The classifications roughly indicate a country's gross domestic product (GDP) and the growth in GDP. The classifications are not exact but they simplify discussions of world trade and investments.

Exhibit 1.2 **Globalization Chronology**

Time	Economic	Political	Technological
1940s	• Establishment of the Bretton Woods System, a new international monetary system (1944–71) • Establishment of GATT (1947) entering into force in January 1948 • Soviet Union establishes the Council for Mutual Economic Assistance (CMEA) for economic cooperation among communist countries (1949–91)	• Foundation of the United Nations (1945) • Launch of the Marshall Plan (1948–57), a European recovery program • Founding of the Organization for European Economic Cooperation (1948) • Decolonization starts (1948–62). Independence of India, Indonesia, Egypt, for example • China becomes a socialist republic in 1949	• Expansion of plastics and fibre products e.g. first nylon stockings for women (1940) • Discovery of large oilfields in the Middle East, especially in Saudi Arabia (1948)
1950s	• Treaty of Rome establishes the European Community (1957). EC and the European Free Trade Association (1959) favor West European integration • Major currencies become convertible (1958–64) • Development of the Eurodollar Market in London which contributed to the expansion of international liquidity	• Korean war (1950–63) • Suez crisis (1956) • Decolonization in Africa (15 countries become independent between 1958 and 1962)	• Increased use of oil from the Middle East in Europe and Japan • "Just-in-time" production implemented by Toyota • Increasing usage of jet engines in air transport (1957–72) • Offshore oil and gas production developed

Exhibit 1.2 **continued**

Time	Economic	Political	Technological
1960s	• Foundation of the Organization of the Petroleum Exporting Countries (OPEC) (1960) • Kennedy Round, 6th session of the GATT (1964–9) • Rapid spread of automobiles and highways in the North accelerates demand and shift in fuels consumption (from coal to oil) • Trade politics of East Asian countries put more emphasis on export-led development than on import substitution • Elimination of last customs duties within EC (1968)	• Erection of Berlin Wall (1961) and Cuban missile crisis (1962) highlight sharp confrontation between East and West	• Green Revolution—transforming agricultural production in developing countries (1960s onwards) • Integrated circuits become commercially available (1961) • First person in space (Yuri Gagarin, 1961) and the first man on the moon (Neil Armstrong, 1969) • First line of Japan's high-speed train system (*shinkansen*) opened in 1964 • Mont Blanc Road Tunnel (1965) • Increasing usage of containerization in ocean transport (1968 onwards)
1970s	• Departure from US dollar exchange rate gold standard (1971) • Tokyo Round of the GATT (1973–9) • Oil price "shocks" (1973–4 and 1979) reverse decades of real oil price declines • Rise of Asian newly industrialized countries • China's economic reform (1978)	• Yom Kippur war (1973) helps to trigger oil price hike • EU enlargement to nine members (1973)	• First single chip microprocessor (Intel 4004) is introduced (1971)
1980s	• Volcker Fed successfully extinguishes US inflation • Developing country debt crisis • Mexico starts market reforms and joins the GATT in 1986 • Lourve Accord promotes stabilization of major exchange rates (1987)	• Enlargement of the EU to 12 members • Fall of the Berlin Wall (1989)	• IBM introduces first personal computer (1981) • Microsoft Windows introduced (1985) • Invention of the World Wide Web by Tim Berners-Lee (1989)
1990s	• Indian economic reforms launched in 1991 • Establishment of the North American Free Trade Agreement (1994) • Establishment of the WTO (1995) • Asian financial crisis (1997) • Adoption of the euro by 11 European countries (1999)	• Dissolution of the Soviet Union (1991) leads to the formation of 13 independent states • Maastricht Treaty (formally, the Treaty on European Union) signed (1992)	• First website put online in 1991 • Launch of the first 2G-GSM network by Radiolinja in Finland (1991) • Eurotunnel opens in 1994 linking the United Kingdom to continent • The number of mobile phones increases due to the introduction of second-generation (2G) networks using digital technology
2000s	• Dotcom crisis (2001) • China joins WTO (2001) • End of the Multi-fiber Agreement in 2005 (quantitative restrictions of textiles lifted)	• Enlargement of the EU to 27 members (2007)	• Number of users rises to 300 million by 2000 • Container ships transport more than 70 percent of the seaborne trade in value terms • Number of Internet users rises to 800 million in 2005

Source: UNCTAD, 2007, *World Investment Report*, New York and Geneva: United Nations, pp. 22–3.

India

In India, soon after the drastic decline in value of the US stock market in 2008, the Bombay Stock Exchange Index, or Sensex, tumbled 6 percent, reaching a two-year low. There is little doubt that the global financial crisis has arrived in India. As the financial crisis unfolded, foreign investors pulled out nearly $10 billion from India. This resulted in less money that Indian banks have to lend to companies and consumers. N.R. Narayanan, of ICICI Bank, India's largest private-sector bank, noted, "We are tightening our lending norms to certain customer segments." ICICI expects a 35 percent drop in loans. The result of such practices is that companies have had to put off expansion plans and consumers now face more difficulty in getting home and auto loans.

Not only is the high cost of borrowing locally a problem, but the financial turmoil in India's main export markets in the US and Europe has resulted in reduced demand. For example, in the IT sector, the US provides more than half of the revenues for Indian IT giants Tata Consultancy, Infosys Technologies, and Wipro. The US financial crisis and economic slowdown will result in fewer orders and delays in long-term investments by US customers. In addition, many of the customers of these IT firms are US banks, among the hardest hit in the crisis.

Source: Adapted from Nandini Lakshman, 2008, "World financial crisis: India's hurting, too," *BusinessWeek Online*, www.businessweek.com, October 8.

Types of Economies in the Global Marketplace: The Arrived, the Coming, and the Struggling

Exhibit 1.3 shows some divisions of the world's economies based roughly on classifications used by the United Nations and the Boston Consulting Group. **Developed economies** have mature economies with substantial per capita GDPs and international trade and investments. The **developing economies**, such as Hong Kong, Singapore, South Korea, and Taiwan, have economies that have grown extensively over the past two decades yet have sometimes struggled recently, especially during the setbacks of the Asian crisis in the late 1990s. Other developing economies to watch are what the UN calls the **transition economies** of the Czech Republic, Hungary, Poland, and Russia, and the developing economies of Indonesia, Malaysia, the Philippines, Vietnam, and Thailand.

Transition economies are countries that have changed from government-controlled, mostly communist economic systems to market or capitalistic systems. The former systems relied on state-owned organizations and centralized government control to run the economy. In the transition to free market and capitalistic systems, many government-owned companies were converted to private ownership. The market and not the government then determined the success of companies. Several of these transition economies, such as Hungary, Poland, Slovakia, and the Czech Republic, developed market economies that allowed them to join the European Union. Furthermore, many multinationals are deciding to locate in transition economies for various reasons. As you can see from the IB Strategic Insight overleaf, transition economies will remain key elements of international business.

Another important aspect of the international business environment are **least developed countries (LDCs)**, which have yet to show much progress in the

developed economies
mature economies with substantial per capita GDPs and international trade and investments

developing economies
economies that have grown extensively over the past two decades

transition economies
countries in the process of changing from government-controlled economic systems to capitalistic systems

least developed countries (LDCs)
the poorest nations, often plagued with unstable political regimes, high unemployment, and low worker skills

Exhibit 1.3 **Types of Economies in the Globe (example countries)**

Developed Countries	Developing Countries			Least Developed Countries (LDCs)
	Asia	Transition Economies	Low-cost Countries (LCCs)	
Australia	China	Czech Republic	Brazil	Afghanistan
Austria	Hong Kong	Hungary	China	Cambodia
Belgium	India	Poland	India	Chad
Britain	Indonesia	Russia	Mexico	Congo
Canada	Malaysia		Russia	Ethiopia
Denmark	Singapore			Niger
France	South Korea			Sudan
Germany	Taiwan			Yemen
Italy	Thailand			
Ireland				
Japan				
Netherlands				
Spain				
Sweden				
Switzerland				
United States				

Source: Adapted from UNCTD, 2008, *Development and Globalization: Facts and Figures*, New York and Geneva: United Nations; Boston Consulting Group, 2004, *Capturing Global Advantage*, Boston: Boston Consulting Group.

Nokia's New Plant in Cluj, Romania

IB STRATEGIC INSIGHT

Nokia will soon close its plant in Bochum, Belgium, as costs have risen steadily and the factory has become very expensive. Nokia has chosen Cluj in Romania to replace the Belgian factory. Cluj was chosen for many reasons. It has a population of 400,000 and most people are relishing the prospect of working for a multinational and making substantial wages. In fact, at a job fair held in June of 2007, Nokia received twice as many applicants as it needed to fill the jobs available. However, Nokia has chosen Cluj for other reasons besides cheap and plentiful labor. Nokia expects to draw heavily from an ample supply of engineering graduates from the well-regarded local technical university. Graduates of the university are well trained and willing to work for a quarter of what similar engineers would be paid in other Western countries. Cluj was chosen also because of its proximity to Nokia's customers. Unlike other handset competitors which manufacture their products in Asia, Nokia can be more responsive to local customer needs and can react very quickly to such changes.

However, setting up operations in Cluj is not without challenges. Nokia will have to deal with poor infrastructure. The local airport is very small and highways in the region are not well developed. Getting supplies to Cluj and getting finished products out of Cluj will therefore be challenging. Furthermore, many multinationals find that wages rise rapidly in transition economies and workers do not hesitate to work for competitors at higher wages. Nokia is therefore providing perks that it hopes will retain skilled workers. It is expected that the Cluj factory will have a cafeteria with free food, a gym, and playing areas.

Source: Adapted from Jack Ewing, 2008, "Nokia's new home in Romania," *BusinessWeek*, January 28, pp. 40–2.

evolving global economy. They are the poorest nations and are often plagued with unstable political regimes, high unemployment, and unskilled workers. Most of these countries are located in Central and South America, Africa, and the Middle East.

Perhaps most important strategically are those countries that the Boston Consulting Group (BCG) calls the **low-cost countries (LCCs).** These are countries with cheap labor that are becoming the manufacturing and service providers for MNCs headquartered in developed nations such as the United States. Led by China and India, these countries are growing fast as low-cost sources for a growing number of business functions, and to a large degree are the recipients of many of the jobs leaving the more developed economies such as the US.

With this overview of the major economies of the world, we can now look more closely at the driving forces of the new world economy.

low-cost countries (LCCs) countries, usually with cheap labor, that are becoming the manufacturing and service providers for MNCs headquartered in developed nations such as the United States

Globalization Drivers

Several key trends drive the globalization of the world economy and, in turn, force businesses to consider international operations to survive and prosper. Some of the most important trends include falling borders, growing cross-border trade and investment, the rise of global products and global customers, the growing use of the Internet and sophisticated information technology (IT), the role of LCCs in the world market, and the rise of global standards of quality and production. Exhibit 1.4 illustrates these important forces. Each of these driving forces is discussed below.

Exhibit 1.4
The Drivers of Globalization

Lowering the Barriers of National Borders: Making Trade and Cross-border Investment Easier

In the mid-1900s, worldwide tariffs averaged 45 percent. By the early 2000s, tariffs on industrial products fell to 3.8 percent.[1] Tariffs are taxes most often charged to goods imported into a country. They have the effect of raising the price of an imported good. As you will see in more detail in Chapters 4 and 9, tariffs tend to make foreign goods more expensive and less competitive with local goods. Trade is reduced because companies cannot compete with domestic producers. After several rounds of tariff negotiations, known as the **General Agreement on Tariffs and Trade (GATT)**, worldwide tariffs on manufactured goods declined from 45 percent to less than 7 percent.

Later negotiations in Uruguay ended with agreements to reduce tariffs even further, liberalize trade in agriculture and services, and eliminate some nontariff barriers to international trade, such as excessive use of health regulations to keep out imports.[2] The Uruguay talks ended in 1993 and established the **World Trade Organization (WTO)**. The WTO now provides a formal organization that promotes continued negotiations and settles trade disputes among nations. There are now 148 nations in the WTO, up from the original 92 in 1986. Over 90 percent of world trade takes place among countries that are WTO members. At least 30 more countries, including Russia, are seeking WTO membership.

The WTO is not the only organization that seeks to eliminate trade barriers. Other organizations based on **regional trade agreements**, such as the **European Union (EU)** and **North American Free Trade Agreement (NAFTA)**, also attempt to reduce tariffs and develop similar technical and economic standards. These regional organizations lead to more trade among the member nations, and some scholars argue that regional agreements are the first step toward complete globalization. Others, however, argue that regional agreements benefit only the trade-group members and often harm poorer nations that are left out of the agreements (such as the Caribbean countries that are not members of NAFTA).[3] From a practical point of view, although they do benefit member countries the most, regional agreements contribute to world trade more than they restrict such trade. Also, the regional agreements, with fewer countries, are more politically achievable than worldwide trade agreements that include many countries.[4] In Chapter 3 you will find out much more about these agreements.

Is free trade a success? The WTO argues that the answer is yes, and the data seem to support their position. Following the early GATT agreements, world trade exceeded the output of the world's gross domestic product by over fourfold.

However, the policies of the WTO do have critics. Some argue that the WTO favors the developed nations, because the developed nations have the resources to outcompete poorer nations in a non-regulated world. Environmentalists also criticize free trade because it allows MNCs to skirt regulations in many of the developed countries by moving environmentally damaging production to poorer countries that often have weaker protection laws. Ethicists argue that such actions give commercial interests priority over the environment, health, and safety. Organized labor sees free trade as a source of job loss and pressure to reduce wages for remaining jobs as MNCs move or threaten to move production from higher-wage countries to low-cost countries. You can see the WTO's response to these criticisms on their website at www.wto.org/.

General Agreement on Tariffs and Trade (GATT) tariff negotiations between several nations that reduced the average worldwide tariff on manufactured goods

World Trade Organization (WTO) a formal structure for continued negotiations to reduce trade barriers and to act as a mechanism for settling trade disputes

regional trade agreements agreements among nations in a particular region to reduce tariffs and develop similar technical and economic standards

European Union (EU) Austria, Belgium, Britain, Bulgaria, Cyprus, Czech Republic, Denmark, Estonia, Finland, France, Germany, Greece, Hungary, Ireland, Italy, Latvia, Lithuania, Luxembourg, Malta, the Netherlands, Poland, Portugal, Romania, Slovakia, Slovenia, Spain, and Sweden, plus Norway and Switzerland in the related European Free Trade Area

North American Free Trade Agreement (NAFTA) a multilateral treaty that links the United States, Canada, and Mexico in an economic bloc that allows freer exchange of goods and services

Locate and Sell Anywhere to Anybody: It's No Longer Only For Manufacturing but Services as Well

The September 11th, 2001, attack on the United States and the resulting world-wide economic stagnation led to a major setback for world trade. For example, double-digit growth in worldwide exporting of merchandise in 2000 was followed by a more than 4 percent decline in the following two years. However, most of the world's trade rebounded in 2003 and 2004 and trade growth neared double digits again by 2007. Some countries, particularly China, have benefited substantially during the post 9/11 period. China is now in third place in imports and exports and is rapidly gaining on Japan, the US and the EU. Exhibit 1.5 shows the current leading countries in terms of import and export total volume. This suggests that the world's economies are increasingly more intertwined and mutually stimulated.

Not only do MNCs trade across borders with exports and imports, but they also build global networks that connect different worldwide locations for R&D, supply, support services like call centers, production, and sales. Setting up and

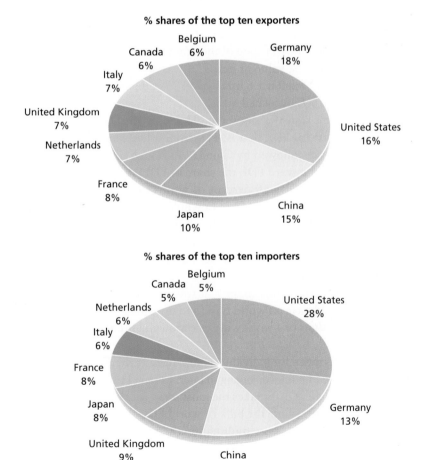

Exhibit 1.5

The World's Top Ten Exporters and Importers: Who's Selling, Who's Buying

Source: Adapted from World Trade Organization, 2007, *International Trade Statistics 2007*, Geneva: World Trade Organization, Table 1.8.

foreign direct investment (FDI)

a multinational firm's ownership, in part or in whole, of an operation in another country

owning your own operations in another country is known as **foreign direct investment (FDI)**. That is, FDI occurs when an MNC from one country owns an organizational unit located in another country. Multinationals often build their own units in foreign countries but they also use cross-border mergers and acquisitions, such as the acquisition of the European company Arcelor for $32 billion by the Indian company Mittal Steel. This was also the largest acquisition ever by a company from a developing nation.[5]

Which countries give and get these cross-border investments in the global economy? The competitive landscape is changing, with the developing nations taking a more active role.

FDI soared to record levels, increasing by over 36 percent between 1996 and 2000 and ultimately topping $1.5 trillion in 2000.[6] However, following a pattern similar to international trade, FDI declined to $735 billion in 2001, less than half of the previous year, and declined another 25 percent in the following two years. Since that time, however, and again like world trade, FDI has regained its steam, growing nearly 40 percent a year.[7]

Even though FDI declined temporarily, there remained a large volume during the recent decade, due in large part to the existence of an estimated 61,000 multinational corporations! These have over 900,000 foreign investments with over 55 million employees, and a stock value of $7 trillion.[8] It is also important to note that in spite of the dramatic slowdown in the growth of FDI starting in 2001, the value of new FDI was and still is the major revenue generator for MNCs.[9] Exhibit 1.6 lists the top 25 companies in the world ranked by the size of their foreign-owned assets.

The most recent statistics show the EU, led by the UK and France, at the top of the list of inward FDI: that is, FDI from other countries going into the EU. The US is second, followed by China.[10] Although the developed countries still lead the world in inward FDI, the share of FDI for developing nations has increased steadily to nearly 40 percent of worldwide inward FDI. However, many LDCs had minimal FDI. Africa as a whole, for example, received less than 3 percent of inward FDI. Outward FDI follows a similar pattern with the EU leading the US, making nearly half the world's investments outside of their own countries. The US is second with less than 20 percent of worldwide FDI, and Japan is a distant third. [11]

At the time of writing this chapter, it was not clear what impact the 2008 financial crisis would have on world trade and investment. However, immediate indicators showed signs of a worldwide recession and declines in both trade and investment.

What does this mean for individual companies? Perhaps the most important implication is that companies engaging in international business now more easily locate and sell anywhere that makes the most sense for their business. Although the EU and the US contribute the bulk of world FDI, and will be likely to do so in the immediate future, astute multinational managers must scan the world continuously for possible profitable investments. The following IB Strategic Insight shows how some major MNCs are moving quickly to take advantage of opportunities in the transition economies.

Exhibit 1.6 **Companies with the Largest Stakes in Foreign Countries**

Rank (foreign assets)	Company	Country	Industry	Foreign Assets ($ millions)	% Foreign Assets	Foreign Sales	% Foreign Sales	Foreign Employees	% Foreign Employees
1	General Electric	USA	Electrical & electronic equipment	412,692	61%	59,815	40%	155,000	49%
2	Vodafone	UK	Telecomm	196,396	89%	39,497	75%	51,052	83%
3	General Motors	USA	Motor vehicles	175,254	37%	65,288	34%	194,000	58%
4	British Petroleum	UK	Petroleum	161,174	78%	200,293	79%	78,100	81%
5	Royal Dutch/Shell	UK	Petroleum	151,324	69%	184,047	60%	92,000	84%
6	ExxonMobil	USA	Petroleum	143,860	69%	248,402	69%	52,920	63%
7	Toyota	Japan	Motor vehicles	131,676	54%	117,721	63%	107,763	38%
8	Ford	USA	Motor vehicles	119,131	44%	80,325	45%	160,000	53%
9	Total	France	Petroleum	108,098	86%	132,960	75%	64,126	57%
10	Eléctricité de France	France	Electricity, gas, and water	91,478	45%	26,060	41%	17,801	11%
11	France Telecom	France	Telecom	87,186	67%	25,634	42%	82,034	40%
12	Volkswagen	Germany	Motor vehicles	82,579	52%	85,896	72%	165,849	48%
13	RWE Group	Germany	Electricity, gas, and water	82,569	64%	23,390	45%	42,349	49%
14	Chevron	USA	Petroleum	81,225	65%	99,970	52%	32,000	54%
15	E.ON	Germany	Electricity, gas, and water	80,941	54%	29,148	35%	45,820	57%
16	Suez	France	Electricity, gas, and water	78,400	82%	39,565	77%	96,741	61%
17	Deutsche Teledom	Germany	Telecomm	78,378	52%	31,659	43%	75,820	31%
18	Siemens	Germany	Electrical & electronic equipment	66,854	64%	64,447	67%	296,000	64%
19	Honda	Japan	Motor vehicles	66,682	74%	69,791	80%	126,122	87%
20	Hutchison Whampoa	Hong Kong	Diversified	61,607	80%	24,721	79%	165,590	83%
21	Procter & Gamble	USA	Diversified	60,251	44%	38,760	57%	69,835	51%
22	Sanofi-Aventis	France	Pharmacy	58,999	57%	18,901	56%	69,186	71%
23	ConocoPhillips	USA	Petroleum	55,906	52%	48,568	27%	15,931	45%
24	BMW	Germany	Motor vehicles	55,308	63%	44,404	76%	25,924	25%
25	Nissan	Company	Motor vehicles	53,747	55%	59,771	72%	89,336	49%

Source: Adapted from UNCTD. World Investment Report: Transnational Corporations, Extractive Industries, and Development. United Nations: New York and Geneva, 2008, Annex table A.1.13, pg. 229.

Automobile Production Moves to Eastern Europe

Louis Schweitzer, CEO of Renault, recently remarked that Toyota's assembly plant in northern France, completed in 2001, is the last of a breed, probably the last new automobile assembly plant that will be built in Western Europe. Recently passing Italy, Russian is now the fifth-largest European automobile assembly country. Why? The cheaper labor costs in the transition economy countries can save Renault around $2,500 per vehicle. This allows companies that build cars in countries like Hungary to sell below competitors manufacturing in Western Europe and still make a healthy profit.

Eastern European production of automobiles grew 27 percent over the last five years while Western European production remained flat. Typical is the new plant in Kolin, Czech Republic, which can produce 300,000 vehicles a year. French Peugeots and Citroëns as well as Japanese Toyotas roll off the line. The Japanese company Suzuki has 24 assembly plants in Central and Eastern Europe. Not only do these automotive companies do final assembly but they also produce many components in smaller plants.

Source: *The Economist*, 2005, "Driving out of the east," www. economist.com, March 3.

Traditionally, most FDI was in manufacturing as MNCs sought low-cost production sites or locations near valued customers. However, in today's global economy, FDI is growing in the service sector as well. Exhibit 1.7 shows the changing distribution of FDI types.

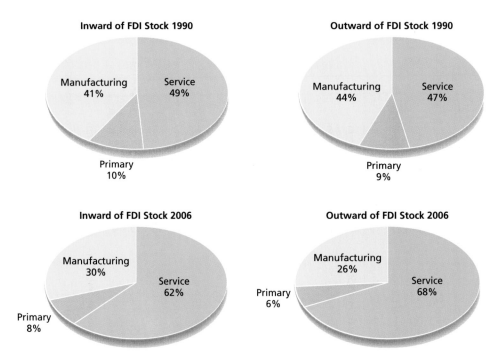

Exhibit 1.7 **Service FDI is Replacing Manufacturing**

Source: Adapted from UNCTAD, 2007, *World Investment Report 2007*, Geneva and New York, Annex A.

The Rise of Low-cost Countries: An Increasingly Important Driver of Globalization

Low-cost countries have two roles as drivers of globalization. First, they fuel trade and investments by MNCs looking for low-cost platforms to manufacture goods or secure services such as information technology and call centers. Second, some low-cost countries are becoming what the Boston Consulting Group calls **rapidly developing economies (RDEs)**.[12] Rapidly developing economies are LCCs such as China, India, Mexico, and Brazil that not only provide a low-cost production site but also have an expanding market for multinational sales. These countries as a whole are expected to see a $2.3 trillion growth in gross domestic product by the next decade as compared to the $3.15 trillion expected for the **Triad** during the same period. However, this growth is a two-way street as RDEs are using the benefits of foreign investments to grow local companies rapidly into world competitors. The Chinese household appliance company Haier Group is a prime example. A $10 billion revenue company and number one in China for full-line appliances, Haier Group already generates 10 percent of its sales from outside of China.[13]

The cost savings of locating in an LCC for a typical manufacturing organization are shown in Exhibit 1.8. This significant cost difference between LCCs and the developed world encourages companies such as Motorola to set up operations in LCCs like China, or companies such as Walmart (previously Wal-Mart) to source their goods or services from local LCC companies. As you will see in later chapters, although a traditional trade theory suggests that we all benefit from moving jobs where the work can be done best or cheapest, there are those who are hurt by the shifting of jobs from the developed economies to the LCCs.

To show the impact of LCCs on the world's competitive landscape, the BCG uses a matrix mapping how much of a country's industrial production is being switched to LCCs through either outsourcing or offshoring. International **outsourcing** is when a company in one country contracts with a company in another country to perform some business function. **Offshoring** is when a company in one country moves a business function such as manufacturing to

rapidly developing economies (RDEs)
LCCs using the benefits of foreign investments to grow rapidly into world competitors

Triad
the world's dominant trading partners: the European Union, the United States, and Japan

outsourcing
when a company in one country contracts with a company in another country to perform some business function

offshoring
when a company in one country moves a business function such as manufacturing to another country, usually to take advantage of lower costs

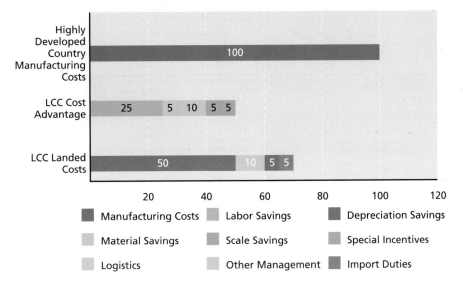

Exhibit 1.8

Saving Big: Cost Advantages of LCC Manufacturing

Source: Adapted from Boston Consulting Group, 2005, *BCG Focus, Navigating the Five Currents of Globalization*, Boston: Boston Consulting Group, p. 5.

another country, usually to take advantage of lower costs. Exhibit 1.9 shows some examples of outsourcing and offshoring, and Exhibit 1.10 the BCG matrix for a variety of industries in the United States.

Exhibit 1.9 **Definitions and Examples of Offshoring and Outsourcing from the United Nations**

Location	Outsourced	Internal to the Company
Offshoring in a foreign country	Production or service done by a foreign company provider (e.g. Infosys in India does software development for Bank of America)	Production or service done by a foreign affiliate of the company (e.g. a US firm produces in its Mexican factory)
Home country	Production or service done by another company in the home country	Production or service done inside the company

Source: Adapted from UNCTAD, 2004, *World Investment Report*, Geneva and New York: United Nations, p. 148, Table IV.1.

Case Study: The United States

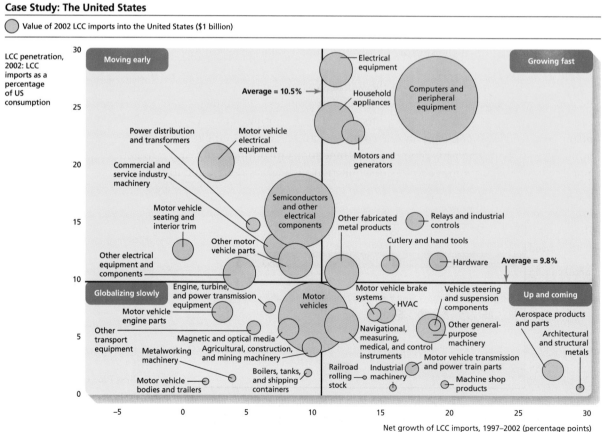

Exhibit 1.10 **The Boston Consulting Group Maps the Influence of LCCs**

Source: Boston Consulting Group, 2004, "Capturing global advantage," www.bcg.com

Drug Testing Made Easier

ETHICAL CHALLENGE

Drug companies around the world have been shifting some pharmaceutical manufacturing and development work to LCCs driven by the same cost savings in other industries. More recently companies such as Pfizer and Eli Lilly of the United States and Roche Holding of Switzerland have started offshoring and outsourcing clinical trials for newly developed medicines in countries like India, Brazil, China, and Mexico. Indian physicians such as Dr Arvind Sosale of Diacon Hospital in Bangalore report no trouble getting volunteers, unlike the case for patients from developed nations, where participants are often more wary and resistant to trying new drugs. In a poor country such as India, people are more likely attracted to the free drugs and special attention one gets for participation.

Although the Indian government has recently instituted more strict control of clinical drug trials, some still think the use of poor and often illiterate subjects is a form of exploitation. Given the fourfold growth from 2001 to 2003, forecasts are that the drug-testing industry will grow even faster.

As a multinational manager for a drug company, how would you respond?

Sources: Based on Sarith Rai, 2005, "Drug companies cut costs with foreign clinical trails," *New York Times*, February 24, p. C5; Andrew Pollack, 2005, "Medical companies joining offshore trend, too," *New York Times*, February 24, pp. A1, C4.

One side of the matrix in Exhibit 1.10 shows the market penetration of low-cost products in the US and the other side of the matrix shows the percentage of growth. This gives you an idea of the types of products that are heavily sourced from LCCs through outsourcing and offshoring and those likely to become more so. A similar matrix could be applied to service areas such as call centers, which are increasingly outsourced or offshored to India.

Outsourcing and offshoring are not without potential harm to the givers and receivers. Most often we hear about the people who lose jobs in one country when their work is transferred to another country. However, that is not the only potential ethical issue. The ethical and institutional systems may differ in host countries in ways that might allow potentially ethically questionable behaviors by MNCs. Above is an example of one possible ethical challenge.

Offshoring and outsourcing are not limited to the large MNCs. Small businesses are also getting into the act. The IB Small Business Insight overleaf gives an example of a Swedish company's efforts to take advantage of the same benefits sought by larger companies.

The shifting of production and services to LCCs is also creating a potential group of new competitors in the world market. As noted above, these are the RDEs including China, India, Mexico, Brazil, and several countries in Southeast Asia and Eastern Europe.

What are some of these companies to watch? A look at the recent *Fortune Global 500* annual scoreboard of the global largest 500 companies shows an increased presence of companies from emerging markets and RDEs. At this point, Korean, Russian, and Chinese companies dominate the top rankings for emerging markets. Although the US leads the list of Global 500, China now has 29 members and Korea has 15.[14]

A Swedish Company Goes Offshoring

The bulk of offshoring of services has so far been undertaken by large firms—but smaller companies are also starting to exploit opportunities created by the increased tradability of services. Global Refund—a market-leading supplier of financial services to enable travelers to collect tax refunds—is a good example.

Global Refund employs 800 people worldwide, in some 35 countries. It has its origin in Sweden, but is legally registered in the Netherlands (mainly for tax purposes). IT has made it possible to locate various headquarter functions to different locations: the chief executive officer (CEO) is based in Switzerland, marketing and finance functions are located in Sweden, IT and transaction processing functions are run from Austria, and certain business segments are managed from Singapore.

As of early 2004, Global Refund was in the process of consolidating back-office work into two "centres of excellence" in Europe. Once consolidated, tried and tested, the company may, as a second step, offshore these functions and establish a foreign affiliate in a lower-cost location in either the CEE or Asia.

The company has also chosen to offshore some services through outsourcing. In one business segment, all transaction processing work has been outsourced to a local service provider in Singapore; software development for the European market has been outsourced to a local company in Bulgaria; and software development to support the Asia-Pacific region is undertaken by a local company in India. There are also plans to establish a captive call center in a low-cost location (a captive call centre is one owned by the company, even if in a foreign location).

The company views the offshoring of services as a necessary process to increase competitiveness. By consolidating certain functions in centres of excellence, it has been able to reap economies of scale, avoid duplication of work, enhance worker skills, and thereby reduce costs as well as improve the quality of the services performed.

Source: UNCTAD, 2004, *World Investment Report*, Geneva and New York: United Nations.

Climbing oil prices helped the Russian company of Gazprom make the top 50 and China's Sinopec make the top 20. Korea's Samsung, known for its memory chips, LCD display panels, and cell phones, also made the 50. According to the recent Boston Consulting Group study of the top 100 global challengers to watch from the RDEs, the majority of the hot companies come from China, followed by India and Brazil. Chinese companies include Chery Automotive, China's leading manufacturer of automobiles now building plants in Eastern Europe and South America, and Changhong Electric, a $2.6 billion operation with plants in Australia, Europe, and the US. Brazilian companies include JBS–Friboi, Latin America's largest beef and pork processor that recently acquired the US-based Swift & Co. From India, there is Suzlon Energy, the fifth-largest company for installed wind energy capacity.[15] There is little doubt that in the near future many of these companies from RDEs will become household names around the world.

Global trade has two important effects in developing new competitors. First, when the large multinationals use developing countries as low-wage platforms for high-tech assembly, they facilitate the transfer of technology. This means that workers and companies in developing countries often learn new skills when

New Competitors on the Move

Indian information technology (IT) services firms such as Wipro and Infosys want to be more than low-cost sources of IT outsourcing for major US and European firms. They want to take on the IBMs and Accentures by becoming the Walmart of IT, turning software engineering and business processes such as running call centers into commodities that can be produced cheaply and sold in great volume around the world. In India, where top engineers cost less than $10,000 a year and top companies meet or exceed global standards, this might be the future. "Almost everything that is done can be done by us faster, cheaper and better," claims Nadan Nilekani, Infosys CEO. India's revenue from business process outsourcing has grown at nearly $4 billion a year for the last few years.

The strategy of Indian firms is to keep 80 percent of the value added in low-cost India while using local consultancies in other countries to deal directly with customers. Wipro, for example, recently acquired NerveWire, a Massachusetts firm, and Infosys established its own business process subsidiary, Progeon, in Australia. Multinationals like IBM and GE Capital counter the low-cost challenge by having their "captive" units in India. Indian managers, however, think they have the competitive advantage since they know their own country better.

Sources: Based on *The Economist*, 2004, "The latest in remote control," www.economist.com, September 9; *The Economist*, 2004, "Faster, cheaper, better," www.economist.com, November 11.

the large multinationals use them as sites for low-cost production and assembly. In countries where the workers are well educated and motivated, the former assemblers often become the creators rather than the builders of advanced technologies. Second, aggressive MNCs from emerging-market countries are also expanding beyond their own borders. Consider the IB Strategic Insight above for the up-and-coming Indian IT service firms. It shows not only how smaller competitors can grow to challenge any company, but also how information and web technology can be used successfully.

Information Technology and the Internet: A Necessary Tool for Globally Dispersed Companies

The explosive growth in the capabilities of information technology and the Internet increases the MNC's ability to reach customers in a global economy and to manage operations throughout the world. Since any website can be accessed by anyone with access to a computer, the Internet makes it easy for companies to go global. That is, with a global online population exceeding 600 million, individuals can shop anywhere and companies can sell anywhere.

Electronic communication (e-mail, the World Wide Web, etc.) allows MNCs to communicate with company locations throughout the world. Information technology expands the global reach of an organization. MNCs can now monitor worldwide operations to an extent never before possible. Text and graphic information can flow to any part of the world nearly instantaneously. Headquarters, research and development, manufacturing, or sales can be located anywhere there is a computer. Because employees, suppliers, and customers are geographically dispersed, organizations are becoming virtual—linked by networks of computers. Information technology makes it all happen.

Information technology is also spurring a borderless financial market. Investors are going global, and companies of the future will get their financing not in local stock or bond markets but in global markets that seek the best companies worldwide.

The decreasing price and increasing sophistication of computer systems also affects globalization. Small companies can now have computer power that only the largest multinationals could have afforded just a few years ago. Similarly, cheap and readily available computer power allows companies in poorer nations to make technological gains previously reserved for the rich.

The use of information technology and the Internet is also speeding up another globalization driver. Since many companies now use the Web to search for suppliers, it is easier to be a global customer. Because of the importance of this growing trend, Chapter 15 in this book discusses the impact of the Internet on **multinational management** in detail.

Increasing Global Products, Services, and Customers

Even though countries differ in national cultures, political, and economic systems, customers in different countries increasingly want similar products and services. For example, aircraft manufacturers such as Boeing and Airbus and fast-food chains such as Kentucky Fried Chicken offer the same or similar products in many different markets. When companies can sell the same product or deliver the same service regardless of the nationality of the customer, the industry has a **global product**. When industries have mostly global products, global competition is more likely.

Perhaps driven by the rise of similar customer needs worldwide, customers are also crossing borders and becoming **global customers**. Global customers look for products or services ignoring national boundaries, seeking instead the best price and quality rather than national location. Companies making industrial purchases are more likely than individuals to become global customers. Seventy percent of the global e-commerce comes from such business-to-business transactions. However, with the increased use of web stores for purchasing consumer goods, any site is available for customers worldwide so anyone with a computer can be a global customer. Many of you seeking better prices may have already become global customers by purchasing books or computer equipment from outside of your home country. The IB Strategic Insight opposite shows how some individuals are becoming global customers to meet their health care needs.

Increasingly, similar customer needs and the willingness of customers to shop globally encourage the speed of globalization because companies are more likely to offer one product for everybody, allowing any customer to buy anything from anywhere. These trends will continue as developing nations move beyond simply serving as low-cost production sites and, instead, become the centers of consumer growth.

multinational management
the formulation of strategies and the design of management systems that successfully take advantage of international opportunities and respond to international threats

global product
the same product or service regardless of the nationality of the customer

global customers
global customers search the world for products or services without regard for national boundaries

Health Care Destinations: Indian Hospitals Seek Global Customers

India attracts about 150,000 medical tourists a year. These are people who look for low-cost medical procedures outside of their own country, namely global customers for health care. A study by McKinsey and the Indian business lobby estimates that foreign customers for medical services could bring to India estimated revenues of $2.2 billion by 2012.

Why go to India for operations? India has large numbers of well-qualified physicians and modern hospitals such as the Apollo hospitals chain. Founded by cardiologist/entrepreneur Prathap Reddy, the Apollo chain has five hospitals in India, all equipped with contemporary medical equipment. Apollo hospitals can do joint replacements, heart by-passes, cataract operations, and elective treatments such as in vitro fertilizations for one-third of the cost of the same procedures in Western Europe.

Right now the target market is overseas Indians who might partake of an elective medical procedure while visiting family, and people from the overburdened health care systems in Britain and Canada, where long waits are required for medical treatments paid for by state insurance and private costs are extremely high. In the long term, however, Dr Reddy hopes to persuade medical insurance companies in the developed nations to seek lower costs by outsourcing to India.

In a developing nation that has only one-fifth as many doctors per capita as the US, not everyone in India sees the allocation of top medical treatments to foreigners as a good thing.

Source: *The Economist*, 2004, "Get well away," www.economist.com, October 7.

Can I Buy it in Germany and Use it in Japan? The Need for Global Standards

Increasingly, especially for technical products, global design standards are common. That is, for example, you can buy a pin drive for your computer in Paris and use it in Nebraska. Why is this so? Probably the most important reason is that, once a product standard is accepted globally or regionally, manufacturers need only produce one or a few versions of a product and still can sell worldwide. Because this is cheaper than making dozens of different versions, one for each country, everyone benefits with a lower-cost product and companies face fewer obstacles to selling outside of their own country. Component makers also become more efficient with fewer product designs. The competitive pressure to save money by developing one product for everyone will likely increase as products are introduced into the world market. A tremendous strategic advantage exists for those companies that can establish their standards as dominant either regionally or worldwide. For example, the company that develops and deploys the next generation standards for video downloads on cell phones will have a dominant position in the market.

Although global standardization has progressed substantially, it is not yet complete. For example, Europe and North America have different formats for TVs and VCRs, and one still needs a tri-band cell phone to access the systems in many countries. And do not forget when you travel that electrical current and plug-ins often differ from country to country. However, at least most laptops are now "smart" enough to adjust automatically for differences in voltage.

Meeting formal standards for consistency in quality is now a requirement to do business in many countries. The International Organization for Standardization (ISO), in Geneva, Switzerland, developed a set of technical standards known as **ISO 9001** for quality in manufacturing and ISO 14000 for environmental management. According to the ISO, "ISO 9000 and ISO 14000 standards are implemented by some 634,000 organizations in 152 countries."[16] Meeting these standards means that a company produces its products exactly as specified technically and environmentally.

ISO compliance is part of product-safety law in many European countries. Many large European multinationals such as Germany's Siemens now require suppliers to be ISO-certified. As a result, in order to do business in the EU, the pressure is increasing for the United States and other countries to adopt ISO quality requirements and standardization.[17]

The above provides an understanding of the many factors making the business environment global. However, as more multinationals are entering the world of international trade and investment, they are being pressured to implement more environmentally friendly practices. Next we discuss issues pertinent to environmental responsibility.

ISO 9001
the current name for the technical and quality standards of the International Organization for Standardization

Environmental Sustainability and Responsibility

Most companies, domestic and international alike, are being pressured to implement sustainable practices. **Sustainable practices** refer to business practices that minimize the impact of business operations on the earth's environment, thereby enhancing the ability of the earth's ecosystems to stay healthy and to continue functioning indefinitely.[18] Consider, for example, that Walmart has been working closely with suppliers to reduce packaging waste, while Nike has been removing toxic chemicals from its shoes. Furthermore, PepsiCo recently gave a sizable grant to the Earth Institute at Columbia University to help the non-profit organization develop local, high-impact activities to help people in less developed countries have access to water.

A recent study of executives by the McKinsey group shows that the environment has become one of the top priorities for most executives around the world. In fact, most executives consider climate change as one of the top issues to consider when crafting their overall strategy. Exhibit 1.11 shows the percentage of executives who felt that climate change is an important consideration when crafting overall corporate strategy.

Why have environmental and sustainable issues become so important? As most societies become concerned about global warming and greenhouse gas emissions, managers are becoming increasingly concerned about the impact of their actions on shareholders, as well as how such actions are portrayed in the media. However, a recent study by PricewaterhouseCoopers also suggests that many executives feel that going green can also present a company with significant market opportunities.[19] Many companies are seeing increased customer demand for their environmentally friendly products. However, beyond economic drivers, many multinationals are engaging in sustainable practices for other reasons. Some multinationals are proactive and are implementing sustain-

sustainable practices
business practices that minimize the impact of business operations on the earth's environment, thereby enhancing the ability of the earth's ecosystems to stay healthy and to continue functioning indefinitely

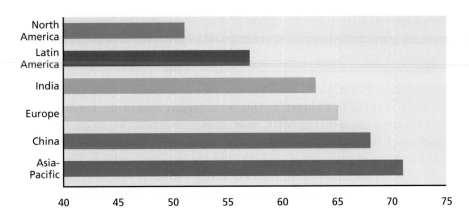

Exhibit 1.11
**Importance of Climate
Change in Corporate
Strategy (% of executives)**

Source: Adapted from *McKinsey
Quarterly*, 2007, December

able practices to avoid future governmental legislation. Other companies are implementing sustainable practices to reduce costs.

This introduction gives you just a brief taste of the exciting world of international business. Before we go on to other chapters, the next section gives you a brief outline of what to expect in this text.

Plan of the Book

The book is divided into five major sections. Each section contains chapters that provide information on essential topics of international business. The intent is to give you an overview of the complex and exciting world of international business.

Part One provides an introduction to the field of international business, including background on globalization and how MNCs compete strategically. It is important that you first understand the strategic choices open to MNCs. With that understanding you will have a better appreciation of the information presented in later chapters that provides essential material for understanding international business.

Part Two of your text is intended to provide you with an understanding of the global context in which MNCs compete. Chapter 1 touched on the issue of how growing international trade and investment, combined with global economic integration, is changing the competitive landscape for MNCs. In this part, two chapters, Chapter 3 on economic integration and Chapter 4 on global trade and investment, will give you more detail on how and why these trends are driving international business throughout the world. Chapters 5 and 6 will show you how money moves across borders to make international transactions possible. Chapter 5 overviews the basics of foreign exchange: that is, what affects the varying values of currency from different countries and how multinational managers manage cross-border money transactions. Chapter 6 discusses how MNCs, in today's global financial systems, get capital from bond and stock markets outside of their own countries.

Part Three looks inside the countries where MNCs do business. Here you will learn how MNCs adjust their strategies and operations to the local context. Chapter 7 looks at how culture influences the conduct of international business. Chapter 8 focuses on social institutions such as the legal and political systems.

This chapter also considers the effects of religion on an MNC's operations and strategies when doing business in countries or areas of the world with particular religious institutions.

Part Four of your text brings you inside the MNC to look at the functional and operational strategies that support the broader multinational strategies that you learned about in Chapter 2. This is the largest part of the book because there are many issues that an MNC must consider in conducting its international businesses. Chapter 9 shows how MNCs actually set up operations in different countries through techniques such as joint ventures or licensing. Chapter 10 looks at how companies adjust their marketing and supply-chain management strategies to support operations in varied countries. The third and fourth chapters in this part, Chapters 11 and 12, show how MNCs develop specialized accounting systems and manage their financial systems to conduct cross-border activities successfully.

Because running an MNC is an organizational challenge, Chapter 13 is devoted to organizational structures for international operations. Similarly, because of the complexities of dealing with managers and workers located anywhere in the world, Chapter 14 is also dedicated to the international human resource management. Part Four concludes with Chapter 15 on e-commerce for the MNC. This chapter focuses on the unique challenges of running an international operation via the Internet.

Part Five, the final part of your text, contains only one chapter, "Managing Ethical and Social Responsibility in an MNC." The challenges of managing ethical issues in varied cultural and institutional contexts cannot be underestimated. While you will not learn how to be ethical by reading this chapter, you will be introduced to the basics of ethical reasoning and some of the issues you need to consider when faced with ethically challenging decisions.

International Business: A Strategic Approach

This book takes a strategic approach to international business. Why? Because strategy focuses on how to compete successfully in the global economy.

Strategy is defined here as the activities that managers use to outcompete other companies by increasing and then sustaining superior organizational performance. Strategy formulation is the process managers use to craft a strategy. Strategy implementation includes all the activities that managers and an organization must perform to achieve strategic objectives.

From the perspective of the MNC and its managers, strategies must include maneuvers and tactics that deal with operating and competing in more than one country, each with its unique culture and political, legal, religious, and financial systems. In turn, more complex strategies require that multinational strategy implementation deal with added challenges, including the need to understand different economic, cultural, legal, financial and ethical systems. Thus, not only do you need to understand the complex systems in which you conduct international business but also, as potential international managers, you must develop the management systems to carry out strategies that reach beyond domestic boundaries.

CHAPTER REVIEW

This chapter has provided you with key background information that supports the study of international management. The chapter defined international management and the MNC. Because we exist in a globalizing world, considerable attention has been devoted to the forces that drive globalization. These are key environmental issues that affect every MNC and its managers. World trade and investments are growing rapidly but not always consistently, making all economies more linked and creating both opportunities and threats for both domestic and multinational companies. New competitors, strong and motivated, are coming from low-cost countries in Asia, the Americas, and Eastern Europe. Customers, products, and standards are becoming more global. The increasing sophistication and lower cost of information technology fuel the development of global companies that can more easily manage worldwide operation.

Multinational managers of the next generation will need skills not always considered necessary for domestic-only managers. Perhaps the most encompassing characteristic is the global mindset. Managers with a global mindset understand the rapidly changing business and economic environment. They can see the world as an integrated market, yet appreciate and understand the wide array of differences in the world cultures and social institutions.

After reading this text, you should have the foundation for understanding the latest challenges and practices of international business. However, the world is dynamic and your learning will never be complete, as the challenges of international business will continue to the distant future.

 DISCUSSION QUESTIONS

1. Discuss how any company can become an MNC. What are some of the options available to companies that allow them to use international markets and locations competitively?
2. Discuss some reasons why reductions in world trade barriers are driving the world toward a global economy.
3. Consider how wars, terrorist acts, SARS, etc., might alter the progression of globalization. What should a multinational manager do to deal with these situations?
4. Discuss the differences between foreign trade and foreign direct investment.
5. Identify some of the competitive threats of RDEs.
6. Discuss the ethics of outsourcing to other countries where the wages are less than one-quarter of the home country.
7. Discuss some of the advantages and disadvantages of setting up production in LCCs. Consider the benefits of market growth and the risk of an example venture.
8. Look at the information on the RDEs discussed in the text. Where do you think the next generation of world-class competitors will come from? Why?

INTERNATIONAL BUSINESS SKILL BUILDER

Pros and Cons of Globalization

Step 1: Do an Internet search on the pros and cons of globalization. You will find throusands of sites. Start your search in the year 2000 and end in the present. See if you observe any trends in different pros or cons. Do people from different countries or regions have differ perceptions of globalization? Do people from different groups (age, gender, job type, race, etc.) view globalization differently?

Step 2: Pair up with a fellow student. One student should take the pro side and the other the con side. Discuss and argue the merits of your position. Alternatively, discuss globalization from the perspective of different groups.

Step 3: Share your positions with your class.

CHAPTER INTERNET ACTIVITY

As you will see, throughout this text there are Internet Activities at the end of each chapter. These activities are designed to expand on important information as well as to enhance your knowledge and understanding of the management resources on the Web. Your instructor may assign these activities or you may choose to complete them on your own. However, while every effort has been made to ensure that the sites you are directed to are stable and live, the Internet is a rapidly changing environment in which it is hard to always keep pace.

For the Internet Activity for this chapter, simply familiarize yourself with the Internet sites identified in this chapter. Many contain valuable up-to-date information on the changing nature of international business and multinational management. Log onto the Web and spend 30–60 minutes searching for multinational management information or resources. What did you find? Was it difficult to locate the information? Compile a list of resources for future use in this class or others.

KEY CONCEPTS

developed economies

developing economies

European Union (EU)

foreign direct investment (FDI)

General Agreement on Tariffs and
    Trade (GATT)

global customers

global product

globalization

international business

ISO 9001

least developed countries (LDCs)

low-cost countries (LCCs)

multinational company (MNC)

multinational management

North American Free Trade
    Agreement (NAFTA)

offshoring

outsourcing

rapidly developing economies
    (RDEs)

regional trade agreements

sustainable practices

transition economies

Triad

World Trade Organization (WTO)

BUSINESS > INTERNATIONAL

McDONALD'S SELLS
HAMBURGERS IN INDIA

CASE 1

page 1

In 1954, a milkshake-mixer salesman named Ray Kroc traveled to San Bernardino, California, to see why one restaurant had ordered so many of his Multimixers. The McDonald brothers had invented a new concept in the restaurant business and Kroc wanted to see for himself why the business was so popular. Dick and Mac McDonald had pioneered fast food based on high volume, low prices, a limited menu, and quick service. The restaurant was a success, and Ray Kroc wanted it. He negotiated an agreement with the McDonald brothers in which he would become the exclusive franchiser of the McDonald name.

In 1955, the first McDonald's franchise opened in Des Plaines, Illinois. The McDonald's empire would be based on four core values, providing customers with *quality*, *service*, *cleanliness*, and *value* (QSCV). Kroc believed that consistency in these core values would allow McDonald's to build a strong brand image throughout the United States. He was right. The concept was a success, and by 1963 McDonald's was selling one million hamburgers a day.

. . .

The first international McDonald's opened in Canada in 1967. McDonald's continued its international expansion into Japan, Germany, Australia, France, and England in the 1970s. Additional outlets were established in Latin America, the Middle East, Central and Eastern Europe, Russia, and China. The motive for McDonald's international expansion was the realization that most potential sales existed outside the United States. As Kroc had said in 1954, when he witnessed the McDonald brothers' original restaurant concept, "This idea can sell anywhere." Based on the need for additional sales growth and the belief that the concept could be exported, McDonald's embarked on an aggressive international expansion effort beginning in the 1970s. Today, McDonald's has restaurants in over 100 countries and derives approximately 60 percent of its profits from sales overseas. On average, the company opens a new restaurant somewhere in the world every five hours, and McDonald's can be found on every continent except Antarctica.

Prior to 1996, McDonald's did not have a restaurant anywhere on the Indian subcontinent. With a population of over one billion, India is viewed by many as a market with enormous potential. India's population is second only to that of China and, with differing birth rates, India will become the most populated country in the world by 2020, according to some estimates.

India represented a big challenge to McDonald's because most Indians could not eat the main menu item: the beef hamburger. Over 80 percent of the Indian population is Hindu and this religion prohibits the consumption of cow products. Also, approximately 40 percent of Indians are strict vegetarians and eat no meat of any kind. A significant percentage of the Indian population is Muslim, which also prohibits the consumption of pork products.

India is a federal republic which gained its independence from Great Britain in 1947. After many years of British rule, Mahatma Gandhi led a mass movement for independence. Since that time, India has been, as its constitution states, a "sovereign, socialist, secular, democratic republic." The economic self-reliance or *swadeshi* begun under Gandhi influenced public policy in India for over 40 years. India finally began to liberalize economic policy after experiencing a severe foreign currency crisis. In 1991, major changes occurred that made foreign investment easier, including reduced tariffs, removed non-tariff barriers to trade, and loosened foreign investment restrictions and currency controls.

India still remains a poor country and a difficult market for Western companies. Per capita GDP is $420 and at least 350 million Indians live on less than a dollar a day. The government recognizes 18 languages, with Hindi being the most widely spoken. English is also spoken, especially in urban areas and among the better-educated component of the population. Violent religious clashes occur between Hindus and Christians and between Hindus and Muslims, and there is a current movement to establish an all-Hindu India. The religious and social class tolerances advocated by Gandhi do not seem to be as well accepted by many in India today. India is a country divided by languages, religion, and caste.

In 1996, McDonald's opened its first restaurant in India. The first McDonald's in India was located in Delhi and was the only McDonald's outlet worldwide not to offer beef on its menu. Because of dietary restrictions imposed by religion,

. . .

McDonald's had to be creative in its product offerings. Without the possibility of serving beef or pork, McDonald's offered the lamb patty and a veggie burger. The Big Mac was named the Maharaja Mac and substituted ground lamb for beef. After opening its second restaurant in India, this one in Mumbai (Bombay), McDonald's had invested $14 million, yet the company was not completely sure of the potential of the Indian market. Although business was brisk at both locations, some concerns were raised.

Some consumers complained about the bland taste of the food. Consumers were accustomed to spicy traditional Indian food, and McDonald's meals seemed too plain for some. There was also a concern about the political stability of the country and long-term acceptance of McDonald's in India. The Indian government did not support the entry of McDonald's into the country and some Indians protested the arrival of the American multinational. Previous American franchises have been the target of vandalism in India in the past. KFC, Domino's Pizza, and Pizza Hut all have several locations in India, and some of the restaurants have experienced difficulties with political mobs. McDonald's is perhaps in an even more vulnerable position because its primary product worldwide (beef) is viewed by many Hindus as not appropriate for consumption. As one protestor remarked, "They are the chief killers of the cow." Other protestors see McDonald's as a symbol of the exploitation of the world's poor by rich American multinationals. In 2005, McDonald's settled a $10 million lawsuit brought by vegetarians in the United States who had charged McDonald's with misleading advertising. McDonald's had been using a beef flavoring for its French fries without telling consumers. The news of this culinary process caused protest in India and some store vandalism; however, McDonald's had been careful not to use the beef flavoring in India.

Faced with the difficulties of product acceptance, low purchasing power among consumers, and the ever-present potential of political conflict, McDonald's must decide if further expansion in India is a good investment.

CASE DISCUSSION POINTS

1. In your opinion, is India a good market for McDonald's? Explain.
2. Has McDonald's responded to the advice often given transnational companies to "think globally and act locally"?
3. Do you think McDonald's will be a success in India? Explain.

Sources: McDonald's corporate website, www.mcdonalds.com; S. Mohanty, 1996, "India's Maharaja Mac has no beef," *Reuters Business Report*, October 11; S. Mohanty, 1996, "Where's the beef? India's McDonald's eschews chuck," Reuters, October 11; *Dallas Morning News*, 1996, "McDonald's goes to India without beef," October 12; K. Cooper, 1996, "Where's the beef? McDonald's menu in India culturally correct, but company's presence cooks up controversy," *Dallas Morning News*, November 10; *Philadelphia Inquirer*, 1998, "Big in Bombay: The Maharaja Mac is one hot item," April 22; US Department of State, 2000, "Background notes: India," March; S. Dutta, 2000, "Domino theory," *Business India*, May 1; L. Kadaba and D. Gardner, 2000, "India's elusive reforms," *Financial Times*, August 4; C. Raghatta, 2005, "McDonald's pays up Hindu veggie group in US," *New Times of India*, July 12.

Case prepared by Charles A. Rarick

2 Strategy and the MNC

After reading this chapter you should be able to:

- Understand the benefits MNCs can achieve using global integration or local adaptation.

- Understand the conflicting pressures of the global–local dilemma faced by international managers in MNCs.

- Know the content of the basic multinational strategies: transnational, international, multidomestic, and regional.

- Choose a multinational strategy by using the diagnostic questions that help MNCs to cope with the global–local dilemma.

The Preview IB Strategic Insight describes a situation showing how even very successful companies such as Starbucks must carefully choose the best strategies to take their products or services international. There are many options for an MNC to take advantage of international opportunities for growth and profits. In this chapter you will find a review of the essential strategies that MNCs use to succeed in this endeavor.

This chapter contains two major sections. In the first section, you are introduced to general strategies regarding international operations. In the second section, you are introduced to some of the questions international managers must answer to choose their best multinational strategies. After reading this chapter you should understand how the choice of a multinational strategy depends on differences in global markets, products, competition, and risks. You should also understand that international management is more complex and challenging than domestic-only management.

Starbucks' International Challenge

It's hard to walk a couple of city blocks in any US city without encountering the green-and-white Starbucks logo. Starbucks is the leading seller of specialty coffee in the world, with close to 9,000 retail stores in 35 countries. After its phenomenal growth in the US, Starbucks went international in 1996, first with two stores in Japan and another 125 in Canada. By 2005, it had nearly 2,500 stores outside the US. However, international sales represent less than 6 percent of Starbucks' gross revenue. International operations did not turn profitable until 2004, and most of that came from Japan.

Can Starbucks successfully sell the "Starbucks Experience" worldwide? Coffee is pretty much a global product, invented by Arabs, brewed with beans discovered by Africans, and consumed everywhere. Even the "Starbucks Experience" was created by now Chairman Howard Schultz's Americanization of his experience in an Italian café (just add music, wi-fi, and host of creative drink names). Such a history would suggest that you could export the Starbucks business model anywhere. The company's goal is at least 15,000 stores outside the US.

However, as Starbucks' bottom line suggests, coffee-drinking culture varies widely and local regulations can be a challenge. "Some countries present more challenges than others," notes Herman Uscategui, who has the responsibility of developing Starbucks' international stores. In Spain, for example, Starbucks prints menus in Catalan and Spanish in response to linguistic and regional sensitivities. Italy has a long traditional of coffee drinking but also has strict regulations regarding food importers. Some analysts also question whether Starbucks can charge twice the local price, a dilemma for Starbucks all over Europe. Capturing the basic issue, Bernard Quartier, an official in the French café owners' industry association, notes, "Coffee and muffins are OK, but we French have such good pastries."

Sources: Adapted from *Business Week*, 2005, "Will Europe warm to Starbucks?" January 24; Knight Ridder/Tribune Business News, 2004, "Starbucks offers glimpse of global strategy," June 12; Business Wire, 2004, "Starbucks lays out global strategy and expanded market opportunity," October 14; Business Wire, 2004, "Starbucks outlines international growth strategy; focus on retail expansion and profitability," October 14; Starbucks, "Company fact sheet," www.starbucks.com.

Strategic Choices for MNCs

Companies engaged in international business, like all businesses, face pressures to respond to the unique needs of their customers. However, when your customers come from different countries and regions of the world, they often have different needs and desires for products and services. When a company decides to focus on meeting customer needs based on national and regional differences, it adopts a **local responsiveness strategy**. Alternatively, when a company decides to de-emphasize local differences and locate its operations anywhere in the world where it is advantageous, it adopts what is know as a **global integration strategy**.

Companies that adopt a local responsiveness strategy stress customizing their organizations and products to accommodate country or regional differences. They focus on satisfying local customer needs by tailoring products or services to meet those needs. Forces that favor a local responsiveness strategy come primarily from cultural differences in consumer tastes and variations in customer needs, as well as differences driven by social institutions such as religion and the political system. For example, government regulations can require a company to share ownership with a local company. Some governments also require companies to produce their products in the countries in which they sell.[1]

MNCs that lean toward a global integration strategy reduce their costs by using standardized products, promotional strategies, and distribution channels in every country. In addition, such globally oriented multinationals seek sources of lower costs or higher quality by locating their operations anywhere in the world. For example, in such companies, headquarters, R&D, production, or distribution centers may be located where they provide the best value added with quality or lower cost.[2] With products like athletic shoes, for example, companies such as Nike and Reebok use low-cost Asian manufacturing sites for all of their manufacturing while keeping most research and design at their headquarters.

However, neither responding to local customer needs nor selling the same product worldwide is a guarantee of success. For example, customers may be willing to pay a higher price for products or services that are tailored to their needs. Alternatively, if customers see no value in unique products or services, they will be more attracted to a product or service that is sourced in low-cost countries and can be priced for less. Multinational firms must choose carefully for each product or business how globally or locally they orient their strategies. The problem of which strategic orientation to choose is called **global–local dilemma**. Later in the chapter you will see some of the questions that managers must answer before selecting an appropriate multinational strategy. Before that, however, consider the IB Strategic Insight opposite, which stories how Sweden's Ikea and Vodafone, the world's largest cell-phone operator, struggle to get the right balance.

The IB Strategic Insight shows two firms struggling to perfect their multinational strategies. For most firms, this is an ongoing process that requires continuous refinements and adjustments to changing competitive conditions. Before we consider more specific applications of the basic multinational strategies, one needs a basic understanding of the value chain. Much of multinational strategy concerns decisions regarding what activities such as production or research and development, for example, should be located in different parts of

local responsiveness strategy
responding to differences in the markets in all the countries in which a company operates

global integration strategy
conducting business similarly throughout the world, and locating company units wherever there is high quality and low cost

global–local dilemma
choice between a local responsiveness or global approach to a multinational's strategies

Vodafone and Ikea Try to Get the Global Thing Right

Ikea, a low-cost furniture company, entered China in the late 1990s with plans to have ten stores by 2010. Ulf Smedberg, director of marketing of Ikea China, noted, "When Ikea first entered China, the store was considered too expensive for its target consumers—young, professional couples" who earn about $400/month. Ikea adapted and cut its prices by 10 percent. Sales increased between 35 percent and 50 percent a year. Ikea sells its 10,000 products in all countries but it changes store layouts to match local sensibilities. In China, it focuses on living rooms since the Chinese consumer gives that room more priority, and even has the balconies typical of Chinese apartments in the stores. Although popular in other parts of the world, the Do-It-Yourself assembly doesn't work in China. So Ikea provides more assembly services. The future, according to Smedberg, is more local sourcing.

When Vodafone acquired J-Phone, a trendy Japanese cell-phone company with a cutting-edge image and already standing at #3 in the Japanese market, the outlook was bright. Two years later Vodafone was struggling. Local companies, #1 DoCoMo and #2 KDDI Corp, were pulling away. Why? Vodafone failed to understand the Japanese market and to give the Japanese cell-phone users what they wanted, mostly fancy features and many choices. DoCoMo, for example, has 38 models while Vodafone has only 15. Instead, Vodafone focused on selling its global brands, good phones but seen as dull and uninteresting—not the priciest, newest, and gadget-filled phones coveted by the Japanese youth, the major cell-phone users.

Sources: Based on Paula M. Miller, 2004, "Ikea with Chinese characteristics," *China Business Review*, July/August, 31(4), pp. 36–8; Ginny Parker, 2004, "Going global can hit snags, Vodafone finds," *Wall Street Journal*, June 16, p. B1.

the world. Such activities are part of a firm's value chain, and the next section gives a basic explanation of this concept.

Competitive Advantage and the Value Chain

A firm can gain a competitive advantage over other firms by finding sources of lower cost or added value in any of its activities. This means that companies can make more money than competitors can by doing things more cheaply or by delivering better value to customers for which they can charge a higher price. Such activities range from getting necessary raw materials, through production, to sales, and to eventual follow-up with after-sales service. For example, a company may find cost savings sourcing cheaper raw materials or cheaper labor in other countries. Taking advantage of the low-cost clothing production in India and the reduction of import quotas into the US and the EU, Sears and the British department store Marks & Spencer are investing in Indian factories to produce their garments. Similarly, an MNC such as Motorola adds value to its products by using R&D produced by its subsidiary located in China, where engineering talent is cheap and of high quality. Many multinational software-design companies, for example, take advantage of the very high number of quality engineers in India and Singapore.

One convenient way of thinking about such activities is called the **value chain.** Harvard University's Michael Porter, a leading scholar and consultant

value chain
a way of identifying all the areas where a firm can create value for customers

in strategic management, uses the term "value chain" to represent all the activities that a firm uses "to design, produce, market, deliver, and support its product."[3] The value chain identifies areas where a firm can create value for customers. Better designs, more efficient production, and better service all represent value added in the value chain. Ultimately, the value a company produces represents what customers will pay for a product or service. Exhibit 2.1 shows a picture of the value chain. Later you will see that the value chain provides a useful way of thinking about how MNCs operate.

Porter divides the value chain into primary and support activities. These activities represent (1) the processes of creating goods or services, and (2) the organizational mechanisms necessary to support the creative activities. *Primary activities* involve the physical actions of creating (or serving), selling, and after-sales service of products. Early activities in the value chain, such as R&D and managing the supply chain, are called *upstream*. Later value-chain activities, such as sales and dealing with distribution channels, represent *downstream* activities. *Support activities* include systems for human resources management (e.g. recruitment and selection procedures), information technology, organizational design and control (e.g. structural form and accounting procedures), and a firm's basic technology. In Chapter 1 we saw how many companies are outsourcing business process support activities such as accounting and information technology activities to low-cost countries such as India. In the IB Strategic Insight opposite, you can see how Dell uses its value chain to produce competitively priced PCs.

The value chain identifies the areas in the input, throughput, output, and support processes where companies like Dell try to achieve higher value or lower costs for their products or services than do rivals. MNCs have the potential to gain advantages over rivals by basing value activities in many countries. How they configure these activities is really the basis of multinational strategy.

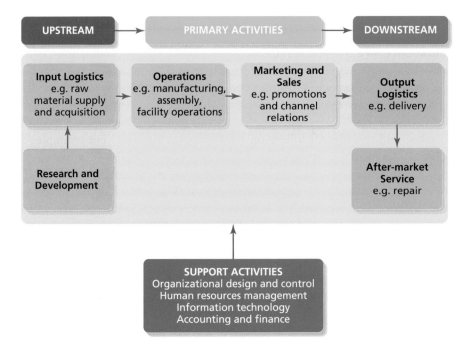

Exhibit 2.1

The Value Chain

Source: Adapted from Michael E. Porter, 1985, *Competitive Advantage*, New York: The Free Press, pp. 35, 37.

How Dell Rules Using its Value Chain

IB STRATEGIC INSIGHT

Unlike competitors Gateway and Apple, Dell has not offshored its computer manufacturing to cheaper plants in Asia. It insists on controlling manufacturing and maintains the only major computer assembly plants remaining in the US. Don't be fooled. Dell's plants are extremely efficient, producing 700 PCs an hour with the expectation that productivity will increase by 30 percent each year. However, the core of Dell's competitive advantage on price is in its ultra-efficient supply-chain management.

Kevin Rollins, who succeeded founder Michael Dell as CEO, considers inventory a four-letter word. Like many companies, Dell once carried 25 days of parts inventory stored in a network of warehouses. Now it has no warehouses and manages to assemble 80,000 computers a day with only two hours of inventory on hand. According to Rollins, "Computer components depreciate anywhere from a half to a full point a week. Cutting inventory is not just a nice thing to do. It's a financial imperative."

How can Dell manage its upstream value chain so well? It has a vast global supply chain that runs on speed. When Dell gets an order over the Internet or phone, signals go to suppliers with warehouses near the plant to deliver. They have exactly 90 minutes to get their products to Dell's assembly line—they can't be early or late. There are 110 cargo bays around the factory and Dell doesn't take ownership until its forklift unloads the supplies.

Source: Adapted from *FastCompany*, 2004, "Living in Dell time," November 9, pp. 88, 86–90.

With a basic knowledge of the value chain you will now see how the global integration and local responsiveness strategies can be refined further.

Exhibit 2.2 shows a graphical presentation of the basic orientations of the global integration and local responsiveness strategies.

The Global Integration Strategy Box

- Similar Products/ Services Worldwide
- Global Sourcing of Supplies based on Low Cost for ≥ Quality
- Global Locations of Activities based on Low Cost/Quality
- Similar Marketing Worldwide

The Local Responsiveness Strategy

- Country Focus
- Regional Focus

Exhibit 2.2
Multinational Strategy Orientations

Global Integration: Where Can We Do Things Best or Cheapest?

We can think of the global integration strategy as a box representing a company's value-chain activities. In the most extreme global integration strategy, all activities from all corners of the box are spread around the globe based on strategic advantages.

The Transnational Strategy

transnational strategy
two goals get top priority: seeking location advantages and gaining economic efficiencies from operating worldwide

location advantages
dispersing value-chain activities anywhere in the world where the company can do them best or cheapest

global platform
country location where a firm can best perform some, but not necessarily all, of its value-chain activities

national advantage
that arising from cost, quality, or resource advantages associated with a particular nation

The more inclusive version of global integration is known as the **transnational strategy**. Its top priorities are seeking location advantages and gaining economic efficiencies from operating worldwide.[4] **Location advantages** mean that the transnational company disperses or locates its value-chain activities (e.g. manufacturing, R&D, and sales) anywhere in the world where the company can "do it best or cheapest" as the situation requires. For example, Intel has manufacturing and testing facilities located in five countries outside of the US, its headquarters. These production facilities offer cheaper but also high-quality labor. Michael Porter argues that, for global competition, firms must look at countries not only as potential markets but also as "global platforms."[5] A **global platform** is a country location where a firm can outperform competitors in some, but not necessarily all, of its value-chain activities. Look at the IB Small Business Insight below to see an innovative use of location advantages by two entrepreneurs.

Like companies, nations have advantages in costs, quality, or other resources available to local and MNCs. Economists call this absolute advantage. Later, in Chapter 4, you will learn more about how the advantages associated with a particular nation influence trade patterns. **National advantage** is different from *competitive* advantage, which refers to the advantages of individual firms over other firms. *Absolute* advantage refers to advantages of *nations over other nations*. For example, countries with cheaper and better-educated labor have absolute advantages over other nations. Germany, for example, is generally considered to have an excellent educational system and thus has an advantage over other nations in the availability of a technical workforce. National advantage is important to local organizations because they can use their nation's advantages to gain competitive advantages over rivals from other nations. Germany is known for producing high-quality technical products such as luxury automobiles (BMW) and appliances (Bosch dishwashing machines).

Traditionally, many international business experts viewed national advantage as something from which only the indigenous or local organizations could benefit in world competition. Many Japanese and Korean organizations, for example, built their early competitive advantages on the cheap, high-quality, and motivated labor available in their countries. However, the transnational strategy has made this view out of date. National advantages no longer give competitive advantages to local companies only. That is, in a globalizing world, any resources available in different nations such as educated workers or raw materials provide the transnational firm with the global platforms to boost location-based competitive advantages in costs and quality. The transnational views *any country* as a global platform where it can perform *any value-chain activity*. Thus, the absolute advantage of a nation is no longer just for locals.

Location Advantages and a Mobile Platform

SeaCode's innovative offshoring solution: buy a cruise ship and anchor it in international waters outside the US border

Offshoring can be literal. To take advantage of the shifting of software engineering tasks to low-cost countries such as China and India, two entrepreneurs, David Cook and Roger Green from San Diego, have come up with an innovative solution. Buy a cruise ship and anchor it in international waters outside the US border. Their company is called SeaCode.

They propose to hire software engineers from India and Russia and have them work aboard ship in four-months-on and two-months-off work cycles. Working in two shifts, Cook and Green say they can charge US firms the rates that they pay for offshoring to India. They also think it's a better deal for the programmers: $1,800/month versus the typical $500 paid in India. Off duty, the programmers can return to their private cabins in the 600-cabin ship, use the ship's amenities, or take the water taxi to shore.

One catch is that the workers will have to be classified as "seamen" to fall under international maritime law and avoid immigration visas and restrictions when entering Los Angeles en route to picking up their water taxi to work. Under maritime law, a seaman is defined broadly as anyone who works on a ship, so this may just work. Cook is a former supertanker captain and Green a former chief information officer, so they may just have the right capabilities to succeed.

Source: Adapted from David Whelan, 2005, "C++ faring lads," *Forbes*, May 9.

With increasingly free and open borders, any firm, regardless of the nationality of ownership, can turn any national advantage into a competitive advantage for the whole company—if the firm has the flexibility and willingness to locate anywhere.

Examples of such transnational strategic activities include:

- Locate upstream supply units near cheap sources of high-quality raw material—approximately 18 multinational oil companies are in Nigeria.
- Locate research and development centers near centers of research and innovation—in 2005 Motorola opened its new R&D center in Bangalore, a growing center of IT development in India.
- Locate manufacturing subunits near sources of high-quality or low-cost labor—Intel has five sites where labor is relatively cheap and well educated.
- Share discoveries and innovations made in any unit regardless of location with operations in other parts of the world—Ford's Taiwan-based design center, named Ford Lio, is working on the next-generation Tierra medium-sized sedan, which shares a chassis platform with the Mazda 323, for the Asia-Pacific market.
- Locate supporting value-chain activities such as accounting in low-cost

countries—GE Capital uses Indian employees to do support activities such as checking eligibility of payments on health plans.
- Operate close to key customers—BWM produces a sport utility vehicle in the US, which is the major market for this type of vehicle.
- Offshore aftermarket support such as call centers to low-cost countries—if you call American Express, Sprint, Citibank, or IBM it is likely your call will be answered in India.

Location advantages provide the transnational company with cost or quality gains for different value-chain activities. To reduce costs even further, transnational strategists strive for uniform marketing and promotional activities throughout the world; these companies use the same brand names, advertisements, and promotional brochures wherever they sell their products or services. The soft-drink companies, such as Coca-Cola, have been among the most successful in taking their brands worldwide. When a company can do things similarly throughout the world, it can take advantage of economies of scale. Thus, for example, it is most efficient to have one package of the same color and size produced worldwide in centralized production facilities.

Of course, it does not always make good business sense to move value-chain activities to other countries even if there are apparent savings in costs or other possible benefits. For example, because wages tend to rise when multinationals enter a country, low-cost local labor is often a temporary advantage. Perhaps more important is that when subunits are spread all over the world the coordination and control of the international operations becomes a significant challenge for international managers. As we saw in the IB Strategic Insight above, Dell prefers to do final assembly of its computers in the US (unlike most of its competitors, despite of higher labor costs) because managers believe that control is better.

What happens if the advantages of a global platform location are based in part in opportunities that may endanger the people in a country of operation? The IB Ethical Challenge opposite confronts this issue for oil companies operating in Nigeria.

International Strategy

international strategies
selling global products and using similar marketing techniques worldwide

The international strategy is a partial global integration strategy. That is, companies pursuing **international strategies**, such as Toys "R" Us, Boeing, Apple, and IBM, take a middle ground regarding the global–local dilemma. Like the transnational strategist, the international strategist prefers, to the degree possible, to use global products and similar marketing techniques everywhere. To the degree that local customs, culture, and laws allow, they limit adaptations to minor adjustments in product offerings and marketing strategies. However, international-strategist MNCs differ from transnational companies in that they keep as many value-chain activities as possible located at home. In particular, the international strategist concentrates its R&D and manufacturing units at home to gain economies of scale and quality than are more difficult to achieve with the dispersed activities of the transnational. For example, Boeing keeps most of its R&D and production in the United States while selling its planes worldwide with a similar marketing approach focusing on price and technology. However, for its most recent plane, the Dreamliner, Boeing become a little more

Getting Oil Cheaply but with Increased Environmental Controls: A Report from the US Government

ETHICAL CHALLENGE

Below is an excerpt from a US government report on oil companies and sustainability practices in Nigeria.

The perceived indifference of both the Nigerian federal government and the oil companies to the environment in the Niger Delta has been exacerbated by Nigeria's lack of coherent pollution control policy. Until recently, there was little incentive for power plants to implement pollution abatement strategies or for oil companies to undertake environmental remediation efforts, as the Nigerian federal government was unwilling or unable to enforce environmental laws. However, the Nigerian federal government has indicated that it is no longer willing to tolerate oil companies absolving themselves of their responsibility to reduce pollution. Chief Ime Titus Okopido, the Minister of State in the Federal Ministry of Environment, noted that future drilling rights will be "closely determined by" companies' environmental compliance, in addition to their submission of an environmental impact assessment for the proposed site.

The Nigerian government has ordered oil companies operating in the country to comply with the Environmental Guidelines and Standards for the Oil Industry, published by the Department of Petroleum Resources (DPR), the monitoring arm of the Nigeria National Petroleum Corporation (NNPC), or risk paying a fine. The 300-page guidelines provide rules to reduce pollution and procedures for environmental monitoring. The DPR also has been tasked with conducting regular health, safety, and environment audits of the oil companies.

The Nigerian government has taken action to show it is serious about enforcing environmental regulations. Recently, the Nigerian subsidiary of Shell was ordered to pay $1.5 billion to the Ijaw tribe for the company's actions in the state of Bayelsa over a 50-year period. A government committee that investigated Shell ruled that the company was responsible for a number of oil spills and environmental incidents, including an epidemic in which 1,400 people were killed that was blamed on a Shell oil spill. The government committee blamed the prevalence of cancer in the region on exposure to the company's oil spills, noting that Shell continually refused to pay compensation for these spills, and where it had, the payment was inadequate.

Oil companies such as Shell have profited substantially by operations in developing countries. Lax environmental regulations often provide an opportunity to lower costs. Are these companies responsible for the negative consequences of their actions, even if they are consistent with the laws in operation at this time?

Source: US Government, 2003, "Country analysis briefs: Nigeria: environmental issues," eia.doe.gov

transnational, outsourcing production and design of some components to Japan and other countries but leaving final assembly in the US. Unfortunately for Boeing, coordination problems resulted in costly delays to the final delivery of the plane.

[When necessary for economic or political reasons, companies with international strategies frequently do set up sales and production units in major countries of operation.]However, home-country headquarters retains control of local strategies, marketing, R&D, finances, and production. Local facilities become only "mini-replicas" of production and sales facilities at home.[6] ⌐Toyota

The Local Responsiveness Strategy: How Far to Go?

The local responsiveness strategy is in many respects a form of differentiation strategy. That is, a company attempts to differentiate itself from competitors by giving its products or services an extra value that attracts customers by closely satisfying their cultural needs and expectations. For example, advertisements, packaging, sales outlets, and pricing are adapted to local practices, with the hope that customers will find this more attractive than something produced similarly for the whole world. Even if a product might seem similar in different countries, there are often local adaptations required to serve local needs. For example, Kentucky Fried Chicken sells tempura crispy strips in Japan and potato-and-onion croquettes in Holland, and its Dutch chicken produce becomes spicier as one goes further inland from the seacoast cities.[7]

As with most uses of a differentiation strategy, it usually costs more for MNCs to produce and sell unique or special products for different countries throughout the world. There are extra costs to adapt each product to local requirements, such as different package sizes and colors. Thus, to succeed, a local responsiveness strategy usually requires charging higher prices to recoup the costs of tailoring a product for local needs. Customers, like the Japanese cell-phone users discussed in the IB Strategic Insight on Vodafone, will pay this higher price if they perceive an extra value in having a company's products adapted to their tastes, distribution systems, and industry structures.

A local responsive strategy is not limited to large multinationals that can afford to set up overseas subsidiaries. Even a small firm that only exports its products may use a local responsive strategy by extensively adapting its product line to different countries and cultures. However, for larger organizations with production and sales units in many countries, using a local responsive strategy often means treating foreign subsidiaries as independent businesses. Headquarters focuses on the bottom line, viewing each country as a profit center. Each country's subsidiary is free to manage its own operations following local customs, but it must generate a profit to get resources from headquarters. Besides having its own local production facilities, marketing strategy, sales staff, and distribution system, the subsidiary of the local responsive company often uses local sources of raw materials and employs mostly local people.

Multidomestic and Regional Strategies

multidomestic strategy emphasizing local responsiveness issues at the country level

regional strategy managing raw-material sourcing, production, marketing, and support activities within a particular region

One important problem for a locally responsive strategist is the question of how fine-grained one should focus. The extreme approach is called the **multidomestic strategy**, which means each country where you do business is treated differently. A similar but more broadly targeted approach is called the **regional strategy**. This strategy attempts to gain some of the economic efficiency and location advantages of the more global strategies combined with some of the local-adaptation advantages of the multidomestic strategy. Rather than having worldwide products and a worldwide value chain, the regional strategist manages raw-material sourcing, production, marketing, and some support activities within a particular region. For example, a regional strategist might have one set of products for North America and another for Mexico and South America. Not only does this allow some cost savings similar to those of the transnational and international strategists, but it also gives the firm flexibility for regional responsiveness. Managers have the opportunity to deal regionally with regional problems, such as competitive position, product mix, promotional strategy, and sources of capital.[8]

Regional trading blocs such as the EU and NAFTA have led to more uniformity of customer needs and expectations within member nations. Trading blocs also reduce differences in government- and industry-required specifications for products. As a result, within the trading bloc, companies can use regional products and regional location advantages for all value-chain activities. The rise of trading blocs has forced some former multidomestic strategists, especially in Europe and the US, to adopt regional strategies. For example, Procter & Gamble and DuPont have combined their subunits in Mexico, the US, and Canada into one regional organization. With this strategy, these companies gain some of the advantages of local adaptation and some of the advantages of transnationalization.

Romania

COUNTRY FOCUS

A marketplace of 22 million, a well-educated workforce, and an expanding economy with access to the Black Sea and Asia has made Romania an attractive location for investment by MNCs. As in most East European countries, the wages in Romania are quite low in comparison to Western Europe. As such, countries like Romania are also often considered as low-cost production platforms for MNCs. However, as with other former communist countries, some of the products produced during the communist years can retain a negative image. Such is or at least was the case for Dacia, a company born during the communist era but with help from Renault. In Romania, the Dacia always had a positive image. However, in the rest of Eastern Europe people remember the brand from communist times, but with a tremble.

Dacia's no-frills inexpensive cars have proved a success in Western markets.

Once Renault owned Dacia (bought in 2004) its plan was to build a cheap car for local use in Eastern Europe and perhaps sell to emerging markets—at best a domestic or regional strategy. The new model was called the Logan, although Romanian workers at the Dacia factory built it. Gérard Detourbet, the Renault CEO, notes that building a no-frills inexpensive car "would not make sense paying French or Spanish wages."

Then something interesting happened. Renault discovered that the car was being sold in France as an unofficial import. It met EU standards, so some entrepreneurs decided to see if the car would sell in the West as well. The result: Renault started selling the Logan in France. With over 80,000 in sales last year, it is a success. Although in North Africa and the EU the Logan is still named as a Dacia brand, it is sold through Renault dealers. With a price of €7,600 for the basic model, Mr Detourbet notes that, even though most French buyers know that it is made in Romania, "they don't really think it's a Dacia." Now it is a stable product of Renault in France and hence the new French word, *delocalization.*

There are benefits to the Romanian Dacia factory workers as well. Last year their salaries were raised an average of 20 percent to about €450 a month.

Sources: Adapted from www.buyusa.gov/romania; *The Economist*, 2008, "The logic of the Logan," www.economist.com, May 29.

For practical considerations, many companies mix regional and country focus. There are simply too many countries, many of which are small markets, for MNCs to treat each one separately as a different market. Consequently, some companies focus on larger market countries such as the US or Japan with a multidomestic approach while treating regions such as Southeast Asia with a regional approach. The Country/Regional Focus on the previous page shows how a regional strategy grew beyond its borders, even creating a new French word, *delocalization*.

A Brief Summary and Caveat

Exhibit 2.3 summarizes the content of the four basic multinational strategies. Students of international business should realize, however, that these strategies are general descriptions of multinational strategic options. Seldom do companies adopt a pure form of a multinational strategy. Companies with more than one business may adopt different multinational strategies for each business. Even single-business companies may alter strategies to adjust for product differences. In addition, governmental regulations regarding trade, the historical evolution of the company, and the cost of switching strategies may prevent a firm from fully implementing a particular strategy. The IB Strategic Insight opposite shows how even the world's largest company, Walmart, must adapt its basic international retailing strategy to local conditions.

Exhibit 2.3 **The Content of Multinational Strategies: From Local Adaptation to Global Integration**

Content Areas	Adaptation Strategy Content		Global Strategy Content	
	Multidomestic	Regional	International	Transnational
Markets	Treat each country as a separate market	Treat regions (e.g. EU) as markets	Maintain flexibility for local adaptation directed from headquarters	Maintain flexibility for local adaptation based on local learning
Products	Tailor products to best serve local customer needs in the country of location	Use similar products within major economic regions but different between regions	Use minimal local adaptation and rely on worldwide brand recognition	Use minimal local adaptation and rely on worldwide brand recognition
Marketing	Focus on local country customers using local practices of advertising, promotion and sales	Focus on customers in the region using regional practices of advertising, promotion and sales	Use similar marketing tactics worldwide	Use similar marketing tactics worldwide
Location of Value-chain Activities	Locate all or most value-chain activities in each country of operation	Locate all or most value-chain activities in the region which can include best sites in different countries	Limit mostly to sales and where necessary use local production replicating home country organization	Locate anywhere based on best value to company—lowest cost for highest quality

Source: Adapted from John B. Cullen and K. Praveen Parboteeah, 2008, *Multinational Management*, Mason, OH: Thomson South-Western, 2008, p. 265.

With nearly $300 billion in sales and 300 million worldwide customers a week, Walmart may be the biggest company in the world but its highly successful business model has not always worked in all countries. Walmart has ventures in Argentina, Britain, Canada, China, Germany, Indonesia, Japan, and Mexico, but with an international division that is hardly 15 years old, Walmart is still an adolescent in the international market.

Walmart is the leading retailer in the close-by countries of the US of Mexico and Canada. In Britain, it immediately gained the #3 position by acquiring the Asda chain. However, its ventures into Germany, Argentina, and Indonesia initially flopped and led to heavy losses. Analysts say Walmart just failed to adapt to local conditions. For example, the "everyday low prices" promotions that work so well in the US turned off the Japanese, who equate low prices with low quality. Walmart CEO Lee Scott described the entry into Germany as "embarrassing." It under-estimated the strength of the entrenched competition, the strength of the unions (not a problem in the US) and

the inflexibility of the suppliers. German workers found Walmart an unattractive place to work, with its low pay and management styles. Many staff members hid in the bathrooms during Walmart cheers, and many of the expatriate managers from the US refused to learn German. Perhaps only a company as big as Walmart can afford the $300 million in losses a year in Germany.

In contrast to Walmart and its major competitor, France's Carrefour, the world's #3 retailer, Tesco, seems most adept at international operations. Tesco's CEO Sir Terry Leahy argues for a multidomestic strategy, changing products and operations in every country. According to Sir Terry, "Despite globalization, local differences still hold sway over mass retailing. What works well in one country does not necessarily work in another." Perhaps Walmart could learn a bit of international strategy from Tesco.

Sources: Based on *The Economist*, 2001, "Wal-Mart around the world," December 6; *The Economist*, 2004, "How big can it grow?" April 15; *The Economist*, 2005, "Growing pains," April 14.

Given the choice, strategic options for international operations means that international managers must carefully analyze the situation for their company and its products or businesses when formulating or choosing a multinational strategy. The next section gives some diagnostic questions that international managers use to help select the best strategy for their company. These diagnostic questions guide MNCs in resolving the global–local dilemma.

Choosing a Multinational Strategy: How to Solve the Global–Local Dilemma

Choosing a multinational strategy, be it transnational, multidomestic, international, regional, or some combination of these options, depends to a large degree on the balance of pressures for local adaptation and potential advantages of cost and quality from global integration. Exhibit 2.4 shows where the basic multinational strategies fall in meeting these often conflicting demands.

One of the best ways to determine whether local adaptation pressures or global integration pressures are more important is to understand the degree of globalization of the industry in which your company competes. According

Exhibit 2.4

Solutions to the Global–Local Dilemma

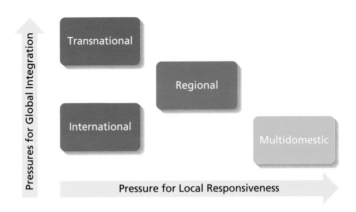

to the multinational strategy expert George Yip, international managers can tell how globalized their industry is by looking at the industry's degree of globalization. You can tell how global your industry is by looking at its globalization drivers.

What are globalization drivers? **Globalization drivers** define the industry characteristics that suggest when an MNC will likely be more successful adopting more globally oriented transnational or international strategies over the MNCs that choose more locally oriented multidomestic or regional strategies.[9] The globalization drivers come from the nature of markets, cost structure of the industry, government policies in countries of operation, and what the competition is doing. For each of these areas the international strategist can ask diagnostic questions that help assess the degree of globalization of the industry and in turn suggest different multinational strategies.[10] The next section outlines these questions.

globalization drivers conditions in an industry that favor transnational or international strategies over multilocal or regional strategies

Global Markets

Do your Customers from Different Countries have Similar Needs? Increasingly, the needs of customers are becoming more similar around the world. However, this convergence is not the same in all industries and for all products. The consumer electronics and pharmaceutical industries tend to have customers with similar needs. For example, antibiotics are needed throughout the world. If you wear soft contact lenses, you have a need for saline solution whether you live in Moscow, Idaho, USA, or Moscow, Russia. Bausch & Lomb can provide you with this solution almost anywhere in the world.

However, in industries where cultural differences, government requirements, income, and physical climate are important, common customer needs are less likely. For example, in spite of the worldwide love of the automobile, no company has succeeded in developing one car for all markets. Difference in income levels, fuel prices, roads and highways, government regulations, and consumer preferences for styles and options have made this a difficult challenge.

Are There Global Customers? Global customers are organizations or people who shop for their goods or services anywhere in the world. Global customers are usually organizations (not individual consumers). They search the world market for suppliers. PC manufacturers are perhaps some of the most global customers for PC components. If you looked inside your PC you would find that the components come from companies located all over the world. As we saw in Chapter 1, an important trend is that many businesses are not only acting as global customers for components but are also shopping for business services such as IT and customer service centers.

Although more rare, individual consumers can be global customers. If you have ever bought software or music from a site outside your country, you are a global customer. Many people are global customers when they fly internationally, picking a carrier based on price and convenient service rather than nationality.

Although soft contact lens wearers may not shop for saline solution worldwide, shoppers in the EU often cross borders to find lower-cost medical supplies.

Can You Transfer Marketing Activities to Other Countries? If you can use the same brand name, advertising, packaging, and channels of distribution, the industry is more global. Brand names like Coke and Microsoft are certainly recognized worldwide and need little adaptation. Although conventional wisdom would suggest that advertisements need adjustments to local cultures, if customers respond similarly regardless of nationality, globally oriented companies can efficiently and effectively use the same strategies worldwide. Some companies like Exxon purposely developed world brands not based on any specific language to benefit from a single global advertising strategy.[11]

Marketing channels represent how products get from the producer to the ultimate consumer. Business-to-business sales (e.g. Boeing or Airbus selling to an airline) are often direct and the channel is similar worldwide. Other channels may be more complex and differ by country.

Take, for example, our example of Bausch & Lomb saline solution for soft contact lenses. Basically just salt water, it is a global product; however, in the US one can purchase saline in grocery stores and a variety of other outlets. In most European countries, saline must be sold through pharmacies so companies like Bausch & Lomb must make local adaptations in distribution. More consistent with the image of a medicine, bottles are also smaller than one might find in a US grocery store. In such cases, the more local adaptation required in the industry, the less it is globalized.

Globalization Cost Drivers

Are There Global Economies of Scale? In some industries, such as the aircraft industry, no one country's market is sufficiently large to buy all the products of efficient production runs. To be cost-competitive, firms in this industry must go global and sell worldwide. Industries where individual unit costs drop substantially with more volume tend to be more globalized. For example, Airbus hopes to sell over 700 A380s, its new super jumbo jet. Just to break even, it must sell over 500. The only way to do this is to sell to airlines all over the world. No one country could produce a demand of 500. Not surprisingly, as a result the civil aircraft industry is one of the most globalized.

Are There Global Sources of Low-cost Raw Materials or Components? Usually it pays to procure your raw materials or components in low-cost countries with absolute cost advantages. The trade-off is that the supplies must be sufficiently less expensive to offset the additional costs of shipping and administration. India's Tata Steel is one of the lowest-cost producers in the world and is a source of steel material for a variety of MNCs. Tata also has access to a native iron ore that is low in phosphorus content, making it ideal for steel used in automobiles, household appliances, and computers.[12]

Are There Cheaper Sources of Skilled Labor? Similar to the case for raw materials, the cost advantage is for companies to manufacture in low-cost countries. The move of many manufacturing plants to Eastern Europe by European companies and the move of many US manufacturing operations to China represent examples of companies seeking global sources of lower costs. Take Tower Automotive, for example. Tower is a supplier of truck frames for both Dodge and Ford. To be closer to Dodge assembly plants in Mexico and to get a much cheaper labor force, Tower moved its Dodge Ram production to Monterey, Mexico, in 2005. Over 500 jobs left Ohio and were transferred to Mexico at a significant cost savings.

Are Product Development Costs High? When product development costs are high, companies often find it more efficient to produce a few products that they can sell worldwide. Sometimes a single country or even regional market is not sufficiently large to absorb the development costs of a unique product produced for that market even if sales are high. For instance, Toyota's sales volume for its higher-end Camry sedan can recover development costs because Toyota sells the car throughout the world using a different name and standard internal components. To be sure, they vary the exterior in different countries to meet local consumer tastes and local regulations. Similarly, the major aircraft manufacturers Boeing and Airbus must sell the same products worldwide to recover the billions of dollars it takes to develop a new plane model.

Governments

Do Many Countries have Favorable Trade Policies for the Industry? As you read in Chapter 1, barriers are falling to trade and investment, encouraging globalization and global strategies. That is, the WTO and trading blocs such as NAFTA and the EU encourage the use of more transnational and international strategies by lowering governmental investment and trade restrictions, at least among member nations. The US government keeps a close watch on trade barriers that directly affect US companies.[13] However, government policies that allow tariffs, quotas, and subsidized local companies still exist and restrict global strategies. Rice farmers in Japan, for example, benefit from import restrictions and heavy subsidies of rice that keep foreign competition out of Japan and allow domestic prices over four times the world market price.

Do Many Countries have Regulations that Restrict Operations in the Industry? Government regulations regarding foreign ownership on the use of foreign components, on the ability of foreign managers and workers to work in the country, and on advertising and promotional content, make the full implementation of a transnational strategy or an international strategy more difficult. Although the general trend of globalization is reducing these regulations, they still exist in many countries for certain industries. Particularly, many countries restrict foreign ownership in defense-related industries or other industries such as agriculture when they are considered essential to the survival of the country. For instance, majority ownership by local citizens is required by airlines in the EU and most North American countries, as well as in the telecommunications industry in Japan. Additionally, foreign ownership is forbidden in the oil industry in Mexico and energy industries in Iceland.[14]

The Competition

What Strategies do your Competitors Use? When transnational or international MNCs outcompete multidomestic and local competitors, it suggests two reasons to follow the more global strategists. First, if uniform products and marketing strategies are successful in a variety of different countries then the pressure is on all firms to follow similar practices. Second, since more global firms are more likely to use low-cost-country sources of raw materials and labor and can price lower than other competitors, others are forced to source from similar locations. For example, the low-cost production facilities in Asia have driven athletic shoe companies such as Nike and Germany's Adidas to move production to match competitors' costs.

What is the Volume of Imports and Exports in the Industry? A high volume of trade in an industry is a strong indicator of a globalized industry and suggests that success is related to cross-borders. That is, it shows an already existing high level of international competition and acceptance of products from different countries. It also suggests that many companies have already taken advantage of strategies that are more global.

A Caveat

Although MNCs are finding the more global strategies increasingly popular and successful, cultural and national differences remain and the astute international manager remains sensitive to these differences. The important thing is to find a proper balance. Managing the degree of local adaptation can also be a challenge, though. The IB Strategic Insight overleaf describes how Metro, the German warehouse company, tries to find the right levels of local adaptation.

A Warehouse Store in India

Although almost unknown in the US, Metro operates in 30 countries besides its home country, Germany. Resembling in style the US-headquartered Costco or Sam's Club, Metro stores have a bare-bones look. Metro, however, is a warehouse store that sells just to businesses. The typical store carries 50,000 items compared to the 4,000 of a Costco. Metro's business model is to source locally, especially for food.

Metro has a cash-and-carry format that works well for small entrepreneurs in emerging markets. In places like India and China, where small enterprises are everywhere, it provides a centralized alternative to traditional specialized markets. The breadth of its product offerings and the cash-and-carry format serve the developing markets exceptionally well. Most of Metro's recent growth is in Asia and the transition economies in Eastern Europe. In addition, as a wholesaler it often avoids prohibitions on foreign retailers.

Although the business model seems to work for most developing nations, local adaptations are usually required.

When Metro opened a store in Saigon, local manager James Scott, a British expatriate, tried to set up Metro's standard procurement systems: sign a contract, send orders by fax, take payments by checks. What he found was that farmers didn't have fax machines, didn't have bank accounts, and had never seen contracts. After fax lessons, he convinced the farmers to open accounts and sign the contracts. With his sourcing set up, Scott still had more to learn. Customers ripped open shrink-wrapped tomatoes. "They thought we were hiding rotten fruit underneath," noted Scott. Fruit is now stacked in open stalls.

Even with success in a variety of emerging market countries, Hans-Joachim Körber, CEO of Metro and the force behind Metro's international strategy, admits "We were a bit naïve" when they set up shop in Shanghai. For example, Körber notes that Metro had to quickly install tanks for live snakes, snails, and frogs. "We learned that in China fresh means alive."

Source: Adapted from Deborah Orr, 2005, "Don't wrap the veggies," *Forbes*, April 18.

How to Make the Transnational or International Choice

When companies compete in more globalized industries, transnational and international MNCs usually are more successful than multidomestic or regional strategists. They can usually offer cheaper or higher-quality products or services by using uniform product/services and marketing, or lower-cost or higher-quality sourcing. How then do international managers decide whether to be more transnational or international in strategy?

To select a more transnational strategy over a more international strategy, the international manager must believe that the benefits of dispersing value-chain activities worldwide offset the costs of coordinating a more complex organization. For example, with a more transnational approach, a company may do R&D in one country, parts manufacturing in another, final assembly in another, and sales in a fourth. Coordination of these activities across national borders and in different parts of the world is costly and difficult. The transnational strategist, however, anticipates that the benefits of these dispersed activities in low-cost or high-quality labor and raw materials will offset the difficulties and costs of coordination to produce better or cheaper products.

In contrast to the transnational strategist, the international business manager adopting a more international strategy believes that centralizing key activities such as R&D reduces coordination costs and gives economies of scale. An economy of scale means that it is more efficient to do all of one activity in one place. The cost savings from economies of scale then offset the lower costs or high-quality raw materials or labor that the transnationalist can find by locating worldwide. Traditionally, Boeing adopted more of an international strategy, doing research and development for commercial aircraft and most manufacturing in its plants in the US.

In the reality of the world's competitive landscape, most major multi-national corporations, such as IBM, GE, and Siemens, do not adopt a pure international or transnational strategy. Instead, they blend both approaches depending on the businesses they own or the products they are producing. However, as information systems and communications systems become more sophisticated, many of the traditional international firms are developing more transnational characteristics. For example, with the Dreamliner—a high-tech plane built from new composite material and new engine technologies—Boeing moved away from its purer international strategy and is manufacturing the majority of the plane's components using supplier composite production expertise located in Japan and China.

Company-Situation Analysis and the Multinational Strategy Choice

Each company faces its own unique situation in the competitive business world. In addition to looking at the globalization of their industry, managers must understand what *their* particular company can and cannot do best, realistically assessing their company's resources and strategic capabilities. In addition, in formulating their multinational strategies, they must identify the opportunities or threats that globalization poses to their company's unique position in the industry. The globalization drivers represent a balance sheet of forces in an industry that suggests the potential success of more transnational or inter-national strategies or more regional or multidomestic strategies. Thus, the diagnostic questions based on the globalization drivers help international man-agers formulate better strategies to compete globally or locally.

In addition to the globalization drivers external to the MNC, the location of the firm's competitive advantage in the value chain influences the choice of a multinational strategy.

When an MNC has competitive advantages from primarily upstream in the value chain, as for example from low-cost or high-quality design, engineering, and manufacturing, it can often generalize these advantages to many markets with similar high-quality products. A transnational strategy or an international strategy usually follows. For example, Mercedes Benz and BMW use their world-class designs to sell similar products in all major markets. In contrast, other types of MNCs generally focus most of their value downstream—in mar-keting, sales, and service. Such MNCs have natural local adaptation strengths and are more likely to adopt a more multidomestic or regional strategy, serving each market uniquely.

Of course, competing internationally is complex and a company's com-petitive strengths may not align directly with the degree of globalization in the industry. Some firms may compete in industries with strong globalization drivers, yet their competitive strengths are in downstream value-chain activities, such as after-market service. Other MNCs may compete in industries with weak globalization drivers and thus weaker pressures, yet be stronger in manufacturing and R&D rather than in customer service. When facing such misaligned situations, MNCs often select a regional strategy as a compromise. For the MNC with upstream strengths, such as high-quality production that faces pressure for local adaptation, a more regional strategy allows: (1) some use of similar products, and (2) some downstream adaptation to regional differences. For the MNC with downstream competitive strengths, such as after-market service, facing pressure for globalization, a more regional strategy allows: (1) some adaptation of customer interactions to more local markets, and (2) some ability to respond to the globalization driver of lower costs by the economies of scale produced by activities such as centralized purchasing and uniform products.

Exhibit 2.5 shows how the location of strengths within the value chain combine with the pressures for globalization or local responsiveness and lead to different multinational strategies.

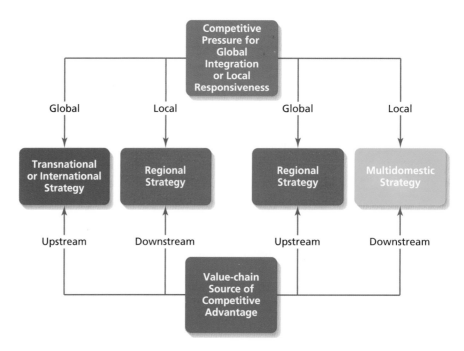

Exhibit 2.5 **Pressure for Global Integration or Local Responsiveness, Value-chain Sources of Competitive Advantage, and Multinational Strategy Choices**

Successful firms monitor not only their industry, which is usually called the operating environment, but also the broader environment, which is usually called the general environment. The general environment includes all the social institutions (e.g. economy, political system) and cultural context discussed earlier as the national context. It also includes broad issues of technological change, such as the evolution of the Internet that has provided opportunities for many new business forms as well as threats to established organizations.

CHAPTER REVIEW

Beyond the traditional strategic questions facing all managers, the international manager, in both large and small companies, must confront the global–local dilemma. Markets, costs, governments, and the competition drive the choice of a solution. As the world becomes more globalized (see Chapter 1), we are seeing more companies choosing transnational or international strategies to compete with low cost and high quality. However, cultural and other national differences remain, and these will continue to provide opportunities to companies with more local or regional orientations.

As a form of differentiation—meeting unique customer needs—there are benefits to favoring the more local responsiveness-oriented strategies. That is, the multidomestic or regional strategy tailors the product or service to meet the unique needs of customers in a country or region. Because you deliver unique products or services for each country, the pure multidomestic strategy is the most costly. However, it allows an MNC the most latitude to handle differences in culture, language, and political and legal systems. The regional strategy is less costly as it is only a partial adaptation to local differences, allowing the use of more similar products and lower-cost or higher-quality production within the region. In this way, adaptation to regional differences is balanced against the efficiencies of doing things similarly within the region.

The goal for international and transnational strategists is to produce high-quality products as efficiently as possible. Typically, MNCs using these strategies or a mix of the two try to have global products with global marketing. Differing from the international strategist, the MNC with a more transnational strategy uses worldwide locations or platforms for its value-chain activities to maximize efficiency and quality. That is, the more transnational strategies will look to do anything anywhere if it makes good business sense. They are particularly attracted to offshoring activities to the low-cost countries.

The complexities of choosing multinational strategies in an ever-globalizing economy represent considerable challenges to international managers. To name only a few issues, for example, in choosing a multinational strategy the international manager must consider the type of the product or service (e.g. can it be global?), the government and political systems where the MNC has units (e.g. how safe are the assets?), the financial risk of the investment (e.g. what are the expected returns?), and the needs of the company to control operations (e.g. can we really do it right 2,000 miles away?). The IB Strategic Insights in this chapter have shown you several examples of how practicing international managers in real companies faced and responded to the challenges of formulating multinational strategies.

MNCs execute multinational strategies in a dynamic global context related to relationships among governments, patterns of trade and investments, foreign exchange markets, and global capital markets. This chapter dealt very briefly with some of these issues in terms of multinational strategy formulation and content. In the next section, you will see in much more detail how this dynamic global context influences the playing field in which companies compete internationally.

DISCUSSION QUESTIONS

1. Discuss the conditions where a multidomestic or regional strategy might perform better than a transnational or international strategy.
2. Explain how global integration and local responsiveness might be successful in the same industry.
3. Contrast the transnational and international strategies in their approach to location advantages.
4. Using the diagnostic questions in the chapter, analyze the globalization potential of the "big box" (e.g. Walmart, Costco, Metro) retail trade industry.
5. Do the same as in Question 4 but for an industry of your choice.
6. Discuss how a small manufacturing company might adopt some aspects of international and transnational strategies.

INTERNATIONAL BUSINESS SKILL BUILDER

Identifying the Value-chain and Multinational Strategies

Step 1: Choose a global industry such as the automobile industry or the cell-phone industry and identify two major competitors in the industry.

Step 2: Research the selected companies in the popular business press and make a list of their major value-chain activities.

Step 3: For each company, using the matrix below, identify the major geographical locations of these value-chain activities. Are they in the home country? Or are they dispersed around the globe?

Value-chain Activity	Home Country	Location 1	Location 2	Location 3
R&D				
Input Logistics				
Global Products				
Operations				
Marketing and Sales				
Output Logistics				
After-market Service				

Step 4: For each company, write an analysis showing how the company attempts to gain a competitive advantage by its choice of value-chain locations. What is its predominate multinational strategy?

CHAPTER INTERNET ACTIVITY ——————

Explore the Internet sites of three companies noted in the chapter. Go to the investor relations section in the sites and look for information on their multi-national strategies. Often, the annual report contains a description of the company's strategy. See if you can tell the degree to which the company uses primarily a local responsiveness or global integration strategy.

KEY CONCEPTS ——————————

global integration strategy

global platform

global–local dilemma

globalization drivers

international strategies

local responsiveness strategy

location advantages

multidomestic strategy

national advantage

regional strategy

transnational strategy

value chain

WALMART OR CARREFOUR

WHO WILL BE MASTER OF PLANET RETAIL?

CASE 2

page 1

Sam Walton began Walmart, the world's largest retailer, in 1962. Headquartered in Bentonville, Arkansas, Walmart was built on the policies of "everyday low prices" and a 100 percent customer satisfaction guarantee. Walton provided the lowest prices, on average, among American retailers, and directed the organization to achieve superior customer satisfaction. He had previously worked for the JC Penney Company and it has been reported that Mr Penney once told Sam that he did not have a future in retailing. Walton's views on retailing were iconoclastic and industry-defining in the United States.

With over 3,000 stores in the United States, Walmart has begun an aggressive expansion into the international marketplace. Walmart has over 1,500 stores in Canada, Mexico, the UK, Germany, South Korea, China, Brazil, and Argentina. It also operates a small number of stores in a few other countries through joint ventures. Walmart's recent entry into the European market (primarily through acquisition) has caused anxiety, and in some cases panic, among European retailers. Walmart is larger (sales) than its major competitors Carrefour, Metro AG, and Ahold combined. Approximately 80 percent of Walmart's stores are in the United States.

Carrefour, the second-largest retailer in the world, was started in France when two brothers, Jacques and Denis Deforey, who were in the grocery business, partnered with Marcel Fournier, who owned a department store. Known for its extreme attention to detail and the ability to cater to local tastes, Carrefour established itself as the major retailer in Europe. Carrefour now has over 6,000 stores in Europe, South America, and Asia, and is planning expansions into the Caribbean, Africa, and the Middle East. Carrefour attempts to localize its operations as much as possible and uses few expatriates. Approximately 80 percent of store sales come from outside its home country, France.

Carrefour's global strategy involves careful study of local markets and careful attention to local customs. For example, in China Carrefour cuts its vegetables vertically, not horizontally, to avoid an image of bad luck among its Chinese customers. Carrefour has been a pioneer in the concept of "store clustering" internationally, altering its product mix, store facilities, and prices to suit different economic regions. Carrefour is the largest foreign retailer in China and sees the Asian market as critical to its continued success. Carrefour has 226 stores in Asia, compared to Walmart's 59 stores. One-quarter of Carrefour's new store growth comes from the Asian market.

. . .

CASE 2

page 2

Walmart is a much stronger company financially and it has deep pockets for international expansion. Its everyday low price concept has been a very viable strategy, and Walmart pioneered creative and successful approaches to supplier management and technology integration. In the United States, Walmart has huge scale economies and excellent logistical operations. In terms of domestic operations, Walmart has a very impressive 22 percent return on shareholder equity.

Internationally, Walmart has experienced less success. International sales account for only about 20 percent of Walmart's total revenue, and its return on assets for international operations has been considerably lower than for its domestic operations. In Europe, Walmart faces strong unions, increased regulatory constraints, and weak scale economies. The ability to export its everyday low price concept to Europe is being challenged, especially in Germany. The everyday low price concept has also not been effective in Japan, where Walmart operates a joint venture with Seiyu. Many Japanese associate low prices with lower-quality goods.

The world's largest retailer hopes to match its domestic success internationally, and many analysts believe it has the financial and managerial ability to do so. On the other hand, Walmart lacks the international experience of Carrefour and is a latecomer in many markets where Carrefour is well established.

CASE DISCUSSION POINTS

1. Which international strategy does Walmart follow? Which international strategy does Carrefour follow? Which do you feel is a better strategy for global expansion?
2. Can Walmart learn anything from Carrefour? Can Carrefour learn anything from Walmart's success? Explain.
3. Which retailer, in your opinion, will win the battle for global leadership?

Sources: *The Economist*, 2000, "Wal-Mart: Chimera," January 29; *Fortune*, 2000, "Who's afraid of Wal-Mart?" June 26; *Financial Times* (London), 2000, "Wal-Mart at centre of prices probe in Germany," June 28; *The Economist*, 2005, "Business: Growing pains," April 16; Wal-Mart, 2005, *Annual Report*; www.carrefour.com

Case prepared by Charles A. Rarick

The Global Context of

The Global Context of Multinational Competitive Strategy

part two

Multinational Competitive Strategy

3 Global and Regional Economic Integration

An Evolving Competitive Landscape

After reading this chapter you should be able to:

- Know the history of GATT and the WTO.

- Understand how WTO agreements can influence your company and its multinational strategies.

- Understand the possible trade implications of regional trade agreements.

- Know the types of regional trade agreements.

- Be familiar with the nature and structure of the major regional trade agreements in the world.

The Preview IB Strategic Insight shows how changes in trade barriers can open up new markets for different products. Of course, as you learned in Chapter 1, trade has never been as open as it is today. However, not all products or services are free from government restrictions regarding importing or exporting. Some governments use trade regulations to protect key or emerging industries such as defense contracting. Not all countries, including some big countries such as Russia, participate fully in the efforts to reduce world trade barriers. As such, since trade regulations change frequently, international managers must monitor and understand how evolving government trade policies affect their operations. In this chapter you will see some of the history of how we arrived at our present system and how world trade negotiations are structured and continue to evolve.

Let the Wines Pour In

Prior to its joining the World Trade Organization, selling wine in China was difficult. Changyu, Dynasty, Great Wall, and Tonghua, the top Chinese wine brands, controlled over 60 percent of the wine market. Why? Import tariffs on foreign wine were 65 percent, making it very difficult for foreign wine makers to sell wine at a price the Chinese consumers could afford.

Although wine making in China can be traced back over 8,000 years, the oldest in the world, and alcoholic drinks are a ritual part of Chinese celebrations, wine now makes up only a small percentage of the alcoholic drinks market. However, in the booming Chinese economy wine is becoming a fashionable drink for the emerging affluent Chinese. The World Wine Industry Association forecasts a 7 percent group rate per year up to 2008 as compared to the world average of less than 1 percent.

The reduction in tariffs combined with the growing Chinese attraction to wine is encouraging foreign vintners to go to China. For example, marketing and sales director Doyle Hinman of Henry Estate Winery in Roseburg, Oregon, notes, "If we can get just a fraction of a fraction of a fraction of their 1.3 billion people to buy our wines, it will be huge business for us." However, convincing consumers to spend high prices for top-quality wine remains a challenge in a country where the average bottle costs less than two dollars and a culture of wine drinking is a novelty. Consider the experience of Sam Featherston, a US American who owns a wine import business in Beijing. He brought 12 bottles of Chateau Lafite Rothschild, one of the world's top wines, to entertain a group of Chinese businessmen. Instead of savoring the taste like French wine connoisseurs, they poured the $200-a-bottle wine into pitchers, and added Sprite and some fruit.

Sources: Adapted from Yilu Zhao, 2003, "Inroads in China for wine importers," *New York Times*, December 28, pp. 3, 5; *Columbian*, 2004, "Oregon wine hits China," December 12, p. E2; Zhang Lu, 2004, "Low tariffs help foreign wines pour in," *China Daily*, December 23, p. 11; Justine Lau, 2005, "Domestic wines hit the spot: Changing tastes have opened up the market for Western-style wines," *Financial Times*, January 19, p. 9.

Dropping Barriers to World Trade: GATT and the WTO

tariffs
taxes applied to imported or exported goods

In 1947, faced with the prospect of rebuilding world trade after World War II, several nations began negotiating to limit worldwide tariffs and to encourage free trade. **Tariffs** are taxes applied to imported or exported goods. A tariff is also known as a customs duty. The word "tariff" comes from Tenerife, which is the name of an island in the Canary Islands. Folklore suggests that local Tenerife pirates forced passing ships to pay a fee to sail in the local waters around the island.[1]

Immediately after World War II, tariffs averaged 45 percent worldwide, adding a huge price increase for goods from other countries and severely limiting world trade. Eight rounds of tariff negotiations reduced the average worldwide tariffs on manufactured goods from 45 percent to less than 7 percent. These negotiations were known as the **General Agreement on Tariffs and Trade (GATT)**.

General Agreement on Tariffs and Trade (GATT)
eight rounds of tariff negotiations that reduced the average worldwide tariffs on manufactured goods from 45 percent to less than 7 percent

During this time, world trade grew dramatically. That is, much like the entry of import wine companies into China, as shown in the Preview IB Strategic Insight, reduced tariffs prompted more companies to see opportunities to enter foreign markets where they could compete on an equal footing with domestic companies.

GATT created the basic principle of nondiscrimination, with the intent to put all the signing nations on an equal footing for trade and to reduce trade barriers. The **principle of nondiscrimination** requires that trade agreements between any two nations apply to all GATT signers. That is, signing nations must give to all other GATT members the same favorable treatment that they give to any other nation. This favorable treatment is now called normal trade relations, although it was once called most favored nation treatment. Nondiscrimination also means that participants must treat industries from other nations no differently than the same industries in one's own country. Once foreign products enter the market they must be treated the same as domestic products.

principle of nondiscrimination
requires that trade agreements between any two nations apply to all GATT signers

Exhibit 3.1 shows the chronology of the GATT negotiations and the subjects covered at each stage.

After the initial success of the Geneva round of negotiations, progress on tariff reductions slowed considerably. This occurred because many tariff negotiations became bilateral. Bilateral trade negotiations take place between pairs of countries agreeing to reduce tariffs on particular products. An important change occurred in the Kennedy round, so named after President Kennedy, who was the driving force behind the negotiations. At the Kennedy round, negotiations became multilateral, meaning several countries at once. Multilateral trade negotiations are more efficient because all the group members agree at once to reduce tariffs on broad categories of goods.

Prior to the Tokyo round of negotiations, the GATT countries worked only on reducing trade barriers based on tariffs. A significant change with this negotiation round was the reduction in trade barriers of other forms. Tariffs are not the only barriers countries use to protect domestic industries. Non-tariff barriers to trade include, for example:

* State subsidies that give some companies an advantage in the international market. Boeing accuses Airbus of having unfair subsidies from European countries to design new aircraft.

Exhibit 3.1 **A Chronology of GATT and the WTO**

Name of Round	Year	Countries Participating	Major Focus of Negotiations
Geneva	1947	23	Tariffs
Annecy	1949	13	Tariffs
Torquay	1951	38	Tariffs
Geneva	1956	26	Tariffs
Dillon	1960–1	26	Tariffs
Kennedy	1964–7	62	Tariffs and anti-dumping measures
Tokyo	1973–9	102	Tariffs, non-tariff measures, partial agreements by some countries on more general frameworks for trade
Uruguay	1986–94	123	Tariffs, non-tariff measures, rules, services, intellectual property, dispute settlement, textiles, agriculture, creation of WTO, etc.
Doha	2001–present	153	Tariffs, agriculture, services, intellectual property, government procurement, anti-dumping, regional trade agreements, e-commerce, trade and environment, small economies

Source: Adapted from www.wto.org/english/thewto_e/whatis_e/tif_e/fact4_e.htm#rounds

- Quotas that limit the amount of imports and/or exports. The US has often used quotas to limit the amount of imports of certain product types. As a strategy to avoid more restrictive trade barriers, the Japanese with automobiles in the 1970s and more recently the Chinese with textiles used voluntary quotas to restrict their imports into the US.
- National regulations related to health and safety. The European Union restricts the sale of genetically modified foods or beef treated with growth hormones. This prevents the sale of many US-produced agricultural goods.
- "Buy national" policies. These can require governments to procure from own-country suppliers and can also be nationalistic campaigns to encourage citizens to buy local.
- These and other trade-restricting techniques were addressed in the Tokyo round.

The final round of the GATT was the Uruguay round. Negotiations in Uruguay began in 1986 and ended in 1993 with agreements to reduce tariffs even further, liberalize trade in agriculture and services, and eliminate some non-tariff barriers to international trade, such as excessive use of health regulations to keep out imports.[2] Most importantly, the Uruguay talks also established the **World Trade Organization (WTO)** to succeed GATT.

Differing from GATT, which, as we have seen, is a series of governmental agreements, the WTO is a formal organizational structure for continued negotiations and for settling trade disputes among member nations. There are now 153 nations in the WTO, up from 92 when the 1986 GATT talks began, including 29 of the UN-classified least developed countries. Thirty

World Trade Organization (WTO)
a formal structure for continued negotiations and for settling trade disputes among nations

more countries, including Russia, seek WTO membership, called ascension in WTO terminology. Since 1995, tariffs on industrial products have fallen from an average of 6.3 percent to 3.8 percent.[3] Nearly all of the world's trade occurs among WTO member countries.

As an organization the WTO has several objectives.[4] These include:

- administering trade agreements based on GATT and those negotiated later;
- cooperating with other international organizations such as the UN and the World Bank;
- providing technical assistance and training for developing countries;
- monitoring the trade policies of member nations;
- providing a forum for current and future trade negotiations;
- adjudicating trade disputes.

Exhibits 3.2 and 3.3 show, respectively, descriptions of the basic functions and agreements of the WTO and its organizational structure

The most recent series of talks began in 2001. Members met in Doha, Qatar, in what are now called the Doha talks, with the wide-ranging objectives of trade reduction, but with particular emphasis on reducing trade barriers for food and reducing the developed world's subsidies for farmers. The talks are ongoing. However, the goal of reducing agricultural subsidies has proven difficult to attain as the developed nations such as the US have resisted eliminating subsidies to farmers, a sensitive political issue in many countries.

The US pays farmers approximately $20 billion in subsidies per year. In 2000 the subsidies reached a peak at $32.3 billion, according to the US Department of Agriculture. The EU is even a bigger spender, paying out

The Textile Industry in India

IB STRATEGIC INSIGHT

Globally the textile industry is big business, averaging around $500 billion a year. This approximately equals the national income of India and is just about one-third that of China. By 2010, global exports of textiles are projected to pass the $1,200 billion mark. Most recent attention has focus on the huge growth of textile imports into the US and the EU from China. However, India, along with other low-cost-labor countries, is also a player in this market.

Immediately after the end of quotas in 2005 Indian textile exports increased by 50 percent, and companies like Sears and Gap Inc. have begun looking to India as a source for clothing imports. Forecasts of the growth of Indian textile exports range from $20 to $80 billion by 2010.

Typical of entrepreneurial Indian managers is Sudhir Dhingra. He is chairman of Orient Craft, one of the largest Indian textile exporters. In a typical operation, such as one of his factories in Gurgaon, just near Delhi, he has 3,800 workers. They labor on a modern assembly-line, which is clean and well-lit. Typical of the products are dresses and skirts that Orient Craft sells at $4 a piece. Retail value in the US is $45.

With margins like this it is not surprising that global garment manufacture is expected to move entirely to developing countries over the next few years.

Source: Adapted from Kaushik Basu, 2005, "Winners and losers in textile shake-up," BBC News, http://news.bbc.co.uk/2/hi/south_asia/4294679.st, March 5.

Exhibit 3.2 **WTO Agreements and Functions**

WTO Functions	Goods	Services	Intellectual Property
Basic Agreements	GATT General Agreements on Tariffs and Trade	GATS General Agreement on Trade in Services	TRIPS Trade Related Aspects of Intellectual Property Rights
Dispute Settlement	DISPUTE SETTLEMENT BODY		
Transparency	TRADE POLICY REVIEWS OF COUNTRY COMPLIANCE		

Source: Adapted from www.wto.org, 2005.

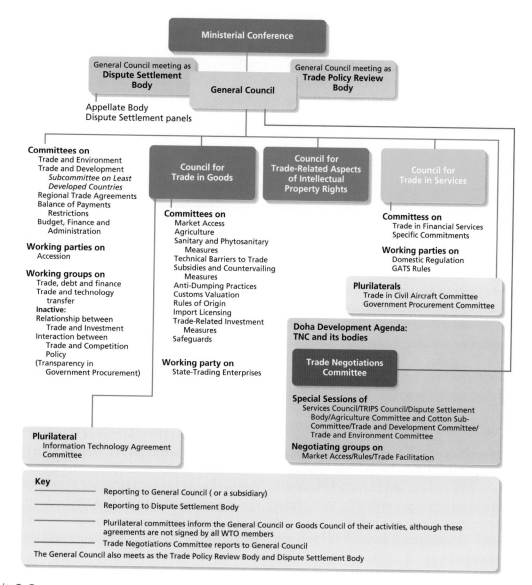

Exhibit 3.3 **WTO Structure**

All WTO members may participate in all councils, committees, etc., except Appellate Body, Dispute Settlement panels, and plurilateral committees.

Source: www.wto.org/english/thewto_e/whatis_e/tif_e/organigram_e.pdf

farmers roughly $50 billion. Japan is another big farm subsidizer, particularly in rice. Recently, Brazil, Argentina and India took the issue of US cotton subsidies to the WTO, arguing that the United States exceed allowable subsidy levels. According to the International Food Policy Research Institute, a Washington DC group funded partly by the World Bank, subsidies by industrialized nations cost developing countries about $24 billion annually in lost income.[5]

Quotas on textiles (fabrics for clothing and other cloth goods), in contrast to the continuing battle over agricultural products, ended on January 1, 2005. The result was an immediate surge in textile imports into the US and the EU. However, so large was this growth that both the EU and the US negotiated or imposed import limitations under WTO rules that allow temporary controls to avoid extreme market disruption.[6] The IB Strategic Insight on page 66 shows how the dropping of trade barriers can spur the growth of certain industries in different countries. The paradox, of course, is that these same forces can shift entire industries such as textile manufacturing from developed countries such as the US to low-cost countries such as China and India.

Two Examples of How the WTO Can Influence Your Strategy

IB STRATEGIC INSIGHT

Pharmaceutical research companies are springing up in India. Why? India now has a patent-protection law that follows WTO standards. Indian research centers are producing drug patterns at a rate of nearly 1,000/year, up from near zero ten years ago. It's now safe to invest in new drugs. Prior to the change to conform to WTO standards, patent laws allowed many Indian drug companies to produce generic versions of popular drugs. No one would do research in India because they could not protect their patented drugs from being copied.

Although conforming to WTO standards has produced an opportunity for Indian companies to join the world competition in drug research, WTO standards have also reduced the barriers to foreign investments. Multinational drug companies that left India in fear of losing their prized drugs to Indian copies are now, protected by the patent law, coming back. The rising Indian drug research industry must face this strong competition at home.

In the battle of the big two aircraft manufacturers, Boeing and Airbus, WTO rules are part of their strategy. Both Boeing and Airbus accuse each other of getting unfair subsidies and tax breaks from their governments. Boeing points at the "launch aid" given by EU countries to help Airbus launch new models. Totaling $15 billion over the life of the company, it includes $3.2 billion to launch the A380, the 550-seat new super jumbo. Airbus points out that Boeing gets similar support for its military aircraft and also gets tax breaks from states in the US. One difference, however, is that Airbus does not have to pay back the loan if the super jumbo fails to make money.

Airbus spent most of its R&D money to develop the A380 and has little left over to develop a competitor to the super-efficient Boeing Dreamliner 787. With the threat of a WTO complaint from Boeing over launch money, Airbus was forced to revamp an older model A330 into an A350 rather than build a new plane from scratch. The result is that Boeing's sales of the 787 are booming and Airbus may have to surrender the midsize market.

Sources: Adapted from *BusinessWeek Online*, 2005, "Boeing vs Airbus: Time to escalate," www.businessweek.com, March 21; *BusinessWeek Online*, 2005, "Boeing: A comeback in the air," www.businessweek.com, April 13; *BusinessWeek Online*, 2005, "India: Bigger pharma," www.businessweek.com, April 18.

Is free trade working? The WTO thinks so and the data seem to support its conclusion. Since the early GATT agreements, world trade has grown at more than four times the output of the world's gross domestic product. This suggests that the world's economies are increasingly more intertwined and mutually stimulated.

There are, however, critics. Some argue that the WTO favors the developed nations, because it is more difficult for poorer nations to compete in a non-regulated world. Environmentalists note that free trade encourages large MNCs to move environmentally damaging production to poorer and often environmentally sensitive countries. That is, commercial interests have priority over the environment, health, and safety. Labor unions see free trade leading to the migration of jobs from higher-wage countries to lower-wage countries. You can see the WTO's counter-arguments on their website at www.wto.org/.

The WTO trade agreements alter the competitive landscape for MNCs. International managers must be aware of how trade policies influence their industries and companies. The IB Strategic Insight opposite shows how the WTO influences the strategies of Airbus, Boeing, and several Indian pharmaceutical companies.

Free trade also brings into conflict different policies on the protection of the environment and sustainability practices. In the IB Sustainability Practices

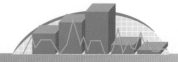

Trade and the Environmental Threat of Genetically Modified Organisms (GMOs)

IB SUSTAINABILITY PRACTICES

Often called genetic engineering or biotechnology, GMOs are created by taking genetic material from one organism and merging it with another. This is different from selective breeding that people have used for centuries to allow us to have different varieties of food and animals. It is different because it is possible to take genetic material from one species and merge it with another: for example, put a plant gene into a fish. In traditional selective breeding, only closely related species can be interbred.

Because GMOs are relatively new, countries disagree on how to protect the environment and health from potential and perhaps yet unknown dangers that might occur as these organisms enter the food chain and our diets. When countries have different regulations to test and approve procedures to take GMOs and their products on the market, trade problems can occur. Companies from countries who hope to sell GMO plants, food, and animals argue that blocking GMOs is just another form of trade protection.

In such a case, Argentina, Canada, and the United States sued the European Union at the WTO, after the WTO ruled that a de facto EU ban on imports of genetically modified foods between 1984 and 2004 was illegal. In particular, Austria has refused to allow imports of two genetically modified corn types produced by Monsanto of the United States, a leading GMO producer in the world. More recently, EU Environment Commissioner Stavros Dimas was potentially starting another conflict with the United States when he proposed a European ban on the cultivation of modified corn made by Dow Agrosciences, Pioneer Hi-Bred, and Syngenta. Dimas claims that the products potentially harm the environment. This is in spite of US claims that EU scientists found that the corn had no impact. In addition to the GMO companies, US farmers claim that the EU ban cost them $300 million a year in lost sales.

Sources: Adapted from: GM WATCH daily, 2006, "EU steadfast in rejecting genetically engineered food, despite WTO pressure," www.gmwatch.org, February 7; James Kanter, 2007, "WTO gives EU more time on genetically modified foods," *International Herald Tribune*, November 22; www.wto.org

box on the previous page you will see how different perspectives on the environmental and human safety of genetically modified organisms come into conflict in a WTO trade dispute.

Regional Trade Agreements (RTAs)

Are RTAs Friend or Foe to World Trade?

regional trade agreements (RTAs)
agreements among groups of nations to reduce tariffs and develop similar technical and economic standards

The WTO is not the only group encouraging the elimination of trade barriers. **Regional trade agreements** (RTAs) are agreements among groups of nations to reduce tariffs and develop similar technical and economic standards. Such agreements have usually led to more trade among the member nations. Some argue that these agreements are the first step toward complete globalization. Others criticize the agreements as benefiting only trade-group members and harmful for the poorer nations left out of the agreements (such as the Caribbean countries that are not members of NAFTA).[7] From a practical point of view, regional agreements benefit world trade more than they hurt it. Although they do benefit member countries the most, such agreements are more politically manageable than worldwide trade agreements.[8]

Technically, the WTO is not fully comfortable with regional trade agreements. While many regional agreements have paved the way for later WTO multilateral agreements (agreements among all WTO members), the fear is that regional agreements can lead to unequal treatment of nations that are not members of the region. Because of this, under Article XXIV of the GATT, members of the WTO are required to notify the WTO when they enter into an agreement. These agreements must be notified to the WTO to be checked for compliance with the GATT–WTO regulations. Not all nations follow this rule, so not all agreements are notified, but most of the major agreements have WTO approval.[9]

Within the last few years, the number of regional trade agreements notified to the WTO approached 180, more than double the number that existed in 1992.[10] In addition, more than 70 potential agreements are under consideration for approval by the WTO.[11] It should be noted that the majority of regional trade agreements came into existence after 1990.[12] By 2008 there were over 240 notified agreements, and some experts anticipate that regional agreements may total more than 500 by 2010. See Exhibits 3.4 and 3.5 for a look at the trends in notified agreements since the founding of GATT and the geographical spread of those agreements today.

Not all regional trade agreements have the same form or structure of their agreements. In the next section you will see the types in use today and the consequences for trading or doing business within and between these types.

Types of Regional Trade Agreements

preferential trade agreement
preferential trade relations granted to a group of nations, not necessarily reciprocal

Typically, experts look at the types of agreements as a hierarchy, with each level involving more complex relationships and economic integration. Exhibit 3.6 summarizes the various options.

The most basic agreement is called a **preferential trade agreement**. With this type, nations grant preferential trade to a group of nations. These are not

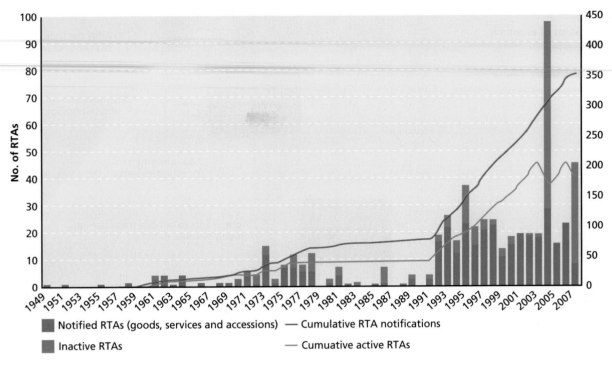

Exhibit 3.4 **The Evolution of Regional Trade Agreements**

Source: www.wto.org/english/tratop_e/religion_e/regfac_e.htm

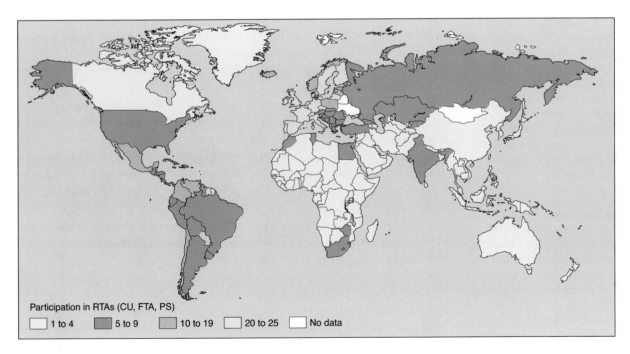

Exhibit 3.5 **RTAs Around the World: A Geographical Picture of Regional Trade Agreements**

Source: Jo-Ann Crawford & Roberto V. Fiorentino, 2005 "The changing landscape of regional trade agreements." *Discussion Paper No. 8*, World Trade Organization.

Exhibit 3.6
The Steps of Economic Integration

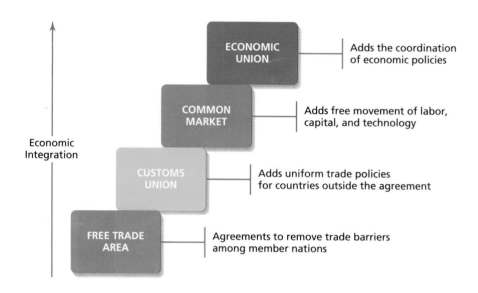

Economic Integration

ECONOMIC UNION — Adds the coordination of economic policies

COMMON MARKET — Adds free movement of labor, capital, and technology

CUSTOMS UNION — Adds uniform trade policies for countries outside the agreement

FREE TRADE AREA — Agreements to remove trade barriers among member nations

free trade areas
reciprocal agreements among groups of nations to remove tariffs and other trade barriers among members, but each nation is free to impose any barriers or preferential treatments to other nations

trade deflection
occurs in free trade areas when companies from nonmember countries enter the free trade area through a member country with low trade barriers

rules of origin
specify how much of the content or valued added of a product must be produced in a member country to count as "produced" in the country

customs union
a free trade area with the additional provision that members use uniform treatment of outsiders with regard to trade policies

necessarily reciprocal. One example, called the "Bolivarian alternative," is an agreement between Bolivia and Cuba to eliminate tariffs on imports and allow state-owned companies unrestricted operations in both countries. Already, Bolivia sells Cuba, with preferential treatment, nearly a quarter of the oil consumed in the island.[13] Part of the motivation for this "alternative" is the potential of a new US-backed Free Trade Area of the Americas.

Free trade areas are reciprocal agreements among a group of nations, usually from one region of the world, to remove tariffs and other trade barriers (e.g. quotas) affecting trade with each other. Each nation, however, remains free to impose any barriers or preferential treatments to other nations outside of the area. The most famous free trade area is the North American Free Trade Agreement (NAFTA) between the United States, Canada, and Mexico. Later in this chapter you will get more information on how this and other major regional trade agreements operate.

One weakness of a free trade area is called **trade deflection**. Trade deflection often occurs in free trade areas when companies from nonmember countries enter the free trade area though a member country with low trade barriers. They then can re-export their goods to the other countries in the area and avoid the other countries' trade restrictions. This is an attractive strategy for companies located outside the area because they can price their goods much more cheaply in their target countries.

To prevent trade deflection, countries often agree to **rules of origin**. Rules of origin specify how much of the content or valued added of a product must be produced in a member country to count as "produced" in the country. Specifying how these rules work can be quite complex. For example, in NAFTA, the rules of origin for textiles require that fabrics or clothing be spun from yarns or fibers produced in NAFTA countries. Rules also require that they and the fabrics or clothing be cut and sewn within the NAFTA area.[14] Such rules of origin prevent trade deflection of third-country goods from one NAFTA country to other NAFTA countries.

The next level of regional trade integration is called the **customs union**. The oldest customs union in the world is the Southern African Customs Union

(SACU), which includes the countries of South Africa, Botswana, Lesotho, Namibia, and Swaziland.

Customs unions are similar to free trade areas regarding relationships among members. All members get the same benefits of reduced tariffs and other trade barriers with each other. What makes customs unions different from regional trade agreements is that country members also agree to use uniform treatment of outsiders with regard to trade policies. This means, for example, that South Africa and Botswana in the SACU must impose the same tariff rates or other import restrictions on goods imported from the US or EU.

From an international manager's point of view, this means that the company from a country outside the union will pay the same tariffs regardless of which country is chosen as the entry into the union. That is, unlike the free trade area, there is no possibility of a back-door low-tariff entry point into the union. As such, this type of agreement avoids the possibility of trade diversion without resorting to complex rules-of-origin laws. Although customs unions have free trade among members and treat outsiders with similar trade policies, there are still barriers between the countries. To take the next step in the economic integration ladder, countries form **common markets**. Common markets allow free movement of labor, capital, and technology across member nations' borders. From the strategic point of view, this allows companies to locate any value-chain activity in any fellow common market country without restrictions. For example, the best available managers and workers can be hired from anywhere within the common market and be stationed at any of the company's locations. Ideally, as you learned from the discussion of transnational activities in Chapter 2, this increases the efficiency and effectiveness of companies because they can use the best platforms in their market in terms of price of quality. The European Union moved to a common market status in 1992.

common markets
add to the customs union the free movement of labor, capital, and technology among member nations

The final step typically achieved in economic integration without becoming a new country is called the **economic union**. The economic union includes all of the integration mechanisms of a common market but goes a step further. Member countries agree to coordinate economic policies, which include such factors as monetary policies, taxation, and currencies. The European Union is making strides toward becoming an economic union as member countries adopt the use of a single currency, called the euro (€). You will see more detail about the euro in the discussion of the European Union, below.

economic union
adds to the common market the agreement to coordinate economic policies, which include such factors as monetary policies, taxation, and currencies

Motivations for Regional Trade Agreements

Countries seek to join RTAs not only for economic reasons associated with trade and investment growth possibilities but also for political reasons. In addition, regional trade agreements are often easier to create than the multilateral trade agreements favored by the WTO. That is, fewer countries, especially when they are located close to each other, have less trouble finding common trading grounds.

The major motivation is economic growth with access to larger markets, more foreign investment, and more efficient use of local resources. Smaller nations such as Mexico are also attracted to agreements that lock in trade relationships with large countries such as the US. Political gains from joining regional trade areas can include benefits such as solidifying support for local reforms. For example, many of the transition economies of Eastern Europe used the requirements of regional agreements to lock in reforms such as the privatization of government-owned businesses that moved them toward more capitalistic economies. Political considerations also relate to enhanced security in the region. That is, some governments seek regional trade agreements to strengthen relationships among nations as a basis for increased security. Many experts point to the history of conflicts among European countries and note that economic integration reduces political friction among partners. Governments use agreements as rewards to other countries that conform to political goals. Some of the rationale for the US entering agreements such as the Free Trade Area of the Americas and the Central American Free Trade Agreement is to use access to the US market as a reward for economic liberalization and democratization.

Are Regional Trade Agreements Good for Business?

In general, experts see RTAs as having both positive and negative effects on trade. These two opposing forces are called **trade creation** and **trade diversion**.

trade creation
occurs when higher-cost production in one member country is replaced with lower-cost production from another member country

Once member nations eliminate protectionist barriers such as tariffs, quotas, and non-tariff barriers such as subsidies, there are economic incentives to increase trade among the members based on the advantages member nations have in the production of certain goods or services. That is, trade creation occurs because the lower-cost or higher-quality production from one member country can now be exported freely to replace the higher-cost or lower-quality production in other member countries. Consumers benefit by getting better products or services at lower prices. For individual companies, enhanced trade increases the competitive environment as all companies must compete against the most efficient and effective producers from any member country.

trade diversion
occurs when high-cost trade among member nations replaces trade with lower-cost producers who are outside of the agreement

However, the increased trade among RTA partners can also lead to potentially higher prices and less efficient use of resources and capabilities. As you will see in Chapter 4, economic theory suggests that if we all traded freely, nations would produce what they do most efficiently or best and would trade this output with other nations in exchange for what the other nations do cheapest or best. Because RTAs promote free trade only with their members and not with outsiders, there is a chance that trade barriers with outsiders may block what might otherwise be the most beneficial trade relations. This is called trade diversion: the trade among member nations replaces trade with lower-cost or higher-quality producers who are outside of the agreement. In general, economists see the net effect of trade creation and trade diversion as an indication of how the regional trade agreement contributes to world trade.

Regional Trade Agreements: A Look Inside

There are many regional trade agreements and most nations belong to more than one. Exhibit 3.7 shows the membership of all existing major agreements. However, new agreements are being created all of the time.

Next, to look more closely at how free trade agreements work, we will look at the structure and organization of three groups. These groups are: the European Union, the North American Free Trade Agreement, and Asia-Pacific

Exhibit 3.7 **Regional Trade Agreements and Member Nations**

Andean Group (ANCOM)	ASEAN (Association of South-East Asian Nations)	APEC (Asia-Pacific Economic Cooperation)			CEPGL (Economic Community of the Great Lakes Countries)	Baltic countries
Bolivia	Brunei Darussalam	Australia	China, Taiwan Province of	Peru	Burundi	Estonia
Colombia	Cambodia	Brunei Darussalam	Indonesia	Philippines	Democratic Republic of the Congo	Latvia
Ecuador	Indonesia	Canada	Japan	Republic of Korea	Rwanda	Lithuania
Peru	Lao People's Democratic Republic	Chile	Malaysia	Russian Federation		
Venezuela	Malaysia	China	Mexico	Singapore		
	Myanmar	China, Hong Kong SAR	New Zealand	Thailand		
	Philippines		Papua New Guinea	United States of America		
	Singapore			Vietnam		
	Thailand					
	Vietnam					

CACM (Central American Common Market)	Bangkok Agreement	BSEC (Black Sea Economic Cooperation)		COMESA (Common Market for Eastern and Southern Africa)		EFTA (European Free Trade Association)	EU (European Union)	
Costa Rica	Bangladesh	Albania	Romania	Angola	Rwanda	Iceland	Austria	Lithuania
El Salvador	China	Armenia	Russian Federation	Burundi	Seychelles	Norway	Belgium	Malta
Guatemala	India	Azerbaijan	Turkey	Comoros	Sudan	Switzerland	Denmark	Poland
Honduras	Lao People's Democratic Republic	Bulgaria	Ukraine	Democratic Republic of the Congo	Swaziland		Finland	Romania
Nicaragua	Republic of Korea	Georgia		Djibouti	Uganda			
	Sri Lanka	Greece		Egypt	Zambia			
		Moldova, Republic of		Eritrea	Zimbabwe			
				Ethiopia				
				Kenya				
				Madagascar				
				Malawi				
				Mauritius				
				Namibia				

CARICOM (Caribbean Community)	ECO (Economic Cooperation Organization)	EU (European Union)	UMA (Arab Maghreb Union)	CIS (Commonwealth of Independent States)
Antigua and Barbuda	Afghanistan		Algeria	Armenia
Bahamas	Azerbaijan		Libyan Arab Jamahiriya	Azerbaijan
Barbados	Iran, Islamic Republic of		Mauritania	Belarus
				Georgia

Exhibit 3.7 **continued**

CARICOM (Caribbean Community)	ECO (Economic Cooperation Organization)	EU (European Union)	UMA (Arab Maghreb Union)	CIS (Commonwealth of Independent States)
Belize	Kazakhstan	France	Morocco	Kazakhstan
Dominica	Kyrgyzstan	Germany	Tunisia	Kyrgyzstan
Grenada	Pakistan	Greece		Republic of Moldova
Guyana	Tajikistan	Ireland		Russian Federation
Jamaica	Turkey	Italy		Tajikistan
Montserrat	Turkmenistan	Luxembourg		Turkmenistan
Saint Kitts and Nevis	Uzbekistan	Netherlands		Ukraine
Saint Lucia		Portugal		Uzbekistan
Saint Vincent and the Grenadines		Spain		
Suriname		Sweden		
Trinidad and Tobago		United Kingdom		
		Recent:		
		Cyprus		
		Czech Republic		
		Bulgaria		
		Estonia		
		Hungary		
		Slovakia		
		Slovenia		

FTAA (Free Trade Area of the Americas)			GCC (Gulf Cooperation Council)	ECOWAS (Economic Community of West African States)
Antigua and Barbuda	Dominican Republic	Saint Kitts and Nevis	Bahrain	Benin
Argentina	Ecuador	Saint Lucia	Kuwait	Burkina Faso
Bahamas	El Salvador	Saint Vincent and the Grenadines	Oman	Cape Verde
Barbados	Grenada	Suriname	Qatar	Côte d'Ivoire
Belize	Guatemala	Trinidad and Tobago	Saudi Arabia	Gambia
Bolivia	Guyana	United States of America	United Arab Emirates	Ghana
Brazil	Haiti	Uruguay		Guinea
Canada	Honduras	Venezuela		Guinea-Bissau
Chile	Jamaica			Liberia
Colombia	Mexico			Mali
Costa Rica	Nicaragua			Niger
Dominica	Panama			Nigeria
	Paraguay			Senegal
	Peru			Sierra Leone
				Togo

LAIA (Latin American Integration Association)

Argentina, Bolivia, Brazil, Chile, Colombia, Cuba, Ecuador, Mexico, Paraguay, Peru, Uruguay, Venezuela

MSG (Melanesia Spearhead Group)

Fiji, New Caledonia, Papua New Guinea, Solomon Islands, Vanuatu

SADC (Southern African Development Community)

Angola, Botswana, Democratic Republic of the Congo, Lesotho, Malawi, Mauritius, Mozambique, Namibia, Seychelles, South Africa, Swaziland, United Republic of Tanzania, Zambia, Zimbabwe

MERCOSUR (Southern Common Market)

Argentina, Brazil, Paraguay, Uruguay

SAARC (South Asian Association for Regional Cooperation)

Bangladesh, Bhutan, India, Maldives, Nepal, Pakistan, Sri Lanka

ECCAS (Economic Community of Central African States)

Angola, Burundi, Cameroon, Central African Republic, Chad, Congo, Democratic Republic of the Congo, Equatorial Guinea, Gabon, Rwanda, Sao Tome and Principe

NAFTA (North American Free Trade Agreement)

Canada, Mexico, United States of America

MRU (Mano River Union)

Guinea, Liberia, Sierra Leone

OECS (Organization of Eastern Caribbean States)

Anguilla, Antigua and Barbuda, British Virgin Islands, Dominica, Grenada, Montserrat, Saint Kitts and Nevis, Saint Lucia, Saint Vincent and the Grenadines

CEMAC, former UDEAC (Economic and Monetary Community of Central Africa)

Cameroon, Central African Republic, Chad, Congo, Equatorial Guinea, Gabon

EMOA (West African Economic and Monetary Union)

Benin, Burkina Faso, Côte d'Ivoire, Guinea-Bissau, Mali, Niger, Senegal, Togo

Source: Adapted from UNCTAD, 2007, *Trade and Development Report 2007*, New York and Geneva: United Nations.

Economic Cooperation. These three largest free trade groups account for nearly half of the world's trade.

European Union

European Union
a group of 25 countries that act as a common market with the goal of being a complete economic union

Initially, the **European Union** (EU) included just six countries. By 1995 the EU totaled 15 countries: Austria, Belgium, Britain, Denmark, Finland, France, Germany, Greece, Ireland, Italy, Luxembourg, the Netherlands, Portugal, Spain, and Sweden. In 2004, with its biggest expansion, the EU added ten new countries and nearly doubled in population served. It now represents more

Member states of the European Union (2007)

Candidate countries

Exhibit 3.8 **The Countries of the European Union**

Source: © European Community 2008.

than 450 million people. The newest member countries include many from the former Eastern Bloc, including Poland, the Czech Republic, Hungary, Slovakia, Lithuania, Latvia, Slovenia, Estonia, Cyprus, and Malta. Croatia, Macedonia, and Turkey are also candidates to join. Norway and Switzerland are closely aligned with the EU countries by their membership of the related European Free Trade Area.

The €100 note

Note the map in Exhibit 3.8 that shows the current make-up of the EU and the location of its countries.

Since 1992, the EU countries have allowed goods and services to move across borders without customs duties and quotas, and more recently, as noted above, some of the countries have adopted the euro as their national currency. The 12 countries now using the euro are part of the European Economic and Monetary Union or, as it is more often called, the **European Monetary Union** (EMU). Eventually, all countries in the EU, with the exception of Great Britain and Denmark, are required to join the EMU and will have the euro as their national currency. Britain and Denmark chose to stay out of the EMU prior to it becoming a requirement. Not only must all new EU member countries eventually use the euro but they also must manage their economies to satisfy the preconditions to adopt the euro, as spelled out in the Maastricht Treaty.[15] One important precondition is that the accession countries must achieve exchange-rate stability between the value of their current national currencies and the euro for at least two years. Full integration including adopting the euro or common currency may not occur for some time. With full integration, this new mega-Europe will have an economy of nearly $10 trillion that rivals the United States[16]

European Monetary Union (EMU)
the EU countries that use the euro as a common currency

Euro users can be seen on the map in Exhibit 3.9 overleaf.

As the IB Strategic Insight on page 81 shows, the use of a common currency can have different impacts on countries and business. International managers must be aware of how such forms of economic integration can affect their companies and industries now and in the future.

In addition to a common currency, another important step in the economic integration of the EU was the creation of the European Central Bank. This bank took over the role of the central banks in euro countries that previously managed local currencies and monetary policies such as interest rates. The European Central Bank now manages euro and monetary policy for the Union. As more members take on the euro and if EU members can ever agree on a common constitution, the European Union will move even closer to becoming a true economic union.

History and Organization of the EU   The seeds for the idea of a European Union were proposed in a speech on May 9, 1950, by French Foreign Minister Robert Schuman. Although May 9 is now considered the birthday of the EU, Mr Schuman's proposal was modest. He only suggested that coal and steel industries be integrated. The result was the European Coal and Steel Community

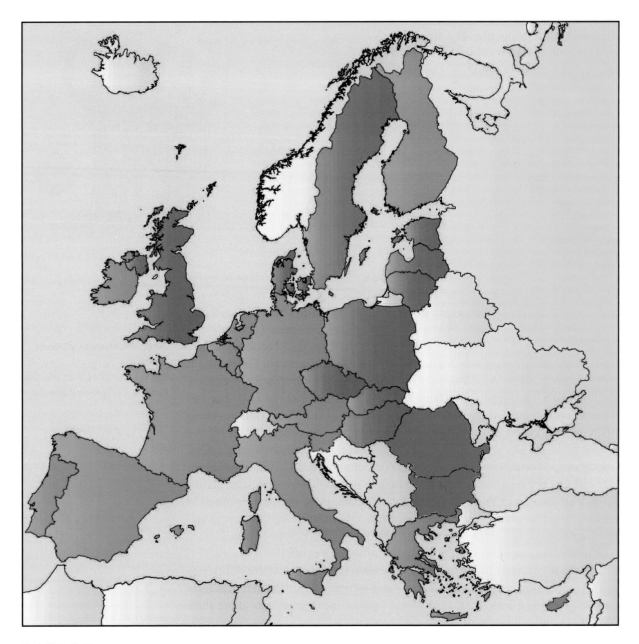

Exhibit 3.9 **Currencies within the European Union**
Key: Red shows euro users; blue shows users of other currencies.

Source: © European Community 2008.

(ECSC), which included six members: Belgium, West Germany, Luxembourg, France, Italy and the Netherlands. Further integration followed and the original six countries signed the Treaties of Rome, creating the European Atomic Energy Community (EURATOM) and the European Economic Community (EEC).

To simplify managing these agreements, in 1967 participating countries created a Commission, a Council of Ministers, and the European Parliament. By the late 1970s, the Parliament became a legislative body elected directly by the citizens of member states every five years.

Pluses and Minuses of the European Monetary Union

The European Monetary Union represents those EU countries that have adopted the euro as their national currency. It represents an important step in the EU becoming a true economic union. Now, several years after its January 1, 1999, launch, countries and companies are starting to take stock of its impact.

A big benefit is that the risk associated with changing exchange rates among euro countries is gone. For individual companies this can really pay off. Rick Simonson, the chief financial officer of Nokia, the Finnish cell-phone company, estimates that they have a $6 million saving by not having currency transaction costs in the Euro zone. He also estimates that "It makes the whole supply chain more efficient," because Nokia's suppliers also benefit.

Unfortunately, not all countries and companies benefit from the euro. Monetary policies set by the European Central Bank that keep down the supply of euros and thus make them more valuable have resulted in a strong euro relative to other currencies such as the dollar. This makes European goods more expensive and less competitive on the world market. If the Euro is worth more than the dollar,

it takes more dollars to buy European goods. Countries like Germany, France, and Italy have inflexible labor markets, making wage adjustments difficult and making it costly if not impossible to fire workers. That is, they cannot easily reduce costs to make their goods cheaper on the world market. When these forces combine, European companies face severe strategic challenges.

In Italy, even upscale fashion designers such as Giorgio Armani are looking to China to produce their lower-level items such as jeans. However, in spite of the difficulties of inflexible work arrangements and a highly valued currency, some companies still thrive. The innovative fitness-equipment maker Technogym is a $285 million company growing at nearly 15 percent a year. Eighty percent of its sales are from exports. Nerio Alessandri, founder and president, notes, "If you have an innovative product, the strong euro and the Asians [low-cost competitors] are not a problem . . . change [cut costs or innovate] or die."

Sources: Adapted from *BusinessWeek Online*, 2005, "Italy: The Euro-zone's sickest patient," www.businessweek.com, June 6; *BusinessWeek Online*, 2005, "Squeezed by the euro," www.businessweek.com, June 6.

Originally, the members of the European Parliament were chosen by the national parliaments. But in 1979 this changed and the first direct elections were held, allowing the citizens of the member states to vote for the candidate of their choice. Since then, direct elections have been held every five years.

Continuous political and economic integration led eventually to the formal creation of the EU with the Treaty of Maastricht in 1992 and the creation of a common market. During the 1990s most countries abolished customs borders and more and more products and services crossed borders freely. As noted above, the Maastricht Treaty also created the EMU and the introduction of the euro.[17]

Perhaps because the EU is the most integrated of the regional trade agreements its governing structures are complex and resemble those of parliamentary democracies with legislative and executive branches of government. There are three major organizational units used to govern EU activities: the European Parliament, the Council of the European Union, and the European Commission.

The *European Commission* is somewhat like an executive branch (law-enforcing and daily management) of government, with the exception that it is appointed. The European Commission proposes legislation to the legislative (law-making) branches of the organization, which include the *Parliament* and the *Council*. It also manages and implements EU policies and the budget, enforces European law (jointly with the Court of Justice), and represents the EU in its dealings with other countries.

Exhibit 3.10 **Number of Elected Representatives to the European Parliament**

	1999–2004	*2004–7*	*2007–9*
Austria	21	18	18
Belgium	25	24	24
Bulgaria	—	—	18
Cyprus	—	6	6
Czech Republic	—	24	24
Denmark	16	14	14
Estonia	—	6	6
Finland	16	14	14
France	87	78	78
Germany	99	99	99
Greece	25	24	24
Hungary	—	24	24
Ireland	15	13	13
Italy	87	78	78
Latvia	—	9	9
Lithuania	—	13	13
Luxembourg	6	6	6
Malta	—	5	5
Netherlands	31	27	27
Poland	—	54	54
Portugal	25	24	24
Romania	—	—	36
Slovakia	—	14	14
Slovenia	—	7	7
Spain	64	54	54
Sweden	22	19	19
United Kingdom	87	78	78
(MAX) TOTAL	**626**	**732**	**786**

Source: http://europa.eu.int

The European Parliament is the one legislative branch elected directly by the people. It shares its legislative authority with the Council. The Parliament and the Council legislate laws and rules that have EU-wide applications. The Parliament also has the authority to approve or reject the nomination of Commissioners and, somewhat like the US House of Representatives, it shares with the Council the authority over the EU budget. Exhibit 3.10 shows the number of elected representatives from each EU country during different time periods.

In addition to its legislative functions shared with the Parliament, the Council co-ordinates the broad economic policies of the EU, develops the EU's Common Foreign and Security Policy, and coordinates legal issues with the member states. Ministers in the Council are appointed by their governments and not elected directly. They also have the power to commit their government to EU actions without further consultations.

You can check the current status of the EU at http://europa.eu.

North American Free Trade Agreement

The **North American Free Trade Agreement (NAFTA)** links the United States, Canada, and Mexico in an economic bloc that allows freer exchange of goods and services. After the agreement went into effect in the early 1990s, all three countries saw immediate increases in trade. However, the Mexican economy soon went into a tailspin, with inflation running as high as 45 percent. Emergency loans from the United States helped stabilize the situation, and by 1996 Mexico had paid back the loans—before the due date. The next step for NAFTA may be to expand, as we have seen with the EU. The proposed FTAA or the Free Trade Area of the Americas will include not only the United States, Canada, and Mexico, but also most other Caribbean, Central American, and South American nations.

North American Free Trade Agreement (NAFTA) links the United States, Canada, and Mexico in an economic bloc that allows freer exchange of goods and services

Governance of NAFTA NAFTA has two major governing bodies, the Free Trade Commission and the NAFTA coordinators, and one major dispute resolution body, the NAFTA Secretariat.

The *Free Trade Commission* consists of cabinet-level representatives from the three member countries. It meets annually. The Commission supervises the implementation of the NAFTA agreement by subordinate committees and working groups.

The *NAFTA Coordinators* are in charge of day-to-day management of NAFTA. This is a shared leadership role among three senior trade department officials assigned by Canada, Mexico, and the US. NAFTA also uses over 30 working groups and committees to manage specific areas of the agreement. These include, for example, trade in goods, rules of origin, customs, agricultural trade and subsidies, standards, government procurement, investment and services, and cross-border movement of business people (e.g. visa standards and work permits).

The *NAFTA Secretariat* is responsible for dispute settlement between member nations. The Secretariat has Canadian, US, and Mexican sections. They coordinate the investigation and resolution of disputes under NAFTA. Information on the Secretariat is available from www.nafta-sec-alena.org/.

Two Canadian Companies Succeed because of NAFTA

IB STRATEGIC INSIGHT

KDM Electronics Inc. (www.octasound.com) of Scarborough, Ontario, is a family-owned company with only six employees. It produces speaker systems and music sound systems for commercial use in gymnasiums, convention centers, sports arenas, shopping malls, warehouses and factories. "Being highly specialized and niche-oriented, we need a sizable market," says Ron Bull, president of KDM. He notes, "With an industrial and commercial market eight times the size of Canada's, the United States fits the bill. And it's all one level playing field, due to NAFTA."

Since the signing of NAFTA, KDM's exports to the US have increased to 85 percent of the company's total production. Bull says, "And as long as you're competitive, the border is transparent. For KDM that's crucial, as we often deal with small, family-owned businesses who don't want the hassles of regulations and tariffs. What they do require is a stable trading relationship, and with NAFTA that's what we have."

Like KDM, the Quebec-based freight carrier SGT Inc. (www.sgt.qu.ca) saw a boom in business after NAFTA. Fleet size grew to 1,600 vehicles, up from 100, and the company now employs 750 people, up from 30. SGT ships from Alaska to the Yucatan. It has terminals and sales offices throughout Canada, the US, and Mexico.

SGT President Denis Coderre notes, "Since NAFTA came into effect, we have a lot more traffic from Mexico to Canada and the US. By easing restrictions and reducing tariffs, the agreement has facilitated the transportation of all kinds of products. For us, it has meant a boost in volume and more jobs."

Source: Adapted from www.itcan-cican.gc.ca/menu-en.asp

As with all types of trade agreements, from the WTO to the regional trade agreements, some gain from the openness while others lose. In the IB Strategic Insight above you can see two different perspectives on the effects of NAFTA. Both show the positive effects for two Canadian companies.

Having seen how NAFTA benefited KDM and SGT, consider the IB Ethical Challenge opposite, which takes a more negative position on the effects of NAFTA.

The final example of a regional trade agreement considered in this chapter looks at the major agreement for countries in the Asia and Pacific region. It also shows a type of relationship that is less structured than the EU or NAFTA.

Asia-Pacific Economic Cooperation

Asia-Pacific Economic Cooperation (APEC)
a loose confederation of 21 nations with nonbinding free trade area agreements

When compared with the EU or NAFTA, the **Asia-Pacific Economic Cooperation (APEC)** is a looser confederation of 21 nations with less specific agreements on trade facilitation. However, ultimate goals call for total free trade in the Pacific region by 2020.[18] Member nations in APEC include: Australia; Brunei Darussalam; Canada; Chile; the People's Republic of China; Hong Kong, China; Indonesia; Japan; the Republic of Korea; Malaysia; Mexico; New Zealand; Papua New Guinea; Peru; the Republic of the Philippines; the Russian Federation; Singapore; Chinese Taipei; Thailand; the United States of America; and Vietnam.

ETHICAL CHALLENGE

Public Insight, Ralph Nadar's Consumer Advocates' Group, Takes a Negative Position on NAFTA

Not all people support multilateral trade agreements and regional trade agreements because they believe that certain groups are particularly hurt. Below is a quote from *Public Citizen's Global Trade Watch*, which looks at the downside of NAFTA for many Mexican workers.

Mexico suffered many negative economic effects as a result of NAFTA. Sharp cuts in farm subsidy programs combined with the near-elimination of import restrictions on corn and other commodities resulted in dumped US corn flooding the Mexican market, forcing over 1.5 million *campesinos* or peasant farmers whose livelihoods were based on small-scale farming off their land. Many US agribusiness multinationals also used NAFTA investment and service sector rules to buy corn-processing and tortilla-making factories in Mexico. Yet instead of falling (as "free" trade theory predicts), retail prices for food products increased sharply. The cost of tortillas rose by 50 percent in Mexico City and more in the countryside, even as prices paid to Mexican farmers for corn plummeted. At the same time, the purchasing power of the average Mexican worker has also dropped. Since NAFTA, a combination of factors—including the migration of so many *campesinos* to the cities—has caused Mexican industrial wages to decline by approximately 25 percent. The economic fallout from NAFTA has also been shown to have had particularly harsh consequences for Mexican women; a recent study found that the poverty rate for female-headed households in Mexico has increased by 50 percent since NAFTA went into effect.

Source: Labor Council for Latin American Advancement, 2004, "Another Americas is possible: The impact of NAFTA on the US Latino community and lessons for future trade agreements," *Public Citizen's Global Trade Watch*, August, p. 4.

In addition, other trade groups in the Pacific region often participate in APEC activities as observers. These include the Association of South East Asian Nations (ASEAN) Secretariat, the Pacific Economic Cooperation Council (PECC), and the Pacific Islands Forum Secretariat (PIF).

APEC is unique when compared to other regional trade agreements. It operates on the basis of non-binding commitments. That is, unlike the WTO or other RTAs, APEC has no treaty obligations that govern member nations. Instead, trade agreements are voluntary and are reached by consensus.

Although APEC does not have the treaty authority to enforce compliance with trade rules that are part of other treaty-based agreements, it is important because of its coverage of major sections of the world's economy. APEC nations have more than a third of the world's population (2.6 billion people) and produce 60 percent of the world's GDP ($19,254 billion) and nearly half of world trade. Moreover, in spite of the lack of binding agreements, it seems that APEC has, at least in part, helped the growth of trade and investment in the region. Since its founding, exports for APEC countries have increased by 113 percent to over $2.5 trillion, and FDI grew by 210 percent overall and by 475 percent in lower-income APEC countries.[19]

A summary of the structure and activities of APEC is shown in Exhibit 3.11. You can see that its organization is somewhat similar to other RTAs even without the formal binding agreements among members.

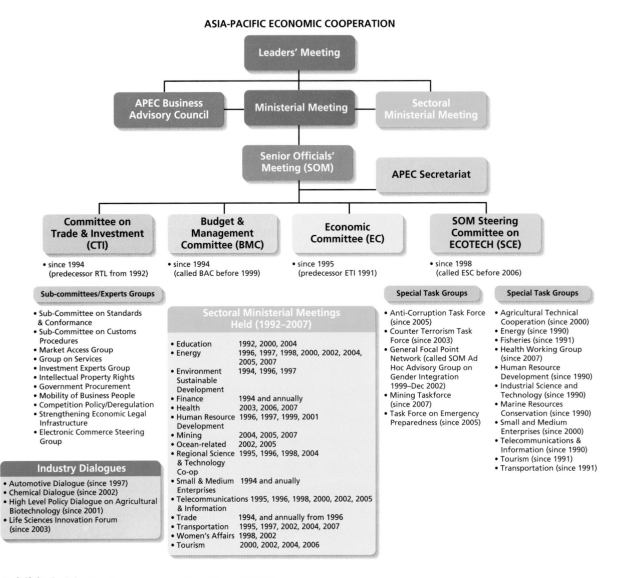

Exhibit 3.11   **The Structure and Activities of APEC**

Source: www.apec.org/apec/about_apec/structure.html

CHAPTER REVIEW

This chapter provided you with an overview of the existing mechanisms for global and regional integration. These agreements are important for international business people because they define the context of international competition and the extent of globalization. As barriers to trade drop, MNCs are more likely to adopt transnational, international, or regional multinational strategies because crossing borders becomes easier. Companies can source raw material or sell anywhere more advantageous when barriers to trade fall.

The chapter began with a history of GATT and how this basic agreement led eventually to the creation of a permanent organization, the WTO, to manage the reduction in trade barriers around the world. Importantly, the WTO also added a mechanism for dispute resolution when countries came into conflict over violations of agreements. Prior to GATT and the WTO, most trade agreements were bilateral, that is just between two countries. Now such agreements tend to be multilateral, agreements between groups of countries who are members of the WTO or of the many regional trade agreements.

The goal of the WTO is to reduce trade barriers worldwide. However, there are many other groups involved in trade barriers reduction. These regional trade agreements vary widely in membership and structure. Most countries belong to several groups in addition to the WTO. The RTAs range from simple agreements for preferential treatment to the more complex agreements of the customs union and economic union. The customs union not only treats members preferentially but also treats all outsiders with a uniform trade policy. The economic union goes even further by combining under one monetary policy.

To look inside the operations of RTAs in action, the chapter described the history and structure of the EU, NAFTA, and APEC. The EU is the most integrated of all RTAs and is now approaching a true economic union with the use of the euro as a common currency at least among some members. NAFA is a less integrated preferential trade agreement but may at some time become more like the EU, with new agreements such as the Central American Free Trade Agreement. APEC is a loosely configured preferential trade agreement where members do not sign binding treaties. Nevertheless, APEC seemingly has succeeded in reducing trade barriers among its member nations.

In all cases, the astute international manager will understand the implications of the various agreements for the types of goods or services produced by his or her company. Each new agreement creates both opportunities and threats for companies in different countries and different industries.

DISCUSSION QUESTIONS

1. Describe how GATT evolved into the WTO. What are the major differences between these agreements?
2. What are the differences between multilateral and bilateral trade agreements?
3. Describe how a company might use trade deflection or trade diversion to gain a strategic advantage over competitors.
4. Describe the basic types of regional trade agreements. Discuss some of the advantages and disadvantages of MNCs doing business in each type.
5. Discuss some of the implications (costs and benefits) of a common currency for companies operating in countries that formerly had their own currencies.

INTERNATIONAL BUSINESS SKILL BUILDER

Understanding the WTO Debate

Not everyone agrees that the WTO is beneficial for the people of the world. The WTO is founded on the economic belief that free trade is more efficient and that on aggregate most people will be better served in a free trade environment. Critics argue that the multinational corporations are the prime beneficiaries with an array of negative effects for some countries and people.

For this exercise, consider both sides of the debate.

Step 1: Investigate some of the organizations that are critical of the WTO and most other trade agreements. Some examples are:

www.globalexchange.org/campaigns/wto/
www.citizen.org/trade/wto/
www.globalissues.org/TradeRelated/Seattle.asp

Step 2: Consider the WTO's positions regarding many of these criticisms. You can find the WTO's perspective on their website, www.wto.org/. Search the WTO site and read Chapter 1 of *The Future of the WTO*. Also look at *Ten Benefits of the WTO Trading System* and *Ten Common Misunderstandings about the WTO*. These publications can be downloaded in PDF or read online.

Step 3: Consider the merits of each side and be prepared to defend and debate your position.

Step 4: Form teams of pro and con WTO positions and debate the issue in class.

CHAPTER INTERNET ACTIVITY

In this project you will get to explore the effects of different tariffs on different products. As an international manager considering exporting:

1. Pick a product that you intend to export. Imagine that you will export that product to one of the APEC nations.
2. Explore the APEC tariff database at **www.apectariff.org/** to see what trade barriers exist. You will need to register but registration is free.
3. Identify the countries with the lowest and highest tariff barriers.
4. Write or present a report dealing with your findings.

KEY CONCEPTS

Asia-Pacific Economic Cooperation (APEC)

common markets

customs unions

economic union

European Monetary Union (EMU)

European Union

free trade areas

General Agreement on Tariffs and Trade (GATT)

North American Free Trade Agreement (NAFTA)

preferential trade agreement

principle of nondiscrimination

regional trade agreements (RTAs)

rules of origin

tariffs

trade creation

trade deflection

trade diversion

World Trade Organization (WTO)

BUSINESS > INTERNATIONAL

SUNSHINE FARMS

WITHERING SINCE NAFTA

Sunshine Farms Inc. is a fourth-generation family business located in south Florida. Sunshine began as a small farm devoted to citrus fruits and vegetables, and over the years the company has prospered. Sunshine Farms now grows and markets limes, lemons, mangos, snap beans, tomatoes, and other "row crops." Sunshine Farms has endured hurricanes, tropical flooding, freezes, and plant diseases; however, its most recent challenge appears to be its greatest.

Since the passage of the North American Free Trade Agreement (NAFTA), a number of Florida farms have been closed. With the reduction of tariffs on agricultural products, farmers have had difficulty competing with Mexican producers. Many Mexican farm products are imported into the United States and sold at a price that is considerably below the cost of domestic products. Row-crop farmers, as compared to nurseries, have been particularly hard hit by the Mexican competition.

Domestic producers complain that lower labor costs and fewer environmental regulations in Mexico allow Mexican farmers to export their products into the United States at a price that will not allow American farmers to make a profit. Without tariffs on these goods, and given the inability to differentiate their products, some American farms have not been able to make a profit and stay in business.

Sunshine Farms possessed a strong competitive advantage prior to NAFTA. Florida weather allows for a growing season that is much longer than that in other parts of the United States. Florida farmers were able to grow products in December and January when much of the country was experiencing frigid temperatures. Mexican farmers were exporting agricultural products into the United States prior to NAFTA; however, the tariffs assessed on those products made Sunshine's prices competitive. With lower production costs, longer growing seasons, and the elimination of tariffs, Mexican farm products have become a significant threat to the survival of some domestic farmers.

Ben McDonald, CEO of Sunshine Farms, is worried about not only the survival of his business, but the survival of the entire Florida farming community. "In 20 years you won't have a single row-crop farmer left in Florida," McDonald predicts. Since farm products are commodities, it is difficult to brand the products and extract a premium price. "Consumers are usually not aware of where their tomatoes come from, and in most cases they simply don't care. All they care about is price," says McDonald. He has stated on several occasions that "We should learn from the country's dependence on foreign oil and the disruptions in supply. Just wait until this happens in food production."

. . .

CASE 3

page 2

Some have recommended that Ben and others shift their focus toward the nursery business. The nurseries of South Florida have been doing very well with the construction increases in the US, and they seem less vulnerable to foreign imports. Others have recommended that American farmers begin to brand their products or place a "Grown in the USA" label on them in order to charge a higher price. Few row-crop farmers have successfully made the shift into nurseries or seem willing to brand their products. As more farms continue to close each year, Ben wonders if Sunshine Farms can survive in a free-trade environment.

CASE DISCUSSION POINTS

1. Is NAFTA unfair to American farmers? Explain.
2. Could Sunshine Farms differentiate its products by placing a "Grown in the USA" label on them in order to charge a premium price?
3. What would you recommend to Ben McDonald in order to save the farm?

Source: This case is fictional; however, it is based on actual situations as reported in *Miami Herald*, 2001, "Farming on faith," January 1.

Case prepared by Charles A. Rarick

4 Global Trade and Foreign Direct Investment

After reading this chapter you should be able to:

- Understand the history of trade theory.

- Appreciate how the knowledge of trade theory can help you select better multi-national strategies.

- Understand the concepts of absolute and comparative advantage.

- Appreciate the benefits and costs of international trade.

- Be familiar with the basic theories that explain foreign direct investment.

The Preview IB Strategic Insight shows how Boeing uses the international trade system to benefit from global supply sources. Boeing can take advantage of the engineering and manufacturing strengths located in countries like Japan and build an entirely new airplane quicker and more efficiently than doing it completely in the US. This is only possible because trade occurs between countries.

In this chapter, you will see why such international trade as well as cross-border investments often make sense and work to the general benefit of most people. The chapter begins this exploration by a look at the history of trade theories.

Boeing's New 787 Dreamliner is 70 Percent Imported!

**PREVIEW IB
STRATEGIC INSIGHT**

At the heart of globalization is increasing trade between companies from different countries. Companies use world trade to find both suppliers and customers. No company probably illustrates this trend more than the US aircraft manufacturer, Boeing. For Boeing, things have changed drasti- cally in the world of commercial jet manufacturing and sales. In the 1960s, the Boeing 727 was the company's prize product. Only 2 percent of its components came from outside the US. By the mid-1990s, components for Boeing's 777 were 30 percent foreign. The new 787 will be 70 percent

Company/Business Unit	Main Location	787 Work Statement
Alenia/Vought Aircraft Industries	Italy, Texas	Horizontal stabilizer, center fuselage, aft fuselage
Fuji Heavy Industries	Japan	Center wing box, integration of the center wing box with the main landing-gear wheel well
Kawasaki Heavy Industries	Japan	Main landing-gear wheel well, main wing fixed trailing edge, part of forward fuselage
Mitsubishi Heavy Industries	Japan	Wing box
Rockwell Collins	Iowa	Displays, communications/surveillance systems
Smiths	United Kingdom	Common core system, landing-gear actuation and control system, high lift actuation system
Messier-Dowty	France	Landing-gear structure
Dassault Systèmes	France	Global collaboration tools/software
FR-HiTemp	United Kingdom	Pumps and valves
Rolls-Royce	United Kingdom	Engines
Thales	France	Electrical power conversion, integrated standby flight display
Labinal	France	Wiring
Messier-Bugatti	France	Electric brakes
Latecoere	France	Passenger doors
Panasonic	Japan	Cabin services system
Bridgestone	Japan	Tires
Ultra Electronics Holdings	United Kingdom	Wing ice-protection system
GKN Aerospace	United Kingdom	Composite mat for the wing ice-protection system
Ipeco	United Kingdom	Flight-deck seats
Diehl Luftfahrt Elektronik	Germany	Main cabin lighting
Jamco	Japan	Lavatories, flight deck interiors, flight deck door and bulkhead assembly

foreign and most of that Japanese. Japan's three major aerospace manufacturers, Fuji, Kawasaki, and Mitsubishi, will build approximately 35 percent of the plane. These companies will also subcontract component manufacturing to other Asian countries.

The table on the previous page shows the international component suppliers Boeing intends to use for the 787.

Although not as extensive as with the Dreamliner, importing components for commercial aircraft production is common. Even the European Airbus planes often have nearly 50 percent of US-produced components. One-third of Boeing's 3,500 world fleet of planes has major parts and assemblies built in China. Boeing has contracts valued at $1.6 billion with the Chinese aviation industry for components for all of its major models.

Boeing's Dreamliner 787 is a completely new design and represents a radical departure in commercial aircraft production. Built almost entirely of ultra-light composite materials, the plane will be lighter and more efficient than contemporary aircraft. Boeing hopes that this efficiency will offset the massive carrying capacity of its rival, Airbus's A380.

Another radical shift in Boeing's strategy is that suppliers are not just building components based on exact specified designs delivered to suppliers in final form. Boeing is using the talents and money of suppliers to produce components from the design to final production. Boeing then becomes more of a virtual company coordinating the design and production process remotely. The goal is for a 787 to take only three days of final assembly when the components reach the Everett, Washington, plant.

Sources: Adapted from *Flight International*, 2005, "787 suppliers sign deal," May 31–6 June, p. 8; www.boeing.com; *The Economist*, 2005, "How Japan learned to fly," June 25, p. 68.

History of Trade Theory

Although trade between countries is as old as the existence of nation-states, the development of modern trade theory came much later. Below you will see some of the important historical developments in our understanding of how trade works.

Mercantilism: Early Thinking

zero-sum game
when one side loses, another side gains

mercantilism
the objective of between-country trade is for a country to win by exporting more than it imports

favorable trade balance
a surplus of exports over imports overall or applied to a particular country

During the seventeenth and early eighteenth centuries, the common belief was that trade between countries was a **zero-sum game**. A zero-sum game is like a tennis match: when one person wins a point, the other person loses. In the **mercantilism** philosophy, the objective of between-country trade was for a country to win by exporting more than it imported.

This trade philosophy prospered at a period of nation-building and the expectation that each state would accumulate as much gold and silver as possible. Gold and silver was the currency of trade, and nations that exported more than they imported accumulated more gold and silver. One nation's gain was another nation's loss. Economists call this surplus of exports over imports a **favorable trade balance**. The belief was that there was a fixed amount of gold and silver in the world and the nation that had the most of these precious metals would be the most powerful.

By the mid-1700s, the mercantilists were under attack. David Hume pointed out the basic flaws in the mercantilism reasoning.[1] He noted two problems. The first was a very practical one. How would you like to live in a country that has lots of gold and silver buried deeply in secure areas like Fort Knox in the US, but fewer goods or services to buy? Hume argued that most people want the things that gold or silver or any other form of money can buy.

The second problem relates to what economists call the **specie-flow mechanism**. What this means is that when the supply or amount of money in a country increases, the prices in that country tend to go up as well. Since gold and silver represent the money supply, this means that more of these metals that a country accumulates from exporting, the higher prices become in the country. As people generally get more affluent, they purchase more goods and services. Thus, as the demands for these goods and services go up, so do the prices.

But what is the impact on trade? Consider if France and Germany were trading partners, with France having a favorable trade balance with Germany

specie-flow mechanism
when the supply or amount of money in a country increases, the prices in that country tend to go up as well

Neo-mercantilism: Should the US and EU Protect their Textile Industries from Chinese Imports?

IB STRATEGIC INSIGHT

In spite of the efforts of the WTO and the general opinion of economists that mercantilism does not work, variants of the mercantile position are often popular for the companies in industries hurt by international competition and with politicians who support those industries.

With the US trade deficit to China reaching $160 billion in 2004 and the EU deficit reaching $98 billion (certainly a favorable trade balance for China), protectionist sentiment is rising in Europe and Washington. China alone accounts for 26 percent of the trade gap in the US, and many politicians and workers in industries where China competes with imports see China as the culprit for lost jobs and stagnant wages.

Nowhere is this more apparent than in the textile industry. When the quotas on the amount of Chinese textile imports based on the Multi-Fiber Agreement ended in January of 2005, Chinese textile imports jumped immediately and dramatically. In some categories, increases exceeded 1,000 percent in the first quarter of 2005 (e.g. cotton trousers 1,492 percent). In Europe, imports of men's trousers quintupled and prices fell by nearly one-quarter. With the end of the Multi-Fiber Agreement, no longer were the largest textile markets in the world, the EU and the US, able to enjoy the comfort of a protected market, a luxury for 40 years.

For Jeff Johnson, 44 years old and a worker for 28 years at the same North Carolina mill where his grandfather and farther worked, and the nearly 700,000 US textile workers, trade theory seems far removed. "We are apprehensive," says Johnson. Given such fears, pressure on the US and the EU to impose a growth rate of 7.5 percent on Chinese textile imports is rising. China agreed to this possibility when it joined the WTO. To blunt such possible actions, the Chinese voluntarily raised export taxes on clothing products.

However, there is another side. Those companies that use or sell the cheaper textile imports can be more competitive, domestically and internationally, with less expensive supplies. When industries that use the restricted product pay higher prices for protected goods, then they pass those costs along to consumers. Therefore, if we restrict textile imports, companies that make products from textiles pass along those price increases to consumers. For example, producers—from those making cloth automobile seats to your local clothing shops—will charge higher prices. Look at Exhibit 4.1 to see estimates of the costs in higher prices paid by society as a whole to save jobs. They are often more expensive than the wages of the jobs saved and consider the costs and benefits of saving jobs that must be borne by the society as a whole.

Exhibit 4.1 **The Cost of Protection**

How much does it cost to protect a job? An average of $231,289, figured across just 20 of the many protected industries. Costs range from $132,870 per job saved in the costume jewelry business to $1,376,435 in the benzenoid chemical industry. Protectionism costs US consumers nearly $100 billion annually. It increases the cost not just of the protected items but of downstream products as well. Protecting sugar raises candy and soft-drink prices; protecting lumber raises home-building costs; protecting steel makes car prices higher; and so forth. Then there are the job losses in downstream industries. Workers in steel-using industries outnumber those in steel-producing industries by 57 to 1. And the protection doesn't even work. Subsidies to steel-producing industries since 1975 have exceeded $23 billion; yet industry employment has declined by nearly two-thirds.

	Protected Industry	Jobs Saved	Total Cost (in $ millions)	Annual Cost per Job Saved ($)
1	Benzenoid chemicals	216	297	1,376,435
2	Luggage	226	290	1,285,078
3	Softwood lumber	605	632	1,044,271
4	Sugar	2,261	1,868	826,104
5	Polyethylene resins	298	242	812,928
6	Dairy products	2,378	1,630	685,323
7	Frozen concentrate orange juice	609	387	635,103
8	Ball bearings	146	88	603,368
9	Maritime services	4,411	2,522	571,668
10	Ceramic tiles	347	191	551,367
11	Machine tools	1,556	746	479,452
12	Ceramic articles	418	140	335,876
13	Women's handbags	773	204	263,535
14	Canned tuna	390	100	257,640
15	Glassware	1,477	366	247,889
16	Apparel and textiles	168,786	33,629	199,241
17	Peanuts	397	74	187,223
18	Rubber footwear	1,701	286	168,312
19	Women's nonathletic footwear	3,702	518	139,800
20	Costume jewelry	1,067	142	132,870
Total		191,764	44,352	
Average (weighted)				231,289

Sources: Adapted from Paul Blustein, 2004, "On pins and needles; As quotas expire, US textile industry braces for change," *Washington Post*, December 31, p. E1; Laura D'Andrea Tyson, 2005, "Stop scapegoating China—before it's too late," *BusinessWeek*, May 2, p. 26; C.P. Chandrasekhar and Jayati Ghosh, 2005, "The Chinese bogeyman in US clothing," *Macroscan*, May 25; *The Economist*, 2005, "The great stitch-up," www.economist.com, May 26; *The Economist*, 2005, "Europe's new protectionism," www. economist.com, June 30.

(France exports more to Germany than Germany does to France). As France accumulates gold and silver, its money supply, and hence prices, will go up in France. This has two effects. It makes French goods more expensive for Germans, reducing French imports into Germany, and it makes German goods cheaper for the French, increasing German imports into France. The result is that, in the end, trade surpluses disappear and mercantilist policies provide a country only a short-term advantage.

Foundations of Modern Trade Theory

Absolute Advantage: The World According to Adam Smith

In 1776, Adam Smith published his famous book, *The Wealth of Nations*.[2] In this book, he attacked the mercantilism belief that the amount of wealth in the world is fixed and trade surpluses or deficits are a zero-sum game where one trading partner must win at the other's expense. Smith argued that the world's wealth is not fixed because when nations engage in international trade world productivity increases (everyone is wealthier). This happens because individual nations do what they do most efficiently and pass on the gains from this efficiency to all trading partners. Next, we can see how this works.

For Smith, the organizations in each nation should specialize in producing those things that they can do at the lowest cost. In Smith's view, costs are based on the value of labor, and the cost to produce a good depends on the amount of labor to produce the good. Thus, country A has an **absolute advantage** in the production of a good when it takes fewer units of labor to produce the good than in country B. According to Smith, for the world to benefit from absolute advantages, a country should produce goods for which it has absolute advantage and import those goods in which it has absolute disadvantage.

absolute advantage when the production of a good in country A takes fewer units of labor than production of the good in country B

For a personal example, let us imagine that you and one other person (call her Jane) are marooned on an island. You do not trust each other very much so both of you try to survive on your own. The island has fertile soil so you can grow fruits and vegetables, and it has a good supply of fish so you can also fish for your food. You come from a family of farmers and have been successful at growing all the fruit and vegetables you need. Unfortunately, you are not very good at fishing and it takes a lot of time and effort for you to catch any fish. Jane has just the opposite problem. She comes from a fishing family and is very good at fishing but has trouble getting her fruits and vegetables to grow.

What should you do? According to Smith you should specialize in what you do best—farming—and the other person should specialize in what she does best—fishing—and you should trade. If things work as Smith predicts both of you will have more fish and fruit and vegetables than you did before. Now we can look at a more formal example of how these numbers work out.

You can see the benefits from trade using absolute advantage in labor costs in a simple example of a two-nation, two-product world. Exhibit 4.2 shows an example of French wine production and US wheat production. For a unit of labor, French wineries produce 15 liters of wine, three times the 5 liters produced by US wineries. The French have an absolute advantage in wine production. US farmers, however, are more efficient than French farmers at producing wheat. They produce twice as many bushels of wheat for a unit of labor as do the French farmers. As you can see in Exhibit 4.2, if countries simply produce for their own consumption of wheat and wine, the total worldwide production in our example "world" is 20 liters of wine per unit of labor and 30 bushels of wheat with two units of labor.

What happens when we specialize? That is, what happens if US farmers just produce wheat and French farmers just produces wine? When the French shift their inefficient wheat production to wine, for every freed-up unit of labor that previously produced wheat they get 15 liters of wine. Similarly, when the US shifts its inefficient wine production to wheat, it gets another 20 bushels of wheat. The result of this shift in production to specialize in areas of absolute advantage is shown in the bottom part of Exhibit 4.2. Without using any more labor, total world production increases, and if the US imports wine and the French wheat, everyone in those countries can drink more wine and eat more bread than they did before.

Of course, this example makes many simplifying assumptions to show how trading based on absolute advantage can be beneficial to all trading partners. For example, in the real world it is not always possible to shift agricultural production from one product to another. The best soil and climate for wheat production may not produce wine at all, or the viniculturists who produce wine may no know nothing about wheat farming. As we will see in our journey through the history of trade theory, scholars have expanded on these basic ideas to explain better what happens in the real world of international trade.

One of the problems of trading based on absolute advantage is that it eliminates many potential trading partners. For our small two-product, two-country world, what happens if one country has absolute advantage in both products? Although it does not seem to make as much intuitive sense as Adam Smith's view on trade based on absolute advantage, David Ricardo made the

Exhibit 4.2 **Two-nation Wine and Wheat Production Possibilities with and without Trade under Conditions of Absolute Advantage**

Absolute Advantage with No Specialization				
	Output from Units of Labor			
Nation	*Wine*	*Units of Labor*	*Wheat*	*Units of Labor*
France	15 liters	1	10 bushels	1
United States	5 liters	1	20 bushels	1
Two-nation world totals	20 liters	2	30 bushels	2

Absolute Advantage with Total Specialization				
	Output from Units of Labor			
Nation	*Wine*	*Units of Labor*	*Wheat*	*Units of Labor*
France	30 liters	2	0 bushels	0
United States	0 liters	0	40 bushels	2
Two-nation world totals	30 liters	2	40 bushels	2

insightful observation that trade can benefit both partners even if one is more efficient in producing both goods.[3] In the next section, we will see how this is possible.

Comparative Advantage: The World According to David Ricardo

Within any particular nation the companies and industries do some things better than they do other things. That is, for example, one nation may be twice as good at making computers as it is at growing corn. Another nation may be better at growing corn than at producing computers. The principle of **comparative advantage** explains how these relative differences within countries can lead to beneficial trade between partners.

Returning to our example of the island, imagine that you and Jane both are still fishing and farming to survive. She spends half a day fishing and one day farming and she gets all the food she needs for a week. Since you do not fish very well it takes you a whole day to get a week's fish. It takes you a day and half to get your farming done. Jane is more efficient than you are in both tasks since she spends less time in both tasks. She has absolute advantage in both tasks. However, because Jane is better at fishing than farming she spends twice as much of her time farming as she does fishing. Because you are better at farming than fishing, you spend 1.5 as much time fishing as farming.

Because both Jane and you are relatively better at one task than another task, there are comparative advantages. Jane's is fishing and yours is farming. Does it make sense for you to specialize in what you do best and for Jane to specialize in what she does best, and trade fish for fruits and vegetables? Let us look at a simple example as shown in Exhibit 4.3 to show how trade in such a situation can work for both sides' benefit.

In this example, we compare US and Chinese production of computers and bicycles. Many people in the US and Europe now fear that production of many goods will go to developing nations, with their low-cost labor and increasingly sophisticated production technologies. However, even if, for example, the Chinese can do most things more cheaply, the theory of comparative advantage suggests that trade can still be beneficial to the world's trading partners.

To illustrate the point, we arbitrarily make the Chinese television and bicycle manufacturers more efficient than their US counterparts. For the example of absolute advantage shown in Exhibit 4.3, we considered only labor costs and input, but since we know that much more than labor goes into producing something, we generalize in this example to consider broadly the input of

comparative advantage
the relative advantage in production efficiency that a nation has internally over another

Exhibit 4.3 **Comparative Advantage and Opportunity Costs when One Country has Absolute Advantage in Both Goods**

	Resource Inputs		Opportunity Costs	
	Computer	Bicycle	Computer	Bicycle
China	10	2	5	0.2
United States	100	4	25	0.04

resources. Thus, in this illustration, the Chinese use 10 units of resources (e.g. labor, materials, capital, machinery, etc.) to produce one computer and 2 units of resources to produce a bicycle. In comparison, the US producers use 100 resource units for a computer and 4 units for a bicycle. The Chinese have absolute advantage in the production of both products because they use fewer resources.

opportunity costs
the choice to produce one good requires you to give up the opportunity to produce another good

Comparative advantage relates to the idea of **opportunity costs**. Opportunity costs mean that when you choose to produce one good, you have to give up the opportunity to produce another good. Thus, there is a trade-off each country makes when it decides to produce one good in place of another. A country has comparative advantage in good A if it has to give up producing fewer units of good B than does another country. This means that within that country it is relatively more efficient to produce one product than another product.

We estimate opportunity costs by comparing the relative resource inputs into producing a good. That is, how many resources would you have to switch from one product to produce another product? In our example, you can see that if the Chinese want to produce another computer with the required 10 units of resources, they must give up production of five bicycles. The opportunity costs are 10/2, or 5. That is, for every computer produced instead of bicycles they lose about five bicycles. US manufacturers must give up 25 bicycles for each computer since they are comparatively less efficient than are the Chinese in computer production. For the US producers, however, an additional bicycle costs only a very small fraction of the resources that produce a computer (4/100 = 0.04). This is relatively better than the Chinese output (2/5 = 0.2). Thus, although the Chinese have absolute advantage in both products, the US has comparative advantage in bicycle production and the Chinese have comparative advantage in computer production.

Comparative Advantage and Production Gains   The theory of comparative advantage suggests that countries should specialize not only in those products for which they have absolute advantage but also in those products for which they have comparative advantage. With specialization and trade it becomes possible with comparative advantage for both trading partners to gain.

Exhibit 4.4 shows how it works out. In this Exhibit, we show how each country could use 10,000 resource units in the production of bicycles and computers.

autarky
the absence of trade

With no trade between the US and China, which economists call the state of **autarky** or lack of trade, each country would have to produce and consume its own output. Each country would then produce a mixture of computers and bicycles by allocating its 10,000 resource units between the two products. The Chinese could produce up to 1,000 computers with no bicycles or up to 5,000 bicycles with no computers. US manufacturers could produce up to 100 computers with no bicycles or 2,500 bicycles without any computers. These are the extremes of the production possibilities; more realistically, each country would produce a mix of products depending on consumer tastes. It is unlikely that there would be no demand for at least some bicycles or some computers in each country.

For the sake of illustration, let us assume that each country divides its 10,000 resource units equally between bicycle production and computer

Exhibit 4.4 **Production and Consumption Possibilities for Computers and Bicycles Using 10,000 Resource Units in China and the US**

Production Gains from Trade						
	Before Specialization		After Specialization		Net Gain (Loss)	
	Computers	Bicycles	Computers	Bicycles	Computers	Bicycles
China	500	2,500	700	1,500	200	−1,000
US	50	1,250	0	2,500	−50	1,250
Total	550	3,750	700	4,000	150	250

Consumption Gains from Trade						
	Before Trade		After Trade		Net Gain (Loss)	
	Computers	Bicycles	Computers	Bicycles	Computers	Bicycles
China	500	2,500	575	2,625	75	125
US	50	1,250	125	1,375	75	125
Total	550	3,750	700	4,000	150	250

production. Using the required resource units per computer and per bicycle, Exhibit 4.4 shows the production from 10,000 resource units spread equally between products based on the required resource inputs for each country (see Exhibit 4.3 for the resource units required to produce each product). Chinese manufacturers can produce 500 computers (5,000/10) and 2,500 bicycles (50,000/2) in China and 50 computers (5,000/100) and 1,250 bicycles (5,000/4) in the US.

If each country specializes in its area of comparative advantage, as shown in Exhibit 4.4, production becomes greater in both bicycles and computers! Unlike for absolute advantage, total specialization by each country does not always produce more in both products. Had the Chinese completely specialized in computers and the US in bicycles, the world would have many more computers and slightly fewer bicycles than before specialization. However, the Chinese could increase world production output using only 70 percent of their resources and still allocate the remaining 30 percent to bicycle production. With the US totally specializing in bicycle production, worldwide production is now higher than before in both products.

Comparative Advantage and Consumption Gains With the production gains, there are now 150 more computers and 250 more bicycles available for Chinese and US American consumers. However, in order to get these goods, China and the US must trade.

Without trade, Chinese and US consumers were limited in what they could purchase by the range of production possibilities in the trade-offs between computers and bicycles. Exhibit 4.4 shows the net gains in consumption possibilities for the two-country world assuming they were divided equally between China and the US. With trade and the right forms of specialization, consumers in both countries now can consume more than would be possible in a world without trade. Theoretically, at least, everyone benefits.

Free trade advocates rely heavily on the theory of comparative advantage to offset arguments that low-cost countries such as China will eventually produce everything, leaving the developed world with nothing but local service industries and many lost jobs. The argument is that no country can have comparative advantage in everything.

Ricardo's theory of comparative advantage looks at the efficiency of production primarily through labor costs as the basis of comparative advantage. For example, it is easy to see in today's world that countries like Mexico, China, and the Czech Republic have lower wages than the US or Germany, and thus are more efficient at producing some products. However, there are other sources of comparative advantage besides the efficiency of resource inputs. In the next section, we consider other sources of comparative advantage as outlined by two Swedish economists, Eli Heckscher[4] and the Nobel prizewinner Bertil Ohlin.[5]

The Heckscher–Ohlin Theory and the Role of Factor Endowments

Heckscher–Ohlin theory (HO)
a nation's comparative advantage comes from the relative abundance of its factor endowments

The **Heckscher–Ohlin theory (HO)** argues that a nation's comparative advantage comes from the relative abundance of its factor endowments. Factor endowments are resources that a nation's businesses use to produce their products or services. There are two basic types of factor endowments. One is capital, which in trade theory refers to inputs that go into making a product or delivering a service, such as land, energy, machines, buildings, or tools. The other is labor. Not all nations have equal factor endowments. For example, the US has abundant supplies of natural resources such as land and energy. Japan has limited factor endowments in land and natural resources such as coal.

As in traditional views of comparative advantage based on the *relative* costs of inputs to production, the HO theory uses the *relative* abundance of capital versus labor to define comparative advantage. That is, a nation would have a comparative advantage in labor if it has more labor available than capital, even if it has less labor and capital than another nation. Like the theories of Ricardo and Smith, the HO theory argues that free trade is beneficial to all partners. However, for HO theory, international trade is driven not by relative differences in production efficiency but by relative differences in the factor endowments of countries.

With unrestricted trade, nations will export goods that require factors in which they have comparative advantage and import goods that require factors in which they are relatively less endowed. For example, Brazil exports coffee and France exports wine because they have the factor endowment of the right soil and climate conditions for growing coffee beans and grapes. China exports huge numbers of garments and textiles to the US and Europe because it has comparative advantage in cheaper labor.

Consider again our example of your lost island. When your ship sank, not only you but also your friend managed to swim to shore on the same island. When Jane's ship sank she was the only one to swim to the same island as you. However, her boat's fishing equipment washed ashore. On your half of the island, with two people, you have more factor endowments in labor. On Jane's half of the island, with her fishing gear, Jane has more factor endowments in capital. Even if Jane were a great farmer, HO theory would predict that Jane should use her superior factor endowments and specialize in fishing while you use your superior labor force and do farming. You can then trade.

One additional prediction of the HO theory is that trade will lead to factor price equality among partners. What this means is that the prices of the capital and labor that goes into producing something in both countries will gradually become equal. Prior to trade, the price of goods produced from the rarer factor—say, for example, industrial products in agricultural countries—would cost more. This makes sense because we usually have to pay more for things that are in short supply. After trading with nations endowed with industrial production capacity, the supply of industrial goods in the agricultural nation goes up. Again, based on simple supply and demand, we would expect prices for industrial products in the agricultural nation to decline. Thus, for example, HO theory would predict the reduction of wages for unskilled workers (a reduction in labor costs) in the US when the types of goods produced by these workers are imported from countries like China or Mexico with high endowments of unskilled labor. As you will see from some of the strategic insights in this chapter, the likelihood of this happening is one reason why many unskilled workers look to the government to protect their industries from low-cost country competition.

Exhibit 4.5 shows World Bank statistics on the capital per worker endowments of various countries. Based on the HO theory, which countries would you predict to export and import goods that involve capital-intensive production?

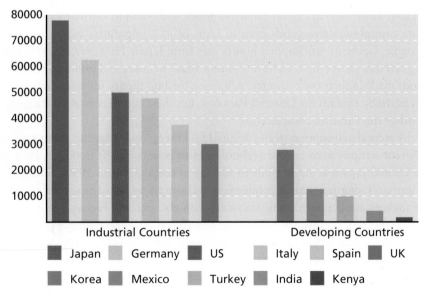

Exhibit 4.5

Capital Stock per Worker in Selected Industrial and Developing Countries

Source: A. Heston, R. Summers, and B. Aten, 2002, Penn World Table Version 6.0, Center for International Comparisons of Production, Income and Prices at the University of Pennsylvania, January.

For approximately two decades after the introduction of the HO theory, most economists took intuitive examples like capital-intensive Germany exporting technical machinery as evidence that the HO theory was correct. In the early 1950s, Wassily Leontief produced the first comprehensive test of the HO theory and found some unusual results.[6] The next section details the findings of this study.

The Leontief Paradox According to the HO theory, a capital-intensive country such as the United States should export capital-intensive goods and import labor-intensive goods. To test this hypothesis, Leontief looked at 200 industries in the US. Contrary to expectations, he found that the US was exporting relatively more labor-intensive goods and importing capital-intensive goods. Much to the surprise of economists, the US exports were about 30 percent more labor-intensive than its imports. This result was so contrary to expectations that this finding became known as the **Leontief Paradox**.

Leontief Paradox
when a capital-intensive country exports more labor-intensive goods and imports capital-intensive goods

Updating the HO Theory Although the Leontief Paradox showed that the simple form of HO theory could not fully explain world trade, economists up to the present time have continued to modify and update the theory. Current empirical tests of the theory show that, in its updated versions, the HO theory can explain many aspects of trade quite well.[7]

One assumption of the HO theory is that tastes in countries are identical. That is, people in different countries enjoy the same products. Given equal tastes, countries will import goods for which they have a comparative disadvantage. But what happens if a capital-intensive country, for example like Germany, has consumers that have strong preferences for capital-intensive goods such as high technology cars? Such a taste bias may completely offset the German comparative advantage in capital-intensive goods and result in Germany importing more capital-intensive goods even in areas of its comparative advantage. For example, Germany still imports luxury cars from Japan. However, research also suggests that most countries have a "home bias" in tastes and prefer to consume goods made in their own country. Adjusting the HO theory for taste differences can partially explain the Leontief Paradox, but these differences are not enough to offset the Paradox completely.

A second assumption of the original HO theory was that the companies in different nations used similar technologies to produce their goods. A look at the US and Japanese automobile producers in the 1970s and 1980s shows this as untrue. Using innovative production and supply technologies, the Japanese car makers outcompeted their US rivals with cheaper and higher-quality vehicles. Their imports into the US rose so fast that the US government convinced the Japanese to adopt voluntary quotas to limit Japanese competition. Although US manufacturers managed to increase quality and efficiency of production to compete with their Japanese rivals, companies like Toyota continue to use manufacturing technologies that are more efficient than those used by US companies. Most recent economics research suggests that trade is best explained by both Ricardo's comparative advantage in efficiency of production (in part due to superior technologies) and the relative factor endowments identified by HO theory.

Another advance in the HO theory is a refinement of the two factors of capital and labor into more detailed classifications. Most economists now consider factor endowments as farmland, raw materials or natural resources, human capital or skilled labor, manmade capital such as transportation systems, and unskilled labor. The HO theory works much better with a more precise breakdown of resources. For example, it then makes more sense that the US is a big exporter of agricultural products (based on the large endowment of arable land) and also outputs like super-computers (based on large endowments in university and industry research and development).

Exhibit 4.6 shows the relative factor endowments of selected countries as a percentage of world totals. Note that the US and the EU are highly endowed with capital and skilled labor but lack unskilled labor endowments. India and China dominate with unskilled labor, but the Chinese have more skilled labor endowments than does the US. Recent US trade data suggest a pattern consistent with the HO theory. The US exports more goods and services requiring skilled labor than it imports, and it imports more low-skilled labor-intensive manufactured goods such as athletic shoes and textiles. For a specific case, look at Exhibit 4.7 to see if this pattern holds for the trade between the US and India. This Exhibit shows the trade balance of exports and imports of the US with India. The positive numbers show the top ten product categories in which the US exports more to India than it imports. The negative numbers show the top ten product categories in which the US imports more than it exports to India, hence a negative trade balance.

Most economists believe that the continuing modifications to the HO theory produce a reasonable explanation of a significant amount of world trade. However, the model is still not a complete explanation and one needs to understand alternative models to grasp more completely the complexities of world trade. We now turn to examine some of these complementary and alternative views.

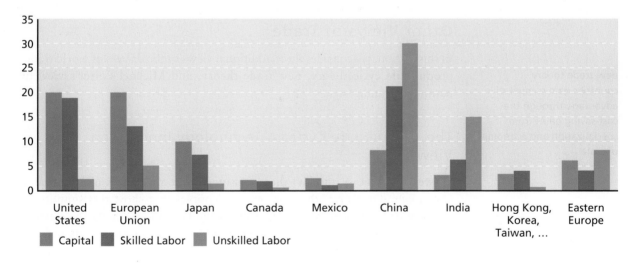

Exhibit 4.6

Types of Factor Endowments of Countries and Regions (percent of world total)

Source: Adapted from William R. Cline, 1997, *Trade and Income Distribution*, Washington, DC: Institute for International Economics.

Exhibit 4.7 **The US Trade Balance with India by Top Ten Positive and Negative Product Categories: Exports–Imports ($,000)**

Positive Product Categories		Negative Categories	
Nuclear reactors, boilers, machinery, etc.; parts	754,842	Furniture; bedding, etc.; lamps not elsewhere specified or included, etc.; prefab bd	−256,379
Electric machinery, etc.; sound equipment; TV equipment; parts	374,670	Vehicles, except railway or tramway, and parts, etc.	−261,198
Aircraft, spacecraft, and parts thereof	371,677	Fish, crustaceans and aquatic invertebrates	−378,142
Optic, photo, etc., medical or surgical instruments, etc.	315,357	Articles of iron or steel	−433,200
Miscellaneous chemical products	190,829	Iron and steel	−482,638
Fertilizers	118,449	Carpets and other textile floor coverings	−496,386
Wood pulp, etc.; recovered (waste and scrap) paper and paperboard	111,404	Apparel articles and accessories, knit or crochet	−679,115
Mineral fuel, oil, etc.; bitumin substances; mineral wax	43,005	Textile art not elsewhere specified or included; needlecraft sets; worn text. art	−832,167
Photographic or cinematographic goods	38,183	Apparel articles and accessories, not knit, etc.	−1,596,883
Printed books, newspapers, etc.; manuscripts, etc.	23,705	Natural, etc. pearls, precious, etc., stones, precious metal, etc.; coin	−3,934,088

Source: Data reported in Trade Stats Express, Office of Trade and Industry Information http://tse.export.gov/NTDChartDisplay.aspx?Unique URL=ohyney45fficcz452vfrvgmc-2008-11-10-19-32-15

Other Views of Trade

new trade theory
countries gain comparative advantage through the cost-saving gains from specialization and economies of scale

In this section, we consider three additional views of the drivers of world trade, product life cycle theory, **new trade theory**, and Michael Porter's view of national advantages.

The Product Life Cycle: A Technology Innovation View

As we noted above, the HO theory assumed that all nations used the same technology. Of course, there are many examples that show this simplifying assumption as incorrect. For example, in the US and especially the western states, the availability of many large rivers allows US companies to take advantage of hydroelectric power at a very low cost. This technology is not available in Saudi Arabia or other desert countries. Nations keep other technologies secret for security reasons. The US government restricts the exportation of technological equipment or computer software, such as the encryption programs designed by Microsoft, which may have military applications. Interestingly, the Dutch satellite company New Skies Satellites NV lobbied the US Congress to ease rules that limit exports of satellite technology to companies outside the US. New Skies wants to obtain US satellite technology that is not readily accessible to foreign-based companies such as them. New Skies argues that companies from North Atlantic Treaty Organization (NATO) countries should be exempt from the US Export Control Act. Similarly, patent and copyright laws attempt to restrict the flow of technologies across borders and can be a source of competitive advantage for companies in particular nations

One aspect of technology that may determine trade patterns is not what the technology is but who gets it first and who eventually produces it most efficiently. This viewpoint, first proposed by Raymond Vernon, focuses on the life cycle of a product from its initial innovation and introduction to its eventual standardization. For an example of a product life cycle, consider the history of electronic calculators. When first introduced, even with simple functions such as square root, they were quite expensive (often over $1,000) and innovative products. This was the new product stage. After a period, many companies learned to produce calculators with increasing efficiency. As competition drove down prices, more and more people could afford a calculator. This was the growth product stage. Of course, now one can have that once-$1,000 calculator for a few dollars. Calculators are now a mature product. Can you think of any other products going through this life cycle? Plasma TVs seem to be in the growth stage now. Why should this relate to trade?

In what became known as **product life cycle theory**, Vernon[8] proposed that the major industrial economies, such as the US, Japan, and Germany, focus on new product development and innovation. Such countries with their highly skilled workforce and large capital resources provide the fertile ground for companies to develop new and innovative products. Typically, companies like Apple begin small and gradually refine the production process and the product. Apple began with the Apple I prototype in a garage. This was soon followed by the Apple II, which became the first commercially successful personal computer.

If the product is successful, companies first serve domestic markets and then move to export markets. As long as the innovating company controls the technology, it has little fear of competition from companies from other nations. Eventually, as the production of the product becomes standardized, companies consider moving production of the entire product or its components to other countries such as China. No longer are the companies willing to pay for the highly skilled labor needed initially in the product's early development. Once production of a product becomes routine, it makes sense to replace higher-paid, higher-skilled workers with lower-skilled and lower-paid workers in other countries. At the same time, foreign competitors in the low-cost countries begin to develop the skills necessary to produce the product.

Eventually imports from foreign companies rather than domestic production serve the innovating countries' markets. In summary, many manufactured products go through the following stages:

1. Introduction into the home market.
2. Export sales are added to domestic sales.
3. Foreign production begins in lower-cost countries.
4. Domestic industry loses its competitive advantage in price and innovation.
5. Foreign competition serves the domestic market with imports.

product life cycle theory
major industrial economies focus on new product development and innovation and less-developed countries focus on production of mature products

Exhibit 4.8 shows how these processes work over time.

Products that seemingly have followed Vernon's hypothesis include the pocket calculator, radios, televisions, and VCRs. Initially producers from the major industrialized countries dominated the production of these products. Eventually, through standardized production and the movement of the technologies first to Japan (when it was a low-cost country) and then to other low-cost countries, the US now imports most of these goods. For example, consider the history of the TV. Prior to 1970, single manufacturers designed, produced and assembled each component of their TVs. Most TVs came from the US, Japan, and Germany, at the time among the top industrialized nations. Now almost all TVs purchased in the US come from other low-cost countries, most recently from China. Even Japanese imports into the US are manufactured in low-cost countries under Japanese brand names.

Although the product life cycle theory seems to explain the post-World War II product development innovations in the US and the eventual migration of the production of these products to low-cost countries, its application to today's more integrated global economy may be less strong. MNCs often introduce new products simultaneously in many countries. In addition, MNCs such as Dell

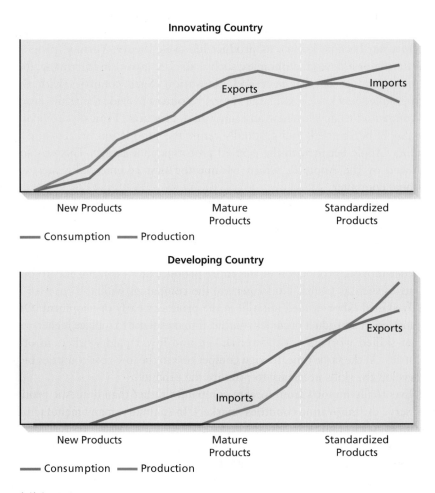

Exhibit 4.8 **Vernon's Product Life Cycle Theory**

Source: Adapted from R. Vernon and L.T. Wells, 1986, The Economic Environment of International Business (4th edn.), Upper Saddle River, NJ: Pearson Education.

Computer may still produce in developed countries using highly automated assembly plants. Yet, Dell sources its PC components worldwide from manufacturers in lower-cost countries such as China and Taiwan.

Product life cycle theory adds another consideration regarding how to look at specialization of production based on absolute or comparative advantage. That is, according to this view, some countries are more likely to develop companies that are good at creating new products when other countries are more likely to develop companies that are efficient at producing mature products. Next, we will look at an additional explanation of trade that considers specialization in production based on a different type of efficiency.

New Trade Theory

One limitation of traditional views of comparative advantage is their failure to explain why nations with similar resources engage in so much trade. The US, for example, imports and exports more to Canada and the EU than any other country or region. During the 1980s, several economists developed what is now called new trade theory.[9]

New trade theory looks at how companies and industries in a nation can take advantage of **economies of scale**. Economies of scale mean that each additional unit of production costs less to produce than did the previous unit. Companies gain economies of scale most often when they can spread large fixed costs over more units of output. For example, the new Airbus super jumbo jet required huge investments in development costs. Airbus must sell nearly 600 planes just to break even, but after that the development cost per plane gets progressively smaller. Pharmaceutical companies face similar problems. It often takes years of research and development and millions of dollars to bring a drug to market. As with commercial airplanes, when companies spread these costs over a larger volume of sales, the cost per unit drops. Not only do larger production runs allow companies to spread fixed costs over more units, but they also allow workers to learn the production skills, both of which lead to reduced costs.

economies of scale
each additional unit of production costs less to produce than did the previous unit

Firms can also get economies of scale from the nature of the industry. These are often called external scale economies. As industry output increases, suppliers get larger and can pass on some of their economies to the producer. In addition, the pool of skill labor grows with the industry and companies can gain efficiencies from this labor pool. Many experts link the availability of skilled labor in an industry to what experts call industrial agglomeration. This means the tendency of companies in an industry to cluster in one location. Some examples of industrial agglomeration include the movie industry in Hollywood, the financial industry in London and New York, and computer-related industries in Silicon Valley and Bangalore, India. Although, to some extent, historical accident has led to this clustering, the benefits are often apparent. Once the clustering begins, new companies in an industry locate closer to competitors to take advantage of the local supply of skilled labor. In addition to skilled labor, companies in industrial clusters sometimes benefit from lower transportation from suppliers and to customers. Clusters can also increase competition, which forces companies to be more innovative and technologically advanced. Close proximity also seems to increase the amount of learning companies get from each other. People move from one company to another, shared projects are more likely, and the competition encourages related companies (e.g. supplier and manufacturer) to share more information.

How do economies of scale, whether internal or external to the company, relate to trade? The basic answer points to the cost-saving gains from specialization. If a nation, by accident or through the encouragement of government policy, can develop an industry that can produce in great quantities, then it can produce at lower costs and trade the excess production beyond domestic needs to other countries. Thus, two nations with equal endowments of resources who, based on other trade theories, would have no reason to trade, may specialize in products they produce with economies of scale. They can then trade with each other, and consumers in both countries will get access to less expensive goods.

Next, we will see an alternative view of trade offered by the renowned Harvard University strategy professor Michael Porter.

Michael Porter and the Competitive Advantage of Nations

Porter asks the question, "Why does a nation become the home base for successful international competitors in an industry?"[10] For example, he asks, "Why is Switzerland a leader in pharmaceuticals and chocolates?" "Why is Germany a leader in luxury cars and chemical production?" "Why is Finland a leader in mobile phones?" "Why is Japan a leader in automobile production?"

Porter rejects the notion that comparative advantage is sufficient to explain world trade. More importantly, he sees trade theories based on existing endowments as assuming away what managers do to compete: strategize, improve technology and management practices, and differentiate products. As such, he is more concerned with what makes industries competitive in different national settings and how companies can take advantage of these conditions.

Porter sees four broad areas in a nation that lead to international competitive companies in different industries. These include:

- *Firm strategy, structure, and rivalry:* how a company is run and how it competes.
- *Related and supporting industries:* the existence of suppliers and related talents.
- *Demand conditions:* the home country demand for the industry's output.
- *Factor endowments:* similar to HO theory but with additional possibilities.

national diamond
includes: firm strategy, structure, and rivalry; related and supporting industries; demand conditions; and, factor endowments

He argues that these areas form a **national diamond** of interrelated factors, and that an industry must have advantages in most or all to achieve and maintain competitive success. Exhibit 4.9 shows a picture of the national diamond as illustrated by Porter.

Firm Strategy, Structure, and Rivalry   No one management system is appropriate for all industries, and different countries support different types of management. For example, in Germany, many top executives hold PhDs in technical areas and this produces a superior ability to improve product designs and production processes. Porter contrasts this with the US management emphasis on finance, to which he attributes the US decline in some manufacturing industries.

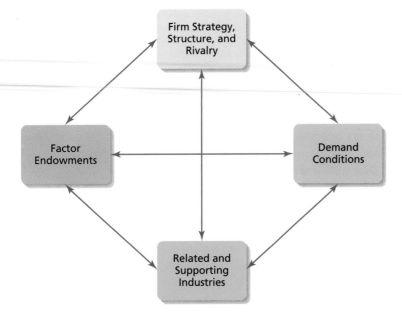

Exhibit 4.9

Porter's National Diamond: Determinants of National Competitve Advantage

Source: Michael E. Porter, 1990, *The Competitive Advantage of Nations*, New York: The Free Press.

Also important for developing internationally competitive companies is the existence of high levels of rivalry in a domestic industry. This competition drives companies to achieve superior performance just to compete locally. For Porter, national competition is a driver of innovation, and this innovation makes these companies better international competitors. Without such rivalry, companies are more likely to stay in their domestic market. For example, the local competition in Japan for flat-panel TV displays is fierce. Four companies dominate the Japanese market: NEC, the Fujitsu/Hitachi consortium, Pioneer, and Matsushita Electric, Japan's largest consumer electronics company. This competition at home helps drive innovations in flat-panel display technologies and manufacturing efficiencies. In turn, it makes these companies better competitors in the world market.

Related and Supporting Industries   When suppliers are superior and more innovative, companies in the industry are more likely to gain knowledge about the processes of innovation and upgrading from these relationships. That is, suppliers help companies see new methods of operations and perceive opportunities to use new technologies. This is a spin-off of ideas and innovations from one industry to another. For example, Italian firms produce the majority of the jewelry-making machinery in the world. Italian jewelry-manufacturing companies such as New Silver in Vicenza, Italy, are leaders in the gold and silver jewelry industry in part because they have more ready access to the latest jewelry-producing machines.

Porter discovered that internationally competitive industries in a country tend to cluster into groups of related industries. Often this cluster is in one geographical area. Related industries transfer knowledge and innovation to each other. For example, many Japanese companies are world leaders in

A Look at the Italian Furniture-manufacturing Cluster in Milan

The furniture industry in Milan, Italy, shows extensive cooperation among material suppliers, component manufacturers, and furniture producers. Over 6,500 small to medium-sized wood furniture companies cluster in the Brianza area and 7,200 small to medium-sized non-wood furniture companies cluster in the Cantu area. Both of these clusters are close to Milan. Thousands of small business suppliers and subcontractors that are highly specialized support them.

Italian companies such as Driade, Magis, and Kartell can compete globally because these clusters of suppliers, subcontractors, and associated human resource talents allow for the "diffused factory" concept of organization. The "factory" focuses on research designs and prototyping and does testing of raw materials. Production work is outsourced to the specialized suppliers and subcontractors.

Furniture-machine manufacturers are also located close by the clusters. These related companies work directly with the suppliers to custom-make equipment that can produce furniture that would be impossible to make with standardized manufacturing equipment.

Source: Adapted from information available at www.cawp.ubc.ca/cawp/index_cawp.html

the production of synthetic textile fibers. The technologies used in producing these synthetic fibers are similar to those used in the production of textiles made from silk. This just happens to be another industry in which the Japanese are internationally competitive.

Italian furniture makers are among the world's leading suppliers. The IB Strategic Insight above shows how the situation in Milan, Italy, gives an example of how related and supporting industries in Milan allow Italy to be a major competitor in the world furniture market.

Demand Conditions   The core design of products usually first reflects the nature of the home country's demand. For example, to accommodate highly congested areas, high fuel costs, and a strong cultural value for quality, Japanese consumers have demanded smaller, high-quality and highly efficient automobiles. For example, when Toyota introduced its hybrid (gas and electric) sedan Prius, its success set the stage for world competition with hybrid technology. Not surprisingly, Japanese automobile manufacturers are among the world leaders in many areas of automobile production, including hybrid technology. Porter argues that companies gain competitive advantage when the demand in the home country gives them a clearer or earlier picture of buyer needs from other nations.

Factor Endowments   Porter also argues that created and not inherited factors are the most important for competitive success. He calls these created factors the specialized factors of production, and they include skilled labor, capital, and the country's infrastructure. Non-key or general-use factors are unskilled labor and raw materials. He does not see these factors as leading to competitive advantage because companies can easily get these inputs. For example, although Japan and Korea have little natural endowments of raw materials such as iron ore or coal, they get these on the world market. Instead, they use their endowments of skilled and motivated labor to produce worldwide competitive products. Because specialized factors such as educating a skilled workforce require heavy and sustained investments, they are difficult to imitate. Hence, countries like Germany, even with the most highly paid workers in the world, can have competitive companies because the German educational system does an excellent job at producing technologically skilled workers. Approximately 70 percent of German secondary school graduates continue in some type of specialized occupational training. Many times this combines on-the-job training paid for by companies with part-time vocational education paid for by the government.

Evaluating Trade Theories: What Do They Tell Us?

The economic theories of trade generally tell us that free trade between nations is, on average, beneficial for all of the involved countries. Although limited by simplifying assumptions, the theories of absolute and comparative advantage provide the mathematical logic that trade works to produce more products and give consumers more options.

The world is not as simple as the two-country, two-product examples typically used to illustrate absolute and comparative advantage. When applied to the real world that is multi-country, multi-product, culturally diverse in tastes, and diverse in economic structures and affluence, we see that the fundamental trade theories are incomplete. Contemporary theories of trade attempt to fill in the blanks by providing explanations of the missing links in explaining the growing world trade phenomena.

Traditional theories of trade focused on explaining the importing and exporting of goods. In today's global economy, international business people are also concerned with the exporting and importing of services. Although we have no reason to assume that trade in services will not follow similar patterns to trade in goods, we do not have the extensive scientific research to know for sure.

Trade theories, with the partial exception of Porter's diamond, tend to look at the nation as the unit of analysis. However, individual companies make the strategic decisions to import or export. Later chapters in the text will deal more thoroughly with the strategic rationale and decision-making processes regarding how and when to procure or sell your products or services in other nations.

At this point, we can note that the prime strategic reasons to import are to get cheaper or otherwise unavailable services or supplies for a company. For example, in the computer industry, companies like Dell and Compaq source their chips, LCDs, and keyboards from all over the world. Similarly, the global automobile industry imports automotive components from all over the world. Although we seldom can track the sources of all the components of our cars, some might come from companies such as Hella KgaA Hueck located in Lippstadt, Germany. Tomas Hedenborg, Hella's president and CEO, notes that they are "the only company worldwide specializing in front-end modules." They supply components to VW's plant in Puebla, Mexico; to Ford's plant in Hermosillo (the Ford Fusion, Mercury Milan, and Lincoln Zephyr); and for

Chrysler in St Louis and Windsor, Canada. According to Hedenborg, Hella is the world leader with 23 percent of the global market share for outsourced front-end modules.[11]

From the company's perspective, exporting is an opportunity to increase sales and revenues. Besides this obvious motivation, companies may export because of saturated markets at home, unused production capacity, or difficulty in overcoming the advantages of a market leader at home. For example, AMD, the computer chip manufacturer and competitor of market leader Intel, exports more products to South America, where it gained an early advantage over Intel.

With a booming export business to China, and counter to the trend of moving US manufacturing jobs to low-cost countries, BTU International is a growing Massachusetts small business. The IB Small Business Insight below presents the picture of BTU's success in the export market.

An important strategic concern of all international companies is to understand the impact of government policies regarding trade on their industry's position in the world economy. When governments choose to join free trade areas or choose to impose tariffs or other barriers to trade, particular industries

Exporting as an Opportunity for Small Businesses

IB SMALL BUSINESS INSIGHT

BTU International is a member of the *Fortune* Small Business 100 list. This Massachusetts-based company is a maker of furnaces for semiconductor and electronics manufacturing. Consistent with Porter's diamond model, Massachusetts has a cluster of successful technology companies specializing in producing sophisticated manufacturing products needed by growing Chinese industries, such as the machines that produce and package the silicone wafers used in computer chips. Recent exports to China from these mostly small Massachusetts companies grew at over 89 percent during the last year. The state has a trade office in Shanghai and over 800 companies have contacted the office for help with China exports.

Sixty percent of BTU's sales come from Asia and most of that from China. Recent sales growth is over 50 percent a year and the company just recently added 65 jobs to its original 300 employees.

In general, exporting is an opportunity not overlooked by US small to medium-sized companies. The chart in Exhibit 4.10 shows that most exporters are small businesses.

Size Composition of US Exporting Companies, 2002

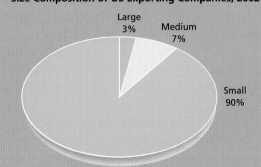

Large 3%
Medium 7%
Small 90%

Exhibit 4.10

Nearly 97 Percent of US Exporters are Small and Medium-sized Enterprises

Note: Definitions: small = less than 100 employees; medium = 100–400 employees; large = 500 or more employees.

Source: US Department of Commerce. Exporser Database.

Sources: Adapted from Robert Gavin, 2004, "Exports to China give bay state firms a boost." *Boston Globe*, August 28, p. A1; www.fortune.com.

may benefit or be hurt. For example, big box retailers like Walmart benefit greatly from clothing and television imports from China. At the same time, the EU and US textile industries are calling for restrictions on Chinese imports to protect their local companies. In the next section, we will consider some of other anti-free trade arguments.

Arguments against Free Trade

While most economists are free trade advocates, there are counter-arguments to a system based mostly on efficiency and less on political and socio-cultural considerations. Those who hold these positions typically call on their governments to impose tariffs or other import restrictions on foreign imports. Several of these arguments follow.

Free Trade as a Threat to National Sovereignty

This position, often adopted by anti-free trade politicians such as Pat Buchanan in the US, reflects the worry that if a nation loses its production capacity in key products it may be in danger of losing its core national identity. Sometimes this position reflects a challenge to the unique nature of a national culture. In France, for example, there exists a concern for protecting the uniqueness of French culture and language. In particular, there is a concern for the use of English in advertising, the naming of products, and workplace terms. For example, labor unions at General Electric Medical Systems in France recently challenged in court the company's right to use a technical manual published only in English. The unions won their case—French law requires that all workplace manuals be translated into French.[12] MNCs that work in France must be aware of the laws regarding language use.

Other areas of concern related to national sovereignty focus on security. Leaders often believe that some industries are too important for national security to allow a reliance on imports. For example, the US government supports industries essential for the military, such as fighter aircraft production, because many consider it bad policy to become reliant on other countries for military-related equipment. An arms supplier could become a future enemy or be conquered by an enemy. In Japan, consumers pay several times the world market price for rice because the Japanese government believes that rice is essential for Japanese survival.

Protecting Infant Industries

The basic point of this argument is that new industries need a temporary shield from foreign competition. This position is not totally against free trade but holds that an infant industry will never develop if the government allows more mature and efficient foreign companies into a country without some tariff or other trade barrier. Similar arguments are often used to temporarily protect industries such as the US steel industry, which in 2002 benefited from a 30 percent increase in tariffs on steel imports based on the US government's reasoning that the industry was not competitive because of inefficient facilities and costly labor agreements. Less than two years later the tariffs were lifted, based in part on WTO pressure and the claim that the industry had used the time wisely to retool factories and become more efficient.

Fair Trade

The fair trade argument proposes that free trade takes advantage of cheap labor that does not have the protection of minimum wages, child labor prohibitions, and worker safety protections. Advocates of fair trade or, as it is sometimes called, the trade justice approach often promote voluntary standards so that consumers can know that the product was produced according to minimum standards for workers' protection. Coffee imported from South and Central America to the US often has fair trade labeling. Starbucks offers fair trade coffee in its selections.

Protecting the Environment

This argument is related in some respects to the fair trade argument, in that companies in countries with stronger environmental protection laws are often more costly producers than are companies in countries with weak protection laws. From a broader perspective, the "green" augment is that decisions made for pure economic efficiency push production to countries with less concern for the environment, often because they have little choice if they wish to attract business. The conclusion is that the world will eventually pay the price. Economists call this a social cost that is often not borne by the seller. For example, when factories in China produce goods under less strict pollution controls than in the US or Europe, they save money. Consumers around the world get these goods at cheaper prices. However, the pollution also adds to global warming and potentially costly climate changes such as a reduced ozone layer (more cancer) and possibly more violent and damaging weather (Katrina in the US in 2005). As such, although it is not part of the original exchange, pollution is not free and the world must pay such social costs.

The IB Sustainability Practices box opposite gives an example of the environmental costs and benefits of transferring operations to a low-cost country.

Job Loss

Probably the most emotional appeal against free trade is the job loss argument. Even the most supportive of free trade accept that some jobs will be lost to a country when another country can produce the product or service with absolute or comparative advantage. The US has lost approximately one in six manufacturing jobs since the year 2000. Proponents of the job-loss argument see most of these jobs lost to imports that outcompete local companies, forcing them to close or reduce production, or US companies moving production to the low-cost countries. The IB Ethical Challenge on page 118 gives one poignant example of this situation.

As you saw earlier in the chapter, free traders counter that protecting jobs costs the society generally. They also argue that manufacturing job loss is not all attributable to trade. Alan Greenspan, in recent testimony to a US Congress worried about the rising trade imbalance from Chinese imports, perhaps sums up the counter-argument:

IB SUSTAINABILITY PRACTICES

Exporting Absolute Advantage while Reducing the Local Carbon Footprint

In the northern Chinese city of Handong, residents often complain that clothes hung out to dry end up covered in black fallout from pollution generated from nearby Handan Iron and Steel. Although separated by 5,000 miles and a decade in time, neighbors of a former ThyssenKrupp steel mill in Dortmund, Germany, used to have similar complaints.

Not so in Germany any more. In late 1990s ThyssenKrupp's hulking blast furnace was plucked from the heartland of Germany's old industrial district, the Ruhr Valley, disassembled and shipped to Handong in Hebei Province, China's now equivalent of the German Ruhr Valley. This transfer was just one of dozens which have made China a steel producer that exceeds the combined output of Germany, Japan, and the United States. Chinese mills now provide about 38 percent of the world's total steel output.

Why the growth? Chen Kexin, an economist from the Ministry of Commerce, notes that, perhaps even more than cheap labor, weak environmental laws and cheap power allow Chinese steel producers to have the lowest prices. Mr Chen notes, "The shortfall of environmental protection is one of the main reasons why our exports are cheaper." As the *New York Times* points out, "China has become the world's factory, but also its smokestack."

Exporting jobs to China has been costly to Dortmund and other Ruhr cities. These cities still face high unemployment rates because of the migration of jobs to lower-cost countries like China. Dortmund's unemployment rate is 15 percent, which is 50 percent higher than the national average. Dortmund now has barely 3,000 working in steel mills; in 1960, there were 40,000. However, switching to what is often seen as a comparative or absolute advantage of German technology, the region now has 12,000 new jobs in information technology and 2,300 in nanotechnology. Where once there were no universities, there are now six universities and eight technical colleges.

There is also a cost to the residents of Handong. While Germany has reduced its annual carbon emissions by 19 percent, China's coal-fired power plants contribute heavily to the country's rising emissions of sulfur dioxide and carbon dioxide. In Handan, residents live in a sea of smoke and dust that spills from the steel plant, which even Chinese authorities acknowledge contains carcinogens. Only after public protests did Handan Iron and Steel agree to pay an annual "pollution fee" as compensation to its neighbors.

A paradox for the world and increasing carbon levels is that China's steel mills emit three times as much carbon dioxide per ton of steel as did the German producers. This is in a significant degree because about 85 percent of even the newer Chinese plants burn coal as their fuel.

To see a video or slide show regarding this factory, see www.nytimes.com/interactive/2007/12/21/world/asia/choking_on_growth_9.html#story3 or www.nytimes.com/interactive/2007/12/21/world/asia/choking_on_growth_9.html#story2.

Source: Adapted from Joseph Kahn and Mark Landler, 2007, "China grabs West's smoke-spewing factories," *New York Times*, www.nytimes.com/2007/12/21/world/asia/21transfer.html?_r=3&hp&oref=slogin&oref=slogin&oref=slogin, December 21.

More generally, any significant elevation of tariffs that substantially reduces our overall imports, by keeping out competitively priced goods, would materially lower our standard of living . . . New hires in the United States currently average more than a million per week, half resulting from voluntary job change. At the same time, during a typical recent week, about 150,000 workers are temporarily laid off and another 225,000 are subject to permanent job loss. Any effect of trade with China on US employment is likely to be very small relative to the scale of job creation and job loss in our economy . . . A policy

What Do You Do when over 4,000 People in One Town Lose their Jobs on the Same Day?

Kannapolis, North Carolina, used to be a company town. Founded in the early 1900s, Cannon Mills produced nearly 300,000 towels a day at the height of its operations. Cannon developed a reputation for quality and at its height employed 22,000 workers. Although beset by labor relations problems toward the end of its existence, the founder's son established a paternalistic relationship with workers when the company flourished. After World War II, Cannon built 150 houses for returning veterans. Rent was $5 every two weeks and electricity was free.

Later acquired by Pillowtex, Cannon met its final demise when, citing foreign competition and especially the Chinese, Pillowtex filed for bankruptcy and abruptly closed all 15 of its US factories. In Kannapolis alone 4,300 people lost their jobs. North Carolina has lost over 90,000 jobs in textiles and expects to loose more as Chinese textile imports increase.

Such stories of human suffering feed the calls for protectionism. However, the service and technology sections in North Carolina are booming. Consistent with trade theories, a loss in one sector often comes with gains in another. The problem is that one-third of the Cannon workers never finished high school, one in ten is illiterate, and nearly 50 percent are over age 50. These are hardly the kind of workers that can move easily into the technology and service sectors.

What can be done? The US Trade Adjustment Assistant program provides income and support for training but it remains questionable what the success rate will be.

Sources: Adapted from *The Economist*, 2005, "The human cost of cheaper towels," www.economist.com, April 21; www.wheredoyoustand.info/timeline.html; www.ci.kannapolis.nc.us/welcome_1.asp; http://greenvilleonline.com/news/business/2003/07/30/ 2003073011279.htm

to dismantle the global trading system in a misguided effort to protect jobs from competition would redound to the eventual detriment of all US job seekers, as well as of millions of American consumers.[13]

However, the IB Ethical Challenge above gives a more human insight to the issue of job loss.

To this point, we have considered the incentives for trade between companies from different countries. However, companies can achieve many of the same benefits by setting up operations in another country. The next section explores broadly the rationale for investing in assets in other countries.

Foreign Direct Investment

foreign direct investment (FDI)
having ownership or control of at least 10 percent or more of an enterprise in another country

The US Department of Commerce defines **foreign direct investment (FDI,** as it is commonly referred to) as having ownership or control of at least 10 percent or more of an enterprise in another country.

As you remember from Chapter 2, a major issue in formulating a multinational strategy is using location advantages to find lower-cost or higher-quality inputs (supplies or labor) and to expand sales and service to customers. Later, in Chapter 10, you will see how international managers make the strategic choice to export/import or to engage in FDI, or to do both. Consequently, this chapter will provide only a brief overview of some of the theoretical reasons to engage in FDI.

One general observation is that worldwide FDI, like international trade, has grown substantially over the last few decades. Exhibits in Chapter 1 give the latest worldwide statistics on both the growth of FDI and international trade. Although the tragedy of 9/11 affected both trade and investment after the year 2000, statistics that are more recent suggest a return to higher levels of FDI. In any case, in spite of a large drop in the post-2000 years, worldwide FDI remains higher than that of the previous decade. Similar to the situation for world trade, where companies seek to buy exports from low-cost countries, FDI in low-cost countries is also growing for similar reasons. Exhibit 4.11 shows the changes of FDI for China over the last few years.

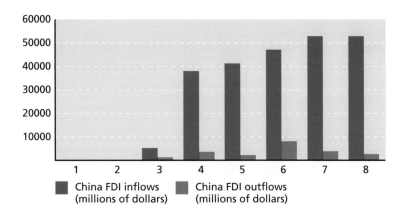

Exhibit 4.11 **Recent FDI Inflows and Outflows for China**

Source: Adapted from United Nations Conference on Trade and Development Database.

As noted above, some of the same drivers of exporting and importing influence the choice of companies to engage in FDI. Next, we review briefly some contemporary theories of FDI.

Monopolistic advantage theory is an economic view of FDI that argues that FDI should occur only when foreign companies have unique competitive advantages over local companies.[14] That is, FDI occurs when the foreign company is superior in areas such as technology, management, economies of scale, brand name, or financial assets. The prime motivation for FDI then is to keep control of these competitive advantages while using them in other countries. Intel, the computer chip manufacturer, is a good example of this type of FDI motivation. Intel has superior knowledge of chip-manufacturing technology. For its assembly and testing facilities, Intel uses only a few carefully selected sites in low-cost countries, but always as fully owned operations. Intel has a hierarchical and integrated international production system based on tightly controlled subsidiaries.[15] This means that Intel not only produces computer chips but also owns the companies that supply the raw materials for chips, such as silicon wafers.

Internalization theory also asks the question of why FDI exists. Internalization theory begins with the assumption that operating in a foreign country is likely more costly than operating at home. Foreign companies are unlikely to have the local contacts and same knowledge of local customs,

monopolistic advantage theory
argues that FDI should occur only when foreign companies have unique competitive advantages over local companies

internalization theory
asks the question of when it is less costly to do something yourself in another country rather than selling your product or service

cultures, and business practices as local competitors. If a company has something of value, why not export the product or license the production process to local companies to take advantage of their local expertise?[16]

transaction costs
the costs associated with negotiating, monitoring, and enforcing contracts

Exporting and licensing are types of market relationships that usually require contracts. Internalization theory uses the concept of **transaction costs** to point out that contracts are not free. To make market transactions one must negotiate, monitor, and enforce contracts. Some companies decide that the transaction costs are too high to use the market to sell their goods, services, and procedures. Instead, they adopt the strategy that it makes more sense (in terms of costs) to internalize (do it yourself) the international operation.

Internalization theory would further explain the rationale for Intel's FDI. With its proprietary technology of chip development and manufacturing, Intel would need to invest considerable effort in monitoring any contracted manufacturer of its chips. It would also face great risk if future foreign competition appropriated its advanced design and production technology.

Dunning's eclectic theory
focuses on three advantages that a company must have to succeed with FDI: ownership, internalization, and location

Dunning's eclectic theory focuses on three advantages that a company must have to succeed with FDI.[17] These advantages consider both the internal characteristics of the MNC and the local environment in which it operates. They also combine the ideas suggested by earlier FDI theories.

1. *Ownership advantages* As with monopolistic advantage theory, the eclectic theory argues that a company must have some strategic competitive advantages over local companies. Otherwise, without something like a superior technology or internationally recognized brand name, a foreign competitor could not compete with the locals. Toyota has an internationally recognized brand name for quality and has superior manufacturing technologies to its competitors. These are two reasons why Toyota owns production facilities throughout the world.

2. *Internalization advantages* A company must gain some cost savings over exporting its product or service or licensing its production processes or brand name.

3. *Location advantages* This means that there must be some profit motive to produce in another country. Usually, this comes from lower-cost production that can serve either local or home markets. Cost saving, and thus higher profits, can also come from reduced transportation costs in serving local markets. BMW, for example, manufactures its X5 sport utility and Z4 roadster in the US. Profits are higher because transportation costs to serve the US market are lower than if these products were shipped from Germany or other BMW plants in England or South Africa. This is important because of the strong demand for sport utility vehicles in the US. However, because US wages are lower than the approximately $30/hour paid to German workers, the US plant produces all of BMW's X5s and Z4s not only for the US market but also for exporting to the rest of the world.

These theories broadly explain some of the motivations for FDI. However, the strategic decision on how to enter a market is quite complex, and you will see more detail later in the text. Among the many factors that companies take into account when considering FDI include better local image, availability of required natural resources, closer access to customers, and closer access to suppliers.

CHAPTER REVIEW

Traditional theories of trade help explain the importing and exporting of goods among nations.

The economic theories of trade generally tell us that free trade between nations is, on average, beneficial for all of the involved countries. However, the gains from trade are not distributed equally in all industries. Undoubtedly, some people and industries suffer. Trade theories suggest that if you are in an industry that is less efficient than that same industry in another country, your company will face stiff international competition. However, trade does not occur in a vacuum and government interventions are common. As such, an important strategic concern for international managers is to understand the impact of government policies regarding trade on their industry's position in the world economy.

Modern trade theories began as reaction to mercantilism. In the mercantilism philosophy, the objective of between-country trade was for a country to win by exporting more than it imported. One nation's gain was another nation's loss. Economists call this surplus of exports over imports a favorable balance of trade. Although limited by simplifying assumptions, and counter to the mercantilist view, the theories of absolute and comparative advantage provide the mathematical logic that trade works to produce more products and give consumers more options.

Adam Smith argued that the world's wealth is not fixed because, when nations engage in international trade, world productivity increases (everyone is wealthier). According to Smith, for the world to benefit from absolute advantages, a country should produce goods for which it has absolute advantage and import those goods in which it has absolute disadvantage.

The theory of comparative advantage suggests that countries should specialize not only in those products for which they have absolute advantage but also for those products in which they have comparative advantage. With specialization and trade, it becomes possible with comparative advantage for both trading partners to gain.

The Heckscher–Ohlin theory argues that a nation's comparative advantage comes from the relative abundance of its factor endowments. Like Ricardo and Smith, the HO theory argues that free trade is beneficial to all partners. However, international trade is driven not only by relative differences in production efficiency but also by relative differences in the factor endowments of countries. Most recent economics research suggests that trade is best explained by both Ricardo's comparative advantage in efficiency of production (in part due to superior technologies) and the relative factor endowments identified by HO theory.

Product life cycle theory adds another consideration regarding how to look at specialization of production based on absolute or comparative advantage. That is, according to this view, some countries are more likely to develop companies that are good at creating new products, while other countries are more likely to develop companies that are efficient at producing mature products. Once a production of a product becomes routine, it makes sense to replace higher-paid, higher-skilled workers with lower-skilled and lower-paid workers in other countries. At the same time, foreign competitors in the low-cost countries begin to develop the skills necessary to produce the product. Eventually imports from foreign companies rather than domestic production serve the innovating countries' markets

During the 1980s, several economists developed what is now called new trade theory. New trade theory looks at how companies and industries in a nation can take advantage of economies of scale. Economies of scale mean that each additional unit of production costs less to produce than did the previous unit. Economies of scale are another form of comparative advantage.

Harvard strategic management professor Michael Porter rejects the notion that comparative advantage is sufficient to explain world trade. His diamond model notes that local demand, the existence of related and supporting industries, as well as factor endowments, give industries in certain countries an international competitive advantage.

The chapter considered several arguments against free trade. These included free trade as a threat to national sovereignty, the need to protect infant industries, the argument that trade must be fair, and the protection of local jobs. Different interest groups and industries hurt by international competition often appeal to governments for protection based on these arguments.

Exporting and importing are not the only strategies for companies to engage in international operations. Foreign direct investment (FDI) is another option. This chapter considered some of the theoretical reasons for FDI. In later chapters, you will see more information on how to use FDI as a strategic option for an international company.

Monopolistic advantage theory is an economic view of FDI that argues that FDI should occur only when foreign companies have unique competitive advantages over local companies. Internalization theory looks at the relative efficiency of using the market (e.g. import or export) to go international contrasted with building or acquiring your own organization in another country. Dunning's eclectic theory focuses on three advantages that a company must have to succeed with FDI. Ownership advantage means that a company must have some strategic competitive advantages over local companies. Internalization advantage means that a company must gain some cost savings over exporting its product or service or licensing its production processes or brand name. Location advantage means that there must be some profit reason to go into a foreign location.

DISCUSSION QUESTIONS

1. Compare and contrast the theories of absolute and comparative advantage.
2. How does the Heckscher–Ohlin (HO) theory build on the earlier work of absolute and comparative advantage?
3. The Leontief Paradox finds opposite trading patterns for the US to those predicted by the HO theory. How can you resolve this paradox?
4. Although economists generally discredit mercantilism, can you find any examples in the popular press where politicians or business leaders use similar arguments to protect an industry?
5. Identify some products initially produced in the US, Germany, or Japan that followed the product life cycle theory. Where are they produced now?
6. Present arguments that saving jobs in one industry is a cost that should be shared by everyone in a society.
7. Present alternative arguments about saving jobs, looking at how saving jobs in one industry might eventually hurt another industry.
8. Based on your knowledge of trade theory, discuss the usefulness of limiting textile imports from China and other developing countries.
9. In deciding whether to export from another country or build their own sales or production site, based on your knowledge of trade theory and theories of FDI what are the major considerations for international managers making this choice?
10. Boeing is using world-class manufacturing facilities in Japan to supply components for its new Dreamliner. Should Boeing consider building production plants in countries like India and China, where there are many excellent lower-wage engineers? What factors should they take into account?

INTERNATIONAL BUSINESS SKILL BUILDER

A Simulation of International Trade

Step 1: Review the theory of comparative advantage.
Step 2: Go to the website http://desertislandgame.com/.
Step 3: Play the simple and advanced trade games.
Step 4: Compare your performance with other students and discuss the implications for world trade.

CHAPTER INTERNET ACTIVITY

In this project, you will explore the absolute advantage of labor costs.

1. Go to the International Labor Organization's website (**http://laborsta.ilo.org/**) and look at the wages of manufacturing workers in your own country and two or three others. Note whether these countries have lower or higher wages.
2. Now go the World Trade Organization's statistics website (**www.wto.org/english/res_e/statis_e/its2008_e/its08_toc_e.htm**) and examine the trade patterns in manufactured goods between your country and the other countries.
3. Write a brief report or prepare a presentation that examines whether the trade flows make sense in terms of which countries have the absolute advantage in terms of labor costs. If the trade patterns do not reflect trade based on absolute advantage, consider why this might not be working. For example, there may be cultural, political, manufacturing capacity or other factors involved.

KEY CONCEPTS

*absolute advantage

autarky

*comparative advantage

Dunning's eclectic theory

economies of scale

favorable trade balance

foreign direct investment (FDI)

Heckscher–Ohlin theory (HO)

internalization theory

Leontief Paradox

mercantilism

monopolistic advantage theory

national diamond

new trade theory

opportunity costs

product life cycle theory

specie-flow mechanism

transaction costs

zero-sum game

LEVI STRAUSS & COMPANY

NO LONGER "MADE IN THE USA"

CASE 4

page 1

Levi Strauss & Company (LS&C) of San Francisco, California, has been in the clothing business for 150 years. The company developed and set the standard for denim jeans and has been manufacturing them for over 130 years. Throughout most of LS&C's existence its clothing has been manufactured, at least in part, in the United States. The firm recently announced that it will no longer manufacturer its products in North America, shutting down its one remaining plant in the United States and two in Canada. For most of its history, the company founded by Levi Strauss proudly manufactured clothing in the United States.

Levi Strauss was born in Bavaria in 1829. He immigrated to the United States with his mother to join other family members in a dry goods business in New York. At age 24 Strauss moved to San Francisco to open a west-coast branch of the family business. While the dry goods business was successful, Strauss stumbled upon a product line that would make Levi's a household name in the United States, and much of the rest of the world.

Jacob Davis, a tailor in Reno, Nevada, was a customer of Levi Strauss. Davis wrote Strauss in 1872 telling him of an invention in which he might be interested. Davis had developed a new way of ensuring that men did not rip the pockets of their pants. He had installed metal rivets at the corners of the pants pockets to strengthen them, and he found that customers liked the new product. Davis sought a patent on this process; however, he did not have the money required for the legal protection of his invention, so he sought the financial aid of Strauss. Realizing that riveted pants might have potential, Strauss provided the $68 needed to obtain the patent. Using denim to create work pants, the partnership of Strauss and Davis created the "original, authentic jeans."

Today, Levi Strauss & Company is privately owned by the Haas family, descendants of Levi Strauss. LS&C sells its products in over 100 countries. The firm continues to sell its traditional product under the Levi brand, and has added the successful Dockers brand of khaki-type products to its product offerings. LS&C also sells a value-oriented brand called Signature that it markets through mass merchandisers such as Walmart. While the company enjoyed enormous success throughout many years of its existence, it has suffered in recent years as competitors have significantly eroded market share. The company, once the premier supplier of clothing for America's youth, has witnessed sizable decreases in sales and earnings over the past few years. A new strategy of product development is underway in an effort to recapture the loyalty of the youth market. At the same time, LS&C is attempting to reduce its costs through a change in its product sourcing.

. . .

CASE 4

page 2

In the past, LS&C relied on its own manufacturing capability to source its product. The company operated many manufacturing facilities in the United States. Eventually foreign manufacturing was established and production capability began to shift to lower-cost countries. The company also began to contract the manufacturing of its products to independent producers. The decision in 2003 to end all North American production caused some to question the ethical orientation of a company well known for being a socially responsible organization. The change in strategy will allow LS&C to focus on product design and marketing, and to free resources previously devoted to manufacturing.

LS&C was built on four core values: empathy, originality, integrity, and courage. The company feels that these core values have served the organization well, and they continue to be the driving forces for change at LS&C. Levi Strauss has been a pioneer not only in clothing design, but also in other areas of business as well. The firm's progressive employment policies predated the civil rights movement in the United States, and LS&C has been listed as one of "America's 50 Best Companies for Minorities" by *Fortune* magazine. LS&C has been awarded the Excellence in Ethics designation by *Business Ethics* magazine, and the company was a pioneer in establishing and supporting employee volunteers through its Community Involvement Teams. In addition, the Levi Strauss Foundation awards $15 million annually to community-based organizations. LS&C was an early supporter of ethical guidelines for contractors. In 1991 the Company created the Global Sourcing and Operating Guidelines that regulate its contractors in areas of worker health and safety, environmental standards, and general employment practices.

Critics of the company contend that LS&C is simply following other American companies in outsourcing its production to lower labor-cost countries. This practice reduces the employment opportunities available in the United States and further erodes the industrial base of the country. It is felt by some that the company relies on the important US market for sales; however, the company does not provide employment opportunities to support those sales. LS&C has responded to these charges by stating that outsourcing of production is necessary in order for the company to survive. As CEO Phil Marineau states, "We're in a highly competitive industry where few apparel brands own and operate manufacturing facilities in North America." The company also counters its critics with the fact that a Community Trust Fund has been established by the company to aid the communities affected by the plant closures, and that comprehensive separation packages will be offered to the terminated employees. Some critics feel that Levi, an American icon, has a greater responsibility in stopping the deindustralization of America.

. . .

CASE 4

page 3

CASE DISCUSSION POINTS

1. Do you feel that LS&C is acting in a responsible manner in closing its North American production operations? Explain.
2. Do American companies like LS&C that transfer production to lower-wage countries hurt or help the economy of the United States?
3. Evaluate the soundness of the strategic shift away from production and towards a focus on design and marketing.

Sources: L. Foster, 2003, "Levi to end North America production," *Financial Times*, September 26; S. Matthews, 2003, "Levi to fire 1,980, shut plants," *Miami Herald*, September 26; www.hoovers.com (accessed September 29, 2003); www.levistrauss.com (accessed September 26, 2003).

Case prepared by Charles A. Rarick

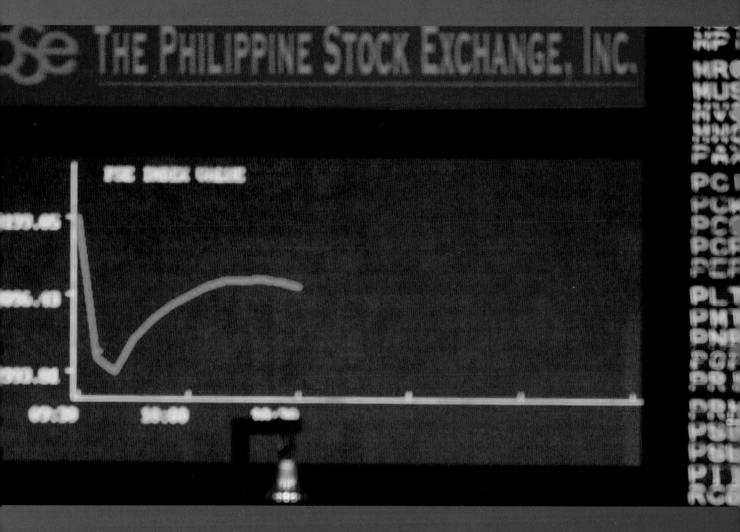

After reading this chapter you should be able to:

- Understand the nature of the foreign exchange market.

- Know the history of financial exchange systems.

- Understand what determines exchange rates.

- Know how MNCs manage exchange-rate risks.

- Be familiar with the nature of foreign exchange arbitrage.

The Preview IB Strategic Insight shows that even individual exchanges using foreign currencies can have large effects on the value of purchases or sales made across borders. MNCs must deal with many of the same issues because, as this case shows, exchange rates can have dramatic effects on the bottom line.

In this chapter, you will see how exchange-rate systems operate, and you will see how MNCs can use this knowledge to mitigate the dangers fluctuating rates have on international commerce.

Living on US Dollars and Buying a Car in France

When your author arrived in France for a sabbatical to teach and do research at the Catholic University of Lille, I was still receiving my sabbatical pay of 75 percent of my Washington State University salary. The French university provided lodging as payment for local teaching. Twice a month my WSU salary was deposited into my account at the Washington State Employees' Credit Union.

Of course, to live in France we needed euros, the common European currency, to buy goods and services. A little bit of research showed that the most efficient way to get euros was through the ATM. Since local French ATMs were not charging any fees at the time, this was much cheaper than exchanging dollars for euros at a bank. But how many euros could I get in a day became the question. The credit union had a limit of $300/day withdrawal in cash. On arrival in France, I checked the approximate exchange rate for credit card purchases and found that $1 could buy €0.963. Therefore, this meant that $300 would buy €0.963 × 300 = €288.9, and one could ask for that many euros from the ATM. Of course, the exchange rate changed daily, so on some days €288.9 could exceed the $300 limit.

After a few weeks in France, we decided to buy a used car. I contracted with a local shop owner to buy a Renault 5, commonly known as a Super

Cinq, for €1,000. It took us a few days to withdraw enough euros to pay for the car. Buy what did it cost me? Fortunately, while we were in France, the dollar was appreciating against the euro, meaning that $1 could buy more euros. By the time I paid for the car, I was getting €105 for every dollar. This means that the car cost about $952 (1,000/1.05), where it would have cost $1,038 (1,000/0.963) on the day we arrived!

Fortunately, we got progressively richer on my WSU salary as the year progressed. During our stay, $1 bought as many as €1.23, making everything European much cheaper than the day we arrived.

When we left France, the local garage owner agreed to sell the car on consignment. A month after we left France, he sent me a check for €700. I brought the check to the credit union; they checked the exchange rate at the time ($1 = €1.11) and deposited $660.63 into my account (€700/ 1.11). Had the exchange rate returned to the same value as on the day we entered France ($1 = €0.963), I would have made more money on the car: €700/0.963 = $726.90! A few months later the exchange rate was below 0.963 euros/dollar; maybe I should have waited to sell the car.

Source: Personal experience, John Cullen.

What is the Foreign Exchange Market?

Because each country, or group of countries in the case of the EU, has its own currency, cross-border business requires that companies exchange their home currency for the currencies of other countries in which they do business. If, for example, a European company wants to invest in a factory in Japan or buy supplies from Japanese companies, it will usually acquire Japanese currency (yen) to make its purchases. It is the foreign exchange market that provides the European company with the ability to exchange euros for yen and then use the yen to do business in Japan. Similarly, if Japanese companies were to accept payment in euros they would not have much use for euros in Japan and would need to use the foreign exchange market to replace this foreign currency with yen.

Thus, international trade and investment requires that people and companies from one country can convert their currencies into the currencies of another country. Rather than buying and selling currencies to each other, tourists, investors, exporters and importers buy and sell foreign currencies primarily through banks. The **foreign exchange market** is a combination of national central banks, private banks, and foreign exchange dealers and brokers through which people and companies can sell or buy foreign currencies.[1]

The foreign exchange market is the biggest market in the world, with transactions exceeding $1.8 trillion a day. Unlike a stock market, it is not an organized structure with a centralized meeting place. Rather, exchanges in currencies take place all over the world and some exchange is open nearly every hour of the day. London, Tokyo, and New York are the biggest markets. The market opens in Hong Kong on Monday morning (which is Sunday evening in New York) and progresses across the world via Tokyo, Frankfurt, London, New York, Chicago, and San Francisco. An hour after banks on the US west coast close on Monday, Hong Kong is opening for business on Tuesday morning.

An **exchange rate** represents the price of one currency in terms of the value of another currency. Every exchange rate has two sides, the value of currency X in terms of Y, and value of currency Y in terms of X. For example, a US dollar might buy or be worth 0.5738 British pounds, whereas, at the same rate, the pound would be worth 1.7429 US dollars. This is called a bilateral exchange rate. When multiple currencies are considered in terms of each other's values, this is called currency cross rates. You can see a brief video on the exchange rate at http://videos.howstuffworks.com/discovery/28735-assignment-discovery-currency-exchange-video.htm.

Exhibit 5.1 shows example currency cross rates among eight often-traded currencies.

Like any market, the value of currencies in terms of other currencies changes continuously, often up to 20 times a minute. Currencies may depreciate or appreciate against each other. For example, when it takes more US dollars to buy Swiss francs (CHF), one would say that the dollar has depreciated against the Swiss franc. Imagine yesterday's exchanges rates are in the table in Exhibit 5.1; yesterday one dollar could buy 5.9404 Swiss francs. Today, however, the US dollar can buy only 5.34636 Swiss francs. This means that the dollar has depreciated by 10 percent (5.9404 –5.34636/5.9404 = 0.1). Conversely, since a Swiss franc can buy more dollars today than yesterday, we say the Swiss franc has appreciated relative to the dollar. You can also check current trends in exchange rates at the *Economist* website, www.economist.com/markets/currency/map.cfm.

foreign exchange market
a combination of national central banks, private banks, and foreign exchange dealers and brokers through which people and companies can sell or buy foreign currencies

exchange rate
represents the prices of foreign currencies in terms of other currencies

Exhibit 5.1 **A Sample of Currency Cross Rates**

	USD	EUR	JPY	GBP	CHF	CAD	AUD	HKD
HKD	7.76	9.2433	0.0659	13.5248	5.9404	6.7183	5.7331	
AUD	1.3535	1.6123	0.0115	2.3591	1.0362	1.1719		0.1744
CAD	1.155	1.3758	0.0098	2.0131	0.8842		0.8534	0.1488
CHF	1.3063	1.556	0.0111	2.2768		1.1309	0.9651	0.1683
GBP	0.5738	0.6834	0.0049		0.4392	0.4967	0.4239	0.0739
JPY	117.695	140.1924		205.1306	90.098	101.896	86.9531	15.167
EUR	0.8395		0.0071	1.4632	0.6427	0.7268	0.6202	0.1082
USD		1.1912	0.0085	1.7429	0.7655	0.8658	0.7388	0.1289

Note: HKD = Hong Kong dollar; AUD = Australian dollar; CAD = Canadian dollar; CHF = Swiss franc; GBP = Great Britain pound; JPY = Japanese yen; ERU = Euro; USD = US dollar.

The exchange rates you see in Exhibit 5.1 and reported daily in the business press such as the *Wall Street Journal* or the *Financial Times* are the midpoints between what banks and other exchange dealers call **the bid and the ask spread.** Banks and others dealing with currency exchange often do not charge for their services but make money by buying at one price, the bid price, and selling currency at a higher price, the ask price.

the bid and the ask spread
the difference between the price a bank buys a currency, the bid price, and price a bank sells a currency, the ask price

For example, Franz from the University of Berlin is going to come to the US to study for a semester at the University of Washington. He has saved €2,000 to use as spending money. Becky, an exchange student from the University of Washington, has just arrived in Germany with $2,000 cash. After meeting Franz, Becky suggests that they go to the bank together to exchange their money, Franz to exchange his €2,000 for dollars and Becky to exchange her $2,000 for euros. A quick check on the Web before they go shows that €1 = $1.1912. However, when they arrive at the bank, Franz is quoted a rate of €1= $1.1902. This is the bid price or the number of US dollars the bank is willing to give Franz for his euros. However, Becky finds that the bank asks her to give $1.1917 for each euro. This is the ask price or the number of US dollars you would have to pay the bank to get euros. This is an example of the bid/ask spread. Sometimes this is expressed as a percentage, which is called the margin, where bid–ask margin = ask price–bid price/ask price × 100. Using the figures above, this would be 1.1907–1.1902 × 100 = 0.15.

Economists often look at the foreign exchange market as a tiered system.[2] First is the wholesale tier, which includes the commercial banks that directly serve the businesses and individuals who wish to buy or sell a foreign currency. Second is the retail tier, which consists of the small agents who buy and sell foreign exchange.

The wholesale tier is an informal, geographically dispersed network of about 2,000 banks and currency brokerage firms. Approximately three-quarters of the $1.5 trillion a day in exchanges is between banks. SWIFT (Society for Worldwide Interbank Financial Telecommunication) is the primary clearing system for international transactions. Banks involved in a foreign currency transaction transfer bank deposits through SWIFT to settle a transaction.[3] Occasionally, banks use brokers who provide a wholesale interbank market for foreign exchange. Brokers buy and sell currencies to banks that may not have enough of a desired currency in their possession to conduct a transaction. The broker would receive a commission for their services.

Tourists, exporters, importers, and foreign investors usually do not have stores of foreign currency to purchase products or services, or to make investments in other countries. Similarly, when companies and individuals receive foreign currencies, they usually wish to convert those currencies to their own currencies for use in their home countries. For example, if you returned to your home in France with ¥200,000 remaining from your trip to Japan, your money would not be very useful in the land of the euro and you would likely want to exchange your yen for euros.

Most often, MNCs buy and sell the foreign currencies they use to conduct their cross-national businesses from large commercial banks such as Citibank. This allows them to buy and sell goods and services in other countries in the local currency. For example, consider that a US motorcycle dealer wants to buy Japanese Kawasaki motorcycles to sell in California. Kawasaki charges ¥1,332,000 for each bike. The dealer does not own any yen and does not have a checking account based in yen. Instead, she goes to Citibank's foreign-exchange department in Los Angeles, and Citibank debits her Citibank account for $15,000 based on an exchange rate of ¥111/dollar. In turn, Citibank pays Kawasaki the ¥1,332,000 from its branch office in Tokyo.

The IB Small Business Insight below shows how changing exchange rates can influence the business of two US entrepreneurs.

Two Entrepreneurs: One Gains and Another Loses from the Weakening Dollar

IB SMALL BUSINESS INSIGHT

Recently, the US dollar has weakened against other currencies. This means that the US dollar buys less of other currencies like the euro or, conversely, it takes fewer euros to buy a US dollar.

For entrepreneur Ted Koh, owner of Amtech, the weakening US dollar is a competitive advantage over his European rivals. His medical equipment export business did $1.2 million in sales in 2006. Amtech sells diagnostic and rehabilitation products to customers in Hong Kong, Japan, Korea, and Taiwan. Most of Koh's competitors come from Europe, and because of the strength of the British pound and euro his products are cheaper for his Asian customers. As Koh noted, "The euro is really higher than most other countries' currencies, and the pound is

also quite strong. With the US dollar really low, it really helps me."

Fred Hall, president and owner of California-based New Zealand Seafoods Inc., faces the other side of the coin. When the US dollar fell in value by 50 percent against the New Zealand dollar, Hall had to pay twice as much for the fish from his New Zealand suppliers—even though they didn't raise their prices. To lower costs, he is now importing some of his fish from Greece, Tunisia, and some South American countries, where the exchange rates are more favorable.

Source: Based on Kate Berry, 2005, "Dealing with the dollar," *Los Angeles Business Journal*, February 2.

Types of Foreign Exchange Transactions

Foreign exchange transactions can take different forms. The **spot transaction** is an immediate transaction at a specific exchange rate. By convention, when banks engage in spot transactions two business days are allowed to complete the transaction. This allows time to debit and credit bank accounts in the countries involved. The exchange rates reported in the popular business press represent the spot rates. They also usually are for transactions of a million dollars or more, so the exchange rate the individual tourist is going to receive is not as favorable. The example of the Kawasaki dealer's bike purchase is an exchange based on the spot rate.

International businesses have other options regarding their transactions. Say, for example, our Kawasaki dealer knows in August that she will need approximately $15 million worth of yen on September 15, when she will receive a major shipment of motorcycles. Fearing that the yen might appreciate in terms of dollars over the next month (and thus cost her more dollars to buy each motorcycle), she contracts with a bank to buy the necessary yen on September 15 at an agreed-upon exchange rate. She and the bank then know the exchange rate, and she takes delivery of the yen on September 15. This is known as a **forward transaction**. Later we will see how MNCs use forward transactions to cover the risk of exchange-rate changes.

A third type of transaction, which typically occurs between banks, is called a currency swap. A swap involves two exchanges. First, the banks agree to exchange a certain amount of currency for another currency at a set exchange rate. Second, they agree to re-swap the currencies back in the future at a set exchange rate. Banks do this to make sure they have enough of a particular currency to serve their customers. For example, if the Bank of Tokyo is running short of dollars needed by its Japanese customers to pay for US imports, it may arrange a dollar–yen currency swap with Citibank. Citibank sells the Bank of Tokyo dollars for yen and then later buys the dollars back with its accumulated yen. Exhibit 5.2 shows the relative extent of spot, forward, and swaps in the global market.

spot transaction
an immediate transaction at a specific exchange rate

forward transaction
an agreed-upon future exchange rate

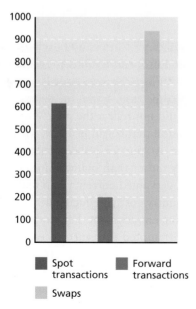

Exhibit 5.2

Types of Transactions in the Global Market (in billions of US dollars/year)

Source: Bank for International Settlements, 2005, *Triennial Central Bank Survey: Foreign Exchange and Derivatives Market Activity in 2004*, March.

The History of Exchange-rate Systems

There is a variety of rules that countries can use to govern the value of their currencies relative to the values of other nations' currencies. These rules are called the **exchange-rate system.**[4] Historically, there have been three major exchange-rate systems: the gold standard, the Bretton Woods system, and the floating system.

exchange-rate system
a variety of rules that countries can use to govern the value of their currencies relative to the values of other nations' currencies

The Gold Standard

Starting in the mid-1800s and lasting to the 1930s, many countries established the value of their currencies relative to one ounce of gold. An ounce of gold for the US dollar, for example, was valued at $20.646 until 1933. During the same period, one ounce of gold cost 86.672 German marks or 107.008 French francs. Thus, national policies stabilized the values of currencies needed to purchase gold from each nation's stocks of gold. That is, countries guaranteed to exchange gold for their currencies at a specific rate. Theoretically, at least, one could exchange the gold "coin" note for $100 worth of gold in 1923. Thus, the term "gold standard" means a standard value of a currency in terms of gold.

How did this result in an exchange-rate system? The reason that this established an exchange-rate system is that all countries adopting the gold standard established a value of the currency relative to the same commodity: gold. Thus, for example, if you know that one ounce of gold = $20.646 = DM 86.672 = Ffr 107.008, you also know that $1 = (DM 86.672/$20.646) or $1= DM 4.198. Similarly, $1 = (Ffr 107.008/$20.646) = Ffr 5.183. Thus, using this system, you know that you could buy the same amount of gold in any of the countries by exchanging your home country's currency at the set price of gold.

One important point about a commodity-based exchange rate such as gold is that a nation must hold substantial amounts of gold in reserve to legitimate the value of its currency in gold. This means that to have more money in a country's economy you must mine or otherwise secure more gold. The value of the money in circulation and the value of the gold need not match exactly, but must remain stable. For example, during early 1900s, the US had approximately eight times more money in circulation than the value of the gold held by the government.

Although the gold standard resulted in a stability of prices and exchange rates, after the beginning of World War I most European nations prevented their currencies from being converted to gold. When the war ended, some nations tried to return to the earlier fixed exchange rates based on the gold standard. However, the value of the currencies did not reflect the post-World War I economic realities and the ensuing depression that began in 1929. Most industrialized nations began to pursue polices such as increasing employment levels rather than maintaining the value of their currency. An overvalued currency can make the goods and services in a country costly, reducing demand from outside and thus lowering employment. For example, when the United Kingdom attempted to return to earlier gold standard currency values, the price of goods produced in the UK became artificially high relative to other countries. This led to a decrease in demand for UK products and an

The 1022 series $100 bill

accompanying rise in unemployment. By 1931, the UK abandoned the gold standard. When the value of a country's currency depreciates relative to other currencies, the country's products become cheaper on the world market. This often leads to increased international and domestic sales because foreign goods become more expensive to local consumers, and local goods become cheaper on the international market. In turn, employment levels tend to rise.

The Bretton Woods Agreement

After World War II, most governments realized that rebuilding the economies of Europe and Japan would require stable exchange rates. With this realization, representatives from over 40 nations met in 1940 at a small resort in Bretton Woods, New Hampshire. The agreement on exchange rates that emerged from this conference is called the **Bretton Woods Agreement.**

To help keep currency exchange rates stable, the Bretton Woods participants agreed to adopt a **pegged exchange-rate system**. When nations participate in a pegged exchange-rate system, they agree to fix the value of their currencies relative to another currency rather than to a commodity such as gold. The US dollar was chosen as the base currency and all the countries agreed to keep the value of their currency within plus or minus 1 percent of a specific value of the dollar. The German mark was pegged to the dollar at DM 4.20 per dollar and the British pound was pegged to the dollar at £2.80 to the dollar. In contrast to all the other nations, the US currency maintained a relationship with gold fixed at $35/ounce. Thus, because the US dollar remained fixed to gold, this was an indirect gold standard, but nations used US dollars rather than gold to settle international transactions. The US, on the other hand, still agreed to exchange dollars for gold at the $35/ounce value.

The Bretton Woods Agreement also created the **International Monetary Fund (IMF)**. The IMF is a multination organization that helps manage international money exchanges. Members agreed to follow specific exchange-rate policies such as the pegged exchange-rate system.

By the early 1970s, speculators and some governments were exchanging dollars for the US-held gold at increasing rates. Speculators noted that the US's trade imbalance (the US was buying more from other countries than other countries were from the US) was increasing the supply of dollars abroad. This suggested that the US might devalue the dollar by requiring more dollars to buy an ounce of gold. The dollar would have less value because it would require more dollars to buy the same amount of gold. Thus, speculators tried to buy gold at $35 an ounce with the hope of selling back the gold later for more dollars and a profit.

With gold outflows increasing daily, President Nixon suspended the convertibility of the dollar into gold on August 15, 1971. This effectively ended the Bretton Woods Agreement and the world's exchange-rate system was in turmoil. Various attempts to re-establish a pegged exchange-rate system met with little success and a floating-rate system emerged. This was eventually formalized at the Jamaica Accords. There, IMF member nations agreed to change the IMF constitution to allow the new system. A **floating-rate system** allows each nation to use market forces to determine the value of its currency. Today, most major economies use a floating-rate system, but it is certainly not the only system encountered by MNCs.

Bretton Woods Agreement the agreement on exchange rates to peg currencies to the US dollar that emerged from the conference at a small resort in Bretton Woods

pegged exchange rate fixing the value of a currency relative to another currency rather than to a commodity such as gold

International Monetary Fund (IMF) an international organization that helps manage international money exchanges

floating-rate system allows each nation to use market forces to determine the value of its currency

Other Currency Exchange-rate Systems

In addition to the floating-rate system and the pegged-rate system discussed above, there are several different systems in use by countries in today's global economy. Exhibit 5.3 shows the distribution of exchange-rate systems in use.

In the managed-float system, countries reserve the right to intervene to influence the value of their currency on the open market. Remember that the independent-float system allows the market to determine the value of a currency relative to another currency. As you will see later in this chapter, the value of a currency is determined in part by the supply of the currency in the market. For example, if the national banks of many countries hold many dollars, the supply is plentiful and the value of the dollar faces downward pressure. One way the US can influence the supply of dollars is to buy dollars from other countries with different currencies. The result is that the supply will decrease and the value will increase.

We saw earlier that the Bretton Woods Agreement resulted in many currencies pegged to the US dollar at a fixed rate. Many smaller nations still peg their currencies to other currencies, often because they are close trading partners or interact via tourism. For example, many of the Caribbean island nations peg their currencies to the US dollar, including Antigua, the Bahamas, Barbados, Grenada, the Netherlands Antilles, and St Vincent and the Grenadines. Pegging currencies reduces the volatility of exchange rates and encourages trade. However, economic conditions often differ between countries and this leads to difficulties in maintaining the peg. To adjust for these differences some countries adopt a **crawling-peg system**. With this system, the peg is allowed to adjust within boundaries over time. Nicaragua, for example, allows its currency to adjust in value by 1 percent a month relative to the US dollar.

Rather than pegging their currencies to a single country, some nations choose to peg their currencies to an average of several currencies, usually six or fewer. This approach is called the **currency-basket peg**. To visualize a currency basket, imagine you have a basket with five coins, each from a different country. The sum value of the coins in the basket should equal a unit of your currency. That is, the exchange is based on a combination of the exchange rates for each currency. All of the five currency exchange rates can be given equal weighting. However, similar to selecting one currency for pegging, some currency exchange rates might be more important to your country because of economic relation-

crawling-peg system
system in which the currency peg is allowed to adjust within boundaries over time

currency-basket peg
to peg currencies to an average of several currencies

Exhibit 5.3 **Distribution of Exchange-rate Types by Country Type (%)**

Country Groups	Peg	Limited Flexibility	Managed Floating	Freely Floating	Total
Advanced	32.32	25.46	13.72	28.5	100
Emerging	39.52	0.63	43.97	15.87	100
Transition	35.06	0	34.32	30.63	100
Developing	72.84	1.11	14.32	11.73	100

Source: Peter Clark, Natalia Tamirisa, and Shang-Jin Wei, with Azim Sadikov, and Li Zeng, 2004, *Exchange Rate Volatility and Trade Flows–Some New Evidence*, Washington, DC: International Monetary Fund, May.

Exhibit 5.4 **Dollarization around the World**

Nation	Political status	Currency	Since
American Samoa	US territory	US dollar	1899
Andorra	Independent	Euro (formerly French franc, Spanish peseta), own coins	1278
British Virgin Islands	British dependency	US dollar	1973
Cocos (Keeling) Islands	Australian external territory	Australian dollar	1955
Cook Islands	New Zealand self-governing territory	New Zealand dollar	1995
Cyprus, Northern	De facto independent	Turkish lira	1974
East Timor	Independent	US dollar	2000
Ecuador	Independent	US dollar	2000
El Salvador	Independent	US dollar	2001
Greenland	Danish self-governing region	Danish krone	before 1800
Guam	US territory	US dollar	1898
Kiribati	Independent	Australian dollar, own coins	1943
Kosovo	UN administration	Euro	1999
Lichtenstein	Independent	Swiss franc	1921
Marshall Islands	Independent	US dollar	1944
Micronesia	Independent	US dollar	1944
Monaco	Independent	Euro (formerly French franc)	1865
Montenegro	Semi-independent	Euro (partly "DM-ized" since 1999)	2002
Nauru	Independent	Australian dollar	1914
Niue	New Zealand self-governing territory	New Zealand dollar	1901
Norfolk Island	Australian external territory	Australian dollar	before 1900?
Northern Mariana Islands	US commonwealth	US dollar	1944
Palau	Independent	US dollar	1944
Panama	Independent	US dollar, own balboa coins	1904
Pitcairn Island	British dependency	New Zealand, US dollars	1800s
Puerto Rico	US commonwealth	US dollar	1899
San Marino	Independent	Euro (formerly Italian lira), own coins	1897
Tokelau	New Zealand territory	New Zealand dollar	1926
Turks and Caicos Islands	British colony	US dollar	1973
Tuvalu	Independent	Australian dollar, own coins	1892
US Virgin Islands	US territory	US dollar	1934
Vatican City	Independent	Euro (formerly Italian lira), own coins	1929

Sources: Kurt Schuler, 1999, "Encouraging official dollarization in emerging markets," staff report, Office of the Chairman, Joint Economic Committee, US Congress, April; CIA World Factbook 2005; press reports.

ships. In that case, these currencies are often given added weight. For example, in 2005, China moved to break from its 8.3 yuan/dollar peg to a basket peg of currencies including the euro, the yen, the won, the Singapore dollar, the pound, and the Malaysian ringgit. The dollar, however, still dominates the weighting.[5] The IB Strategic Insight below shows how this managed exchange rate can benefit Chinese companies and US consumers.

One final way a nation can manage its exchange rate is to adopt the currency of anther country. Since the US dollar is most often the currency of choice, this practice is called **dollarization**. The IMF reports that over 20 percent of its members use the currency of another nation as their own. Exhibit 5.4 shows a list of countries that use the dollarization approach to managing their currencies.

dollarization
to adopt the currency of another country

What Determines Exchange Rates

Purchasing Power Parity

Purchasing Power Parity (PPP)
ignoring tax differences, transportation costs, and trade restrictions, goods and other services in any two countries should have the same prices after converting each of their currencies into a common currency

Purchasing power parity (PPP) means that, ignoring tax differences, transportation costs, and trade restrictions, goods and services in any two countries should have the same prices *after converting each of their currencies into a common currency*. This is also called the Law of One Price.

For example, you buy your favorite tennis racquet in Los Angeles for $200. Your friend, who is studying in France for the year, buys the same racquet for

| Competitive Advantage through Exchange Rates | IB STRATEGIC INSIGHT |

From 1995 to July of 2005, the Chinese government kept the value of the yuan pegged or fixed against the dollar. This was called a "revised" Bretton Woods system. Many US manufacturers complained that the value of the yuan was kept artificially low to make Chinese products cheaper than those of their US competitors.

They claimed an undervalued yuan gave Chinese exporters an unfair advantage, and put China under pressure to revalue its currency, preferably moving to a floating-rate system. Most experts believe that the Chinese are a long way from adopting a floating system, as it would possibly hurt the export growth that is driving the growth of the Chinese economy.

The move to the basket peg resulted in only a small revaluation against the dollar of 2.1 percent. That is, a dollar buys 2.1 percent fewer yuan, so Chinese goods become more expensive for US purchasers. However, experts believe that Chinese manufacturers reducing their profit margins mostly absorbed this revaluation. Only some of the increased export prices for Chinese goods reflected the actual selling prices. To make the Chinese exports represent the real value of their currency, some Western governments are calling for a 25–30 percent revaluation, and this would certainly send the price of Chinese goods up. The result would be higher prices for US consumers at stores like Walmart that import many products produced in China, but higher prices for Chinese goods would allow US, European, and Japanese manufactures to compete more successfully on price.

Sources: *The Economist*, 2005, "From T-shirts to T-bonds," www.economist.com, July 28; *The Economist*,

Exhibit 5.5 **The Big Mac Index**

	Big Mac prices		Implied ppp[†] of the dollar	actual exchange rate	Undex (–)/over (+) valuation against dollar
	In local currency	in dollars*			
United States[‡]	$3.57	3.57	–	–	
Argentina	Peso 11.0	3.64	3.08	3.02	+2
Australia	A$3.45	3.36	0.97	1.03	–6
Brazil	Real 7.50	4.73	2.10	1.58	+33
Britain	£2.29	4.57	1.56	2.00[§]	+28
Canada	C$4.09	4.08	1.15	1.00	+14
Chile	Peso 1,550	3.13	434	494	–12
China	Yuan 12.5	1.83	3.50	6.83	–49
Czech Republic	Koruna 66.1	4.56	18.5	14.5	+28
Denmark	DK28.0	5.95	7.84	4.70	+67
Egypt	Pound 13.0	2.45	3.64	5.31	–31
Euro Area**	€3.37	5.34	1.06[††]	1.59	+50
Hong Kong	HK$13.3	1.71	3.73	7.80	–52
Hungary	Forint 670	4.64	187.7	144.3	+30
Indonesia	Rupiah 18,700	2.04	5,238	9,152	–43
Japan	Yen 280	2.62	78.4	106.8	–27
Malaysia	Ringgit 5.50	1.70	1.54	3.2	–52
Mexico	Peso 32.0	3.15	8.96	10.2	–12
New Zealand	NZ$4.90	3.72	1.37	1.32	+4
Norway	Kroner 40.0	7.88	11.2	5.08	+121
Poland	Zloty 7.00	3.45	1.96	2.03	–3
Russia	Rouble 59.0	2.54	16.5	23.2	–29
Saudi Arabia	Riyal 10.0	2.67	2.80	3.75	–25
Singapore	S$3.95	2.92	1.11	1.35	–18
South Africa	Rand 16.9	2.24	4.75	7.56	–37
South Korea	Won 3,200	3.14	895	1,018	–12
Sweden	SKr38.0	6.37	10.6	5.96	+79
Switzerland	SFr6.50	6.36	1.82	1.02	+78
Taiwan	NT$75.0	2.47	21.0	30.4	–31

Exhibit 5.5 **Continued**

	Big Mac prices		Implied ppp† of the dollar	actual exchange rate	Undex (−)/over (+) valuation against dollar
	In local currency	in dollars*			
Thailand	Baht 62.0	1.86	17.4	33.4	−48
Turkey	Lire 5.15	4.32	1.44	1.19	+21
UAE	Dirhams 10.00	2.72	2.80	3.67	−24
Colombia	Peso 7000.00	3.89	1960.78	1798.65	9
Costa Rica	Colones 1800.00	3.27	504.20	551.02	−8
Estonia	Kroon 32.00	3.24	8.96	9.87	−9
Iceland	Kronur 469.00	5.97	131.37	78.57	67
Latvia	Lats 1,55	3.50	0.43	0,44	−2
Lithuania	Litas 6.90	3.17	1.93	2.18	−11
Pakistan	Rupee 140.00	1.97	39.22	70.90	−45
Peru	New Sol 9.50	3.35	2.66	2.84	−6
Philippines	Peso 87.00	1.96	24.37	44.49	−45
Slovakia	Koruna 77.00	4.03	21.57	19.13	13
Sri Lanka	Rupee 210.00	1.95	58.82	107.55	−45
Ukraine	Hryvnia 11.00	2.39	3.08	4.60	−33
Uruguay	Peso 61.00	3.19	17.09	19.15	−11

* At current exchange rates
† Purchasing-power parity; local price divided by price in the United States
‡ Average of New York, Chicago, Atlanta and San Francisco
§ Dollars per pound
** Weighted average of prices in euro area
†† Dollars per euro

Source: *Economist.com*, "The Big Mac Index, Sandwiched" July 24, 2008

€180 at a Lille sporting goods store. Applying the logic of PPP, these prices should be the same when we factor in the exchange rate between the dollar and the euro. Assume that the exchange rate = 0.8 $/€. Your friend can then convert the price you paid in dollars for your racquet to the price she should pay in euros as $200 × 0.8 = €180.

However, because currencies can be "overvalued" or "undervalued," the Law of One Price does not always hold. Overvalued means that the currency is worth more than would be predicted by an economic model. Undervalued means the currency is worth less than would be predicted by an economic model. The use of PPP since the sixteenth century makes it perhaps the oldest economic model used to estimate how over- or undervalued is a currency.

Based on the theory of PPP, *The Economist* publishes each year an index of currency overvaluation and undervaluation based on the price of a McDonald's Big Mac. This has become known as the **Big Mac Index**. The logic is that the price of a Big Mac should be the same everywhere if exchange rates are correct. However, as you can see from the recent index in Exhibit 5.5, and based on what you must pay for a Big Mac in many countries, most currencies are over- or undervalued relative to the US dollar.

Look at the price of a Big Mac in China. It is less than half that in the US. This suggests that the Chinese currency is undervalued by over 50 percent.

Of course, the Big Mac Index is a simple way of looking at currency values regarding PPP. Numerous other factors that come into play determine exchange rates. We discuss some of those drivers below.

Market Factors

Exchange rates reflect the price of money bought and sold in a market. As such, like most markets, the supply and demand for a currency affects its price in terms of other currencies. Of course, not all exchange rates are allowed to respond to market forces (see the history of exchange rates in this chapter) and governments often intervene by buying or selling currencies to influence their value. However, supply and demand remain the major drivers of currency value.

The demand for a currency is based on **derived demand**. That means, for example, that demand for the euro comes from the degree to which people from other countries wish to purchase European products or services or invest in European companies. That is, for example, if US consumers buy European automobiles (a demand for a European good) then US dollars must be converted into euros to buy these automobiles. Consequently, the demand for euros increases.

Exhibit 5.6 shows the relationship between the exchange rate and the demand for euros. The *x*-axis on this chart shows the quantity of euros demanded and the *y*-axis shows hypothetical exchange rates. Note, as the number of dollars it takes to buy euros drops, there is an increase in the quantity of euros demanded. This occurs because US consumers and companies are encouraged to buy more European goods when it takes fewer dollars to do so.

Big Mac Index \
an index of currency overvaluation or undervaluation based on the price of a McDonald's Big Mac, published by *The Economist* each year

derived demand \
demand that comes from the demand for goods and services

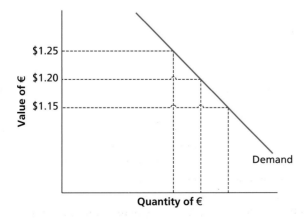

Exhibit 5.6 **Demand Curve for Euros**

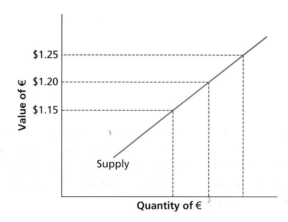

Exhibit 5.7 **Supply Curve for Euros**

Demand goes up, because to buy more European goods, people and companies need to purchase more euros.

The foreign exchange market also includes the supply of, for our example, euros available for sale or for exchange with US dollars. Similar to the US demand curve for euros, we can look at a supply curve for the sale of euros in the foreign exchange market relative to the exchange rate with US dollars.

As shown in Exhibit 5.7, as the ability of euros to buy more US dollars increases, the supply of euros for sale increases. The supply of euros increases when euros can buy more US dollars because US goods and services become cheaper and European consumers and companies do not have to use as many euros to satisfy their needs. That is, because they use fewer euros, there are more euros available.

The point where demand and supply curves intersect is the equilibrium point. As shown in Exhibit 5.8, this is the point where the demand for euros equals the supply of euros, and the result is the price of each currency in terms of the other: namely, the exchange rate. This simple supply/demand view of exchange-rate determination begins with the logic of international trade activities determining the demand or attractiveness of the products and services in another country, and shows how changes in price (exchange rates) increase the demand and supply of currencies to complete these transactions. Of course,

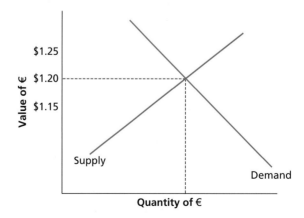

Exhibit 5.8 **Equilibrium Point for the Exchange Rate**

many other factors influence the nature of these demand and supply curves and we will consider some of these factors below.

Effects of Other Factors on Exchange Rates

Inflation   Imagine that the US economy is experiencing a period of inflation. That means that prices are increasing rapidly. In Europe, however, inflation is low so prices are rising more slowly. These price differences make European goods cheaper and more attractive to US businesses and consumers and, conversely, make US goods more expensive and thus less attractive to European companies and consumers. Exhibit 5.9 shows a shift in the demand curve reflecting the increased demand from the US to purchase European goods and thus demand more euros. This increase in demand due to differences in inflation rates brings a new equilibrium point that reflects a higher price (exchange rate) in dollars/euros.

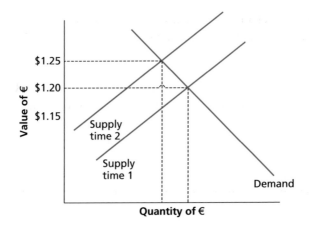

Exhibit 5.9   **Equilibrium Points for Exchange Rates with Rising US Inflation**

Relative Interest Rates   Another factor that influences the demand and supply for currencies is the interest rate. The interest rate is important because investors tend to put their money into countries where they can get the highest rate of return. Thus, if interest rates in the US are higher than in Europe, both European and US investors would find the potentially higher returns a motivation to buy US stocks and bonds. For example, imagine that a typical US company must issue bonds paying 8 percent when it needs to finance its operations with debt. Companies issue or sell bonds to raise money, with the promise to pay back the money with interest in the future to those who buy the bonds. However, similar European companies need only pay 4 percent for their bond issues. US bonds are more attractive because the return is higher.

Attracted by the differences in returns, investors will demand fewer euros than dollars, since they will need dollars to invest in the US. As shown in Exhibit 5.10, when investors seek fewer euros to invest in Europe, the demand for euros drops. Also, in this example, because European investors exchange euros for dollars to take advantage of the higher US interest rates, the supply of euros increases, and the supply curve shifts to the right (more euros are

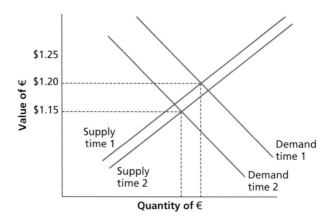

Exhibit 5.10 **Equilibrium Points for Exchange Rates with Rising US Interest Rates**

available) while the demand curve shifts to the left (fewer euros are sought by investors). The situation reduces or depreciates the value of the euros relative to the dollar.

Because an increasing interest rate often accompanies an increasing inflation rate, the effects on the value of a currency can be offset. Rising interest rates attract investors and increase the demand for a currency. Rising inflation increases prices and reduces the demand for a currency. To consider these effects in combination, economists often look at the **real interest rate**. Sometimes called the Fisher effect, the real interest rate is represented as:

Real interest rate = interest rate – inflation rate

real interest rate
the inflation rate subtracted from the interest rate

Income Levels Of course, not all countries have similar income levels so the relative income levels between trading partners can affect the amount of imports from a country. When a country's income levels rise relative to a trading partner's (assuming this is not just inflation but also a real rise in purchasing power), that country will likely buy more goods from its partner. For example, if US incomes levels rise, US consumers are likely to buy more European automobiles. Like all the other factors that can increase the demand for a currency, this would make the price of the European euros rise.

Government Controls Governments can and often do intervene with the market forces that determine exchange rates. Governments and their central banks have several tools to influence exchange rates. The choice of an exchange-rate policy that is not free-floating limits the effects of market forces. For example, as we saw above, the Chinese RMB (also called the yuan) is pegged or fixed to several currencies including the US dollar at a fixed rate. Many claim that this artificially keeps the value of the RMB weak and makes Chinese imports cheaper than local competition in Western countries.

Other options include barriers on foreign trade and investments. Tariffs or restrictions on imports reduce the demand for a foreign currency. Similarly, a government can tax foreign investments at a high rate, offsetting the effects of higher interest rates in other countries. Thus, for example, if investors wish to buy bonds in Europe because the interest rate is better than that in the US, this would increase the demand for euros and, in turn, the dollar would weaken requiring more dollars to buy euros. However, if the US government taxes the returns on European bonds at a higher rate than US bonds, the demand for euros will drop, as will the effects on the exchange rate. Finally, governments often purchase or sell currencies in the exchange market for the sole purpose of influencing supply and demand and thus the exchange rates. For example, during September 2000, several central banks, including the US Federal Reserve and the European Central Bank (the central bank of the EU), purchased about $4 billion worth of euros to strengthen the euro.

Exhibit 5.11 gives a graphic summary of the major factors affecting exchange rates.

Exchange-rate Risks and Hedging

Because exchange rates vary continuously, MNCs necessarily face continuous uncertainties regarding how to value in their own currency what they own in other countries, what they buy from other countries, and what they sell to other countries. Imagine, for example, that your company agrees to buy 1,000 LCD screens a month from Toshiba for a security monitoring system you produce. Toshiba charges you ¥11,800 for each screen. For the first month, the exchange rate is ¥118.00/dollar so you are paying $100 for each LCD. When you go to pay for your next month's LCDs, you find that a dollar only buys ¥112.38, and now the cost of an LCD = (11800/112.38) or $105. Even though Toshiba has never changed its price, your cost for this component of your security monitoring system has gone up 5 percent.

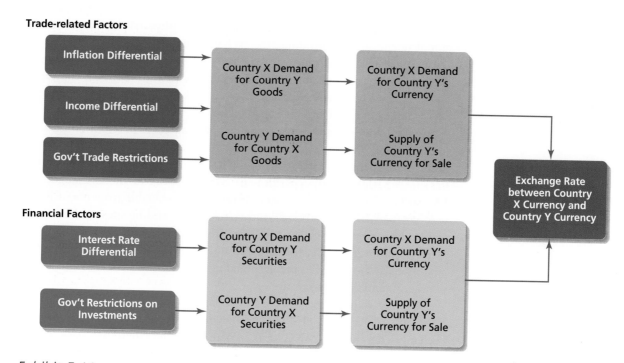

Exhibit 5.11 **Factors Influencing Exchange Rates**

transaction exposure
a risk that MNCs face that involves uncertainty regarding: the value of their own currency for what they own in other countries, what they buy from other countries and what they sell to other countries

translation exposure
a risk that involves the financial characteristics of an MNC with assets and liabilities in different currencies that can look quite different depending on the exchange rates

hedging
offsets risk by making future exchange rates predictable

forward exchange contract
an agreement to purchase a foreign currency in the future between independent parties

currency futures contracts
an agreement to purchase a foreign currency in the future based on contracts traded in a market

The type of exchange-rate risk in the example above is called **transaction exposure**. Formally, transaction exposure occurs when the MNC agrees to a transaction in a foreign currency—selling or buying—in the future. In our example, the company agreed to a price for LCDs in yen in the future. The risk is that the costs, such as the example above, or the proceeds from a sale, can change to the detriment of the organization in question.

A second problem dealing with exchange rates for MNCs is how they value foreign assets (e.g. an asset might be a factory owned in Munich, Germany, by an Australian company) and liabilities (e.g. debt owed to a Swiss bank by an Australian company) in their home country currency, in this case Australian dollars. As the relationships among these currencies change, the worth of the company changes in its home currency. For example, if the Australian dollar depreciates against the Swiss franc, the Australian company's debt, in Australian dollars, increases because it will take more dollars to pay off the debt. For publicly owned companies, US law requires that assets and liabilities be translated into US dollars at the existing exchange rate at the end of the reporting period. If you look at annual reports for MNCs, you can see how companies do this in their financial statements. Since foreign currencies are translated into the home currency for financial statements, this type of risk is called **translation exposure**. The risk is that the financial characteristics of an MNC with assets and liabilities in different currencies can look quite different, depending on the exchange rates.

What can companies do to offset these risks? Companies attempt to offset exchange-rate risk by hedging. **Hedging** offsets risk by making future exchange rates predictable. How can companies do this? There are several mechanisms.

Imagine that you are working for a company that buys a lot of land for a greenfield investment in Poland. A greenfield investment means that you are going to start the company from scratch (imagine building a factory in a green field). Your company agrees to the sale price of 31,786,395 Polish zloty, which on the day of the contract is worth approximately US$ 10 million. The problem for your company is that real-estate transactions often take a few months to complete and, in the meantime, the exchange rate between the zloty and the dollar will likely change. One way to reduce your uncertainty is to buy a **forward exchange contract** from a commercial bank. The forward exchange contract is an agreement to purchase a foreign currency in the future, say three months for this example, at a specified exchange rate.

In this hypothetical contract, your company agrees to purchase Polish zloty in three months at the exchange rate of 1 Polish zloty = 0.3146 US$. Now you know that your cost for the property is $10 million (31,786,395 Polish zloty × 0.3146 = $10,000,000) regardless of what happens to the exchange rate. Forward exchange rates for major currencies are available from major banks (e.g. www.ny.frb.org/markets/fxrates/tenAm.cfm) and business publications. Unlike the example above, forward rates are seldom the same as current or spot rates. To a large degree, forward rates are based on anticipated economic conditions in the countries involved and may be less (a discount) or greater (a premium) than the current rate.

Another way to hedge on the future changes in exchange rates, similar to a forward contract, is called the **currency futures contracts**. Like the forward exchange contract, the MNC locks into an exchange rate to purchase foreign currency in the future. For the forward contract, the agreement is usually between two parties such as a bank and an MNC, with size and delivery date

A Sample of Hedging Strategies

With stores in over 120 countries and 65 percent of its revenue derived from outside the US, McDonald's has a large exposure to the risk of currency value changes. At McDonald's, the Financial Markets group develops hedging strategies for managing foreign exchange risks. One way to hedge naturally is to buy local assets with locally borrowed money, and McDonald's has more than $8 billion in debt, with over 50 percent of the debt denominated in a foreign currency. In this way, they can pay the debt with locally generated money and not worry about the value of the US dollar in local currency. However, for the other 50 percent, they use forward options contracted on a basket of currencies.

Like McDonald's, Walmart uses some natural hedging by borrowing in local currencies to fund local operations. However, since Walmart buys almost nothing from Europe but over $20 billion in goods from China, its major concern is the Chinese yuan. Because the yuan remains essentially pegged to the US$ (even with its now small rate of gain on the dollar), Jay Fitzsimmons, Walmart's treasurer, notes, "The actual impact of currency on the merchandise we buy is minimal."

Yoiehi Hojo, Honda's general manager of the finance division, says that Honda takes a conservative approach, using the same natural hedges as McDonald's and Walmart, as well as forward contracts. However, not all strategies work, as one-quarter showed Honda losing ¥54 billion in operating income (10 percent) due to the impact from a declining dollar in its major market, the US.

Sources: Based on Ed Zwirn, 2005, "Dollar doldrums: Multinationals are hedging currency risk, but they may need to do more," *CFO*, May; FinancialCAD Corporation, 2002, "Increasing the effectiveness of hedging interest rate and foreign exchange risks," www.fincad.com/pdfs/mcdonalds.pdf

tailored to the parties' needs. For the futures contract, contracts to buy or sell currencies in the future at a fixed exchange rate are traded in a regulated market with standardized lots, delivery dates, and only in major currencies. The world's largest currency futures market is the International Monetary Market of the Chicago Mercantile Exchange. Large MNCs with close relationships with banks usually use forward contracts to tailor the exchange to their exact currency needs. Smaller operations prefer the futures market. Hedging strategies used by some major MNCs are described in the IB Strategic Insight above.

Forward contacts make exchange rates predictable for MNCs. However, there is always a chance that exchange rates will move in a direction favorable to the company, as they did for your author in the opening case. Because of this, many companies attempt to forecast future exchange rates to anticipate whether the rates will move in a favorable direction. For example, if a company anticipates that the dollar will appreciate against the yen, it may be willing to agree to a price in yen for a future delivery, hoping that the future price in dollars will be less.

The techniques of forecasting exchange rates are complex and beyond the scope of this text. However, you can see forecasts available from various services on the Web, such as www.forecasts.org/exchange-rate/index.htm.

There are also opportunities to make money on small differences in exchange rates. This is called foreign exchange arbitrage and it is covered in the next section.

Foreign Exchange Arbitrage

Because currencies trade in markets all over the world, exchange rates may differ in different markets. When exchange rates do differ, there is an opportunity to make money by buying lower and selling higher. In fact, the word "arbitrage" means buy low and sell high.

Suppose the exchange rate for the Mexican peso and the US dollar was 40.5 peso/dollar in New York. However, in Tokyo the exchange rate was 40.75 peso/dollar. If both markets are open and there are no restrictions on trade, there is an arbitrage opportunity. Arbitrageurs with substantial dollars or with substantial credit lines in dollars can purchase more pesos per dollar in Tokyo and then immediately sell the pesos in New York for more dollars than they paid. For example, $1,000,000 would buy 40,750,000 pesos in Tokyo. These pesos could then buy $1,006,173 in New York (40,750,000 pesos/40.5 = $1,006,173) for a profit of $6,173.

Of course, when arbitrage opportunities exist, currency traders move quickly to take advantage of the exchange-rate difference. Because an increase in demand for the cheaper currency will cause its value to rise, markets quickly adjust, eliminating arbitrage opportunities. Because rates often differ by a very small amount, it takes very large transactions to show a profit. Although it is mostly currency speculators that try to take advantage of arbitrage, MNCs also do so when opportunities arise.

CHAPTER REVIEW

To buy, sell, or invest across national borders, MNCs must be able to exchange their home currencies for the currencies of the nations in which they do business. The foreign exchange market is where these currency exchanges take place. The foreign exchange market is the biggest in the world. The dollar value of daily exchanges exceeds $1.8 trillion. Thus, having a basic understanding of how currency exchange works is an important step in conducting international business.

The price of one currency in terms of another represents the exchange rate between the two currencies. Major business publications publish the ending daily exchange rates among major currencies each day. However, the values of currencies change continuously, often up to 20 times a minute.

Early efforts to manage and stabilize exchange rates among currencies led to the development of the gold standard. When countries used the gold standard, they set the value of their currency in terms of an ounce of gold. The US set the price of gold at $20.646, and technically you could buy an ounce of gold from the US Treasury at that price. This system broke down after World War II and many countries then fixed the value of their currencies to the US dollar. Although some countries still fix the value of their money to the US dollar or to several other currencies, most major economies in the world now use a floating-rate system. Market forces set the value of currencies.

People and companies tend to buy and invest in other countries where their own currency has greater buying power, so they need more of the foreign currency to do this. This is the demand side of the currency market. The supply of a currency is also influenced by the exchange rate since if you need less of currency X to buy currency Y then the supply of currency available increases. When the demand and supply curves of a currency cross, that is the equilibrium point and reflects the exchange rate. However, other market forces that determine the value of currencies include a country's inflation rate, interest rates, income levels, and government controls. These factors shift the supply and demand curves and thus change the exchange rates.

Because exchange rates change so much, MNCs face exchange-rate risks. When a company buys or sells something and gives or takes payments in the future, costs or income from these exchanges are often different from those existing at the time of the initial agreement. This is called transaction exposure. Similarly, the values of investments and debts in other countries vary with the exchange rates. This is called translation exposure. To hedge against these variations, MNCs can fix the rates of exchange in the future by buying forward exchange contracts or currency future contracts.

Because the foreign exchange market is a worldwide operation and because markets do not always value currencies at the same rates, there exist opportunities for foreign exchange arbitrage. This means that one buys the currency in one market at a cheaper price and then sells in another market at a higher price. Since currency values change continuously, arbitrage opportunities are often fleeting and companies must move very fast with large amounts of money to succeed before the markets adjust.

All international business people must keep a vigil on the foreign exchange market as it affects all cross-border transactions as well as the value of one's company. Tactics such as hedging allow managers to have some reducibility in their transnational operations. However, in parts of the world where currencies are highly unstable, the exchange-rate risks can make international business a challenging financial management problem.

DISCUSSION QUESTIONS

1. Describe the foreign exchange market. Discuss why it exists and why it is necessary for international trade and commerce.
2. What is an exchange rate and how does it relate to the bid and the ask spread?
3. Compare and contrast the basic types of foreign exchange transactions.
4. Explain how the gold standard worked and why it led to stable exchange rates. What might be some advantages and disadvantages of returning to the gold standard?
5. Describe the relationship between purchasing power parity and the Big Mac Index.
6. What is derived demand and how does this relate to the value of one currency in terms of another?
7. What are the advantages of hedging for an MNC? How do MNCs hedge?

INTERNATIONAL BUSINESS SKILL BUILDER

Formulating a Hedging Strategy

Step 1: Find a local small business that buys or sells internationally.
Step 2: Interview the manager/owner to find out how they manage their exchange-rate risk. If you cannot contact a real business, create a simulated company that engages in foreign transactions. See www.forecasts. org/exchange-rate/index.htm.
Step 3: Create a hypothetical (or real, if you have the information) anticipated purchase or sale a few months into the future.
Step 4: Recommend to the company whether to hedge on exchange rates or to trust forecasts that may show beneficial exchange rates in the future. In formulating your strategy, check the future rates at Chicago Mercantile Exchange, www.cme.com/trading/dta/del/globex.html and compare with forecasted rates from sites such as www.forecasts.org/ exchange-rate/index.htm.

CHAPTER INTERNET ACTIVITY

Open a practice account at **https://fxtrade.oanda.com/** and explore the world of currency trading. Explore this site for all kinds of currency exchange information, including current and historical rates.

KEY CONCEPTS

Big Mac Index

Bretton Woods Agreement

crawling-peg system

currency futures contracts

currency-basket peg

derived demand

dollarization

exchange rate

exchange-rate system

floating-rate system

foreign exchange market

forward exchange contract

forward transaction

hedging

International Monetary Fund (IMF)

pegged exchange rate

Purchasing Power Parity (PPP)

real interest rate

spot transaction

the bid and the ask spread

transaction exposure

translation exposure

CASE 5

page 1

BUSINESS > INTERNATIONAL

TRADING PESOS FOR GREENBACKS

THE DOLLARIZATION OF SAN MIGUEL

With its economy shrinking and inflation being the highest in the western hemisphere, the president of San Miguel has decided that his country should abandon its own currency in favor of the US dollar. The president of this small, South American country reasons that the dollar will bring economic, and perhaps political, stability to San Miguel. He feels that having the American dollar as its official currency will restore investor confidence in San Miguel's economy and force fiscal and monetary responsibility on the part of the government.

Last year, the economy of San Miguel contracted 7 percent and inflation is currently running at over 60 percent. The San Miguel peso has lost 20 percent of its value in the past six months and foreign reserves are rapidly being depleted. It is hoped that by adopting the dollar as the official currency of the country, inflation will be eliminated, foreign investment will increase in the country, and economic growth will occur.

The president is using the example of Argentina as his model; however, he plans to go further than this neighbor did: Argentina now pegs its currency to the dollar on a one-for-one basis. The president's plan calls for San Miguel to slowly replace all its pesos with American dollars and only use its own currency for small transactions. All San Miguel pesos would be exchanged for dollars at a set exchange rate and all financial statements would be issued in dollars. No new national currency would be created.

The idea has the support of the business community and the International Monetary Fund (IMF); however, there is opposition from indigenous groups and others who worry that the plan would have an adverse effect on the poor. Others worry that such a plan would also remove some national sovereignty and put the United States in charge of monetary policy in San Miguel. At present both sides are strengthening their positions. The president and the business community are pushing for a rapid conversion and the opposition is planning demonstrations against the plan. There has been a call for work stoppages and mass protests on the part of the opponents. The president dismisses the concerns of the opposition as foolish and points to Panama, which uses the US dollar as its currency. He states that Panama is a completely independent country with economic stability and that Panama is poised for strong economic development. San Miguel should learn from the Panamanian experience, states the president.

. . .

CASE 5

page 2

CASE DISCUSSION POINTS

1. How would replacing the peso with the dollar affect monetary policy in San Miguel?
2. What are the advantages and disadvantages of a country adopting the US dollar as its currency?
3. Other than replacing its currency, what else could be done to help solve San Miguel's economic problems?
4. What would you recommend?

Note: This is intended to be a fictional case; however, it is based on an actual recent situation.

Case prepared by Charles A. Rarick

6 Global Capital Markets

After reading this chapter you should be able to:

- Understand the nature of capital markets.

- Know the terminology and basic structure of a bond issue.

- Understand stocks and stock markets from a domestic and international perspective.

- Know the basics of how banks make money and the effects of regulations.

- Be familiar with the motivations to seek capital outside of one's home country.

- Understand the implications of regulations for the choice of country of stock market listings.

- Be prepared for the changing nature of international stock markets.

The Preview IB Strategic Insight shows you how companies such as Baidu and Hurray! can get money needed for expansion and growth outside of their own country. It shows one of many options companies use to get needed funds. In this chapter, you will find some basic background on the array of sources that all companies use to get needed funds. However, more importantly, you will learn how these sources of funds are becoming more globalized.

Chinese Companies Seek Capital for Expansion in the US

PREVIEW IB
STRATEGIC INSIGHT

Hurray! is a Chinese wireless-services provider and a leader in China for wireless music distribution and other wireless value-added services including artist development and music production. To expand its wireless music-related businesses, Hurray! needed additional cash. Rather than taking on debt from loans from banks, Hurray!'s management decided to raise $70.5 million by selling Hurray! stocks in the US. According to Steven L. Toronto, a managing partner of the Beijing office of Morrison & Foerster, a San Francisco law firm that advised Hurray! on how to enter the US equity (stock) markets, Hurray! chose to sell its stocks on NASDAQ (National Association of Securities Dealers Automated Quotation system) rather than on the older New York Stock Exchange. The rationale was that NASDAQ has a global reputation for listing technology and less established companies.

The biggest Chinese company on NASDAQ is Baidu.com Inc. Baidu is a Beijing company that sold its first stocks to the public on NASDAQ in 2005. Baidu is the Chinese Google and the leading Chinese-language Internet search engine. Its first public offering of 4,040,402 American depositary shares, or ADSs (the mechanism used to sell shares of foreign companies in US stock exchanges), sold for US$ 27 per ADS on the NASDAQ under the symbol "BIDU." Later the price rose to over $150. According to the Baidu website,

the name "Baidu" was inspired by a poem written more than 800 years ago during the Song Dynasty. The poem compares the search for a retreating beauty amid chaotic glamour with the search for one's dream while confronted by life's many obstacles. [A verse in the poem states] "hundreds and thousands of times, for her I searched in chaos, suddenly, I turned by chance, to where the lights were waning, and there she stood." Baidu, whose literal meaning is hundreds of times, represents persistent search for the ideal.

Recently, HP has started preloading the Baidu search engine on its PCs. One of Baidu's innovations is the "pin-yin" search, which allows users to type in Chinese keywords using English letters.

Other Chinese companies recently seeking capital in the NASDAQ market include online games company Shanda Networking Development Co., whose initial public offering raised $152 million, and 51job Inc., a recruitment website company, which raised $73.5 million largely because US investors see a huge demand for job-search services in China with its rapidly growing labor market. Over 300 Chinese companies are now listed on stock markets outside the mainland, although some Chinese academics think that this allows foreign investors to reap the benefits of the growth of Chinese companies.

Sources: Adapted from *BusinessWeek Online*, 2004, "New rules for China's IPO game," www.businessweek.com, August 8; www.hurray.com.cn/english/home.htm; http://ir.baidu.com; People's Daily Online, 2006, "Overseas listings of big companies causes controversy," March 14; Joseph Weber and Brian Bremner, 2005, "A Chinese banquet for NASDAQ," *BusinessWeek Online*, www.businessweek.com, September 12.

There is an old saying that "it takes money to make money." So, if companies want to buy the raw materials needed for production, expand into new markets, develop new products or services, or build or remodel their factories, it takes money. Of course, very profitable companies might take all of their profits and reinvest them to accomplish such goals. However, this is somewhat like saying to individuals who want to buy a new house or a new car that they should save the money from their earnings until they have sufficient money to buy the car or house. Not many people can do this, so instead, if for example an individual wants to buy a new house and does not have the $120,000 plus in savings that almost any house will cost, he or she will usually go to a bank or credit union and get a loan for 80–90 percent of the value of the house. With a fixed interest rate, they pay back the loan over 15 to 30 years with one constant payment per month. At the end of 15 to 30 years, they own the house but have also paid the bank a lot of money in interest. For example, imagine that your friend Juan takes a $100,000 25-year mortgage at 6 percent interest. Juan will pay $639.81 per month for 25 years. At the end, he will have paid off that $100,000 by making a total of $191,943 in payments.

Like most individuals, companies at some time also need cash beyond what their profits and savings can generate. Companies can go to commercial banks for similar loans to home loans, but they usually do not do this as companies use banks mostly for short-term cash needs. Instead, for large cash needs over longer terms, companies get money from other sources. These other sources for cash are known as **capital markets,** and in the next section you will learn about the options companies use to get needed money.

What are Capital Markets?

In simple terms, a capital market is a market where individuals, governments, and businesses that do not have an immediate use for their money transfer that money to individuals, governments and businesses that do have a need and a use for that money. Check out a video concerning capital markets here: http://video.msn.com/video.aspx?mkt=en-US&vid=ef8e2373-afda-4b8d-95ce-498a619d6dea.

Businesses have short-term needs for money, for example if they need to buy raw material to produce their products or are waiting to be paid by customers but still must pay their employees. Most often, they meet these short-term cash needs by short-term loans from commercial banks.

Commercial banks are banks that specialize in making loans to companies rather than to individuals as customers. However, as the banking industry has been deregulated, many commercial banks offer bank services to consumers as well. The major commercial banks in the US are Citigroup, Bank of America Corp., J.P. Morgan Chase & Company, and Wells Fargo. Since companies most often use bank loans for short-term financing, many have lines of credit, similar to a credit card, so they can cover cash needs quickly.

One problem that became apparent in the 2008 financial crises is that, when banks stopped loaning money to other banks, banks had less money available to loan to companies. In this situation, companies that depend on short-term financing to fund current operations (e.g. payroll, raw materials, etc.) suffer

capital markets
markets where individuals, governments, and businesses that do not have an immediate use for their money transfer that money to individuals, governments, and businesses that do have a need and a use for that money

most. In general, in such situations, banks reduce companies' revolving credit (like the limit on your credit card) and charge high rates to borrow money.

When companies need money for longer-term investments such as opening a new factory, they usually turn to the major capital markets. These markets are the bond market and the stock market. When we think of markets we often think of people buying and trading commodities such as wheat or livestock or gold and silver. However, in financial markets people and organizations can buy and trade financial instruments that represent either debts owned by companies (bonds) or partial ownership of companies (stocks). Now let us consider how each of these financial markets works.

The Bond Market

The **bond market** is where companies can take on debt using a financial instrument called a bond. Companies have used bonds for a long time.

Bonds are a form of debt, somewhat like a loan from a bank but with a slightly different relationship to investors. Although bonds are loans, the terminology is different from what we usually hear regarding loans that an individual might take to buy a car or a new house. The **bond issuer** is the borrower. The **bondholder** is the lender and the **coupon** is the interest rate. Unlike getting a loan from a single bank, issuing bonds allows bondholders to come from a large group of potential investors. Pension funds and banks often purchase corporate bonds, but individuals can do so as well. Thus, when a company has a bond issue it is usually not dependent on one lender but can have many lenders. Issuing bonds allows companies to finance long-term investments using external funds.

Bondholders receive interest payments from the company until the redemption date, which is the end of the loan period. At the redemption date, the company agrees to pay the bondholder the value of the bond. For example, following the illustration in Exhibit 6.1, assume a company issues $20,000 bonds with a ten-year maturity and a 7 percent coupon or interest rate. If you buy or hold one of these bonds, you will receive $1,400 (7 percent of $20,000) each year for ten years. Most bonds are paid in semiannual installments (in this case it would be $700 twice a year) for each bond held by an investor, but some are paid at other periods. At the end of ten years, you would get back the face value of your bond ($20,000). Like stocks, bonds can be traded or sold to other investors.

bond market
a market where companies can take on debt using a financial instrument called a bond

bonds
a form of debt like a loan from a bank but with a slightly different relationship to investors

bond issuer
the company borrowing money

bondholder
the individuals or institutions lending money to a company

coupon
the interest rate for a bond

Exhibit 6.1 **Illustration of a Bond Payment**

A bond from the Dutch East India Company (Vereenigde Oostindische Compagnie), dating from 7 November 1623, for the amount of 2,400 florins; written out and authorized in Middelburg but signed in Amsterdam.

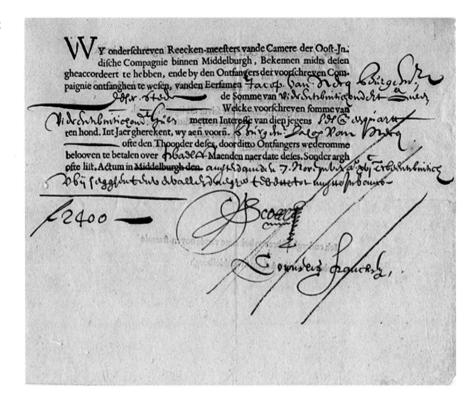

The Stock Market

Like individuals, who can only make payments on a limited number of credit cards, auto loans, and home loans, there is a limited amount of debt that companies can tolerate. For example, mortgage payments on a house can often be as high as 30 percent of a family's take-home earnings. Similarly, for a company, both bank loans and bonds require paying back interest, which can sap a company's cash.

In place of taking on debt and having to pay back the amount of the loan or bond with interest, a company can get needed funds in a stock market by selling shares of ownership to the general public or private investors. A **stock market** is a financial institution where companies can sell shares of ownership and investors also can trade these shares to other investors. That is, for example, a company can sell shares of its ownership to get needed cash. Once purchased, these shares of ownership can be sold to other investors.

Stocks are known as equities because the stock owners have an equity or ownership position in the company. The first stock offering by a company is called the IPO, or initial public offering. Companies can later issue more stocks or buy back stocks from investors. The first known stock issue was by the Dutch East India Company in 1602.

When investors buy shares or equity ownership in a company, as partial owners of the company they are entitled to share in the profits of the company. To share the profits most companies pay **dividends**. That is, a certain percent of the profits of a company is paid out to the owners (stockholders) in the form of dividends. The more shares owned, the greater the ownership of the company, and the greater the share of the profits in dividends. Once stocks are issued they are often traded among investors in a secondary market such as the New York

stock market
a market where companies sell shares of ownership and investors trade shares of ownership to other investors

dividends
the proportion of a company's profits paid to the owners (stockholders)

Stock Exchange. If the stock price rises, investors can sell them to other investors at a profit or, if the price falls, selling would be at a loss. Companies usually like to see the price of their stock going up, because if they issue more stock they can get more money more easily.

Global Financial Markets

Most companies look first to home country banks and capital markets for loans or to issue bonds or stock. However, companies are increasingly attracted to the benefits of capital markets outside of their own countries. Why would companies leave the comfort of doing business at home? As it turns out, there are many benefits to getting needed funds outside of your own country.

The major benefit of seeking needed capital (i.e. money) outside of your own country, be it from banks, bond markets, or stock markets, is that there is often a lower cost of capital for the borrower. What this means is that if you can shop for loans or issue stock in many different countries, you are likely to find more investors, lower interest rates, or perhaps less costly regulations. As such, companies can often borrow needed funds at a lower cost than available to them domestically.

When there are more investors, there is more competition among lenders, and it is likely that you can find a lower interest rate for your loans or bonds. When issuing stocks in many countries not only are there more potential investors, there are also chances of being in markets that are performing better than a home country's stock market. Also, and perhaps more importantly, international capital markets often have minimal regulations, which helps to lower the cost of capital that lenders must charge to make a profit.

Global Banking

How do government regulations influence bank loan rates? The story goes back to the collapse of banks in the 1929 depression. But first let us consider how banks operate as businesses.

Banks make money by first holding money deposited by savers and paying them interest. They then lend some of the money received from the savers to borrowers. To make a profit, banks charge borrowers a higher interest than they pay the savers. Of course, if banks are lending the money you deposit to other people, they never have all of your money available at any time. This works fine as long as not everyone tries to withdraw his or her money at one time. When too many people try to withdraw all their money at once, as happened in 1929, banks cannot meet the depositors' demands and banks fail. To make sure this does not happen, bank regulators want to ensure that at least the banks in their own country have enough money on hand should a large number of people want to withdraw their money at one time.

As such, most countries closely regulate the lending of their own currencies. They do this by limiting the amount of money a bank can lend relative to the amount it receives in deposits. That is, a bank cannot lend 100 percent of the money people deposit. Although banks must keep some money on hand in case people want to withdraw their money, they also must place a certain percentage of the money they do not lend out in national banks such as the Federal Reserve in the US and the Bank of England in Great Britain.

The US government's requirement for deposits to the Federal Reserve can be as high as 10 percent, depending on the value of the deposit.[1] In contrast, most countries do not place the same restrictions on the lending of currencies from other countries, so banks can lend more of the foreign money they receive, making the cost of doing business cheaper for the bank. In turn, that reduced cost is passed onto the borrower in lower interest rates. Later you will see an example of just how this works.

The market for getting loans in a currency that is different from the lending bank's home currency is called the **Eurocurrency market**. When companies borrow money in a country using a currency other than the local currency, they are borrowing a Eurocurrency. Any currency held by banks outside of its country of origin is a Eurocurrency.

The most common currency banked outside of its country of origin is the US dollar, known as **Eurodollars**.[2] For example, US dollars held by a Japanese bank are a Eurocurrency deposit or, more specifically, a Eurodollar deposit. If a US company borrows these dollars from the Japanese bank, it is borrowing Eurodollars. Because the Japanese bank is lending dollars and not yen it does not have to follow Japanese or US regulations regarding loans.

The concept of Eurocurrency can be a bit confusing since the European Union adopted the euro as its currency, but they are not related. Eurocurrency has existed since the early 1950s, long before the euro, which went into effect in 1999. The "Euro" in Eurocurrency comes from its European origin. During the Cold War, the Soviet Union and other Eastern bloc countries withdrew much of the dollar deposits that they had made in US banks. They had used this money to finance trade with the US. However, they did not want to keep their dollars in US banks, fearing loss of the money to the US government for political reasons. During the communist era, many US citizens lost money when communist governments took over US-owned assets (companies, land, etc.) without adequate payments. Leaders from these communist bloc countries feared that any money they left deposited in the US might be confiscated to pay back US citizens for their losses or for other political reasons. To safeguard their money, the strategy was to deposit their dollars outside of the US, with most of these US dollars banked in London. London bankers were willing partners, seeing this as an opportunity to dominate financial markets.[3]

Currently, countries such as China and Japan, which have large reserves of US dollars, provide much of the supply of Eurodollars available to MNCs to finance their operations.

Eurocurrencies generally have the following characteristics:[4]

- *Little or no disclosure requirements* In contrast, the Securities and Exchange Commission in the US requires that firms disclose financial information and financial reports that meet US accounting standards.
- *No reserve requirements* Deposits made in Eurocurrencies do not have to have a certain percentage held back from being loaned to others.
- *Avoiding interest rate regulations* There are no caps or other regulations on interest rates.
- *No deposit insurance requirements* In the US, deposits in commercial banks are insured up to $100,000.

Eurocurrency market
the market for getting loans in a currency that is different from the lending bank's home currency

Eurodollars
US dollars banked outside the US for loans to companies without the restrictions of borrowing within the US

Exhibit 6.2

How a Eurocurrency Deposit Can Pay Higher Interest to Depositors and Result in Cheaper Loans for Borrowers

	Deposit	Reserve	Interest Rate for Depositors	Interest Paid to Depositors	Available to Loan	Interest for Borrowers	Interest Received from Borrowers	Gross Profit
US bank	$100,000.00	$10,000.00	3.0%	$3,000.00	$90,000.00	5.0%	$4,500.00	$1,500.00
Eurocurrency bank	$100,000.00	$0.00	3.25%	$3,250.00	$100,000.00	4.75%	$4,750.00	$1,500.00

Why do these characteristics of Eurocurrencies lead to a separate market from deposits and borrowing in domestic currencies? As you learned before, banks make money by taking deposits, for which they pay interest to the depositors, and then lend the money to others, for which they charge a higher interest rate than they pay to depositors. Imagine that a bank takes deposits for which it pays 3 percent interest to the depositors. It then loans this money to businesses for 5 percent. The 2 percent difference is called the **spread**. In the Eurocurrency market, however, banks offer higher deposit interest and lower loan interest. Because of efficiencies in dealing with Eurocurrencies, in particular the lack of reserve requirements, banks can accept a smaller spread and still make money.

spread
the difference between the interest a bank pays its depositors and the interest it charges borrowers

You can see how this works by looking at Exhibit 6.2. On a $100,000 deposit, when compared to a US bank loaning dollars the bank dealing in Eurocurrency pays its depositors a quarter of a percent higher interest and charges its borrowers a quarter of a percent less interest and still makes the same gross profit because it has more money to lend.

The rates for Eurocurrency deposits and loans are often quoted based on rates offered by London banks, since about 50 percent of the Eurocurrency transactions take place in London. The **London Interbank Bid Rate (LIBID)** is the interest rate the London banks are willing to pay other banks to make deposits in Eurocurrencies and the **London Interbank Offer Rate (LIBOR)** is the interest rates the London banks are willing to charge other banks for loans in Eurocurrencies. The rates that companies receive when they borrow Eurocurrency are higher than the LIBOR charged to other banks. Usually companies must pay an additional 0.15 to 0.25 percentage points above the interbank rate, depending on the credit rating of the company. To check the current LIBOR rates, go to www.bba.org.uk/.

London Interbank Bid Rate (LIBID)
the interest rates the London banks pay other banks to make deposits in Eurocurrencies

London Interbank Offer Rate (LIBOR)
the interest rates the London banks charge other banks for loans in Eurocurrencies

Now that we have considered how MNCs can get loans based on foreign currencies, we can look at how bonds and stocks are traded internationally.

The International Bond Market

As with the domestic bond market, for longer-term debt companies can issue bonds outside of their own country. Recall that the bond issuer is the borrower and the bondholder is the lender. Just as in their own country, issuing bonds outside the home country allows companies to finance long-term investments using external funds rather than cash or profits. There are several types of international bonds issued by MNCs. These include: foreign bonds, Eurobonds, and global bonds.[5]

foreign bonds
bonds issued by a foreign company in a local currency (i.e. the country in which they are doing business)

Eurobonds
bonds issued in a currency other than the local currency

global bonds
similar to Eurobonds but issued in several currencies at once

When a foreign company issues bonds in the local currency (i.e. the country in which they are doing business), these bonds are **foreign bonds**. For example, if a US company issues bonds in Japan in Japanese yen, this is a foreign bond. Foreign bonds often have nicknames to show the country of origin. Samurai or sushi bonds are issued in Japan by foreign companies, and Yankee bonds are issued in the US by foreign companies. **Eurobonds** are like Eurodollars. That means that any bond issued in a currency other than the local currency is a Eurobond. For example, an MNC might issue bonds denominated in yen in Great Britain and these would be Eurobonds. The most common Eurobonds are issued in US dollars, Japanese yen, British pounds, and the euro. **Global bonds** are similar to Eurobonds but are issued in several currencies at once, which can include the currency of the country in which they are issued.

Exhibit 6.3 shows the extent of international bond issues by non-financial corporations over several years in numerous countries. In the last quarter shown, the largest corporate issue was by Ras Laffan Liquefied Natural Gas Company, a Qatari natural gas company, for $1.6 billion.[6]

The IB Strategic Insight opposite describes how many companies sought samurai bonds during the 2008 financial crisis, when credit dried up in Europe and the US. However, when companies fail, investors can lose out.

The incentives to issue Eurobonds and global bonds are similar to the incentives for borrowing Eurodollars. That is, companies can shop for the best deals in interest rates and they can avoid local regulations that increase the costs of

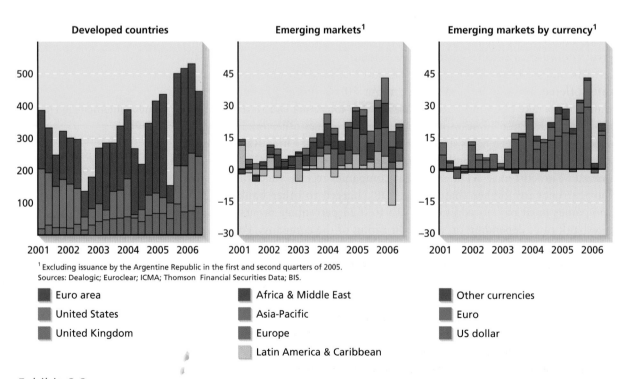

[1] Excluding issuance by the Argentine Republic in the first and second quarters of 2005.
Sources: Dealogic; Euroclear; ICMA; Thomson Financial Securities Data; BIS.

■ Euro area
■ United States
■ United Kingdom

■ Africa & Middle East
■ Asia-Pacific
■ Europe
□ Latin America & Caribbean

■ Other currencies
■ Euro
■ US dollar

Exhibit 6.3 **Net Issuance of International Bonds and Notes (by nationality of issuer, in billions of US dollars)**

Source: Ryan Stever, Goetz von Peter, and Christian Upper, 2006, "Highlights of international banking and financial market activity", *BIS Quarterly Review*, December, p. 23.

In the Financial Crisis, Big Companies Sought Samurai Bonds, but Some Investors Still Lost Out

Japan's financial system has always been a source of quick funding where MNCs can raise billions of dollars in a matter of days. When the financial crises hit the US banks in the summer of 2008, credit dried up in the US and Europe. So Japan became the source of funds for corporate borrowers such as Walmart, UBS, and Daimler. By September of 2008 bond issuances exceeded ¥2.4 trillion, exceeding the ¥2.25 trillion ($20.9 billion) sold for all of 2007. This, combined with low interest rates for borrowers, yet rates higher than Japanese investors could get from than other yen-denominated debt, led to a boom.

Japanese investors felt safe since most of the bond issuers were big-name companies with strong credit ratings, However, when the US brokerage firm Lehman Brothers filed for bankruptcy, essentially defaulting on $2.7 billion in loans, many Japanese lenders learned that they will likely recoup only a fraction of their investments. Not only did big Japanese banks suffer, but regional banks, life insurers, and pension funds also were hit since they held nearly all of Lehman Brothers' $1.8 billion in yen-denominated, or samurai, bonds.

Source: Adapted from *BusinessWeek Online*, 2008, "Lehman collapse hits Japan bond market," www.businessweek.com/print/globalbiz/ content/sep2008/gb20080919_257977.htm, September 19.

them getting needed cash. Most often, MNCs use Euro or global bonds to avoid paying higher taxes. This is often a very complex decision as the tax laws in the country of issue and the home country can be complex and subject to change.

Because of the differences in tax laws and other restrictions on bond issues and loans, multinational managers must always consider carefully the legal and ethical consequences of their actions. Below in the IB Ethical Challenge you can see how companies operating in Islamic nations get needed financing while remaining true to Islamic law, which prohibits the charging of interest.

Global Stock (Equity) Market

Just as with bonds, MNCs in need of capital can issue stock or equity (ownership) in their company, not only in their own countries but also in foreign countries. The major stock markets of the world are listed in Exhibit 6.4. The exchanges are ranked by market capitalization, which means the market value of the stocks traded on the exchange during a year.

Again, like bonds, most companies issue stock or sell equity shares in their companies in the stock exchanges located within their countries. This is convenient and managers often feel most comfortable dealing with markets in their own country and culture.

However, the world is seeing more companies issuing stock outside of their home countries. Why is this becoming more popular? There are several reasons why companies choose to list stock in foreign markets. Companies can list in large efficient markets such as the New York Stock Exchange or the London Stock Exchange and have access to a large pool of investors. More investors often means that the company has a greater potential to get a higher value for its stock. Some companies may try to anticipate which markets are performing

How Can You Issue Bonds when Interest is Forbidden?

ETHICAL CHALLENGE

Under the Shari'ah or Islamic law, charging or paying interest, or *riba*, is forbidden. It is not allowed to make money from just money alone. Thus, issuing or buying bonds, where the seller pays interest and the purchaser makes money only from interest, is not allowed. Credit cards are also not permitted. Yet, to compete in increasingly globalized markets, companies that wish to adhere to Shari'ah need access to money. The financial certificate that provides the Shari'ah-compliant function of a bond is called the Sukuk.

The prohibition on interest raises the question of why one would buy a Sukuk when there is not payment in interest. However, the Sukuk does provide a potential return to the investor. To be acceptable under Islamic law, the Sukuk must be linked to some tangible asset, such as a factory. The investors are then paid back the loan based on the performance of that asset. If it makes money, the investors

get a return; if not, the investors may lose money. This is something like the risk one takes by owning stock in a company—you may make or lose money—but without the ownership position in the company.

Because they function similarly to bonds, Sukuks are controversial. Conservative Islamic scholars argue that the Sukuk is simply a mechanism to evade the restrictions on *riba*, or interest. However, the market for Sukuks is estimated at over $400 billion and growing at 15 percent a year. The takeover of Britain's P&O, a seaport management company, by DP World of Dubai, was financed by $11.4 billion in Sukuks. This is so far the largest Sukuk issue and half the investors were international. "This is another pool of money" to tap, notes Matthew Sapte, an expert on Islamic finance.

Sources: Adapted from *The Economist*, 2006, "Finance and economics: Call the faithful: Islamic finance," December 9, p. 86.

Exhibit 6.4 **The World's Largest Stock Exchanges by Market Capitalization**

Exchange	Market Capitalization ($ billion)	% growth from previous year
NYSE/Euronext	19,129	19.42%
Tokyo Stock Exchange	4,614	0.90%
Nasdaq	3,865	7.20%
London Stock Exchange	3,794	24.10%
Hong Kong Exchange	1,715	62.60%

Source: Adapted from World Federation of Stock Exchanges, www.world-exchanges.org/.

best (highest stock prices) and list in those markets. Another reason to list in a different market is to avoid regulations that may be costly. You will learn more about how regulations can increase costs after we consider alternative ways of listing on an exchange.

An Alternative Way to List on a Foreign Exchange There is an alternative way for companies to list on foreign exchanges and sell equity in their companies without actually selling stock directly. This way of raising capital indirectly from the stock market is called a depository receipt. A depository receipt is a certificate issued by a bank called the depository bank. The depository bank actually holds the stocks and then allows certificates (i.e. the depository receipts) to be sold or traded in a stock market. The most popular depository receipt is the **American Depository Receipt (ADR)**, which allows foreign companies to sell their stocks indirectly and raise capital in the US. The ADR is the way most foreign companies trade their stock in the US

For example, say a Polish company wishes to raise capital in the US without directly listing on the New York Stock Exchange. To use ADRs, the Polish company would sell its shares to a broker—brokers are agents who help people conduct transactions, such as a real-estate broker who helps sell a house. The broker would then deposit the shares in a branch bank of a US bank located in Poland, usually the Bank of New York. Once the Bank of New York certifies that it now owns shares of the Polish company, it begins trading the shares in the US as ADRs. Investors who purchase ADRs have the right to the original stocks if they wish. ADRs make it easier for US Americans to invest in foreign companies because they do not have to buy stock directly in another currency. ADRs make it easier for the foreign company to get investors from the US

American Depository Receipt (ADR)
allows foreign companies to sell their stocks indirectly and raise capital in the US

Managing in Stock Issues in the Regulated US Market: The Sarbanes–Oxley Act

IB STRATEGIC INSIGHT

In response to several scandals involving companies such Enron, Tyco International, and WorldCom, the US Congress determined that publicly traded companies and their accounting firms needed stricter oversight. Sponsored by Senator Paul Sarbanes and Representative Michael G. Oxley, the legislation became known as the Sarbanes–Oxley Act. The objective of the Act was to make sure that stockholders are protected from those unethical practices that had resulted in many people losing money by investing in the suspect corporations. The legislation established new or enhanced standards for all US public companies and, importantly, also applies to those foreign companies selling stocks in the US. The Act's 11 sections (see Exhibit 6.5) identify important responsibilities and reporting procedures for corporate boards, executives, and accounting firms. The Act also specifies penalties for failing to follow these procedures.

Some of the major provisions of the Sarbanes–Oxley Act include:

- It specifies an obligation that public companies evaluate the effectiveness of their financial reporting.

Independent auditors must confirm the effectiveness of these procedures.

- It requires chief executive officers and chief financial officers to certify financial reports.
- It regulates the type of work accounting firms can do for their company clients if the firm also acts as the auditor. Some accounting firms were acting as both auditors and consultants, resulting in potential conflicts of interest. This helps ensure independence.
- It creates a new government agency called the Public Company Accounting Oversight Board (PCAOB) to monitor the accounting firms.
- It requires fully independent audit committees for companies that wish to list stock exchanges.
- It increases the criminal and civil penalties for violations related to managing stock transactions.
- It increases the maximum jail sentences and the fines for corporate executives found guilty of knowingly and willfully falsifying the financial statements of their company.

Source: Adapted from US Congress House Resolution 3763.

for case study

American Depository Shares (ADS)
individual shares of a foreign company represented by an ADR

Global Depository Receipt (GDR)
like ADRs, but traded in several countries at once

Sarbanes–Oxley Act
law passed by the US Congress that requires increased disclosure of financial practices designed to protect stockholders from the unethical practices in financial reporting

because the company does not have to register with and meet the regulations of the US Securities and Exchange Commission regarding accounting practices. Individual shares of a foreign company represented by an ADR are called **American Depository Shares (ADS)**.[7] Sometimes an ADR can represent more than one share. You can see ADR listings at www.adrbny.com/.

Other depository receipts include **Global Depository Receipt (GDR)**. GDRs are like ADRs, except that they are traded in several countries at once. For example, the Polish company described above might use GDRs in Europe and the US at the same time.[8] When DRs are priced in Euros, they are often called European Depository Receipts. Recently, companies in China are using Chinese Depository Receipts (CDRs) to raise capital for Chinese companies by making it easier for foreigners to buy stock indirectly using the CDR rather than directly buying the Chinese stock.

Although ADRs traditionally dominated the depository receipt market, GDRs are gradually taking over the market. By 2005, more than half of the capital raised worldwide came from GDRs.[9] Why is this happening? Much of the shift away from the US stock market, both for direct listings and ADRs, stems from controls put into place after Enron and other companies' failures led to great loses among investors. Listing in the US requires following provisions in the **Sarbanes–Oxley Act**. The IB Strategic Insight on the previous page describes some of the provisions and consequences of this legislation.

Listing your company in a foreign exchange is not just for the big MNCs. The IB Small Business Insight below discusses how and why one US small business chooses to list stock outside of the US.

Even Small Businesses Cross Borders to Issue Stock

IB SMALL BUSINESS INSIGHT

One stock market that is attractive to smaller US companies is called AIM or Alternative Investment Market. It is run by the London Stock Exchange and aimed primarily to provide a stock market for smaller businesses.

One recent listing on AIM is XL TechGroup. XL is a Florida company that manages a group of companies in the biotech, ecotech, and medtech areas. The business model is to build new companies in these areas.

Had XL listed in the US they would have been considered an investment company even though they do not buy companies but build them from scratch. Investment companies have to report extensive information to the US government's Securities and Exchange Commission. Chief financial officer Davis Szostak called this "onerous, but well outside the character of our business model." In addition, unlike in the US, AIM did not mandate a minimum value for the company in terms of stock ownership or a minimum number of shares owned by the public rather than those inside the company.

CFO Szostak noted that the more flexible regulations of AIM were only part of the reason to list in London. Two XL companies, Tyratech and AgCert, have products in environmental areas that are in demand in Europe. Tyratech produces insecticides with minimal environmental impact and AgCert provides farmers with techniques to reduce greenhouse gas emissions. In a region with over 300 restricted pesticides and strict environmental protection laws, both of these companies have a big customer base in Europe. As such, European investors were quick to see value in the companies. Since their IPO in 2004, XL raises about $25 million a year in the AIM.

Source: Adapted from Helen Shaw, 2005, "Small-caps eye listings abroad," www.cfo.com, August 9.

Exhibit 6.5 **Table of Contents of the Sarbanes–Oxley Act**

H.R. 3763

To protect investors by improving the accuracy and reliability of corporate disclosures made pursuant to the securities laws, and for other purposes.

Be it enacted by the Senate and House of Representatives of the United States of America in Congress assembled,

SECTION 1. SHORT TITLE; TABLE OF CONTENTS

(a) SHORT TITLE.—This Act may be cited as the "Sarbanes–Oxley Act of 2002."

(b) TABLE OF CONTENTS.—The table of contents for this Act is as follows:

Sec. 1. Short title; table of contents.
Sec. 2. Definitions.
Sec. 3. Commission rules and enforcement.

TITLE I—PUBLIC COMPANY ACCOUNTING OVERSIGHT BOARD

Sec. 101. Establishment; administrative provisions.
Sec. 102. Registration with the Board.
Sec. 103. Auditing, quality control, and independence standards and rules.
Sec. 104. Inspections of registered public accounting firms.
Sec. 105. Investigations and disciplinary proceedings.
Sec. 106. Foreign public accounting firms.
Sec. 107. Commission oversight of the Board.
Sec. 108. Accounting standards.
Sec. 109. Funding.

TITLE II—AUDITOR INDEPENDENCE

Sec. 201. Services outside the scope of practice of auditors.
Sec. 202. Preapproval requirements.
Sec. 203. Audit partner rotation.
Sec. 204. Auditor reports to audit committees.
Sec. 205. Conforming amendments.
Sec. 206. Conflicts of interest.
Sec. 207. Study of mandatory rotation of registered public accounting firms.
Sec. 208. Commission authority.
Sec. 209. Considerations by appropriate State regulatory authorities.

TITLE III—CORPORATE RESPONSIBILITY

Sec. 301. Public company audit committees.
Sec. 302. Corporate responsibility for financial reports.
Sec. 303. Improper influence on conduct of audits.
Sec. 304. Forfeiture of certain bonuses and profits.
Sec. 305. Officer and director bars and penalties.
Sec. 306. Insider trades during pension fund blackout periods.
Sec. 307. Rules of professional responsibility for attorneys.
Sec. 308. Fair funds for investors.

TITLE IV—ENHANCED FINANCIAL DISCLOSURES

Sec. 401. Disclosures in periodic reports.
Sec. 402. Enhanced conflict of interest provisions.
Sec. 403. Disclosures of transactions involving management and principal stockholders.
Sec. 404. Management assessment of internal controls.
Sec. 405. Exemption.
Sec. 406. Code of ethics for senior financial officers.
Sec. 407. Disclosure of audit committee financial expert.
Sec. 408. Enhanced review of periodic disclosures by issuers.
Sec. 409. Real time issuer disclosures.

Exhibit 6.5 **Continued**

H.R. 3763

TITLE V—ANALYST CONFLICTS OF INTEREST

Sec. 501. Treatment of securities analysts by registered securities associations and national securities exchanges.

TITLE VIII—CORPORATE AND CRIMINAL FRAUD ACCOUNTABILITY

Sec. 801. Short title.

Sec. 802. Criminal penalties for altering documents.

Sec. 803. Debts nondischargeable if incurred in violation of securities fraud laws.

Sec. 804. Statute of limitations for securities fraud.

Sec. 805. Review of Federal Sentencing Guidelines for obstruction of justice and extensive criminal fraud.

Sec. 806. Protection for employees of publicly traded companies who provide evidence of fraud.

Sec. 807. Criminal penalties for defrauding shareholders of publicly traded companies.

TITLE IX—WHITE-COLLAR CRIME PENALTY ENHANCEMENTS

Sec. 901. Short title.

Sec. 902. Attempts and conspiracies to commit criminal fraud offenses.

Sec. 903. Criminal penalties for mail and wire fraud.

Sec. 904. Criminal penalties for violations of the Employee Retirement Income Security Act of 1974.

Sec. 905. Amendment to sentencing guidelines relating to certain white-collar offenses.

Sec. 906. Corporate responsibility for financial reports.

TITLE X—CORPORATE TAX RETURNS

Sec. 1001. Sense of the Senate regarding the signing of corporate tax returns by chief executive officers.

TITLE XI—CORPORATE FRAUD AND ACCOUNTABILITY

Sec. 1101. Short title.

Sec. 1102. Tampering with a record or otherwise impeding an official proceeding.

Sec. 1103. Temporary freeze authority for the Securities and Exchange Commission.

Sec. 1104. Amendment to the Federal Sentencing Guidelines.

Sec. 1105. Authority of the Commission to prohibit persons from serving as officers or directors.

Sec. 1106. Increased criminal penalties under Securities Exchange Act of 1934.

Sec. 1107. Retaliation against informants.

It is estimated that the Sarbanes–Oxley Act costs US companies $6 billion a year to comply with the law, according to a study by AMR Research in Boston. The result is that the average company spends approximately $4 million to comply. Smaller companies—those with a stock value of less than $75 million—were initially exempt from the law, but eventually all companies listed on US stock exchanges will be expected to comply. The direst and most negative predictions come from the consulting firm McKinsey. McKinsey anticipates that the law will eventually cost New York its spot as the world's financial capital. Consider that, at its peak, NASDAQ had 57 percent of the world's IPOs in 1999. By 2005, just a couple of years after the passage of Sarbanes–Oxley, NASDAQ had only 18 percent.[10]

Not all predictions are so pessimistic. Professor Sharad Asthana, an expert on the law's impact, notes, "Despite the increased costs, it's [the law] improved public perceptions about the markets. Investors see requiring the signing off by the CEO and CFO as being positive and that they can feel more secure in the quality of earnings."[11] In addition, the tightening up of rules in the US has caused other countries to follow suit. Australia, Brazil, Canada, the EU, Germany, and the UK are introducing laws that make the audit committees on boards of directors more accountable for monitoring the financial practices of companies listed on their exchanges. Listing outside the US may not always offer companies havens from oversight and regulations.

Of course, as with many international business activities, local country regulations may become less important. In the next section, you will see how stock markets are consolidating into multinational operations, making local regulations less important.

A Changing Future for the World's Stock Markets

Like many companies in today's global economy, stock markets are also becoming more globally connected and concentrated. The US financial crisis in 2008 resulted in almost immediate drops in the prices of US stocks, and this was followed within hours by stock markets around the world. In addition, beyond financial linkages, organizational links are expanding as well. For example, in 2007, the New York Stock Exchange acquired the Paris-based exchange

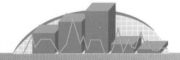

Led by the EU, a New Trading Market Emerges

IB SUSTAINABILITY PRACTICES

In the EU, the control of carbon emissions has serious financial consequences for both local and multinational companies. Companies will have strict limits to outputs. However, the EU system is not just a company-by-company restriction but allows companies to buy and trade carbon credits. Under the EU Greenhouse Gas Emission Trading Scheme (EU ETS), companies receive a set number of carbon allowances. They can sell or buy these credits on the open market. The theory is that the market creates a financial incentive to monitor carbon emissions. If a worldwide cap-and-trade CO_2 agreement becomes reality, the experience of European and other MNCs working in the EU could be a competitive advantage.

Carbon trading is already a reality. According to World Bank estimates, the global market for carbon trading was valued at about $64 billion in 2007. Point Carbon, an industry consultant, predicts that the market will reach $3 trillion by 2020 if large polluters such as China and the US introduce cap-and-trade schemes similar to the EU ETS.

Sensing an opportunity, the stock market company NASDAQ is building a trading platform for this new market. The transatlantic exchange operator acquired Nord Pool, a former Norwegian power exchange, to provide the business model. Nord Pool has experience in carbon dioxide contracts under the European Union trading scheme. It also deals with global carbon contracts through the United Nations' Green Development Mechanism. NASDAQ chief executive Robert Greifeld says that his company will develop products for businesses looking to trade allowances for greenhouse gas emissions. He expects NASDAQ to be the leader in developing standards for this trading. "We believe a standardization of contracts is necessary for the carbon market," he said, pointing to issues such as unit size that remained to be resolved. "Things need to be perfected, and then the carbon market can develop in ways we don't envisage today."

Perhaps in the future markets such as this will become equally important to other capital markets.

Sources: Adapted from *BusinessWeek Online*, 2008, "Is Europe leading or losing on CO_2 emissions?" www.businessweek.com/print/globalbiz/content/aug2008/gb2008084_780404.htm, August 7; Doug Cameron, 2008, "NASDAQ to get in on emissions contracts: New energy-trading platform aims to capitalize on a hot market," *Wall Street Journal*, www.wsj.com, October 22; Andrew Donoghue, 2008, "NASDAQ bets on emissions trading market—Markets might be up and down, but greenhouse gases still look a good bet," www.businessgree.com, October 22.

Euronext NV. In the same year, the New York Stock Exchange also acquired a 20 percent stake in India's largest exchange, the National Stock Exchange. As a first step to a possible merger, the Tokyo and New York Stock Exchanges announced an alliance in the same year to offer common financial products and mutual listings.

Cross-border consolidation among stock markets will make stock markets MNCs in their own right. With a presence in many countries, the former national stock exchanges will attract investors from more nations. Local economic conditions will have less impact in attracting investors because multinational exchanges, like MNCs, can locate in the most favorable conditions.

What this means for companies is that they will have increased access to the global capital markets without ever leaving their home countries. Also, managers will not have to learn the operation of foreign exchanges as they can do one-stop global financing at one exchange. A listing on a multinational exchange will attract investors from everywhere in the world as well. Like companies that seek the advantage of raising capital without concern for local economic conditions, investors will be able to shop for stocks in the best companies in the world without concern for a company's nationality.

In the future, MNCs may need more than financial capital to operate. Limits on the consumption of or potential damage to environmental resources may result in new markets where companies can purchase or trade credits for environmental impacts that result from their operations. Such trading is already taking place in a market for carbon trading. CO_2, or carbon dioxide, is generally considered a major contributor to global warming, and one strategy is to limit companies' output but also to allow them to trade carbon credits, buying if they need more or selling if they have extra. The box on IB Sustainability Practices on the previous page gives you some insights into this issue. You can also look at videos on carbon trading here: http://video.msn.com/video.aspx?mkt=en-US&vid= 4dbb8148-4ec7-465d-be27-048cabd85487.

CHAPTER REVIEW

This chapter has provided you with an overview of how capital markets work in today's global economy. In simple terms, a capital market is a market where investors that do not have an immediate use for their money transfer that money to individuals, governments and businesses that have a need and a use for that money. The two major capital markets for long-term financing are the bond market and the stock market. For the shorter term, financial companies often use loans from commercial banks.

In the bond market, companies issue bonds to borrow money from bondholders. This is a loan and is known as debt financing. In the stock market, companies sell shares of ownership to investors and these investors have equity in the company.

In today's global economy, companies are no longer constrained to borrow money or sell stocks in their company within their country of origin. Often, companies can get cheaper loans in the Eurocurrency market: that is, the market for getting loans in a currency that is different from the lending bank's home currency. Similarly, companies can issue bonds in countries where they do business (foreign bonds) or in other currencies (Eurobonds, global bonds).

In this chapter, you also learned that the world of global finance is changing. Concerns over the unethical practices of some US corporations, which led to great losses by investors, led the US government to pass the Sarbanes–Oxley Act. The law forces companies to reveal more of their financial operations and holds managers responsible for these disclosures. While this has caused some flight of stock listings from the US to other countries, similar regulations are spreading around the world. Stock markets are also consolidating across borders, making them MNCs in their own right. This will also result in a convergence of global standards of stock market operations and further the increase of money flowing across borders. Companies will find it easier to seek capital worldwide and investors will find it easier to buy stock from any company regardless of nationality.

The chapter concluded with an observation that issues such as CO_2 trading may become an important market where, in order to survive and prosper, future MNCs may need to seek not only financial capital but environmental capital.

DISCUSSION QUESTIONS

1. What is a capital market?
2. Why do companies use capital markets to finance growth, new products, R&D, etc.? Would it be better just to keep profits and reinvest them in the company?
3. Discuss the basics of how the bond market works. How does this differ in structure and terminology from the types of loans people get to buy their homes?
4. Discuss the basics of how a stock market works. What are the advantages and disadvantages of listing on a foreign exchange?
5. Discuss the advantages and disadvantages of dealing with Eurocurrencies.
6. Discuss the competing perspectives regarding increased regulations, especially regarding financial reporting, for companies. What are the effects of country differences, and what do you anticipate will result as stock markets converge across borders?

INTERNATIONAL BUSINESS SKILL BUILDER

Understanding how Stock Markets Work

For this exercise, you will play the game called "The Stock Market Bakery." You will assume the roles of companies by producing "chocolate-chip cookies." The companies will sell stock to raise money for new equipment and research. The companies then make the "cookies" and use some of their earnings to pay dividends to stockholders. Students also take the roles of savers who invest in the stock market.

CHAPTER INTERNET ACTIVITY

In this project, you will explore how several companies use the Eurobond market to raise capital.

1. Google search "raising capital with Eurobonds."
2. Search within these results for companies from three different countries (e.g. Russia, Japan, and China).
3. Prepare a paragraph for each company describing how it used the Eurobond market.

KEY CONCEPTS

American Depository Receipt (ADR)

American Depository Shares (ADS)

bondholder

bond issuer

bond market

bonds

capital markets

coupon

dividends

Eurobonds

Eurocurrency market

Eurodollars

foreign bonds

global bonds

Global Depository Receipt (GDR)

London Interbank Bid Rate (LIBID)

London Interbank Offer Rate (LIBOR)

Sarbanes–Oxley Act

spread

stock market

BUSINESS > INTERNATIONAL

WALL STREET OR GREAT WALL?

THE CHALLENGE TO MAINTAIN DOMINANCE IN THE GLOBAL FINANCIAL MARKETS

CASE 6

page 1

On September 29, 2008, the American equities markets lost an estimated $1.2 trillion in market capitalization. This astonishing figure represents the single biggest one-day loss in the history of the country. The major market index, the Dow Jones Industrial Average, lost 777 points, representing its largest single-day decline. The incredible drop in the equities market was believed to be caused by the failure of the United States' Congress to enact legislation which would support the ailing financial sector. While the market made an impressive rebound on September 30, the lingering problems of the financial sector have caused some to wonder if the United States will be able to maintain its dominance in the global financial markets.

. . .

CASE 6

---

page 2

The New York Stock Exchange (NYSE), or Big Board, is the largest stock exchange in the world in terms of market capitalization. The United States has maintained its dominant position through its strong economy and its financial and political stability. The financial centers of London and Frankfurt (also major players) have also been shaken by the troubles in the United States. The traditionally strong economies of the West are facing new challenges. Increased oil prices have poured enormous amounts of capital into oil-rich economies, such as those of the Gulf States, and some of these countries are using this money to develop their financial industries. Dubai, for example, hopes to become the center of Islamic finance and challenge Wall Street in that increasingly important niche market. With increased oil revenue, Russia could also become a more significant player in the market, especially for the emerging economies of Eastern Europe. Even sub-Saharan Africa, not often thought of when discussing rising capital markets, has over 500 companies listed with a market capitalization in excess of $100 billion on its dynamic stock exchanges.

While Dubai and Moscow, and perhaps Africa, may be of some concern, the greatest threat to dominance of the financial sector comes from Asia. In recent years the world has seen the development and growth of financial markets in emerging economies such as China, India, and other Asian countries. The Bombay Stock Exchange is the oldest in Asia and has grown as the Indian economy has advanced. The greatest concern, however, is China. China has two mainland stock exchanges—the Shanghai Stock Exchange and the Shenzhen Stock Exchange. With the return of Hong Kong, China also has a larger exchange in the Special Administrative Region (Hong Kong), the Hong Kong Exchange. Although the Chinese exchanges have experienced a significant correction recently (after a period of rapid increase), given China's continuing economic growth some feel that Shanghai will replace Wall Street as the world's main financial center.

Q3 [According to Fan Dizhao, an investment manager at Guotai Asset Management, it is only a matter of time before China dominates the global capital markets. According to Fan, "It is inevitable that we will take the US's place as the world leader." China is aggressively recruiting financial specialists from the United States to help the country build its financial institutions. China has the money to attract such talent, and to offer opportunities that many feel have been lost in the United States. With the failure of banks, brokerage firms, and insurance companies, surplus talent in the US may find the lure of large salaries, education stipends, and personal tax exemptions tempting enough to relocate to China to help build its financial services industry.]

With the world's fastest growing economy, China is in a good position to challenge the United States and Europe for the dominant position in the global equities markets. Growing companies need capital, and the rising incomes of the Chinese now make it possible for individuals to invest. The troubled economy of Q1 the United States, coupled with the increased cost to companies to be listed on an American stock exchange due to the Sarbanes–Oxley Act, may make US equity markets less desirable. After passage of the Act, foreign listings on American exchanges began to decline. Increased costs, greater financial uncertainty, and

. . .

CASE 6

page 3

decreased liquidity put Wall Street at a competitive disadvantage in the global market. At the same time, China has some significant disadvantages of its own, including government-mandated capital controls, concerns about the integrity of the Chinese legal system, and a less developed financial structure. The tendency of the authoritative Chinese government to quickly change investment rules also causes concern among investors and companies, such as the recent decision by China's Securities Regulatory Commission to require a greater dividend payout for listed companies. Recently, however, China has begun to relax some of its restrictions on foreign ownership of Chinese class A shares, which previously could only be owned by Chinese citizens. With China rising and Wall Street stumbling, the competition is on for dominance in the global capital markets.

CASE DISCUSSION POINTS

1. From your understanding of the Sarbanes–Oxley Act, explain how you feel it may negatively affect America's stock exchanges.
2. What advantages would China offer foreign companies to list on its exchanges? Are these advantages greater than the disadvantages? Explain.
3. Do you feel that China will eventually control the world's financial industry? Explain your answer.

Sources: *China Briefing*, 2008, "Foreigners now allowed to list on Shanghai Stock Exchange," June 2; L. Peck, 2008, "Controls may hurt China's stock market," *New York Sun*, August 26; *The Economist*, 2008, "The new champions," September 18; J. Bush, 2008, "Russian stocks in free fall," *Business Week*, September 29; A. Cha, 2008, "Financial hubs see opening up at the top," *Washington Post*, October 1.

The Institutional and Cultural Context

The Institutional and Cultural Context of Multinational Competitive Strategy

part three

of Multinational Competitive Strategy

7 Culture and International Business

After reading this chapter you should be able to:

- Understand the importance of culture and the need to appreciate cultural differences.

- Know two of the most popular cultural frameworks (Hofstede and GLOBE) and how they explain differences between countries.

- Appreciate these cultural differences and implications for international business and specifically the business culture.

- Be aware of cultural paradoxes and some of the dangers of making broad generalizations based on culture.

- Learn about how multinational managers can prepare for cultural differences.

The Preview IB Strategic Insight describes three situations where cultural mishaps occurred. Such mistakes can be costly to MNCs as potentially important contracts are lost. However, the most important point about these situations is that you can easily avoid them. This chapter provides you with a basic understanding of national cultures and how to prepare for cultural differences in international business activities. By properly preparing for cultural differences, an international manager can be more successful by behaving in ways consistent with local expectations.

This chapter contains four major sections. In the first section, you are introduced to some of the major reasons why cultural differences need to be understood. In the second section, you are exposed to two of the most important frameworks that have been developed to understand culture. In the third section, you look at some of the ways national cultures affect business through a special emphasis on business cultures. Finally, you will examine some ways MNCs and their employees can prepare for cultural differences.

After reading this chapter you should understand how cultural differences impact behaviors and attitudes of people in a country. You will look at how national culture relates to and influences the business environment and business culture for any MNC. You will also be made aware of some of the dangers of making broad generalizations based on the cultural differences we discuss. Finally, you should be able to recognize what can be done to prepare for such challenges.

International Cultural Blunders

You are sent to Malaysia to close an important contract. In a flashy ceremony, you are introduced to an important potential customer you thought was named Roger. You spend the negotiations calling that person Roger and even Rog. You find that your hosts are insulted and you realize later that the potential client was actually a rajah, a noble title. You also find out that many states in Malaysia are actually headed by rajahs.

You arrive in Beijing hoping to have an important real-estate transaction signed. You meet with your potential customers and spend the evening socializing. After a few days, you start losing interest as you find that the negotiations are not progressing as smoothly as you wished. At the end of the third day, you produce a detailed contract hoping to get the contract signed. Your hosts decide to abruptly end the negotiations and you are unable to get them back to the negotiation table.

You work for an important firm on Wall Street and arrive in Paris to discuss an important deal. You meet your French counterparts for a three-course meal. You start the meal and you feel that every time you start discussing business, your French hosts change the conversation. Your hosts seem to be more interested in talking about art, politics, and even your background. Unfortunately, both you and your hosts eventually get frustrated and the deal is never concluded.

Sources: Adapted from *Financial Times*, 2007, "Excuse my French, but pleasure before business," February 13; *Nation's Business*, 1989, "Blunders abroad," March; *Real Estate Issues*, 2006, "The impact of cultural mistakes on international real estate negotiations," Fall.

National Culture

national culture
pervasive and shared values, beliefs and norms that guide life in a society

National culture is the pervasive and shared values, beliefs and norms that guide life in any society.[1] It tells people who they are, what behaviors are appropriate and what behaviors are not acceptable in any society. It adds predictability and ensures behaviors of people are not random. For instance, you regularly hear about the American dream or about rags-to-riches stories. They reflect the cultural belief that anyone has the potential to become very successful if he or she works very hard in the United States. This represents a cultural aspect of US society.

National Culture Components

cultural beliefs
people's perception of what is true

cultural norms
shared understanding of what people can and cannot do

cultural symbols, stories and rituals
manifestations of culture through monuments, stories, or other practices

customs
behaviors or habits that are passed from generation to generation

A country's national culture is reflected in many different ways. For instance, as just discussed, culture can be manifested in **cultural beliefs,** which represent people's perception of what is true. Culture can also be shown in terms of cultural norms. For example, while it is acceptable to jump line in countries such as India or China, people are expected to respect lines in other countries such as Germany. This is an example of a **cultural norm,** a shared understanding of what people can do and what they cannot do. Culture can also manifest itself in **cultural symbols, stories and rituals,** which represent physical manifestations of culture. Symbols may take the form of monuments or buildings, such as the Great Wall of China as a reflection of China's past. Stories are passed on from generation to generation to reinforce the culture. Finally, rituals are activities such as baptisms that are used to reinforce cultural messages. Culture can also manifest itself through customs. **Customs** are behaviors or habits that are passed on from different generations and are appropriate in different situations. For example, in many Islamic countries, women are expected to wear the *burka* or veil as a reflection of the custom. Furthermore, some Islamic states also have customs preventing women from being in the same room with men.

Culture can therefore manifest itself in various ways. But why should you be concerned with culture? As you saw in Chapter 1, no one is immune to the forces of globalization. A good understanding of culture is necessary for anyone to navigate the workplace. Most countries are seeing an influx of workers from other countries, and understanding culture can be helpful in understanding diversity in the workplace. A basic understanding of culture can be helpful in navigating the very diverse local workplace environment.

Even with the US, consider that the projected population growth in the US is predicted to come from such groups as Hispanics, African-Americans and Asians. If an MNC wants to be able to sell successfully to these different groups, multinational marketers need to understand the cultural subtleties of each group and design appropriate marketing campaigns. Consider, for instance, the finding that the majority of Hispanic consumers prefer advertisements either in Spanish or including both English and Spanish.[2] Such findings are not possible without appropriate cultural understanding. Most companies will find that they are better able to target different ethnic groups if they have a good understanding of culture.

Many MNCs now realize that the key to success is the ability to hire the best individuals regardless of background. Consider that many of the best ideas for new product innovations are now coming from employees located around various parts of the world.[3] However, having employees of diverse backgrounds collaborate can sometimes result in conflict and cultural misunderstanding. Understanding culture can help the MNC build a work environment where cultural differences are respected and diversity is used as the means to contribute to profitability.

Many human resource management experts also agree that having cultural and international experience will be an important asset in the future. Because of global expansion, many companies are looking for employees with international experience to deal with diverse cultural backgrounds. Consider that, for instance, IBM has a global workforce of over 375,000 on six continents and has hired over 90,000 workers from low-cost countries such as India, China, and Brazil just over the last three years.[4] To succeed, IBM needs managers who have an appropriate understanding of the various cultures it operates in. Understanding the local culture can therefore be a source of competitive advantage for promotion opportunities in the future.

Experts also argue that the competitive landscape is changing dramatically and that the future will see global companies with headquarters located in emerging markets.[5] Consider India's Tata Motors, Brazil's Embraer or Mexico's Cemex, all major global multinationals that are competing with the traditional multinationals from Western countries. To be able to compete successfully with these new challengers, a strong cultural understanding of the various consumers around the world is needed.

Furthermore, you will find that most companies you choose to work for will have some form of international operations. Even if your company is not involved in international markets, it will still have to compete with MNCs

McDonald's and Doing the Right Thing in India

IB STRATEGIC INSIGHT

In 1996, McDonald's opened its first restaurant in India. Today, it has over 56 restaurants and employs around 2,000 Indians. How did McDonald's manage such a feat? It carefully examined cultural differences and found ways to address these cultural challenges. For instance, recognizing the more vegetarian nature of Indian society, McDonald's developed many vegetarian menu items while also integrating local foods. It also recognized the very diverse nature of Indian society and has the appropriate regional foods offered in different regions. McDonald's understood the family- and child-centric nature of Indian society. It strives to target children with many programs such as birthdays, children's parades, free polio vaccination and even low-height children-friendly counters in some locations. McDonald's also understood India's colonized

past and the need to counter potential conflict. McDonald's has made a large effort to hire only local managers while also playing an important role in the community: for instance, it donates to local environmental causes. McDonald's has worked hard to develop relationships with local suppliers, going so far as helping local suppliers improve their processes. Finally, McDonald's is very aware of pricing issues in India and provides products that target a wide range of incomes.

While McDonald's will surely encounter challenges in the future, its actions show deliberate attempts to understand and adapt to local cultural conditions. Such actions probably explain why McDonald's is doing so well in India.

Sources: Adapted from "McDonald's in India," www.mcdonaldsindia.com/aboutus/index.html, 2008.

operating within your local country. As such, it is important to understand a country's culture as it will give you a better appreciation of what people value in other countries. This appreciation can be very useful as it allows you to avoid some of the cultural blunders we discussed earlier. Furthermore, an appropriate understanding of culture can help you avoid conflict with workers from other countries and also put you in a better position to understand the local market. Consider the IB Strategic Insight on the previous page and how McDonald's became successful in India.

The IB Strategic Insight above shows how McDonald's took great pains to understand the local Indian culture and to adapt its operations to fit cultural dispositions. Such actions are surely more likely to increase the likelihood of success. How can you understand which aspects of culture to pay attention to, though? In the next section, we look at some of the most important ways societies differ in terms of culture. National culture affects many aspects of international business. However, one of the most important influences of culture is on human behavior. You will notice that many of the examples discussed pertain to discussion of the influence of culture on individual behaviors.

National Culture: Hofstede and the Global Organizational Behavior and Leadership Studies

To understand how countries differ on culture, we will consider two of the most popular cultural frameworks. There are many cultural models that have been proposed over time (e.g. Trompenaars's cultural framework or Ronen and Shenkar's framework). However, we focus on the Hofstede framework and the GLOBE framework. We consider the Hofstede model as it is by far the most popular cross-cultural model and has generated important understanding of cross-cultural management.[6] However, Hofstede's cultural framework was conducted in the 1970s and is sometimes seen as outdated. We therefore also consider the GLOBE studies as one of the most up-to-date cultural frameworks.[7] The GLOBE studies complement Hofstede's study and suggest that there are several other cultural dimensions that explain how societies differ. In the next few pages, we consider these cultural dimensions and implications for various aspects of international business.

Hofstede's Model of National Culture

Hofstede model of national culture
cultural dimensions based on surveys of IBM employees from over 50 countries

Hofstede,[8] a Dutch social scientist, developed the **Hofstede model of national culture** by surveying over 88,000 employees in IBM subsidiaries from 72 countries.[9] However, he reduced the number of countries to 40 based on responses and later added ten more countries and three regions to his findings. He developed his cultural model primarily on the basis of differences in values and beliefs regarding work goals. Thus, it has easily identifiable implications for international business by providing a clear link between national and business cultures. You will see later in the text numerous examples of Hofstede's ideas providing the background to understand differences in international business practices.

power distance
degree to which people accept power and authority differences in society

The first cultural dimension proposed by Hofstede is power distance. **Power distance** refers to the degree to which societies accept power differences and authority in society. In societies with high power distance, people are more likely to accept that inequality is good and acceptable. In such societies, people are also more likely to accept that there are some people who are in charge and that these powerful people are entitled to privileges. Exhibit 7.1 shows selected countries and their ranking on Hofstede's power distance function. It should be noted that the Hofstede scores range from 100 (high) to 0 (low).

As Exhibit 7.1 shows, many Latin American, Latin European and Asian countries have high power distance. In these countries, the concern for hierarchy and inequality in organizations is rooted in early socialization in the family and school. In high power distance cultures, children are expected to obey their parents and elders. In schools, teachers assume the role of dominance and are often seen as father figures. Children must not challenge a teacher's authority. Later in life, organizations assume many of the roles of parents and teachers. In contrast, countries such as the US, UK, and Germany have lower power distance. There are no expectations that hierarchy and power differences are appropriate.

Power distance has important implications for many aspects of international business. For instance, MNCs operating in high power distance societies will

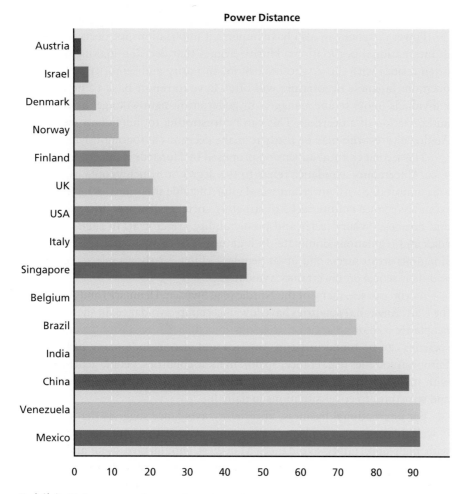

Power Distance

Exhibit 7.1 **Power Distance for Selected Countries**

Source: Based on G. Hofstede, 2001, *Culture's Consequences: Comparing Values, Behaviours, Institutions, and Organizations Across Nations* (2nd edn.), Thousand Oaks: Sage.

often have to hire managers who can show their leadership qualities. Employees are more deferential to their supervisors and will expect more explicit directions about what needs to get done. Managers are therefore expected to show their position in the company. Consider the experience of a US vice president, who was meeting with vice presidents from the Indian affiliate of the company.[10] When the US vice president entered the room, she saw a room in disarray. She asked for help from one of the Indian executives to arrange the chairs but was ignored. Later the Indian told her that he couldn't believe that she was moving chairs when she could have delegated this task to the office staff. The Indian executive couldn't believe that she was engaging in a task that was perceived as below her skills. Because of the Indian culture's high power distance, those at the executive level of the organization are expected to behave accordingly.

MNCs also often find that they need to send older employees when negotiating with their counterparts in high power distance societies. Age tends to be equated with wisdom and experience. Consider Exxon Mobil's experience when they sent some of their employees from Angola and Russia for cross-cultural training in Canada.[11] Both Angolans and Russians equated age with authority, a characteristic of high power distance societies. Exxon Mobil had to train these workers to accept that younger employees may sometimes have authority.

Power distance can also have important implications for decision making in international negotiations. Hurn[12] argues that decision-making authority often resides with those who have more authority and seniority in the organization. Japanese negotiators will often have to report back to more senior individuals (more senior managers or government figures) to get approval for authorization of a decision. This can be frustrating to individuals from more Anglo cultures who may be ready to make decisions autonomously.

The second cultural dimension proposed by Hofstede is uncertainty avoidance. **Uncertainty avoidance** refers to the degree to which people in a society are comfortable with uncertainty and unpredictable situations. A higher uncertainty avoidance culture seeks to structure social systems (politics, education, and business) where order and predictability are crucial. In such countries, rules and regulations dominate. In high uncertainty avoidance societies, risky situations create stress and upset people. Exhibit 7.2 shows selected countries and their scores on uncertainty avoidance.

As you can see, many of the Nordic (e.g. Sweden, Denmark) and Anglo (e.g. the USA, Australia) countries have low uncertainty avoidance. In such societies, people are comfortable with change and ambiguity. In contrast, high uncertainty societies can be found in Latin America and also include many of the Latin European societies (e.g. France, Spain). In these countries, people generally react with stress and anxiety when rules of behavior are not clear. They prefer order and structures to cover situations in daily life.

For international business, uncertainty avoidance suggests that the MNC is well advised to provide structure and order if they operate in societies with high uncertainty avoidance. Managers should give clear and explicit directions to subordinates. Such clear instructions make subordinates less anxious, since subordinates know exactly what is expected of them. This reduces ambiguity regarding job expectations. The boss tells workers exactly what to do. Similarly, organizations in these cultures have many written rules and procedures. Like the situation produced by the task-directed leader, extensive

uncertainty avoidance
degree to which people are comfortable with uncertainty and unpredictable situations

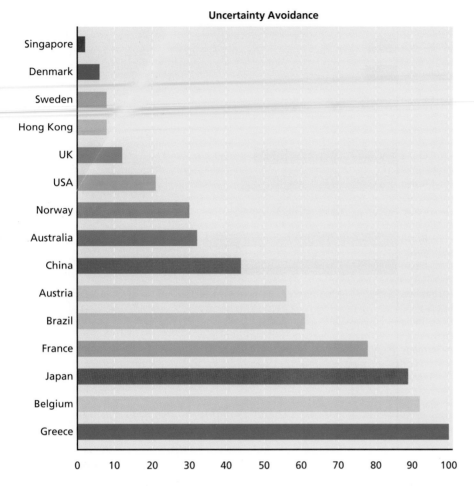

Uncertainty Avoidance

Exhibit 7.2 **Uncertainty Avoidance for Selected Countries**

Source: Based on G. Hofstede, 2001, *Culture's Consequences: Comparing Values, Behaviours, Institutions, and Organizations Across Nations* (2nd edn.), Thousand Oaks: Sage.

rules and procedures tell employees exactly what the organization expects of them. Consequently, employees believe that these rules should not be broken.

A third important cultural dimension proposed by Hofstede is the individualism dimension. **Individualism** refers to the degree to which society focuses on the relationship of the individual to the group. In more individualistic societies, people are viewed as unique and are valued for their achievements. In contrast, in societies that are low on individualism, the individual is seen as being part of a wider group such as the family, social class or even team. In more collectivistic societies, rewards and recognition go to groups rather than any single individual. Exhibit 7.3 shows selected countries and their rankings on the individualism dimension.

As you can see from Exhibit 7.3, the US has the highest individualism scores. In fact, many of the Anglo cultures, such as the UK and Australia, also have very high individualism scores. In these countries, people are rewarded and recognized for their achievements. In contrast, many of the Asian and Latin American societies have low individualism scores. In these countries, social groups such as the family and the organization are emphasized over each individual.

individualism
refers to the degree to which society focuses on the relationship of the individual to the group

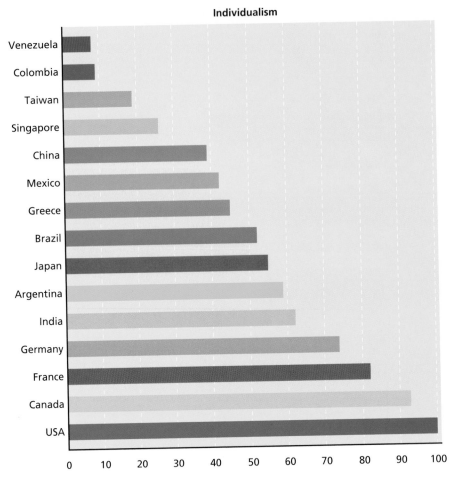

Exhibit 7.3 **Individualism for Selected Countries**

Source: Based on G. Hofstede, 2001, *Culture's Consequences: Comparing Values, Behaviours, Institutions, and Organizations Across Nations* (2nd edn.), Thousand Oaks: Sage.

Individualism has important implications for international business. In countries with low individualism, MNCs will find that employees are hired and promoted mostly on the basis of association with a larger group such as a university or high school. In such societies, emphasis is placed on loyalty, seniority and age. As mentioned earlier, MNCs operating in more collectivistic societies need to appreciate the importance of the larger social group. Consider Procter & Gamble's Canada subsidiary and their effort to understand diversity in their workforce. Because of the emphasis on the group and group harmony, they realized that in more collectivist cultures it is necessary to reward groups rather than individuals in some cases.[13] If they were to reward individuals within a team, they would potentially create conflict among the team members. The following Small Business Insight provides some understanding of the implications of individualism for brand management.

The IB Strategic Insight clearly shows that for the collective culture, the pressure coming from collective norms cannot be ignored. In the workplace, it is important for the MNC to respect collective norms and values.

The fourth cultural dimension proposed by Hofstede is masculinity. **Masculinity** refers to the degree to which a society emphasizes masculine cultural

masculinity
degree to which society emphasizes masculine cultural characteristics such as emphasis on advancement and earning

Branding in Collectivistic Societies

You are a small company interested in marketing to collectivist societies. What do you pay attention to? Understanding the relationship people have with brands has been an important challenge for most marketers. While for the individualistic person from the UK or the US the personal brand meaning is as important as the public meaning, the situation is different for the more collectivistic Asian societies. People in these societies often build their self-definitions based on what others think of them. As such, Asians are more likely to use or wear something that conforms to accepted group norms. Furthermore, collectivistic societies tend to be slower to risk trying new products but, for fear of being left out, will catch up much faster once a critical mass of people is using the new product. Marketers also find that products used in private have less important branding effects as no one sees these products being used. In the case of private products, price becomes more important than branding.

Sources: Adapted from Brand Strategy, 2006, "Asian marketing: East meets West," July 17, p. 38.

characteristics such as emphasis on advancement and earnings. In societies with a high degree of masculinity, work tends to be very important and central to people's lives. Furthermore, these societies tend to see occupations clearly categorized by gender. In contrast, less masculine societies tend to value quality of life over a job and earnings. Work tends to be less central and important in people's lives. Exhibit 7.4 shows selected countries and their respective scores on masculinity.

Exhibit 7.4 depicts that many of the Anglo countries such as the US and the UK have high levels of masculinity. This suggests that MNCs operating in these countries will encounter employees who see work as very important in their lives. In these societies, people tend to work very long hours and recognition on the job is seen as an important motivator. The Exhibit also shows that many of the Nordic societies such as Sweden, Denmark and Norway have low levels of masculinity. In these societies, people tend to work less and take longer vacations. MNCs operating in these countries should expect a workforce that is less dedicated to work and more focused on quality of life. Consider France, for instance, where employees typically get around 40 days off compared to only 15 in the US.[14] Many French employers actually offer company-owned ski cabins or beach houses as benefits to motivate employees. Such practices are consistent with the emphasis on quality of life in France because of the low levels of masculinity.

Low levels of masculinity have also been implied to mean less inequality between genders regarding occupations. In more masculine societies, jobs are clearly defined by gender and some jobs are automatically reserved for males. However, in less masculine societies, occupations tend to be less gender-based. Low levels of masculinity are also perceived to be associated with a better work environment for women. Is this accurate? Consider the Country/ Regional Focus overleaf.

However, despite the important understanding the Hofstede model has generated, it has also received some criticisms.[15] First, some have argued that

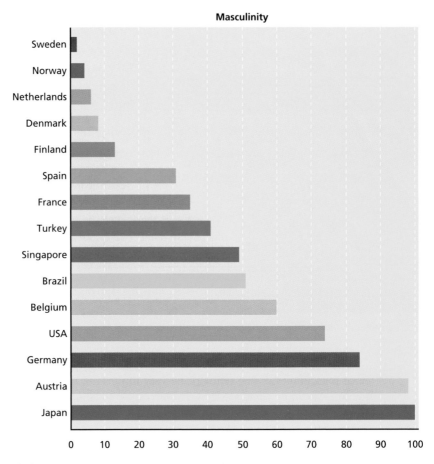

Exhibit 7.4 **Masculinity for Selected Countries**

Source: Based on G. Hofstede, 2001, *Culture's Consequences: Comparing Values, Behaviours, Institutions, and Organizations Across Nations* (2nd edn.), Thousand Oaks: Sage.

Sweden

COUNTRY FOCUS

Sweden has one of the lowest masculinity scores on Hofstede's cultural dimension and is considered by many as one of the bastions of gender equality. In fact, Sweden has one of the highest rates of women parliament members in the world. However, the cultural preference for gender equality and quality of life has actually resulted in a paradox. The generous government benefits to make lives better for working mothers have created an unwanted ceiling for women and less gender equality. Although it is believed that longer maternity leaves and state-funded childcare make it easier for women to have careers, Swedish private employers have been more reluctant to hire Swedish women in managerial and more powerful positions because they don't want to deal with maternity disruption. In fact, while women hold around 45 percent of managerial positions in the US, only around 29 percent of such positions are held by Swedish women. This situation has become a hot topic and politicians are considering legislation similar to that in Norway, where companies will be required to have at least two women on their board of directors. Furthermore, requiring men to take at least a portion of the maternity leave is also being seriously considered.

Sources: Adapted from *Newsweek International*, 2006, "The gender gap: Moms not wanted," www.newsweek.com, January 9.

Culture and Sustainability

IB SUSTAINABILITY PRACTICES

It is undeniable that multinational corporations have a critical role to play in promoting environmental responsibility and sustainability. However, the multinationals' ability to implement sustainable programs is dependent on the local culture and the acceptance of such programs by the local population. Multinationals must therefore design programs that are tailored to cultural preferences of the local population.

A recent study by Husted[16] shows the importance of understanding Hofstede's national culture dimensions and their influence on sustainability. Husted found that the main driver of environmental sustainability in societies is wealth. However, he also found that countries that are wealthy and have low levels of power distance, high levels of individualism and low levels of masculinity are more likely to encourage and support environmental sustainability. Such egalitarian, individualist and feminine societies tend to have more green or sustainable values.

Multinational managers may thus consider cultural dimensions and adopt policies consistent with the local culture. For instance, in collectivistic societies that don't value sustainability, programs that show that environmental degradation can harm the in-group's interests will be more effective.

Based on Bryan W. Husted, 2005, "Culture and ecology: A cross-national study of the determinants of environmental sustainability," *Management International Review*, 45 (3): 349–71.

Hofstede's model is too simplistic and that cultures cannot be reduced to a few dimensions. As you will see later, understanding a country's culture is indeed very difficult and takes long periods of training. Second, Hofstede's data was from IBM managers. There is some concern over whether IBM managers in a country are sufficiently similar to the average person in that country to make conclusions about the country's culture. Third, Hofstede's model is also seen as static as it cannot detect how culture changes over time. For instance, many countries in Eastern Europe have experienced dramatic changes in the last decades. Hofstede's cultural dimensions may not necessarily be able to reflect such changes. The final critical aspect of Hofstede's model is that the data was collected in the 1970s and that the model is outdated.

Despite the above criticisms, Hofstede's study has been very useful in helping multinational managers navigate cultural differences. Hofstede's dimensions have been shown to influence many key aspects of multinational strategic management. These dimensions have also been shown to help understand differences in environmental management. Consider the IB Sustainability Practices above.

Because of the many criticisms against Hofstede's model, a large team of researchers conducted the GLOBE studies. We will consider that model next.

The Global Leadership and Organizational Behavior Studies Model of Culture

The Hofstede model discussed earlier provides a good understanding of many of the critical ways countries differ on culture. However, while the Hofstede data was collected more than three decades ago, a more recent study by the Global Leadership and Organizational Behavior Studies researchers (GLOBE) provides additional insight into understanding culture.[17] The GLOBE project involves 170 researchers who collected data on 17,000 managers from 62 countries around the world. Many of the cultural dimensions studied by the GLOBE researchers are similar to the ones studied by Hofstede. Specifically, the GLOBE researchers found evidence of nine cultural dimensions such as power distance, uncertainty avoidance, societal and institutional collectivism (similar to Hofstede's individualism and collectivism dimensions), assertiveness (similar to Hofstede's masculinity), and gender egalitarianism (similar to Hofstede's femininity). Given the similarity with Hofstede's dimensions, many of the implications discussed earlier for Hofstede's cultural dimensions would also apply for the similar GLOBE dimensions.

However, three of the dimensions the GLOBE researchers studied are fairly unique. Below we consider these three dimensions, namely future orientation, humane orientation and performance orientation.

Future orientation deals with the degree to which individuals believe that their current behavior will impact their future. This dimension was developed to reflect how people use time to organize their experiences and events. It is actually similar to another of Hofstede's dimensions known as the Confucian dynamism or more long-term orientation. However, we focus on GLOBE's future orientation measure as it is most recent and covers a wider range of societies than Hofstede.

Cultures that are low on the future orientation scale (present orientation) tend to be more spontaneous and prefer enjoying the current moment. In contrast, societies that have high future orientation tend to think more of the future and engage in planning and strategies in order to achieve future goals. Exhibit 7.5 shows selected countries and their scores on future orientation. The GLOBE scale runs from a 1 (low) to 7 (high).

As you can see from the chart, many of the former communist societies such as Poland, Russia and Hungary have relatively low future orientation scores. It is possible that decades of communism have resulted in individuals preferring instant gratification rather than planning ahead. Given the relative deprivation that people in many of these societies had to endure, they probably prefer the present rather than planning for an uncertain future. It is also interesting to note that many of the Nordic societies score relatively high on this dimension. It seems possible that the relative periods of wealth they have enjoyed make it possible to plan for the future.

Future orientation has important implications for international business. MNCs should expect less preference for strategic planning and more inflexible management systems in societies with low future orientation. Furthermore, people may also be more interested in what the MNC has to offer in the immediacy (job security) rather than future prospects. However, in higher future orientation societies, there tends to be more of a future-looking perspective.

Performance orientation refers to the degree to which the society encourages societal members to innovate, to improve their performance, and to strive for excellence. This dimension is similar to Weber's Protestant work ethic and reflects the desire for achievement in a society. Countries such as the United States and Singapore have high scores on performance orientation, while countries such as Russia and Greece have low scores on the dimension.

future orientation
degree to which people believe that their current behavior will impact their future

performance orientation
degree to which the society encourages societal members to innovate, to improve their performance, and to strive for excellence

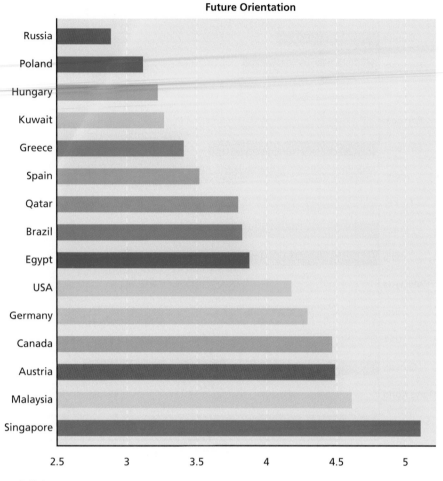

Future Orientation

Exhibit 7.5 **Future Orientation for Selected Countries**

Source: Based on R.J. House, P.J. Hanges, M. Javidan, P.W. Dorfman and V. Gupta (eds) 2004, *Culture, Leadership and Organizations: The GLOBE Study of 62 Societies*, Thousand Oaks: Sage.

An important reflection of the performance orientation cultural dimension is how status is conferred in society. High performance societies tend to be more similar to achievement societies where people are evaluated on the basis of their accomplishments. In contrast, low performance societies are ascription societies where status is given to people based on characteristics such as age, family connections, gender and education.

Exhibit 7.6 shows selected countries and their scores on performance orientation.

Countries that have high performance orientation scores tend to favor training and development, while in countries low on performance orientation, family and background are more important.[18] In societies with high performance orientation, people are encouraged to take initiative and are rewarded for performing with the belief that one can succeed by trying hard. In contrast, low performance orientation societies reward harmony with the environment, emphasizing loyalty and integrity while regarding assertiveness as unacceptable.

The final cultural dimension we discuss is humane orientation. **Humane orientation** refers to the degree to which people within a society are expected

humane orientation
degree to which people are expected to be friendly, generous and caring

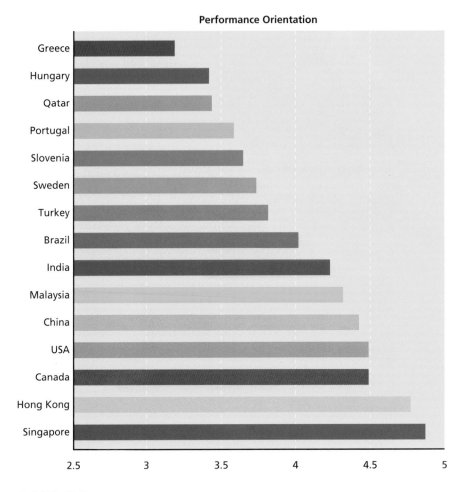

Exhibit 7.6 **Performance Orientation for Selected Countries**

Source: Based on R.J. House, P.J. Hanges, M. Javidan, P.W. Dorfman and V. Gupta (eds) 2004, *Culture, Leadership and Organizations: The GLOBE Study of 62 Societies*, Thousand Oaks: Sage.

to be friendly, generous and caring. In societies with high humane orientation, people see others as very important and value kindness, benevolence, generosity and love. In contrast, low humane orientation societies tend to place emphasis on self-interest and value material possessions. Exhibit 7.7 shows selected societies and their scores on the humane orientation dimension.

As the chart shows, many of the Asian societies score highly on humane orientation. It is surprising to see Zambia has the highest score on the dimension. However, high humane societies are characterized by the expectation that members of the society will help each other and provide material and financial help. This is typical of many Asian and African societies where the individual can rely on the extended family for support. The US has a fairly moderate level of humane orientation, while many of the Latin European countries and Germany have lower levels of humane orientation.

Humane orientation affects international business in that MNCs should expect to provide an environment that is based on relationships in more humane oriented societies. Such societies tend to be characterized by more informal relationships among people. From a human resources perspective, MNCs in

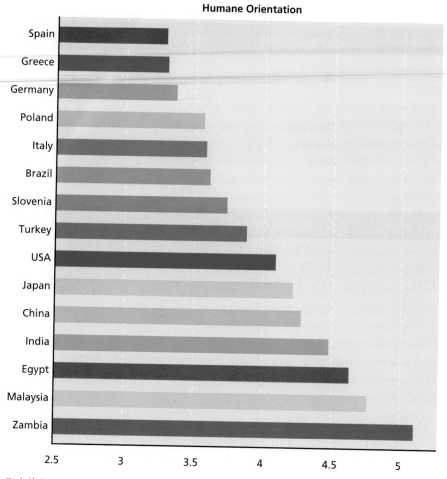

Exhibit 7.7 **Humane Orientation for Selected Countries**

Source: Based on R.J. House, P.J. Hanges, M. Javidan, P.W. Dorfman and V. Gupta (eds) 2004, *Culture, Leadership and Organizations: The GLOBE Study of 62 Societies*, Thousand Oaks: Sage.

such societies will tend to be more trusted. In contrast, low humane orientation societies tend to be more formal, and MNCs should expect more control from the state and unions.

Although the GLOBE data provides many insights into a large number of countries, further analysis has shown that the cultural dimensions' implications can be simplified when applied to country clusters. **Country clusters** are groups of countries, such as Anglo, Latin American, and Latin European, with roughly similar cultural patterns. Ten clusters were found in the GLOBE project and include the Anglo cluster, the Confucian Asia cluster, the Eastern Europe cluster, the Germanic Europe cluster, the Latin America cluster, Latin Europe cluster, the Middle East cluster, the Nordic Europe cluster, the Southern Asia cluster, and the sub-Saharan cluster. Exhibit 7.8 shows the various clusters and corresponding countries in the cluster.

Country clusters share many similarities with regards to cultural patterns. Exhibit 7.9 shows the various clusters and where these clusters stand on selected GLOBE cultural dimensions.

Why should you be concerned with country clusters? Although cultures

country clusters
group of countries with similar cultural patterns

193

Exhibit 7.8 **GLOBE Country Clusters**

Anglo	Latin Europe	Eastern Europe	Latin America	Confucian Asia
Australia	Israel	Albania	Argentina	China
Canada	Italy	Georgia	Bolivia	Hong Kong
Ireland	Portugal	Greece	Brazil	Japan
New Zealand	Spain	Hungary	Colombia	Singapore
South Africa (White)	France	Kazakhstan	Costa Rica	South Korea
United Kingdom	Switzerland (French)	Poland	El Salvador	Taiwan
USA		Russia	Guatemala	
		Slovenia	Mexico	
			Venezuela	

Nordic Europe	Germanic Europe	Sub-Saharan Africa	Middle East	Southern Asia
Denmark	Austria	Namibia	Qatar	India
Finland	Switzerland	Nigeria	Morocco	Indonesia
Sweden	Netherlands	South Africa (Black)	Turkey	Philippines
	Germany (former East)	Zambia	Egypt	Malaysia
	Germany (former West)	Zimbabwe	Kuwait	Thailand
				Iran

Source: Based on Vipin Gupta, Paul J. Hanges, and Peter Dorfman, 2002, "Cultural clusters: Methodology and findings," *Journal of World Business*, 37, pp. 11–15.

differ within these broad classifications, such summaries are useful for condensing cultural information. They are useful to predict likely cultural traits when specific information is not available on a national culture. Clusters are important as they provide important information to multinationals regarding similarity of cultures. Multinationals may find it less risky to enter other countries with cultures that are similar to their own, and clusters provide readily available information.

How important are country clusters? Consider the IB Strategic Insight on page 196.

The information discussed in this section shows the importance of understanding national culture in international business. Nevertheless, it should be noted that the GLOBE model has also been criticized for many of the same points as the Hofstede model. As you will see later, cultures are extremely complex, and some argue that research based on questionnaires can never accurately assess a country's cultural profile. However, using the Hofstede and GLOBE cultural models is a good starting point and provides crucial information about how countries differ on critical cultural dimensions. National culture affects how individuals behave and think, and an appropriate understanding of culture reduces the chance of making cultural blunders. Furthermore, national culture has an undeniable influence on the business culture and etiquette within any society. In the next section, we consider some of the linkages between national culture and business culture.

Exhibit 7.9 **GLOBE Country Clusters and Cultural Dimensions**

Cluster	Performance Orientation	Assertiveness	Future Orientation	Humane Orientation	Institutional Collectivism	In-group Collectivism	Gender Egalitarianism	Power Distance	Uncertainty Avoidance
Comparison with Hofstede	Unique	Masculinity	Long-term orientation	Unique	Collectivism	Collectivism	Femininity	Power Distance	Uncertainty Avoidance
Anglo	High	Medium	Medium	Medium	Medium	Low	Medium	Medium	Medium
Confucian Asia	High	Medium	Medium	Medium	High	High	Medium	Medium	Medium
Eastern Europe	Low	High	Low	Medium	Medium	High	High	Medium	Low
Germanic Europe	High	High	High	Low	Low	Low	Medium	Medium	High
Latin America	Low	Medium	Low	Medium	Low	High	Medium	Medium	Low
Latin Europe	Medium	Medium	Medium	Low	Low	Medium	Medium	Medium	Medium
Middle East	Medium	Medium	Low	Medium	Medium	High	Low	Medium	Medium
Nordic Europe	Medium	Low	High	Medium	High	Low	High	Low	High
Southern Asia	Medium	Medium	Medium	High	Medium	High	Medium	Medium	Medium
Sub-Saharan Africa	Medium	Medium	Medium	High	Medium	Medium	Medium	Medium	Medium

Source: Based on Mansour Javidan, Peter W. Dorfman, Mary Sully de Luque, and Robert J. House, 2006, "In the eye of the beholder: Cross-cultural lessons in leadership for project GLOBE," *The Academy of Management Perspectives*, February, 20(1), pp. 67–90.

Country Clusters and the GLOBE Project

IB STRATEGIC INSIGHT

Exhibit 7.10 **GLOBE Country Clusters and Preferred Leadership Attributes**

	Latin America	Confucian Asia	Anglo	Sub-Saharan Africa	Germanic Europe	Middle East
Charisma	High	Medium	High	Medium	High	Low
Team-oriented	High	Medium/High	Medium	Medium	Medium/Low	Low
Participative	Medium	Low	High	Medium	High	Low
Autonomous	Low	Medium	Medium	Low	High	Medium

Source: Based on Mansour Javidan, Peter W. Dorfman, Mary Sully de Luque, and Robert J. House, 2006, "In the eye of the beholder: Cross-cultural lessons in leadership for project GLOBE," *The Academy of Management Perspectives*, February, 20(1), pp. 67–90.

Country clusters represent a simple but powerful way to summarize information about countries with similar cultural profiles. Javidan et al.[19] provide some evidence of the usefulness of country clusters. They examined the cultural backgrounds of the ten country clusters and whether people in specific clusters preferred leaders with specific profiles. They considered such leadership profiles such as charisma (ability to inspire and motivate others), team-oriented (ability to motivate employees to work as a team), participative (degree to which the leader involves others) and autonomous (degree to which the leader behaves in individualistic manner), and found definite preference for specific leadership traits among clusters.

Consider their findings for the Latin American cluster. The Latin American cluster has countries where people frown on individualism. Furthermore, Latin American countries have high power distance and high levels of uncertainty avoidance. As such, those leaders who do well are typically those who make decisions collectively, those who treat their subordinates with formality and those who are less inclined to invite others to make decisions. It is therefore not surprising to see that the preferred leader in the Latin American cluster displays a high level of charisma, is team-oriented and has moderate levels of the participative profile.

In contrast, consider the Middle East cluster where countries tend to score low on uncertainty avoidance and high on collectivism, while medium on power distance. Because of the low levels of uncertainty avoidance, subordinates are often reluctant to make decisions that involve risk. As such, preferred leaders are those who display low levels of the participative dimension. Furthermore, the good leader in this cluster behaves in a collectivistic manner and tries to maintain harmony because of the high levels of collectivism.

As you can see from the above, country clusters are crucial tools to understand cultures. Exhibit 7.10 shows selected leadership profiles and appropriateness in different clusters.

Source: Based on Mansour Javidan, Peter W. Dorfman, Mary Sully de Luque, and Robert J House, 2006, "In the eye of the beholder: Cross-cultural lessons in leadership from project GLOBE," *Academy of Management Perspectives*, February, pp. 67–90.

National Culture and Business Culture

business culture
values, beliefs and norms regarding how to conduct business in a society

A society's **business culture** reflects the values, beliefs and norms regarding how business is conducted in any society. It reflects the appropriate and inappropriate behaviors when conducting business in any society. Understanding business culture is extremely critical as, similar to national culture, it provides insights regarding appropriate aspects of doing business in a culture. Obviously, a country's business culture is heavily influenced by its national culture. Such aspects of the business culture tend to be manifested in **business etiquette**, the range of expected acceptable and unacceptable behaviors when doing business. In this section, we consider a few key aspects of business etiquette and how they are affected by national culture.

business etiquette
range of acceptable and unacceptable behaviors when doing business

One of the most important aspects of business etiquette is whether to use a person's formal title and last name when meeting that person. In the US, the business culture tends to be more informal and managers seldom use last names and titles to refer to each other. However, in other societies such as China and Germany, it is expected that titles and formality are respected when addressing someone. One of the important cultural differences that explains the degree of formality is power distance. Because of the emphasis on hierarchy and privileged position of the powerful in countries with a high degree of power distance, there is an expectation that this hierarchy will be respected through the appropriate use of titles.

High power distance tends to be associated with formality in many other aspects of the business environment. For instance, in a high power distance society, business people are expected to dress more conservatively, to be punctual for appointments, to make more formal presentations, and to value the use of a business card. Additionally, when negotiating with individuals in high power distance societies, it is very likely that those with the highest seniority are the decision makers. It therefore makes sense to know the seniority and rank of those involved in negotiations.

Another important aspect that pertains to the business environment in a society is the nature of relationships between business partners. In some societies such as China, it is expected that business partners will be patient and consider any partnership through a long-term perspective. However, in the US business negotiators may not necessarily view a business partnership as long-term. The cultural dimension of collectivism provides some explanation for these differences. In more collectivistic societies, personal relationships are extremely important. It is therefore expected that US companies negotiating with Chinese companies will want to develop relationships first. Unlike the US preference for completing negotiations in as timely a fashion as possible, Chinese negotiators often prefer to socialize and to cultivate the relationship before getting to business matters. This also suggests the importance of being properly connected to undertake business operations. To give you further insight on how business etiquette works, consider the IB Small Business Insight overleaf on small businesses attempting to establish contacts in China.

As the IB Small Business Insight shows, the cultural dimension of collectivism has a strong influence on the business culture in China. The implications for business etiquette are that people should expect to engage in non-business conversations with individuals from more collectivistic societies. During meetings, more time can be spent talking about non-business issues so that the partners get to know each other.

Furthermore, care must be taken to give opportunities for collectivistic individuals to avoid loss of face. For instance, it is important to understand that a "yes" in Japan may not have the same connotation as a "yes" in the US. In the US, if someone says "yes," that person is indicating agreement with your

Business Culture in China

Many smaller companies rely on Chinese companies for manufacturing and prototyping purposes. Chinese experts suggest that small-business employees keep in mind the many aspects of Chinese business culture:

- Handle business cards with two hands and delicately. Chinese business people tend to view handling of business cards as a sign of respect. It is also polite to have business cards with Chinese lettering on the other side.
- Dress conservatively.

- Show up on time for meetings.
- Cultivate personal relationships.
- Try to get consensus on decisions rather than create conflict.
- Be patient but persistent with negotiations.
- Don't use slang with your hosts.

Sources: Adapted from Dave Archer, 2006. "Doing business in China," *Journal of Commerce*, October 30, p. 1; Dave Hannon, 2006, "The dos and don'ts of doing business in China," *Purchasing*, May 18, pp. 52–4.

statement. Disagreement is simply indicated with a "no." However, the Japanese negotiator may be reluctant to say "no." In fact, the Japanese negotiator may say "yes" when, in reality, the "yes" means "possibly" or even "no." As such, it is important not to place collective individuals in such precarious positions. Consider, for instance, that ITT China was facing high employee turnover in its Shanghai sales office.[20] Local managers soon found out that the performance ratings were influencing turnover. Employees who were rated a 3 on a 1–5 performance scale were more likely to quit shortly thereafter. These employees could not face their peers as they were losing face when receiving such low ratings. For them, it made more sense to quit. ITT decided to drop such performance ratings altogether in most of the collective countries where it was operating.

Because of the focus on the collective, it is also important to know that teams are very important in collectivistic societies. In teams, people strive to reach consensus and generally avoid conflicts. Teams would rather show consensus than disagreement in front of their hosts. As a reflection of the business culture, it is important for individuals from more individualistic societies to realize that they may have to deal with teams rather than individuals.

It is important to understand the impact of the masculinity dimension on business etiquette. Because work is a big aspect of an individual's life in more masculine societies, you can expect a strong work ethic and discussion of work-related matters long into the night. However, for the more feminine societies, such as the Danes, meetings are expected to end in the afternoon. Danes prefer to work intensely on the job and end work early so that they can spend time with their families.

A final critical aspect of the business culture of a country is the use of language in the communication context. The anthropologist Edward T. Hall identified an important distinction among the world's languages based on whether communication is explicit or implicit. Hall focused on how different cultures use the context or the situation in which communication takes place to understand what people are saying. Languages in which people state things

Kiwi Companies and China

IB STRATEGIC INSIGHT

For Kiwi companies based in New Zealand, the Chinese market offers tremendous potential. As these Kiwi companies negotiate with Chinese companies, e-mails are often used to communicate. However, experts agree that the language context has important implications, even for e-mails. For New Zealanders living in a low-context culture, e-mails are usually very direct and to the point. However, such e-mails can be very offensive to the Chinese, who live in a high-context culture. Chinese prefer e-mails that tend to be longer, first discussing the weather or family before getting to the point. Furthermore, what a low-context New Zealander may see as a binding contract in an e-mail may be only the starting point for the Chinese, who are more interested in developing long-term relationships. People from low-context cultures are therefore well advised to write in a more formal, lengthy and complex style when communicating with people from high-context cultures.

Source: Based on Reuben Schwartz, 2006, "Cultural divide in e-mails," *Dominion Post*, May 8, p. C10.

directly and explicitly are called **low-context languages**. The words provide most of the meaning. You do not have to understand the situation in which the words are used. Languages in which people state things indirectly and implicitly are called **high-context languages**. In the high-context language, communications have multiple meanings that one can interpret only by reading the situation in which the communication occurs.

Most northern European languages, including German, English, and the Scandinavian languages, are low context. People use explicit words to communicate direct meaning. Thus, for example, if a German manager says "yes," she means "yes." In addition, most Western cultures attach a positive value to clear and direct communication. This is particularly apparent in negotiations, where low-context languages allow clear statements concerning what a negotiator wants out of the relationship. In contrast, Asian and Arabic languages are among the most high-context languages in the world. In Asian languages, often what is left unsaid is just as important as what is said. Silent periods and the use of incomplete sentences require a person to interpret what the communicator does not say by reading the situation. Arabic introduces interpretation into the language with an opposite tack. Extensive imprecise verbal and nonverbal communication produces an interaction where reading the situation is necessary for understanding.

Why is it necessary to understand whether communication in a country is high or low context? Consider the following IB Strategic Insight.

low-context languages people say things directly and explicitly

high-context languages people state things indirectly and implicitly

National Culture: Some Cautions and Caveats

The preceding paragraphs discuss some of the ways countries are different based on culture and how the national culture affects business culture. However, you need to keep in mind that these are broad generalizations that provide the basis to understand how people are different across countries, and that not

subcultures
groups of people with similar culture within a culture

all individuals within a society will fit the cultural profile for that country. Furthermore, most countries have **subcultures**, which represent the ways of life of groups of people within a culture. For example, considering India as a homogeneous culture can be damaging for any multinational. There are significant differences among regions and among castes. McDonald's adjusted its menu significantly to address such regional subcultures. It tailored its menu to address regional variations in terms of preference of meat and vegetarian menus as well as preference for local fares. In this section, we therefore discuss some of the dangers of making broad generalizations and how to better prepare to understand such differences.

Cultures do not determine exactly how each individual behaves, thinks, acts, and feels. Assuming that all people within one culture behave, believe, feel, and act the same is known as **stereotyping**. Using a cultural stereotype to understand another culture is not necessarily wrong, if it is used carefully. Broad generalization about a culture can serve as a starting point for understanding the complexities of cultural differences. Another important danger related to understanding culture is **ethnocentricity**. Ethnocentricity is the belief that one's own culture is superior to others. Many international business projects fail because multinational managers are ethnocentric and they ignore the benefits of other cultures.

stereotyping
assuming that all people within a particular group behave, believe, feel and act the same

ethnocentricity
belief that one's own culture is superior

Even when an effort is made to understand culture, experts often find that there are a lot of exceptions to the generalizations we discussed earlier.[21] For instance, consider that although the US is one of the most individualistic societies, it has one of the highest percentages of charitable giving in the world. Similarly, although Japan is very high on uncertainty avoidance, business partners often find that Japanese contracts tend to incorporate significant ambiguity clauses compared to specific and direct US contracts. Such **cultural paradoxes**, where observations often contradict cultural expectations, suggest that you need to be very careful when you are trying to understand culture in any society.

cultural paradoxes
refers to situations that contradict cultural expectations

The cultural differences we outlined earlier are very useful tools for understanding how countries differ on culture. However, they can be limited in understanding the wide variations in cultural patterns within a country. It is therefore imperative for you to be very attentive to situations or contexts that may make an individual behave contrary to cultural expectations. In other words, you cannot assume that all business people in the US prefer participative management styles because of low power distance. In fact, although the US generally prefers a more egalitarian culture, CEOs are often allowed to be authoritarian and people accept an unequal degree of power. As you can see, this reflects a cultural paradox where US Americans accept inequality and power characteristic of higher power distance societies.

How can you prepare for the subtleties of understanding culture? Culture experts suggest using the cultural dimensions we discussed earlier as basic tools. Beyond that, you need to understand that cultures are incredibly complex and cannot be reduced to simple do's and don'ts. For instance, appropriate understanding of a country's history and a country's logic can be very helpful. Through cultural mentors, culture students can also get a more in-depth understanding of cultural nuances. Finally, you should always remain open-minded and try to understand the reasoning behind cultural paradoxes. Consider the following IB Strategic Insight.

MTV Networks International and Saudi Arabia

For Bill Roedy, the chief of MTV Networks International, getting the mayor of Mecca, Saudi Arabia to support MTV Arabia was very important. Expanding in the region would give MTV the opportunity to reach over 200 million Arabs. However, he also knew that he would face significant hurdles given the many stereotypes key Saudi Arabian decision makers had about MTV and the potential to offend local sensibilities.

How did Bill Roedy prepare before his meeting with the mayor? He spent significant time understanding the history that shapes the local Saudi Arabian context. However, he also spent significant time in Riyadh and even attended recording sessions of leading Arab rappers. Through such experiences, he got better insights into the lyrics and found that most popular groups emphasized the themes of family and religion.

His extensive preparations and visit were very helpful as he was able to provide guarantees that MTV Arabia would respect many local cultural requirements, such as educating the young, providing a call for prayers, and not showing bare skin in any of the programs. The mayor gave his blessing and MTV Arabia will become a reality.

Source: Based on Tom Lowry and Frederik Balfour, 2008, "It's all about the face-to-face," *BusinessWeek*, January 28, pp. 48–51.

As you can see above, fully understanding the local cultural context is important. Consider some of the examples of cultural paradoxes mentioned earlier. Why would the US have the highest levels of charitable giving when this is clearly a behavior that contradicts the high levels of individualism? US history shows that the US prospered based on a communal tradition of religions and cultural values. It is therefore not surprising to see such high levels of charitable giving.[22] Similarly, the more ambiguous clauses contained in Japanese contracts reflect the more collectivistic nature of Japanese culture. The Japanese believe that they can rely on and trust others, and such aspects take precedence over any uncertainty about the contract. Therefore, they do not need to specify all aspects of a contract as they leave some flexibility to deal with contingencies. Both examples suggest that a more in-depth appreciation of the cultural context can bring better cultural understanding.

National Culture: Cross-cultural Training

It is obvious from this chapter that understanding cultural differences is crucial to today's global manager. You should not be surprised to be asked to take an international assignment when you start your career. For the company sending personnel into the international arena, there are significant costs involved. Consider that an expatriate may often require a salary premium of 10 to 25 percent above his or her salary on international assignments. Furthermore, extra expenses are incurred through the provision of housing, a company vehicle, cost-of-living adjustments, medical and other benefits (private school, spousal support) to support the family.[23] With such high costs, it is imperative that the MNC ensures that the expatriate has a chance to succeed. A big factor contributing to success is cultural training.

There is enough evidence that cross-cultural training is extremely valuable for multinationals.[24] Cross-cultural training provides the recipient with better skills to adjust to the new culture. Such adjustment enhances the likelihood that the person will do well at the job. Furthermore, appropriate training also reduces the likelihood that an expatriate will leave the job. Cross-cultural training also increases self-confidence and well-being in the new culture.

In the final section, we therefore examine some of the ways MNCs can prepare their employees to understand new cultures.

Culture Training Methods

There is a range of training techniques available for cross-cultural training.[25] The selection of the technique used depends on the nature of the assignment. For short-term assignments, **low-rigor cultural training programs**, where more limited mental involvement and effort is extended to complete the program, may be adequate. However, for long-term expatriate assignments, **higher-rigor training programs** may be more appropriate. Below we discuss the forms of training and corresponding levels of rigor.

There are two basic forms of cultural training available: simulations and field experiences.[26] **Simulations** tend be of lower rigor, where participants are offered the opportunity to experience the foreign culture through role-playing and other programmed instruction. One of the most basic forms of simulation cultural training can be of the instructional type. In this form of training, employees are exposed to various forms of instructional material such as lectures, tutorials and reading assignments about the new culture. Participants can also engage in role-playing as well as participating in case studies. In some cases, MNCs provide some form of cultural awareness training. The basic assumption behind cultural awareness methods is that someone can better appreciate cultural differences if the person is aware of his or her own culture. Finally, this method may also involve some form of language training whereby participants are taught the basic aspects of the language so that they have a rudimentary knowledge of the language.

The major advantage of these low-rigor methods typical of the simulations discussed above is that they tend to be very cost-effective and typically involve minimal work disruption. Companies can bring cross-cultural experts to the employees' workplace to provide convenient training. Furthermore, these methods are also amenable to delivery via the Internet and can thus involve minimal work disturbances.

The major drawbacks include the fact that instructors have to be very experienced or participants may not take the exercise very seriously. For instance, for case studies and experiential forms of learning, instructors need to have the skills and experiences to provide lessons that are as realistic as possible. Furthermore, because most of the instructions can be offered in a classroom, participants also suffer from the "classroom" syndrome. They may not believe that the exercises are very realistic and may thus doubt the effectiveness of the approach. In some cases, they may just be recipients of static information without having the chance to engage in experiential activities to digest the information.

The **field experiences** techniques are usually of higher rigor and participants are given the opportunity to learn through experience. Employees can

low-rigor cultural training programs
cultural training that necessitates minimal effort and mental involvement

higher-rigor training methods
cultural training that is more involved

simulations
training programs that offer participants the chance to experience a foreign culture through role-playing and other forms of instruction

field experiences
cultural training programs that offer participants the opportunity to learn by experiencing the new culture

participate in field trips, where they visit and experience the host culture first hand for a significant period of time. Some MNCs also offer on-the-job training where the employee is coached and trained on the job. This method allows the trainee to see not only the new culture but also how that culture interacts with the work environment. In other cases, employees get interaction training whereby they learn from the expatriate they will be replacing. This allows the new employee to get firsthand training on the appropriate business behaviors in the country. Furthermore, it allows the person to meet the key people in the new workplace and to learn how to interact with the new community. This method eases expectations regarding daily operation in the new culture.

Most cultural training experts suggest that field experiences are the most effective means of training.[27] Participants get a direct and strong appreciation of the new culture by experiencing the culture firsthand. Furthermore, with on-the-job coaching they experience not only the culture but also the workplace environment, meeting key individuals and getting to know the organizational culture. This learning and experience is valuable in giving the recipient an experience as close as possible to reality, thereby increasing the likelihood of success.

The major disadvantage associated with field experiences is that they tend to be both time-consuming and costly. For instance, sending someone on a field trip may involve significant costs. In many cases, it may also be necessary to send the whole family, costing thousands of dollars more. Additionally, on-the-job training can be very disruptive for the trainer. Expatriates tend to be very busy individuals, and unless they are provided with the additional time and resources they may feel overburdened if they have to train a new person.

Which training method should be used? Researchers argue that the types of training should be based on three main factors: the degree to which the employee's national culture is different from the one she will be experiencing; the degree to which the employee will need to interact with locals; and the length of the cultural assignment. If assignments are short term, for instance when a

De Beers and Culture Training

IB STRATEGIC INSIGHT

When De Beers, the world's leading diamond jeweler, was preparing to open new stores in Japan, it realized that the Japanese market was very complicated. It understood that its own team of employees would need to become more knowledgeable about Japanese culture for the retail stores to succeed. It therefore commissioned Communicaid to devise and provide training for its employees.

Instead of providing uniform training to the 25-employee De Beers team, Communicaid divided the team into smaller groups of five to six members. The teams were

then provided with intensive face-to-face sessions and then developed standardized training programs cooperatively. De Beers' employees were also given tailored training on awareness of cultural differences and the effects on communication and working styles based on their job functions. Such training was very successful, and more De Beers' UK-based employees are now getting such cross-cultural training.

Source: Based on Ross Bentley, 2007, "It pays to be a cross-culture vulture," *Personnel Today*, January 23, p. 28.

person is sent to negotiate in a different culture for a short period of time, low-rigor simulations may work well. However, if a manager is sent for a long period of time, for instance, as an expatriate, higher-rigor types of training may be necessary. How do companies customize training programs? Consider the IB Strategic Insight on the previous page.

Culture Training: Best Practices

In this final section, we examine some of the best practices regarding cross-cultural training based on a review by Littrell and Salas.[28] They argue that any cross-cultural training has many aspects that need to be tailored according to the training needs. Specifically, the three crucial aspects of cross-cultural training include the design, delivery, and evaluation. With regard to design, many of the issues discussed earlier apply here. For instance, the nature of the assignment should play a role in determining the length of the training. More complex international assignments obviously require more rigorous training. Additionally, cross-cultural training works best if it is also offered to the accompanying family. The ability of a manager to succeed on a foreign assignment also depends on the family's level of adaptation to the new culture. Finally, a properly designed program should involve the human resource (HR) management department. The HR department can play a critical role in selecting the best individual and also tailoring the program based on the individual's personality.

With regards to delivery, many methods such as simulations and field experiences are available. Best practices suggest that a combination of the various methods may work best. For instance, employees can be exposed to instructional material about the new culture and also participate in field trips. This combination of methods is likely to enhance learning. Many experts also suggest the use of online facilities and programs to deliver training. For instance, important cultural information can be made available online for viewing at the employee's discretion. It is also advisable to provide training both before and after the employee is on the assignment. Such approaches maximize learning and adaptation to the culture.

Finally, no training program can be complete without adequate evaluation. Experts suggest that programs be evaluated regularly. It is also advisable to use multiple measures of both success and failure. Best practices suggest that successful companies incorporate failure factors such as delayed productivity, lost opportunities, etc. Additionally, employees receiving training should be surveyed to determine their level of satisfaction and improved performance resulting from the training. Finally, human resource management departments of multinationals need to assess whether the cross-cultural training is being applied to the actual work setting.

CHAPTER REVIEW

In this chapter, we discussed how crucial it is to understand cultures and cross-cultural differences. Understanding of culture is becoming more important as the world becomes more global. Not only do companies get a better understanding of their markets and consumers if they have a better understanding of cultures, but their employees also perform better when sent on international assignments. Given the growth of international trade and cross-border operations, no company is immune to these forces, and you will benefit from understanding culture.

To understand how countries differ culturally, we looked at two of the most popular cultural frameworks. The Hofstede framework is certainly the one that has received the most attention and proposes that countries differ mostly on four cultural dimensions. However, we also integrated more recent research by considering the Global Leadership and Organizational Behavior (GLOBE) studies and two additional dimensions. We discussed many international business implications of these cultural differences.

One of the most important ways that national culture affects international business operations is through the business culture. We considered some of the most important cultural differences and implications for business culture. We also emphasized business etiquette as one of the important manifestations of a country's business culture.

We examined some of the dangers of making broad generalizations using these cultural dimensions. The best cultural students stay open-minded and are very careful about their interpretations. Finally, we examined some of the popular types of cross-cultural training and some of the best practices regarding design, delivery and evaluation of such programs.

DISCUSSION QUESTIONS

1. Discuss some of the major reasons why it is important to understand national culture.
2. Discuss three of Hofstede's national culture dimensions. What are some of the implications of these dimensions for international business?
3. What is future orientation? What can an MNC expect when it decides to invest in a country with high future orientation?
4. What is business culture? Does national culture affect business culture? Discuss some implications of national culture for business culture.
5. Discuss how national culture affects the business culture and the business etiquette in a country.
6. What are cultural paradoxes? How can one prepare against making wrong assessments of culture?
7. How can multinationals prepare their employees to understand cross-cultural differences?

INTERNATIONAL BUSINESS SKILL BUILDER

Designing a Cross-cultural Training Program

Step 1: You have been approached by a large MNC with no operations yet in China or India. Research the selected countries in the popular press and make a list of cultural differences compared to the US.

Step 2: For each cultural difference, discuss some of the implications for someone who will conduct negotiations in that country.

Step 3: For each country, design a training program that will allow a negotiator to prepare him or herself for cross-cultural differences.

Step 4: Discuss how the training program will be different if you are asked to develop a program for expatriates.

 CHAPTER INTERNET ACTIVITY

Visit the Executive Planet website by going to **www.executiveplanet.com**. Explore the business etiquette of the countries listed.

 KEY CONCEPTS

business culture	Hofstede model of national culture
business etiquette	humane orientation
country clusters	individualism
cultural beliefs	low-rigor training methods
cultural norms	low-context languages
cultural paradoxes	masculinity
cultural symbols, stories and rituals	national culture
customs	performance orientation
ethnocentricity	power distance
field experiences	simulations
future orientation	stereotyping
high-rigor training methods	subcultures
high-context languages	uncertainty avoidance

BUSINESS > INTERNATIONAL

TRYING TO DO BUSINESS IN MEXICO, GRINGO STYLE

CASE 7

page 1

Ted Dorman was looking forward to his new assignment as plant manager at a newly formed American–Mexican joint venture in Guadalajara, Mexico. The American company, Sterling Metal, produced hardware and decorative fixtures for furniture manufacturers in the United States and Mexico. The new joint venture was an attempt to lower labor costs by operating in Mexico.

Ted had worked at Sterling Metal since graduating from college with a degree in accounting. He had worked his way up in the company through accounting, and eventually shifted his career focus to production. Ted found the challenges of managing the production function very interesting, and he was successful in this area. His position at the new company, SterMexicana, would be a promotion for him, and he looked forward to the opportunity of building a new company.

Although Ted had not worked outside the United States before, he felt confident that his managerial abilities would transfer "south of the border." He and his wife enjoyed vacationing in Cancun and they both liked Mexican food, so the idea of spending a few years building a new company in Mexico appealed to him. Ted's wife, Kim, was not as excited about the move, since she and their two small children would have to leave family and friends. Kim would also probably not be working in Mexico, as she had done in the United States.

Before the move, both Ted and Kim read travel books on Mexico and visited Guadalajara to select suitable housing. While Kim had reservations about the move, she felt that it would be a good opportunity for Ted and that she and the children would learn to adapt to their new surroundings. After all, she reasoned, they were only planning on living in Mexico for two years, just long enough for Ted to get the plant up and running and profitable. None of the Dormans spoke Spanish fluently; however, Kim thought that she could get by, since she had taken three years of Spanish in high school. She had heard that Guadalajara was home to a large expatriate community, and that she could isolate herself and the children from Mexican culture if she felt the need. Ted would be working with English-speakers mostly, and many people at the plant could do translating for him. A number of SterMexicana managers had been to the United States and were familiar with its culture. Ted and Kim concluded that cultural adaptation would not be difficult, and no matter how hard the assignment, its short duration was manageable.

When the family arrived in Guadalajara, Manuel Angel Menendez Mata met them at the airport. Manuel would be Ted's Mexican counterpart, acting in the official capacity of assistant plant manager and unofficially as a cultural mentor. Ted and Kim were surprised by the warmth and friendliness of Manuel and his

. . .

wife Adriana, and they felt very welcomed by their new Mexican friends. Over the next few days Manuel and Adriana helped the new expatriates get settled in and become familiar with their new home. Ted appreciated the personal attention Manuel was giving him and his family; however, Ted was anxious to begin discussing the needs of the new business. It sometimes seemed to Ted that Manuel didn't care to discuss the business and that he was not very excited about the new opportunity. Manuel seemed more interested in showing Ted and his family the city and discussing its history, politics, and culture.

Once the Dorman family had settled in, Ted was able to turn his attention toward the business. He had many matters to attend to, including a review of the preliminary work Manuel had done in securing the facility, hiring a workforce, and establishing an organizational structure. Manuel explained what he had done and how it would work well. He predicted that the new plant would be fully functional in less than two weeks. Ted was very impressed with Manuel's work and looked forward to the opening of the plant.

During their many conversations, Ted felt that Manuel was very friendly and polite but that he was a bit too formal and not very relaxed. Manuel wore a suit and tie, even when Ted told him that a more casual form of dress would be appropriate. Ted stated that he had no intention of ever wearing a tie the whole time he would be in Mexico. Manuel sometimes referred to Ted as "Mr Dorman," even though Ted had instructed him to call him by his first name. During their meetings with outside business associates, Ted noticed that Manuel was even more formal. Manuel, who had visited the United States many times and spoke English very well, understood that Americans were more relaxed when it came to such matters, but he was not happy when Ted began to call him "Manny." Manuel was also unhappy with Ted's refusal to recognize his title, *Licenciado* (licensed one), and that he sometimes referred to him as Senor Mata.

Although things seemed to be progressing toward the opening of the plant, Ted began to worry that Manuel's estimate of when the plant would be functional was too optimistic. Manuel insisted that everything was on schedule and that there would be no problems. However, it did become obvious as the days went by that the plant was not going to be ready as Manuel had promised. Ted felt that he had been misled by Manny and that he would have to explain to his superiors back in the US why the plant was not going to open on schedule. Manuel finally admitted that some problems had developed with work permits, but he assured Ted that the plant would be operational in an additional week's time. The plant finally opened five weeks past the scheduled date.

This delay had caused tension between Manuel and Ted, and Ted felt that he could not trust Manuel. Manuel felt that Ted was too impatient, and that he was not sensitive enough to the problems sometimes found in conducting business in Mexico. Manuel complained to a friend that Ted was trying to do business in Mexico "gringo style." He offered as an example the failed attempt Ted had made to establish a business relationship with a new supplier. Manuel had arranged for a business lunch between Ted, himself, and representatives from a well-respected metals supplier. Manuel explained how Ted offended the Mexican businessmen by

. . .

attempting to get down to business quickly. The supplier's representatives felt that Ted was too concerned about business matters, especially price, and that he was rushing to close a deal. They were also offended when Manuel offered to take the visiting businessmen on a tour of the city and show them some important cultural sites and Ted refused to come along. Ted later told Manuel that he felt that the suppliers were not really serious about getting SterMexicana's business, and that if they wanted to do business with the company, they would have to send only one representative to his office with samples and a price list. Ted told Manuel that he would no longer spend hours discussing politics, sports, and history without any consideration given to the actual business deal.

The plant had been functioning for about six months without any serious problems when Ted received word from corporate headquarters that the plant needed to improve its efficiency. The quality of the product was considered acceptable, but the American managers were disappointed with the productivity of the plant. Sterling's main incentive for investing in Mexico was the desire to reduce its labor costs and improve its overall operational efficiency. Ted worried that his career mobility was in serious jeopardy if he did not make major improvements. With this in mind, he began to look more carefully at Manuel's work.

From the beginning Ted had turned over to Manuel the day-to-day responsibility for running the plant, but he now felt that he would have to intervene and make some significant changes. After analyzing the situation, Ted concluded that three major changes should be made. He proposed to Manuel that an incentive pay system be introduced, that a more participative approach to decision making be implemented, and that a number of workers be fired.

The productivity level of the plant was considered low by American standards, and Ted felt that there was simply no incentive for workers to do more than the minimum level of work. He proposed a pay-for-performance plan in which workers would essentially be paid on a piece-rate basis. The workers would also be given more responsibility for planning and organizing their work, and in some cases even planning their own schedules. Ted felt that a more flexible scheduling system would eliminate the excessive time off requested by many workers to handle family matters. Ted also created a list of the lowest-performing workers and instructed Manuel to fire all of them immediately. Since the unemployment rate was much higher in Mexico than in the United States, Ted reasoned that he would have no problem replacing the workers.

Manuel was stunned by what he was hearing from Ted. Manuel was upset, first, that Ted had chosen to invade his areas of responsibility, and he was further upset by Ted's recommendations. Manuel felt that Ted was being too aggressive and insensitive in labor relations matters, and that his recommendations would not be successful in Mexico. He told Ted that there would be problems with these proposed changes; however, Ted did not seem to want to listen.

Although Manuel did not agree with the recommendations, he did as Ted had instructed and began by firing some of the employees Ted had targeted as low performers. He then implemented the pay-for-performance plan and attempted

. . .

to explain how it would work. Most workers felt confused by the complex, flexible working hours plan, which involved basic quotas, a two-tiered pay system, and a time-borrowing option which could be used for personal time off, such as doctor's appointments. Manuel simplified the plan so that workers could go home when they had met their quota, or they could continue to work for additional compensation at a slightly lower per-unit rate. Ted felt that workers would be willing to work longer hours even at a reduced rate if their total compensation would rise. After all, he reasoned, "Mexico is a dirt-poor country and people really need money." Finally, Manuel told the plant supervisors about the plan to empower factory workers and allow them some of the decision-making authority that the supervisors had exercised in the past.

Ted had high hopes that his recommendations for change would produce significant improvements at SterMexicana. He was aware that Mexican culture was different from his; however, he felt that business activities were for the most part universal and that efficiency was not a cultural issue. Ted felt that the proposed changes would result in an immediate improvement in overall operating efficiency.

Slowly, however, Ted began to realize that problems were developing with his recommendations. The first problem he confronted was notification that severance pay would have to be paid to the employees he had recently fired. Ted was unaware, and Manuel did not mention, that Mexican law does not operate in the same way as US law, in which workers are considered to be hired at will and subject to at-will termination. Ted was also surprised to learn that not all the employees he had targeted for termination had, in fact, been fired. After investigating the situation further, he discovered that five of the employees whom he had instructed to be fired were still working for the company. Ted was shocked to learn that the five employees were close relatives of Manuel. When confronted with this fact, Manuel just shrugged his shoulders and told Ted that he could not bring himself to fire them.

Although Ted was upset with Manuel's insubordination, he was far more concerned with the lack of any productivity gains at the plant. He was told that most workers did complete their tasks more quickly under the incentive plan; however, they elected to go home rather than work additional hours for more money. Ted was confused by this behavior and asked some of the supervisors to explain it. They didn't provide satisfactory answers so Ted decided that he should conduct interviews with the employees themselves. Working through an interpreter, Ted asked workers about their jobs and what he could do to make them more productive. He was frustrated by the lack of responses he was getting from the employees. When Ted probed more deeply he discovered that the supervisors had not implemented the participative management practices he had ordered.

Faced with poor operating results during the first year of operation, Ted wondered if the decision to take the job in Mexico had been a mistake. To make matters worse, Ted's family was very unhappy about living in Mexico. Ted had been working long hours at the plant and had basically discounted the complaints he

. . .

CASE 7

page 5

had heard from his wife and children. At this point he began to feel that perhaps they were right in their frequent criticisms of Mexican culture. With over a year left in his assignment in Mexico, Ted felt frustrated and wondered what he should do next.

CASE DISCUSSION POINTS

1. What mistakes did Ted make in his management of SterMexicana?
2. Is Manuel responsible for any of the difficulties presented in the case?
3. What should Ted do now to correct the situation?

Sources: R. Malat, 1996, *Passport Mexico*, San Rafael, CA: World Trade Press; P. Beamish, A. Morrison, and P. Rosenweig, 1997, *International Management*, Chicago: Irwin; R Sanyal, 2001, *International Management: A Strategic Perspective*, Upper Saddle River, NJ: Prentice Hall; J. Scarborough, 2001, *The Origins of Cultural Differences and Their Impact on Management*, Westport, CT: Quorum.

Case prepared by Charles A. Rarick

8 The Strategic Implications of Economic, Legal, and Religious Institutions for International Business

After reading this chapter you should be able to:

- Understand the importance of institutions and their impact on both individuals and MNCs.

- Know the basic political and economic systems and implications for international business.

- Appreciate the various legal systems around the world.

- Understand political risk and ways companies can prepare for political risk.

- Learn about the world's key religions and implications for multinational operations.

The Preview IB Strategic Insight portrays the environment facing anyone interested in doing business in China. As another example, consider that Starbucks is currently facing major opposition to its store operating in the "Forbidden City." Chinese officials believe that the store denigrates Chinese culture, and many government officials are pressuring the government to close the store. Understanding of international business is not complete without an adequate understanding of the environment facing any business. Specifically, important elements of the environment such as the political, legal and religious environment are crucial. The Preview IB Strategic Insight shows that both the political environment (shift from a communist regime to a market-based economy) and the legal environment are playing important roles in shaping the business environment facing those doing business in China.

This chapter contains four major sections. In the first section, you are introduced to a basic definition of institutions and the effects they have on both organizations and

Legal Environment in China

China's economy has only recently been progressing from a communist regime to a more market-driven economy. Under communism, the government had a critical role in all business matters. It controlled production and decided where resources would be going. It even controlled employment conditions and hiring and firing of workers. For instance, the 1950s Iron Rice Bowl policy provided workers with the right to lifetime employment and a wide range of social programs such as housing, schools, and medical care.

However, as China has been transitioning to a more market-based economy where economic decisions are governed by demand and supply, MNCs have faced significant hurdles. For instance, consider that China has presented investors with significant challenges related to government interference, such as allowing investments only in some industries. Foreign investors have often found it very difficult to predict, verify, and even control such interference. To further complicate the problem, greater decentralization and deregulation has meant that investors also have to deal with local governmental interference as well as interference from the central government agencies.

Recent events, however, suggest that things may be changing. China's leadership have been working

hard to create a legal system that supports a market-based economy. For instance, they recently considered passing legislation to give individuals the right and protection to their own private property. Although many individuals own their houses and businesses, there has not been much legal protection for such ownership. The government has routinely confiscated land, and the new property legislation will provide a more stable environment for private ownership, a critical element of a market-based economy.

The Chinese government is also considering legislation to modify the taxation structure so that both domestic and foreign companies pay the same rate of taxes. In the past, the Chinese government provided hefty tax breaks to encourage foreign investment. However, many domestic companies have complained about the unfair tax situation and the government is now set to have equal tax treatment.

Sources: Based on Andrew Batson, 2007, "China legal system gains focus in a new economy," *Wall Street Journal*, March 2, p. 10; Maureen Fan, 2007, "China looks to protect private property," *The Washington Post*, March 8, p. A16.

individuals. In the second section, you will be exposed to critical elements of the political environment. In the third section we will look at some of the key aspects of the legal system and the different types of legal systems around the world. Finally, we will examine some of the world's most important religions, another key institution that affects international business. We discuss key international business implications of each institution.

After reading this chapter you should understand some of the key institutions affecting international business. You will be able to comprehend some of the key elements of a country's political environment through an understanding of the various types of economic systems. You should be able to recognize some of the ways legal systems are different around the world. You should also be able to understand some of the basic religions practiced by people around the world. Finally, you should understand the implications of these various aspects of the environment for international business.

Social Institutions

social institutions
complex of positions, roles, norms and values lodged in particular types of social structures

A social institution is "a complex of positions, roles, norms, and values lodged in particular types of social structures and organizing relatively stable patterns of human resources with respect to fundamental problems in . . . sustaining viable societal structures within a given environment".[1] In other words, similar to national culture, social institutions provide boundaries and norms that guide both companies and individuals regarding appropriate behavior.

Why should you be concerned about social institutions? Chapter 7 discussed the many cultural differences impacting international business. However, an understanding of a country's business environment is not complete without an appropriate understanding of social institutions such as the economic system and the legal and religious environment. Each of these social institutions has an important impact on how business is conducted in the country. Without an understanding of these social institutions, it is difficult to have a complete understanding of the environment facing the multinational.

Furthermore, as we discussed in Chapter 7, understanding a country only through culture has some drawbacks. Many of Hofstede's cultural dimensions are outdated, while the GLOBE project also provides a static view of culture. However, changes in many countries today suggest that institutions are gradually changing the way things are done in a country. Such changes suggest that, in addition to an appropriate understanding of culture, we also need to get a solid understanding of institutions in order to better appreciate a country's environment. Consider the IB Strategic Insight opposite about the fate of the Japanese "salaryman."

As the IB Strategic Insight shows, institutional changes have important influences on both individuals and multinationals. In this case, many of these institutional changes could potentially change the traditional Japanese cultural expectations consistent with high levels of collectivism. Institutions thus complement cultural understanding by providing additional understanding of what is appropriate and what is not acceptable. In the next section, we consider one of the most critical institutions, namely the economic system.

The Japanese "Salaryman"

For decades, being employed as a Japanese "salaryman," the equivalent of a Japanese white-collar employee, was an aspiration for most Japanese. Such a position denoted success and guarantee for long-term stability. Most university graduates chose a company and devoted their lives to the company. The typical salaryman started work at 9 a.m. and would often work until midnight. Furthermore, supervisors would also often take their subordinates out for a drink numerous times per week, adding two or three more hours to the workday. Many of the older-generation Japanese believed that the drinking was critical in order to strengthen camaraderie among co-workers. Such camaraderie is necessary to reach consensus decisions that equate with company performance.

This lifetime devotion of the salarymen to the company is not one-sided. In fact, most companies would provide lifetime employment for their employees. In addition, the company provides a salary that is based on seniority, increasing rapidly when employees reach the age of 50. At the age of 50, it is expected that the employee's expenses are likely to increase as his children leave for university. The company also provides numerous perks and benefits, including housing and the use of hot spring resorts.

Consistent with cultural expectations of high Japanese collectivism, the company provides for the salaryman and his family. In return, the salaryman devotes his life loyally to the company.

Recent institutional changes suggest that the salaryman concept will likely fade. For instance, because of mergers and acquisitions, fewer companies are able to offer lifetime employment as competition forces them to employ a more flexible workforce. More companies are hiring part-time or temporary employees instead of the corporate salarymen. Furthermore, as the Japanese population is getting older, there is a heavy strain on the pension system, with fewer people making contributions while more people need access to their pensions. In an effort to reward individual performance, many companies are now basing compensation on a merit system rather than the more usual seniority-based system. The younger Japanese generation is also rebelling against this system. They are less likely to accept that the company and work play a central role in their lives.

Source: Based on *The Economist*, 2008, "Sayonara, salaryman," January 5, pp. 68–70.

Economic Systems

The **economic system** refers to the structures and processes that guide the conduct of business activities that lead to the production of goods and services consumed by the members of a society. The economic system can be characterized according to the degree to which the government or private individuals are allowed to make economic decisions guiding production. At one extreme, the government owns and controls all production resources, thereby resulting in a centrally planned economy. At the other extreme, private individuals are allowed to make the majority of economic decisions, thus describing a capitalist society. Because of the differences in terms of who makes economic and production decisions, multinationals need to be aware of these issues when engaged in international business.

economic system
structures and processes that guide conduct of business

Types of Economic Systems

capitalist or market economy
economic system where private individuals make economic and production decisions

The **capitalist or market economy** refers to an economic system where production activities are "decentralized to private-property-rights holders (or their agents) who carry out these activities for the purpose of making profits in a competitive market".[2] In other words, in capitalist societies private individuals make most economic and production decisions and the government does not interfere in such matters. Examples of capitalist economies include the United Kingdom, Canada, Hong Kong, and the USA.

socialist or command economy
economic system where the government owns production resources and makes production decisions

In contrast, the **socialist or command economy** is one where production resources are owned by the state and production decisions are centrally coordinated.[3] In such societies, the government owns and controls all resources. The government decides what will be produced, in what quantities, and the price at which the products will be sold. Instead of allowing the invisible forces of the market to dictate production, as is the case in a market economy, the government's hand plays a very visible role in all production matters. In its most extreme form, the command economy is found in communist societies. There remain few command economies today and examples include Cuba and North Korea.

Capitalism and socialism are the extremes of the economic system spectrum. In reality, many countries fall in between these two extremes. Such economies are known as the **mixed economy**, which combines aspects of the capitalist and socialist economic systems. In such economies, the state determines that some sectors of the economy cannot be run by private interests and thus intervenes and takes control of such sectors (e.g. health care and education). The state makes resource allocation and production decisions. Countries such as Sweden, France, Denmark, Italy and India are examples of mixed economies.

mixed economy
economic system that combines elements of the capitalist and socialist economies

Mixed economies ideally combine advantages of the market-based and centrally planned economies. Thus, while private decisions about production are allowed, the government controls those sectors that it sees as critical to national stability and security. However, many countries have found that government control of specific sectors has led to waste, economic inefficiencies, and lack of accountability and responsibility regarding cost control. The more recent evidence thus suggests that more countries are moving more towards market-based economies.

International Business Implications of Economic Systems

privatization
process where government assets and resources are sold to private individuals

One aspect of this move towards more market-based economies is **privatization**, whereby former government assets and resources are sold to private individuals. Privatization of state businesses is seen as an effective way to encourage companies to become more efficient. However, privatization is not without its dangers. Consider the case of the Czech Republic and its privatization efforts. In an effort to make formerly state-owned assets available to ordinary Czech citizens, the government started a scheme that sold vouchers that could be converted into shares of companies on the new Prague Stock Exchange. However, most ordinary citizens did not have much experience investing and lost their money through various programs devised by those who did have experience investing. One notorious fraudster, Kozeny, created a fund and encouraged ordinary Czechs to invest in it, promising that he would increase their investment ten times. However, he eventually fled the Czech Republic owing 240,000 investors over US$ 403 million.[4]

However, despite the dangers, privatization has been very beneficial to companies. Private owners are given a new powerful incentive to turn around formerly state-run businesses, namely profits. In fact, emerging markets present tremendous potential as the massive privatization wave continues. As the pace of privatization slows in stable countries such as Poland, the Czech Republic, and Hungary, other countries such as Slovakia, Romania, Bulgaria, Serbia, and Croatia all present tremendous opportunities. For instance, foreign investors have been able to participate in privatization efforts of the Bratislava and Kosice airports and the local electricity provider in Slovakia.[5] The banking sector in Romania also represents tremendous opportunities for foreign investors.

Economic systems thus have important implications for international business. At a fundamental level, MNCs should expect an environment conducive to business in more market-based or capitalist economies. In such economies, governmental interference is minimal and MNCs can operate freely within the boundaries of the law. In such countries, labor regulation also tends to be minimal and multinationals usually face a favorable labor market. However, that's not the case for many of the mixed economies. Decades of job security and fair treatment in the labor market have resulted in environments where workers expect some rights to be protected. Consider the following Country Focus on France.

France

COUNTRY FOCUS

Although France has a mixed economy, its economic system has mostly been one where the government has had a major role to play in terms of economic decisions. Decades of an economic system focused on protecting worker interests have resulted in a situation where most individuals see certain forms of worker protection and rights as guarantees. However, beyond the effects of the economic environment, students in high schools are also taught that the perfectly competitive market in capitalism is inherently impossible. Most economics lectures tend to focus on how the state or the government can intervene to address the limitations of a market-based economy. In fact, some teachers will actually avoid using the term "capitalism," as it has such negative connotations, and prefer the term "market economy."

Given the above, it is not surprising to see resistance against measures that seem to target traditional employee rights. For instance, France saw major demonstrations in its attempt to introduce labor flexibility by making it easier to fire young workers. The French population thinks very fondly of the post World War II welfare state, where the government's role was to use its visible hand to protect workers by exercising authority and control over exploiting companies. In fact, polls around the world show that the French were the only group of people to disagree with the statement that the "free market economy is the best system." While around 71 percent of respondents in the US and 74 percent of respondents in China agreed with the statement, only 33 percent of the French respondents agreed with the statement.

Source: Based on K. Bennhold, 2006, "Economics, French style. Looking behind the rebellion on jobs law," *International Herald Tribune*, April 8, p. 1.

As the Country/Regional Focus shows, MNCs operating in mixed economies have to be aware of some of the resistance against free markets. In many cases, these mixed economies had governments that were involved in protecting workers. MNCs need to be aware of the labor market environment that they face.

Another critical international business implication pertaining to economic systems applies to transition economies. **Transition economies** are those societies that are moving from socialism to a more market-based system. The post 1980s saw a large number of countries in Russia, Eastern Europe, and Asia (i.e. China and Vietnam) undergo governmental efforts to promote capitalism. For most MNCs, such open-market policies have presented incredible opportunities as they provide these companies with new markets and access to skilled but relatively cheap labor. For example, Nokia is currently setting up a plant in the city of Cluj, Romania. The company chose that location because it will have access to a plentiful supply of workers, including a steady flow of engineering graduates from the local well-regarded university.[6] It has been very easy for Nokia to find willing workers as individuals from all over Romania queued up for its job fair.

An important challenge for most MNCs in transition economies has been to understand the lingering effects of communism and its effects on workers and companies. Under socialism, most enterprises were factories with no need for cost control, lacking strategic planning, accounting or marketing departments. The government often guaranteed the survival and inefficiencies of these firms by setting up prices that were not accurate reflections of costs. Banks also were managed according to the needs of central planners, where loans were

transition economies
economies that are transitioning from socialism to capitalism

Doing Business in Russia

IB STRATEGIC INSIGHT

Russia remains one of the most difficult places to do business. A recent survey of multinationals in over 50 cities placed Moscow as the worse place in the world to do business. As in many transition economies, setting up a business requires significant paperwork and many businesses consider such efforts as wasted time. Furthermore, because of the lack of clear rules and guidelines, government officials and bureaucrats will often make decisions based on their whims and personal relationships. Such lack of clear guidance is often a major deterrent for multinationals interested in investing in Russia.

However, despite these significant challenges, many multinationals are finding that Russia can present a very profitable market. For instance, Ford and GM are now the top-selling foreign brands of car in Russia. Procter & Gamble (P&G) also sells more than 70 of its brands there. P&G was even able to make significant investments into a formerly state-owned plant to make it the leading detergent manufacturing plant. As such, both companies have made significant investments in the Russian economy and have large numbers of Russian employees. Even the services company Deloitte-Touche is hiring hundreds of Russian college graduates as it has enjoyed double-digit growth rates recently.

Source: Based on Alan M. Field, 2007, "Russia in the fast lane," *Journal of Commerce*, September 3, p. 1.

often made to enterprises on the basis of connections and personal relationships rather than credit-worthiness.

These traditional approaches to doing business have resulted in significant hurdles for many of the transition economies. For example, workers may not necessarily trust MNCs as they no longer have the same job security as in the past. Furthermore, significant effort has to be devoted to encourage workers to trust each other to function effectively in teams. Multinationals also have to deal with inefficient financial systems and corrupt individuals. Transition economies also still experience significant governmental interference. Consider the IB Strategic Insight opposite.

As the IB Strategic Insight shows, although transition markets present challenges, these challenges can be dealt with. To address such challenges, MNCs operating in transition economies have to implement measures to turn around inefficient companies into profitable ones. Additionally, managers' thinking has to be changed completely so that they understand management functions and the necessity to be cost-effective. Furthermore, employees have to be treated with care to make the smooth transition from a secure job to a labor market influenced by the market. Finally, the financial system and firms (and price) have to be left unregulated to more accurately reflect the forces of the market.

Economic systems thus have many important implications for international business. Different economic systems present different environments regarding decision making for resources and production. However, one other important component of the economic system is the degree of governmental interference in the conduct of business. In that context, MNCs may consider the **index of economic freedom**, which refers to "the absence of government coercion or constraint on the production, distribution, or consumption of goods and services beyond the extent necessary for citizens to protect and maintain liberty itself."[7] Since 1995, the Heritage Foundation, a US-based research foundation, has been

index of economic freedom
index reflecting the ease of doing business in any given country

Exhibit 8.1 **Index of Economic Freedom**

Free	Mostly Free	Moderately Free	Mostly Unfree	Repressed
Hong Kong	Luxembourg	Czech Republic	Fiji	Togo
Singapore	Canada	Mauritius	Senegal	Venezuela
Australia	Chile	South Korea	Poland	Bangladesh
USA	Netherlands	France	Ghana	Belarus
New Zealand	Japan	Thailand	India	Angola
United Kingdom	Bahamas	Namibia	China	Turkmenistan
Ireland	Taiwan	Peru	Russia	Libya
	Spain	Switzerland	Algeria	Cuba
	Norway	Tunisia	Vietnam	Sierra Leone
	Finland	Lebanon	Nigeria	Burundi

Source: Based on Heritage Foundation Index of Economic Freedom, http://www.heritage.org

constructing the index. The index includes ten indicators, ranging from trade policy (i.e. the degree to which the government hinders free trade through tariffs), taxation policies, and the level of governmental intervention in the economy to property rights (freedom to accumulate private property) and regulation (i.e. ease of obtaining a business license).

Exhibit 8.1 shows selected countries and where they stand on the index of economic freedom. Representative countries are listed for each of the five categories of economic freedom, namely those nations that are (1) free, (2) mostly free, (3) moderately free, (4) mostly "unfree," and (5) repressed. MNCs can use the index to determine their presence in different countries. Obviously, they can expect higher levels of difficulty as they move into countries with less economic freedom.

In this section, you were exposed to critical aspects of the economic system and how they influence business operations. In the next section, we consider another critical institution, namely the legal system.

Legal Systems

legal system
represents the unique
systems of regulations, rules
and laws of a country

The **legal system** refers to the unique systems of regulations, laws and rules that affect the choices made by individuals in any society and that govern the ways these individuals are responsible for their decisions and actions. For the MNC, of more importance is the international business law system representing the law and rules of any nation that affect the types of business decisions made in that country.[8] Consider the following IB Strategic Insight.

| Multinational Business Decisions | IB STRATEGIC INSIGHT |

MNCs and individuals alike regularly face decisions with legal implications. Consider the following examples:

- Through your international website, you find that there is significant demand for your product in Asia. You decide that it may be useful to set up a sales office in Singapore. However, you wonder how easy it will be to set up the sales office in Singapore.
- You work for a multinational that has operations in India. However, you find that if operations are moved to China, your company can enjoy significantly cheaper labor costs. Furthermore, unlike India, where most workers belong to trade unions, you find that Chinese

workers seldom belong to unions. You ponder about the ease of closing the plant in India and opening a new plant in China.

- You currently have a contract with a sales distributor in Houston, Texas. You clearly specify that if performance sales goals are not met, you will terminate the contract. You also know that there are interests from French distributors for your products. However, you are unsure whether you can have a similar contract with a French distributor.
- You decide that you want to start a business in Indonesia. You are curious about how easy it will be compared to starting a business in the USA.

The IB Strategic Insight shows how important it is to understand the laws and regulations in any society if one wants to be able to compete internationally. Consider, for example, that in India, it is extremely hard to fire workers. Similarly, in France a multinational may be liable to specific laws that make it more difficult to terminate the contract.[9] Finally, consider that an entrepreneur needs to go through 12 procedures that may take up to 97 days if they want to start a business in Indonesia.[10] Ignoring aspects of the legal environment can be very costly and may doom the business from the start. In this section, you will be exposed to some of the most popular legal systems around the world, namely common law, civil law, and Islamic law. We then look at some international business implications of these legal systems.

Types of Legal Systems

Common law originated in England and is practiced by many of the former British colonies, including the US. **Common law** is based on the concept of precedent, whereby the law is applied after an examination of past cases.[11] In common law, the judge tends to be very neutral and will allow lawyers for parties to demonstrate their cases. The lawyers will examine prior cases and make their arguments to convince a jury of their position. In common law, the choice of lawyers plays a critical role in successfully defending a case.[12]

common law
legal system based on the concept of legal precedence

Civil law, which can be traced back to the Romans, is based on a very detailed set of rules and regulations that forms part of a country's legal code. Cases are decided based on the legal code and there is usually no interpretation of laws according to previous cases. In contrast to common law, where the judge is more neutral, in civil law the judge is a key element in cases, taking on the role of lawyer in deciding what information is to be presented in deciding a course. The judge typically determines the extent of guilt. The jury is not used in civil law countries. Because of the use of established codes, civil law often tends to ignore specific circumstances of cases.

civil law
legal system based on detailed set of rules and regulations that form part of the legal code

Another legal tradition practiced in many nations today is known as Islamic law. **Islamic law** is based on the Shari'ah, the Law taken from the Qur'an, Islam's sacred texts. Islamic countries believe that all humans must live according to the structures prescribed in the Qur'an. The Qur'an expresses Islamic ethic and the ethical duties in life. However, as you will see later, it also contains rules that apply to conduct of business, such as general guidance regarding the need to honor contracts and appropriate behaviors in commercial transactions. We will discuss Islamic law and implications for international business in greater depth later when we examine religions.

Islamic law
legal tradition based on the Qur'an, Islam's sacred text

Exhibit 8.2 shows selected countries and their respective legal system.

Although one should be aware of the limits of generalizing legal system differences around the world, it is important to recognize the implications of a country's particular legal system on international business. For instance, it is usual for business contracts in common law countries to be very lengthy. The latter is necessary to ensure that all contingencies are covered. It is therefore important for MNCs to devote significant resources to understand a common law country's legal system through legal advice. Because of the need to interpret laws based on precedent, multinationals typically employ legal teams to navigate the legal environment.

Exhibit 8.2 **Legal Systems Around the World**

Common Law	Civil Law
Australia	Armenia
Bahamas	Azerbaijan
Cyprus	Belarus
Fiji	Belgium
Hong Kong	Cameroon
India	Denmark
Ireland	France
Japan	Luxembourg
Mexico	Montenegro
New Zealand	Panama
Tonga	Portugal
United Kingdom	Russia
USA	Serbia
Zambia	Taiwan

Source: Based on CIA World Factbook,
http://cia.gov/cia/publications/factbook

In civil law countries, the legal system is less confrontational compared to common law countries. Instead of lawyers colliding to interpret the law, there is more reliance on written rules and regulations. As a consequence, fewer resources tend to be devoted to understanding the law. For instance, multinationals tend to be more concerned about precise wording in contracts to ensure consistency with the relevant codified laws.

Other Aspects of the Legal Environment: The "Doing Business" Project

"Doing Business" project
project undertaken by the World Bank providing important information about the ease of conducting business in various nations

While it is difficult to provide a comprehensive treatment of differences in the legal systems around the world, the World Bank, through its **"Doing Business" project**, provides valuable insight into the key issues that need to be taken into consideration when doing business in any nation. The World Bank provides objective measures of the various aspects of the legal infrastructure in a society. Specifically, the World Bank considers various aspects of the regulative environment of any society. Here, you are exposed to four key aspects pertaining to international business, namely starting a business, employing workers, getting credit and enforcing contracts.

Any form of involvement in a new country requires an understanding of the various legal and bureaucratic requirements that need to be fulfilled. The "Starting a Business" measure provides an objective view of the various issues

an entrepreneur or multinational needs to consider when starting a commercial or industrial business with over 50 employees. It includes the number of procedures that are needed to register a firm, the time spent for each procedure, the expenses associated with each procedure and the minimum capital required as a percentage of income. This gives a good indication of what you may face when you decide to open a business in any selected country. Consider the following Small Business Insight.

A second important aspect of the regulatory environment is dealing with the hiring and firing of workers. Most MNCs need to be aware of the various regulations pertaining to employing workers. This measure considers areas such

Where to Start a Business

IB SMALL BUSINESS INSIGHT

You have developed a product prototype that you believe will do very well. You also believe that you can manufacture and sell the product anywhere in the world. Where do you start your business and set up a plant? Consider Exhibit 8.3.

As you can see, starting businesses in countries in Latin America and North Africa tends to be more difficult. For instance, starting a business in the Latin American/Caribbean region can take an average of around ten procedures, with each procedure lasting over 70 days.

Similarly, both Latin America and the Middle East/North Africa region have the highest costs associated with starting a business. In contrast, the members of the Organization for Economic Cooperation and Development (OECD), including most industrialized nations such as Canada, the UK, Germany, Italy, and the US, among others, have environments that are very conducive to setting up new businesses.

Source: Based on Doing Business website, www.doingbusiness.org.

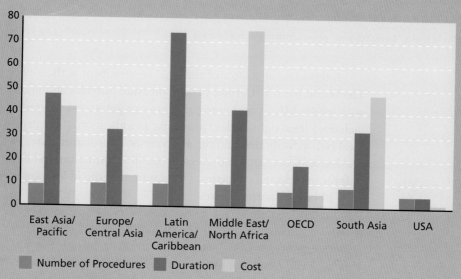

Exhibit 8.3 "Starting a Business" Index

Source: Based on World Bank's "Doing Business" project, http://doingbusiness.org

as the difficulty of hiring workers, the difficulty of expanding or reducing current workers' hours, the difficulty of laying off workers, and the cost of firing workers. As you will see in Chapter 14, properly understanding the labor force regulatory environment is important to developing an effective workforce. Exhibit 8.4 shows selected countries with the difficulty of hiring index and the difficulty and expense of firing workers. Higher numbers indicate higher difficulties of hiring or firing.

As Exhibit 8.4 shows, many of the more socialist European countries, such as Sweden, France, and Italy, pose more difficulties with regards to hiring or firing workers. It is also interesting to note that the emerging economies such as China and India also have fairly rigid labor regulations. In contrast, countries such as the US and Australia have very flexible work environments where workers can be hired or fired easily. MNCs therefore need to be aware of such issues if they decide to hire employees in any society.

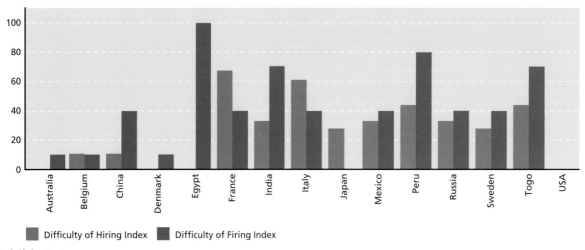

Exhibit 8.4 **"Employing Worker" Index**

Note: No values mean that there are no difficulties in hiring or filing in the noted countries.

Source: Based on World Bank's "Doing Business" project, http://doingbusiness.org

A third crucial aspect of the legal environment is the ability to get credit. The World Bank's "Getting Credit" measure provides an indication of the ease with which MNCs and entrepreneurs can get access to credit. The measure includes a legal rights index, providing an indication of the degree to which the legal system facilitates lending, and a credit information index, which indicates the degree of accuracy and access to credit information. Exhibit 8.5 shows the indexes for selected countries. Please note that the index ranges from 0 to 10, with 10 being a perfect score.

Exhibit 8.5 shows that getting access to credit is much easier in many of the OECD countries, such as the USA, the UK and Japan. However, it is also important to note that a good number of the transition economies, such as the Czech Republic and Hungary, have implemented many legal changes to ensure a more efficient banking system. Such efforts have paid off as many of these countries have an environment that facilitates getting access to credit. In contrast, countries such as India and China still have an underdeveloped credit market.

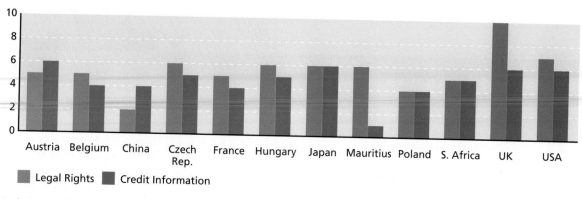

Exhibit 8.5 **"Getting Credit" Index**

Source: Based on World Bank's "Doing Business" project, http://doingbusiness.org

A final indication of a country's legal environment is the degree to which contracts can be enforced. "Enforcing Contracts" provides an indication of the time and resources needed to resolve commercial disputes in courts. Many MNCs use strategic alliances or other forms of agreement to enter a new country. Most of these agreements are based on contracts, and a multinational's ability to have contracts respected is dependent on the degree to which a country enforces these contracts. Exhibit 8.6 shows the number of procedures from the day an individual goes to court until payment, and the number of days it takes to resolve the commercial dispute by region.

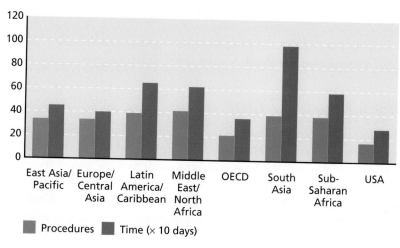

Exhibit 8.6 **"Enforcing Contract" Index**

Source: Based on World Bank's "Doing Business" project, http://doingbusiness.org

Exhibit 8.6 shows that contract enforcement is much more difficult in the South Asian, sub-Saharan Africa and North Africa/Middle East regions. Often these regions have less developed legal systems to deal with business matters. In contrast, the OECD countries, as well as Europe and the US, have a more developed infrastructure to enforce contracts.

As the above section on the legal systems shows, adequate understanding of the legal context in any society is extremely important for any multinational

225

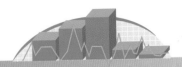

Germany and Alternative Energy

As more countries struggle to wean themselves from non-fossil forms of fuel, Germany is enjoying a global leading position in solar and wind power technology. For instance, Q-Cells, a German company based north of Leipzig, is now the world's leader of the photovoltaic cells widely in use in solar cells. How can a company based in a country that is not viewed as generally sunny be the leader in solar energy technology? More important, how did Germany achieve this global leadership in green energy?

Many experts credit Germany's energy laws as the major reason they have achieved such prominence. The energy laws require that utilities buy energy from renewable sources at premium prices. For instance, anyone with a solar panel on their house can sell the electricity produced back to the utilities and make a significant profit. Such incentives have encouraged the growth of a number of small and larger companies developing energy from renewable sources.

The philosophy behind Germany's law is that major utilities will never bother developing alternative sources of energy as they continue to rely on traditional fossil fuels. Before the law was passed in 2000, the market price for energy from renewable sources was too low to justify the research and development and equipment investment. However, forcing utilities to buy energy from renewable sources has resulted in a significant growth and is now the leading destination for green technology investment (roughly $14 billion in 2007).

Source: Based on M. Blake, 2008, "Germany's key to green energy," *Christian Science Monitor*, August 21, p. 24; *The Economist*, 2008, "German lessons: Renewable energy," April 5, 8574, p. 75.

operating in that country. To provide further evidence of the role of laws and the legal system, consider the IB Sustainability Practices above.

Political Risk

Earlier in this chapter, you read about the various economic and legal systems. One aspect of the combined effects of the economic and legal system in a society is political risk. As such, in this section we look at political risk, some elements of political risk and what companies can do to minimize political risk.

political risk
threat of a country's social, political or economic factors affecting a company's profitability

Political risk refers to the "threat that social, political or economic factors in a foreign country may affect the feasibility and profitability of an organization's global operations".[13] As more multinationals engage in foreign investments, they are being increasingly confronted with political risk. MNCs run the risk of destruction of their foreign plants or even the ability to repatriate currency. Nevertheless, many countries with high levels of political risk often offer the best opportunities.[14] The challenge for the multinational is to accurately predict and manage such risks.

Political risk can impact a multinational negatively on many levels. For instance, political risk can influence the degree to which currency can be freely converted to other currency for use. Host governments may restrict the transfer of local currency into a freely usable currency, thereby limiting the multinational's access to its own capital. Furthermore, host governments can also place conditions on an MNC's ability to control its own plant, thus leading to governmental interference. Additionally, countries with high levels of political risk may also have higher levels of political violence and more contracts breached. Political risk may also influence the degree to which the government has the power or desire to enforce the legal and bureaucratic system to support business operations. Finally, in countries with high political risk, governments may sometimes confiscate a multinational's assets by nationalizing the industry. Host governments may also force multinationals to sell their operations, thus resulting in expropriation. Consider the IB Strategic Insight below.

As the IB Strategic Insight shows, accurately understanding political risk is critical for survival. How can a multinational assess the level of political risk? Various issues contribute to the political risk of any country.[15] For instance, you can examine the degree of political stability, the ease of transitioning to new governments, the freedom of non-governmental institutions such as trade unions, the degree of social unrest, and the level of political violence. Other factors contributing to the level of political risk include issues such as the resilience of the political system, the level of social inequality and unemployment, the level of corruption, the threat of terrorism and other threats to security, and even infrastructure risk.

Political Risk in South America

IB STRATEGIC INSIGHT

Back in the 1990s, Venezuela did not have the necessary capital to exploit its many natural resources. The Venezuelan government encouraged many foreign companies to invest in local key industries such as oil and gas exploration and telecommunications. At one point, there were around 60 companies, many based in the US, operating in the Venezuelan oil sector. These companies would operate the oilfields and sell the oil to the Venezuelan government.

However, things are now changing rapidly with President Hugo Chavez's vision of "twenty-first-century socialism." As the price of oil has risen, Venezuela has enjoyed dramatic growth. The government now wants a bigger share of revenues and it has been forcing multinationals to either sell their stakes in local industries or renegotiate their contracts. Recently, the Venezuelan government gave one year to foreign companies to enter into joint ventures with the Venezuelan government oil company so that the local company would own at least 60 percent of the joint venture. When Total, a French oil company, refused, the Venezuelan government seized the oilfields and started operating both companies. As such, many of the companies such Exxon Mobil, Total and Eni SPA had no recourse but to satisfy the government demands. Verizon was also forced to sell its stakes in local telecommunications operations to the Venezuelan government for $100 million less than the originally agreed price. Similarly, AES, a power company based in Virginia, USA, purchased a stake of around 82 percent in Venezuela's largest electric utility in 2000. However, new laws passed by the Venezuelan Congress forced AES to sell its stakes at $550–$650 million below book value.

Similar changes are taking place in other countries such as Bolivia and Ecuador. New governments intent on nationalizing critical industries will present multinationals with significant political risks.

Source: Based on N. Popovic and A. Lathrop, 2007, "Recovery tactics: Outlines for foreign takeover losses," *Oil & Gas Journal*, June 25, pp. 20–4.

While some companies such as Royal Dutch Shell or AIG have departments dedicated to understanding political risk, other MNCs rely on services provided by assessment firms such as the Economist Intelligence Unit (www.eiu.com) or the Political Risk Services Group (www.prsgroup.com) to determine the level of political risk in a nation. Such information can be very useful as the MNC contemplates expansion in new regions. Furthermore, the index of economic freedom discussed earlier can also provide an idea of the degree to which governmental interference can be expected.

Although accurately assessing a country's political risk can be very tricky, MNCs can be proactive and take some steps to minimize the potential disruption of political risk. Consider the IB Strategic Insight below, which discusses some of the steps a company can take to minimize political risk in China (and any other country).

The IB Strategic Insight provides some critical ways in which a multinational may try to prevent political risk. However, as a last resort, multinationals may also seek arbitration. For instance, in the case of the multinationals that lost their assets in Venezuela, many experts see such occurrences as forced expropriation. However, most countries abide by international laws that prohibit expropriation or unfair compensation. These multinationals can thus resort to international laws to receive adequate compensation for their lost investments.

Political Risk in China

IB STRATEGIC INSIGHT

China presents tremendous opportunities for multinationals. However, China also presents significant political risk in the form of dislocation of large populations, widening incomes, and potential for large industrial accidents that can result in social unrest. How can an MNC or entrepreneur operating in China protect its business from political risk? While accurately predicting political risk is difficult, there are some possible actions that can hedge against such risks. These include:

- Obtaining political risk insurance. Private companies offer insurance against various risks, such as political violence, foreign currency inconvertibility risks, expropriation risks, and other interference with business operations. The US governmental agency Overseas Private Investment Corporation (OPIC) (www.opic.gov) also provides such insurance.
- Creating emergency plans. Any business can anticipate potential disruption by planning for such circumstances.

By having emergency plans in place, an MNC is in a better position to respond to problems associated with political risk.

- Diversifying political risk. Any multinational is strongly advised to have different business activities in different parts of China. Concentrating all activities in one region may make the business more vulnerable.
- Being socially responsible. Companies that are socially responsible and contribute to local charities tend to build stronger relations with local communities. Such efforts may mitigate effects of political risk.
- Having an exit strategy. MNCs must have emergency plans for the eventuality of their needing to leave China. Although China's economy presents opportunities, there are potential long-term difficulties and having a plan to leave rapidly is useful.

Source: Based on I. Bremmer and F. Zakaria, 2006, "Hedging political risk in China," *Harvard Business Review*, November, pp. 22–5.

In the next and final section, we look at religion and its implications for international business.

Religion

Religion, the shared set of beliefs, activities, and institutions based on faith in supernatural forces,[16] remains a critical force in most countries. Although religion has a significant influence on culture, most experts see it as an institution that needs to be examined on its own merit. Most countries are now seeing a strong growth in popularity of religions. For instance, the rise of Islam in many parts of the world, the tremendous growth of Protestantism in Latin America, the sustained influence of Buddhism in Asia, and the continued role of Hinduism in Indian society all suggest that religion has significant influences on how most societies and individuals within them operate.[17] Furthermore, even countries such as Russia and China, where religion was banned, are now seeing dramatic increases in the popularity of religions. It is therefore critical to understand religion and its impact on international business.

How does religion impact international business? At a fundamental level, religions provide guides regarding the appropriate way to deal with societal expectations. Religions provide individuals with a set of principles to live by. However, through its effects on people, religion also affects both MNCs and their operations through its influence on business procedures. As an example, consider that any MNC needs to be acutely aware of religious holidays in the many countries where they operate. For instance, many Islamic countries, such as Saudi Arabia and Pakistan, have lower levels of productivity during the months of the Ramadan fast. Similarly, Asian countries slow down considerably during celebrations for the Chinese New Year, while the pace of work in many European nations will slow down during the Easter holidays. As you can see, an appropriate understanding of religion is extremely important if an MNC wants to function efficiently.

To understand the impact of religion on international business, the next few paragraphs consider some of the most popular religions around the world. Specifically, you will be exposed to the four major religious traditions, namely Buddhism, Christianity, Hinduism, and Islam. Judaism and Confucianism will also be considered briefly because they also have impact on international business. You will also see how each religion affects the business environment. Exhibit 8.7 shows the various religions and the percentage of people who practice these religions.

Buddhism

Buddhism refers to a religious tradition that focuses primarily on the reality of worldly suffering and on the ways one can be freed from such suffering.[18] Gautama Buddha, born as a prince around the six century BC in India, founded Buddhism. The basic teaching of Buddhism argues that there is no "self" or "I." Every person and everything in the world is assumed to be interconnected and the impact of one's actions affects others. Today Buddhism is very popular in Europe and the US, although most of its followers are found in countries such as Cambodia, China, Japan, Korea, Laos, Sri Lanka, and Thailand.

religion
set of beliefs, activities and institutions based on faith in supernatural forces

Buddhism
religious tradition based on the teachings of the Buddha

229

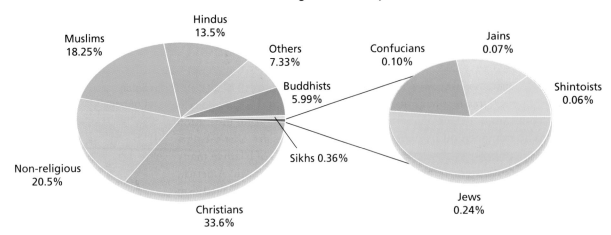

Percentage of World Population

Exhibit 8.7 **Religions Around the World**

MNCs operating in Buddhist societies will find that Buddhism has strong influences on the work environment. Buddhism is based on the philosophy that all beings are interconnected and interdependent. Such beliefs have important bearings with regards to how people treat each other. Buddhists see boundless compassion and love as important goals in life. Furthermore, Buddhism provides actual practical guidance to living according to such high ethical standards and selflessness. Multinationals operating in Buddhist environments should be aware of the consequences of their actions and ensure that decisions are made within such ethical boundaries. Although Buddhism does not necessarily condemn wealth creation and profit, multinationals nevertheless need to understand that a company exists for the betterment of society and other beings.

Additionally, Nanayakkara's interpretations of the Buddha's teachings suggest that the Buddha saw poverty as the major reason for ethical behavior decline in society.[19] Buddhism therefore prescribed a strong work ethic that encouraged workers to engage in their best efforts, while laziness is seen as a very negative quality and heavily discouraged. Multinationals should expect workers to have a generally positive view of work. It is also important for multinationals to be aware that Buddhism emphasizes teamwork and ethical means to achieve success at work. MNCs need to provide the environment where workers can flourish.

Christianity

Christianity
faith based on the teachings of Jesus

"**Christianity** is a faith based on the life, teachings, death and resurrection of Jesus"[20] and is clearly the most practiced religion around the world. Christians all share the same belief that Jesus is the incarnation of God who was sent to clean the sinfulness of humanity. Jesus is often associated with love and the possibility of humans to connect with God through penance, confessions of one's sins, self-discipline and purification.

The impact on the development of capitalism of Protestantism, a branch of Christianity developed by Martin Luther, a German monk, is seen as major evidence of the link between religion and the economic structuring of societies. Protestantism emphasized wealth and hard work for the glory of God and allowed the focus on goals attached to economic development and wealth accumulation. This explained the sustained development of capitalism in the Western Protestant societies.

Multinationals are very likely to have access to environments that encourage the conduct of business in most Christian countries. In general, Christians generally support the freedom to accumulate wealth and possessions. However, human greed and selfishness is nevertheless viewed with contempt and attempts are made to ensure that there is equality of opportunity and fairness for the less fortunate.

However, despite the general support of international business and profits, MNCs should respect Christian beliefs and values when operating in Christian countries. For instance, consider that the church authorities in many countries are blaming global companies for enticing people to consume more than they need through ad campaigns. Similarly, any use of Christian religious imagery in ad campaigns tends to be considered offensive. Consider Ryanair's experience when it used someone resembling the pope in one of its ad campaigns. The Church accused Ryanair of serious blasphemy in portraying the pope.

Hinduism

Hinduism is a broad and inclusive term referring to those individuals who mostly respect and accept the ancient traditions of India, "especially the Vedic scriptures and the social class structure with its special respect for Brahmans (the priestly class)."[21] The quest for Brahman, the ultimate reality and truth and the "sacred power that pervades and maintains all things" is the ultimate quest for many Hindus. There are currently around 760 million Hindus residing in India, Malaysia, Nepal, Surinam, and Sri Lanka. Many of the Hindus outside of India share ancestors from India.

Hinduism
religious traditions and beliefs originating in the ancient traditions of India

One aspect of Hinduism that is most likely to have international business implications is the caste system, which refers to the ordering of Indian society based on four occupational groups. The highest caste includes the priests, followed by the kings and warriors, and merchants and farmers. The fourth caste includes the manual laborers and artisans. Unfortunately, the lower castes have been seriously discriminated against and many people of the lower caste still live in poverty. A recent survey by the Indian government suggests that around 70 percent of the Indian population is from the lower castes.

Although many are hoping that the caste system is slowly disappearing, the reality is that the caste system is still very strong. A recent study found that many Indian and US multinationals still prefer to hire higher-caste applicants.[22] Furthermore, although the Indian government has implemented affirmative action programs, both the government and businesses have viewed hiring quotas as burdens.[23]

Multinationals operating in India thus have to be aware of the caste system. These MNCs will need to be aware of caste conflicts when hiring employees. As an example, having a lower-caste member supervise higher-caste individuals can be a major source of conflicts. Furthermore, when meetings are held, it is important to consider how the various castes interact. Such considerations are necessary if a multinational wants smooth operations in India.

231

ETHICAL CHALLENGE

McDonald's and the French Fries Controversy in India

As you saw in Chapter 7 on culture, McDonald's has been very successful in understanding and adapting to the Indian market. In a country where 200 million people are strictly vegetarian while around 500 million seldom eat meat, McDonald's serves mostly vegetarian meals. Furthermore, because India's Hindus don't eat beef while the Indian Muslims don't consume pork, McDonald's does not serve beef or bacon products. However, to get to this point, McDonald's was involved in an ethical controversy that severely damaged its reputation.

The case began in the US when three vegetarians (two of them Hindus) sued McDonald's for concealing the use of beef in their French fries. Although McDonald's claimed that their French fries are cooked in 100 percent vegetable oil, they were in reality using beef flavoring. Given that devout Hindus don't eat beef, they felt that McDonald's

had fraudulently induced them to eat something that was clearly not vegetarian. Furthermore, when this controversy was revealed in India, it resulted in strong demonstrations where windows were smashed at many franchises. Many Hindu fundamentalists even called for the government to close all 27 McDonald's outlets in India. In the face of such controversy, McDonald's eventually settled the suit and agreed to pay $10 million to charitable groups supporting vegetarianism. It also issued a public apology and appointed a committee to look into vegetarian needs.

Source: Based on Laurie Goering, 2007, "Young carnivores in a veggie nation," Knight Ridder Tribune News Service, March 21, p. 1; H.D.S. Greenway, 2001, "Arches not so golden to some in India," *Boston Globe*, June 4, p. A11; Ameet Sachdev, 2002, "McDonald's nears settling vegetarians' lawsuits," Knight Ridder Tribune News Service, March 6, p. 1.

Despite these challenges, multinationals can nevertheless play a critical role in facilitating change by hiring Indians from lower castes. Consider, for example, Infosys, India's leading software giant, and its training program geared towards lower castes. Infosys started a special seven-month program to train low-caste engineers who had failed to get jobs. When the program started, the trainers had to give lessons in basic self-presentation and table manners. However, with time, the trainees gained confidence and started scoring as well as other higher castes. At the end of the program, only four of the 89 low-caste trainees did not have jobs.[24] Such programs suggest that multinationals can play an important role in helping change the caste system in India.

MNCs should also respect traditional Hindu beliefs when operating in India. While the Indian middle class is growing and has significant purchasing power, companies need to be careful when treading in the Indian environment. For instance, Hindus generally consider cows as sacred animals and do not consume beef. Furthermore, some regions of India have predominantly vegetarian populations and investing companies are well advised to take such issues into consideration. Consider the IB Ethical Challenge above.

Islam

Islam
religious traditions based on the submission to the will of Allah, or God

The essence of **Islam** as described in the Qur'an is the submission to the will of Allah (God). Islam is currently the second largest of the world's religions and has adherents in countries in Africa, the Middle East, China, Malaysia, and the Far East. It continues to grow rapidly in many countries, especially in Europe.

Today, the Muslim lives in a society that is heavily influenced by Islamic standards and norms. Islam provides encompassing guidance in all spheres of life, both social and economic. An important aspect of living in an Islamic society is the presence of Islamic law. Islamic law is based on the Qur'an, Islam's holy book. The Qur'an is not necessarily a code of law. Rather, it expresses the Islamic work ethic and the rules that should guide Muslims as they encounter situations in their daily lives.[25]

Islam has implications for MNCs on many levels. For instance, Islam has clear rules for commercial transactions. The *riba* strictly forbids receiving or giving interest. Such practices of forbidding interest are not just ideals but are actually respected in many countries, including Pakistan. In such countries, governments have instituted financial laws that see interest as illegal. For an MNC operating in a Muslim country, the prohibition of interest presents a serious challenge. However, many Muslim societies have been working in profit-sharing plans to avoid the payment or receipt of interest. Additionally, companies operating in countries with Muslim populations have also found creative ways to circumvent interest. Consider the following IB Strategic Insight.

Islam and Interest

IB STRATEGIC INSIGHT

As the middle class in many Islamic nations grows and as the Muslim population grows in Europe, Western-based companies are finding it increasingly important to devise programs satisfying Islamic law when they engage in financial transactions. Consider the following examples.

- There are currently two million Muslims living in England. However, for a long time, many British Muslims were not able to use traditional British banking services because of their belief. Many British banks have started offering Shari'ah-compliant services to respect Islamic laws regarding interest. Banks such as HSBC, Bristol & West and specialist banks all offer Islamic-compliant bank accounts. Lloyds Bank is now the largest provider of Islamic banking. It now offers mortgages where Lloyds buys property on behalf of its Islamic customers, providing 90 percent of the purchase price. Customers pay the 90 percent over time until they own the property. However, rather than pay interest on the mortgage, the customers pay rent on a monthly basis. Similarly, many banks offer savings

accounts where the money is invested only in Shari'ah-compliant investments. Profits are then shared between the bank and its customers.

- Middle Eastern countries are also facing significant challenges as the growing population and middle class need to get increased access to home ownership. Traditional banking services in these countries have failed because of the forbidding of interest. Consequently, many banks in Turkey and Egypt are now working to offer "Islamic mortgages." Similar to the British banks, the Islamic banks enter into promise-to-purchase agreements with their customers. The banks agree to buy the property for their customer and then rent the property to their customer. However, part of the payment is also applied to the purchase of the property.

Source: Based on S. Bergsman, 2006, "Mortgages for the Middle East," *Mortgage Banking*, 66(8), p. 50; J. Brown, 2006, "Banks home in on Islam," *Sunday Times*, June 18, p. 7; *Birmingham Post*, 2006 "Lloyds looks to Islam for profit," June 14, p. 23.

In addition to the above rule regarding interest, Muslims can live the pious life according to the Shari'ah based on five pillars, namely confession, prayer, alms-giving, fasting, and the pilgrimage to Mecca.[26] These pillars have important implications for international business. For instance, if an MNC is operating in a Muslim country, it has to accommodate the Muslim's need to pray five times a day. Muslims need to pray in the early morning, noon, mid-afternoon, sunset and evening.[27] Furthermore, during Ramadan, the month of fasting, multinationals will face some decline in productivity. During that month, Muslims are not allowed to eat, drink, smoke, and even take medicines from dawn till dusk. As such, multinationals are advised to take the necessary steps to ensure that business activities are not disrupted.

The alms-giving pillar also has critical implications for multinational strategic management and how Islam views business. In general, the Qur'an is supportive of entrepreneurship and earning of profits through legitimate business activities while also allowing accumulation and protection of wealth. However, Muslims are naturally concerned with issues of social justice and fairness. As such, Muslims are likely to condemn the pursuit of profits through exploitation of others. Multinationals thus have to ensure that their business activities are conducted in a socially just manner.

Judaism

Judaism
religious traditions associated with Jewish people

Judaism, which has no single founder or leader, represents the family of religious traditions associated with Jewish people. It represents an evolution of religious tradition starting with the Tanakh—called the Old Testament by Christians—culminating in a compilation of Jewish law and lore in the Talmud. Although it is difficult to discuss central tenets of the Jewish faith, several common themes can be extracted from the Torah (the first five books of Moses), namely the concept of one God and love for God, the sacredness of human life and appreciation of suffering.[28]

Like the other religions we have discussed, Judaism also has important implications for international business. For instance, Judaism has clear laws regarding many aspects of business. Multinationals are well advised to respect such rules and laws when operating in predominantly Jewish countries. Human resource managers need to be aware of the Sabbath where work schedules have to be adjusted. Practicing Jews do not work or travel during the Sabbath, which lasts from sundown on Friday until sundown on Saturday. Retailers should also be aware of banned foods. For instance, devout Jews don't consume pork. Finally, it is also important to note that Judaism has a very positive view of work. Most Jews view a hard work ethic as associated with living the pious life.

Confucianism

Confucianism
school of thought developed by Confucius and based on ancient Chinese beliefs

Confucianism refers to the school of thought developed by Chinese philosopher K'ung Fu-tzu (or Confucius), based on ancient Chinese beliefs. From these traditional Chinese roots, Confucius developed a religion that emphasizes moral virtues and the importance of political involvement to make changes in the world.[29] It is crucial to understand Confucianism as it is the dominant religion in many of the economically advanced Asian nations such as Japan, South Korea and China. Confucianism is also important in countries with a significant ethnic Chinese population, such as Singapore.

Confucianism has important implications for international business. For instance, because of its emphasis on hierarchy, piety and order, management systems based on loyalty, relationships and placing the interest of the group over the individual have developed. Some even argue that such qualities have led to the economic transformation of countries such as Japan, South Korea and Singapore. Another important aspect of Confucianism in China is *guanxi*, a network of relationships linking individuals with families and clans.[30] Similar networks can also be found in South Korea (*chae bol*) or Japan (*keiretsu*). Because of the Confucian emphasis on loyalty and relationships, business deals tend to be typically arranged among businesses that have already developed a relationship with each other. *Guanxi* thus represents these networks of relationships where businesses trust each other, support each other and even reciprocate on past favors. As such, it is crucial for MNCs interested in doing business in China to have access to such *guanxi*.

Another aspect of Confucianism that has generated recent controversy is intellectual property. While Western societies have legal systems that guarantee intellectual property rights, the Chinese legal system based on Confucian ethics has a different view of intellectual property. Under Confucianism, knowledge is seen as contributing to society's well-being. Rather than protecting intellectual property, knowledge is seen as something that should be disseminated and shared with others in society. MNCs should therefore take appropriate measures to prepare for this environment.

CHAPTER REVIEW

Chapter 7 discussed some of the important aspects of the cultural environment of a country. However, the business environment of a country is not complete without an understanding of social institutions. In this chapter, social institutions were defined and you saw some of the potential effects of institutions through regulative, cognitive and normative aspects.

The first social institution examined in this chapter was the economic system. You were exposed to the various types of economic system (market-based, command, and mixed economies) and their implications for international business. That section also discussed the unique challenges facing countries that are transitioning from a socialist economic system to a more capitalist market system.

You also looked at the world's dominant legal systems. Specifically, international business implications of common law and civil law were examined. Crucial elements of the World Bank "Doing Business" project were also discussed. Finally, because political risk combines elements of the economic and legal system, we discussed some key elements of political risk. You were also exposed to some of the ways MNCs can minimize political risk.

In the final section, the world's major religions were discussed. Specifically, Buddhism, Christianity, Hinduism and Islam were covered and international business implications detailed. Finally, we also looked at two other important religions, Judaism and Confucianism. This final section should give you a good background on the international business implications of the world's major religion.

Altogether, this chapter provides you with some crucial information pertaining to the business environment facing any MNC. An appreciation of these factors is very important if any organization wants to maximize its chance of success. The chapter also discusses some of the important ways multinationals can prepare for and adapt to these institutions.

 ## DISCUSSION QUESTIONS

1. What are social institutions? What effects do social institutions have on people?
2. Discuss the three most important influences of social institutions. Give some examples of each of the three forms of influence.
3. Discuss the main types of economic systems. How do they affect the conduct of international business?
4. What are transition economies? What are some of the important changes occurring in transition economies?
5. Discuss some of the major legal systems that exist around the world. What are some of the most important differences between common and civil law?
6. Discuss some of the key elements of the World Bank's "Doing Business" project.
7. What is political risk? What are the important elements of political risk? How can companies prepare for political risk?
8. Discuss three of the world's major religions. What are some implications of these religions for international business?

 ## INTERNATIONAL BUSINESS SKILL BUILDER

Where to Start a Business?

Step 1: Find a local business interested in expanding internationally.
Step 2: Interview the company executives to find out what products they make and where they want to sell their products.
Step 3: If you cannot find a real business, create a hypothetical company with a hypothetical product.
Step 4: Using the many resources provided in the text, recommend to the company which countries make most sense for them to enter. Focus your recommendations on the institutions discussed in the text.

CHAPTER INTERNET ACTIVITY

Go to the World Bank "Doing Business" project website at **www.doingbusiness. org** and the Heritage Foundation website at **www.heritage.org**. Locate the various measures related to ease of doing business. Explore the many components of both websites. Select ten countries and compare measures from both websites. Are they similar? Why or why not?

 KEY CONCEPTS

Buddhism

capitalist or market economy

Christianity

civil law

common law

Confucianism

"Doing Business" project

economic system

Hinduism

index of economic freedom

Islam

Islamic law

Judaism

legal system

mixed economy

political risk

privatization

religion

social institutions

socialist or command
   economy

transition economies

BUSINESS > INTERNATIONAL

TONIA MOTORBIKES

CHINESE PIRACY

CASE 8

page 1

Tonia Motorbikes is the third largest manufacturer of motorized scooters in Japan. The company sells its product, a 125cc vehicle, in Japan, Taiwan, Korea, Vietnam, and other Asian markets.

In an effort to reduce labor costs and to penetrate the Chinese market, Kenichi Hoskia, CEO of Tonia, decided to establish a manufacturing operation on the Chinese mainland. Tonia invested $17 million in a state-of-the-art production facility. The Chinese government had insisted on Tonia making a major commitment in order to enter China, including the establishment of a facility equipped with Tonia's most advanced manufacturing technology.

Tonia formed a joint venture with China's Happy Motors, a large state-owned motorbike manufacturer. Tonia was required to share its technology secrets with Happy as a condition of the joint venture agreement. At first Kenichi resisted; however, the Chinese government assured him that it was in the best interests of both partners to keep the information secret. The Chinese government guaranteed that no one outside the partnership would be allowed access to any of Tonia's trade secrets. Since this guarantee came from high levels of the Chinese government, Kenichi felt more comfortable letting Happy Motors gain insight into the recent advances Tonia had made in small engine design. The thought of a market with 1.25 billion consumers was also a factor in his decision to share critical trade information.

After only five months of producing motorbikes in China, a Tonia employee noticed the Tonia 125 model being sold over the Internet for $2,200. Since the machine sold for $3,400 in Japan and $2,600 in China, the employee questioned how a new bike could be sold so cheaply. Further investigation led Tonia to Yiwu, China, where the seller was located. It was learned that Yiwu is the counterfeit capital of China, a place where counterfeiters from all over the country come to distribute their goods. Upon investigation, Tonia employees learned that the motorbikes being sold under the Tonia brand name were indeed counterfeit products.

With the help of an investigator in China, Tonia learned that not only were counterfeit bikes being sold in China, but they were being exported to other Asian countries and some were even being exported to the United States and Europe. It was obvious to Kenichi that someone at Happy Motors had sold Tonia's technology. Not only was Tonia losing sales through the counterfeit goods, but Kenichi also worried that if the quality of the product were inferior, consumers in important markets would be lost for future sales. Kenichi feared that if this situation were left unchecked, the potential existed to ruin the strong brand name Tonia had established.

. . .

CASE 8

page 2

Kenichi continued to investigate the source of the counterfeited goods but was unable to determine where the products were being manufactured. Rumor had it that a former Taiwanese counterfeiter, who had been expelled from Taiwan when the government cracked down on product piracy, had moved to the Guangdong Province of China and was manufacturing Tonia brand scooters there. It was also rumored that this individual had connections with Chinese government officials; however, there was no proof that these rumors were true.

After six months of investigation, Kenichi still could not determine the source of the counterfeit bikes and it was becoming clear that further investigation would probably not reveal the source. Kenichi did learn that, regardless of official government policy, product piracy was rampant in China. Weak laws, poor enforcement, and light penalties made counterfeiting a very lucrative and attractive business in China. Kenichi sat in his office and pondered his next move.

CASE DISCUSSION POINTS

1. Do you find it conceivable that state-owned enterprises in China are engaging in product piracy? Explain.
2. What effect has China's entry into the World Trade Organization (WTO) had on product piracy?
3. What should Kenichi do about this problem?

Note: This case is fictional; however, some source material is from *Business Week*, 2005, "China's Piracy Plaque," June 25.

Case prepared by Charles A. Rarick

[handwritten note:] Product piracy: the illegal use of signs, names, logo, and brand names that business manufactures use to distinguish their products. — imitating or copying goods

Multinational Operational

Multinational Operational and Functional Strategies

part four

and Functional Strategies

9 Entry Strategies for MNCs

After reading this chapter you should be able to:

- Understand an MNC's options for exporting.

- Know how MNCs use licensing and franchising to enter foreign markets.

- Understand when and how companies use international strategic alliances.

- Know the differences between equity joint ventures and cooperative alliances.

- Appreciate the benefits and potential risks of FDI as an entry strategy.

- Choose an appropriate entry strategy based on the strengths and weaknesses of each approach and the needs of the MNC.

- Understand the relationship between multinational strategies and entry strategies.

To carry out their multinational strategies, whether it be multidomestic, transnational, international, or regional, international managers must choose exactly how they will enter each country in which they wish to do business. The Preview IB Strategic Insight describes a situation showing one option of how the Australian company, TPAS, chose to take its product international. For TPAS, the logical entry strategy was exporting since they fish for their high quality prawns in South Australian waters. So, to sell internationally they must ship this product to other nations.

In this chapter, you will see that multinational companies have many options, including the exporting strategy of TPAS, regarding how to sell or do other business functions outside of their own country. The strategies that deal with the choices regarding how to enter foreign markets and countries are called **entry strategies**. For example, international managers must decide: Will we export only? Will we have our products or services manufactured or provided by foreign companies? Will we use licensing or franchising so that foreign companies that use our business models or technologies pay us a fee? Or, will we build our own manufacturing plant in another country? This section reviews several entry strategies popular with multinational companies, including exporting, licensing, strategic alliances, and foreign direct investment.

entry strategies
options MNCs have to enter foreign markets and countries

Australian Prawns a Greek Winner

In the Greek islands, seafood is a part of the staple diet. Adelaide, Australia-based Theo Parissos and Sons Pty Limited (TPAS) provides the Greek market with high quality South Australian prawns. Says Parissos, "Our prawns are larger and of a consistently higher quality than our competitors, this has helped get our product on tables in the Greek islands, cruise ships, and resorts." In spite of charging higher prices than local Greek competitors charge, Parissos hopes the size and quality of his prawns will provide a winning edge for this Australian product. Greek competitors just cannot match the qualities of the prawns from South Austrialia.

How did TPAS get to Greece? Faced with an increasing supply of seafood in Australia, many Australian seafood retailing and wholesaling company began to look beyond their traditional local market. For Greek-speaking Theo Parissos, exporting was the logical step and the Greek market was an attractive target. Parissos used Austrade for help. Austrade is an Australian government organization that helps small to medium sized firms chooses foreign markets for markets for their products or services and the entry strategies into these markets. Parissos noted that "Austrade's Athens office was excellent, providing us with the names of potential customers who we were able to negotiate a supply contract with." Many other countries such as Canada, the UK (https://www.uktradeinvest.gov.uk), and the United States have similar government agencies that help businesses of all types find international customers.

With annual sales growth of over 60% a year, TPAS's revenues reached $1.2 million in just three years after beginning exporting. Their five-year goal is to ship up to 250 tons of prawns a year to Greece with an expected value $5 million. With stagnant markets at home, and after their success in the Greek market, TPAS is looking to expand into other countries and continue to grow its export business.

Source: Adapted from www.austrade.gov.au; www.ec21.com/westernkingprawns.

MNC Entry Strategies

As you remember from Chapter 2, MNCs can locate any of their value-chain activities anywhere in the world. This means, for example, that a company might do R&D in one country, manufacture in another country, sales in a third country, and after-market service in a fourth country. The basic function of entry strategies is to provide mechanisms to conduct the various value-chain activities in other locations.

For example, let us look at how Apple Computer Company uses entry strategies in its European operations.

Apple originally entered Ireland in the early 1980s to manufacture the Mac for the European market. At that time, Apple managers decided it was most efficient to build their own plant close to the European market rather than ship from the US or other locations. Today, due in part to the high-quality labor force in Ireland, that plant has evolved into the European headquarters, providing not only manufacturing and regional management but also other value-chain activities such as research and development and after-market service.

From the sales perspective, Apple Ireland is primarily an exporter to the rest of Europe. From the manufacturing, research and development, and service perspectives, Apple, as a US company, is a foreign investor in Ireland. This example shows how one company can use a variety of entry strategies for sales and other activities in different countries. The placement of these activities, based on location advantages, allows Apple to use aspects of a transnational strategy in the intensely competitive world of PCs and other electronic devices.

In the following sections, we will explore in more depth the nature of entry strategies and consider the conditions that suggest the use of each. First, you will see how companies use exporting for international sales.

Exporting

passive exporters
companies that treat and fill overseas orders like domestic orders

Exporting is the easiest way to sell a product to customers in another country. Often companies begin as **passive exporters**, where the effort can be as little as treating and filling overseas orders like domestic orders. A company gets an order over its website or while showing its goods at a trade fair and just treats the foreign customer the same as any other customer. Many small businesses start out as passive exporters and then progress to more involved programs. However, even some larger businesses such as REI, the sporting goods retailer, is a passive exporter. REI fills international orders from its catalogue and website sales but makes no particular effort to target any international market.

Alternatively, an MNC can put more resources into exporting using, for example, a dedicated export department or division or an international sales force. In the United States, most export sales in dollars go to large companies. The aircraft manufacturer Boeing, for example, sells very expensive products (e.g. a 747) and makes over half of its revenues from exports. However, in terms of number of MNCs, most US exporters are small companies.

The chapter next discusses other export options beyond passive exporting.

Active Export Strategies

Once a company moves beyond passive exporting, there are two general export strategies for the MNC: indirect and direct exporting.

Indirect exporters use go-between companies to provide them with the knowledge and contacts necessary to export into different countries. Smaller companies and beginning exporters that are looking for an export option without the complexities of doing it alone often favor this approach.

The **export management company (EMC)** and the **export trading company (ETC)** are the most common intermediaries or go-between companies.[1]

When a company uses an EMC, it is outsourcing the functions that the company otherwise does internally with an export unit or international sales force. That is, instead of the exporting company, the EMC promotes the company's products to international buyers and distributors. An EMC can conduct business in the name of the producer it represents or in its own name for a commission, salary, or retainer plus commission. EMCs usually specialize in selling particular types of products or understanding the cultures and markets of particular countries or regions. Some have both product and country specializations. Thus, they provide a beginning export company with ready-made access to particular international markets.

For example, an EMC might specialize in fruit products for the Asian market, and an apple producer who wished to export to Japan would seek an EMC with that specialization. Good EMCs know their products and countries very well and have strong links to networks of foreign distributors.

Typical EMC functions include:

- attending trade shows to promote their client's products;
- providing market research to locate new markets;
- adapting packaging for local tastes;
- local advertising and translations;
- finding the overseas representatives, distributors and suppliers;
- managing export documentation, customs forms, logistics, regulation compliance, and payment.

Export Trading Companies provide many of the same services as EMCs. They differ, however, in that the ETC usually takes title to the product before exporting. Taking title means that the ETC buys the goods from the exporter, and then resells them in another country. ETCs most often act as independent distributors that link domestic producers and foreign buyers. Rather than representing a manufacturer in a foreign market, the ETC identifies what products or services are in demand in a foreign market. It then seeks out domestic companies that can provide what the foreign market desires.

The most important advantage for an exporting company using an EMC or an ETC is that the company enters a foreign market quickly, but at a low cost in management and financial resources.

The IB Strategic Insight overleaf shows how one Japanese sake producer company found success in indirect exporting using a US export trading company.

indirect exporter
uses intermediaries or go-between firms to provide the knowledge and services necessary to sell overseas

export management company (EMC)
intermediary specializing in particular types of products or particular countries or regions

export trading company (ETC)
intermediary similar to EMC, but it usually takes title to the product before exporting

245

Exporting Upscale Sake to the US

Miyasaka Brewing is a 340-year-old family business located northwest of Tokyo at the foot of the Japanese Alps. Miyasaka produces high-quality prizewinning sake, Japan's traditional rice wine made from fermented rice. However, as managing director, and the most recent in his family to run the business, Naotaka Miyasaka notes, "It's a very dark period for small brewers." Sake consumption in Japan is down to half its postwar peak as drinkers switch to imported wine, beer, and other spirits.

Along with many of Japan's 2,000 other small sake producers, Miyasaka is looking to the US to expand his market. Most sake currently imported to the US comes from large brewers and is generally considered lower quality. The business model of Miyasaka and other boutique breweries is similar to the small wineries and microbreweries in the US. Producers emphasize the artesian traits of their trade, noting that their *jizake*, or microbrews, are produced using techniques honed by centuries of experience. Award-winning bottles can cost over $100 and are often described by connoisseurs with terms similar to wine-drinkers, such as "nutty" or "crisp."

Because Miyasaka is not experienced in international business, he uses export-trading companies such as

Honolulu's World Sake Imports LLC to get his product to market in the US. World Sake Imports' president Chris Pearce notes, "Good sake does a good job of selling itself." One of his customers, Haru, is a New York Asian restaurant that Americanizes sake with "saketinis." However, Haru also sells the high-end sake for as much as $130 a bottle.

Source: Adapted from *BusinessWeek Online*, 2006, "Selling sake like single malts: Japan's microbrewers are out to sell Americans on the good stuff," www.businessweek.com, April 26.

direct exporting
more aggressive exporting strategy, where exporters take on the duties of intermediaries and make direct contact with customers in the foreign market

Contrasting with indirect exporting, **direct exporting** is the more active exporting entry strategy. Direct exporters take on the duties of the intermediaries, the ETCs and EMCs, performing them within the company. That is, the exporters make direct contact with customers located in foreign countries. To get their products to end users in foreign markets, direct exporters often start out by using local sales representatives, distributors, or retailers. Direct exporters that wish to sell direct to end users may set up their own branch offices in foreign countries.

Local sales representatives work in the target foreign markets by using the company's promotional literature and samples to sell the company's products to local buyers. Sales representatives are not usually employed by the direct exporters but, rather, have a contract relationship with the exporter. Such contracts define the sales representatives' commissions, assigned territories, length of agreements, and other details. They may work for several exporters at once. Foreign distributors differ from foreign sales representatives in that they buy products from exporting sellers at a discount and then resell the products in a foreign market to make a profit.

The IB Small Business Insight below shows how a small Australian wine exporter uses a foreign distributor to sell its wines in Hungary.

Direct exporters can sell directly to foreign retailers. For example, some Korean and Japanese companies such as Samsung and Sony sell electronics products directly to large retailers, such as Walmart. Depending on their resources and local laws, direct exporters can also sell directly to foreign end-user customers. However, this direct sales approach is more common for companies selling industrial products to other companies than for an exporter trying to sell consumer products like toothpaste or shampoos to individual consumers. An industrial sales example is Schweitzer Engineering Laboratories from Pullman, Washington. They sell special circuit breakers that allow utility companies to identify the location of breaks in underground cables. Their customers are utility companies from all over the world. One technique that does work to sell to individual customers through exporting is using catalog sales or website catalogues. Examples of successfully marketing internationally using this approach include Austad (golfing equipment), Dell Computer (PCs), and L.L. Bean (outdoor clothing).

Experience Helps: Direct Exporting for Aussie Red Wines to Hungary

IB SMALL BUSINESS INSIGHT

Australian John Curnow was managing director of Coca-Cola in Hungary for three years during the 1990s. After leaving Coke, he and his wife Sue decided to apply their passion for wines to a new business as a start-up wine producer. Just three years after buying two vineyards in South Australia's Barossa Valley, the Curnows' signature "1847" label is on the tables of the best restaurants in Budapest. How did this come about?

At first, the Curnows chose to sell their grapes to more established Australian wine producers such as Southcorp's Penfolds, who used the grapes for their own premium wines. When, after a couple of years, they bottled their own vintage "1847" label, they immediately planned export sales to Hungary. John Curnow had extensive international management experience with Coke and he knew the Hungarian business culture and economic system well. He also had local contacts.

A friend in the Australian trade commission introduced him to a local Budapest distributor with the skills to find the right market for a premium wine, and local sales quickly took off. Promotional samples sent to Hungary even found their way to the Hungarian prime minister's table.

Future plans call for Curnow Family Vineyards to target niche markets in other countries including the USA, Canada, New Zealand, Poland, and the Czech Republic. Curnow recommends that small-business exporters sell to countries that they enjoy visiting. He says, "A lot of business is about the enthusiasm that you have for your product and the location you're involved in. If you feel it's a chore to go to these places, this reflects in how you present yourself and your product."

Source: Adapted from www.austrade.gov.au, August 2005.

Which Way to Go—Passive or Direct?

Although exporting is the easiest and cheapest entry strategy, it may not always be as profitable as other entry strategies. However, export is often the first step to internationalize a company or, for more established MNCs, the way to minimize risk or to test new markets. Consequently, most MNCs continue exporting, often used in combination with more sophisticated entry strategies. However, every MNC that wants to export must answer the question of which form of exporting it should choose.

As with most business decisions, both types of export strategies have some advantages and some disadvantages. Basically, the international manager must consider whether the greater potential profits of direct exporting can offset the greater financial risk and commitment of resources associated with this strategy.[2] In addition, international managers must consider whether the needs and capabilities of their company warrant the bigger investment in direct exporting. International managers can use the following diagnostic questions to help select the export strategy that best fits their company:[3]

- *How important is the control of foreign sales, customer credit, and the eventual sale of the product and customer?*

The more important the control of these activities, the more likely the international manager should choose direct exporting. In direct exporting, the company does not pass off these functions to EMCs or ETCs as in indirect exporting.

- *Does the company have the resources, both financial and human, to design and run an effective export department to manage its export operations?*

Indirect exporting often makes more sense for smaller companies that do not have people with international expertise in their employment. Even for a larger company, creating a new unit can involve substantial costs that may not be offset until exporting becomes a larger share of the business. In the short term, EMCs or ETCs allow the company to outsource export functions (for a price) and avoid the investment of its own resources.

- *Does the company have the resources, both financial and human, to design and execute international marketing activities (for example, create foreign-language advertisements, deal directly with foreign customers, etc.)?*

Managers must ask whether they have anyone in their company that can write ads in foreign languages and can travel to trade shows and successfully promote their materials in foreign languages. If they do not have such skills, or resources to hire people with such skills, companies usually rely on the expertise of intermediaries and choose indirect exporting.

- *Does the company have the resources, financial and human, to support extensive international travel for sales or an expatriate sales force located in the foreign market, and the time and expertise to develop its own overseas contacts and networks?*

Extensive travel takes managers away from company activities and may require hiring additional managers for the home office. Expatriates may cost three times their home country salaries. Yet, if the exporting business is substantial, companies may still find it more profitable to do these functions themselves and avoid the commissions and discounts required by intermediaries.

The next option we will consider of how to enter a foreign market is licensing and franchising.[4]

Licensing and Franchising

International **licensing** is a contractual agreement between a licensor in one country and a licensee in another country. A licensor has some valuable asset that it will allow the licensee to use for a price. This asset might include a valuable patent, trademark, technological know-how, or company name that the licensor provides to the licensee in return for a payment. For example, imagine a small Australian surfboard company with a unique new material, that wants to enter the US market. One option would be to license the use of this technology to a US manufacturer who would produced the boards in the US, paying a royalty fee for each board produced using the Australian technique.

Like exporting, licensing provides one of the easier, lower-cost, and least risky mechanisms for going international. As such, it is often an attractive option for small companies or for companies with limited capital. However, when the conditions are right, even very large MNCs use licensing as an entry strategy.

The licensing agreement or contract specifies the legal nature of the relationship between the licensee and the licensor. Exhibit 9.1 shows some the contents that you will find in a typical licensing agreement. As you can see in the Exhibit, these contracts can be complex. Because of these complexities, most MNCs will hire specialized attorneys from both countries to prepare an agreement that is valid in the legal systems of both countries.

> **licensing**
> contractual agreement between a domestic licensor and a foreign licensee (licensor usually has a valuable patent, technological know-how, trademark, or company name that it provides to the foreign licensee)

International Franchising: A Special Licensing Agreement

International franchising is a comprehensive licensing agreement between a franchisor (licensor) and a franchisee (licensee). The international franchisor licenses to the franchisee the use of a whole business model. The business models usually include trademarks, business organization structures, technologies and know-how, and training. Franchisors, such as McDonald's, may even provide company-owned stores.

Most multinational franchise operations require the franchisee to follow strict rules and procedures. This provides a standardized product or service. In return for a known business model, the franchisor receives compensation, typically based on the franchisee's revenues. Dominant players in the use of franchising as an international entry strategy include companies such as Holiday Inn, Kentucky Fried Chicken, McDonald's, and 7-Eleven.[5]

The IB Strategic Insight overleaf gives some background on Gap's new franchising strategy.

> **international franchising**
> comprehensive licensing agreement where the franchisor grants to the franchisee the use of a whole business operation

Exhibit 9.1 **What is in a Licensing Agreement?**

What you get to use	How can you use it?	How do the licensors get paid?	Other issues to consider
• Trademarks: Brand names such as Hilton	• Who: Which companies have the right to use the licensed asset?	• Currency: In what currency are payments made to the licensor?	• Law: In what country will the contract law apply?
• Designs: The right to use the same design or production processes of the licensor	• Where: Identifies the nations in which the licensee is allowed or prohibited from operating	• Method: Types of payments, which can be lump sum, installments, royalties as a percentage of profits	• Language: What is the official language of the contract?
• Patents: The right to use otherwise legally protected processes or inventions such as a cancer drug	• Performance: What exactly is required of the licensee?	• Minimum payments: Agreements stating the minimum payment	• Disputes: What type of dispute-resolution mechanism will be used?
• Copyrights: The use of intellectual property such as computer software or written material	• Improvements: What happens if the licensee or licensor makes improvements in licensed property?	• Other: Fees for product improvements, technical assistance, training, etc.	• Reports: What and when must the licensee report?
• Knowledge: Access to special knowledge or technology such as a reservations system in a hotel group	• Duration: How long does the license contract last?	• Schedule: When payments to the licensor are due	• Penalties: What penalties are in place if either party fails to live up to the agreement?
	• Confidentiality: Specific provisions in the agreement that require the licensee to protect trade secrets or designs from others		• Inspections and audits: What are the rights of the licensor to monitor the licensee?
			• Termination: How to end the agreement

Sources: Adapted from Paul Beamish, J. Peter Killing, Donald J. Lecraw, and Allen J. Morrison, 1994, *International Management*, Burr Ridge, IL: Irwin, pp. 110–17; Franklin Root, 1994, *Entry Strategies for International Markets*, New York: Lexington, pp. 129–30.

Gap Goes Franchising

Although well known in the US, Gap Inc. has had only modest success with its international operations for its Gap and Banana Republic stores. Gap's company-owned stores in Britain and France (in place since the early 1990s) have had spotty performance with revenues down 6 percent last year. Its Japanese stores showed only a modest 2 percent revenue growth during the same time. After struggling for years, Gap left the German market in 2004. Industry analysts have noted that using company-owned stores as an entry strategy has been expensive and unwieldy for Gap.

Given its past experience, and rather than managing company-owned stores in new international markets, Gap has decided to use franchising as the entry strategy for further international expansion. Working with local franchisees allows Gap to reduce its financial risks, and avoid the difficulties of dealing with local real-estate markets and having to hire and train store-level employees.

Gap's most recent franchise agreement is with Dubai-based retailer Al Tayer Group and targets the Middle Eastern market. Al Tayer plans Gap and Banana Republic franchise stores in the United Arab Emirates, Kuwait, Qatar, Bahrain, and Oman. The target for Al Tayer is to open up to 35 stores by 2010. As franchisee, Al Tayer will find locations, hire employees, and operate the stores. As the franchisor, Gap keeps control of marketing and product design. Outside of the Middle East, Singaporean franchisee F.J. Benjamin will operate franchised stores in Singapore and Malaysia. Joshua Schulman, Gap's vice president of international alliances, is optimistic. He notes, "We know from our stores here [in the US] that we attract many (overseas) customers when they're traveling here. In Asia, in particular, Gap has tremendous brand recognition."

Source: Adapted from Louise Lee, 2006, "Gap Goes Global," *BusinessWeek Online*, www.businessweek.com, April 18.

When to Choose a Licensing Entry Strategy

When considering international licensing, international managers often look at three factors: the characteristics of their product, the characteristics of the target country in which the product will be licensed, and the nature of their company.

The Product Companies that license older technologies avoid giving potential competitors their innovations, while using the license to continue to profit from earlier investments. As such, the MNC should consider licensing if it has products that are older or are using a soon-to-be-replaced technology.

Another consideration in the licensing decision is if the company has a product that no longer has domestic sales potential, perhaps because of the domestic market saturation or domestic buyers anticipating new technologies. However, older technologies may remain attractive in different countries. Potential countries as licensing candidates include those where there are no competitors with recent technology, which may lead to strong demand still existing for a licensed product. In other countries, particularly in developing nations, foreign licensees may not have production facilities capable of producing the latest technology and may welcome the opportunity to learn production methods or other information from a licensor's older technology.[6]

Characteristics of the Target Country Characteristics of a local market that add costs to a product often make licensing more attractive than exporting or other entry strategies. For example, if a country has trade barriers such as tariffs or quotas, these add costs to finished goods. These costs increase the price of your goods, reduce demand, and can often make exporting them to a high-tariff country unprofitable. In this situation, rather than transferring a physical product, an MNC can transfer the intangible know-how through a license. For example, a brewing company that exports beer may face complex bottling and labeling regulations as well as high import tariffs. This might make exporting unprofitable. However, if the brewer licenses the brewing process to a local brewer—licensing know-how—regulations and tariffs are avoided and the licensee can still make some money from the royalties.

Another issue that can make licensing a consideration is the distance between two countries. Exporting long distances, especially with products that are heavy or perishable, can add significantly to costs and make the produce unattractive locally. For example, the international managers working in the brewery from the example above realize that their product is about 90 percent water—making it quite heavy to transport. Beer also has a limited shelf life. In considering a target market some distance from their home country, these managers also realize that overseas shipping will be bulky, heavy, and probably too expensive. In such cases, when transportation costs can make a product prohibitively expensive in a target country market, international managers often decide to license the technology to local producers. For example, in the real brewing industry, the Baltika Brewery in St Petersburg, Russia, produces the Australian beer Fosters and Danish beer Carlsberg under licenses.[7]

Another factor that makes licensing a good entry choice includes government requirements. For example, for sensitive military and high technology products, local governments require local production to avoid dependence on production facilities located in other countries. In other situations, licensing minimizes risk associated with a country. Political instability in the target country can make the lower risks of licensing attractive. In an unstable political environment, since licensing does not require the MNC to contribute equity or transfer products to the host country, the only risk is losing the licensing income. Finally, for some target countries, their market are small and do not warrant any investment other than licensing.[8]

The Nature of the Company If your company lacks adequate financial, technical, or managerial resources to export or to invest directly in foreign operations, licensing can be an attractive entry strategy. With licensing, the company does not have to invest much to manage international operations. There is no need to hire EMCs or ETCs. There is no need to spend the money to create an export department, manage a foreign sales force, or build or buy an overseas unit. The company's managers need only limited expertise regarding operations in the target market or how to adapt their product to local needs. As such, with a license the licensor transfers to the licensee the costs and risks associated with these tasks and responsibilities. Thus, because licensing is a low-cost option, demanding little from the licensing company, small MNCs often find it the most attractive.[9]

MNCs with several products may find it advantageous to license when some of its products are more peripheral or sideline products. Since such products are not their key or most important products, their use in licensing does not give outsiders access to the core of the company. This prevents licensees, who are often potential competitors as well, from copying core technologies. However, it still allows the licensing MNC to get additional profits from licensing some less important products.

When to Choose Franchising

Although not all types of businesses can be franchised, many are good candidates for both domestic and international franchising. Candidates for international franchising include companies with the following attributes:[10]

- Newer or unique business models must meet customer needs in many markets. The product or service must catch the eye of potential franchisees because it is different or new.
- A high degree of control over the products or services must be possible. Franchises succeed when they produce consistent output to their customers.
- Brands that are easily identifiable and travel well cross-culturally, such as the Subway brand, succeed in international franchising.
- Systems must be easily copied and able to be replicated many times.
- Systematic operating systems and procedures must be well developed and easy to train cross-culturally.
- There must be predictable high profitability potential for each unit so that the franchisor can attract franchisees. Franchisees that follow the system should be able to achieve high returns on their investment. They must be able to pay the royalties to the franchisor and still have a reasonable profit.
- The franchises must be affordable in the countries of operation. Franchises under $100,000 are popular in the US because many people can afford investments of that size.

Some Disadvantages of Licensing and Franchising

Although these entry strategies are low cost and low risk, certain disadvantages are possible for MNCs that use them.

First and most important, granting a license may create *a new competitor*. A licensee may use the knowledge about your product or service to compete against you, not only in the licensee's country but also in other countries. Even when a licensing contract prohibits future use of the licensed asset, local laws may not support this restriction or may not be enforced. In addition, even with the protection of local laws, foreign litigation to compel the licensee to give up copying your product or service may prove too costly. Similarly, franchisees may copy the business model and open their own stores with only slight modifications if local laws are not strong regarding brand protection. As Tony Chen from Tricon Greater China (parent company of KFC, Pizza Hut and Taco Bell) notes, "We get copycat restaurants all the time. There is a Taiwanese restaurant chain in China with very similar branding—the look is the same down to the old gentleman, he just doesn't have the Colonel's beard." [11]

Second, licensing or franchising can give up or weaken *control*. Once a licensing or franchise agreement is signed and the asset (e.g. trademark, technology, know-how, or business model) is transferred, controlling the behavior of the licensee/franchisee can be problematic, short of revoking the agreement. For example, a licensee may not price a product appropriately or correctly, or the franchisee may not follow the quality requirements. Much depends on local laws regarding licensing and franchising regarding how the contracts can be enforced, so caution is advised.

Third, licensing or franchising may result in *lower profits* for the licensee or franchisor. If licensees have their own products besides those that are licensed, they are less motivated to sell a licensed product with its shared profits than to sell their own, homegrown products. To attract good franchisors, franchising fees need to be low enough so the franchisees can make a sufficient profit. The fees can be lower than the profit a company might make in its own store.

Fourth, licensing or franchising have *opportunity costs*. That is, the typical agreement gives licensees or franchisees the exclusive legal right to use business models, trademarks, or technologies in their countries. This excludes even the licensor or franchisor. The result is that the licensee or franchisee cannot enter the country of the licensor or franchisor through potentially more profitable entry strategies, such as foreign direct investment—a least for a specified period. This is a potential lost opportunity for making more money than provided by licensing should the country prove profitable.

For example, say a company like Jamba Juice opens a franchise operation in New Zealand. If the franchised stores do extremely well, the company may realize that it could be making a lot more money with its own stores. However, if its franchise agreement restricted it from using company stores to compete with franchised stores then this would be a missed opportunity.

In the next section you will see how MNCs develop closer relationships with foreign partners by using strategic alliances.

International Strategic Alliances

international strategic alliance
agreement between two or more firms from different countries to cooperate in any value-chain activity from R&D to sales

international joint venture (IJV)
an agreement where two or more firms from different countries have an equity (or ownership) position in a new, separate company

international cooperative alliance (ICA)
an agreement for cooperation between two or more companies from different nations that does not set up a legally separate company

When two or more companies from different countries agree to engage jointly in business activities, we call this an **international strategic alliance**. These cooperative ventures may include any value-chain activity, from joint R&D, to joint manufacturing, to joint sales and service. The international business manager has two basic options for an international strategic alliance: the equity international joint venture, typically called an IJV, and non-equity-based alliances, typically called international cooperative alliances.

To form an equity **international joint venture (IJV)** two or more firms from different countries must have an equity (or ownership) position in a new, separate company. Although 50/50 ownership between two companies is the most common form, some IJVs have several participants and any individual company may have a majority, minority, or equal ownership in the IJV. To form a non-equity-based **international cooperative alliance (ICA)**, all that is necessary is that two or more firms from different countries agree to cooperate in any value-chain activity. Unlike the IJV, an ICA does not require the participating companies to set up a separate company. Instead, the participants usually sign a contract agreeing to cooperate in some venture. For example, the French company Renault and the US company Ford jointly design, produce, and sell utility vans in Europe for the commercial market. Although quite profitable on per unit sales, the market for commercial vans is not big enough to warrant

General Motors' Strategic Alliances in China

Shanghai General Motors Co. Ltd. (Shanghai GM) is a 50/50 joint venture with Shanghai Automotive Industry Corp. Group (SAIC), a leading passenger car manufacturer in China. Shanghai GM was formed in June 1997. Shanghai GM has a current annual production capacity of 320,000 vehicles operating on two shifts. It builds and sells a comprehensive range of products, which currently include the Buick, Chevrolet, and Cadillac lines. It also produces engines and transmissions. In 2005, Shanghai GM sold a total of 325,429 vehicles, which represented a 28.7 percent increase from the previous year, and ended the year as number one in terms of passenger car sales in China.

Pan Asia Technical Automotive Center (PATAC) is a $50-million, 50/50 joint venture between GM and SAIC. It provides automotive engineering services including design, development, testing, and validation of components and vehicles.

SAIC–GM–Wuling Automobile Co. Ltd (SAIC–GM–Wuling) is a $99.6-million joint venture that was launched in November 2002. GM China holds a 34 percent stake, while SAIC holds 50.1 percent and Wuling Automotive holds 15.9 percent. The joint venture is situated in Liuzhou, Guangxi Zhuang Autonomous Region, in southwestern China. It manufactures a range of Wuling brand mini-trucks and minivans as well as the Chevrolet Spark mini-car.

Shanghai GM (Shenyang) Norsom Motors Co. Ltd is a joint venture formerly known as Jinbei General Motors. Shanghai GM holds a 50 percent stake and oversees management. GM China and SAIC each hold 25 percent stakes in the facility, which is located in Shenyang, Liaoning. The joint venture has an annual designed production capacity of 50,000 vehicles. It manufactures the Buick GL8 and FirstLand executive wagons.

Shanghai GM Dong Yue Motors Co. Ltd is a $108-million joint venture manufacturing facility situated in Yantai, Shandong. Shanghai GM holds a 50 percent stake and oversees management. GM China and SAIC each hold 25 percent stakes in the facility, which manufactures the Chevrolet Epica, Aveo and Sail vehicle families. The plant has an annual designed production capacity of 100,000 units operating on two shifts.

Shanghai GM Dong Yue Automotive Powertrain Co. Ltd is a joint venture located in Yantai, Shandong. Shanghai GM owns 50 percent and oversees management. GM China and SAIC each own 25 percent. The facility has an annual designed manufacturing capacity of 375,000 engines operating on two shifts. Since regular production started in June 2005, the company has been supplying a family of 1.6-liter engines for vehicles manufactured by Shanghai GM.

GMAC–SAIC Automotive Finance Co. Ltd became China's first approved and operational automotive financing company when it opened for business in August 2004. The joint venture between General Motors Acceptance Corp. (GMAC) and Shanghai Automotive Group Finance Co. Ltd (SAICFC) provides retail financing for vehicles manufactured by GM's joint ventures with SAIC. It also supports Shanghai GM dealers by providing wholesale financing for their vehicle inventories.

Yulon GM Motors Co. Ltd (Yulon GM) is a joint venture for the sale and distribution of GM vehicles in Taiwan with Yulon Motor, one of the largest automotive companies in Taiwan. Yulon GM was formed in July 2005. With a 51 percent equity stake held by Yulon Motor and 49 percent by GM, registered capital is NT$ 2 billion (approximately US$ 62.5 million).

GM–Shanghai Jiao Tong University Technology Institute is a cooperative institution established by GM and Shanghai Jiao Tong University. It focuses on joint research and development, and technical training.

Source: www.gm.com/company/corp_info/global_operations/asia_pacific/chin.html

single companies investing in design and production and then competing with each other.

During the last decade, international strategic alliances have become one of the more popular entry strategies for MNCs. Even those largest MNCs that have the financial resources and international expertise to operate directly in foreign countries have turned increasingly to using international strategic alliances as entry strategies.[12] In an example of a major MNC using alliances, the IB Strategic Insight on the previous page describes GM's IJV and cooperative alliances in China.

When to Choose Strategic Alliances

MNCs use strategic alliances for several reasons. Most reasons derive from the logic that when two or more companies have different capabilities their combined efforts can lead to competitive advantages. Some of the reasons for forming alliances follow.

The Local Partner's Knowledge of their Market MNCs, especially the smaller ones, often use alliances when they are newly arrived in a country and want to tap a local partner's knowledge of the local market. This works particularly well when an MNC can find a local partner with similar products or services. Naturally, such a partner would have more insights regarding needs of local customers and the local mechanisms, such as government regulations, necessary to get a product or service to market. Often such partnerships begin only as sales and marketing agreements. For example, Jochen Zeitz, CEO and chairman of the German athletic shoe and sporting goods company PUMA AG, notes:

> Swire Pacific [their joint venture partner in Hong Kong] possesses very valuable market know-how that, combined with our knowledge, will allow us to further accelerate our rapid expansion in this highly important area. Our goal is to at least quadruple sales in the next five years and to firmly establish PUMA in the top three of the industry's global brands in China.[13]

Alliances may later progress to joint manufacturing and sourcing of raw material when the foreign partner is confident that its products or services will succeed in the local market.[14]

Local Government Regulations and Requirements Especially in developing countries, local governments often want to ensure that their nationals have an ownership position in any foreign venture. Local governments may even require MNCs to use joint ventures as a condition of entry into the country. For example, the United Arab Emirates requires that 51 percent of the ownership be local. In countries such as China and in many of the former Eastern bloc countries, the government itself is often a joint venture partner. Some countries do not require joint ventures but, instead, make it more attractive by giving favorable treatment in areas such as lower taxes.

Local government regulations can also be difficult for a foreign firm to understand and manage. Just as local partners can bring knowledge of the local market, they can also bring a good knowledge of how to deal with local government bureaucracies. When equity positions are not required by the government, non-equity-based alliances may also provide necessary contacts and information regarding the local government.

Sharing Risks among Partners   Sometimes, a potential venture is too risky for one company to take on by itself. An alliance allows partners to share not only the potential profits of the venture but also the risks. Factors that might increase risk include, for example, projects using a new or untested technology or when the start-up costs of the project require a heavy investment. Some projects are so expensive relative to the size of the firm that a failure would doom a single firm to bankruptcy. For example, in the commercial airline industry, no one European company was willing to take on the US giant Boeing—one failed project would doom the company. Instead, several European companies formed a joint venture, which became the Airbus consortium. Spreading the risks over more than one company allowed each participant in the alliance to take on a project that would otherwise have been too risky.

Sharing Technology   Not all companies have the same technological strengths. As a result, many MNCs use alliances with companies from other countries that have complementary technological strengths. In combination, two or more companies often can bring a new product to market more quickly and with higher quality. One example is Sony Ericsson. This is a 50/50 joint venture between the Swedish telecommunications company Ericsson and the Japanese consumer electronics company Sony Corporation. After forming the joint venture, both companies stopped making their own cell phones. The logic is to let the joint venture company use Sony's knowledge in consumer electronics and Ericsson's expertise in cellular technology. The joint venture's management is located in London. Sony Ericsson has R&D sites in Sweden, Japan, China, the United States, and the United Kingdom.[15]

Economies of Scale   Strategic alliances can often provide the most efficient size to conduct a particular business. For example, Ford uses Nissan's design for a front-wheel-drive minivan. Nissan and Ford then share the production costs at Ford's Avon Lake, Ohio, truck-assembly plant. Ford gets the design faster and cheaper and can produce a product that otherwise might not have been cost-effective. Small businesses may team up to compete successfully with larger global firms.[16]

Although IJVs involve ownership of foreign assets, MNCs often choose to go it alone and set up their own operations in a foreign country. The next section explores the nature of such decisions regarding foreign direct investment.

Foreign Direct Investment

Foreign direct investment (FDI) is the highest stage of internationalization. FDI means that the MNC owns, in part or in whole, a business unit in another country. Although IJVs also involve ownership, the IJV is a separate organization

foreign direct investment (FDI)
multinational firm's ownership, in part or in whole, of an operation in another country

257

from the parent companies while FDI usually means that the foreign unit is an internal part of the MNC.

MNCs use FDI to set up any kind of subsidiary along the value chain. This might include units for R&D, sales, manufacturing, etc., located in a country other than the headquarters country. When a multinational sets up a company from scratch, this is called a **greenfield investment**. The term is meant to convey the image of a company building a brand new factory on a previously green field. Of course, in reality, most companies buy land or buildings for their factories or offices just as local companies, and the lots need not be green. FDI also occurs when MNCs buy existing companies in another country, called an acquisition, or merge with existing companies in another country.

According to the United Nations' *World Investment Report*,[17] cross-border mergers and acquisitions (M&A) are a major driving force for FDI having a value that grew at a rate of over 50 percent during the last decade. As opposed to the greenfield investments, the M&A provides speed and access to business assets. Examples of some mega M&As worth over $1 billion include: John Hancock Financial (formerly US) acquired by Manulife Financial Corp. (Canada); John Labatt brewery (formerly Canadian) acquired by Ambev (Brazil); Dial Group (formerly US) acquired by Henkel KgaA (Germany); and JC Penney (formerly US) acquired by Jean Coutu Group, Inc. (Canada).[18] Perhaps the most famous and largest of single mergers is that of US Chrysler and German Daimler Benz to create the company DaimlerChrysler (worth $54.6 billion)—although some would say that it was a merger of unequals as Daimler took full charge of the company soon after the merger. Unfortunately for Daimler, this acquisition failed to meet expectations and less than ten years later Daimler sold 80 percent of its ownership to a private investment group in the US. By late 2008, Daimler still held a 19.9 stake in Chrysler, however.

The rapid pace of technological change and the liberalization of foreign investment policies by numerous countries are the major driving factors leading to more M&A as a form of FDI. Exhibit 9.2 illustrates the driving forces behind cross-border M&A activity based on a United Nations report of worldwide levels of FDI.

Acquisitions can sometimes result in partial ownership of a foreign company. For example, in the automobile industry, Ford has a controlling ownership of Mazda (33.4 percent). A controlling ownership means that Ford owns enough of the company to control the everyday management of Mazda. Renault owns 40 percent of Nissan. GM owns 10 percent of Isuzu, 20 percent of Suzuki, and 20 percent of Subaru.

FDI can occur anywhere in the value chain. For example, some MNCs use foreign operations only to extract raw materials that may not exist in their home countries. Further in the value chain, they use these raw materials to support production at home. This type of FDI is common in what are known as the extraction industries, where raw materials such as iron and oil are refined to produce steel and gasoline. Other MNCs use their foreign operations for production using low-cost or high-quality labor or because of proximity to suppliers. Products or components produced in the manufacturing country can then be shipped to the home country or to other markets anywhere in the world. Ford, for example, assembles some automobiles in Mexico that are returned to the US, and some in Thailand primarily for export to other Asian markets.

greenfield investment
starting foreign operations from scratch

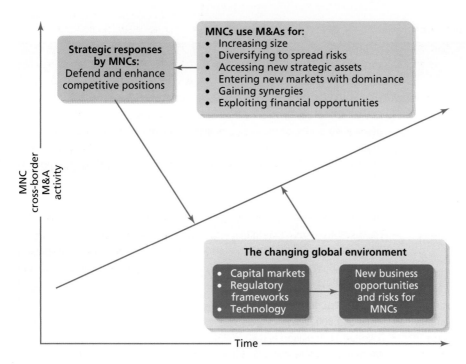

Exhibit 9.2 **The Driving Forces of Increasing MNC Cross-Border (M&A)**

Source: Adapted from: World Investment Report, 2000, *Cross-border Mergers and Acquisitions and Development*, Geneva, Switzerland: United Nations Conference on Trade and Development, p. 154.

Exhibit 9.3 gives examples and the locations of companies that have significant FDI for R&D in China.

Although there are many uses in the value chain for FDI, the most important is developing a foreign market for direct sales in that country or region. That is, the major motivation to invest abroad is a base for production or sales in their target countries.[19]

The scale of FDI often changes as firms gain greater returns from their investments or perceive less risk in running their foreign operations. For example, a multinational manufacturing firm may begin with only a sales office, later add a warehouse, and still later add a plant or acquire a local company with the capacity only to assemble or package its product. Ultimately, at the highest scale of investment, the MNC builds or acquires its own full-scale production facility.[20]

Deciding in which country to invest and the choice of local partners are often part of the FDI and alliance decisions. In addition to the strict business reasons for choosing a country or partner, issues regarding corporate social responsibility (CSR) are increasingly important for the MNC's investment decisions. The IB Sustainability Practices box overleaf shows results from a recent World Bank study showing how this issue is gaining in importance.

Exhibit 9.3 **Foreign R & D in China**

Company	Number of R&D centres in China	Location	Features
General Electric	1	Shanghai	• China Technology Centre, opened in Shanghai in 2003, is the third global R&D centre of the company after those in the United States and India. • Invested $640 million and centralized its previous existing R&D units in China. • 500 R&D engineers (planned to increase to 1,200 in 2005).
Microsoft	5	Beijing Shanghai	• Invested $130 million. • Microsoft Research Asia (MRA), established in 1998, is the company's basic research facility in the Asia and Oceania region and the fifth largest research centre in the world. • MRA employs over 170 researchers.
Motorola	15	Beijing Shanghai Tianjin Suzhou Nanjing Chengdu	• The first TNC R&D centre in China (set up in 1990). • Total of 1,300 R&D engineers. • Invested $300 million in R&D in China until 2001. • Motorola China Research Institute (MCRDI) was established in 1999. • Will invest $500 million in a new R&D centre in Beijing.
Nokia	5	Beijing Shanghai Hangzhou	• Nokia China R&D Centre, established in 1998, employs 300 R&D engineers. • Hangzhou R&D Centre, established in 1998, employs 180 R&D engineers (will increase to 400).

Source: UNCTAD, based on company press information.

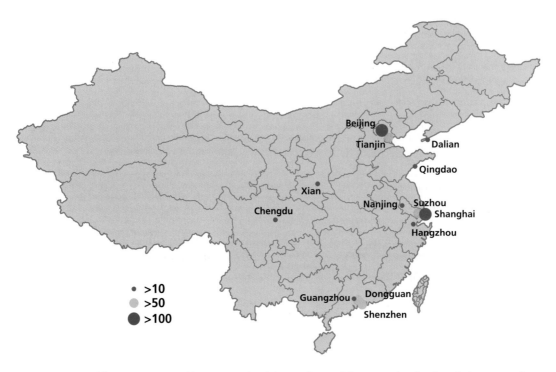

Source: UNCTAD, 2005, *World Investment Report 2005: Transnational Corporations and the Internationalization of R&D*, New York: UNCTAD.

Corporate Social Responsibility and Sustainability in the Location Choice

IB SUSTAINABILITY PRACTICES

A recent World Bank study identified how corporate social responsibility influences the investment decisions of MNCs. The study interviewed executives from 107 MNCs in extractive, agribusiness, and manufacturing industries. Companies came from Africa, Australia, Canada, Japan, Latin America, the Middle East, Russia, South Asia, the United States, and Western Europe.

While many assume that MNCs seek locations for lower-cost production because of weak laws on environment, labor, and other CSR issues, the majority of executives in this World Bank study felt that strong local laws regarding CSR issues help them conduct business more effectively. According to the World Bank, "Over 80 percent of respondents reported that they look at the CSR performance of potential partners and locations before they close the deal on a new venture." More than half of the MNCs noted that the analysis of the CSR readiness of the country and partner begins immediately in the investment decision. Nearly all of the MNCs require some level of CSR performance from local partners.

The charts in Exhibit 9.4 show that environmental management dominated the CSR considerations both at the board of directors level and in the time spent in making

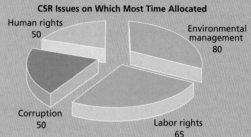

Exhibit 9.4 **CSR Considerations**

internationalization decisions regarding countries and partners.

Source: Adapted from World Bank, 2003, *Race to the Top: Attracting and Enabling Global Sustainable Business—Business Survey Report*, Washington, DC: World Bank, October.

FDI Advantages and Disadvantages

Usually, but not always, MNCs try exporting, licensing, or alliances prior to FDI. Experience with these other entry strategies helps prepare the MNC and its managers for the complexities of FDI and helps minimize the risks associated with failure. As such, all but the most experienced MNCs usually try other forms of entry strategies before they select direct investment. Regardless of a company's international experience, however, the advantages and disadvantages of FDI should be considered prior to making an entry decision. The IB Strategic Insight overleaf gives an example of how even a huge company like Airbus can be challenged with managing an investment successfully.

Exhibit 9.5 summarizes the advantages and disadvantages of FDI that the international managers should consider.

Airbus Struggles to Succeed in China

The commercial airline giant Airbus plans to open its first assembly plant outside of Europe in China. The Chinese offered free land, low-cost labor, and the possibility of more orders of Airbus planes. On face value, it looked like a good deal. However, experts point out that many components such as wings and fuselages are beyond the capability of Chinese plants. Some estimate that only 5 percent of the components will be sourced locally in China. When the added costs of shipping these components to China are combined with the challenges of training a local Chinese workforce, any cost advantages could be gone.

Another disadvantage of the Airbus deal is that the Chinese will only manufacturer the A320, a narrow-body plane that costs much less than the new wide-body A350, which competes directly with Boeing's new Dreamliner. Unfortunately for Airbus, the Chinese aerospace industry has neither the financial strength nor the technical competence to produce the larger and more profitable plane. Boeing, on the other hand, will source many of its Dreamliner components from Japanese manufacturing giants Mitsubishi and Kawasaki, both of whom have expertise in the advanced composite materials that will go into the Dreamliner.

Although Airbus may succeed, FDI manufacturing of aircraft in China has had limited success. Brazil's Embraer, which produces smaller jets for regional airlines, only managed to deliver nine planes in four years. Prior to its acquisition by Boeing, McDonnell Douglas abandoned production in its Shanghai plant after only 55 planes because of quality and logics problems.

Source: Adapted from Carol Matlack, Stanley Holmes, and Frederik Balfour, 2006, "Airbus may hit an air pocket over China," *BusinessWeek Online*, www.businessweek.com, April 13.

Exhibit 9.5 **FDI: Advantages and Disadvantages**

Advantages	Disadvantages
• Usually more profitable	• Increased costs of capital investment
• Easier to adapt products to the local markets	• Can require expensive expatriate managers to staff FDI or to train local management
• More control of marketing and local strategy	• Higher cost to coordinate units located in different countries
• Improved local image of the product or service	• Increased exposure to local political risks
• Easier to provide after-market service	• Increased exposure to financial risks
• Reduces costs of selling locally in host countries or regions	
• Avoids tariffs or import quotas on finished products or supplies	

Source: Adapted from Franklin R. Root, 1994, *Entry Strategies for International Markets*, New York: Lexington Books.

Selecting the Entry Strategy: Some General Strategic Considerations

Before finalizing the choice of an entry strategy, international managers must consider several broader strategic issues as part of formulating such a strategy. In particular, international managers must consider: (1) their company's strategic intent regarding short- and long-term goals such as profits versus learning; (2) the international capabilities of their company to conduct business in the target country markets; (3) local government regulations relevant to their company's products or services in the target countries; (4) the cultural and institutional characteristics of the target product and market; (5) geographic and cultural distance between the home country and target country or region; and (6) the trade-off between risk and control. (This section relies heavily on Root.[21])

Strategic Intent

If the strategic goal is immediate profit, then multinational managers often look at the best immediate return on their investment. As you will see in Chapter 11 in this text, managers can project the estimated revenues for projects using particular entry strategies (for example, licensing versus exporting). Using the forecast revenues and costs associated with the investment options yields a forecast profit for each entry strategy. If the immediate goal is a profitable return on the international investment (and other considerations are similar), the international managers usually choose the most profitable entry strategy.

Certainly, profit must be the major goal of all companies if they are to survive. However, other goals such as learning a new technology or management approach or beating a competitor into a new market encourage companies to internationalize their operations. For example, many MNCs have entered China and India with the realization that profits may not materialize immediately. Instead, the long-term potential in these markets is so attractive that the MNCs focus on learning about the local market and developing the business contacts necessary to take advantage of potential opportunities. In such cases, joint ventures are often a mechanism for learning because of the direct association with a local partner.

Company Capabilities

The first question that governs almost every entry choice is: What can the MNC afford? For many and especially smaller companies, exporting is the only financially possible option for internationalization. A second issue considered by international managers concerns the human resource capabilities of the company. For example, a company might consider whether it has or can recruit managers with the necessary skills to transfer to a joint venture, to run a wholly owned subsidiary in a different nation, or even to supervise a local export department. A third consideration for international managers, beyond financial and human resource capabilities, concerns whether their company has the home country production capabilities to produce the types of products in demand in foreign markets. Or, perhaps the international managers should consider finding a partner company or an FDI investment to meet to build these capabilities.

Local Government Regulations

A company that decides to go international confronts a whole new set of regulations in the target market countries. Many issues must be decided. Consider the examples we note below. What kinds of import or export tariffs, duties, or restrictions exist? Excessive import tariffs, for example, may inflate the price of components for products produced in a foreign country or home country products exported into the foreign country. Laws might restrict foreign ownership or entry in local firms. For example, in some countries, majority ownership by foreign companies is not possible under local laws. Other legal and regulatory issues that demand careful consideration in the entry strategy decision might include, depending on the company, product, and industry, patent laws, consumer-protection laws, labor laws, tax laws, and local-content laws (how much of the product or raw material must be produced or supplied locally).

Target Market and Product Characteristics

Factors related to the targeted international market affect the entry decision in several ways. Consider just a few examples. One major concern is how and where the product is sold. This means that international managers must figure how to get the product or service to its customers. For example, a small winemaker in Argentina might need to figure out how to get the wine on to the shelves of stores or into restaurants in Tokyo. Can they use local channels of distribution, such as having local distributors sell their wine to the sales points? If not, our wine company example might consider using a joint venture to let a local alcohol company navigate the often complex steps from producer to end user.

Characteristics of products are equally important. For example, a product such as beer that is mostly water and difficult to transport might not be a strong candidate for exporting. Perhaps this is why Heineken exports only its formula and yeast and uses local water for production. Depending on customer needs, some products may need extensive adaptations in packaging, labeling, coloring, taste, etc. In such cases an MNC may lean toward using a joint venture or FDI to get closer to the customer and to be better able to understand local needs.

Cultural and Geographic Distance

Large distances between two countries, in either geography or culture, affect the entry decision.

Cultural distance is the degree that two national cultures differ on fundamental beliefs, attitudes, and values. For example, the US and Saudi Arabia have greater cultural distance than do the US and Australia. A large cultural distance usually encourages the foreign MNC to avoid direct investment, at least initially. In such situations, joint ventures are often attractive entry strategies because the local partner can deal with many local cultural issues. McDonald's, for example, uses joint ventures in the Middle East because McDonald's management feels that local cultures are so different from that of the US that it is safer to allow a joint venture partner to operate its local franchises. Licensing and exporting are entry strategies that also remove the foreign MNC even further from the necessity of dealing directly with the local culture.

Physical distance also raises entry strategy considerations for the international manager. For example, a long distance between producing and consuming countries may discourage an exporting strategy because of excessive transportation costs. Even with direct investment for production, as in the Airbus IB Strategic Insight above, it is sometimes necessary to ship components or raw material from another country to the producing country. Distance also has a psychological component for the MNC's managers. Even in today's electronic world, a lack of proximity making it more difficult for face-to-face communication may cause local managers to feel "out of the loop" in corporate decision making and limit the quality of their interactions with headquarters.

Political and Financial Risks of the Investment

Not all potential or otherwise attractive international markets have stable political systems. Governments change, and policies toward foreign companies can change just as quickly. Usually, foreign companies hold off on equity investments (that is, direct investments or joint ventures) until governments show some degree of stability. However, MNCs that take risks in unstable political environments can sometimes gain first-mover advantage in new international markets.

Like political systems, economic systems can be unstable and risky for MNCs. Take, for instance, international trade, and thus exporting, which is more complex and difficult when currencies fluctuate widely in value. In Chapter 12 you will learn some techniques available for international managers to manage such situations. Another consideration for the entry strategy focuses on the general economic situation regarding inflation or recession. Rapidly rising local prices or decreases in spending can affect the profitability of local investments making an FDI or joint venture entry more risky and less attractive. This is why most MNCs stick to licensing or exporting in risky economic environments unless a joint venture or direct investment has a potential for extremely high profits.

Need for Control

When an MNC selects an entry strategy, its managers must determine how important it is that their company control operations directly in the international operation. Potentially important areas for control include product quality and price, advertising and promotional activities, where and how the product is sold, and after-market service. Franchising companies such as McDonald's, Subway, and some hotel chains that use their uniform product quality as a competitive advantage over local competition necessarily have high needs for control. Franchisees must follow very specific regulations to maintain their franchise membership. In countries with well-developed contractual laws, such as most of Europe, the franchise contract provides adequate control. In other countries, even these companies that predominately franchise may use FDI and build company-owned stores as they usually provide the most control.

Exhibit 9.6 summarizes the preferred entry strategies for companies facing different conditions for the issues just discussed. Ultimately, and perhaps most importantly, entry strategies must align with the multinational strategy. Next, we address this final issue in the section on formulating an entry strategy.

Exhibit 9.6 **A Guide for Formulating Entry Strategies**

Participation Strategies	MNC's Situation									
	Strategic Intent		Need for Control	Company Resources		Product		Local Government	Geography	Culture
	Immediate Profit	Learn the Market	High	International Expertise	Strong Financial Position	Easy to Adapt	Difficult to Transport	Favorable Regulatory Environment	Long Distance between Markets	Large Cultural Distance
Indirect Export	✓✓						✓✓			✓✓
Direct Export	✓✓✓	✓		✓		✓✓		✓		✓
Licensing	✓✓	✓✓		✓✓✓	✓✓	✓✓	✓✓	✓	✓✓	✓✓
IJVs/ Alliances	✓	✓✓	✓✓	✓✓✓	✓✓	✓	✓✓	✓✓	✓✓	✓✓✓
FDI	✓	✓✓✓	✓✓✓	✓✓✓	✓✓✓	✓	✓	✓✓✓	✓	✓

Key:

✓ = Good situations for entry strategy

✓✓ = Better situations for entry strategy

✓✓✓ = Best situations for entry strategy

Source: Adapted in part from Franklin R. Root, 1994, *Entry Strategies for International Markets*, New York: Lexington, pp. 36–8, and John B. Cullen and K. Praveen Parboteeah, 2008, *Multinational Management*, Mason, OH: Thomson, p. 286.

Entry Strategies and Multinational Strategies

Most MNCs do not use a single entry strategy for all markets or for all products. Rather, they use combinations of entry strategies that reflect the best strategic choices for local conditions that best support the more general multinational strategy of their company.

The first question most international managers ask is, "Why do we want to be in this country?" Potential answers might include getting raw materials, manufacturing products or selling products, or perhaps any combination of these. More importantly, however, the answer to the question why a company is in a specific country follows from the understanding of how the country provides the right platform to carry out the multinational strategy. In this sense, entry strategies represent the "nuts and bolts" (e.g. sales, production, etc.) regarding how and why an MNC uses specific country locations to carry out its more general multinational strategies.

Because transnational strategists seek location advantages more than other strategists do, they use any entry strategy for any value-chain activity that can minimize costs or increase quality. Because multidomestic and regional strategists seek more local adaptation, the issue becomes whether the multinational uses modified home-country exports or uses FDI that locates the entire value chain in each country or region. Thus, the basic diagnostic question for the international manager is what entry strategy best serves the company's strategic objectives for being in a given country or region.

Exhibit 9.7 gives a summary of how companies with the various multinational strategies might use the different entry options.

Exhibit 9.7 **Choosing Entry Strategies to Support Multinational Strategies**

Multinational Strategies	Entry Strategies		
	Exporting	*Licensing*	*IJVs/Cooperative Alliances*	*Foreign Direct Investment*
Multidomestic	Export unique products/services to each country	License local companies allowing flexibility to adapt to a country's unique conditions	Employ when partner's knowledge of country's conditions such as adaptation for product or service is necessary	Own full value-chain activities in each country, from raw materials to service
Regional	Export similar products to each region served	License regional companies allowing flexibility to adapt to the region's unique conditions	Employ when partner's knowledge of regional conditions such as adaptation for product or service is necessary	Own full value-chain activities in regions, distribute activities within regions for location advantages
International	Export worldwide global products produced in the home country	License as a substitute strategy if local requirements or import barriers rule out exports from home country	Employ IJVs or alliances for upstream value-chain activities to complement or supplement own resources (e.g. shared investment costs); employ downstream under same conditions as licensing	Employ for downstream value-chain activities such as sales and aftermarket service activities
Transnational	Export global products/services worldwide from most advantageous cost or quality locations	License under similar conditions to the international strategy if other conditions prevent imports from optimal production locations or if local risk factors or other barriers counter-indicate FDI	Employ IJVs or alliances for upstream value-chain activities to complement or supplement own resources (e.g. shared R&D knowledge); use downstream under same conditions as licensing	Employ FDI for any value-chain activity anywhere in the world where location advantages are possible

Source: Adapted from John B. Cullen and K. Praveen Parboteeah, 2008, *Multinational Management*, Mason, OH: Thomson, p. 287.

CHAPTER REVIEW

Companies of all sizes have the option to go international and must choose the appropriate mechanisms to do so. With the growth of global competition, more and more companies seek international locations for R&D, raw materials, manufacturing, and sales. This chapter reviewed entry choices that companies can use to operate in the international marketplace. It also addressed major issues that an international manager must consider in selecting an entry strategy.

The selection of an entry strategy depends on a complex array of factors, including, but not limited to, the company's multinational strategy, its strategic intent, and its need for control of its products. Most MNCs will choose a mixture of entry strategies to fit different products or different businesses.

For the MNC, entry into the international market may occur anywhere in the value chain from R&D to after-market service. The majority of MNCs go beyond sourcing on the international market and thus must choose entry strategies that focus on the downstream value-chain activities of selling their products or services. Sales can take place using all entry strategies, from exporting to FDI. Although it can provide other strategic benefits such as learning about the market, exporting focuses primarily on sales. In addition to sales, the other entry strategies, including licensing, strategic alliances, and FDI, can serve other value-chain activities. For example, an MNC might use FDI for R&D and manufacturing in one country and use a joint venture for sales in a third country.

The complexities of choosing an entry strategy that complements the company's multinational strategy or strategies represent significant challenges to international managers. To name only a few issues, you saw that the nature of the product, the financial and political risks of the operation, the nature of the governmental regulations where the company locates, and the needs of the international managers to control operations must be considered when formulating entry choices for the MNC. To illustrate these complexities in the real world, the IB Strategic Insights showed you how practicing international managers react to the challenges of formulating successful entry strategies.

DISCUSSION QUESTIONS

1. Discuss some of the major issues to consider when choosing between an active or passive exporting strategy.
2. You work for a small company that has an innovative low-cost production method for high-capacity jump drives. A Japanese firm approaches your CEO to license the technology for use in Japan. Assume that your CEO has just asked you to write a report detailing the risks and potential benefits of this deal.
3. You work for a company with no international experience that has an efficient production method for small engines. A Vietnamese company approaches your CEO with a proposal to form a joint venture with your company in Vietnam. Assume that your CEO asks you to write a report detailing the risks and potential benefits of this deal.
4. Discuss some advantages and disadvantages to consider when considering FDI in a developing nation.
5. Identify a business that is not already franchising but has potential for international franchise success. Support your position.
6. As you saw in the chapter, China is attracting an increasing level of FDI for the R&D of MNCs. What are the drivers of this attraction and what are the major risks?
7. Look in your local business press and identify some local businesses that may have potential for international operations. What entry strategies would you advise and why?

INTERNATIONAL BUSINESS SKILL BUILDER

Identifying the Value-chain Activities and Entry Strategies

Step 1: Choose a global industry such as the automobile industry or the cell-phone industry and identify two major competitors in the industry.

Step 2: Research the selected companies in the popular business press and make a list of their major value-chain activities.

Step 3: For each company, identify value-chain activities located outside of the home country.

Step 4: For each company, write an analysis showing the entry strategies used in each location.

CHAPTER INTERNET ACTIVITY ——————

1. Explore the following websites: **www.franchise.org/; www.franchise opportunities.com/; www.franchisegator.com**
2. Compare and contrast international franchising opportunities in different industries.

KEY CONCEPTS ————————————

direct exporting

entry strategies

export management company (EMC)

export trading company (ETC)

foreign direct investment (FDI)

greenfield investment

indirect exporter

international cooperative alliance (ICA)

international franchising

international joint venture (IJV)

international strategic alliance

licensing

passive exporters

MOONBEAM ELECTRONICS

PROFITING FROM A FOREIGN TRADE ZONE

CASE 9

page 1

Located in southwest Missouri, Moonbeam Electronics is a manufacturer of small electrical appliances, such as toasters, toaster ovens, can openers, mixers, and blenders. Moonbeam assembles these products in its Springfield, Missouri, facility using a number of foreign suppliers for component parts. Virtually all products are assembled from parts from Japan, Taiwan, Korea, and China.

All of Moonbeam's production occurs in the Springfield facility, and the company employs over 400 people. Although labor costs might be lower in Mexico or Asia, Moonbeam has never considered moving its production operations out of the country. Wages and benefit costs are moderate and the workforce is productive. Moonbeam exports approximately 25 percent of its production output to Latin America, Europe, and Asia. The company hopes to increase its export potential with some product design changes and increased international marketing efforts.

Jim Harrison, vice president of logistics for Moonbeam, has been communicating with an old college friend who recently took a job at the Toyota production facility in Kentucky. Jim's friend told him that Toyota utilizes a foreign trade zone (FTZ) and that Moonbeam could benefit from one as well. After further discussions on the telephone, Jim decided to fly to Kentucky to see the Toyota facility and learn more about the FTZ concept.

Jim learned that Toyota imports from Japan component parts for its automobile manufacturing, and that by utilizing an FTZ the company avoids paying any customs duties on the component parts until the cars leave the FTZ. If the autos are exported out of the United States, then Toyota pays no tax on the component parts at all. It was explained to Jim that an FTZ is an area in the United States that is considered to be international territory, and therefore US customs duties do not apply.

Jim has further learned that there are two types of FTZ, a general-purpose trade zone and a subzone. The general-purpose trade zone operates for the benefit of several different companies and the subzone is established for one company's use exclusively. Toyota has a subzone for its production operations in Kentucky. From his visit Jim has decided that there are three benefits to operating in an FTZ: (1) delay of payment of custom duties, (2) possible elimination of custom duties, and (3) the bypassing of US Customs regulations. He is confident that Moonbeam can realize all three benefits, but he wants to further investigate this idea before he formally presents a proposal for adoption to senior management.

...

CASE DISCUSSION POINTS

1. Research foreign trade zones and determine if Jim is correct in his assertions concerning the potential benefits.
2. Specifically, how might Moonbeam benefit from the establishment of an FTZ? Are there any disadvantages?
3. Would you recommend that Moonbeam establish a subzone? Explain.

Sources: G. Hanks and L. Van, 1999, "Foreign Trade Zone," *Management Accounting*, January 1; J. Daniels and L. Radebaugh, 2001, *International Business*, Upper Saddle River, NJ: Prentice Hall,.

Case prepared by Charles A. Rarick

CASE 9

page 2

10 International Marketing and Supply-chain Management for MNCs

After reading this chapter you should be able to:

- Understand how complex global markets can be and the need for relevant information on foreign markets.

- Understand market responses in terms of the global–local dilemma.

- Understand how the marketing mix can vary in global markets.

- Understand the implications of the global–local dilemma in the marketing mix.

- Understand the implications of global supply chains and outsourcing.

What makes products successful in foreign markets? Why do some products succeed and others fail? How does the international manager know what makes a product valued in one culture compared to another? How does the international manager communicate with potential customers in various cultures? What makes a product's packaging appealing? Do customers in a foreign market prefer to buy products in large modern department stores or in small family-owned corner stores? What sorts of services do they

Zeno and the Global Market for Acne Treatment

PREVIEW IB
STRATEGIC INSIGHT

Tyrell, Inc. a Houston, Texas, based company, is pioneering an exciting new product category of home-based medical devices. The first of these groundbreaking products is the acne treatment device, Zeno™. Zeno is a hand-held portable electronic device for clearing mild to moderate individual inflammatory acne pimples. Zeno works through a precisely controlled application of heat to the acne pimple. When applied for a specific amount of time the heat causes acne bacteria to self-destruct and the pimple disappears.[1] The product has met with significant success in the US, but should Tyrell consider taking Zeno global?

The global appeal of such a product depends on many factors. The first is cultural values. Some national cultures, for example Turkey, see acne as a natural course of life, and unless it is chronic, would not be responsive to aggressive and expensive acne treatment for a normal teenage case. Other cultures, such as the US, see people as more in control of nature and the environment[2] and would respond well to a product that controls acne. In the US, people tend to feel that they can and should be able to control many aspects of nature such as normal teenage acne and the effects of aging.

The second factor affecting the success of Zeno in global markets is demand and spending power. This involves not only the population of a potential foreign market in terms of the number of people who would be interested in purchasing such a product but also how the income is distributed across the population. Countries with large middle classes, where a large part of the population makes enough money to spend something on products that are not essential to live, are highly attractive markets in general. The presence of a sizable middle class with middle-class and upper middle-class incomes would mean that there is sufficient market potential for Zeno. Beyond this, of course the specific market segments still must be researched and understood.

The third major influence in taking a product like Zeno global is infrastructure. Zeno sells for US$ 200, and in the US it is sold through dermatologists, dermatology clinics, medical spas, and trained aestheticians. In other words, people buy this product because a trained professional, a doctor, nurse, or medical technician, specializing in skin disorders, recommends it. And quite often the customer sees the product promoted in the doctor's office or skin treatment center. While Zeno does not require a prescription, because of its cost it benefits from being "sold" through the medical community. If Zeno is to be successful in foreign markets, there need to be the right medical clinics, the right medical specialists, and treatment centers through which Zeno can be recommended and distributed. The Korean (Brazilian, Chinese, etc.) consumer interested in acne treatments must have access to information about the existence of the product, how it works, and its effectiveness through medical establishments. A country without the medical infrastructure to provide this would not be viable for Zeno.

So Tyrell must understand consumer preferences and address the segment of consumers that would appreciate and value acne treatments. It must research its potential markets and make sure the economy is developed to the level that there are enough people with enough money to buy Zeno. Tyrell must further research its potential markets to make sure that the medical infrastructure is advanced enough to support the marketing of Zeno. In addition, it must research all medical and import regulations in each market that will affect Zeno. All of this is a daunting and complex task. Yet the potential success of a product like Zeno makes the idea quite attractive.

marketing mix
the combination of an MNC's product offering, distribution, pricing, and all marketing communication components

want when they buy a product? As the Preview IB Strategic Insight shows, these questions involve everything the international manager does to connect, communicate, and deliver products to customers—this is marketing. We can understand the way marketing works in terms of the **marketing mix**, which is (1) the product offering, (2) distribution, (3) pricing, and (4) all the components of marketing communications.

Of all the areas where the global–local dilemma affects international business, marketing may be the one where it is the biggest factor. All the cost and management advantages of a global integration strategy where the marketing mix is standardized across every country are still great. Yet, the greatest pressure for a local-responsiveness strategy comes from important differences in what customers want and how customers respond from country to country. One of the key factors in helping the international manager figure out the balance of where and when to respond locally and where and when to standardize is knowledge about the markets in question.

Market Research—The Knowledge Advantage

When you were deciding on the college you wanted to attend, where did you start? Rather than simply tossing a coin, you most likely started by systematically gathering information on various colleges to consider. Gathering this information gave you a knowledge advantage as it helped you understand many of the factors involved in making the best decision for your future. International managers approach decisions associated with marketing in foreign countries in much the same way. **International marketing research** is the systematic gathering of objective information in and about foreign markets that will help the international manager understand customer wants and needs. This research provides a knowledge advantage because it provides a critically important guide to the international manager in balancing the global–local dilemma, developing the appropriate marketing mix, and, as we discuss below, segmentation, targeting, and market growth decisions.

international marketing research
the systematic collection of objective information in and about foreign markets that helps international managers understand customer wants and needs

secondary data
data that already exist and were gathered for some previous purpose, sometimes by governments, the UN, the World Bank, or other agencies and trade associations

One of the first issues in building the knowledge advantage is to understand what kind of marketing information is needed. This comes directly from the questions that the international manager needs answered. Some questions about foreign markets can be answered with secondary data. **Secondary data** are data that already exist and were gathered for some previous purposes, sometimes by governments, the UN, the World Bank, or various agencies and trade associations. For example, an MNC considering marketing an acne treatment device in Asian countries might look at income levels from government data and the sales of pharmaceuticals of certain types available from the UN. This would provide the international manager with information about whether people can afford to buy such a device and whether such products are acceptable in a culture.

If the international manager cannot answer his or her questions regarding a foreign market with secondary data, primary data may be needed. **Primary data** are gathered specifically to provide the information needed by the international manager; they did not previously exist. Primary data most often involve surveys asking customers, for example: how satisfied they are with the product; what types of services are most important; what they believe is a reasonable price for the coffee; and how much they would be willing to spend for a movie. Another form of primary data involves customer panels, where the same set of customers are surveyed to measure changes over time, for example in product awareness or product knowledge, or in responses to advertising messages.

Primary data can be gathered in person by trained interviewers, by mail, by e-mail, or by websites. Regardless of how the data are collected, there are a number of complications in international marketing research, most of which involve language and cultural differences. Developing questionnaires in a different language requires more than simple translation. To avoid serious mistakes in interpretation, back translation can be used. **Back translation** is when the questionnaire is repeatedly translated back and forth between the two languages until all of it agrees and is consistent between both languages.

Other problems in international marketing research can come from cultural biases. In some cultures, there can be a bias to respond in a certain way regardless of how you really feel. For example, the Japanese find it extremely difficult to say "no" directly or to disagree, so the agree–disagree statements often used in market research must be avoided in Japan. Besides Japan, there is a cultural bias against saying "no" or disagreeing in a number of other counties. Likewise, many cultures have a courtesy bias. That is, the person responding will strive to be polite and give you the answer that they believe you want, which may be totally unrelated to how they really feel about the product. In other cultures, getting customers to respond and participate in market research at all can be problematic. There can be strong biases against revealing any information about feelings and opinions. There may also be gender issues. For example, in the Middle East, it is often difficult to get the opinions of female consumers.

Another important marketing research tool is focus groups. A **focus group** is a small group of actual or potential customers that are gathered especially to discuss and talk about the topic or idea that the international manager needs to understand. For example, an MNC attempting to market an acne treatment device in Korea might gather a group of six to eight teenagers to discuss the whole notion of acne and acne treatment. The **moderator**, the trained professional who runs the focus group, might show the teenagers the actual device and ask them to discuss various features or aspects of the actual product. Again, some of the same biases are a problem for focus groups: a cultural norm of always agreeing or of seeing different opinions as discourteous, or of getting consumers to participate and provide information at all.

primary data
data that did not previously exist and were specifically collected to directly provide the information needed by a manager, and often involving surveys of customers or customer panels

back translation
the repeated translation, back and forth, between two languages until a common meaning is consistent between both languages

focus group
a small group of actual or potential customers specifically brought together to discuss and talk about a particular topic or idea that a manager needs to understand

moderator
a trained professional who leads and facilitates a focus group

The IB Strategic Insight below shows an example of how the use of a focus group can provide the wine industry insights into the Chinese market for wines.

In sum, to build a knowledge advantage, it is critical to adapt research procedures to local conditions so that valid and useful information results. Because cultural sensitivity is so important in market research, sometimes hiring a local market research company is the best alternative. Local market research companies have the specialized understanding and experience with local conditions that are necessary in certain countries such as China and the Arab states. The international manager must carefully screen local research agencies to ensure that they provide high-quality information.

While international market research is typically much more expensive than domestic research, the quality of information should be the focus and must not be compromised because of cost. Another issue is the ability to integrate the new market research information with the MNC's programs. International

Focus Groups on Wine in China

IB STRATEGIC INSIGHT

The enjoyment of drinking wine is growing in popularity and thus presents a huge market opportunity in many countries. The US wine industry is working to develop markets on a number of fronts: young adult age groups, ethnic groups, and international markets. Research is being done to understand what the preferences are in these various groups and what drives consumer response. Of particular concern is trade dress. Trade dress refers to the physical appearance of the product and suggests what marketers can do to make it more appealing. In wine, this is the color and shape of the bottle, and of particular concern is the label. Wine labels have become much more colorful, artistic, and sometimes even whimsical, with cartoon-like images and various depictions of animals (this trend is called "critter" labeling).

One of the fastest growing wine markets is China,[3] but little is understood about that market in terms of mainstream customer response to wine labels. As such, to gain some knowledge about market preferences so that companies can develop this quite large and potentially rich wine market, marketing researchers have begun using focus groups. In one study, researchers assembled groups of 20-something Chinese men and women. Several key challenges immediately emerged. The first involved the

gender mix of groups. In mixed groups, the interactions and levels of participation were imbalanced. Often, regardless of how the moderator tried to direct interaction, one gender, typically the females, dominated the discussion, while the other gender was quiet. To gain reliable information, the focus groups had to be split by gender.

The second problem was the entrenchment of traditional perspectives on the product category. The moderator had to remind and reinforce to participants that the subject was *grape* wine and not rice wine, as is the traditional type in China. Results from the focus groups indicated that wine drinking among younger people is evolving into what looks like more mainstream, widespread practice. Wine drinking in this group seems to emulate Western practices that are perceived as hip and sophisticated. In older generations, wine drinking is seen as medicinal. Wine drinkers in this group would drink smaller amounts regularly, for example one small glass every day for health benefits. This group is not concerned about variety, taste, or image. Importantly, the views of this older generation of wine drinkers are consistent with Chinese cultural views of nontraditional, holistic, and herbal medical practices. One last interesting issue that emerged is that the Chinese still believe that good wine can only come from France.

market research provides important information to develop global plans and strategies and to help decide the extent of local adaptation that is necessary.

The knowledge advantage is very important in the first basic decision that the international manager makes—is the foreign market large enough so that the MNC can make profits by offering its products or services there? This question involves estimating the market potential and forecasting demand in the local market. Before deciding to enter the market, the MNC needs an understanding of whether or not local consumers would buy the product and how much of the product they would buy. Some large international research companies, such as ACNeilsen, can provide estimates of market demand, but such information is expensive. Various methods that rely on secondary data published by local governments, the World Bank or the UN can also be useful. Here again, local market research companies can be very helpful.

Understanding Global Demand—Segmentation

Segmentation drives our understanding of market demand. Segmentation, the process of grouping consumers according to their preferences and needs, allows the MNC to tailor marketing programs and products that focus on filling those particular needs. Segmentation is based on any characteristic that associates with how consumer decides to spend his or her money. For example, incomes and spending power, gender, profession, or the presence of children all associate with the types of products needed in various segments.

Sometimes market research uncovers segments that are global. Global segments are made up of customers with similar needs regardless of their country. For example, consumers throughout the world have a need and preference for reliable, convenient, and accessible communication. Advances in communications technology have made it possible for cell-phone companies such as Nokia to tap into these global segments. As the largest cell-phone manufacturer in the world, Nokia offers its products in Europe, Africa, the Middle East, Asia Pacific, Greater China, and North, South, and Latin America.[4]

Market research can also reveal regional segments where customer needs and preferences are similar within regions that cross several countries. This can be seen in certain regions such as Central America or Southern Europe. Also as an example, Aafia, the Saudi Arabian food company, has capitalized on consistent preferences for its products across Persian regions.[5]

On occasion, market research reveals that segments are unique by country: that is, customer preferences are so diverse that cross-border grouping is not possible. How consumers' preferences cluster and group together across and within countries is a key consideration in global–local. When segments are global or regional, it is possible to take advantage of standardized marketing programs. However, when segments are unique within a country, offerings must be adapted specifically for those unique local needs. As you will see below, this is related directly to how to solve the global–local dilemma introduced in Chapter 2.

segmentation
the process of grouping consumers according to any characteristics that influence their buying and consumption behavior, allowing MNCs to tailor marketing programs and products to satisfying the particular needs of distinct consumer groups

Products and Brands—Global or Local?

product
a set of benefits that satisfies needs for the consumer, including all physical or tangible components as well as all intangible components, such as service, reputation, prestige, and other elements that the customer cannot feel and see

For the marketer, a **product** provides a set of benefits that satisfy needs for the consumer. It consists of all the physical or tangible components, such as color, as well as all intangible components, such as service, reputation, prestige, and other elements that the customer cannot feel and see. All these components and characteristics, whether they are tangible or intangible, can bring value to the consumer, and taken as a whole are the product. In international business, the MNC can extend its products, adapt its products, or it can develop new products to take to foreign markets. Of course, this relates back to the research that shows you whether or not and how consumer needs and preferences group across foreign markets.

direct extension
marketing the same product to customers across foreign markets with only minor modifications like language changes on the label or instructions, or no changes at all

When the MNC's product meets the needs of customers in foreign markets with little or no change, marketers say it can be extended directly. **Direct extension** may involve only language changes on the label or instructions, as with soft drinks or bicycles, for example. However, sometimes even that is not necessary and a completely standardized product can be offered. The most famous example of direct extension is Coke. In many markets, it is not even necessary for Coke to change the language in product labeling. **Standardization** means that the product is uniform and consistent from country to country. Sometimes standardized products can be extended directly to only one or a few countries when there are regional segments. Direct extension works when consumers have highly common needs and common conditions of use and purchase in many countries. In such cases, the MNC's existing product can fill needs with little or no change. For example, the French luxury bag marketer Louis Vuitton directly extends its product offering with no modifications to consumers throughout the world. You can buy the same bag in New York, Paris, or Tokyo.

standardization
maintaining a product's uniformity and consistency from country to country

While there are many cost advantages to standardized products, much of the time, entering foreign markets means that some product changes are necessary. In some markets, these can be substantial. When consumer wants and needs differ from country to country, or when the conditions when or how the consumer uses the product differ, an **adaptation strategy** is appropriate. Adaptation means that the MNC customizes and adapts its products to local wants, needs, and conditions. Adaptation is rarely a question of "yes" or "no," but instead it involves questions of what features to customize, how much and in which ways to customize them for which countries. Too much customization is costly and may not necessarily better serve consumer needs. Too little customization may ignore important differences in needs from country to country, and cost the MNC sales and market share.

adaptation strategy
customizing or adapting an MNC's products to the local wants, needs, and conditions of different foreign markets

When entering foreign markets, the MNC may decide to develop a new product from scratch. In the case of new product development for multiple foreign markets, the decisions of standardization or adaptation are not eliminated. There are still concerns over where and how much local adaptation is appropriate from market to market. Also, there are still decisions about the extent and scope of advantages to be gained from standardization. However, because the new product begins with a global scope, the global–local dilemma is managed from the very beginning. For example, when the product is "born global," from the very beginning there is a strong focus on tapping the commonalities across various foreign markets. Likewise, from the beginning, the new product formulation can be designed so that adaptation to local situations and local market preferences is accomplished more easily. Certain components and features are easily changed out or added in for various markets.

Experts often refer to the 70/30 rule here, meaning that at least 70 percent of a global product must remain consistent while 30 percent can remain flexible for response to local conditions.[6] For example, BMW's models are configured slightly differently between European and US markets. If you own a laptop computer, you can see that the only local adaptation necessary is to change the cord that plugs into the power converter to adapt to differences in electricity receptacles.

Global and Local Branding

The **brand** is the identity of a product. It includes the name, logo, symbols, terms, song, colors, special packaging characteristics, product appearance, words, or anything else used to establish our association with the product and identify the product. For example, the Nike brand is based on the "swoosh" symbol, the "Just do it" slogan, as well as an array of other things that establish the image of Nike products and our positive association with them. Below, you

brand
the identity of a product embodied in the name, logo, symbols, terms, song, colors, special packaging characteristics, product appearance, words, or anything else used to establish our association with the product and identify the product

Hello Kitty—What Do Brands Mean Across Cultures?

IB STRATEGIC INSIGHT

Since its creation in 1974 by Japan's Sanrio Company, Hello Kitty has grown by leaps and bounds. Hello Kitty ranks as the third most recognized Asian brand and is recognized in more than 40 countries across the world. Kitty's creators purposely did not develop any details about Kitty or her life. With her oversized moon-shaped face, button nose, six whiskers, and dot eyes, she was simply cute. This allowed her beholders, young girls, to make Kitty whatever they needed her to be.

This turned out to be a very smart move, as across the globe the little cat seems to convey a message. Exactly what this message is likely varies from culture to culture. Some experts believe that in collectivist cultures such as China and Japan, where groups such as family, co-workers, and peer groups have great influence on behavior, people react to a brand such as Hello Kitty only because it is what everyone else does. According to these experts, consumers in collectivist cultures are more interested in the concrete product features and do not respond to abstract personality traits and characteristics portrayed in brands.

In individualistic cultures like the US where people tend to "do their own thing," brands such as Hello Kitty have wide appeal precisely because she can mean a variety of things to different people. In individualistic cultures people respond to unique brand personalities and like brand portrayals that are friendly, according to experts.

However, some experts also suggest that these notions of collectivism versus individualism do not necessarily apply across all aspects of a person's life. In their public lives, the Japanese have an aversion to standing out, or challenging authority and social norms. Yet in their private lives, Japanese highly value ideals of self-expression, freedom, and uniqueness—notions they would and could never express at work or in the educational system. So it could be that brand portrayals based on certain personalities and characteristics do appeal across cultures. The challenge in global branding is tapping into these customer responses that cross cultural and national boundaries. The lesson from Hello Kitty is that simplicity may be key.

Source: Adapted from Randall Frost, 2006, "Cultures split over brand personality," www.brandchannel.com, April 19.

global brand
a single brand used for a product throughout the world. A global brand has a consistent identity with customers in all markets, using the same product benefits and characteristics, the same brand name, logos, and slogans, with the same meaning for consumers in all countries and markets

can see an example of how dolls from Japan can have different brand images in different cultures.

In branding strategies and decisions, the MNC again faces the global–local dilemma. Whether extending an existing product or developing a new product for foreign markets, the MNC must decide whether to use one brand across all markets or a separate brand for regional markets or even a separate brand for each country market. When a product has a global identity, when there is a single brand for the product throughout the world, it is called a **global brand**. A global brand has a consistent identity with customers in all markets. A global brand has the same product benefits and characteristics, the same brand name, logos, and slogans, all with the same meaning for consumers throughout the world.

As the following IB Ethical Challenge notes, global brands can be so important that they even have ethical implications for an MNC.

There are very few truly global brands. Exhibit 10.1 shows the top 25 brands in the world. Each year, Interbrand, a consulting company, tracks the

Trust in Global Brands

ETHICAL CHALLENGE

Global brands are now battling not only for customers' attention but also more importantly for customers' trust. Trust is built over time by engaging customers and behaving responsibly in business activities. The MNC's brand messages are only one of the many sources of information now available to customers, and out of all those sources the brand information developed and put out by the MNC is the information least trusted by customers. A survey by the World Economic Forum (WEF) found that trust in global companies is at an all-time low. Customers tend to trust just about anyone else more than the MNC. They seem to trust non-governmental agencies (NGOs) such as Greenpeace particularly.

Customer trust provides a mind-blowing competitive advantage that can be hugely leveraged and impossible to replicate. It is easy to lose and extremely difficult to regain once lost. The WEF survey indicates that the global customer is now much less likely to be "taken in" by branding messages produced and put out by MNCs. Importantly, customers seem to trust MNCs that are seen as contributing to the best interests of society and those that place themselves in a position of accountability for their actions.

To build trust, customers must believe that the MNC is responsible and accountable in its brand building and branding messages. The MNC must develop brand images that openly reflect authenticity and genuineness. Importantly, the MNC must build in notions of customer responsiveness and receptivity to larger issue of global ethics.

The twenty-first-century global customer is street savvy and very good at spotting inconsistencies in branding activities and messages. These customers look for discontinuities in brand information provided by the MNC and that provided by the multitude of other sources now available, for example blogs. MNCs can protect themselves against possible damage to their brands in incidences where their ethical behavior is being questioned by a powerful NGO such as Greenpeace. However, to be an effective defense, the MNC's image of responsibility, accountability, responsiveness, and integrity must be in place before any incidents occur.

Source: Arlo Brady, 2006, "Corporate responsibility: The role of the brand," www.brandchannel.com, March 13.

Exhibit 10.1 **The 25 Top Global Brands**

2007 Rank	2008 Rank	Brand	Sector	Country of Origin	2008 Brand Value ($m)	Change in Brand Value
1	1	Coca-Cola	Beverages	United States	66,667	2%
3	2	IBM	Computer Services	United States	59,031	3%
2	3	Microsoft	Computer Software	United States	59,007	1%
4	4	GE	Diversified	United States	53,086	3%
5	5	Nokia	Consumer Electronics	Finland	35,942	7%
6	6	Toyota	Automotive	Japan	34,050	6%
7	7	intel	Computer Hardware	United States	31,261	1%
8	8	McDonald's	Restaurants	United States	31,049	6%
9	9	Disney	Media	United States	29,251	0%
20	10	Google	Internet Services	United States	25,590	43%
10	11	Mercedes Benz	Automotive	Germany	25,577	9%
12	12	HP	Computer Hardware	United States	23,509	6%
13	13	BMW	Automotive	Germany	23,298	8%
16	14	Gillette	Personal Care	United States	22,689	8%
15	15	American Express	Financial Services	United States	21,940	5%
17	16	Louis Vuitton	Luxury	France	21,602	6%
18	17	Cisco	Computer Services	United States	21,306	12%
14	18	Marlboro	Tobacco	United States	21,300	0%
11	19	Citi	Financial Services	United States	20,174	−14%
19	20	Honda	Automotive	Japan	19,079	6%
21	21	Samsung	Consumer Electronics	Republic of Korea	17,689	5%
New	22	H&M	Apparel	Sweden	13,840	New
27	23	Oracle	Computer Software	United States	13,831	11%
33	24	Apple	Computer Hardware	United States	13,724	24%
25	25	Sony	Consumer Electronics	Japan	13,583	5%

Source: Interbrand, "Best global brands," www.interbrand.com/best_global_brands.aspx

performance of top global brands. As we can see, these global brands can be extremely valuable for the MNC. A major part of the advantage of global brands comes from economies of scale. The development and marketing costs for a global brand can be spread over large sales volumes in many markets. Global brands are much more visible than local brands because of their consistent identity. When customers travel around, they see the product in other countries as well as their own. In addition, global brands gain from media overlap. Potential customers in the US can view many Canadian TV channels and listen to many Canadian radio stations. With the advanced communications technology making satellite TV and radio more and more common, this media overlap will become commonplace and even more beneficial to global brands.

In spite of the powerful advantages of global brands, global branding strategies are not always possible and not always the most desirable approach. Local branding strategies may be necessary because the brand name may have some undesirable associations or offensive meanings in the local culture. Likewise, certain terms may have a specific meaning that is not consistent across cultures. For example, product brand names do not contain the term "diet" in association with caloric content in France because diet is a specific medical term requiring sale in a pharmacy. Brands like Diet Coke must be sold as Coke Light. In Japan, the diet is the national legislature. There are many examples of brand names that have restricted global use. For example, the Chevy Nova translates into "no go" in Spanish. The IB Strategic Insight below gives another recent example.

Local brands can be a great asset. Local branding can signal that the company is sensitive to cultural differences and committed to serving the local market. Customers may feel resentment toward a certain country or toward big MNCs in general. In such cases, local brands are preferable. Local brands can sometimes enjoy more support from local retailers when they advise customers on product choices. Local brands may also have wider distribution with more local retailers. This means that after-sales services, such as product repair and maintenance, are more available and easier for customers. Finally, even though it may not always be true, buyers may believe that global or regional brands offered by well-known MNCs are more expensive than local offerings. Customers in local markets may see local brands as better value for their money. For example, in Turkey consumers see appliances produced by the Turkish company Arcelik as providing better value for their money than the better known, more prestigious brands from Western MNCs.

Cultural Sensitivity Issues Show up in Surprising Ways for Adidas

IB STRATEGIC INSIGHT

The German company Adidas-Salomon used a caricature of an Asian boy on their "Yellow Series" shoe that was released in April 2006 in Paris, Tokyo, Hamburg, Denmark, San Francisco, New York, and Los Angeles. The shoes sell for $250 and depict a boy with buckteeth, a bowl haircut, and slanted eyes. American Asians find the caricature offensive, suggesting that it is racist and demeaning. The avant-garde artist who drew the character has a Chinese mother and noted that the caricature looks like he did when he was eight years old. Adidas is attempting to tap into a younger hipper market and believed that this group would understand the image as art. This was a serious misjudgment as American Asians do not see it as art and continue to be angered by the product.

Source: Adapted from Michael Tunison, "Asians Decry Adidas Shoe as a Misstep," 2006, *Washington Post*, April 14, p. D01.

When an MNC decides to take its products to foreign markets a big issue is the **country of origin (COO) effect**. This means that consumers can take strong messages based on the location where the product is made and marketed. The COO influence can be positive if the country is viewed positively, or negative if the country is viewed negatively. Sometimes the COO signals quality, as with French wines. Sometimes it signals less desirable cues such as the unfair competitive practices associated with China or substandard quality. The COO effect often comes from the "made in" label, but it can also come from the customer's perceptions about where the product originates. The following IB Strategic Insight examines the COO of the "made in China" label.

country of origin (COO) effect

the meanings and messages consumers derive from where a product is made and marketed. The influence can be positive if the country is viewed positively and negative if the country is viewed negatively

Country of Origin Effects of "Made in China"

IB STRATEGIC INSIGHT

What does the "made in China" tag mean in the marketplace? A recent survey of marketing executives showed that country of origin (COO) effects are strong for Chinese products. Importantly, a vast majority of these marketing experts believe that the strong effect of the "made in China" label is negative and harmful in the marketplace. They reported that Chinese products are seen as cheap, poor value, poor quality, unreliable, and unsophisticated (i.e. very basic). Importantly, this is not a perception confined to Western countries, because these executives came not only from the USA but also from Europe, Latin America, and even the Asia/Pacific regions. Also, it is not an impression limited to specific product categories because it includes cars, furniture, food, appliances, clothing, toys, and computers, among others. Interestingly, China is seen as the land of original equipment manufacturers (OEMs). This likely has some basis in reality because so many Chinese companies mass-produce unbranded and unidentified parts and components designed and developed by MNCs as ingredients in their own global brands.

Believe it or not, this situation is very similar to the one for the "made in Japan" tag in the 1960s and 1970s. The Japanese undertook an aggressive strategy to upgrade their low-quality image and successfully transformed it to the extent that beginning in the 1980s and continuing through today, the label "made in Japan" now stands for extremely high-quality and highly innovative products. The Chinese see this as a road that they intend to follow and have embarked on a carefully orchestrated and coordinated strategy. First, Chinese companies have acquired a number

of brands that are well established with strong brand equity. Second, with each acquisition they are absorbing the expertise in brand development and management that comes with the acquired brand and then incorporating it throughout their companies. These Chinese companies are gaining not only the equity and credibility of established brands but also the knowledge and talent to apply to their own homegrown brands.

Chinese-owned brands are already benefiting from this strategy and are expected to climb in status and equity in the next five years. As noteworthy example, Lenovo acquired the IBM PC division late in 2004 and plans to use that brand as a platform for marketing its products, while at the same time using the acquired brand expertise to build its own capabilities in brand creation and management. Another Chinese brand on the move is Bird, a mobile phone company. Bird has positioned itself as the first and only Chinese brand to become a top ten mobile phone brand as it currently ranks number eight and it is expected to continue challenging established names such as Samsung, Sony Ericsson, Panasonic, and Mitsubishi.

While current perceptions of China are clearly hurting Chinese brands, the Japanese demonstrated that such perceptions can indeed be overcome. Given the newly acquired expertise coupled with the established brand names and the ingrained low-cost production capacity, powerful Chinese brands may come sooner than we think.

Source: Jeff Systun, Fred Burt, and Annie Ly, 2005, "The strategy of Chinese brands," Interbrand White Paper.

Although COO effects can be quite strong, they can change over time. Products from Japan were once thought to be of poor quality but are now seen as among the highest-quality products in the world. In formerly communist countries such as the Czech Republic, US brands such as Nike and Reebok are associated with freedom. Interestingly, COO effects remain intact even when they do not actually apply to the product. With the increased economic connections between countries and the increasingly globalized supply chains we describe below, products may actually come from several countries. A consumer may buy a Dodge Ram pickup truck thinking that it is an American product. Yet the truck may have been manufactured in Mexico with components from Germany and Taiwan as well as the US! What should the "made in" label say? In fact, the sticker on a Dodge pickup now indicates the percentage of parts and components that originate in the US.

Delivering Products across the Globe—Distribution and Supply Chains

Have you ever thought about how products in the supermarket—say, for example, Tillamook cheese—find their way to you? All the companies that help get the cheese from the dairy farmer to you make up the distribution channel for cheese. A **distribution channel** consists of intermediaries, mostly wholesalers and retailers that do all the work to get products to you, the end user. In addition to traditional retail stores, more and more these days the company's products reach the consumer through e-tailers, stores that sell products through websites on the Internet. In rare cases, the company may act as its own distribution channel. This is called **direct distribution** because the company sells its products directly to the consumer. When this happens, it is most often through the Internet. A majority of the time, however, it is just too expensive for the company to sell product items one at a time to customers when intermediaries (wholesalers and retailers) can do it at a much lower cost. In taking its products to foreign markets, a company may use multiple distribution channels as shown in Exhibit 10.2.

distribution channel
the set of intermediaries, mostly wholesalers and retailers, that help get products to end users but do not manufacture the products

direct distribution
MNCs selling products directly to consumers with no wholesale or retail intermediaries

Retailing in Global Markets

Retailers are intermediaries who are closest to the customer and serve the customer directly. Because of this, retailing is most often a localized activity. There are vast differences in retailing from country to country. People in the US are used to seeing mostly large stores with a vast array of products, such as Walmart superstores. In some countries, more retail stores are small mom-and-pop stores, sometimes carrying only a very limited line of items. This is the case for Italy, Algeria, and many parts of France, for example. In some countries, much retailing activity still happens through temporary open-air markets or bazaars. The merchants rent a spot and set up their temporary shop, sell their products for the afternoon, day, or evening, then pack up and repeat the same routine the next week or next evening.

In any case, although retailers always interact directly with customers, there is variance from country to country in the services provided to consumers. In many stores in the US, customers do not get any attention from salespeople,

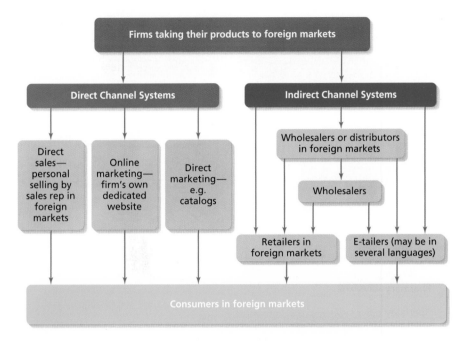

Exhibit 10.2 **Possible Combinations of Distribution Channels with Various Intermediaries That May Be Involved in Global Distribution**

who are there only to complete transactions at the cash register. In Japan, certain components of retail service are legendary and contrast decidedly with the US. For example, at the checkout, the clerk typically wraps the product, boxes it, artistically wraps the box again, and then puts the package in an attractive shopping bag. In France, it is not unusual for the customers to bring their own shopping bags.

Though retailing varies greatly from country to country, overall it is rapidly changing worldwide. These changes involve three major trends: increasing retailer size, increases in e-tailing, and the growing importance of global retailers. First, although there are still many countries where small, specialty shops, or mom-and-pop stores predominate, there is a strong trend of larger retail stores developing a stronger presence worldwide. In China, for example, consumers can shop in large supermarkets and department stores more than ever before.

Exhibit 10.3 shows how retail establishment size has increased recently in China. Even in France, where traditional small merchants have been preferred historically, large *supermarchés* and department stores are seen more and more frequently—and their parking lots are jammed!

As mentioned earlier, MNCs can use their websites as a promotional tool. Increasingly, the Internet also is used in all types of buying and selling and various business transactions. This is generally known as **e-commerce**. The MNC can sell its products through its own website; however, for efficiency reasons, more often Internet distribution intermediaries, virtual retail stores, are used. These intermediaries are called **e-tailers**. Probably the most famous example of an e-tailer is Amazon.com. Importantly, MNCs can benefit from the spillover as communications technologies, e.g. the Internet, have freed up the access to foreign products. Consumers from all over the world can log on

e-commerce
buying and selling transactions conducted through the Internet

e-tailers
Internet distribution intermediaries (virtual retail stores)

287

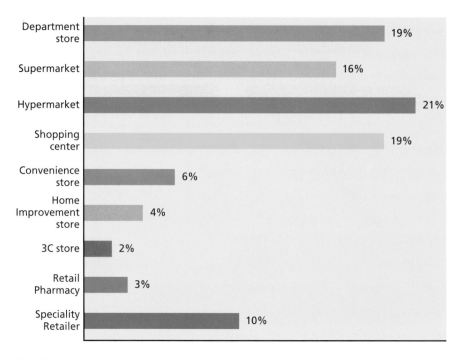

Exhibit 10.3 *Retailing in China*

Notes:

Hypermarket—usually defined as being 2,500 square meters or bigger; similar to the Super Wal-Mart in the US.

3C store—a semi-specialty type of store carrying communication products, information technology products and digital products.

to Amazon.com to view and purchase products. MNCs taking their products to foreign markets have an increased chance to serve those markets through the Internet and various e-tailers. To ensure success in foreign markets, websites should be designed with cultural sensitivity in mind, just as print or television ads are, and even developing websites in other languages. Later, in Chapter 15, you will learn more about e-tailing in international business.

global retailers
large-scale retailing MNCs that have locations throughout various regions of the world

The third important trend in international distribution is the growth and increasing importance of global retailers. **Global retailers** are large-scale retailing MNCs. Not only are these individual retail establishments larger, they are located throughout various regions of the world and some of them are truly global. For example, Walmart has stores in China, Europe, Latin America, the Caribbean, Canada, Japan, and Korea. IKEA, the Scandinavian home furnishing retailer, has stores in Europe, Asia, and the United States. Carrefour, the French *hypermarché*, has opened stores in Latin America, China, and other parts of Asia. The

number and influence of these mega-retailers continues to increase in the global market.

Wholesaling in Global Markets

Often, especially in international markets, the MNC's products do not go directly to a retailer. The MNC first sells its products to a wholesaler or distributor located in that country or at least in that region. These wholesalers or distributors are companies that transfer products from the manufacturer down the distribution channel so that they eventually get to a retailer and then to you, the consumer. The distributor in the local market sells the foreign product to the local retailers in the local markets. Several wholesalers may be involved in the distribution of a product before it gets to the retailer. For example, in Japan, products pass through three or sometimes even more wholesalers. Countries differ in the services provided by wholesalers to retailers. In Japan, retailers expect to be able to return all unsold goods to the wholesaler.[7] Oftentimes, local conditions make it necessary for MNCs to use wholesalers in foreign markets. These challenges can involve getting products through regulation in the foreign market or negotiating the complexities of local infrastructures such as transportation and warehousing.

Global Supply-chain Management

Distribution channels closely relate to supply-chain management. **Supply chains** involve all the tasks and services that connect everything that happens to a product from raw material to the consumer. Distribution channels are the later part of the supply chain that delivers the product to the end user. However, the sourcing of subcomponents and subassemblies components and raw materials used to make the products also are part of the supply chain.

Supply chains involve all the linkages between the origination of raw materials, to the various processing points of raw materials, to the production facilities and then to the distribution channels described above. Supply chains involve transporting of goods and materials, inventory management and flows, order processing, materials handling, and warehousing. Many parts and subcomponents used in products, as well as raw materials, are sourced from other countries. Thus in many ways it is hard to find a business where the supply chains are not in fact global supply chains. For example, the Ford Crown Victoria is assembled in Canada; 75 percent of the Toyota Avalon assembly is done in the US; and the PT Cruiser is a product of Chrysler that is assembled in Mexico. Exhibit 10.4 shows a simplified example of Nikon's global supply chain. Many of these global networks between MNCs are much more complex.

An increasingly important issue for MNCs includes the complexities of managing an ethical supply chain. Consumers are increasingly aware that an MNC's brand image rests not only on the ethical management of their own company but also on how their suppliers deal with issues such as child labor, fair pay, working conditions, and environmental impact. The IB Sustainability Practices box overleaf shows how a UK company takes care in sourcing sustainable wood products for its home improvement business.

supply chains
all the tasks and services that connect everything that happens to a product from raw material to the consumer. Distribution channels are the later part of the supply chain that delivers the product to the end user

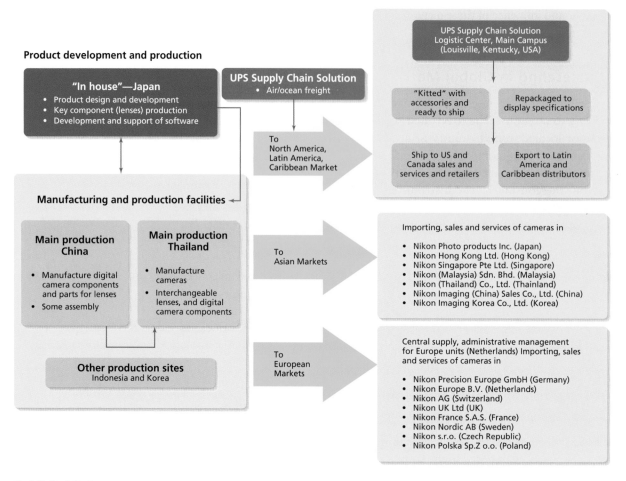

Exhibit 10.4 **Nikon Corporation - Digital Camera Supply Chain**

outsourcing

MNCs buying subcomponents and subassemblies needed in their own finished products from other companies

Rather than just buying raw materials such as steel or plastic and producing a product entirely on their own, many MNCs now buy completed subcomponents and subassemblies needed in their own finished products from other companies. This is called **outsourcing** in the supply chain. GM, the auto-maker, provides an example of outsourcing when it buys electronically controlled car seats from Johnson Controls rather than making the seats itself.

There are several reasons for the growth of global outsourcing. The first is cost savings. As you might imagine, a share of this comes directly from cheaper overseas labor costs. However, because outsourcing allows for the concentration of specialized skills, specialized companies that provide outsourced production to many companies gain economies of scale, often saving even more. Also, this concentration of specialized skills increases the quality and reliability of outsourced goods. For example, companies in India have made massive investments in the most advanced communication technologies and in language training that ensures that customers can hear no traces of Indian accents. This has facilitated extensive and high-quality outsourcing of customer service functions by a vast range of companies from American Express to Delta Airlines.[8] As an additional but very important benefit, because outsourcing allows the MNC to minimize investments in its own plants, equipment, training, and manufacturing facilities, and thus limit its fixed costs and overheads, the MNC that outsources can be

Stewarding Sustainable Forestry in Bolivia

IB SUSTAINABILITY PRACTICES

Almost half (47 percent) of Latin America is covered by natural forest. However, the forest is shrinking dramatically as unsustainable and often illegal logging takes an estimated 58 million hectares of forest every year. Counter to this trend, Bolivia has become a leader in providing sustainable wood products to world markets.

Bolivia has over five million acres, more than a quarter of the country's forest coverage, certified under Forest Stewardship Council (FSC) rules. Sixteen of the major forest harvest operations in Bolivia are certified according to the FSC's rules. FSC rules not only cover protection of water and other natural resources, but also require respect for the rights of indigenous people and protection of the economic well-being of local communities and forest workers.

Bolivia is now Latin America's leading sustainable timber producer. Notes Daniel Arancibia, Latin American representative of the Forest Stewardship Council, "One of the key successes of Bolivia was the willingness of the government, private sector and non-profit groups to work together to establish a system-wide arrangement that would in turn create the preconditions for sustainable forest management."

The "Bolivia certified" label now has an impact in the overseas markets for Bolivian wood products, mostly tropical hardwoods sold as doors, furniture, floorboards, chairs, and sawn timber in the EU and the US. Exports now exceed $20 million a year.

Typical of the Bolivia certified wood importers is the UK retailer B&Q, a home-improvement store. B&Q is one of the main importers of Bolivia certified forest products and yearly sources over 1,700 cubic meters of round wood, mostly used in its garden furniture. B&Q has a commitment to ensuring all its wood and paper products come from sustainable forests or recycled material. Explains George Padelopoulos, B&Q's social responsibility adviser, "We want to offer our customers a choice of sustainable products at affordable prices and our timber-buying policy is aimed at achieving this."

Source: Adapted from *The Ethical Corporation*, 2006, www.ethicalcorp.com/content.asp?ContentID=4174, March 28.

more flexible in important strategic areas. This increased flexibility allows the MNC to be adaptable and deal with changing conditions so that it can remain competitive.

To gain all of the advantages of a global supply-chain network, the MNC must understand the many complexities involved. First, outsourcing increases the importance of the purchasing and acquisition function in the company. When the MNC is purchasing important subcomponents from outside manufacturers, the international purchasing managers buying those subcomponents are making decisions that are much more important than if they were simply reordering paper for the copy machine. The management of key sourcing decisions has made purchasing a core strategic function. Second, the supply chain must be viewed and managed as a system with full understanding of how all the linkages affect one another. The MNC can no longer focus only on vendors with whom it deals directly, but must also consider its suppliers' suppliers and its customers' customers. Third, because of the complex interconnections between all the MNCs in the supply chain, data and tracking information has become much more important. In managing global supply chains, MNCs are tending to rely more and more on software platforms such as those dedicated

Dell's Global Supply Chain

The customer, Mr Friedman, phones Dell's 800 number with his request for a laptop computer. The one Mr Friedman wants has been co-designed by engineers in Austin, Texas, and Taiwan. Dell's customer service representative types the order into the order management system and this sets off a sequence of events that spans the globe and involves activities and transactions in as many as 15 different countries. The final step is completed when Mr Friedman receives his computer about two weeks later.

After Mr Friedman's shipping information is obtained and his credit card information verified, the order is released to Dell's production system. Dell has factories in Ireland, China, Brazil, Tennessee, Texas, and Malaysia. Mr Friedman's order goes out by e-mail to Dell's notebook factory in Malaysia. From there, all the parts for his computer are ordered from the supplier logistics centers (SLC) near the Dell factory. These SLCs are located around all Dell factories and are owned and operated by Dell suppliers. Their job is to keep a supply of all the parts needed so they can be trucked over to the factory for just-in-time manufacturing.

As soon as a computer is ordered, Dell suppliers get the signal. These suppliers know exactly what Dell needs to produce its computers on a minute-by-minute basis. Once the needs are known, the supplier delivers the required parts to the Dell factory within 90 minutes. When the supplier delivers the parts, it takes Dell employees 30 minutes to unload the parts and enter the information in Dell's production tracking system. Dell managers know the location of every part in every SLC in the Dell system at all times.

So from where do the parts for the laptop flow into the SLC? Keep in mind that there are 30 or so major components in the computer. The Intel microprocessor comes from a plant in the Philippines, Costa Rica, Malaysia, or China. The memory comes from Korea, Taiwan, Germany, or Japan. The graphics card, motherboard, and modem come from China. The cooling fan comes from Taiwan. The displays come from South Korea, Japan, or Taiwan. The wireless card comes from China, Malaysia, or Taiwan. The battery comes from Mexico, Malaysia, China, or South Korea. The disk drives come from Singapore, Thailand, Indonesia, China, Taiwan, or the Philippines. The power adapter comes from Thailand, Taiwan, or China. The power cord comes from Malaysia or India. The removable memory stick comes from Israel or Malaysia. And finally, the carrying bag comes from China. The list above indicates where the supplier's manufacturing plants are located so this is where the parts actually originate. Importantly, while some of these manufacturing facilities are owned by companies located in the same country, a number are also owned by companies in England, Ireland, the US, Japan, Korea, and Germany, expanding the global scope of this supply-chain symphony even more.

Keep in mind that the 30 components above are only the main part of the picture. There are a number of smaller components as well. In fact, the total supply chain for Mr Friedman's computer involves about 400 companies from start to finish. Likewise, keep in mind that Dell uses multiple suppliers for each part. That way, if one supplier breaks down or cannot meet Dell's needs, others can step in. This keeps the flow going continuously. A Dell manager noted that keeping this huge and complex network working smoothing requires a lot of collaboration between the MNCs. Dell works constantly on process improvements and real-time demand/supply balancing.

Source: Adapted from Tomas L. Friedman, 2005, *The World is Flat: A Brief History of the 21st Century*, New York: Farrar, Straus and Giroux

specifically to supply-chain management, but also on others such as CRM (customer relationship management) and EPS (enterprise management systems). These specialized management information systems accumulate the data necessary to track the flows of goods and products through the global supply chains. They help ensure that the goods and products arrive on time at the right locations, many of which are often dispersed throughout the world.

Perhaps one of the most sophisticated global supply chains is that used by Dell Computer. In the Strategic Insight opposite you can see how this system works for the competitive advantage of Dell.

Pricing—Global or Local?

Pricing in foreign markets is a critically important element of the marketing program because its effects on the MNC are very direct in terms of revenues and profits. While, of course, the price must cover product costs, beyond that the international manager must understand how the consumer in a foreign market values the MNC's product: that is, what the customer is willing to pay. These two factors set the lower and upper boundaries of the price, as Exhibit 10.5 shows. Other factors in foreign markets, such as competitors, distribution channels, and government policies, make the pricing decision quite complex.

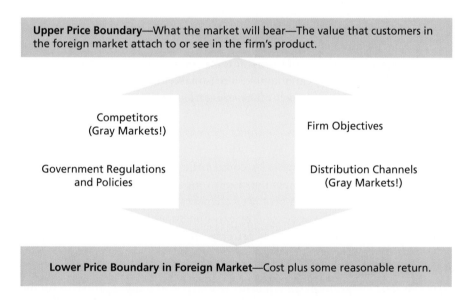

Upper Price Boundary—What the market will bear—The value that customers in the foreign market attach to or see in the firm's product.

Competitors
(Gray Markets!)

Firm Objectives

Government Regulations
and Policies

Distribution Channels
(Gray Markets!)

Lower Price Boundary in Foreign Market—Cost plus some reasonable return.

Exhibit 10.5 **Pressures and Factors Influencing Global Pricing**

For several reasons, competitors play a big part in an MNC's pricing decisions. First, the number of competitors can vary greatly from country to country. In some countries there are only a few competing products, while in other foreign markets there may be many others competing for the same customers. Second, the form or type of competitors can be quite different in various local and regional markets. Some competitors may be small, others may be state-owned, and still others may be large MNCs. Third, the support competitors enjoy can differ greatly across the various foreign markets. Even if competitors are not state-owned, they may enjoy preferential treatment from the local governments. They may get cheap loans, subsidies, better access to land and materials needed, for example.

Distribution channels in the foreign market are another important factor in pricing decisions. The margins demanded by wholesalers, distributors, or retailers are often higher in foreign markets than in the home country market. Yet, if the MNC wants to compete, it must pay the margins and pass as much of the costs as possible on to the consumer in the price. Complex distribution channels with more layers can also increase costs. For example, as noted above, in Japan, products must pass through several wholesalers before they finally reach the retailer, where the customer may purchase them. The retailer in turn must offer more services than would a similar store in the US. The result is that similar goods sold in the US and Japan are often more expensive in Japan, even when they are Japanese goods. For example, the most expensive Toyota Camry would cost about $32,500 before taxes in Japan but only $27,500 in the US.

Finally, government regulations and policies influence pricing. Some governments, even those that are seemingly friendly, find ways to keep foreign products off the shelves, and they often do this through pricing. Some countries are openly protectionist, with steep taxes on foreign products and heavy red tape and bureaucracy meant to bog down and limit market access to foreign products. For example, because China is trying to develop its own wine industry, foreign wines there are heavily taxed and heavily burdened with forms and bureaucratic red tape. This greatly inhibits the ability to market wines in China. Some countries directly regulate the price of foreign products through price controls. Sometimes these controls can force foreign companies to price their products so low that they cannot make a reasonable return. Some governments are even quite tolerant of knock-off or counterfeit products that can be priced to undercut foreign products.

If the marketer misjudges the upper price boundary and sets the product price too high in a foreign market, customers will avoid the product and the MNC will lose sales. Alternatively, competitors may see a high price as an opportunity to introduce cheaper knock-off versions of the company's product. This can undercut the foreign product's chances to make gains in the market

However, setting the price too low can sometimes be an even bigger problem. Local governments can see low prices as an attempt at dumping. **Dumping** occurs when a foreign competitor sells products in a local market at prices that are below local product costs. Because dumping puts local companies at a serious disadvantage, local governments will step in and cause problems for the foreign company. Alternatively, low prices can attract the attention of governments and encourage them to tax or regulate MNCs to protect their domestic companies. Foreign customers may also associate a low price with low quality and stay away from the product.

Another possible harmful outcome of setting the price too low is gray markets. A **gray market** is created when a low-priced product in one market is bought up by unauthorized distributors at the lower price and resold in another market at a higher price. Low prices in one market lead unauthorized dealers to make money by selling the MNC's product in another market at a higher price.

All of these factors make pricing decisions in foreign markets very complex. In terms of the global–local dilemma, these factors among others we discussed in earlier chapters, such as currency movements and transfer pricing, make

dumping
foreign competitors selling products in a local market at abnormally low prices that are below product costs

gray market
unauthorized distributors buying a low-priced product in one market and reselling the product in another market at a higher price

coordination and standardization of pricing extremely difficult. Of all the elements in marketing, pricing may be the one that is most driven by local considerations.

Talking to Customers across the Globe— Marketing Communications

How do you hear about products? What gets you interested in trying a different product? Sometimes you hear about products from your friends or family, but most often you hear about products through the MNC's communication mix. Advertising in the mass media, whether it is print, radio, the Internet, or TV; promotions such as coupons, point-of-purchase displays (in-store displays or signs), event sponsorship, or contests; and personal selling by someone in the store or someone who calls on you in your home—all are part of the MNC's **communication mix**. As the term indicates, the communication mix is anything that the MNC uses to inform customers about its products, promote its products, and persuade customers to buy and use its products. When products are being taken to foreign markets, the communication mix brings a number of unique and special challenges for the MNC. Again, the global–local dilemma heavily influences communication strategies and programs.

Advertising in the mass media may be the most visible component of the MNC's communication mix. The MNC's biggest problems often happen with language. It is more than a matter of simple translation. For example, marketing experts note that there are five different Spanish words for "tire."[9] Often, words, phrases, or terms have subtle meanings that are unique to the culture. For example, in Quebecois French, *ma blonde* means "girlfriend," not "my blond," as it would in the US, and *ma chum* means "boyfriend," not "buddy." It is wise to remember that words do not always translate directly and can have meanings that the MNC never intended. Also, animal sounds vary by culture. In the US a pig says oink. In Japan a pig says ruff-ruff.

In advertising, there are strong cultural taboos that must be avoided, especially when dealing with religion and gender issues. The use of images and drawings of religious deities is strictly forbidden in Islam, for example. Appeals to women and girls are greatly restricted in Arab countries. In Turkey, L'Oréal recently used naked female body images in ads for its cellulite treatment products. The conservative Turkish government banned the ads and imposed heavy penalties on the company. Likewise, despite the huge influence of Western culture in China and India, these societies remain extremely conservative regarding gender-related issues. Any messages that include even the slightest sexual connotation or image meet with a negative reception in these countries. In France, it is highly desirable for advertising to have a strong artistic component, with more music, drama, and flourish in the product presentation in ads. The French see US advertising as stark and clinical.

In addition to language and cultural differences, advertising regulations and access to advertising media, such as TV, radio, newspapers, and magazines, differ widely from country to country. In some countries, media are not available because they do not exist, while in others they are less developed. For example, the postal system in China is highly limited when compared to the US, so the international manager must allow for this in any advertising that depends on

communication mix
anything that an MNC uses to inform customers about its products, promote its products, and persuade customers to buy and use its products. Communication mix includes advertising (print, radio, the Internet, or TV); promotions such as coupons, point-of-purchase displays, event sponsorship, or contests; and personal selling

postal delivery. Even when media for advertising are abundant, some countries limit the use and access. In Germany, for example, TV advertisements can appear only at certain times. The content of advertisements is highly controlled in certain countries such as Malaysia. Exhibit 10.6 shows how spending on the major forms of advertising varies from country to country and reflects how MNCs must adapt marketing communications to local contexts.

Regardless of all these differences in the existence and use of mass media for advertising, advancements in communication technologies are bringing great changes. Satellite TV and radio are blurring national boundaries at an astounding rate. These technologies have resulted in worldwide spillover of advertising messages. A message designed and intended for a local or even regional audience can be viewed all over the world. Another great equalizing force in the communication mix is the Internet. Earlier, we discussed the impact of the Internet

Exhibit 10.6 **Advertising Spending in Selected Nations**

	Advertising expenditures ($ Billion)[1]	Media Usage (% of advertising expenditure)					
		Television	Radio	Print	Cinema	Outdoor	Online
North America							
Canada	6.9	34.3	14.1	47.1	0.1	4.4	N/A
United States	159.4	35.7	14.1	42.3	0.2	2.9	4.9
Latin America							
Argentina	1.9	41.8	4.6	44.8	1.5	4.6	3.1
Brazil	3.8	51.7	10.1	27.1	N/A	5.8	5.3
Chile	0.7	44.9	10.1	37.7	0.0	5.8	N/A
Asia							
China	8.9	55.2	5.2	39.6	N/A	N/A	N/A
Hong Kong	2.0	33.5	7.0	50.5	0.0	8.0	1.0
India	2.4	43.4	4.1	39.3	2.5	9.8	0.4
Japan	39.7	46.0	4.2	34.3	N/A	12.7	2.8
Singapore	1.1	43.2	8.1	42.3	0.9	5.4	N/A
South Korea	7.5	50.5	5.0	44.4	N/A	N/A	N/A
Australia	6.4	36.6	9.3	49.2	0.8	3.3	0.8
New Zealand	1.2	33.6	13.4	49.6	0.0	2.5	N/A
Europe							
France	12.5	32.0	8.0	47.3	0.7	11.5	0.6
Germany	23.4	24.4	3.2	65.5	0.8	4.4	1.7
Italy	10.3	55.9	4.6	33.9	1.0	3.8	0.8
Spain	7.3	40.4	9.3	39.0	0.7	9.6	1.0
Sweden	2.3	20.8	2.7	62.8	0.4	5.3	7.5
Switzerland	3.3	13.6	3.3	64.2	0.9	16.9	1.2
UK	20.1	31.8	4.1	53.7	2.0	6.3	2.1
Russia	3.9	48.5	4.1	26.3	0.5	20.1	0.5

Source: Calculated from Global Market Information Database, 2006, *International Marketing Data and Statistics.*

[1] Calculated with year-on-year currency exchange rate.

in retailing, but it also serves as a powerful device for promoting the MNC's products. MNCs can use banner advertisements placed on popular sites to attract and inform potential customers. These potential customers can then seek additional product information from the MNC's dedicated websites. While the difficulties with the global–local dilemma will always be with us in advertising, it seems that communication technologies are making global strategies more and more viable.

Promotions, devices such as coupons, contests, or point-of-purchase displays, are generally growing in popularity in markets. Point-of-purchase displays are displays or signs that are set up in the retail store, often at the end of the aisle. The use of point-of-purchase displays has greatly increased in China as the size of retail establishments has grown. In other countries, where many stores are still smaller, e.g. Japan and France, point-of-purchase displays are not appropriate.

The use of coupons, probably the most common promotional device in the US, varies greatly from country to country. Some countries, such as Germany and Austria, currently have laws forbidding the use of coupons. In France, Sweden, and Great Britain, for example, any promotional devices that involve or hint at games of chance, such as lotteries, sweepstakes, or contests, are greatly restricted or forbidden.[10] In addition to the laws, infrastructures and cultural acceptance of promotions vary. For example, as mentioned earlier, though it is rapidly improving the postal service in China is still not well developed, making the delivery of coupons by mail impractical. In addition, Chinese consumers are somewhat embarrassed to use coupons.

In terms of the global–local dilemma, promotions are much more effective when managed locally. Given the vast differences in laws and regulations, as well as cultural acceptance of various promotions, there are few opportunities for global programs. Sponsorship of high-profile world sporting events may be the most compelling exception. For example, sponsorship of the Olympic Games offers such an opportunity. Exhibit 10.7 shows the sponsors of some recent Games. It is probably no accident that several of these sponsors are found on our list of top global brands. Such sponsorship, while highly effective in building the MNCs' brands and communicating the MNCs' products, is extremely costly.

Because marketing communications practices and local country laws vary so greatly, it is especially important to have local guidance and information, and this often comes in the form of an advertising agency. Advertising agencies design print, television, and radio advertisements and buy spots in media so that the ads are aired on television and radio programs and placed in magazines and newspapers. In many countries, local advertising agencies are quite rare. This may explain why, in the last decade or so, global or world advertising agencies such as Densu or J. Walter Thompson Co. have become increasingly important. These MNCs establish local operations, with local personnel and in-depth understanding of local conditions from country to country. While, they can be expensive, they may be worth the cost if they can prevent costly mistakes. Importantly, because of their global perspective these agencies can help develop and coordinate standardized communications programs where possible and appropriate.

Personal selling, where the MNC's representative interacts one-on-one with customers to sell the MNC's product, is an expensive but powerful communication tool for the MNC. It is often used for selling large and complex products

promotions
devices such as coupons, contests, or point-of-purchase displays

personal selling
an MNC's representative interacts one-on-one with customers to sell the company's product

Exhibit 10.7 **Olympic Sponsors**

Sponsors of the Beijing 2008 Summer Olympic Games			
Coca-Cola	Atos Origin	Bank of China	China Netcom
GE	Johnson-Johnson	Sinopec	China National Petroleum Corporation
Kodak	Lenovo	China Mobile	Volkswagen
Manulife	McDonalds	Adidas	Omega
Panasonic	Air Chine	PICC	Samsung
Visa	State Grid	UPS	Haier
Budweiser	Sohu	Yili	Tsingtao
Yanjing Beer	Bhpbilliton	Heng Yuan Xiang	Uni-President

Sponsors of the Turin 2006 Winter Olympic Games			
Coca-Cola	Altos Origin	GE	Kodak
Samsung	Lenovo	Manulife	McDonalds
Omega	Panasonic	Visa	FIAI Group
Sanpaolo	Telecom Italia	TIM	AXEM
Alpha Romeo	Elpitour	ACICS	Berloni
Budweiser	Eutelsat	Ferrovi International	Hnmeccanica
IVECO	Jet Set	Johnson-Johnson	Kyocera
Lancia	Reale Mutua		

such as airplanes or steel plants. For example, when Boeing signed the contract for $6 billion in airplanes to six Chinese airlines late in 2005, no doubt a lion's share of the work in that deal involved various elements of personal selling.

For the most part, personal selling efforts for MNCs take place within countries. The MNC hires local sales representatives because they are invaluable in bridging cultural differences. In working with Korean companies, for example, the sales directors of a Northwest semiconductor design company noted how important it is to "have someone on the ground" so that the company has a full understanding of the customer, their needs, and the local situation. This extends beyond language differences into understanding laws, regulations, local infrastructure, and cultural traditions.

Cross-cultural negotiation is one of the biggest challenges in global selling. Even with a strong local representative, managers from local buying companies and foreign selling companies often must get together to negotiate agreements. Successful negotiations depend on how well the international managers adjust and accommodate cultural differences. Exhibit 10.8 shows the stages in the cross-cultural negotiation process; they include preparation, building the relationship, exchanging information and the first offer, persuasion, concessions, agreement, and post-agreement. Preparation involves gathering information on the issues and objectives, the people involved as negotiators, the company, and the setting. Relationship building begins when the people from the two companies actually meet. The focus is on simply getting to know one another and developing a sense of trust.

The real work in cross-cultural negotiation begins with information exchange and the first offer. This stage is where each company reveals its needs and objectives. In this stage, the negotiators lay out the technical limitations and standards for the product features, characteristics, price, and quality. Here both sides present their first offer, which is the first proposal of what they would like to get in the agreement.

The next step, persuasion, is the heart of the negotiation process and where each side attempts to get the other side to see its own position and agree with it. Concessions and agreement is where the final agreement is reached after some modification of demands. Usually both sides must relax some of their

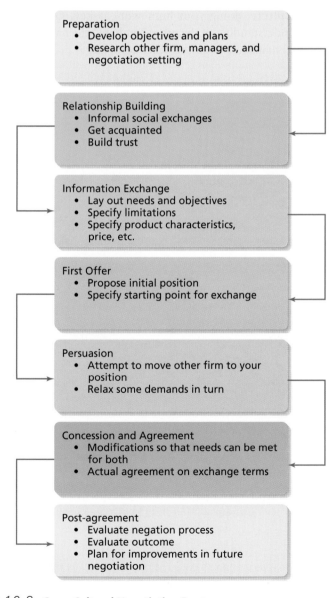

Exhibit 10.8 **Cross Cultural Negotiation Process**

demands to satisfy each other's needs. Post-agreement is where the process is re-evaluated so that the negotiators can see what worked and understand what did not work so that better negotiation can result the next time.

These steps are all important, but it is even more important to remember that there is great variance from culture to culture in the role of each stage and when and how they occur. For example, in the US the early informal stages are short and less important, while in Japan the social non-business parts of the process are critical in setting the stage for any success later on. This is the most important stage and cannot be rushed because it builds the personal context on which the whole negotiation process relies. In China, the later parts of the process are key because important agreements and concessions do not take place until very late in the process. The international manager must be highly flexible in terms of ending times when negotiating with the Chinese. Some cultures, such as Japanese, are quite comfortable with silence in the negotiation process while others, such as the Brazilians and Americans, tend to speak constantly. No matter what the culture, doing your homework is key. Gathering as much information and understanding of the other company, the national culture, and even the individual managers from the other company is necessary.

CHAPTER REVIEW

The global–local dilemma may play out in the biggest way in marketing. To succeed in global markets, the MNC manager must understand when and how to be sensitive to the differences in global markets. At the same time, international managers can gain key cost and competitive advantages if they understand how and when to capitalize on the similarities across markets, both regionally and globally. The first step in developing marketing programs that effectively respond to these differences and similarities involves gathering information and gaining a knowledge advantage with regard to foreign markets. International market research including primary and secondary data can answer important marketing questions about demand, market segmentation, and consumer preferences to help international managers develop effective programs.

Effective global marketing programs rely on the marketing mix that consists of the product, distribution, pricing, and marketing communication to reach customers in foreign markets. Decisions about the extent to which the product offering and product brand development are standardized or adapted are among the first decisions that need to be made by the MNC manager when going global. At times, MNCs may extend a product and brand directly to other markets with little or no change. However, most of the time there must be at least some minimal adaptation—some changes made to the product and branding in response to local conditions in various markets. Rather than a question of "yes" or "no," adaptation and standardization in products and brands is a matter of the right amount in the right places. For example, sometimes products and brands can be standardized across regions but not throughout the world. Global brands are products where the offering and branding are pretty much standardized across the world. In reality, these are quite rare as some level of cultural sensitivity and adaptation to local conditions is usually necessary.

Distribution and supply chains comprise an important element of global marketing. The international manager must develop a system for delivering the product in local markets so that it is readily available to the customer. There are times when direct distribution, most likely through the Internet, works well. However, usually indirect distribution through retailers and wholesalers in the foreign market is needed to get the product to the customer. The Internet is increasingly important in providing customers with access to products from MNCs across the globe. This e-commerce is sometimes done through e-tailers, which are Internet retailers. In addition to e-tailing, other trends are affecting retailing throughout the world. For example, global retailers, large-scale retailers with stores throughout the world, are becoming more important and retail establishments are getting much larger generally.

Global supply chains are an important aspect of global distribution and of global business in general. Supply chains have become more important because companies now outsource much more than in the past. Technology, cost savings, and flexibility have made global outsourcing very attractive. All the components and parts in a Dell computer can come from companies in dozens of countries, for example.

Global pricing is influenced by a number of factors in foreign markets, for example the type and extent of local competition, margins demanded in distribution channels, and government regulations. If the price is set too low in foreign markets, the MNC can be seen as dumping or gray markets can be created. If the price is set too high, customers in the foreign market will turn to local products or products of competing MNCs.

The marketing communication mix consists of advertising, promotions, and personal selling, everything that the MNC uses to talk to its customers. If personal selling is needed, having local sales personnel in place in the foreign market is critical. However, advertising may become more standardized because of spillover in all the communication technologies. The Internet and satellite television and radio allow customers from all over the world to access whatever information they want. Nonetheless, cultural norms, laws, and regulations regarding promotions and advertising vary greatly from culture to culture.

 DISCUSSION QUESTIONS

1. What are the major strategic differences between marketing domestically and marketing internationally?
2. Discuss the importance of marketing research for international marketing. What challenges face marketing researchers when they enter other countries?
3. Describe the choices in the marketing mix in relationship to the global–local dilemma.
4. Explain how and why the marketing mix can vary in global markets.
5. Explain why consumer products often require more adaptation than industrial products sold in business-to-business markets.
6. Discuss the incentives for MNCs to develop global supply chains such as that described in the chapter for Dell. What are the major management challenges for managing such global supply chains?

INTERNATIONAL BUSINESS SKILL BUILDER

Test Your Cross-cultural Advertisements

Step 1: Pick three popular television advertisements that you think are a reflection of popular culture and tape them.

Step 2: Find three students who have arrived in your school this last year from a foreign country—try to pick someone from Asian countries, from Arab countries, the Americas, or from Europe, as appropriate.

Step 3: Play the ads for the students and interview them to get their impressions about the advertisements. First, ask each student to directly interpret the advertisements in their own language and then back-translate it.

Step 4: Apart from the direct interpretation, ask each student what the commercials would mean, what the message would be, to a typical person from their country.

Step 5: Ask each student if there would be anything offensive to their culture or to subgroups (e.g. genders) in their cultures.

CHAPTER INTERNET ACTIVITY

1. Look at the websites for VW, Toyota, GM, and BMW in different countries.
2. Translate if necessary using **http://babelfish.altavista.com/**.
3. Analyze the differences in how these famous brands are presented to local customers.
4. How does the marketing communication differ by country?

KEY CONCEPTS

adaptation strategy	gray market
back translation	international marketing research
brand	
communication mix	marketing mix
country of origin (COO) effect	moderator
direct distribution	outsourcing
direct extension	personal selling
distribution channel	primary data
dumping	product
e-commerce	promotions
e-tailers	secondary data
focus group	segmentation
global brand	standardization
global retailers	supply chain

BUSINESS > INTERNATIONAL

FRITO-LAY ADAPTS TO THE CHINESE MARKET

In the 1930s, two men in different parts of the United States began businesses that would eventually come to dominate the global snack food market. In 1932, Elmer Doolin, an ice cream salesman, stopped for lunch at a local San Antonio café. He noticed a package of corn chips at the café and purchased it for five cents. This small purchase would come to change his career and his life. The chips Doolin purchased were made from corn dough, used for centuries by Mexicans to bake bread. Impressed with the product, Doolin sold his ice cream business and purchased the corn chip producer's business for $100. The brand, Frito, was created in the kitchen of his mother, along with the early production of the corn chips. Doolin would bake the chips at night and sell them during the day. Early sales were in the range of $8–10 a day. As business expanded, the company was moved from San Antonio to Dallas. Frito became a major chip producer in the southwestern United States.

Around the same time, an entrepreneur in Tennessee named Herman W. Lay was selling potato chips produced by an Atlanta company. Lay sold the chips from his personal automobile until 1938, when the chip manufacturer fell on hard times. Lay managed to buy the business and changed its name to H. W. Lay and Company. The company's products became popular with consumers for their good taste and convenience, making Lay the dominant producer of snack foods in the southeastern United States.

After World War II, the two companies began to cooperate in the area of product distribution. At this time they were still limited to their respective geographic markets, with Frito in the southwest and Lay in the southeast. In 1961, the two companies merged to form Frito-Lay, Inc., and in 1965 the company was merged again, this time with the Pepsi-Cola Company. The Pepsi-Cola Company became PepsiCo and consisted of the Pepsi-Cola Company, the Frito-Lay Company, and Tropicana Products. The company now also markets the popular brands Quaker Oats and Gatorade.

Although the US market is the largest market in the world for snack foods, because of its saturation Frito-Lay has expanded significantly into international markets. The company tries to capitalize on its economies of scale and global brand image to compete with local brands. The typical entry strategy is to first learn which company is the leading snack company in the foreign market, and then attempt to purchase that company. If that fails, Frito-Lay aggressively competes against that local company. Frito-Lay's international operations add $9 billion to PepsiCo's $25 billion revenue. International markets have in many cases been more profitable for PepsiCo than the domestic market of the United States.

. . .

Pepsi entered China in 1981 to sell soft drinks, and since that time has invested more than $1 billion. In 1994 Frito-Lay entered the Chinese market with its popular Cheetos brand snack. Potato chips were not introduced into the Chinese market until 1997, because of the Chinese ban on potato imports. Frito-Lay had to establish its own farms in order to grow potatoes acceptable to company standards. Early adaptation to local markets required Frito-Lay to make significant changes. For example, Frito-Lay's Cheetos sold in China do not contain any cheese, because of the propensity of the Chinese to be lactose intolerant. Instead of cheese flavoring, Cheetos are offered with barbecue or seafood flavoring. In addition, the packaging was made smaller so that the price would be more acceptable. Other international adaptations had previously been made in other markets by Frito-Lay, including the popular Thai product, Nori Seaweed Chips.

Frito-Lay found that the Chinese market was not a single entity. Regional tastes and preferences had to be considered and products altered accordingly. Chinese living in Shanghai, for example, prefer sweeter foods, and Chinese living in the northern region prefer a meaty taste. Frito-Lay also has found that having a good understanding of culture helps sell products. The Chinese belief in the Great Unity, or yin and yang, has marketing and product development implications. Yin and yang are the opposing forces in the universe and seek balance. The Chinese also seek balance, including balance in their foods. Fried food is seen as hot and not appropriate in the summer months, so Frito-Lay developed a new product, cool lemon potato chips. This product consists of chips dotted with lime specks and mint and packaged with cool climate images to connote winter months.

Promotion in China has required other adaptations, including advertisements showing the peeling of potatoes to indicate the product's basic ingredient. Promotion in China has successfully related the collectivist tendencies of the Chinese people and the desire of the Chinese to try new products outdoors in a conspicuous fashion. Early adopters in China want others to see their consumption of Western products. As with many Western products, young consumers are the first to try the product, and in the case of Frito-Lay the focus has been on young women. As Jackson Chiu, sales director for Frito-Lay, states: "We market to girls and the boys follow." Frito-Lay has been very creative in its promotion efforts in China; however, one advertisement resulted in a small problem. Using the picture of Mao Zedong's cook in its promotion resulted in the company being ordered to offer an apology and to pay the cook 10,000 yuan (US$ 1,200) for violating a Chinese law that requires getting permission before using someone's picture.

Frito-Lay's entry into the Chinese market has also caused some controversy. Some critics charge that companies like Frito-Lay have caused the Chinese diet to become unhealthy. Many Chinese can remember when food was rationed, long food lines existed, and consumers were offered little choice. Today the Chinese have a large variety of food options, and snack foods are a popular choice. As a result of their dietary changes, the Chinese have become more overweight. In the

. . .

past ten years, the percentage of the Chinese population considered overweight has risen from almost none to a little under one-third of the population. A common way of greeting someone is the Chinese equivalent of "Have you eaten yet?" The Chinese are now able to answer "yes" more often to that question, and many are selecting foods that are considered by some to be unhealthy.

Concerned with the health effects of its products, not only in China but also in health-conscious markets such as the United States, PepsiCo has begun to change its product offerings. Based on medical advice, PepsiCo has divided its products into three groups: (1) "Good for you" foods such as Gatorade and oatmeal; (2) "Better for you" foods such as Nacho Cheesier Baked Doritos; (3) "Fun for you" foods such as Pepsi-Cola. The "Good for you" foods are naturally healthy or engineered to be healthy. The "Better for you" foods contain more wholesome ingredients or have reduced fat and sugar. The fun food isn't considered to be especially healthy. PepsiCo is moving product development towards the "Good for you" and "Better for you" groups. According to nutrition expert Professor Marion Nestle of New York University, "Frito-Lay products are still high in calories, salt, and rapidly absorbed carbohydrates." For now the Chinese do not seem too concerned and Frito-Lay continues to develop this rapidly expanding market.

CASE DISCUSSION POINTS

1. Evaluate the approach Frito-Lay used as it entered the Chinese market. Would you consider the approach to be ethnocentric, polycentric, or geocentric? Explain your answer.
2. In your opinion, is the company being socially responsible by selling products that may be considered unhealthy?
3. What lessons can be learned by examining the experiences of Frito-Lay in China?

Sources: *Economic Times*, 2004, "Frito-Lay sees crunchy business for chips here," June 3; China Economic Net, 2004, "Chairman Mao's cook wins lawsuit vs Pepsi," July 23; R. Flannery, 2004, "China is a big prize," *Forbes*, May 10; E. Kurtenbach, 2004, "Urban Chinese struggle with battle of the bulge," www.latimes.com, July 18; T. Parker-Pope, 1996, "Custom-made: The most successful companies have to realize a simple truth—all consumers aren't alike," *Wall Street Journal*, September 26; P. Sellers, 2004, "The brand king challenge," *Fortune*, March 21; "Using potato chips to spread the spirit of free enterprise," 2004, www.abcnews.com, September 9; www.fritolay.com (accessed on July 12, 2004); www.pepsico.com (accessed on July 12, 2004).

Case prepared by Charles A. Rarick

11 Financial Management for MNCs

After reading this chapter you should be able to:

- Understand the nature of country risk.

- Understand how country risk relates to international investments.

- Know how to estimate the cost of capital and the future value of an international investment.

- Understand how international managers decide on the mix of debt and equity for the capital structure of an MNC's subsidiary.

- Know the basic methods of payment in international trade.

- Be familiar with export financing options.

As you can see in the Preview IB Strategic Insight, Tesco is taking a major financial risk by simultaneously opening numerous Fresh & Easy stores in the US all at once. Tesco's managers and outside investors are betting on the strategy to pay off. Like Tesco's investment, all financial investments involve risk. That is, for example, whether a person starts a new business, an MNC opens a factory in another country, an individual buys stock in an existing company, or a company manufacturers a new product, there is a chance that the company or project will not produce enough money to meet financial

Tesco Comes to the US: Weighing the Financial Risks of a Major International Investment

PREVIEW IB
STRATEGIC INSIGHT

Third in the world behind Walmart and Carrefour, the UK retailer Tesco plans to open Fresh & Easy local groceries at a rate of more than three a week. This is a $500 million/year campaign and a big test for Andy Higginson, who holds the dual roles as the company finance director and strategy director. Entering the US will be Tesco's biggest international investment and Higginson is anxious to show that the investment will pay off.

Although it will take up to £1.5 billion investment to start Fresh & Easy in the US, Higginson notes, "If it all goes horribly wrong, even if you assume there's no residual value—and of course with shops there's always residual value—a billion-and-a-half is something the company could afford," adding, "I'm not sure our careers could, but the business could certainly afford it." On the payoff side, he notes that if the strategy succeeds they will have "a business that could go national in the United States, [generating] billions and billions of shareholder value." The big risk is that entering the US market is not easy and many have failed in the past. The UK's Sainsbury bought Shaw's but eventually sold it to Albertsons in 2004. Marks & Spencer and the French giant Carrefour, in spite of being number two in the world, also abandoned the US market.

Tesco kept its strategy as secret as possible, even to the extent of setting up the first mock store in a warehouse in Santa Monica, California, and telling curious people that it was a film set. The secrecy was necessary because Tesco's strategy is entering the market fast with as many stores as possible

before competitors can copy the model. Tesco's Fresh & Easy stores will be about the size of a Walgreens and focus on convenience, including readymade dinners. With a model that can be easily copied, Tesco is striking for first-mover advantage. But by beginning big, the risks are higher. As Sir Terry Leahy, Tesco's chief executive, notes, "In retailing there aren't huge barriers to entry. That's one of the reasons you can't hang around and trial this thing. You have to launch and go."

Tesco's managers are fully aware of the risks. "We've made it as hard as we can," notes Higginson, while explaining that Tesco is taking a big step by starting a new business from scratch in a foreign country. He is quite aware that Tesco will need "an awful lot" of its Fresh & Easy convenience stores to perform quickly or the investment may fail. Outside investors seem to think the risk is worth the return in the potentially lucrative US market. Admiring the careful planning of Tesco, Warren Buffett, now the richest man in the world and certainly one of the most successful investors, now owns 3 percent of Tesco and is one of its largest shareholders. Stock analysts such as London's Blue Oar Securities give Fresh & Easy high marks as a strategically viable concept with the potential to become "hugely scalable."

Sources: Adapted from Tim Burke, 2008, "US Open," *CFO Europe Magazine*, www.cfo.com, March 3; *The Economist*, 2007, "Tesco, fresh, but far from easy," www.economist.com, June 21.

obligations. If a company or project does not produce sufficient cash then the business may go bankrupt or the project may be abandoned and the investors may lose money. Moreover, even if the project does make money, investors may make less money than they would have from other investments.

International investments often have more and different kinds of risk than domestic investments. As part of the strategic and financial decision to enter a country, the international manager must know how the unique characteristics of a country make it more or less of a risky environment in which to do business. Broadly speaking this type of risk is often called country risk. **Country risk** pertains to how a country's business environment might influence the MNC's profits or the value of its assets (e.g. factories, inventory) within the specific country. Many factors affect the risk of doing business in different countries for the MNC. How do international managers assess the risk in various countries? The first starting point is often to use one of several companies that specialize in developing risk ratings for different countries.

country risk
how a country's business environment might influence the MNC's profits or the value of its assets (e.g. factories, inventory) within the specific country

Exhibit 11.1

Country Risk in Central and South America

Source: Aon Political Risk Services

One popular risk rating service is the International Country Risk Guide (ICRG).[1] The ICRG's ratings focus on three types of risk. **Economic risk** considers a country's economic strengths and weaknesses and how these might affect investments. **Financial risk** considers the ability of the country to finance its trade debt and commercial obligations. **Political risk** assesses political stability in areas such as civil unrest, war, terrorism, and changing regulations. *The Economist*[2] and Aon Global[3] produce similar risk ratings. An excerpt from Aon Global's world risk map appears in Exhibit 11.1.

An increasingly important but nontraditional risk category is **sustainability risk**. Sustainability risk refers to factors that may increase the cost of capital or reduce profits due to changing environmental conditions or changing regulatory environments. When considering either domestic or foreign investments, the next-generation international manager will likely factor sustainability risk into any investment decisions. Exhibit 11.2 highlights some of the sustainability risk areas and their potential impacts on capital performance. The box on IB Sustainability Practices, overleaf, gives examples of how MNCs consider sustainability risk in their investment decisions.

economic risk
considers a country's economic strengths and weaknesses and how these might affect investments

financial risk
considers the ability of the country to finance its trade debt and commercial obligations

political risk
the political stability of a country in areas such as civil unrest, war, terrorism, and changing regulations

sustainability risk
the factors that may increase the cost of capital or reduce profits through changing environmental conditions or changing regulatory environments

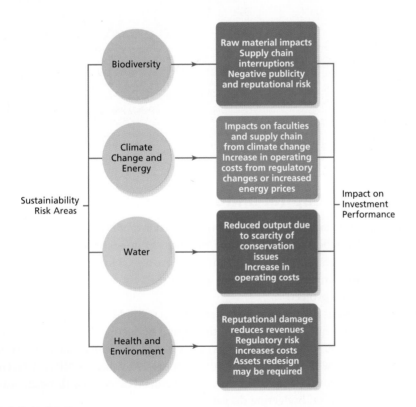

Exhibit 11.2

Sustainability Risk Areas and the Potential Impact on Investment Performance

Source: Adapted from EXCEL Partnership and The Delphi Group, 2005, A Sustainability Lens for Capital Decisions, Duralid: EXCEL Partnership.

In later sections of this chapter you will see more detail on how risk must be factored into the MNC's international investment decisions. First, however, you will learn some basic techniques that companies use to estimate the financial returns from investments.

The Case for Building Sustainability Risk into the Capital Investment Decision

IB SUSTAINABILITY PRACTICES

Unilever buys 5 percent of the world cod supply to support its "Bird's Eye" brand of frozen fish. Unilever has invested heavily over the years in this key capital asset that now represents 2 percent of Unilever's total sales. It seems unlikely that Unilever considered the biodiversity risk exposure when they first decided to invest in the cod brand of frozen fish (advertising, processing facilities, distribution network). Cod stocks, the consumers' choice in fish, are declining worldwide and have collapsed in some areas. Costs for cod have increased by 50 percent and when this is combined with consumer unwillingness to absorb the increases, Unilever has seen a 30 percent reduction in profit for this product. Had Unilever factored biodiversity into its investment decision perhaps it would have found this investment less attractive.

Texas Instruments produces semiconductors in Germany, Japan, and the United States. According to the company, water quality and availability are important factors in the investment decision to build new plants. In addition, the company invests heavily in water conservation. Globally, TI recycles nearly 40 percent of its freshwater consumption, almost four million gallons, every day. In new plants, TI's investments in state-of-the-art water reclaiming systems allow the plant to use 35 percent less water than a similar-sized traditional facility. Presently, TI is considering the long-term financial benefits of retrofitting its larger plants worldwide with the latest water conservation technology.

Sources: Adapted from EXCEL Partnership and the Delphi Group, 2005, *A Sustainability Lens for Capital Decisions*, Ontario: EXCEL Partnership; JP Morgan, 2008, *Watching Water: A Guide to Evaluating Corporate Risks in a Thirsty World*, www.jpmorgan.com, April 1.

The Cost of Capital and Project Valuation

As you saw in Chapter 6 regarding capital markets, MNCs can finance their operations using both debt (usually in the form of bonds) and equity (issuing stock or using retained earnings from their profits). However, the decision making is more complex than simply getting the required money and going forward with the project.[4]

capital budgeting decision
the process of determining whether a project should be financed based on its expected financial returns

The process of determining whether a project should be financed based on its expected financial returns is called the **capital budgeting decision**. Financial managers use several methods to predict the viability of an investment decision. We will review one popular method called **net present value, or NPV**. A recent study[5] found that over 75 percent of US chief financial officers use this technique for evaluating capital budgeting decisions.

net present value, or NPV
a technique used to estimate whether and when an initial capital investment will lead to future cash flows that exceed the cost of the capital

The NPV approach gives managers a way of estimating whether and when an initial capital investment will lead to future cash flows that exceed the cost of the capital. Later in the chapter you will learn more about the cost of capital. However, for this section, just consider it as the cost a company must pay to get money now, like the interest you must pay on a credit card if you want to buy something right away but do not have the available cash.

NPV is usually estimated by the following formula:

$$Net\ Present\ Value = \sum_{t-1}^{n} \frac{CF^t}{(1 + k)^t} - 10$$

Where CF^t = the predicted cash flows in year t,

    k = the required rate of return for the investment,

    n = lifetime of the project in periods (years, months, weeks, etc.),

    IO = the initial investment for the project.

To understand how NPV works, we can look at an example of a hypothetical US MNC called Sportif that is considering opening a subsidiary in the EU. Look at Exhibit 11.3. It contains two scenarios for NPV that multinational managers might consider in deciding whether to go forward with the project. In each scenario you will see when a project pays off based on different circumstances. You will also see how financial information enters into the formula.

In both scenarios, the assumption is that all profits will be returned to the parent company and that the parent company's initial investment (IO) will be $10,000,000. In the examples, we are looking at four years for the lifetime of the project (n), although we could do the calculations for any length of time.

In Scenario 1, managers have decided that they need a return of 15 percent on the investment. This means that, in order to make this project worthwhile from a purely financial point of view, the managers have to decide how best to invest any money they have from retained earnings, stock issues, or bond issues. If, for example, other possible projects can return up to 14 percent, then this project may need a return of 15 percent to become the investment of choice.

Risk also is a factor. Less risky projects may make sense with lower rates of return because there is more certainty that the company will make money. Conversely, more risky projects require projecting higher rates of return to compensate for the gamble of the investment.

All capital budgeting decisions begin with an estimate of how much money the project will generate over several periods. Sales forecasts for the product or service at various price levels help the financial managers estimate future revenues. You can see the project revenues projected for Sportif's subsidiary in line 1 in the example. Of course, all operations have expenses and have to pay local taxes, so what is remaining after these expenses is the cash flow to the subsidiary (line 4). For simplicity, we assume that all of the subsidiary's earnings after taxes and expenses are returned to Sportif's headquarters back in the US (line 7).

To understand the concept of NPV, one has to also understand that the future cash flows shown on line 7 must be valued for their worth today given a specified rate of return. Because there are alternative investments with potential returns, the future value of money is always lower than its face value. This is called the present value of the cash flow (PV) and is shown on line 9. In Scenario 1, this means that the $5,000,000 Sportif received from its subsidiary in year 1 is discounted or reduced based on a chosen rate of return (line 8) that Sportif's managers judged necessary to make this investment versus others.

For each year, line 9 shows the present value of the cash generated by the subsidiary for that year. Again, because of the need to discount or reduce the value of the cash in the future, each dollar has less value as each year passes. To compute the cumulative NPV, these discounted cash flows are subtracted from the initial $10,000,000 investment that Sportif uses to fund its subsidiary in the EU. Thus, in Scenario 1, it is not until the third year that Sportif would be expected to cover its initial investment.

The general rule of thumb is that the investment should be made if the cash flows are positive assuming that no better investment exists, say for example,

Exhibit 11.3 **Capital budget analysis for Sportif Shoes**

Scenario 1	Year 0	Year 1	Year 2	Year 3	Year 4
1 Subsidiary revenue		€21,000,000	€21,000,000	€36,000,000	€38,000,000
2 Expenses		€16,000,000	€16,000,000	€29,000,000	€30,000,000
3 Host government tax (20%)		€1,000,000	€1,000,000	€1,400,000	€1,600,000
4 Cash flow to subsidiary		€4,000,000	€4,000,000	€5,600,000	€6,400,000
5 After earnings remitted to parent		€4,000,000	€4,000,000	€5,600,000	€6,400,000
6 Exchange rate of the $		$1.25	$1.25	$1.25	$1.25
7 Cash flow to parent		$5,000,000	$5,000,000	$7,000,000	$8,000,000
8 Required rate of return (discount rate)	15%				
9 *PV* of parent cash flows		$4,347,826	$3,780,718	$4,602,614	$4,574,026
10 Initial investment by parent	−$10,000,000				
11 Cumulative *NPV*		−$5,652,174	−$1,871,456	$2,731,158	$7,305,184

Scenario 2	Year 0	Year 1	Year 2	Year 3	Year 4
1 Subsidiary revenue		€21,000,000	€21,000,000	€36,000,000	€38,000,000
2 Expenses		€16,000,000	€16,000,000	€29,000,000	€30,000,000
3 Host government tax (20%)		€1,000,000	€1,000,000	€1,400,000	€1,600,000
4 Cash flow to subsidiary		€4,000,000	€4,000,000	€5,600,000	€6,400,000
5 After earnings remitted to parent		€4,000,000	€4,000,000	€5,600,000	€6,400,000
6 Exchange rate of the $		$0.75	$0.75	$0.75	$0.75
7 Cash flow to parent		$3,000,000	$3,000,000	$4,200,000	$4,800,000
8 Required rate of return (discount rate)	20%				
9 *PV* of parent cash flows		$2,500,000	$2,083,333	$2,430,556	$2,744,416
10 Initial investment by parent	−$10,000,000				
11 Cumulative *NPV*		−$7,500,000	−$5,416,667	−$2,986,111	−$241,696

in this case, investment in a subsidiary in another location. If the cash flows are negative, the investment should not be made. It is a strategic choice based in part on the financial strength of the company regarding the time international managers are willing to wait for positive cash flows.

Capital budgeting analyses are not unique to MNCs. However, a variety of issues can make the decision more complex for the multinational. Scenarios 1 and 2 give an example of how an MNC might come to a different decision, even though the projected revenue for the subsidiary is the same. In Scenario 1, the assumption was made that the $/€ exchange rate would remain at $1.25/€1.00. It was also assumed that a 15 percent rate of return was sufficient to choose this project. In Scenario 2, the exchange rate was set at $0.75/€1.00.

As you can see comparing lines 6, the exchange-rate differences significantly reduce the cash returned to Sportif from $5,000,000 to $3,000,000. In addition, the multinational managers in Scenario 2 increased the required rate of return to 20 percent, perhaps because of different alternative investment opportunities or greater risk in the country of location for the subsidiary. The result is that with these different assumptions, Sportif will not recover its initial investment by year 4. Other things being equal, multinational managers would be more likely to go forward with building the subsidiary under the conditions in Scenario 1 than Scenario 2. Of course, this is only a simple example, as other factors such as local government tax rates or local government regulations regarding taking money from the country can affect the multinational manager's decisions. For example, if Sportif negotiated a more favorable local tax rate of 10 percent rather than the 20 percent shown in the Exhibit, the NPV in year 4 would be positive.

Once international managers determine that an investment is worthwhile financially, the next issue they must consider is how to get the needed cash to make the investment. As you learned in Chapter 6, companies get money from issuing debt, selling stocks, or by keeping some of their profits as retained earnings. The next section of this chapter considers how MNCs decide the best mix of financing options.

MNC Capital Structure

A major decision for the chief financial officer of an MNC is assessing the best mixture of debt and equity for his or her company. This mixture of debt and equity is called the **capital structure**.

The main objective of managing the capital structure is to reduce the cost of capital. As you learned in Chapter 6, there is a cost to getting money from others, and there are costs to the owners (stockholders) of using retained earnings since this reduces their dividends. All these factors are called the **cost of capital**. Bondholders expect to receive interest payments and stockholders expect dividends. Since more retained earnings reduce dividends, the cost of retained earnings comes from the lost opportunities of the owners to invest their money elsewhere.

Nearly 50 years ago, Nobel prizewinners Franco Modigliani and Merton Miller published research showing that it does not matter whether a company finances its activities with equity or debt or some combination. However, they noted that there is often an advantage to using debt because most countries allow tax deductions for interest payments.[6] That is, interest payments can be deducted from revenues, thus lowering a company's taxes. However, when a company takes on debt it has to make the interest payments, and these payments, just like the payments a college student who has large credit card balances must make each month, can drain available cash. Moreover, companies that have more debt relative to their equity are considered more risky to outside investors resulting in higher interest payments and lower stock prices.

capital structure
a company's mixture of debt and equity

cost of capital
the cost of getting money for projects either from owners' (stockholders') retained earnings, from issuing new stocks, or by borrowing

Generally, the cost of capital in terms of debt is estimated by the interest that must be paid, adjusting that value by the tax savings from interest deductions. For example, a company issues bonds to buy a new machine and pays €10,000 in interest payments to bondholders in a year. The company then takes a €10,000 tax deduction, reducing its reported profits by that amount. If the corporate tax rate is 30 percent, the company reduces its taxes by €3,000, which makes the cost of the capital in terms of debt equal to €7,000.

Calculating the cost of equity is a little more complex. To put a value on the cost of equity, financial managers use the logic that stockholders give up the opportunity to invest their money in other ventures. Therefore, the cost is what shareholders might have earned had they invested the funds themselves. One way of estimating the cost of new equity (issuing stocks) is known as the **constant dividend growth model**. As you can see below, the formula uses the current stock price and current and future dividends to estimate the opportunity costs (i.e. the money that could be earned from other investments) for investors. The cost of capital new equity is always more expensive than using retained earnings because of flotation costs. Flotation costs are the additional costs related to the expenses of selling new stock in the company. The formula for the constant dividend growth model is:

constant dividend growth model
a technique to estimate the cost of new equity (issuing stocks)

$$\frac{Cost\ of}{Equity} = \frac{Dividends\ per\ Share}{(Current\ Market\ Value\ of\ Stock - Flotation\ Costs)} + \frac{Growth\ Rate}{of\ Dividents}$$

Cost of Capital for the MNC

The cost of capital for an MNC is often different from domestic-only companies. There are several factors and risks associated with being multinational that can make the cost of capital different from that of domestic companies. Most of these differences relate to how MNCs deal with cash flow. **Cash flow** means the availability of cash to pay bills. Its relevance to the cost of capital is the MNC's ability to have enough cash to pay interest owed to bondholders and dividends to stockholders. Next, you will see a series of issues that MNCs encounter when considering the cost of capital. Exhibit 11.4 summarizes the factors that cause the cost of capital to be different for the MNC than for domestic firms.[7]

cash flow
the availability of cash to pay bills

Access to International Capital Markets   Unlike a purely domestic company, the MNC is more likely to take advantage of issuing bonds or selling stock in different capital markets. The regulations in different countries make the mixture of debt and equity financing complex for the MNC, but taking advantage of these regulations can reduce its cost of capital and thus make the company more valuable. For example, local subsidizers of the MNC may have access to local capital markets, where the subsidiary is often treated like a domestic company and gains advantages similar to local companies, such as lower interest rates or fewer regulations to list on local stock exchanges. However, capital markets in different countries can differ fundamentally, letting the MNC seek the best deal in any country.

Why are there country differences in the cost of debt and the cost of equity? Differences in the cost of debt are determined by two components of interest rates, the risk-free rate and the risk premium.

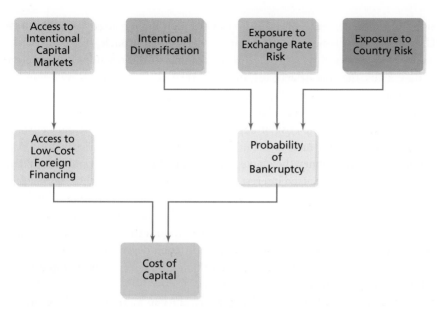

Exhibit 11.4 **Factors that Make the Cost of Capital Different for the MNC**

Source: Adapted from Jeff Madura, 2003, *International Financial Management*, Mason, OH: South-Western, p.512.

The **risk-free interest rate** is the cost of borrowing money determined by the supply and demand for funds. Like all supply–demand relationships, if there are more funds available for a level of demand the price will be lower. Similarly, if the demand for funds increases at a fixed level of supply, the price will rise. For example, the demand for borrowing might be greater in one country because tax laws allow companies to make deductions on interest paid. On the supply side, countries with older populations or cultural traditions of high savings provide more money for financial institutions to lend to companies, thus reducing interest rates. Central banks also control the supply of money, which can lower or increase interest rates. Economic conditions, such as those faced in many emerging economies with high rates of inflation, require higher interest rates to compensate investors for the potential decline value of currencies.

The **risk premium** is the additional interest creditors must charge borrowers to offset any characteristics of the company or their situation that may increase the likelihood of a default. Just as you have a credit rating, which can affect the interest rate a credit card company charges you, a company's bond rating is based on its financial strength and affects the interest charged. However, oftentimes more important for the MNC is that country risk also affects the risk premium. For example, if the probability of a recession is high in a particular country, borrowers face a greater chance of defaulting so creditors add to the risk premium. You can explore calculations of the risk premium charged by the Export–Import Bank of the United States, which offers financing and insurance of US importing and exporting operations, at www.exim.gov/tools/fee_calc.cfm.

In some countries, such as Japan and Germany, financial institutions have a greater tolerance for debt carried by their borrowers. That is, even though the chance of default increases when a company has more debt (as it does for an individual), financial institutions in some countries may not increase the risk premium as much as in other countries. In contrast to Japan and Germany,

risk-free interest rate
the cost of borrowing money determined by the supply of and demand for funds

risk premium
the additional interest creditors must charge borrowers to offset any characteristics of the company or their situation that may increase the likelihood of a default

similar companies in the US would pay a much higher interest rate because US financial institutions have a more risk-averse approach, due in part to a decreased likelihood of the government coming to the rescue of failing companies. Thus, the cost of debt for an MNC relates not only to its own bond or credit rating but also to the local risk-free interest rate and local country factors that affect the risk premium charged by lenders.

Fundamentally, the cost of capital derives from the opportunity costs of investors who could have invested their money elsewhere. For example, if investors took the money they have in the value of their stocks and invested in, say, a bank with guaranteed interest rates, then the baseline for the cost of equity is the level of potential returns from this other possible investment. This is the same risk-free interest rate considered in the cost of debt. Likewise, because the risk-free interest rates vary across countries, so does the cost of equity. Again, because companies and countries also have different degrees of risk to the stockholder, just as they do to those who lend them money, a risk premium must be added to cost of equity.[8]

Another factor that affects the cost of equity in a country is the extent of other opportunities for investing. More opportunities in a country mean that, since investors have more choice in purchasing stocks, it is likely expected returns will be greater and this will increase the cost of equity.

International Diversification   One of the advantages of being an MNC is that your profits and cash flows are not dependent on the economic conditions in a single country. To the extent that economies are independent, it is likely that the MNC located in many countries has a more stable cash flow to meet its debt needs, since good and bad economic conditions tend to cancel each other out. This is attractive to investors because they have more certainty that an MNC can take funds from high-profit units and transfer them to struggling units, giving even the struggling units the ability to cover interest payments. For example, if your European subsidiary is having a profitable year but your Japanese subsidiary is losing money, as long as the net cash flow is positive for the MNC, it can cover it debts and pay dividends in both countries. Thus, the cost of capital can be lower for the MNC.[9]

Exchange-rate Risk Exposure   As you learned in an earlier chapter, MNCs must manage their operations in two or more currencies. While setting up operations in several countries can make cash flows more stable, it also has the potential of being more volatile if a company does business in a foreign country with an unstable exchange rate with the parent company's country. For example, if a US company sets up operations in several emerging markets that have unstable currencies, the company could find that the earnings from these subsidiaries decrease if the US dollar gets stronger against these currencies. Thus, from the perspective of the cost of capital, costs are higher when a company faces more exchange-rate risk exposure.

Country Risk   Unstable political systems, weak enforcement of laws and contracts, changing tax systems, local wars, environmental or health disasters, and government policies regarding MNCs are, as you saw above, just a few of the factors that make up country risk. When MNCs enter countries with greater risk, MNC finance officers realize that investors will require a greater return on their investments to offset the greater likelihood that the company could lose money or fail because of the local country situation. Thus, when country risk increases, investors require higher returns, and the cost of capital is greater.[10]

How MNCs Decide on the Mixture of Debt and Equity in their Capital Structure

The capital structure is a company's choice of how much debt or equity to use to finance its operations. For the MNC this is more complex because the capital structure may differ for subsidiaries located in other countries. The characteristics of the company and the characteristics of the country influence the choice of more debt or equity.[11]

Company Factors

- *Cash flows* Of course, just like for individuals where richer people can take on more debt, companies with more cash can handle more debt. However, the stability of the cash flows is also important. Interest payments on bonds and bank loans must be made periodically over the year. Therefore, in order for a company to have sufficient cash to pay these debts when they are due, company managers must be confident that cash will be coming into the company when needed. From a personal point of view, consider that your credit card company wants payments every month and is not willing to wait until the payer gets a summer job in a few months.
- *Credit risk* You probably see the many advertisements today telling people to check their credit scores. Credit scores are based on your history of paying your debts and the amount of debt you have. If you have a lot of debt or you do not have a good record of paying on time, then you have a lower score and you are a higher credit risk. Credit risk is the estimate of the probability that you will not be able to pay off a loan. Similarly, companies have degrees of credit risk. When they use bonds to finance debt, their credit rating score is the bond rating. In any case, the logic is similar for individuals and companies. The higher the credit risk, the higher the interest a lender will charge, or possibly the loan may even be denied. As such, companies with a lower credit risk have more access to debt financing at lower interest rates and therefore are more likely to use more debt in their capital structure.
- *Availability of retained earnings* If a company is profitable, the managers have a choice. They can pay all the profits to the owners in terms of dividends or they can keep some of the profits to use to fund company activities as retained earnings. Thus, profitable companies can use this type of equity financing—remember, it is still equity because it is the owners' money. The use of retained earnings is often adequate to fund smaller projects, but when companies want to grow rapidly or make major investments in plants and equipment, they usually have to look to debt or issuing new stock.
- *Parent company guarantees* Subsidiaries of MNCs can often get lower interest rates on loans when their parent company agrees to back the debt. This means that the parent company will pay the debt should the subsidiary

default. This reduces the risks for the lenders and increases the lenders' willingness to give more favorable terms. This same thing sometimes happens to people when they do not have the financial resources to get a loan to buy a car or a house. For example, parents might back the loan for a young couple so that they can buy their first house. However, this is a two-sided coin. When an MNC backs a subsidiary, the parent company may see its credit risk increase because it is now liable for more debt.

The IB Strategic Insight below gives some insight on how MNCs can take advantage of different options for financing their projects.

Country Factors   Except for the ability of the parent company to back the debt of a subsidiary, the company factors that influence the capital structure of an MNC are similar to those of a domestic company. However, unlike a domestic company that must respond only to one country's context, the MNC must consider country conditions everywhere it operates. Some country factors to consider include the following:

- *Stock market regulations* Types of financial reporting required by local stock markets (see the chapter on accounting), restrictions on foreign companies, and reluctance of local investors to invest in foreign companies can sometimes make it difficult to raise capital through equity in some countries.

Using the Global Capital Markets: US-based Intel and Swiss-based STMicroelectronics find Money in Italy for their Joint Venture

IB STRATEGIC INSIGHT

Original plans for Swiss-based Numonyx, a joint venture between Intel and Geneva-based chipmaker STMicroelectronics, called for debt financing of $1.55 billion to start this company. The new company is a spin-off of the parent company's NOR and NAND flash microprocessor businesses. The processors drive popular devices such as cell phones, MP3 players, and digital cameras. However, unstable capital markets and declining demand in the NAND flash market made it harder to find lenders willing and able to close the deal. Analyst Brian Piccioni of BMO Capital Markets noted, "Overall, it just hasn't been a strong context to accommodate a spinout such as this." However, several months after the proposed founding date of Numonyx, the parent companies were able to get $450 million of debt financing from Italian banks Intesa Sanpaolo and Unicredit Banca d'Impresa, in addition to $100 million in revolving credit. To cover this debt, the parent companies agreed to guarantee 50 percent of the value of the loans. There is some advantage to less debt, notes Brian Harrison, president and CEO of Numonyx: "The basic structure of the deal hasn't changed and Numonyx will be leaner and in a better position to add funds in the future."

STMicroelectronics holds a 49 percent share in the new company and Intel a 45 percent share. Francisco Partners holds a 6 percent share, buying into the venture for $150 million in cash. Numonyx is estimated to become the third-largest nonvolatile memory manufacturer in the world after Samsung and Toshiba, with annual revenues of $3 billion.

Sources: Adapted from Agam Shah, 2007, "STMicroelectronics, Intel delay launch of joint venture," IDG News Service, December 26; Agam Shah, 2008, "Intel STMicroelectronics open doors to Numonyx," IDG News Service, March 31; Benjamin Pimentel, 2008, "Intel, STMicro launch joint flash venture," MarketWatch, April 1.

Alternatively, if a country's laws restrict investments in other countries or otherwise create barriers such as unfavorable tax rules for investing in foreign markets, local investors may have fewer opportunities to buy stocks. This restricted supply of local investment opportunities makes the prices of stocks higher and makes it more attractive for an MNC to use equity rather than debt financing in such locations.

- *Strength or weakness of local currencies* If the currencies in a host country are weak relative to the currency of the parent company's country, there is an incentive to use local debt financing rather than borrowing from the parent company's retained earnings. The reason that this makes sense is that, from the perspective of the parent company, paying interest in a weaker currency means that the MNC gets cheaper loans That is, interest paid in a weaker currency provides cheaper loans than with a stronger currency. Alternatively, if the financial officers of the MNC believe that the host country's currency will appreciate relative to the home country's, there is an incentive to invest more of the parent company's retained earnings in the subsidiary as those investments will grow in value based on the home country currency. Similarly, there is also an incentive to have the subsidiary retain more of its earnings so that investment will grow in value based on the home country currency.

- *Host country risk* High degrees of country risk encourage multinational managers to find ways to increase local investors' commitment to the success of the company. The common tactic is to use more local debt financing. In this case, should a local government do anything that hurts the performance of the MNC's subsidiary, it puts local investors at risk. Since local citizens rather than foreigners are at risk, there is more pressure on the government to look out for the welfare of the local subsidiary.

- *Local tax laws* Countries often require MNC subsidiaries to pay taxes on earnings that they return to their parent company. Most countries also give tax reductions for interest payments on loans from local financial institutions. This situation encourages local debt financing because it reduces the taxes on money returned to the parent company. It is particularly attractive in high tax rate countries because the deductions for interest payments reduce taxes even more.[12] Exhibit 11.5 summarizes the effects of country conditions on debt financing.

Exhibit 11.5 **The Impact of Host Country Conditions on MNC Subsidiary Financing**

Host Country Conditions	Financing with Local Subsidiary Debt	Financing with Parent Company Debt
Higher risk	Higher	Lower
Higher interest rates	Lower	Higher
Lower interest rates	Higher	Lower
Currency expected to weaken	Higher	Lower
Currency expected to strengthen	Lower	Higher
Higher local taxes	Higher	Lower

As you learned in the chapter on international strategies, MNCs not only have investment opportunities in other countries but also often engage in exporting or importing. In the next section, you will learn some of the procedures used in the financial transactions of this international trade.

Financing International Trade[13]

As you saw from the statistics reported in Chapter 1, international trade continues to grow and is often a part of an MNC's international business transactions. In this section, we review some of the major points regarding financial transaction in international trade.

Methods of Payment in International Trade

For companies to engage in international trade, the importer, the exporter, or financial institutions must provide credit in the sense that there is a lag between when payments are made and when goods or services are delivered. There are four basic methods of payments to settle an international trade transaction, each with different levels of risk for the importer or exporter. The type of payments used in specific transactions depends on how well the participants trust each other, the countries involved, and the competition that may require giving one side or the other more favorable terms to make the sale.

The most common terms of purchase are as follows:

1. Cash-in-advance (pre-payment)
2. Letters of credit
3. Documentary collections
4. Open account.

Exhibit 11.6 gives an overview of each payment method and Exhibit 11.7 shows the balance of risks for each side in the exchange. We discuss each method in more detail below.

cash-in-advance
a payment method when the exporter does not ship the goods until payment is received

Cash-in-advance Under the **cash-in-advance** or pre-payment method, the exporter does not ship the goods until payment is received. Thus, the exporter avoids credit risk or the risk of not being paid. Bank wire transfers provide a common and secure cash-in-advance option for exporters. However, foreign buyers must then take the risk that the goods may not be sent after they have made their payment in advance. Exporters who demand such terms may lose customers to competitors who offer more favorable payment terms and do not insist on pre-payment. Experts suggest this type of payment is best for high-risk trade relationships.

letter of credit
a commitment by a bank on behalf of the importer to pay the exporter when all required shipping documents are presented

Letters of Credit A **letter of credit** (LC) is a commitment by a bank on behalf of the importer to pay the exporter when all required shipping documents are presented. Banks deal only in documents and not the actual goods shipped. The importer makes no payment until the bank receives documents showing that the goods were shipped or otherwise delivered as promised. Because documents are the key to the transaction, an LC is also called a documentary credit.

Exhibit 11.6 **Payment Methods in International Trade**

Method	Time of Payment	Goods Available to Importer	Risk to Exporter	Risk to Importer
Cash-in-advance (pre-payment)	Before shipment	After payment	None	Completely dependent on exporter to ship goods as ordered
Letters of credit	When shipment is made	After payment	Little or none	Shipment is assured but dependent on exporter to ship goods as noted in documents
Documentary collections	When the importer receives documents that shipment has been made	After payment	If the importer does not pay, exporter must do something with the shipped goods	Same as above except that the importer can inspect the goods prior to payment
Open account	As agreed	Before payment	Completely dependent on importer to pay as agreed	None

Source: Adapted from Jeff Madura, 2003, *International Financial Management*, Mason, OH: South-Western, p. 561.

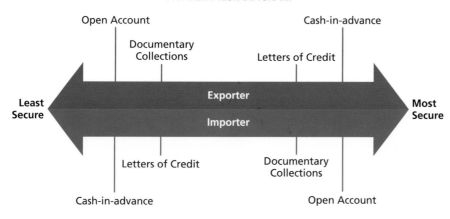

PAYMENT RISK DIAGRAM

Exhibit 11.7 **Balance of Risks for Importers and Exporters**

Source: US Department of Commerce, 2007, *Trade Finance Guide*, Washington, DC: US Department of Commerce, p.3.

Typical documents include a draft, a commercial invoice, and a bill of lading. A **draft** states that one party will pay the other party immediately or at some future date. A **commercial invoice** is a document that identifies the parties involved, the terms of payment, price, shipping information, and quantity, weight, packaging, etc., associated with the product. The **bill of lading** is the receipt issued to the exporter by the transportation carrier showing that the merchandise has been shipped. A bill of lading serves three purposes: as a receipt that the carrier has taken the merchandise listed; as a contract between the exporter and the carrier to provide transportation services of the merchandise for an agreed fee and deliver to the importer; and as a document of title, so that

draft
a document that states that one party will pay the other party immediately or at some future date

commercial invoice
a document that identifies the parties involved, the terms of payment, price, shipping information, and quantity, weight, packaging, etc., associated with the product

bill of lading
the receipt showing that the merchandise has been shipped; it is usually required that the importer present this receipt to get the merchandise

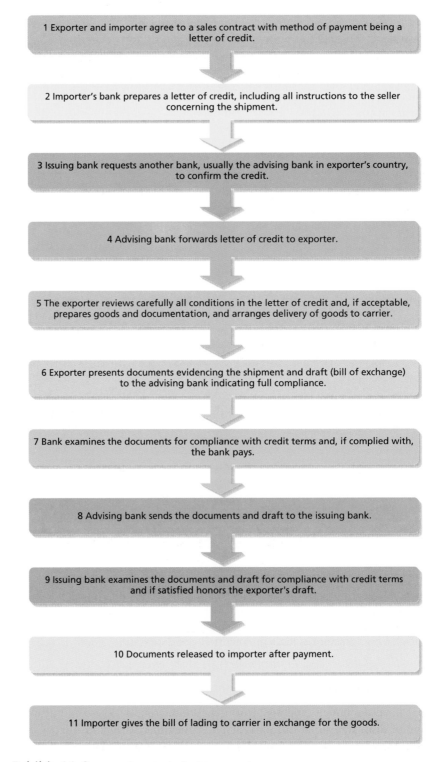

1 Exporter and importer agree to a sales contract with method of payment being a letter of credit.

2 Importer's bank prepares a letter of credit, including all instructions to the seller concerning the shipment.

3 Issuing bank requests another bank, usually the advising bank in exporter's country, to confirm the credit.

4 Advising bank forwards letter of credit to exporter.

5 The exporter reviews carefully all conditions in the letter of credit and, if acceptable, prepares goods and documentation, and arranges delivery of goods to carrier.

6 Exporter presents documents evidencing the shipment and draft (bill of exchange) to the advising bank indicating full compliance.

7 Bank examines the documents for compliance with credit terms and, if complied with, the bank pays.

8 Advising bank sends the documents and draft to the issuing bank.

9 Issuing bank examines the documents and draft for compliance with credit terms and if satisfied honors the exporter's draft.

10 Documents released to importer after payment.

11 Importer gives the bill of lading to carrier in exchange for the goods.

Exhibit 11.8 **Steps in a Typical LC Transaction**

Sources: Adapted from www.export911.com/e911/gateway/summary.htm; www.zeromillion.com/business/international/export-payment.html

the exporter can obtain payment (or written promise of payment) before the merchandise is released to the importer.

In the transaction, the bank in the importer's country, called the issuing bank, authorizes a bank in the exporter's country, called the advising bank, to make payment to the exporter when they receive the agreed-upon documents. Two major types of LCs include an irrevocable letter of credit and a confirmed letter of credit. An irrevocable LC means that it may not be changed or cancelled without the agreement of both the buyer and the seller. A confirmed letter of credit means that the exporter's advising bank guarantees to pay the exporter if the foreign bank fails to do so. This type of LC makes sense when the exporter is worried about the credit risk of the foreign bank or the political risk of the importing country. It is a type of insurance for the exporter.

An LC is somewhat of a complex transaction. As such, as an aid in understanding this type of payment, Exhibit 11.8 shows the sequence of a typical LC transaction.

Documentary Collections In **documentary collections** (DCs), the exporter's bank (called the remitting bank) collects the payments for the exporter. After shipping goods to the importer, the exporter receives documents from the importer and provides them to its bank. The exporter's remitting bank then sends these documents to the importer's bank (called the collecting bank) along with instructions for payment. Upon receipt of the payment, the collecting bank releases the documents to the importer. The collecting bank then sends the money paid by the importer to the exporter's remitting bank, and this bank credits the exporter's account when the money is received. To receive the shipped goods, the importer goes to the shipping carrier and presents the documents.

documentary collections
when the exporter's bank (called the remitting bank) collects the payments for the exporter

Open Account Just the opposite of a pre-payment, an **open account transaction** means that the exporter ships the goods before payment is due. Usually, the importer agrees to pay within 30 to 90 days. This is the highest-risk option for an exporter. Ideally, to accept an open account, the exporter should be confident that the importer will pay at an agreed-upon time, and that the importing country is a low-risk political, economic, and commercial environment. However, in competitive export markets, foreign buyers often demand open accounts if they can get open accounts from the exporter's competitors.

open account transaction
means that the exporter ships the goods before payment is due

Export Financing

Like a company that needs capital to finance building a plant in another country, exporters also need access to funds to finance their operations. Remember, it is often a long time between when the exporter begins building a product and when the exporting company finally receives its payments from the importers. Below are some types of financing available to exporters.

Working Capital Financing

When an exporter needs to cover the entire cash cycle from purchase of raw materials through the ultimate collection of the payments, one option is the use

export working capital
money loaned to an exporter so that the exporter can buy the raw materials and build the products to ship to importers in foreign countries

of **export working capital.** Commercial banks usually provide export working capital facilities so that the exporter can buy the raw materials and build the products to ship to importers in foreign countries. The bank can provide this money in the form of a loan or revolving line of credit. A revolving line of credit is like a credit card that allows companies to borrow money up to some preset limit over a period of time. The IB Small Business Insight below shows how two small businesses from Alabama succeed in the export business by getting working capital export financing.

Export Factoring

export factoring
occurs when an exporter transfers title or ownership of its short-term foreign accounts receivables to a factor for cash but less the face value of the account receivables

Another option that exporters can use to get needed funds is called **export factoring.** As you remember from your accounting class, accounts receivables are payments due the company from customers who have been billed but who have not yet paid. Export factoring focuses on short-term receivables (payments due in up to 180 days). In this system, the exporter transfers title or ownership of its short-term foreign accounts receivables to a factor, which is a bank or a specialized financial firm that purchases account receivables. The factor then gives the exporter cash but less the face value of the account receivables. The

**Two Alabama Small to Medium-sized Enterprises (SMEs)
Find Financing to Propel their Exporting Success**

**IB SMALL
BUSINESS INSIGHT**

Weichai Power Co. Ltd, Weifang City, Shandong, China, put out a call for bids for a contract to engineer and build a cupola-melt facility and emission control system for a diesel engine manufacturing plant. A cupola is a vertical furnace used to melt iron. After several companies contacted Weichai Power about the project, the Chinese company came directly to Gregory R. Bray, president and CEO of Electric Controls and Systems Inc. (EC&S) of Birmingham, Alabama, asking for a bid on the project. Weichai Power recognized that EC&S has an excellent reputation for engineering and producing machinery for heavy industrial processing plants. Bray agreed to bid, offering a price of $11.8 million and getting the contract over a German competitor.

However, noted Bray, "One of our challenges was financing, but with the assistance of First Commercial Bank and the Alabama International Trade Center, we were able to obtain a working capital guarantee from the Export–Import Bank of the US for the issuance of a performance bond required for the project." Weichai Power's cupola is

now running and there are other possible projects in China for EC&S.

Thomasville Lumber Company is an Alabama lumber mill that produces high-quality Southern Yellow Pine for export to international markets. Thomasville exports to the Caribbean, Japan, and Western Europe. Thomasville began humbly when two former employees from a closed lumber mill and the mayor contacted the Alabama International Trade Center and asked for assistance to restart the mill as an export production facility for customers in Europe. The two former employees managed to buy the abandoned mill at a bargain price and then secured a $1,000,000 export working capital loan from the Small Business Administration. This gave sufficient funds to purchase logs and carry short-term receivables. The company is now prospering, and in less than five years of existence sales have grown to over $10 million.

Source: Adapted from Alabama International Trade Center, University of Alabama, www.aitc.ua.edu/success.html

amount it falls below the face value of the receivables is called the discount and this is like the interest on a loan. Thus, the exporter gets less money than the face value of the account receivables, but the company gets the money right away and does not have to wait for payments from customers. It is like a loan but with the additional benefit that the factor handles the collections and risks of nonpayment. You can find factors at Factors Chain International (FCI), www.factors-chain.com.

Forfaiting

Forfaiting is similar to factoring except that it focuses on the sale of medium-term receivables (180 days to seven years). However, unlike factors, forfaiters typically work with exporters on larger projects, typically over $100,000. As such, mostly larger established companies use forfaiting. More recently small and medium-sized companies are using forfaiting when they deal with importers from countries considered high risk. You can find forfaiters by going to the website of the International Forfaiting Association (IFA), www.forfaiters.org.

forfaiting
occurs when an exporter transfers title or ownership of its medium-term foreign accounts receivables, typically for larger projects, to a factor for cash but less the face value of the account receivables

CHAPTER REVIEW

This chapter began with a discussion of risk. You saw that country risk related to how a country's business environment might influence an MNC's profits or the value of its assets in that country. Before MNCs enter a country, the international managers must consider how risk might affect their investments. Tesco's managers, for example, decided that entering the US market with many stores all at once was risky but worth the potential financial loss because the potential pay-off is high. Thus, risk plays an essential role in considering any financial investment, but assessment of risk is more complex when the investment crosses borders.

Although there are many strategic reasons to consider a major project such as entering a new country, ultimately companies need to make money and the investment needs to return more than the cost. This process is called the capital budgeting decision, and one popular technique to estimate when an investment will pay off is called net present value or NPV. Importantly for the international manger, NPV calculations allow considerations of how much return is necessary to match the risk and how issues such as changing exchange rates and local tax rates influence the expected outcomes.

Of course, once international managers decide that an investment makes sense strategically and financially, they must decide the best way to get the money to fund the venture. As you remember from previous chapters, they can do this with debt or equity. The challenging decision is to decide the capital structure, which is the mixture of debt and equity. The basic criterion is based on which will cost the company more, the interest paid on debt or the dividends lost to the stockholders. However, many factors come into play when international managers determine the capital structure of their foreign subsidiaries. One important factor is the degree to which the local tax structure and laws allow deductions of interest payments on bonds and thus reduce taxes. However, numerous other issues such as available cash flows and local country risk are also considered.

The MNC faces financing issues not only when considering foreign investments but also in import and export transactions. For MNCs involved in international trade, financial institutions, importers, or exporters must provide credit to cover the lag between when goods are delivered and when payments are made.

There are various methods of payments in international trade. In this chapter, you learned about cash-in-advance or pre-payments, letters of credit, documentary collections, and open accounts. Each of these has varying degrees of risk for the exporter, importer, or participating financial institutions, depending on which party receives the payments or goods first.

The chapter concluded with a discussion of the types of financing that exporters often use to cover cash flow needs between the time when the exporter begins production of goods and when the company finally receives payments from an importer. Working capital financing from commercial banks allows companies to borrow up to certain amounts, often with revolving credit similar to a credit card. Other forms of financing, export factoring and forfaiting, allow export companies to sell their accounts receivables at a discount in order to receive the money prior to the payments from the exporters.

Chief financial officers, or CFOs, in MNCs have very complex jobs to manage financial operations often in many countries, each with its own unique financial environment. It is the duty of the CFO to work with other top international managers to provide the technical expertise to help determine the best financial options in implementing international strategies.

 ## DISCUSSION QUESTIONS

1. Identify political factors that might affect the risk to do business in a country.
2. Identify financial factors that might affect the risk to do business in a country.
3. Discuss the statement: Any level of risk can be OK if the potential returns are sufficiently high.
4. SEL in Washington State plans to establish a European subsidiary. SEL's financial managers expect that the euro will appreciate over the next few years. How might this affect SEL's decision regarding the use of headquarters' retained earnings or its subsidiary's retained earnings as sources of capital?
5. Discuss factors that must be considered for capital budgeting for an MNC's foreign subsidiary that might not be considered for a domestic investment.
6. Consider investments in Brazil, Hungary, and Germany and discuss the factor of risk in making a capital budgeting decision regarding investments in these countries.
7. Discuss reasons why the capital structure of an MNC's subsidiary might differ from the parent company.
8. Why might the capital structures of companies from different countries differ?
9. What is the role of commercial banks in international trade transactions?

10. Discuss situations where an MNC might prefer a debt-intensive capital structure or an equity-intensive capital structure.
11. Discuss the risks or benefits to the exporter and important contrasting accounts receivable financing and factoring.
12. Discuss the role of the factor for the exporter. How does the factor help an exporter?
13. Contrast the options of forfaiting and factoring.
14. Identify and discuss the basic documents used in international trade transactions.

INTERNATIONAL BUSINESS SKILL BUILDER

Making NPV Decisions

Practice making NPV decisions for investments under different exchange rates and required rates of return. Go to http://spreadsheets.google.com/ccc?key=pfiFjc0K9uyyj1FpTTU29Kg or to your text's website support, where you can download the Excel spreadsheet for Exhibit 11.3, which shows two different scenarios for NPV for a hypothetical company. In the example, the host government's tax rate is 20 percent; the exchange rate of the dollar is 1.25 (shown in line 6); the discount rate is shown as 15 percent in line 8; and the initial investment is shown as $10,000,000 (entered as a negative) in line 10. You can change any of these values or other values in the colored cells and experiment with what happens to NPV.

CHAPTER INTERNET ACTIVITY

Search the web for export factoring companies. Identify at least three companies. You can have a mixture of domestic companies or factor companies in other countries. Compare and contrast their services. Pick one that you would use as a small to medium-sized business and provide a rationale for your choice.

KEY CONCEPTS

bill of lading	constant dividend growth model	economic risk	NPV
capital budgeting decision	cost of capital	export factoring	open account transaction
capital structure	country risk	export working capital	political risk
cash flow	documentary collections	financial risk	risk premium
cash-in-advance		forfaiting	risk-free interest rate
commercial invoice	draft	letter of credit	sustainability risk
		net present value, or	

BUSINESS > INTERNATIONAL

WILSON INTERNATIONAL

INTERNATIONAL CAPITAL BUDGETING

Wilson International is a chain of over 100 luxury hotels found mostly in developed countries. George Wilson, a former Chicago sales representative who frequently traveled internationally, started the company. As an international business traveler, Wilson found that hotel quality varied from country to country. He quit his very successful sales job and started a hotel in Dublin, Ireland, a country known for its extensive bed-and-breakfast industry. Wilson felt that business travelers needed a greater selection of hotels in Dublin, particularly in the higher-priced market. The Wilson of Dublin was an immediate success with business travelers and, with the help of a venture capitalist, George was able to expand his hotel concept to 20 countries.

Wilson has always sought hotel opportunities in more developed countries in Europe and Asia. George and his associates felt that the problems found in less-developed countries presented too much risk for his company, thus they avoided most countries of the world. Because the countries in which Wilson operates are considered politically stable and present little political risk, the investment decisions are normally made on the basis of revenue projections using a net present value approach. The firm's cost of capital is used as a means of discounting expected cash flow. If the net present value (NPV) of the investment is above zero, the hotel is constructed. This approach has worked well for the company over the years.

With the possibility of market saturation beginning to rise, George is considering an opportunity to expand into other markets. He has been approached by a trade representative of St Charles, a small and moderately industrialized island in the Caribbean, who proposes that Wilson International build a business hotel in the capital, Dominic. The trade rep has assured George that an additional hotel is needed in the capital because of the country's expanding industrialization. St Charles has always enjoyed a brisk tourist trade, and now the country is diversifying its economy into light manufacturing.

Multinationals from the United States and Europe have established customer service operations on the island, and a number of garment manufacturers have begun operations there as well. The trade representative tells George that managers from these companies frequently visit the island, and they need a more luxurious hotel in which to stay. The hotel would certainly be profitable, reasons the trade rep.

. . .

Financial analysts for the company have created a report indicating that, using the present financial model, a small hotel would be a good investment. Data included in the model can be seen below.

Wilson International—St Charles Operation Preliminary Financial Analysis

Yearly expected cash flow from operations	US$ 750,000
Expected life of the investment	25 years
Wilson International cost of capital	12%
Investment	US$ 5,000,000

(Present value of cash flows–investment) = NPV (5,882,355–5,000,000) = $882,355

Some Wilson analysts argue, however, that a higher discounting factor than cost of capital should be used. It is proposed by some that a more appropriate discounting factor would be 15 percent, because of the higher risks associated with the investment environment.

George is uncertain about the proposed investment. While he sees the need for the company to find new markets, he is also troubled by reports he has read about increasing social unrest on the island. Although George and his associates do not consider St Charles to be a high-risk country, they are concerned about recent increases in petty street crime and social unrest. It has been reported that citizens have resorted to violent street protest to express their displeasure with the increasing prices of some consumer goods. The currency of St Charles, the Caribbean dollar, has been devalued against most hard currencies of the world and, as a result, imported goods have increased in price. On the other hand, St Charles has no currency or foreign direct investment restrictions, and allows for full repatriation of company profits. In recent years, the government has been attempting to promote the island as an attractive location for foreign investment.

With declining opportunities in more stable environments, George must consider the feasibility of this opportunity, and the necessary change of strategic direction it would mean for Wilson International.

CASE DISCUSSION POINTS

1. What additional information might be useful to consider before making this investment decision?
2. Can an international company avoid all political risk? Explain.
3. Would you recommend that Wilson International build a hotel on St Charles? Are there any alternatives to consider other than building the hotel or staying out of the country? Explain.

Case prepared by Charles A. Rarick

12 Accounting for Multinational Operations

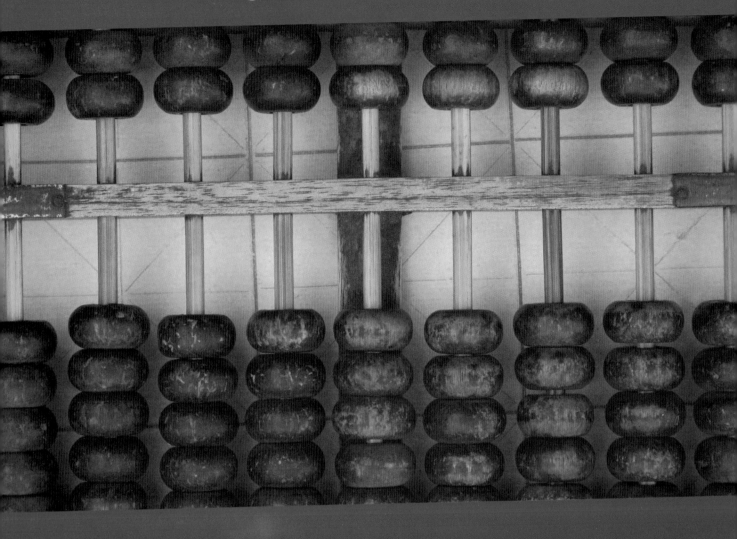

After reading this chapter you should be able to:

- Understand the purpose of accounting and the differences between managerial accounting and financial accounting.

- Understand why nations adopt different accounting systems and the types of systems in use around the world.

- Identify the pressures leading to the harmonization of accounting procedures.

- Understand the basics of International Accounting Standards.

- Know how MNCs account for exchange-rate differences and translate foreign currencies for financial reporting.

- Appreciate the complexities of accounting for transfer pricing between units of MNCs.

- Be able to apply basic tax planning strategies.

managerial accounting accounting information reported for internal used by a company's managers; generally does not have to follow any universal standards

financial accounting provides information to external stakeholders regarding the company's performance

The purpose of accounting is to provide standardized information that helps stakeholders in an organization (e.g. managers, investors) make sound economic and business decisions. As you can see from the Preview IB Strategic Insight, accounting practices can differ widely in their design and implementation in different countries. In this chapter we will explore how these differences influence the activities of MNCs. First, however, let us consider some of the basic types of accounting.

Managerial accounting focuses on the information gathered for internal use by a company's managers and generally does not have to follow any universal standards. In contrast, **financial accounting** provides information to external stakeholders regarding the company's performance. Stockowners, bondholders, and other investors (e.g. banks) need relevant, valid, and reliable (consistently applied to all organizations) information about the financial state of a company. For example, think of yourself as an investor. Before you loan your money to a company or use your money to buy stock, you would want to be certain that the financial reports issued by the company are correct. Like investors, governments are also interested in the quality of financial reports. Since corporations pay taxes based on their profits, governments need to have an accurate assessment of the financial performances of companies in their countries. Unlike managerial accounting, financial accounting follows rules created by standard-setting bodies. In the US, the standard-setting body is called the Financial Accounting Standards

A Cultural Revolution in Accounting

PREVIEW IB
STRATEGIC INSIGHT

In its former planned state economy, accounting in China focused on providing the numbers that state planners needed—mostly production quota numbers. Capitalist information such as costs, debt, and especially profit were ignored. In the 1990s, as China gradually moved to a capitalist economy, the role of accounting changed. To manage and value companies where profit is necessary for survival, accounting numbers had to make sense to investors and managers.

In 2007, the Ministry of Finance directed the 1,200 companies listed on the Shanghai and Shenzhen stock markets to adopt accounting standards and practices similar to International Financial Reporting Standards (IFRS). These or similar standards are gradually replacing local accounting and financial reporting standards in many countries including the EU. The benefits of using IFRS are that investors and managers will be able to tell how well a company is performing. That is, revenues, costs, debts, and profits will be transparent and comparable to other companies. This will not only have local consequences but will allow Chinese companies to attract foreign capital and help Chinese companies wishing to invest in other countries.

The reality, however, is that this change is difficult. There are fewer than 70,000 accountants in China and not many that understand IFRS. Detailing the financial status of companies that have extensive overlapping ownership, common in China, will be extremely difficult and time consuming. This is made all the more difficult because China does not have a tradition of market-based record keeping. However, in the end, this change should lead to more transparency in Chinese companies.

Source: Adapted from *The Economist*, 2007, "Cultural revolution," www.economist.com, January 11; *The Economist*, 2007, "Trust from facts," www.economist.com, January 11.

Board (FASB) and its rules are called the US GAAP or Generally Accepted Accounting Principles. Many countries have their own GAAP standards that reflect the financial accounting rules in use in their country.

Since accounting provides information to make business and economic decisions, the differences in accounting systems used in different nations becomes an important consideration for international business people. Thus, international business managers must be aware of how differences in accounting systems in the countries in which they do business affect issues such as measure of financial performance, cash flows, and taxation. To deal with these issues, the field of international accounting is becoming increasingly important in our globalizing world. International accounting focuses on the differences among countries in accounting principles and reporting practices, the state of international and regional harmonization of accounting principles and reporting practices, foreign currency translation in financial reporting, accounting reporting for taxation, and the financial performance assessments of foreign subsidiaries and companies.[1]

In the remainder of this chapter we will answer several important question related to international accounting. If we are in a world of increasingly global trade and investment, why do accounting standards differ by region and nation? Are there any efforts to make standards similar around the world? What are the implications of having different accounting principles and standards used by different country units for the MNC?

Why do Nations have Different Accounting Systems?

As you have seen for many business practices discussed in this book, the national context of social institutions and national culture provide two drivers of why accounting systems differ.[2] Exhibit 12.1 summarizes the forces that result in different accounting systems. First we will consider cultural issues, and then the institutional context.

National Culture

The classic view of accounting practices and culture links country practices with the Hofstede cultural dimensions that you studied earlier in the book.[3] Some of these accounting values also derive from dimensions of national culture identified by Trompenaars.

There are four major accounting values that studies show are related to national culture.[4] These are:

- *Professionalism versus statutory control* In individualistic, low-power distance cultures and those with low uncertainty avoidance, there is a preference for accountants using individual professional judgment rather than following strict legal requirements.
- *Conservatism versus optimism* In cultures with high power distance, high uncertainty avoidance, and strong affective norms (see Chapter 7), there exists a preference for accountants to take a cautious approach to financial measurement in contrast to being more laissez-faire.

Exhibit 12.1 **Why National Accounting Systems Differ**

- *Secrecy versus transparency* In high power distance and particularistic cultures, there is a preference for accountants to behave with strict confidentiality, only disclosing financial information about a business to managers and those who provide financing. This contrasts with accounting systems that encourage more transparency and publicly available information regarding companies.
- *Uniformity versus flexibility* In high uncertainty avoidance and universalistic cultures there is a preference for accountants to adopt uniform accounting practices applied similarly to all companies at all times. This contrasts with a flexible and particularistic approach to using accounting data that favors flexibility in accordance with the unique circumstances of individual companies.

Social Institutions

In addition to national culture, the institutional context also influences how accounting systems develop and how they are used. In this section, we consider the nature of capital markets, type of tax reporting, the legal system and levels of enforcement of regulations, the types of businesses, the status of the accounting profession and accounting education, and economic and political ties with other nations.[5]

The Nature of Capital Markets As you learned in Chapter 6, companies get needed finances by using debt (bank loans and bond) or equity (stocks). In countries such as Canada and the US, larger companies issue stock to get needed financing. In contrast, in Japan and Germany, it is more common to use bank financing. In equity market countries, there is more pressure to use accounting reports to present the company in the most favorable light. This is more likely to attract more stockholders and keep the price of stocks high. To protect investors there is also pressure from government regulators that requires companies to use more sophisticated accounting methods. For example, as we have seen earlier, the Sarbanes–Oxley Act in the US requires more disclosure of financial information to protect potential investors from the dubious acts of companies like Enron.

The Type of Tax Reporting Countries can be separated on the degree to which there are separate rules for tax reporting and financial reporting. In the US and UK, for example, the rules are mostly independent. Companies file corporate tax returns like individuals and they issue annual reports to their stockholders to show the performance of their companies. In this case, the incentive is to be optimistic to the stockholders and report the lowest earnings possible to the tax collectors. In countries with a single reporting system, within the boundaries of the law, companies will tend to report lower earnings.

The Legal System and Levels of Enforcement of Regulations There are three basic types of legal systems, common law, code or civil law, and theocratic law. The code law system, used in countries such as France, attempts to pre-define rules for acceptable behavior in all situations. For the code to evolve, it must be changed by the governing body. In a common law system, such as that used in the US and the UK, law evolves based on the interpretations of the law by judges and courts. In a theocratic law system, such as that used in Iran, civilian laws must be consistent with religious principles such as those in the Qur'an and religion supersedes civil law. In sum, common law is based on tradition, precedent, and custom; code law is based on codes; theocratic law is based on religious beliefs.

In code law countries, accounting practices also tend to be legislated and are very detailed and procedural. The objective is to protect those who lend money to the company. In common law countries, accounting practices evolve in response to evolving financial systems with the emphasis on presenting a fair and accurate portrayal of the company to shareholders. Theocratic law generally has more broad-based influences on the whole financial system rather than accounting practices.

Regardless of the type of legal system in use, countries differ in willingness and ability to enforce rules and laws regarding accounting practices. The Asian economic crises, some argue, occurred because personal ties between banks and companies kept the financial positions of many companies hidden until they reached crisis proportions. Even in the US, accounting scandals such as Enron and WorldCom have demonstrated that it takes considerable governmental resources to correct such situations.

The Types of Businesses   The financial reporting practices that evolve in different countries reflect the need of the types of companies that exist in the country. In the developed countries of the world, which spawn the large and highly complex MNCs, accounting practices evolve with the complexities of these businesses. In contrast, in much of the developing world there are few large and complex companies. Simple financial reporting is often all that is needed to provide valid and reliable information concerning these companies.

The Status of the Accounting Profession and Accounting Education
The prestige and influence of different occupational groups is not the same in all countries. For example, the role of the physician in Russia does not carry the status and prestige that it does in the US. The accounting profession is no different. In countries where the accounting profession is viewed as largely a book-keeping occupation, its influence is diminished and audit reports have less respect in the business community. In contrast, where accountants are viewed as independent professionals who follow independent professional norms, there is often more trust in what the accountants report. It is also assumed that the companies that are clients of accountants have less influence on the content of the financial reports certified by accountants. For accounting to evolve into a professional status, there must be established educational systems to train accountants. The degrees awarded must be considered legitimate certifications of accounting knowledge by the organizations and the investors in the country. Similarly, there are often licensing or certification requirements from the government or from a professional association that assure the professional competency of the accountants.

Economic and Political Ties with Other Nations   Cross-border trade and investment and membership in trade groups such as the EU and the ASEAN expose different nations to each other's accounting practices. Within trade groups, for example, there is pressure to adopt similar standards to make cross-border transactions simpler and more efficient. For the developing world, there is also pressure to mimic the practices of the developed countries to facilitate trade and investment.

These drivers of national accounting systems result in many different types of systems. In the next section, we consider some basic classifications of systems.

Types of National Accounting Systems

In an attempt to simplify our understanding of differences among national accounting systems, several accounting scholars have developed classification systems that group different nations into similar types. Before we consider these systems, you should realize that national accounting systems change in response to local and global pressures. As such, these are general overviews to help you see the most basic differences. They also give us insights into the historical uses of accounting systems and how such systems developed in different countries.

The traditional way to view differences among accounting systems divides them into two groups: the microeconomic and the macroeconomic.[6] The micro and macro roughly follow the differences in legal systems discussed earlier. The micro systems occur mostly in common law countries and the macro systems occur mostly in codified or rule-based legal systems.

In the macroeconomic approach, accounting practices are developed largely to serve national economic planning and taxing functions. Accounting has a macro function because it most serves macro or nation-level interests. Examples include Italy, France, and Sweden. In the microeconomic approach, accounting serves the need of businesses, hence it is micro or at an organizational level. Examples include the US, Australia, and Canada.

Exhibit 12.2 shows the basic groups of accounting systems based on this classification and more specific historical influences.

However, as noted above, accounting practices are not fixed. Many of the pressures of globalization are leading countries to consider how their accounting practices can fit into an interrelated global economy. The general pressure for accounting practices to become more similar worldwide is called **harmonization** and is the topic of the next section.

Harmonization

Harmonization should not be confused with standardization, which means that all companies and countries use the same accounting practices. Harmonization is more flexible, meaning that differences among national accounting practices should be minimized to make it easy to translate accounting numbers from one system into another.

The pressures for harmonization come from many sources. One driver is that investors will be able to understand a company's accounting numbers and invest in the best companies anywhere in the world. That is, potential stockholders will be less likely to invest in companies in countries where it is difficult to understand the financial position of a company.

A second reason for harmonization is that MNCs have units located in many countries and must expend considerable resources to develop separate financial statements that meet local needs and then reconcile these statements to the practices of their home country. A third driver for harmonization is the needs of tax and investment regulators in different countries. While it might be most simple to make any foreign company conform to local accounting practices, such an approach has the undesirable effect of driving away foreign investors. For example, if a Germany company was considering opening a plant in the US or Canada to serve the North American market, one consideration in the location decision would be how costly and difficult it might be to reconcile German accounting practices with those in the US or Canada.

The fourth major driver for harmonization is the stock exchanges. As you saw in Chapter 6, stock exchanges want foreign companies to list on their exchanges. Stock exchanges are also merging into multination entities that operate in more than one country. Since listing on a stock exchange in a country usually requires the foreign company to adopt local accounting reporting practices, this is often a deterrent if the standards are costly to adopt. As such, exchanges see advantages in harmonized systems that are easy to translate into local general accounting practices.

Setting International Accounting Standards **While many see the benefits of harmonized accounting standards, the process of developing such standards**

harmonization
means that differences among national accounting practices should be minimized to make it easy to translate accounting numbers from one system into another

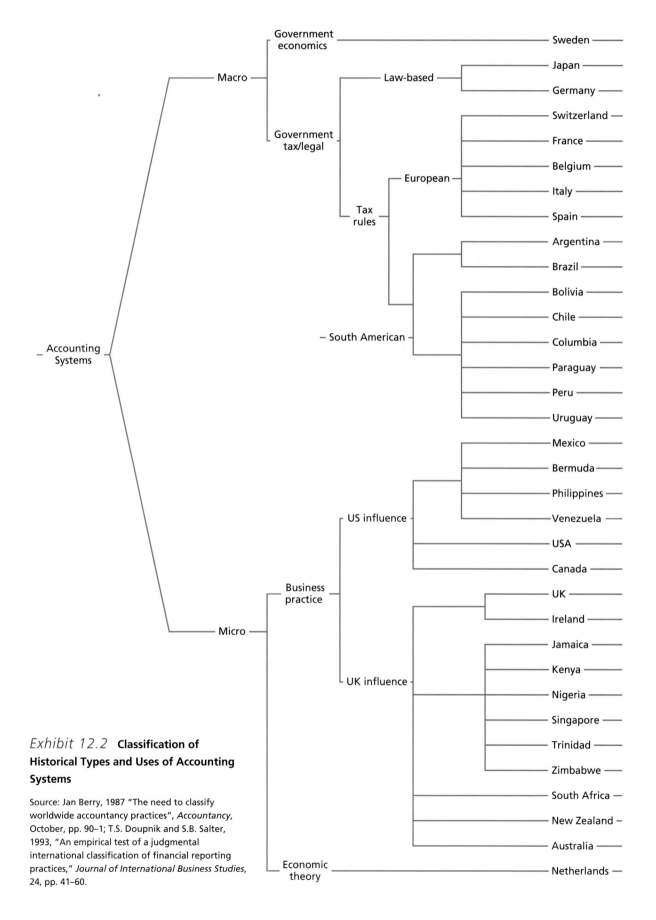

Exhibit 12.2 **Classification of Historical Types and Uses of Accounting Systems**

Source: Jan Berry, 1987 "The need to classify worldwide accountancy practices", *Accountancy*, October, pp. 90–1; T.S. Doupnik and S.B. Salter, 1993, "An empirical test of a judgmental international classification of financial reporting practices," *Journal of International Business Studies*, 24, pp. 41–60.

started with the formation of the International Accounting Standards Committee (IASC) in 1973. Set up by professional accounting organizations from ten countries—Australia, Canada, France, Germany, Ireland, Japan, Mexico, Netherlands, the United Kingdom, and the United States—this body became the major standard-setter for nearly 30 years.

In March 2001, the IASC was reorganized into two units. Incorporated in the State of Delaware, the Accounting Standards Committee (IASC) Foundation is the parent organization of the **International Accounting Standards Board (IASB)**. The IASB is an independent accounting standard-setter located in London, UK, which assumed the accounting standard-setting duties from the IASC on April 1, 2001.

The mission of the IASC Foundation is:

(a) to develop, in the public interest, a single set of high-quality, understandable and enforceable global accounting standards that require high-quality, transparent and comparable information in financial statements and other financial reporting to help participants in the world's capital markets and other users make economic decisions;

(b) to promote the use and rigorous application of those standards;

(c) in fulfilling the objectives associated with (a) and (b), to take account of, as appropriate, the special needs of small and medium-sized entities and emerging economies; and

(d) to bring about convergence of national accounting standards and International Accounting Standards and International Financial Reporting Standards to high-quality solutions.[7]

You can see the structure of the IASC foundation and board in Exhibit 12.3.

International Accounting Standards Board (IASB)
an independent accounting standard-setter located in London, UK

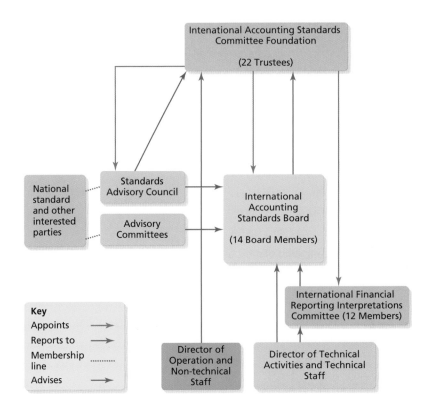

Exhibit 12.3
Structure of the International Accounting Standards Committee Foundation

340

The IASC Foundation has produced two sets of standards. One is for accounting practices, known as International Accounting Standards (IAS), and the other is for financial reporting, known as IFSR or International Financial Reporting Standards. A detailed description of these standards is beyond the scope of an introductory text. However, you can see from Exhibit 12.4 the array of issues considered in financial reporting. Students with more advanced

Exhibit 12.4 Overview of International Financial Reporting Standards (IFRS) and International Accounting Standards (IAS)

International Financial Reporting Standards
• IFRS 1 First-time Adoption of International Financial Reporting Standards
• IFRS 2 Share-based Payment
• IFRS 3 Business Combinations
• IFRS 4 Insurance Contracts
• IFRS 5 Non-current Assets Held for Sale and Discontinued Operations
• IFRS 6 Exploration for and Evaluation of Mineral Resources
• IFRS 7 Financial Instruments: Disclosures
• IFRS 8 Operating Segments
International Accounting Standards
• IAS 1 Presentation of Financial Statements
• IAS 2 Inventories
• IAS 7 Cash Flow Statements
• IAS 8 Accounting Policies, Changes in Accounting Estimates and Errors
• IAS 10 Events after the Balance Sheet Date
• IAS 11 Construction Contracts
• IAS 12 Income Taxes
• IAS 16 Property, Plant and Equipment
• IAS 17 Leases
• IAS 18 Revenue
• IAS 19 Employee Benefits
• IAS 20 Accounting for Government Grants and Disclosure of Government Assistance
• IAS 21 The Effects of Changes in Foreign Exchange Rates
• IAS 23 Borrowing Costs
• IAS 24 Related Party Disclosures
• IAS 26 Accounting and Reporting by Retirement Benefit Plans
• IAS 27 Consolidated and Separate Financial Statements
• IAS 28 Investments in Associates
• IAS 29 Financial Reporting in Hyperinflationary Economies
• IAS 31 Interests in Joint Ventures
• IAS 32 Financial Instruments: Presentation
• IAS 33 Earnings per Share
• IAS 34 Interim Financial Reporting
• IAS 36 Impairment of Assets
• IAS 37 Provisions, Contingent Liabilities and Contingent Assets
• IAS 38 Intangible Assets
• IAS 39 Financial Instruments: Recognition and Measurement
• IAS 40 Investment Property
• IAS 41 Agriculture

Source: www.iasb.org/IFRSs/IFRS.htm

backgrounds in accounting can read the technical summaries available on the IASB's website, http://www.iasb.org/IFRS%20Summaries/Technical%20 Summaries%20of%20International%20Financial%20Reporting%20Standards. htm. Full details of the standards are also available for professional accountants.

Why are the International Accounting and Financial Reporting Standards Important for International Business? The major reason that you, as a potential international business person, should be concerned with international accounting and reporting standards is that they are becoming the world's standard. Consider Exhibit 12.5, which shows areas of the world that have adopted IASC standards or are in the process of doing so.

Importantly, the European Union has moved to adopt international accounting and financial reporting standards.[8] While there remains some variation by country and not all standards are accepted in exact IASB form, this represents a significant step in the move toward harmonization. As the vice chairman of the IASC foundation noted to the European parliament:

> The European Union with the support of the European Parliament took a visionary step when it decided not to choose a uniquely European approach to financial reporting. The result is an effort aimed at establishing an international system relevant for the evolving marketplace. Other countries agreed. It is significant that the major economies of the world are increasingly adopting IFRSs, rather than national accounting standards. Europe is already enjoying the benefits of its leadership position, with Europe attracting an increasing share of the world's capital. As someone who believes strongly in European integration and at the same time the benefits of IFRSs, it is my hope that [the] European

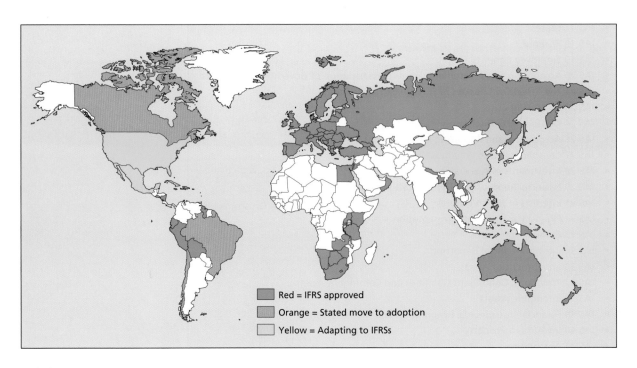

Exhibit 12.5 **The Use of International Financial Reporting Standards around the World**

Union and, in particular, the European Parliament will remain the standard-bearer in promoting consistent application of IFRS.[9]

In another important development, the US has agreed with the EU to allow companies to use either US GAAP or IFRS in either jurisdiction without a requirement for reconciliation. The objective is to have this in place by 2009 or sooner. Multiple stock exchanges in over 50 countries now allow the use of IFRS.

Even if all companies and countries used the same accounting practices and financial reporting, MNCs would still face accounting challenges based to a large degree on the use of different currencies and different national tax laws. In the next sections, you will see how international accountants handle some of these issues.

Accounting for Exchange Rates

As you read in the previous chapters, doing business in different countries requires international managers to deal with different currencies and the changing values of these currencies relative to each other, namely exchange rates. There are two major areas of concern in accounting regarding how to report the effects of exchange rates on financial reports. The first is called **foreign currency transaction** and the second is called **foreign currency translation**. For readers without any background in accounting, the Appendix to this chapter provides an overview of the basic financial reports.

foreign currency transaction refers to the procedures for reporting financial transactions based in a foreign currency, including the possibility of gains or losses due to changing exchange rates

Foreign Currency Transactions

Anytime an MNC has a transaction based in a foreign currency, it faces a possibility of gains or losses due to changing exchange rates. For example, say a US hard disk manufacturer agrees to sell drives to a Japanese PC manufacturer for ¥1,000,000,000 when the exchange rate was ¥115 = $1. The US manufacturer anticipates receiving $8,695,652 in payment when the drives arrive in Japan a month later. However, when the bill comes due, the exchange rate is now ¥120 = $1, meaning that when the Japanese company pays its bill in yen, the US company will now only receive $8,333,333, which is $362,319 less than anticipated.

foreign currency translation refers to the procedures for restating financial statements from a foreign subsidiary into the currency of the country of the parent company

The accounting issue is how to enter data on this sale into a balance sheet. Should it be based on the transaction date, when the agreement is made, or the settlement date, when the payment is made? The US system requires that the accountant enter the information as two transactions:

On the transaction date:

Accounts receivable	8,695,652
Sales	8,695,652

On the settlement date:

Cash	8,333,333
Loss on foreign exchange	362,319
Accounts receivable	362,319

Foreign Currency Translation

Foreign currency translation refers to the procedures for restating financial statements from a foreign subsidiary into the currency of the country of the parent company. For example, BMW has subsidiaries in many parts of the world including the US. However, being a German company, BMW presents its financial statements in euros. As such, for example, the financial statements from its US subsidiary that uses dollars must be translated into euros. Having all financial statements presented in one currency also gives investors a consistent picture of the performance of the company. This is called a **consolidated financial statement**, which means the financial reports treat the MNC as one entity in spite of having locations in different parts of the world that use different currencies. Unlike foreign currency transactions, in which actual money changes hands, no money changes hands in translation.

Of course, if exchange rates among currencies never changed, translation would be easy. However, as you learned in the previous chapter, exchange rates for most currencies vary continuously and this makes the issue of foreign currency translation more complex. To deal with this complexity, accountants have devised four common methods to prepare consolidated financial statements for MNCs, namely the current rate method, the current–noncurrent method, the monetary–nonmonetary method, and the temporal method.[10]

In the **current rate method**, which is the simplest, all assets and liabilities are translated into the base currency on the date of the balance sheet. Dividends are translated based on the exchange rate on the day they are declared. Revenue and expense items on the balance sheet use a weighted average of exchange rates over the period covered. No adjustments are made for differences in accounting principles in different locations. This keeps financial performance ratios (e.g. return on investment; money gained/money invested) the same in the foreign currency and in the parent company currency. The current rate translation method is the most popular method.

In the **current–noncurrent method**, balance sheet items are divided into current and noncurrent types. Current assets include items such as cash, accounts receivable, and inventory that can be converted to cash within one year. Current liabilities are payments that must be made within one year, money owed for interest, accounts payable, short-term loans, and any other debts that must be paid within the year. Any other asset or liability is considered noncurrent. With the current–noncurrent method, translation of current assets and liabilities uses exchange rates on the balance sheet date. Exchange-rate translations for noncurrent assets and liabilities use the exchange rates in existence when the asset was acquired or the liability incurred.

Also using balance sheet classifications, the **monetary–nonmonetary method** divides the balance sheet into monetary and nonmonetary items. Any balance sheet item shown in fixed currency—as, for example, cash and receivables—is considered monetary. Other items such as prepaid insurance are considered nonmonetary. Monetary items are translated based on the exchange rate on the balance sheet date, and historical rates are used for nonmonetary items. Many accounting scholars consider both the current–noncurrent and monetary–nonmonetary methods suspect because they do not believe the classifications are relevant to translations.

The **temporal translation method** translates foreign currency into the parent company financial statement's currency using exchange rates at the date of

consolidated financial statement
a financial report that treats the MNC as one entity in spite of having locations in different parts of the world that use different currencies

current rate method
a currency translation in which all assets and liabilities are translated into the base currency on the date of the balance sheet

current–noncurrent method
a currency translation in which balance sheet items are divided into current and noncurrent types

monetary–nonmonetary method
a currency translation that divides the balance sheet into monetary and nonmonetary items

temporal translation method
a currency translation that uses exchange rates at the date of measurement

measurement. This results in cash, receivables, and payables translated on the balance sheet date. The historical exchange rate in place is used for other items such as fixed assets and inventories.

Exhibit 12.6 presents a summary of the different types of translation methods and their applications to balance sheets and income statements.

Foreign Currency Translation Rules for US Firms and for International Accounting Standards   The Statement of Financial Accounting Standards No. 52 is the regulation that US companies must follow to translate financial statements from their international subsidiaries.[11] This standard allows US companies to translate financial statements using either the temporal or the current rate method. The choice of the method depends on the functional currency of the subsidiary. **Functional currency** is based on selecting the primary

functional currency
the primary economic environment in which the subsidiary or other unit operates

Exhibit 12.6   **Translation Method Exchange Rates for Selected Balance Sheet and Income Statement Items**

| | Exchange Rate for Translation Method | | | |
	Current Rate	Current–Noncurrent	Monetary–Nonmonetary	Temporal
Cash	C	C	C	C
Current receivables	C	C	C	C
Inventory—cost basis	C	C	H	H
Long-term receivables	C	H	C	C
Long-term investments—cost basis	C	H	H	H
Long-term investments—market basis	C	H	H	C
Property, plant, equipment	C	H	H	H
Intangible assets	C	H	H	H
Current liabilities	C	C	C	C
Long-term debt	C	H	C	C
Common stock	H	H	H	H
Retained earnings	B	B	B	B
Revenues	A	A	A	A
Cost of goods sold	A	A	H	H
Depreciation expense	A	H	H	H
Amortization expense	A	H	H	H

Notes
A = Weighted average exchange rate for the current period
B = Balancing or adjustment factor
C = Current exchange rate at the balance sheet date
H = Historical exchange rate

Source: M. Zafar Iqbal, 2002, *International Accounting: A Global Perspective*, Mason, OH: South-Western, p. 48.

economic environment in which the subsidiary or other unit, including divisions, branches, and joint ventures, operates. To use a functional currency other than the dollar, the unit must conduct most of its operations (sales, financing, investing, production, etc.) locally. Making the choice of a functional currency is not always an unambiguous decision. For example, even in the same industry, Texaco uses the US dollar as its functional currency while Exxon Mobile uses foreign currencies, even though both companies have subsidiaries in the same countries.[12]

Exhibit 12.7 shows the decision rule for choosing a translation method based on functional currency. As you can see, the choice of a translation method depends directly on the choice of a functional currency.

The translation method required under international accounting standards is simpler than that required in the US. Assets and liabilities are translated from the subsidiary's functional currency to the currency of the unit's country on the date of the balance sheet. Income and expenses are translated based on the exchange rate existing on the date of transaction.

In the IB Strategic Insight opposite, you can see how a major MNC such as BMW handles the issues of translation.

Up to this point in the chapter, we have considered primarily issues related to international financial accounting. Now we are going to consider some managerial accounting issues related to international operations. As you have seen, financial accounting information deals with providing useful information to investors and others from outside of the company. Managerial accounting, in contrast, is concerned with providing accounting information inside the company to managers for making better managerial decisions.

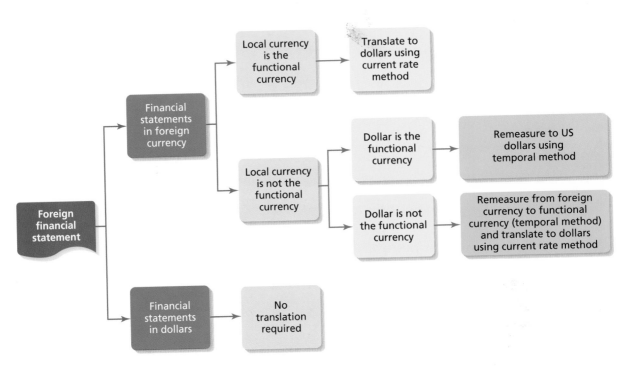

Exhibit 12.7 **Decision Rule for US Companies Choosing a Translation Method**

Foreign Currency Translation at BMW

IB STRATEGIC INSIGHT

With its headquarters located in Germany and thus subject to the EU's adoption of International Accounting Standards, BMW Group reports its translation procedures as follows:

> The financial statements of consolidated companies which are drawn up in a foreign currency are translated using the functional currency concept (IAS 21: The Effects of Changes in Foreign Exchange Rates) and the modified closing rate method. The functional currency of a subsidiary is determined as a general rule on the basis of the primary economic environment in which it operates and corresponds therefore to the relevant local currency. Income and expenses of foreign subsidiaries are translated in the Group financial statements at the average exchange rate for the year, and assets and liabilities are translated at the closing rate. Exchange differences arising from the translation of shareholders' equity are offset directly against accumulated other equity. Exchange differences arising from the use of different exchange rates

to translate the income statement are also offset directly against accumulated other equity. Foreign currency receivables and payables in the single entity accounts of BMW AG and subsidiaries are recorded, at the date of the transaction, at cost. Exchange gains and losses computed at the balance sheet date are recognised as income or expense. The exchange rates of those currencies which have a material impact on the Group financial statements were as follows: based on the group's shareholding. Any difference between the cost of investment and the group's share of equity are accounted for as a general rule using the purchase method. Investments in other companies are accounted for using the equity method, when significant influence can be exercised (IAS 28 Investments in Associates). This is normally the case when voting rights of between 20 percent and 50 percent are held (associated companies).

	Closing Rate		Average Rate	
	31 Dec. 2006	31 Dec. 2005	2006	2005
US dollar	1.32	1.18	1.26	1.24
British pound	0.67	0.69	0.68	0.68
South African rand	9.20	7.47	8.52	7.91
Japanese yen	156.88	139.11	146.06	136.83
Australian dollar	1.67	1.61	1.67	1.63

Source: *BMW Group 2006 Annual Report*, www.bmw-group.de, p. 75.

Major International Managerial Accounting Issues: Transfer Pricing and International Taxation

transfer pricing represents the prices for goods and services that units within a company charge each other

international taxation refers to the need to appreciate the diversity and complexity of tax systems in different nations and their implications for multinational operations

The two major international managerial accounting issues we will examine in this chapter are transfer pricing and international taxation. **Transfer pricing** represents the prices for goods and services that units with a company charge each other. For example, a watch factory in Italy may charge its US parent company €50/watch. The parent company "buys" the watches from its own factory rather than from another manufacturer. **International taxation** refers to

347

the need to appreciate the diversity and complexity of tax systems in different nations and their implications of multinational operations.

Transfer Pricing

As you saw in the chapter on international strategy, MNCs are increasingly more likely to set up units or platforms in any corner of the world. These units exchange services (e.g. call centers), manufactured components, finished goods, and even the results of R&D with each other. One job of the accountant then is how to establish a measurable price for these intra-company exchanges.

Why have Transfer Pricing?   The first question that often comes to mind regarding transfer pricing is why not just exchange goods and services among all units of a company for free? It is the same company, after all. One reason for transfer pricing, for both domestic and MNCs, is to provide a system of management control and evaluation. That is, if a unit of a company pays for its components and services secured internal to the company and external to the company and sells its output either externally or internally to other company units, the unit and thus the managers have profits or losses. However, for an MNC a variety of other factors come into play.

Factors Affecting Transfer Pricing   One very important issue for the MNC is the effects of transfer pricing on taxes. Consider, for example, a US MNC that faces a higher tax rate in the US than its subsidiary faces in Thailand. If the

Taking Advantage of Transfer Pricing

ETHICAL CHALLENGE

Although it is likely that most companies comply with local tax regulations, an investigation by Prem Sikka, Professor of Accounting at the University of Essex, notes the following examples of MNCs stretching the interpretation of "arm's length":

- Some research suggests that the US loses over $50 billion a year in lost tax revenue due to transfer pricing.

- Overpriced imports into the UK used to create losses or lower profits in the home country, thus lowering home country tax payments:

  - From the Czech Republic, $972.98 for plastic buckets
  - From Canada, $1,853 for fence posts

  - From China, $4,121.81 for a kilo of toilet paper
  - From Israel, $2,052 for apple juice
  - From Trinidad, $8,500 for ballpoint pens
  - From Japan, $4,896 for tweezers.

- Underpriced exports that lower profits or create losses for MNC subsidiaries in the UK, thus lowering UK tax payments:

  - To Hong Kong, $1.75 for toilet bowl and tank
  - To Trinidad, $1.20 for prefabricated buildings
  - To Venezuela, $387.83 for bulldozers
  - To Israel, $52.03 for missile and rocket launchers.

Source: Adapted from Prem Sikka, 2003, "Comment: Plastic bucket: $972.98," *Guardian*, June 30.

Thai subsidiary charges the parent company a higher transfer price for its goods sold to the parent, it will make more profit in Thailand. Alternatively, since it is paying a high price for its goods, the US parent will make less profit.

Of course, no country wants its tax base to shrink and lose revenue because of transfer pricing. As such, most adopt tax rules that attempt to have each country get its fair share of the taxes. Many nations, including the US, follow the international guidelines of the Organization for Economic Cooperation and Development (with 30 nation members) that are based on the **arm's length principle**. This means any transfer pricing between units of an MNC should be set as if the units were making the exchange in the open market with other companies.

In spite of the agreements among countries and local tax codes, there remains a temptation for some MNCs to take advantage of reduced taxes by manipulating transfer pricing. In the IB Ethical Challenge opposite, UK accountant Prem Sikka gives some of the more egregious examples.

In addition to taxes, other factors also come into play when an MNC determines the best transfer pricing strategy between the parent and a subsidiary. For example, import or export tariffs and duties may encourage companies to raise or lower transfer prices to adjust for these costs. Similarly, differences in inflation rates may, for example, cause a parent to change a higher transfer price to a subsidiary in a high inflation country to offset the lowering value of local currency. Exhibit 12.8 provides a summary of conditions that encourage under- and overpricing transfers from a parent to a foreign subsidiary.

arm's length principle means that any transfer pricing between units of an MNC should be set as if the units were making the exchange in the open market with other companies

Exhibit 12.8 **Local Conditions for Over or Under Transfer Pricing from a Parent to a Foreign Subsidiary**

Overpricing Condition	Underpricing Condition
Higher local tax rates	Lower local tax rates
Lower tariffs on imports	Higher tariffs on imports
High inflation rate	Low inflation rate
Local government restrictions on profits	Local loans based on financial appearance of subsidiary

The relationship of taxes to transfer pricing is only one area of taxation of concern to MNCs. However, as you can see in Exhibit 12.9, it is considered among the most important.

In the next section, you will see other relevant aspects of taxation for the MNC.

International Taxation

Next to dealing with different currencies, managing the complex and different national tax systems is one of the more challenging areas for managerial accountants. While there is general agreement that MNCs should be taxed similarly to domestic companies for domestic income, there is less agreement on how to tax foreign income.[13]

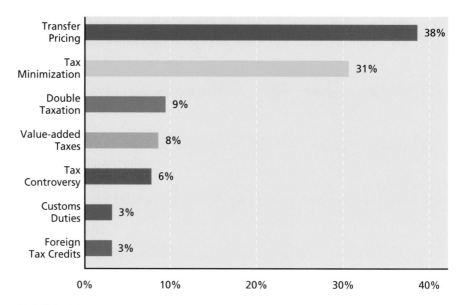

Exhibit 12.9 **Most Important Tax Issues for Tax Directors**

Source: Ernst & Young, 2005, *2005–2006 Global Transfer Pricing Surveys*, New York: Ernst & Young.

territorial tax system
taxes only income earned within a country's borders

worldwide tax system
taxes all profits earned by an MNC, regardless of location

There are two basic types of national tax systems encountered by international managers. The **territorial tax system** taxes only income earned within a country's borders. That is, income earned by the MNC for subsidiaries in other countries is not taxed. An alternative approach is the **worldwide tax system**. In a pure worldwide tax system, MNCs are taxed on their worldwide income, regardless of the country or countries from which the income is derived. To avoid double taxation of foreign income, most countries taking a worldwide approach allow a foreign tax credit. For example, if a US company pays taxes on profits earned in the UK, it does not have to pay these taxes again in the US. In reality, no country has a pure territorial or worldwide system, with all countries having some tax laws that lean to one system or the other. The US, for example, favors a more worldwide system while most European countries favor a more territorial system.

To avoid double taxation of their companies in other countries, many countries negotiate tax treaties. These are agreements among governments as to how to tax companies from each other's countries. A listing of US tax treaties is located at www.ustreas.gov/offices/tax-policy/treaties.shtml.

Tax Planning Strategies for the MNC Of course, all companies want to make as much profit as possible, and one certain way to do this is to reduce expenses. Paying less tax is one strategy that companies and individuals use to have more money. Tax planning should not be confused with illegal activities to avoid taxes. Rather, companies must examine the nature of the operations and the tax codes of the countries in which they operate and use legal strategies to pay the lowest taxes possible. In this chapter, we consider two strategies: thin capitalization and the business model approach.[14]

thin capitalization
occurs when an MNC finances a subsidiary in a foreign country by borrowing money rather than issuing stock

Thin capitalization occurs when an MNC finances a subsidiary in a foreign country by borrowing money rather than issuing stock. As you remember from your readings on capital markets, companies finance new operations not only from profits that they reinvest in the company but also from money they borrow (usually by issuing bonds) or by selling stock. The advantage of borrowing money locally is that most countries give tax deductions for interest paid on borrowed money. This is similar to what happens to individuals who buy a home in the United States. When you borrow money to pay for the home, the interest you pay each year is deducted from your gross income. So, for example, if you make $50,000/year and you buy a new house and pay $4,000 in interest to a bank, your gross income is now $46,000 and you will not pay as much in taxes to the US government.

Increasingly, this thin capitalization strategy is becoming more difficult for companies to implement. Fearing loss of tax revenues, countries are passing laws that make tax deductions more difficult. Exhibit 12.10 shows some of these laws in effect in Europe. As you can see, most of these laws restrict the amount

Exhibit 12.10 *Recent Restrictions on Thin Capitalization in Europe*

Country	Summary of recent laws
Germany	• Revised thin-capitalization rules which affect both cross-border and local debt financing for business years after December 31 2003. • Extension of rules to include partnerships and permanent establishments and loans to partnerships no longer exempt from thin-capitalization limitations. • Introduction of a uniform 1.5:1 debt-to-equity ratio, which is also applicable to holding companies. • *De minimis* rule that allows the deductibility of intercompany interest that is less than €250,000 ($333,892). • Disallowance of interest on intercompany or guaranteed loans where loans arose in connection with the acquisition of shares from a related party.
France	• Extension of the thin-capitalization restrictions to all intercompany financings via a new definition of tainted loans. • 1.5:1 debt-to-equity ratio and disallowance of interest in excess of 25 percent of relevant profits. • Non-deductible interest to be carried forward, reduced by 10%, and deducted in subsequent accounting period (subject to 25 percent relevant profit restriction). • The Charasse amendment re disallowance of interest remains in existence.
Italy	• New thin-capitalization rules introduced for accounting periods. • Limitation on deductibility of interest when debt is used to finance holdings that benefit from the participation exemption. • 4:1 debt-to-equity ratio and complex rules that determine the quantum of the equity element of the computation. • Limitation applies to loans granted or guaranteed by a direct or indirect 10 percent shareholder.
Netherlands	• 3:1 debt-to-equity ratio. • Disallowance of related party interest when funds are used to purchase shares of a company intra-group, fund capital contributions and dividend payments. • Allowance of interest where the interest receipt is subject to "reasonable" taxation in the hands of the lender. • No offset of intra-group interest expense against the operating income of the fiscal unity for eight years after acquisition.

Source: Nick Woodford and Christopher Schreiber, "Debt financing loses appeal as tax planning strategy," *International Tax Review*, April 2005.

of debt a company can take on and thus reduce the amount of interest that can be used as a tax deduction.

As you learned earlier, MNCs can adopt transnational strategies to locate activities anywhere in the world where they can be done cheapest and best. International managers can also extend this general strategic approach to tax planning and strategies. As with labor costs, different countries provide potential tax savings if an MNC locates its operations in a lower tax country. Accountants call this the **business model approach** for tax planning and strategy. Of course, greater tax savings result if the business grows in the lower tax country. Otherwise, the cost savings from lower taxes may be offset by other losses of doing business in a stagnant or declining market.

business model approach seeks location costs advantages by locating in countries with lower taxes

Social Responsibility Reporting and Accounting

With an increasing awareness of the importance of corporate social responsibility, there is also an increasing concern over how to report social performance. That is, evolving beyond the traditional financial reporting of profits and losses, assets and liabilities, there is a growing concern over how to report information on environmental and social performance.

A recent survey by KPMG found

The question is no longer "Who is reporting?" but "Who is not?" Corporate responsibility reporting is now a mainstream expectation of companies. Since more than 80 percent of the world's 250 largest companies now report on corporate responsibility, we can expect this trend to roll out rapidly at the country and sector levels in the coming years.[15]

According to the KPMG survey, 92 percent of the *Fortune* Global 250 companies report the existence of an ethics code or governance code of conduct. Similarly, most of these companies also have a supply-chain code of conduct. However, details on implementation and monitoring are lacking for most of these companies. The majority of companies disclose information about climate risks.

The most common reporting format comes from the Global Reporting Initiative (GRI) (www.globalreporting.org/AboutGRI/WhatWeDo/). The GRI reporting framework provides a consistent method used by over 1,000 companies worldwide to report on their social performance to all stakeholders. The GRI's mission is to make social reporting as common as financial reporting. To address the issue of assurance (i.e. making sure that the reports are accurate and truthful), the International Auditing and Assurance Standards Board (IAASB) has recently set up a group to consider the development of specialized accounting standards on the emerging issues of social reporting.[16]

Environmental sustainability is only one component of social responsibility reporting but it is certainly an important one. Look at this video to appreciate the necessity of companies monitoring their environmental impact: www.accountingforsustainability.org/output/Page93.asp. Also, look at the IB Sustainability Practices box opposite to see some areas of environmental costs that can be consider using an application of managerial cost accounting.

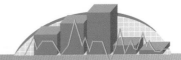

Cost Accounting for Sustainability

The United Nations cost/expenditure categories to account for internal environmental costs are described below.

The first environmental cost category is conventional waste disposal and emission treatment costs. This includes related labor and maintenance materials. Insurance and provisions for environmental liabilities are also included here. This cost category is typical of the traditional definition of environmental costs and deals with the treatment, disposal and clean-up of wastes. This cost category corresponds to the conventional definition of environmental costs for the treatment, disposal, and clean-up of existing waste and emissions.

The second cost category, prevention and environmental management, includes the labor costs and services used for environmental housekeeping as well as any extra costs of using cleaner technologies and green purchases. R&D for environmental projects is part of pollution prevention. Also included in this section are any higher additional costs incurred for using environment-friendly operating materials, low-emission process technologies, and the development of low environmental-impact products.

The third cost category deals with wasted material purchase value. Here, wasted materials are evaluated typically by their purchase value. The fourth and last cost category, production costs of non-product output, considers costs associated with capital and labor due to inefficient production and generating waste and emissions.

The checklist of issues to consider appears in Exhibit 12.11.

---

1. Waste and emission treatment

   - Provisions for clean-up costs, remediation
   - Maintenance, operating materials, services personnel
   - Depreciation for related equipment
   - Fees, taxes, charges
   - Fines and penalties
   - Insurance for environmental liabilities.

2. Prevention and environmental management

   - Personnel for general environmental management activities
   - External services for environmental management
   - Additional expenditure for environmental management technologies
   - Research and development
   - Other environmental management costs.

3. Material purchase value of non-product output

   - Packaging
   - Operating materials
   - Energy
   - Water
   - Raw materials
   - Auxiliary materials.

4. Processing costs of non-product output.

Exhibit 12.11

The United Nations cost/expenditure categories to account for internal environmental costs

Source: Adapted from United Nations, 2001, *Environmental Management Accounting Procedures and Principles*, New York: United Nations.

CHAPTER REVIEW

This chapter provided you with a basic understanding of the accounting function in MNCs. The chapter began with an overview of the purpose of accounting and explained the differences between managerial accounting and financial accounting. For students who have yet to study any accounting, the chapter also has an Appendix that provides an overview of the basics of accounting terminology and financial reports.

National culture and a nation's social institutions influence many business functions and the accounting function is no exception. As such, the chapter provided an explanation of the forces that lead different countries to adopt different accounting practices. However, again as with many business functions, globalization and the increasing importance of doing business anywhere in the world pressures national accounting systems to become more similar. Harmonization of accounting practices is occurring in response to this pressure. Remember that harmonization does not mean that all countries adopt exactly the same accounting standards and practices but, rather, that counties adopt systems that can be more easily translated among various systems.

While harmonization is one step in making accounting numbers universally understandable to investors and managers, there is also increasing pressure on nations and MNCs to adopt accounting practices that are standardized throughout the world. The International Accounting Standards Board promotes two sets of standards for accounting. One is for accounting practices, known as International Accounting Standards (IAS), and the other is for financial reporting; known as IFSR or International Financial Reporting Standards. Importantly, the EU has substantially adopted these standards and practices and there is increasing pressure on other nations to follow suit.

One major problem for MNCs is how to report accounting numbers from units located in different nations that have different currencies. Earlier in the book you learned how exchange rates among currencies are in constant flux. MNCs that buy, sell, and earn profits or losses in other countries deal continuously with the issue of how to value business transactions in their home currency. In this chapter you learned that MNCs use a variety of techniques to account for exchange-rate differences and to translate foreign currencies for financial reporting to their stockholders and managers.

Business units provide each other with goods and services. A common way to account for the value of these transfers is transfer pricing. That is, units buy and sell goods and services as if they are in a market. In this chapter, you learned that the management of transfer pricing becomes much more complex when units are located in different countries with different currencies and different tax laws. Although there is pressure to buy and sell among units so that more profits are earned in lower tax countries (e.g. low transfer pricing to low tax country units reduces costs and increases profits), most local laws require that prices reflect market values—the price the company would pay if it bought the good or service outside the company.

The issue of transfer prices makes it clear that if your company has operations in different countries then differences in tax laws can affect your bottom line. In this chapter, you learned that nations tend to favor worldwide income taxing (tax profits from every location) or territorial taxing (tax only local profits, although no system is pure).

To learn how MNCs deal with taxation, the chapter reviewed two strategies for dealing with international taxation. One is thin capitalization, where companies set up operations by borrowing money rather than issuing stock so that they can get tax deductions based on interest payments on their loans. The other focuses on the business model, which means one of the reasons an MNC chooses a location is favorable local tax laws.

An emerging challenge for the accounting profession is how to develop international standards and assurances for social responsibility reporting. Corporate social responsibility is an increasing concern for investors and other stakeholders. As such, these reports may become as important as financial reports, the traditional province of accountants. In this chapter you learned some of the worldwide trends regarding how the world's largest companies are building social responsibility reporting as a supplement to financial reporting.

As future international business people, you will rely on professional accountants to produce the accurate and reliable financial reports that will help you manage international operations in a financially complex world. Also, investors in your company and local regulatory bodies will rely on your international accountants to report on the state of your company. This brief introduction to the international accounting function should help you better understand the role of accounting professionals in your companies.

DISCUSSION QUESTIONS

1. Discuss several reasons regarding the importance of international accounting.
2. Compare and contrast managerial accounting with financial accounting.
3. Identify differences in the economic role of accounting in different countries. Discuss factors that lead to differences in the use of accounting in these countries.
4. Select two developing nations and discuss how enforcement of accounting rules might affect the nature of financial reporting in these countries.
5. Consider the professionalization of accounting in your discussion.
6. Discuss the pressures that are leading to harmonization of financial reporting. What are the benefits and what are the drawbacks?
7. Discuss the implications of the EU moving to accept most of the IASB standards. How does this affect European companies and how does it affect Japanese and US companies?
8. Identify the accounting issues related to gains or losses from foreign currency transactions.
9. Compare and contrast the different foreign currency translation methods.
10. Identify what is unique for transfer pricing for MNCs as opposed to domestic-only companies.
11. Compare and contrast the types of tax systems used in different countries.
12. Discuss the nature and strategic advantages of thin capitalization.

INTERNATIONAL BUSINESS SKILL BUILDER

Exploring Accounting Standards

Step 1: Select four major MNCs, two from the US and two from the EU. Make sure the companies from the US and the EU are in the same industry. You can have one or two industries.

Step 2: Download their most recent annual reports.

Step 3: Search the annual reports for information on the type or types of accounting standards used in the reports, the impact of foreign currency exchanges on the company, foreign currency translation methods, and foreign taxation.

Step 4: Based on what you have learned in this chapter, prepare a report examining how international accounting information might influence managerial decisions and investor decisions regarding these companies.

CHAPTER INTERNET ACTIVITY

Explore the use of Deloitte Touche Tohmatu's RateFind at **www.deloitte.com/ more/ratefind/ratefind.asp**.

Use this site to look at tax rates and tax treaties. Consider the tax implications of a company from your home country doing business in at least three different countries around the world.

Supplement you information with more general background from **www. deloittetaxguides.com/index.asp**.

KEY CONCEPTS

arm's length principle

business model approach

consolidated financial statement

current rate method

current–noncurrent method

financial accounting

foreign currency transaction

foreign currency translation

functional currency

harmonization

International Accounting Standards Board (IASB)

international taxation

managerial accounting

monetary–nonmonetary method

temporal translation method

territorial tax system

thin capitalization

transfer pricing

worldwide tax system

BUSINESS > INTERNATIONAL

"BAA"ST TRANSFER PRICE[17]

Tara Grant looks out the rain-soaked window of her airplane as it lands at Logan International Airport on a dreary April morning. Exhausted after the long flight, and excited about the opportunity to visit family and friends after spending the past five years in the Australian Outback, she prepares to deplane. Tara has been summoned to corporate headquarters in Boston to confer with her new boss, Alec Young, about a very important issue. Alec is the baby brother of the Young family, the previous owners of Outback Woolworks, the large sheep ranch where Grant is employed as controller. Six years ago, when Outback was acquired as a wholly owned subsidiary of Celtic Sweaters, Alec agreed to join Celtic's management team. Alec has requested that Tara come to the States to help devise an optimum transfer price for the virgin wool produced by her subsidiary company (Outback) and sold to his parent company (Celtic) that would *legally* reduce the combined taxes paid to the Australian and American governments, and thereby maximize consolidated earnings.

Tara is very anxious to make a good first impression with her parent company's top executives, because it is just one year ago that she "blew the whistle" on her former boss, J.R. Wolf, who subsequently was asked to resign because of his unethical practices. Then she feels a sudden calm come over her as she is greeted at the gate by a familiar face and a warm, "G'day, mate." Alec, the newly promoted controller of the United States-based Celtic Sweaters Inc., Outback's parent company, has taken time out of his busy schedule to personally meet Tara at the airport. After exchanging a warm hello, Tara quickly fills Alec in about what his two older brothers are up to back on the Australian sheep ranch.

As the conversation shifts to business, Tara's anxiety level begins to increase again. Before dropping her off at her hotel, Alec cautions her that his predecessor, J.R. Wolf, still has numerous friends at corporate headquarters who are not too happy that he has been forced to resign. This potentially hostile environment could make the task at hand for Tara and Alec even more formidable. So they agree to meet early the next morning to sort out the facts, prior to the afternoon meeting with Celtic's top management. Since Celtic's corporate culture can be best described as a participatory management, consensus building among key executives is crucial to obtaining the necessary approval for business decisions.

The next morning Tara exits her hotel, beaming with confidence as she is greeted with bright sunshine and a rainbow, to hail a cab for her meeting with Alec at Celtic headquarters. Despite the typical hustle and bustle of the city, she smiles as she spots a robin sitting in a tree, thinking about her fond memories of springtime in the Northeast. While riding in the cab, she double-checks her briefcase's contents, to make sure she has the critical data about the projected prices of virgin wool, and her watch, to make sure she will arrive on time.

. . .

CASE 12

page 1

Upon entering Alec's office, Tara is introduced to Kaylee Ann Wright, a CPA tax consultant, who specializes in related-party transactions within consolidated groups. After exchanging pleasantries, Alec informs Tara that Kaylee has been hired to provide technical assistance to make sure their transfer price strategy is in compliance with the US Internal Revenue Code and related Treasury regulations. "What a pleasure to meet you, Kaylee!" exclaims Tara. "I feel so much better about the whole transfer-pricing issue knowing you will review the intercompany transactions. In my opinion, transfer pricing is a complex issue that requires an expert opinion."

Kaylee smiles and replies, "Well, thank you for your vote of confidence, Tara. I tend to agree that these issues are important. In fact, Celtic's 100 percent ownership of Outback (a foreign subsidiary) requires us to file the IRS Form 5472. This form includes information about all intercompany transactions, such as Outback's sale of wool to Celtic Sweaters. Hence, information about transfer pricing between related parties is red flagged.

"Furthermore, the Internal Revenue Code Section 482 and the related Treasury Regulation 1.482 offer specific guidance about 'appropriate transfer prices' for related parties. The most appropriate transfer price is a comparable uncontrolled sales price, if available: for example, the price Outback charges unrelated customers for virgin wool. If a comparable uncontrolled sales price is not readily available, then the next best transfer price is cost-plus, when the parent performs substantial processing: for example, converting raw virgin wool into clothing. This method examines the selling price of Celtic's finished goods (wool clothes) and allows for a 'reasonable' gross profit (industry average) in determining an 'acceptable' cost of goods sold. Since cost of goods sold consists of direct labor and overhead costs incurred by Celtic, plus the 'unknown' cost of raw materials (virgin wool), the transfer price for wool is a plug number to arrive at an 'acceptable' cost of goods sold amount. Finally, any attempts to evade US corporate income taxes through extremely high transfer prices may result in severe penalties ranging from 20 to 40 percent on the additional tax assessments."

Given the relevant tax rules, Tara proposes two transfer-price options, as approved by key executives from Outback. Under the first scenario, the selling price of wool would be increased to reflect market changes, and this cost increase would not be absorbed in the selling price of wool clothing (i.e. consumers would not pay a higher price for a Celtic sweater). According to Aron Young (Alec's oldest brother and vice president of production at Outback), environmental conditions, specifically a devastating "mad sheep" disease in Europe and the Americas, have drastically reduced the world's supply of virgin wool. The limited supply is projected to cause Australian wool prices to rise by up to 50 percent without any objections from the Australian Competition and Consumer Commission (ACCC). Furthermore, Outback plans to increase its prices for virgin wool across the board by 40 percent to all its unrelated customers, if there is any excess product not purchased by its parent company. [However, due to the worldwide shortage, it is doubtful that there will be any excess.] Tara demonstrates the impact of a 40 percent increase with the following projected numbers, presented before and after the change:

. . .

Outback (sales to Celtic, $ million)		Celtic (before consolidation, $ million)	
Sales revenue	100	Sales revenue	320
Operating expenses	90	Operating expenses (incl. wool)	−240
Income before taxes	10	Income before taxes	80
Tax expense (30 percent)	−3	Tax expense (35 percent)	−28
Net income	7	Net income	52

After the proposed 40 percent transfer price increase:

Outback (sales to Celtic, $ million)		Celtic (before consolidation, $ million)	
Sales revenue	140	Sales revenue	320
Operating expenses	−90	Operating expenses (incl. wool)	−280
Income before taxes	50	Income before taxes	40
Tax expense (30 percent)	−15	Tax expense (35 percent)	−14
Net income	35	Net income	26

Under the second scenario, the selling price of wool would be increased to reflect market changes, and this cost increase would be absorbed in the selling price of wool clothing (i.e. consumers would pay a higher price for a Celtic sweater). According to Joe Young (the middle brother and vice president of marketing at Outback), a combination of environmental and economic conditions should justify higher prices for wool products. Unseasonably cold weather around the world for the past few years and major fashion designer preferences have created a very strong demand for wool products despite cost increases in raw materials. Unlike the first scenario, Joe's analysis (based on a thorough market research study) assumes that consumers will accept price increases equal to 31 percent for fine wool clothing. Hence, clothing manufacturers such as Celtic may be able to preserve gross profit margins, while absorbing significantly higher costs for raw material (virgin wool). Under this second scenario, the projected numbers for the upcoming year before the price increase are:

Outback (sales to Celtic, $ million)		Celtic (before consolidation, $ million)	
Sales revenue	100	Sales revenue	320
Cost of goods sold	−50	Cost of goods sold*	−160
Gross profit	50	Gross profit	160
Other expenses	−40	Other expenses	−80
Income before taxes	10	Income before taxes	80
Tax expense (30 percent)	−3	Tax expense (35 percent)	−28
Net income	7	Net income	52

* Where Celtic's cost of goods sold = 100 raw materials + 60 direct labor and overheads.

. . .

Furthermore, the industry average is very similar to Celtic's gross profit margin of 50 percent. After the proposed 31 percent price increase for wool clothing, Outback will be able to increase its transfer price to Celtic by 50 percent:

Outback (sales to Celtic, $ million)		Celtic (before consolidation, $ million)	
Sales revenue	150	Sales revenue	420.0
Cost of goods sold	−50	Cost of goods sold**	−210.0
Gross profit	100	Gross profit	210.0
Other expenses	−40	Other expenses	−80.0
Income before taxes	60	Income before taxes	130.0
Tax expense (30 percent)	−18	Tax expense (35 percent)	−48.5
Net income	42	Net income	84.5

** Where Celtic's cost of goods sold = (100 + 50) for wool + 60 for direct labor and overheads.

Alec notes, "Either of these *legal* options seems reasonable to me." Both women nod in agreement. "However, before claiming victory we had better consider how the rest of the Celtic key executives might interpret the proposed price change." He is referring to the "old boy network" that is prevalent among Celtic's top executives, especially since his predecessor, J.R. Wolf, has two influential friends on the executive board: Sylvester (Sly) Fox, vice president of marketing, and Sam Coyote, vice president of operations. The two labored long and hard over the dismissal of their long-time friend, but finally agreed it was best that J.R. be "offered an early retirement." The real reason Sly and Sam did not support their friend was because they were fearful that his proposed scheme to increase the transfer price of wool from Outback to Celtic by 30 percent (to illegally evade US income taxes one year before) would hurt their profit-sharing bonus. "Can you image how these two will react when a 40–50 percent increase is proposed one year later?" adds Alec.

After careful consideration, the team agree that for the new transfer prices to be accepted by Celtic's executives, the "self-interest factor" has to be addressed. In addition to making a rational presentation about the legitimate price increase, something must be done to offset the price increase's effect on profit-sharing. Hence, Tara suggests replacing the executives' profit-sharing bonus (based on Celtic's domestic income) with a stock-option plan. Her logic is that the overall income tax savings should be reflected in higher stock prices in the future. Since the option will provide executives with the opportunity to purchase stock at a fixed lower price, they should be pleased with the new arrangement. Both Alec and Kaylee agree. Alec congratulates Tara on her stock-option suggestion, especially considering that Celtic has plenty of authorized, but unissued shares of common stock to cover the stock-option plan. They all leave the office feeling adequately prepared for the upcoming big meeting.

. . .

CASE DISCUSSION POINTS

1. How would each of the proposed options regarding the transfer price for wool affect the net income figures for (a) Outback, (b) Celtic, and (c) the consolidated group?

2. Generally, what are the costs or benefits of increasing the transfer price for the following stakeholders under each scenario: (a) Outback's creditors, (b) Celtic's production employees, (c) Australian citizens, (d) Celtic's investors, (e) Celtic's executives, (f) Celtic's customers, and (g) American citizens? Be sure to identify which option each group would prefer.

3. What transfer-price increase for virgin wool would raise the least amount of controversy with respect to the two countries' government regulators, i.e. (a) the ACCC and (b) the IRS? Why?

4. In the spirit of consensus building, if Scenarios 1 and 2 were to be combined, complete the following analysis by calculating (a) the appropriate sales revenue and (b) the increase in wool clothing prices [hint: assume the 40 percent increase in virgin wool would be passed on to Celtic customers in order to preserve Celtic's gross profit margin of 50 percent; the gross margin is equal to gross profit divided by sales revenue]; (b) the increase in wool clothing prices = [(a) less $320] divided by $320 = percent.

Outback (sales to Celtic, $ million)		Celtic (before consolidation, $ million)	
Sales revenue	140	Sales revenue	(a)
Cost of goods sold	−50	Cost of goods sold***	−200
Gross profit	90	Gross profit	200
Other expenses	−40	Other expenses	−80
Income before taxes	**50**	**Income before taxes**	**120**
Tax expense (30 percent)	−15	Tax expense (35 percent)	−42
Net income	35	Net income	78

*** Where Celtic's cost of goods sold = (100 + 40) for wool + 60 for direct labor and overheads.

5. What is a "whistleblower"? If Tara did the appropriate thing by exposing J.R. Wolf's unethical scheme, why does the decision still affect her a year later?

6. While discussing the anticipated reactions of top management to the price changes, Alec, Kaylee, and Tara touched on the "self-interest factor." What were they referring to, and how does it affect business decision making?

Case prepared by Lawrence Hudack, and Suzanne Lowensohn

APPENDIX

A Primer on Accounting Statements[18]

There are four main financial statements. They are: (1) balance sheets; (2) income statements; (3) cash flow statements; and (4) statements of shareholders' equity. Balance sheets show what a company owns and what it owes at a fixed point in time. Income statements show how much money a company made and spent over a period of time. Cash flow statements show the exchange of money between a company and the outside world also over a period of time. The fourth financial statement, called a "statement of shareholders' equity," shows changes in the interests of the company's shareholders over time.

Let us look at each of the first three financial statements in more detail.

Balance Sheets

A balance sheet provides detailed information about a company's assets, liabilities and shareholders' equity.

Assets are things that a company owns that have value. This typically means they can either be sold or used by the company to make products or provide services that can be sold. Assets include physical property, such as plants, trucks, equipment and inventory. They also include things that cannot be touched but nevertheless exist and have value, such as trademarks and patents. In addition, cash itself is an asset. So are investments a company makes.

Liabilities are amounts of money that a company owes to others. This can include all kinds of obligations, like money borrowed from a bank to launch a new product, rent for use of a building, money owed to suppliers for materials, payroll a company owes to its employees, environmental clean-up costs, or taxes owed to the government. Liabilities also include obligations to provide goods or services to customers in the future.

Shareholders' equity is sometimes called capital or net worth. It is the money that would be left if a company sold all of its assets and paid off all of its liabilities. This leftover money belongs to the shareholders, or the owners, of the company.

The following formula summarizes what a balance sheet shows:

ASSETS = LIABILITIES + SHAREHOLDERS' EQUITY

A company's assets have to equal, or "balance," the sum of its liabilities and shareholders' equity.

A company's balance sheet is set up like the basic accounting equation shown above. On the left side of the balance sheet, companies list their assets. On the right side, they list their liabilities and shareholders' equity. Sometimes balance sheets show assets at the top, followed by liabilities, with shareholders' equity at the bottom.

Assets are generally listed based on how quickly they will be converted into cash. *Current* assets are things a company expects to convert to cash within one year. A good example is inventory. Most companies expect to sell their inventory for cash within one year.

Noncurrent assets are things a company does not expect to convert to cash within one year or that would take longer than one year to sell. Noncurrent assets include *fixed* assets. Fixed assets are those assets used to operate the business but that are not available for sale, such as trucks, office furniture and other property.

Liabilities are generally listed based on their due dates. Liabilities are said to be either *current* or *long-term*. Current liabilities are obligations a company expects to pay off within the year. Long-term liabilities are obligations due more than one year away.

Shareholders' equity is the amount owners invested in the company's stock plus or minus the company's earnings or losses since inception. Sometimes companies distribute earnings, instead of retaining them. These distributions are called dividends.

A balance sheet shows a snapshot of a company's assets, liabilities and shareholders' equity at the end of the reporting period. It does not show the flows into and out of the accounts during the period.

Income Statements

An income statement is a report that shows how much revenue a company earned over a specific time period (usually for a year or some portion of a year). An income statement also shows the costs and expenses associated with earning that revenue. The literal "bottom line" of the statement usually shows the company's net earnings or losses. This tells you how much the company earned or lost over the period.

Income statements also report earnings per share (or EPS). This calculation tells you how much money shareholders would receive if the company decided to distribute all of the net earnings for the period. (Companies almost never distribute all of their earnings. Usually they reinvest them in the business.)

To understand how income statements are set up, think of them as a set of stairs. You start at the top with the total amount of sales made during the accounting period. Then you go down, one step at a time. At each step, you make a deduction for certain costs or other operating expenses associated with earning the revenue. At the bottom of the stairs, after deducting all of the expenses, you learn how much the company actually earned or lost during the accounting period. People often call this "the bottom line."

At the top of the income statement is the total amount of money brought in from sales of products or services. This top line is often referred to as gross revenues or sales. It is called "gross" because expenses have not been deducted from it yet.

The next line is money the company does not expect to collect on certain sales. This could be due, for example, to sales discounts or merchandise returns.

When you subtract the returns and allowances from the gross revenues, you arrive at the company's net revenues. It is called "net" because, if you can imagine a net, these revenues are left in the net after the deductions for returns and allowances have come out.

Moving down the stairs from the net revenue line, there are several lines that represent various kinds of operating expenses. Although these lines can be reported in various orders, the next line after net revenues typically shows the costs of sales. This number tells you the amount of money the company spent to produce the goods or services it sold during the accounting period.

The next line subtracts the costs of sales from the net revenues to arrive at a subtotal called "gross profit" or sometimes "gross margin." It is considered "gross" because there are certain expenses that have not been deducted from it yet.

The next section deals with operating expenses. These are expenses that go toward supporting a company's operations for a given period—for example, salaries of administrative personnel and costs of researching new products. Marketing expenses are another example. Operating expenses are different from "costs of sales," which were deducted above, because operating expenses cannot be linked directly to the production of the products or services being sold.

Depreciation is also deducted from gross profit. Depreciation takes into account the wear and tear on some assets, such as machinery, tools and furniture, which are used over the long term. Companies spread the cost of these assets over the periods they are used. This process of spreading these costs is called depreciation or amortization. The "charge" for using these assets during the period is a fraction of the original cost of the assets.

After all operating expenses are deducted from gross profit, you arrive at operating profit before interest and income tax expenses. This is often called "income from operations."

Next, companies must account for interest income and interest expense. Interest income is the money companies make from keeping their cash in interest-bearing savings accounts, money-market funds and the like. On the other hand, interest expense is the money companies pay in interest for money they borrow. Some income statements show interest income and interest expense separately. Some income statements combine the two numbers. The interest income and expense are then added or subtracted from the operating profits to arrive at operating profit *before* income tax.

Finally, income tax is deducted and you arrive at the bottom line: net profit or net losses. (Net profit is also called net income or net earnings.) This tells you how much the company actually earned or lost during the accounting period. Did the company make a profit or did it lose money?

Earnings Per Share or EPS   Most income statements include a calculation of earnings per share or EPS. This calculation tells you how much money shareholders would receive for each share of stock they own if the company distributed all of its net income for the period.

To calculate EPS, you take the total net income and divide it by the number of outstanding shares of the company.

Cash Flow Statements

Cash flow statements report a company's inflows and outflows of cash. This is important because a company needs to have enough cash on hand to pay its expenses and purchase assets. While an *income statement* can tell you whether a company made a profit, a cash flow statement can tell you whether the company generated cash.

A cash flow statement shows changes over time rather than absolute dollar amounts at a point in time. It uses and reorders the information from a company's balance sheet and income statement.

The bottom line of the cash flow statement shows the net increase or decrease in cash for the period. Generally, cash flow statements are divided into three main parts. Each part reviews the cash flow from one of three types of activities: (1) operating activities; (2) investing activities; and (3) financing activities.

Operating Activities The first part of a cash flow statement analyzes a company's cash flow from net income or losses. For most companies, this section of the cash flow statement reconciles the net income (as shown on the income statement) to the actual cash the company received from or used in its operating activities. To do this, it adjusts net income for any non-cash items (such as adding back depreciation expenses) and adjusts for any cash that was used or provided by other operating assets and liabilities.

Investing Activities The second part of a cash flow statement shows the cash flow from all investing activities, which generally include purchases or sales of long-term assets, such as property, plant and equipment, as well as investment securities. If a company buys a piece of machinery, the cash flow statement will reflect this activity as a cash outflow from investing activities because it used cash. If the company decided to sell off some investments from an investment portfolio, the proceeds from the sales would show up as a cash inflow from investing activities because it provided cash.

Financing Activities The third part of a cash flow statement shows the cash flow from all financing activities. Typical sources of cash flow include cash raised by selling stocks and bonds or borrowing from banks. Likewise, paying back a bank loan would show up as a use of cash flow.

13 Organizational Structures for MNCs

After reading this chapter you should be able to:

- Understand the basic components of organizational design.

- Learn about the key organizational designs used by multinationals, namely the export department, international division, worldwide product and geographic structure, matrix and transnational structures.

- Appreciate some of the key approaches to coordinating units within a multinational.

- Learn about global and virtual teams.

- Appreciate the importance of knowledge management to multinationals.

As the Preview IB Strategic Insight shows, MNCs are facing increasing complexities as they strive to become better global competitors. For instance, Boeing had to dramatically change the way it does things to remain competitive and innovative. Such changes were implemented because Boeing had to find the best way to organize its departments and people to build the Dreamliner. Most multinationals are facing such challenges today, and this chapter will discuss some of these important issues.

This chapter first discusses the organizational design options available to implement the various multinational strategies. **Organizational design** represents how organizations structure subunits and coordinate and control mechanisms to achieve their goals. There are many complex and varied choices regarding how to set up an organization. Each organizational design has costs and benefits regarding the appropriate way to deliver a product or service to the customer. This chapter will therefore discuss the many options available to design the organization and will also show how having the right organizational design is crucial for MNCs to achieve their multinational strategic goals.

This chapter first discusses the organizational structures used by MNCs. However, because organizational structure effectively breaks down the organization in terms of

organizational design
represents how organizations structure subunits and coordination and control mechanisms to achieve their strategic goals

---

Boeing and the 787 Dreamliner

In July of 2007, Boeing premiered its latest commercial plane, the Boeing 787 Dreamliner. The Dreamliner is seen as one of the most technologically and environmentally advanced planes at the moment. Built of composite and many other very lightweight materials, the plane is expected to use 20 percent less fuel and offer improved passenger comfort, including better air quality, and make quieter landings and takeoffs compared to similar current planes. As the airline industry sees sustained increases in oil prices and greater demand for customer comfort, such qualities are seen as very desirable by most airlines. It is therefore not surprising to see that orders for the Dreamliner reached 500 in record time and have stayed strong.

Building the Dreamliner has been an exceptional and unique experience for Boeing. For the 777, Boeing decided to micromanage many aspects of its design and production. For the 787, it realized that it couldn't do everything on its own. It therefore built strong partnerships with many of its suppliers in other countries such as Japan and Italy. This represented a major departure from its

traditional way of doing things. Boeing always preferred to be in control and believed that the best ideas could only come from inside the company. With these new partnerships, it had to give up significant control and had to build trusting partnerships with many of its suppliers.

How did Boeing manage the challenges inherent in this new approach? It first had to deal with its managers and their trust in suppliers' progress. Boeing therefore formed a global partner council where senior Boeing managers met regularly with the various suppliers to solve problems. Boeing also sent teams of engineers from one supplier to another to share best practices and act as consultants. Such changes have paid off as development time has shrunk by almost a year and Boeing can charge its customers $130 million for each plane, a price equivalent to what companies are paying for a 1980s plane.

Source: Based on Jena McGregor, Aili McConnon, and Arlene Weintraub, 2007, "The 25 most innovative companies: The leaders in nurturing cultures of creativity," *BusinessWeek*, May 14, pp. 52–5.

logical subunits, it is also necessary to implement various mechanisms to help integrate these entities. The chapter will look at some of the most popular ways that multinationals use to coordinate their various subunits. It will also discuss teams in depth, as many companies are now relying on both virtual and real teams to coordinate their subunits.

Finally, in this chapter, you will also read about knowledge management. As the competitive environment changes and multinationals are being forced to combine knowledge from around the world to innovate, they are feeling increased pressure to adequately manage information and knowledge. Organizational design and coordination aspects are very closely related to an organization's ability to manage information and knowledge. The final aspect of the chapter will therefore discuss some of the key knowledge management issues.

Organizational Design: Challenges, Forms and Basic Designs

Experts see organizational design as the key to success in the future.[1] Many changes are occurring favoring organizational designs that require companies to be more flexible and quick. For instance, many of the traditional boundaries characterizing competition in the past are slowly disappearing. Globalization is erasing national boundaries while strategic alliances are slowly erasing traditional barriers between companies. Furthermore, the increased popularity of e-commerce is also minimizing traditional market boundaries while allowing rapid access to information.[2] All of these changes are requiring that companies design systems that can maximize coordination among their subunits while making rapid use of mass amounts of information. Consider the following IB Strategic Insight on how organizational structure changes are necessary if Nokia wants to stay competitive in the future.

As the IB Strategic Insight shows, organizational design and structure are extremely critical for multinationals. In the next few paragraphs, you will learn about the function of organizational design approaches. In the subsequent sections, you will read about the traditional approaches multinationals use as they enter the global market.

The Functions of Organizational Design

Organizational design addresses two basic questions for an organization: (1) How shall the work among the organization's subunits be divided? and, (2) How shall the efforts of the units created be coordinated and controlled?[3] In very small organizations, most employees have to be involved in all aspects of running the company and organizational design is not necessary. Consider, for example, the hypothetical situation where you decide to open a restaurant. When the restaurant is relatively small, there is little reason to divide the work. For instance, you can act as the cook and waiter, and even perform accounting and finance functions. However, as the restaurant grows you find that you need to hire more cooks, waiters, managers and even someone to answer the phone. You also decide to open restaurants in other locations and you find that you need to begin dividing the work. As such, you may start dividing work first into

New Organizational Structure at Nokia

As of January 2008, Nokia replaced its current organizational structure with a new one focused on taking advantage of new opportunities and becoming more efficient. Nokia is the market leader in mobility, playing an important role in industries combining the Internet and communications. Nokia manufactures a large range of mobile equipment, used by its customers to experience music, navigation, video, television, etc.

Why is Nokia changing its structure? Nokia's current structure reflects an emphasis on separating the various products it offers into different departments. However, current changes in the various industries it operates in suggest convergence and the need to coordinate and integrate the various products it manufactures. For instance, there is strong pressure on companies to integrate mobile communication devices (e.g. cell phones) with the Internet. Consider the launch of Apple's iPhone (integration of Internet, music, movies, etc.) and the new forms of competition that Nokia is facing. Its current organizational structure does not allow it to fully take advantage of such convergence.

The new organizational structure will replace Nokia's current business units with three new departments, namely mobile devices, services and softwares, and a markets division. This change will allow Nokia not only to become more focused on emerging opportunities but also to become more efficient by combining previously separate units. Consider that, for instance, Nokia's current structure includes four separate divisions for its cell phones (low- and mid-tier phones, high-end phones, corporate customers, and networks). By combining all of the cell-phone divisions into the mobile device unit, it can combine its expertise across the range of phones to produce better phones. It can also bring new products to market faster as expertise and skills are shared across its many products.

The new services and softwares division also reflects the pressures on companies to find new markets as the cell-phone industry matures. Furthermore, the new markets division is aimed at increasing its efficiency in marketing and other value-chain activities.

Source: Based on M2 Presswire, 2007, "Nokia to introduce new company structure," June 20, p. 1; and Cassell Bryan-Low, 2007, "Nokia revamps structure in bid for new revenues," *Wall Street Journal Asia*, June 21, p. 6.

specialized jobs. Different people perform different tasks. Later, if one restaurant becomes big enough, with enough people doing the same tasks, a supervisor is required, and managers divide their organizations into specialized subunits. As such, in smaller organizations, the subunits are usually called departments. In larger organizations, divisions or subsidiaries become the major subunits.

Once an organization has specialized subunits, managers must develop mechanisms that coordinate and control the efforts of each subunit.[4] For the restaurant example, the human resource department must work closely with the operations to determine the personnel needs of the company. As another example, a manufacturing company must make sure that the production department produces the goods to be available at the time the marketing department promised the customers. Similarly, an MNC must ensure that its foreign operations support the parent company's strategic goals. Some companies monitor their subunits very closely.

Organizational Designs for Multinationals

To understand how multinationals choose the various options available, it is necessary to understand the process that companies experience as they go international. As such, for a company selling domestically only, the **functional structure**, where departments perform separate business functions such as marketing or manufacturing, is appropriate. The functional structure is the simplest structure for an organization. The major reason to choose a functional structure for a subunit is efficiency through economies of scale in each function, as there are cost savings when a large number of people do the same job in the same place. The downside is that, because functional subunits are separated from each other and serve functional goals, coordination among the units can be difficult. Exhibit 13.1 shows a functional structure.

functional structure
departments perform separate business functions such as marketing, finance, or manufacturing

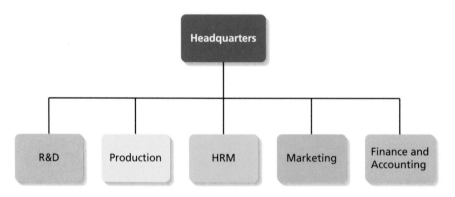

Exhibit 13.1 **A Basic Functional Structure**

When a company goes international, it seldom changes its basic organizational structure. Most companies in such cases are interested in exploiting the international market on a very limited basis. Such organizations tend to act first as passive exporters. Passive exporters simply fill orders using the same structures, procedures, and people used in domestic sales. Furthermore, such companies tend to be relatively small by multinational standards.

However, when international sales become more central to a firm's success, more sophisticated multinational and participation strategies usually become a significant part of a company's overall business strategy. As a result, companies must then build appropriate organizational structures to manage their multinational operations and implement their multinational strategies. The following sections focus on the structural options for MNCs.

The Export Department

export department
separate organizational unit to deal exclusively with exports when the latter becomes a significant percentage of sales

Although passive exporting can be a good way to internationalize operations, certain changes may occur forcing any company to adopt new structures. For instance, exporting over time may result in increased competition from both domestic and international firms. These pressures thus result in a greater threat to the company's market share. As such, when exports become a significant percentage of company sales and a company wishes to have greater control over its export operations, managers often create a separate **export department**. A separate department shows that top management believes that the investment of human and financial resources in exporting is necessary to sustain and build international sales. Exhibit 13.2 shows a hypothetical organization with a functional structure and an export department.

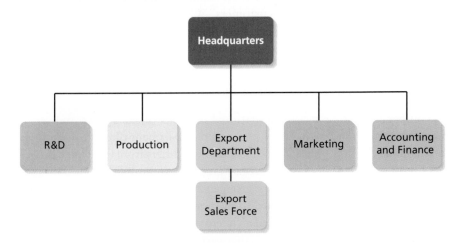

Exhibit 13.2 **Functional Structure with Export Department**

How important is an export department to companies? Consider the following IB Small Business Insight.

Small Firms and Export Departments

IB SMALL BUSINESS INSIGHT

How important is an export department? Many small firms find that exporting can be the key to expanding their business opportunities. In fact, the e-government portal http://export.gov suggests that around 95 percent of the world's consumers live outside of the US. As any small company faces the limits of the domestic market, they can benefit tremendously by exporting and eventually creating an export department. Consider, for example, the success story of Alemite Corporation, leading provider of lubrication and other fluids for equipment lubrication. They made some strategic decisions emphasizing exporting and established an export department. They also decided to attend many trade fairs and shows and made important contacts through such venues. They have since established alliances with many foreign companies and are now present in Central and Eastern Europe as well as the Middle East. They have also expanded their markets tremendously.

As you can see, exports are crucial to small businesses. A few other key points worth remembering are:

- The vast majority of new exporters are small and medium firms.
- Small and medium-sized businesses account for over 97 percent of all exporters of US goods.
- Export helps small businesses grow and become more competitive in their various markets.
- Most small firms export only to one country, suggesting tremendous potential to expand to other countries.

Source: Based on http://export.gov and www.alemite.com

The export department thus deals with all international customers for all products. Managers in the export department often control the pricing and promotion of products for the international market. People within the department may have particular country or product expertise. Export department managers have the responsibility to deal with export management companies, with foreign distributors, and with foreign customers. When the company uses a direct exporting strategy, sales representatives located in other countries may also report to the export department management.

The International Division

As companies become more international in terms of sales force and set up manufacturing in other countries, the export department often grows into an international division.[5] The **international division** differs from the export department in that it is usually larger and has greater responsibilities. Furthermore, all international activities tend to be grouped in a subunit and a senior executive from local headquarters is assigned to the new division.

Besides managing exporting and an international sales force, the international division oversees foreign subsidiaries that perform a variety of functions such as, most often, the sales units. However, other units that provide raw material and produce the company's products in other countries are also common. The international division also has more extensive staff with international expertise. Top management expects these people to perform functions such as negotiating licensing and joint-venture agreements, translating promotional material, or providing expertise on different national cultures and social institutions. Exhibit 13.3 shows a domestic product structure with an international division.

international division
a separate department that groups all international activities and headed by a senior executive from headquarters

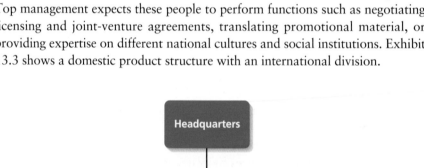

Exhibit 13.3 **International Division with a Product Structure**

When are international divisions appropriate? International divisions work when a company is still at the early stages of internationalizing its markets. In such cases, international sales tend to be comparatively small compared to domestic sales. Furthermore, an international division works well when the company has a limited number of products or a limited number of geographic areas it is serving.

The international division structure has become less popular and for multi-product companies operating in many countries it is not considered an effective multinational structure.[6] However, for companies of moderate size with a limited number of products or country locations, the international division remains a popular and potentially effective organization.

As such, although international divisions tend to be appealing, they suffer from a number of problems. First and most importantly, the creation of a separate international division means that international operations become isolated and are not necessarily integrated within other operations in the multinational. Additionally, too many products can overwhelm the capacities of the international division. In sales, for example, it is difficult for people in the international division to know the whole product line and sell it worldwide. Second, when the number of locations in different countries grows, it is difficult for the international division to manage these various locations. How can a remote headquarters division know local needs and adapt products and strategies accordingly? Finally, some companies start seeing conflict between domestic and international managers as they compete for resources.

To deal with the shortcomings of the international division structure, MNCs have several options, such as the worldwide geographic structure, the worldwide product structure, the matrix structure, and the transnational network structure. We discuss these various options next.

Worldwide Geographic Structure

For domestic-only companies, using **geographic structure** enables the company to serve customer needs that vary by region. Rather than one large functional organization that serves all customers, the smaller, regional organization focuses all functional activities (e.g. marketing, finance, human resources) on serving the unique needs of the regional customer. However, for the multinational, in the **worldwide geographic structure**, regions or large-market countries become the geographical divisions of the MNC. The main reason to choose a worldwide geographic structure is the existence of important differences in an area's product or service needs or in channels of distribution. Because of the significant differences in the product or service, the multinational needs to differentiate its products or services by country or region. Exhibit 13.4 shows PepsiCo's worldwide geographic structure.

The geographic structure differs from the international division in that markets are no longer viewed as domestic and international. Instead, the managers in a worldwide geographic structure view all markets as important and the domestic market simply becomes another market. As such, executives for each region become responsible for developing operations in their own region. Furthermore, executives from each region or area typically work together to develop a coherent plan for the overall multinational.

For all purposes, the geographic structure is appropriate when a country's market size is sufficiently large or important to support a separate organization. Separate divisions often make sense for larger market countries such as the United States, France, Germany, or Japan. Regional divisions combine smaller, similar countries such as a Southern European division for Italy, Spain, and Portugal. Furthermore, as mentioned earlier, PepsiCo also has a worldwide geographic structure (e.g. PepsiCo Asia, PepsiCo Europe, PepsiCo Middle East and Africa, etc.; see www.pepsico.com).

As you may have realized, there are no best organizational structures and the worldwide geographic structure also suffers from a number of drawbacks.

geographic structure
focus of all functional activities on serving unique needs of regional customer

worldwide geographic structure
where regions or large countries become the geographical divisions of the MNC

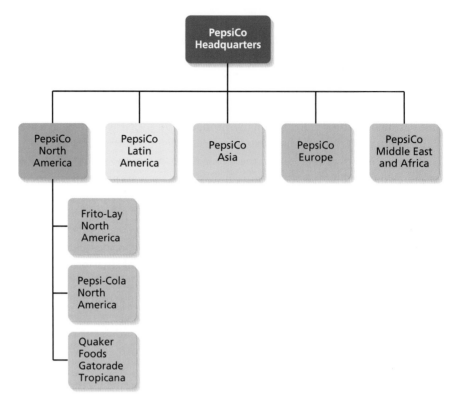

Exhibit 13.4 **PepsiCo's Worldwide Geographic Structure**

Most importantly, the duplication of functions across countries means that the overall cost structure is much higher. However, because of the emphasis on geographic region, the MNC may also find it hard to coordinate the various functions around the world. For instance, if one geographic area develops some specific competencies that reduce costs, this may not always be transferred to other countries. As such, there are significant coordination difficulties in other activities such as research and development, product planning, and so on.

The major drawback of the global geographic structure is that the focus on geographic areas detracts from major developments in the product. To solve such problems, multinationals can adopt a global product structure, which you will read about next.

Worldwide Product Structure

product structure
subdivision of company along product lines

worldwide product structure
subdivision of multinational along product lines where all product divisions are responsible for selling their products around the world

For the domestic company, in the **product structure** the organization is subdivided along product lines. The product structure must still perform the functional tasks of a business (e.g. marketing and accounting), which are duplicated for each product department. Such product divisions also form the basic units of **worldwide product structures** for MNCs. Each product division is responsible for producing and selling its products or services throughout the world. Managers of a worldwide product division are typically in charge of all the functional activities (marketing, finance, human resources) associated with a product or specific product groups. Each product group is also responsible for coordinating and managing both domestic and international operations within that group. However, the corporate headquarters provide the overall

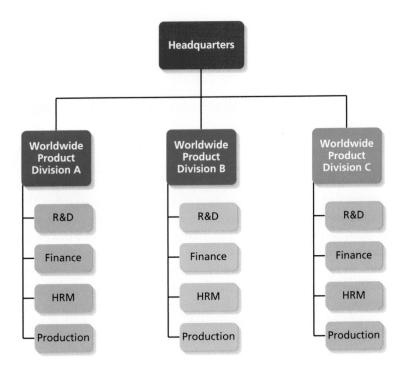

Exhibit 13.5 **Worldwide Product Structure**

strategy to coordinate the various product groups. Exhibit 13.5 shows a worldwide product structure.

Product structures work well when a multinational has a large number of products. Furthermore, as you may realize, a worldwide product structure will fulfill some of the functions that a worldwide geographic structure cannot provide. For instance, if there is a strong need to coordinate and integrate the various functional areas related to a product, the product structure works well. Furthermore, a product structure is appropriate in cases where little adaptation is needed for the various international markets in which the multinational operates.

The global product structure nevertheless suffers from a number of drawbacks. Most importantly, the global product structure requires duplication of functional areas and the associated human resource needs. Such duplication obviously makes the product structure more costly. Furthermore, the focus on products means that managers are more likely to pursue product opportunities at the expense of other characteristics. For instance, a manager may focus more on the domestic aspect of the business if a product is doing well there, and ignore international markets.

Both the worldwide product structure and the worldwide geographic structure have advantages and disadvantages for multinational strategy implementation. As you read earlier, the product structure best supports strategies that emphasize global products and rationalization (worldwide products using worldwide, low-cost sources of raw materials and worldwide marketing strategies). The geographic structure best supports strategies that emphasize local adaptation (managers are often local nationals and are sensitive to local needs). Most MNCs, however, adopt strategies that include concerns for local adaptation as well as for the economic and product-development benefits of globalization. Consequently, most large multinationals have structures that are hybrids, or mixtures of product and area units. You will read about these hybrid structures next.

The Matrix and the Transnational Network Structure

To balance the benefits produced by geographic and product structures and to coordinate a mixture of product and geographic subunits, some multinationals create a worldwide matrix structure. Unlike hybrid organizations, the worldwide **matrix structure**, shown in Exhibit 13.6, is a symmetrical organization: it has equal lines of authority for product groups and for geographic divisions. Ideally, the matrix provides the structure for a firm to pursue both local and more global strategies at the same time. Geographical divisions focus on national responsiveness, and product divisions focus on finding global efficiencies. The matrix structure works well only when there are nearly equal demands from the environment for local adaptation and for product standardization with its associated economies of scale. Without these near-equal demands, the organization tends to evolve into a product or geographic structure, based on whichever side is more important for competitive advantage.

matrix structure
mixture of traditional hierarchical structures, such as product and geographic, where both divisions have equal line of authority

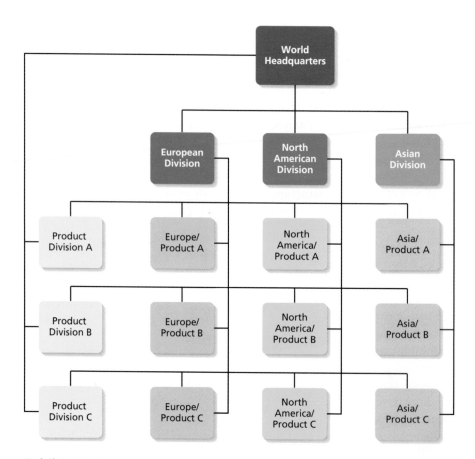

Exhibit 13.6 **Matrix Structure**

On paper, the matrix structure produces quality decisions because two or more managers reach consensus on how to balance local and worldwide needs. It typically allows the multinational to explore new opportunities as the focus is usually on both product and geography. Managers who hold positions at the intersection of product and geographic divisions are called "two-boss managers," as they have a boss from the product side of the organization and a boss from the geographic side of the organization. Product bosses tend to emphasize goals such as efficiency, while geographic bosses tend to emphasize local or regional adaptation. As such, for managers at all levels, the matrix gives the multinational the opportunity to explore both product needs and geographical needs. Furthermore, the matrix structure enables better communication and movement of information.

The major drawback associated with a matrix structure is that it is extremely difficult to manage. For instance, to succeed at balancing the inherent struggles between global and local concerns, the matrix requires extensive resources for communication among the managers. Middle- and upper-level managers must have good human relations skills to deal with inevitable personal conflicts originating from the competing interests of product and geography. The middle-level managers must also learn to deal with two bosses, who often have competing interests. Furthermore, upper-level managers, in turn, must be prepared to resolve conflicts between geographic and product managers. Finally, while decisions that are made may be better, they typically take much longer to reach. Consider the IB Strategic Insight below.

The **transnational network structure** represents another solution to the complex demands of being locally responsive while also taking advantage of global economies of scale and seeking location advantages such as global sources of knowledge. It combines functional, product, and geographic subunits. However,

transnational network structure
network of subsidiaries and divisions that link the company throughout the world

Philips and the Matrix Structure

IB STRATEGIC INSIGHT

Philips, the Dutch electrical multinational giant, was one of the early pioneers of the matrix structure. It set up the matrix structure after the Second World War. Because of its international presence in many countries already by this time, it set up both national and product divisions. As such, the boss of any product in another country would report to the head of Philips in that country as well as to the head of the product at Philips' headquarters. For instance, the head of the washing machine division in Italy would report to both the head of Philips in Italy and the head of the washing machine division in the Netherlands.

However, by the 1990s, Philips realized that the structure was not functioning well. Like most other organizations

using the matrix structure, it faced issues of accountability. Philips had difficulty deciding who should be held responsible for accountability. Should the country head or product head be held responsible for profitability in any division? Furthermore, there were significant conflicts between the product and country heads, which often created barriers to cross-unit collaboration. As a result of these problems, Philips reorganized around its products and the national offices became accountable to the product heads.

Source: Based on *The Economist*, 2006, "The matrix master," January 21, 378, p. 4.

unlike the symmetrical matrix structure, the transnational has no basic form. It has no symmetry or balance between the geographic and product sides of the organization. Instead, the transnational is a network that links different types of transnational subsidiaries throughout the world. Exhibit 13.7 shows the transnational network at Philips, the Dutch multinational.

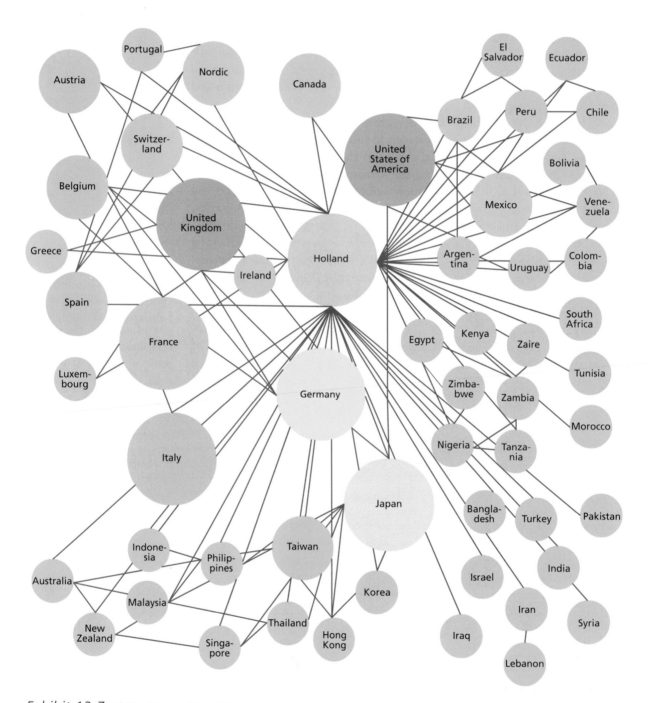

Exhibit 13.7 **Philips Transnational Structure**

Source: Sumantra Goshal and Christopher A. Bartlett, 1990, "The multinational corporation as an interorganizational network," *Academy of Management Review*, 15, pp. 603–25. Republished with permission of the Academy of Management; permission conveyed through Copyright Clearance Center, Inc.

The transnational organization is different from the other forms of organization in a number of important ways. First, while other forms tend to focus on only one aspect (i.e. on the product in the product structure, etc.), the transnational structure tends to provide legitimacy to the various internal perspectives.[7] Furthermore, while the company's physical and human assets are spread globally, there is a very high level of interdependence among these elements. In contrast to other forms where power is concentrated, the transnational structure works by decentralizing authority to the various national units. The local managers are given entrepreneurial freedom to develop new solutions to problems but are also expected to contribute such knowledge to the global operations. As such, managers are expected not only to be creative but also to have the necessary skills to contribute their knowledge for the good of the transnational.

As such, nodes, the units at the center of the network, coordinate product, functional, and geographic information. Different product-group units and geographical-area units have different structures, and often no two subunits are alike. Rather, transnational units evolve to take advantage of resources, talent, and market opportunities wherever they exist in the world. Resources, people, and ideas flow in all directions.

A transnational structure works well when industries become very complex and volatile. As such, a typical hierarchy may not work in such situations. For instance, companies such as Asea Brown Boveri or Philips Electronics operate in extremely complex industries where companies' traditional boundaries have disappeared and where global operations and local operations need to be integrated to build competitive advantage. However, similar to the matrix organization, a transnational structure is extremely complicated to manage. Unlike other structures, there is no set form that a transnational structure can take.

In the next and final section, you will read about which structure a multinational should use.

Choosing the Appropriate Structure: Strategy and Structure

An important point to remember is that there is no one best organizational design. The choice of an organizational design depends mostly on the choice of strategy.[8] That is, some design options are more effective for implementing different strategies. As you read earlier, most small companies act first as passive exporters. They simply fill orders using the same structures, procedures, and people used in domestic sales. Even with greater involvement in exporting, companies often avoid fundamental organizational changes. Instead, they use other companies to provide them with international expertise and to run their export operations. Furthermore, even with licensing, companies do not need complicated structures to collect royalties. However, as we discussed earlier, as exports become more important, an export department works well.

For the multinational extensively involved with international operations, the appropriateness of a structure depends on the basic multinational strategies discussed in Chapter 2. A multinational can pursue each of four main strategies, namely multidomestic, transnational, international, and regional. Each of these strategies requires a different approach to organizational structure. Below, we discuss each strategy briefly (for more detail, please refer to Chapter 2) and the appropriate organizational structure.

A multidomestic structure focuses on local responsiveness where the multinational customizes products for the needs of the local markets. Furthermore, as you may recall from Chapter 2, a regional strategy is also an approach where products are customized for local market needs. The most appropriate structure to implement a multidomestic or regional strategy is a worldwide geographic structure. Since a company with a multidomestic or regional strategy needs to differentiate its products or services by country or region, it needs an organizational design with maximum geographical flexibility. The semi-autonomous regional or country-based subunits of the worldwide geographic structure provide that flexibility to tailor or develop products that meet the particular needs of local or regional markets.

A company pursuing an international strategy attempts to gain economies of scale by selling worldwide products with most upstream activities based at home. Adaptation to local customs and culture, if any, is limited to minor adjustments in product offerings and marketing strategies. Often, the international strategist decides to concentrate its R&D and manufacturing strengths at home, hoping it brings greater economies of scale and quality than the dispersed activities of the transnational. For multinationals pursuing an international strategy, worldwide product structures are appropriate. Worldwide product structures support international strategies because they provide an efficient way to organize and centralize the production and sales of similar products for the world market. The worldwide product structure sacrifices regional or local adaptation strengths derived from a geographic structure to gain product development and manufacturing economies of scale.

Finally, for the company pursuing a transnational strategy, the transnational structure is obviously the most appropriate structure. The transnational strategy gives two goals top priority: seeking location advantages and gaining economic efficiencies from operating worldwide.[9] "Location advantages" means that the transnational company disperses or locates its value-chain activities (e.g. manufacturing, R&D, and sales) anywhere in the world where the company can "do it best or cheapest," as the situation requires. The transnational structure provides the necessary flexibility to achieve transnational strategies.

Next, we examine multinational coordination strategies.

Coordination Mechanisms

As you read earlier, the task of selecting the appropriate organizational design emphasizes breaking down the multinational into subunits to perform specialized tasks and responsibilities. However, top managers must also design organizational systems to coordinate the activities of their subunits. This is a very difficult task. Foreign subsidiaries differ widely by geographical location, local markets, cultures, and legal systems, as well as by the talents and resources available to the subsidiary.[10] However, even subunits within a multinational may have different goals and operate differently. **Coordination mechanisms** become critical for any multinational to coordinate its various subunits. This section therefore reviews coordination systems used by MNCs to coordinate their dispersed activities.

coordination mechanisms
ways to coordinate the various subunits in a multinational

Improving Collaboration at P&G and Raytheon

Procter & Gamble currently has more than 135,000 employees working in around 80 countries. While the number of people involved in research and development had increased, P&G saw its number of technical centers increase from 12 to 25. P&G was therefore concerned about whether dispersing the R&D employees over a larger number of centers was affecting collaboration and knowledge-sharing among these employees. It therefore conducted a social network analysis and asked key R&D personnel to indicate who their closest connections were in the company. The results were very informative for P&G. While it found that many workers were connected to other workers within their unit, it also found that the communities of practice that it had established were also serving an important role in connecting people.

The network study also revealed a few areas of concern for P&G. For instance, it found that its R&D center in China was not as connected with the other centers. The results showed that the China center was always seeking information while its own expertise was not sought after. This was troubling for P&G given the importance of China to its future.

A similar social network analysis at Raytheon showed that the engineers within the company were not collaborating as effectively as possible. Key engineers were not always connected to the right team and the focus on traditional engineering disciplines did not allow collaboration on technology-focused engineering. Results of the study allowed the company to create Centers of Excellence to encourage collaboration among critical individuals.

Source: Based on Jennifer Reingold and Julia Lynn Yang, 2007, "The hidden workplace," *Fortune*, July 23, 156, pp. 98–105.

What's the nature of such coordination? Consider the IB Strategic Insight above, about P&G and Raytheon.

As the IB Strategic Insight illustrates, finding ways to integrate and coordinate various departments in a multinational is critical. The organizational design aspects discussed earlier usually set up the formal nature of the organization. However, the informal aspects of the organization, as you can see from the above IB Strategic Insight, can also be very important in achieving the goals of the multinational. A multinational may need to coordinate various subunits with entities such as cross-functional teams or virtual teams. Furthermore, as argued by Chen and Cannice,[11] appropriate coordination and integration allows a multinational to minimize duplication, thus saving costs. Global integration also allows a multinational to enjoy global economies of scale, thus becoming more globally efficient. Next, you will read about the various coordination mechanisms.

Coordination and Integration

As you read earlier, coordinating and integrating a multinational's subunits is crucial. However, implementing systems to make such coordination and communication happen is not easy. One of the most important barriers to coordination is that different subunits may develop different goals and may thus have their own agendas. For instance, in a functional structure, the various functional areas may develop orientations favoring their own perspectives. Building coordination requires dedicated efforts from multinationals.

According to Jones,[12] there are seven coordination and integration mechanisms. The first and simplest integrating device is the **hierarchy of authority**, depicting who has authority and who reports to whom. Consider, for instance, the worldwide geographic structure discussed earlier. In its simplest arrangement (see Exhibit 13.4), each of the managers from the various functions reports to the area manager. This establishes a hierarchy of authority and responsibility but also coordinates the various geographic areas. However, if a multinational feels that the different geographic areas are too isolated and that several geographic areas may need to coordinate, the hierarchy of authority may be changed whereby a manager is assigned to coordinate the work of two geographic areas and report to higher-level managers.

Another important coordination mechanism is **direct contact**, where managers or workers interact face to face. For MNCs, direct contact often requires sophisticated video-conferencing and knowledge of a common language. Direct contact can be an important way to eliminate barriers among subunits. By establishing personal relationships, a multinational can build the necessary collaborative efforts needed to counter subunit orientations. Consider, for instance, the case of Raytheon, the defense company discussed earlier in the IB Strategic Insight. One of the other findings was that a senior engineer, an expert in systems architecture, was not connected to others with similar expertise. Because systems architecture is such a critical area for Raytheon, the engineer was instructed to make direct contact with other experts in systems architecture. This helped Raytheon create expert groups which has benefited the multinational.

Liaison roles are fulfilled by individuals in one department whose specific responsibility is to communicate with people in another department. For example, in an MNC, one manager in each country subsidiary might be given the responsibility of coordinating marketing efforts within a region of the world. However, some multinationals can also create **full-time integrating roles**. Full-time integrators are similar to liaison roles but have coordination as their sole job responsibility. Product managers are often full-time integrators. In the MNC, they often serve as a link between the production units and local-country operations. Furthermore, some organizations can go as far as creating **integrating departments**. In such cases, rather than have one manager coordinate the work of different subunits, teams of managers are assigned such roles.

Task forces are temporary teams created to solve a particular organizational problem such as entering a new market. They usually link more than one department. A good example stems from Gerstner's efforts at IBM.[13] He launched a diversity task-force initiative and created eight focused teams representing various minority groups at IBM (women, Asians, etc.). These groups were created primarily to help IBM get a better understanding of the market. This initiative has paid off. For instance, the women's task force found that there is a lack of female experts in the technology industry. The task force recommended the creation of technology camps for middle-school girls to encourage interest in math and sciences and to show how these areas can translate into successful careers.

The final coordination mechanism available to multinationals is teams. Because of the importance of teams to most multinationals, you will read about teams in the next section.

---

hierarchy of authority
integrating device depicting authority and accountability

direct contact
face-to-face interaction

liaison roles
specific responsibilities of a person from one department to communicate with people from other departments

full-time integrating roles
similar to liaison roles but with full-time coordination responsibilities

integrating departments
departments responsible for coordination

task forces
temporary teams created to solve organizational concerns or problems

Teams

Teams are the strongest coordination mechanisms, and unlike task forces, which have a short-term life span, teams are permanent units of the organization. Teams come from several organizational subunits to specialize in particular problems. For example, a team doing new-product development might include a scientist from R&D and managers from production and marketing.

teams
permanent groups of people specialized to deal with particular problems

Why are teams so crucial to multinationals? In today's hypercompetitive environment, multinationals often need to develop and launch new products that need to meet local and global needs while at the same time taking advantage of knowledge and expertise located around the world. Teams of individuals located around the world are often used to develop and launch such new products. Teams allow multinationals to bring together important expertise representing both local and global customer needs while also taking advantage of knowledge around the world. Consider the IB Strategic Insight below.

Recent research by Barczak and McDonough also shows that global teams are crucial for multinationals for a variety of other reasons.[14] Teams are often useful in helping multinationals identify common product platforms that can help develop global products. Global products are often desirable because they are cheaper to produce and market. Teams also allow multinationals to bring together key dispersed resources and expertise. By bringing together expertise located around the world (e.g. manufacturing expertise in one country, R&D in another country, etc.), a team is more likely to capitalize on the various strengths and expertise. Furthermore, as you will read later, teams can now exist at the virtual level, thus bringing minimal disruption to the team members' lives and also minimizing costs.

Multinationals and Global Teams

IB STRATEGIC INSIGHT

How important are global teams to multinationals today? Many large multinationals such as Dow Chemical, Nokia and Accenture make extensive use of global teams as they strive to navigate the hypercompetitive environment. They are finding that global teams give them the ability to coordinate activities of globally dispersed workers with special skills and expertise.

As an example, consider the case of Nokia. The company's effort to develop global marketing and product development teams is now paying off. Nokia is developing better products that are successful worldwide. Nokia is now making sure to hire employees who have a collaborative "mindset." Furthermore, they are very careful in creating task forces that reflect the global market they are selling to.

Teams are also critical to Accenture. The company, which spent around $700 million on education in 2006, makes sure that all of its consultants and service workers take collaboration courses. Furthermore, Accenture also picks the most promising managers and puts them through a special leadership course emphasizing collaboration and teamwork. Such efforts are very important as Accenture assigns international teams to work on most of its projects.

Source: Based on Pete Engardio, 2007, "A guide for multinationals. One of the greatest challenges for a multinational is learning how to build a productive global team," *BusinessWeek*, August 20, 4047, p. 48.

Despite the key advantages, global teams suffer from a number of challenges. As argued by Barczak, McDonough and Athanassiou, in a survey of around 300 teams in over 230 companies, global teams face a number of key challenges.[15] First and foremost, global team members are located in countries around the world. Important differences exist in terms of cultural backgrounds, languages used and even the local subsidiary's culture. Such differences can often result in misunderstanding or create other barriers to communication if not addressed properly. However, beyond such differences, global team members have to often deal with logistic and other practical challenges. For instance, a simple video-conferencing with a colleague in South Korea may turn out to be challenging because of the significant time difference. Furthermore, as Kumar discusses, traveling can soon become very tiresome and become very disruptive in terms of both work and family.[16]

What can multinationals do to deal with such challenges? For cultural background differences, it is important to encourage team members to be more culturally aware. Many of the training and other awareness methods discussed in Chapter 7 on national culture can be applied here. However, for the language differences, a team leader can implement various steps to ensure smooth communication.[17] It is important to distribute critical documents ahead of time to allow all team members to comprehend and respond to shared information. It is also advisable for team members to provide a written description of meetings to ensure that everyone is on the same page. Furthermore, it is also critical to make sure that team members are trained regarding potential misunderstandings using a common language. Additionally, because of the challenges of operating in different countries and different time zones, it is important for the team leader to establish clear project goals and to assign appropriate responsibilities. If possible, such goals and responsibilities should be assigned collectively to ensure buy-in and commitment from all team members.

A final but important measure to ensure that global teams function effectively is regular communication. Global team members should be encouraged to communicate regularly through e-mail, telephone and other available technology. However, it is also crucial to have regular face-to-face meetings to build trust and relationships. To get things done, a global team needs to rely on the expertise of its members and their propensity to trust each other to collaborate. Face-to-face meetings can be a good step towards building relationships and trust.

Global Virtual Teams

global virtual teams
groups of people around the world collaborating using information and communication technologies

The new global workplace is also seeing an increased use of **global virtual teams.** Global virtual teams are groups of people who work together from different parts of the world by using information and communication technologies such as intranets, web meetings, WIKIs, e-mails and instant messaging.[18] Global virtual teams are also becoming increasingly important for multinationals. Consider the case of IBM and its goal to make its 360,000 employees work together as a global virtual team.[19] IBM has implemented a global web system where any employee with a new product idea can use online chat boxes to create a team and have access to market intelligence. Employees around the world can collaborate immediately on new product ideas, and develop and test prototypes. This new portal now enables IBM to create a virtual team in as little as 30 minutes, while also shortening the time it takes to create a business from six months to only 30 days. The new web system has also allowed virtual teams to create 70 businesses and ten new products.

Given the importance of global virtual teams to multinationals, it is important to understand some of the key challenges and opportunities facing such teams. According to Brake,[20] virtual teams suffer from many major drawbacks. First, virtual teams suffer from the lack of information richness that is typically afforded by a face-to-face environment. When teams function face to face, team members can pay attention to social and other cues to react or attend to. Such cues are missing in virtual teams. Second, such lack of cues can also result in misunderstanding and confusion. However, Gerke also argues that the virtual team leader faces some challenges such as the difficulty of getting to know team members in a virtual world while also communicating effectively.[21] Other challenges for the virtual team leader include the ability to recognize problems before such problems occur, and also the ability to assign responsibilities and duties and monitor such issues in an environment where team members never actually meet. Furthermore, in addition to the above challenges, virtual global teams also face many of the same challenges that traditional global teams face. For instance, both cultural and language differences may potentially result in misunderstanding and low productivity.

Although virtual teams suffer from a number of potential drawbacks, most experts agree that the most critical step to ensure that a global virtual team works well is to build a social community to ensure that team members don't feel isolated.[22] As such, if possible, team members may want to meet face to face at least once to build relationships. However, if face-to-face meetings are not possible, the team leader should schedule regular conference calls as well as one-to-one phone calls to build trust and collaboration. Furthermore, it is important for virtual team members to discuss other issues than work to build camaraderie. Inquiries about family and other social aspects are more likely to give a chance for virtual team members to get to know each other.

A final key issue pertaining to virtual global teams is staying focused on the task at hand. It is imperative for the team leader to take steps to assign and clarify responsibilities judiciously as well as assigning goals and deadlines. Frequent feedback and updates on the team progress may also be useful. Finally, the team leader should be prepared to modify responsibilities and goals as required.

This section completes consideration of organizational design by showing how managers can coordinate the various types of subunits that multinational organizations employ. In the final section, we look at knowledge management, a design issue that is becoming increasingly crucial for most multinationals.

Knowledge Management

In this chapter, you read about not only how multinationals can break down the organization into subunits, but also how they coordinate these subunits. An increasingly related and important area is knowledge management. As you will read below, the way a multinational organizes its information through its various structures and coordination mechanisms can be very important as it strives to survive in today's global environment.

knowledge management
systems and mechanisms
in place to collect and
disseminate knowledge in
the multinational

Knowledge management refers to the systems, mechanisms and other design elements of any organization to ensure that the right form of knowledge is available to the right individual at the right time.[23] Knowledge management is focused on the processes related to the creation, acquisition and dissemination of critical knowledge and information to enhance learning and performance in the organization. Many well-known multinationals such as HP, British Petroleum, Xerox, Chevron, Ford, etc., have all implemented knowledge management systems.[24]

Why is knowledge management so critical? Many experts agree that knowledge management is critical to successful product innovation and creation of competitive advantage. For example, knowledge management systems allow companies to create and combine critical knowledge that can lead to knowledge creation for new products. Furthermore, many multinationals now have to face forces for both global integration and local differentiation while achieving global innovation. Multinationals need to be able to implement systems that are capable of combining worldwide knowledge from local sources to create and transfer innovation to new products for international markets. Appropriately managing knowledge can give multinationals the means to create the global flexibility they will need to survive.[25]

According to experts, an effective knowledge management is composed of many important tools or mechanisms.[26] In its ideal form, an effective knowledge management system is one where employees are encouraged to share what they know with others while also being able to seek critical knowledge and expertise when needed. One of the important facets of any knowledge management system is the presence of the appropriate technical environment to facilitate storage and sharing of information. In fact, Holsapple argues that a modern knowledge management cannot be separated from computer-based and information

Building Sustainability Knowledge Management Systems

IB SUSTAINABILITY PRACTICES

Experts suggest that knowledge management systems have an important role to play as drivers of sustainability in organizations. Consider that companies such as Volvo, SC Johnson and Sony have all implemented knowledge management systems built around sustainability. Software companies such as Five Winds are working closely with major manufacturers to develop ways to help these multinationals be more environmentally sensitive.

How can knowledge management systems contribute to sustainability? By building knowledge management systems around sustainability and considering all aspects of the life cycle, a company can become more aware of the impact of the various life cycles on the environment. Consider, for example, that when Patagonia decided to use only organic cotton to minimize the environmental impact of its raw materials, it built systems to link closer to growers to show the impact of their actions. A properly designed knowledge management system can also pinpoint to a company where it is lagging in sustainability. However, for multinationals, sustainability knowledge management systems can become critical repositories of information that global managers can access when making decisions.

Source: Based on www.ekosi.com

technology and any knowledge management system needs the appropriate technology to collect, store, and access critical knowledge as needed while also disseminating such information to those who need it.[27] For instance, consider how IBM's intranet portal including global messaging, local information, employee and other human resource-related information has helped IBM become more global and integrated.[28] The portal has provided an environment where IBM employees can chat, collaborate, and contribute knowledge while also allowing them to communicate with critical external groups such as suppliers and other partners. As you will read later in Chapter 15 on e-commerce, a multinational has access to many information technology tools that can help enhance a knowledge management system. Such tools can also be used to enhance a company's sustainability efforts. Consider the IB Sustainability Practices opposite.

Beyond an effective IT system, a properly designed knowledge management system cannot function without the human element. Employees must not only be willing and motivated to contribute and share information, but must also be willing to seek information when needed. As such, it is critical for a multinational to first identify and eliminate human barriers. Riege discusses the many human barriers, such as lack of time to share knowledge, fear of sharing information, differences in experience level, lack of understanding of the critical nature of sharing information, etc.[29] By identifying and eliminating such barriers, a multinational can start building an effective knowledge management

Building a Knowledge Management System at Siemens

IB STRATEGIC INSIGHT

Siemens, the German-based multinational, is one of the largest companies with respect to many information and communication products and services in a large number of industries such as transportation, energy and healthcare. It has more than 417,000 employees based in more than 190 countries. To take full advantage of its vast capabilities in global knowledge, it launched the Siemens ShareNet knowledge management system to connect over 17,000 of its sales and marketing employees around the world.

Siemens' ShareNet is composed of a web-based knowledge library where employees can contribute their experiences from present and past projects based on predefined categories. The system also includes an urgent request forum, where employees can post urgent questions and other users can provide answers to such questions. Finally, the system also includes a forum where knowledge can be shared. Although some knowledge can easily be communicated to others, other forms of

knowledge can be of a tacit nature and Siemens' system has in-built processes to ensure that such tacit knowledge can be communicated to others.

To motivate employees to use its knowledge management system, Siemens developed an incentive system similar to the frequent flyer programs used by airlines to award free flights. Employees were given shares for contributing knowledge to the library, for reusing previously posted knowledge and for responding to urgent requests. Employees could then redeem these "miles" for many gifts and prizes including books, cell phones, computers, etc. This incentive system boosted use tremendously and urgent requests were being answered at a rate of 80 to 90 percent.

Source: Based on Sven C. Voelpel and Zheng Han, 2005, "Managing knowledge sharing in China: The case of Siemens ShareNet," *Journal of Knowledge Management*, 9(3), pp. 51–63.

system. To eliminate such barriers, it is important for any multinational to show the value created by knowledge management systems. Success stories and importance of the knowledge management system should be constantly communicated to the employees.[30]

In addition to removal of potential barriers, employees must also be motivated to participate in a knowledge management system. Employees should not only be made aware of the importance of knowledge management systems but should also be given appropriate incentives and rewards to participate in such networks. Case studies of successful knowledge systems show that identification and support of knowledge "activists" is a key success factor.[31] Such activists will take the initiative of convincing others of the importance of knowledge management systems while also ensuring that the process flows smoothly. Such actions are more likely to motivate others to fully contribute to the new knowledge management system. To give you further understanding of the process, consider the IB Strategic Insight on the previous page.

As the IB Strategic Insight shows, building an effective knowledge management system is very complex and time consuming. Furthermore, many knowledge management systems can also suffer from the same challenges facing global and virtual teams, such as cultural and background differences, language barriers, etc. Any multinational must also be willing to address such challenges. However, if done properly, a knowledge management system can be an extremely important survival tool in today's global environment.

CHAPTER REVIEW

In this chapter, you read about important multinational issues as they relate to organization design and coordination. As the competitive environment gets more complicated for multinationals and as they are pressured to become more innovative while at the same time integrating global and local expertise, organization design and coordination issues will become even more crucial in the future. As the IB Strategic Insights showed, many multinationals are changing their structure or making more effective use of coordination mechanisms to better face the competition.

In the first section, you learned about the many important functions that organizational design plays. Additionally, you read about the various design structures available to multinationals. These include traditional structures such as the export department, international division, worldwide geographic and product structures. However, you also read about mixtures of the more traditional structures including the matrix and transnational structures. You also learned about the appropriateness of each structure based on the multinational's strategy.

While organizational structures show how the multinational can separate subunits, there is also a strong need to coordinate these subunits. The second section of the chapter discussed the many options available to multinationals, including the hierarchy of authority, direct contact, liaison roles and task forces. Because teams are becoming so widely used, you also read about the many challenges facing multinationals as they use both global and virtual teams. Finally, you learned about some of the things multinationals can do to tackle such challenges.

In the final section of this chapter, you read about knowledge management. Because most multinationals are now under pressure to properly manage their information and knowledge to face the hypercompetitive world, you learned about the key roles played by a properly designed knowledge management system. You read about the key aspects of a knowledge management system. Finally, you also learned about the best way to properly design the many aspects of a knowledge management system.

DISCUSSION QUESTIONS

1. What is organizational design? Why is organizational design so important to any multinational?
2. What is an export department? How is an export department different from an international division?
3. Discuss the worldwide geographic structure. When is a worldwide geographic structure appropriate? What are some of the most important drawbacks of a worldwide geographic structure?
4. Compare and contrast a worldwide geographic structure with a worldwide product structure. When is a worldwide product structure more appropriate than a worldwide geographic structure?
5. What is a matrix structure? What are some of the benefits of using a matrix structure? What are some of the drawbacks?
6. What is a transnational structure? When is a transnational structure appropriate?
7. Discuss four coordination mechanisms.
8. What are global teams? What are some of the challenges of using global teams? What can multinationals do to prepare their employees for global teams?
9. What is knowledge management? Discuss some of the most important aspects of a knowledge management system.

INTERNATIONAL BUSINESS SKILL BUILDER

Building a Knowledge Management System

Step 1: A local company, exporting cheese and other dairy products to many locations around the world, has approached you to create a knowledge management system. Advise them on the important aspects of the knowledge management system.

Step 2: Discuss some of the knowledge you believe the company should be collecting.

Step 3: Advise the company on how the collected information can be used to enter new markets or to stay competitive.

Step 4: Advise the company on some ways to motivate employees to contribute knowledge and information to the system.

CHAPTER INTERNET ACTIVITY

Identify four well-known multinationals. Go to their websites and find information about the organizational structure they use. Discuss why such structures are appropriate for these multinationals' strategies.

KEY CONCEPTS

coordination mechanisms	knowledge management
direct contact	liaison roles
export department	matrix structure
full-time integrating roles	organizational design
functional structure	product structure
geographic structure	task forces
global virtual teams	teams
hierarchy of authority	transnational network structure
integrating departments	worldwide geographic structure
international division	worldwide product structure

AIRBUS

TROUBLE GETTING THE A380 OFF THE GROUND

CASE 13

page 1

With great fanfare, the European consortium Airbus announced its plans for building the world's largest passenger aircraft in 1995. With a possible passenger capacity of over 800, but fitted for 525 passengers in different compartments, the A380 was seen as a strong competitor to its American rival Boeing in long-haul passenger travel aircraft. By 2008, very few A380s had actually been produced, and management turnover and allegations of executive insider trading were making newspaper headlines.

Airbus SAS is the aircraft manufacturing division of European Aeronautics Defence and Space Company (EADS). Airbus was formed by the merger of Airbus France, Airbus Deutschland (Germany), and Airbus España (Spain) into a single European entity. Approximately 50 percent of EADS is owned by Daimler of Germany, Sogeade of France, SEPI of Spain, and the remaining ownership is publicly held. Airbus has over 1,500 suppliers in over 30 countries around the world. Because of its Franco-German structure, EADS has two CEOs and two chairmen. The complex organizational structure of Airbus has been described by Richard Aboulafia, aerospace analyst with the Teal Group, as "not the way normal companies are run," and has been seen by some as the source of the production problems with the A380.

The A380 aircraft contains approximately 330 miles of electrical wiring and over 40,000 connectors. Production is divided among different European countries for economic and political reasons. The production delays associated with the A380 were blamed mainly on compatibility problems between its factories in Germany and France. Communication problems between the engineers in France and the plant in Germany led to electrical components not linking up during final assembly. When one group changed design, it did not always tell its counterpart in the other country of those changes. Cultural and language differences may also have contributed to production delays.

Boeing is not immune to production problems itself. While orders for Boeing's new aircraft, the 787 Dreamliner, are impressive, Boeing has fallen behind in production, and was hit by a labor strike in 2008. With over 70 percent of the Dreamliner work outsourced, trouble with contractors produced delays and quality concerns. Both firms have increasing cost pressures and seek to reduce those through outsourcing. Airbus has been especially challenged by the rising value of the euro and has been seeking to outsource more production out of the Eurozone.

. . .

CASE 13

page 2

Airbus has developed an organizational design based on what it calls "Centers of Excellence," or CoEs. Airbus is composed of three parts: operation, programs, and core functions. Within each of these operations are key CoEs. For example, in the operations component there are five CoEs based on wiring and pylon, fuselage and cabin, aft fuselage, empennage, and aerostructures.

With its production problems, in 2007 Airbus reorganized itself, paying particular attention to the transnational integration of the CoEs. Airbus is also seeking to simplify and flatten its organizational structure as it attempts to get more of its flagship product out the production door.

CASE DISCUSSION POINTS

1. Do you think the organizational structure of Airbus is appropriate given its complex and transnational ownership? Explain.
2. What type of organizational design is most appropriate for EADS?
3. Visit the website of Airbus (www.airbus.com) and investigate its Centers of Excellence. Do you think this organizational structure provides a competitive advantage for Airbus? Explain.

Sources: www.airbus.com; "New team pledges to tackle Airbus problems," 2006, www.msnbc.com, July 3; R. Wall, P. Sparaco, A. Nativi, and D. Barrie, 2006, "Tail spin," *Aviation Week*, July; K. Parker, 2006, "Airbus saga the latest on complexity and communications," *Manufacturing Business Technology*, August; K. Done, 2006, "Airbus axes superjumbo chief," *Financial Times*, September 5; J. Ashworth, 2008, "A turbulent year for Airbus and Boeing in race to deliver," *The Business*, January 5; C. Matlack, 2008, "What Airbus learned from the Dreamliner," *BusinessWeek*, April 17; *The Economist*, 2008, "Gathering clouds," June 19; C. Brothers, 2008, "Airbus making headway as Boeing sits idle," *International Herald Tribune*, September 24.

Case prepared by Charles A. Rarick

14 International Human Resource Management

After reading this chapter you should be able to:

- Understand what international human resource management is.

- Know the basic human resource management functions, such as recruitment, selection, training and development, performance appraisal and compensation, and how they apply to international workers.

- Appreciate the various labor and union relations around the world.

- Understand expatriates and how international human resource management applies to expatriates.

- Understand the growth of women expatriates in the future.

The Preview IB Strategic Insight portrays the environment facing any company with international operations. As the MNC hires workers in the different countries in which it operates, it faces significant challenges regarding human resource management practices. However, the human resource management function is an extremely critical aspect of a multinational's ability to successfully implement its strategy. Properly designed human resource management systems provide the company with the critical human resources to enable the company to create the necessary ability to compete successfully.

Why is cross-cultural human resource management so challenging? Countries have widely different human resources environments because of cultural and social institutional differences. To succeed in their operations, MNCs need to be able to understand these differences and the way they affect the human resource management practice. However, beyond differences, the international workforce environment is rapidly changing. Many multinationals are finding that it is difficult to attract and retain talented individuals. Whether a multinational is hiring a middle manager in China or an assembly-line worker in Central Europe or a software engineer in India, many companies are facing significant difficulties in finding such workers.[1] Even if they can hire such individuals, they find it very difficult to keep these workers for a long time. Human resource management is thus becoming an increasingly important aspect of a multinational's ability to succeed, and this chapter will inform you of the key issues for MNCs as they face these human resource management challenges.

Global Human Resource Management and Technology

Global companies are increasingly relying on technology to develop uniform human resources management policy around the world. Having consistent human resource management policies can be beneficial, allowing companies to save on the costs of having multiple licenses of different softwares in different countries. Furthermore, similar human resource policies also allow a company to enforce similar standards around the world, thus making it easier to respect global regulations.

Consider, for instance, the case of Travelport, which is part of the Cendant conglomerate and which also includes Orbitz. Travelport has been implementing an Oracle-based human resource software to harmonize its human resource policies in the 25 countries in which it operates. IBM has also created software that can provide information on the skills, availability and costs of its 90,000 employees around the world.

However, implementing such technology is not without challenge. Many MNCs are struggling to develop systems that can meet country-specific legal and cultural requirements. Consider, for instance, that some recruitment software may not be able to handle names where the format is typically the first name followed by the last name. In some non-Western countries, last names tend to be mentioned first. Similarly, consider that compensation packages may vary widely around the world. While operations in South Africa may include a car allowance as part of the compensation package, workers in Europe may only get an employee loan as part of a similar compensation package. Such widely different practices and policies make it very difficult to maintain a coherent worldwide system.

Source: Based on Workforce Frauheim (ed.), 2006, "Bumps in the road to going global," *Workforce Management*, October 9, p. 29.

This chapter contains several major sections. In the first section, we define international human resource management. You are then exposed to the many human resource management functions, namely recruitment, selection, training and development, compensation, and performance appraisal. These various human resource functions are discussed in the context of MNCs hiring workers in foreign locales. Labor relations and trade unions are also discussed as an important aspect of international human resource management.

In a subsequent section, you are exposed to issues pertaining to expatriates. Most MNCs approach human resource management for expatriates differently compared to domestic workers. In this section, you will be presented with the unique human resource management challenges facing multinationals as they hire expatriates.

After reading this chapter you should understand some of the key issues of human resource management as they are applied internationally. You should be able to understand the important human resource management functions and how they apply to workers for multinationals with foreign operations. You should also be able to appreciate the unique challenges facing companies when they hire expatriates. Finally, you should understand the future of expatriates in terms of growth of numbers of female expatriates.

International Human Resource Management: The International Setting

An MNC cannot function without people or the human assets. From a strategy perspective, human resources are extremely critical as they provide the multinational with the necessary skills and capabilities to outsmart rivals. Managing and developing the human assets are thus the major goals of human resource management. Human resource management (HRM) deals with the entire relationship of the employee with the organization. When applied to the international setting, the HRM functions become **international human resource management (IHRM)**. Consider the IB Strategic Insight opposite.

As the IB Strategic Insight shows, when a company enters the international arena, the human resource management function takes on added complexity. IBM faces significant challenges as it tries to implement human resource management systems to function effectively as a global organization. As you will see later in this chapter, many of the crucial human resource functions are dependent on the cultural and institutional context. It therefore becomes necessary for multinational managers to decide if or how to adapt the company's HRM policies to the national cultures, business cultures, and social institutions where the company is doing business. In the next few sections, we examine the basic HRM functions, including recruitment and selection, training and development, performance appraisal, compensation, and labor relations.

Recruitment and Selection

Recruitment refers to the process of identifying and attracting qualified people to apply for vacant positions in an organization. The recruitment stage usually begins with a company's assessment of its needs in terms of human resources. The company then decides how it will make potential applicants aware of the

international human resource management (IHRM)
application of the various human resource management functions in an international setting

recruitment
refers to the process of identifying and attracting qualified people to apply for vacant positions in an organization

IBM's Global Workforce

IBM has gradually shifted its human resource management focus over the past decade to become a truly global organization. While its subsidiaries used to behave like mini IBM replicas in the past, such an approach created unnecessary duplication and high costs. IBM is now striving to gradually integrate all of its operations through the human resource management function to provide customers with the best service at the optimum cost.

What international human resource management issues does IBM face as it globalizes? With over 375,000 employees across six continents, IBM has been facing significant challenges as it implements a global system. Exhibit 14.1 shows the countries with the largest number of employees.

To become a smooth-running global machine, IBM's chief executive Samuel Palmisano suggests that the major issues IBM face are issues such as "Where do you put IBM employees?" "How do you keep these employees from leaving?" "How can these employees be trained?"

and "How do you move the work to the employees or move the employees to the work?"

To address these issues, IBM has used its expertise in software to develop an elaborate database to track and update all of its workers. For instance, it can now easily assemble a team for projects located around the world. The new database allows IBM to quickly search for employees with relevant skills for the project. This database has also allowed it the ability to develop sophisticated forecasting models to determine its human resource needs within the next six months. IBM has also developed a social networking site similar to Facebook to allow employees to learn about events and to post comments about company events or their private lives. These programs are all contributing to making IBM a truly global organization.

Source: Based on Steve Hamm, 2008, "International isn't just IBM's first name," *BusinessWeek*, January 28, pp. 36–40.

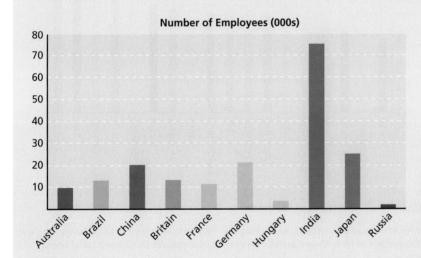

Exhibit 14.1
IBM's Employees Worldwide

Source: Based on Steve Hamm, 2008, "International isn't just IBM's first name," *BusinessWeek*, January 28, pp. 36–40.

job vacancies. There are wide variations in preference for recruitment around the world. To appreciate these differences, you are first exposed to recruitment in the US.

For all types of positions, US companies use a variety of methods to recruit. These include among others, applications and advertisements placed in newspapers or on the Internet, internal job postings where companies post a list of vacancies on their websites or internally, use of private or public agencies and use of recommendations from current employees.

Research shows that US managers see newspaper advertising as one of the most effective recruitment channels, while university recruitment was judged among the most effective only for professional and technical jobs.[2] In contrast, other forms such as employee referral and use of personal contacts for recruitment purposes are not seen as very effective. Such methods can potentially run into legal issues and may not necessarily fulfill the typical US company's goal of finding the best person for the job. For instance, personal contacts can result in potential biases against certain groups, such as women and minorities.

In contrast, other parts of the world don't always prefer open forms of recruitment such as open advertisement in newspapers. Consider, for instance, that for many of the collectivist societies such as Japan, South Korea and Taiwan, referrals from friends or family tend to be much more important. In South Korea, many blue-collar jobs are filled through referrals from friends and family. Such practices are not surprising as collectivist societies place emphasis on harmony and loyalty. By only recruiting from friends and family or other important social groups (e.g. high schools, universities, clubs), an MNC can maximize the chances of finding someone who can fit the organization's culture. Furthermore, friends and family referrals suggest that these individuals can vouch for the potential employees' work ethic and ability to fit.

To get additional insights on recruitment practices around the world, consider Exhibit 14.2.

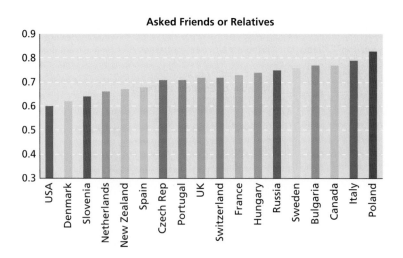

Asked Friends or Relatives

Exhibit 14.2 **Recruitment Methods**

Source: Based on International Social Survey Program, 1999/2000, International Social Survey Program: Work Orientations II, 1997, Ann Arbor: Inter-university Consortium for Political and Social Science Research.

For the Exhibit, data collected through the International Social Survey Program was analyzed.[3] Respondents who were looking for jobs were asked whether they asked their friends or relatives for jobs. As the Exhibit shows, countries such as the US, Denmark and New Zealand tend to have more open recruitment and do not show preference for such methods. In contrast, many former socialist countries such as Poland, Bulgaria and Russia show high scores, as the former communist system emphasized personal relationships and more closed forms of recruitment. People were more likely to get jobs based on contacts rather than openly competing for such jobs.

After an MNC has developed a list of potential candidates for a job, it has to select a person for the job. The process by which a company chooses a person to fill a vacant position is known as **selection.** Similar to recruitment, selection criteria vary widely around the world. Let's first look at selection in the context of US companies.

selection
the process by which a company chooses people to fill a vacant position

In the US, the aim of selection practices is to gather credible information on a candidate's job qualifications. Previous work experience, performance on tests, and perceptions of qualifications from interviews help inform human resource managers about the applicant's qualifications. The US individualistic culture promotes a focus on individual achievements (e.g. education, natural ability, experience) and not on group affiliations such as the family. The ideal selection then results in a match between the specific skills of the job applicant with the specific job requirements.

Similar to recruitment, selection is also affected by cultural practices. One of the most critical differences pertains to more collectivist countries. As Hofstede (1991) notes,

> the hiring process in a collectivist society always takes the in-group into account. Usually preference is given to hiring relatives, first of the employer, but also of other persons already employed by the company. Hiring persons from a family one already knows reduces risks. Also relatives will be concerned about the reputation of the family and help correct misbehavior of a family member.[4]

In selecting employees, collectivist cultural norms value trustworthiness, reliability, and loyalty over performance-related background characteristics. Personal traits such as loyalty to the company, loyalty to the boss, and trustworthiness are the traits that family members can provide. As such, in smaller companies, preference is given to family members.

However, larger and technically oriented companies may need professional managers and technicians with skills not available within the family. In these cases, the selection process still prioritizes personal characteristics over technical characteristics. If one cannot have a family member, then the priority is to find employees who have the personality characteristics and background necessary to fit into the corporate culture. Consider the IB Strategic Insight overleaf, on the Ritz-Carlton's recruitment and selection process for its hotel in Shanghai.

What can a multinational do to ensure smooth recruitment and selection on a worldwide basis? At a basic level, an MNC needs to understand and adapt to local practices. Thus, for example, foreign multinationals in the United States probably have most success using the typical US recruitment practices—advertising in newspapers and going to college campuses. In other countries, the multinational manager will also need to discover and use local recruitment and selection practices. However, adaptation to local recruitment and selection practices is difficult. In societies where backdoor or personal contacts are acceptable recruitment strategies, foreign multinationals may not have access to the appropriate recruitment channels. Furthermore, such recruitment methods may violate ethical codes that require competitive access to all open jobs. However, when a company does not follow local norms in recruitment and selection, it

Recruitment and Selection at Ritz-Carlton

Ritz-Carlton currently operates 59 hotels around the world. Hotels are located in countries in the Americas, Europe, Asia and Africa. However, their operation in Shanghai, China, has attracted significant attention. While some companies struggle to attract good employees, the Shanghai Ritz-Carlton has been very successful in finding good employees and has enjoyed strong financial health. It has been voted "Best Employer in Asia" for three consecutive years and has also been selected as the "Best Hotel in China." The employee satisfaction rate has been among the highest in all of its locations around the world. How does it achieve such success? A big component is careful recruitment and selection practices consistent with cultural demands.

To get the right people, Ritz-Carlton Shanghai spends significant time on the recruitment and selection process. Candidates are carefully chosen based on their personal values. Such practices are important in collectivist societies where employers expect their employees' own values to be closer to the company values. Furthermore, employees are not selected solely on technical qualifications. Most are selected on the basis of their ability to work with others, including both other employees and customers. Such

ability to enjoy contact with others is extremely critical in the hotel industry.

Another reflection of collectivist values is the group interviews. While many companies do not necessarily involve all levels of management in the selection process, Ritz-Carlton ensures that different levels have a chance to interview prospective candidates. This ensures that everyone has the opportunity to find out about potential new employees and the degree of fit with the company's values. Furthermore, even the general manager is involved in the process, demonstrating the group orientation of companies in more collectivist societies.

While all of the practices may not necessarily be true of collectivist societies, the example shows that Ritz-Carlton has nevertheless worked hard to adapt recruitment and selection to the Chinese context. This has greatly helped it have a very satisfied workforce. This satisfaction ensures that workers offer better customer service.

Source: Based on Arthur Yeung, 2006, "Setting people up for success: How the Portman Ritz-Carlton hotel gets the best from its people," *Human Resource Management*, 45(2), pp. 267–75.

may offend local cultural norms or break host country laws. Thus, multinational managers must always assess the trade-off between following home practices that get what they believe are the "right" people for the job against the costs and benefits of following local traditions.

In addition to following local rules and norms, recent trends also suggest that some MNCs may be outsourcing the recruitment and selection process.[5] For instance, the BBC now outsources most of its recruitment, relocation, and compensation functions. Capita is the global provider of such services. The BBC expects to save around £50 million from this outsourcing. While outsourcing can be advantageous, MNCs are strongly advised to carefully consider providers on many aspects such as flexibility, ability to set goals, and having the right chemistry. Exclusive focus on costs or short-term gains can only be disastrous in the long run.

After the MNC has selected individuals for the job, it needs to train these employees. In the next section, we look at training and development.

Training and Development

Training and development refer to the efforts of the MNC to provide education and other programs to better equip its employees to do their job. Such training at work may involve formal training, informal training, learning embedded in the workplace and other forms of learning.[6] With globalization, many countries are seeing an increased emphasis on training as their people are required to learn more than ever before to adapt to the new work environment. However, many multinationals are finding that appropriate training and development can be an asset as they try to retain workers. Furthermore, the ability to identify and train leadership talent is also becoming critical as multinationals face a shortage of talented executives.

Similar to the other human resource management functions you read about, training and development also vary by country. You will first be exposed to the training and development programs in the US. US companies with over 100 employees invest more than $60 billion in training costs per year.[7] The most popular training topics are management development and computer skills, while other training, such as that needed for new methods and procedures, may reach more people on all levels of the organization. Furthermore, a recent analysis of trends between 1970 and 2000 suggests that more women have been receiving training than men in the US.[8] The study also found that more educated employees in the US were more likely to receive some form of training.

How is training different around the world? A recent study provides some insights on the matter.[9] The authors categorize countries on the types of institutional environments based somewhat on the institutions we discussed in Chapter 8. They argue that the emphasis on training is dependent on the institutional environment. In some environments such as those found in Italy or Germany or Japan, companies in these countries have a difficult time hiring or firing workers. Consequently, they have no choice but to focus on cultivating the existing workforce. As such, companies in these countries see a heavy emphasis on training of the employees.

However, in countries such as the UK and the USA, there is emphasis on the short term and on efficiency. There is adversarial competition with employees and a focus on an efficient external labor market. It is therefore not surprising to see that such countries place relatively low emphasis on training and development. Finally, in other countries found in Central and Eastern Europe, there is a focus on the need to control costs. Such costs control is often achieved by reducing the number of employees in companies that frequently had too many employees. These countries also don't place much emphasis on training.

The above clearly shows that there are wide variations in terms of the importance of training around the world. However, the nature of training can also be different. For instance, consider the dual system, which is probably the most important component of vocational training in Germany. The dual system combines in-house apprenticeship training with part-time vocational-school training leading to a skilled-worker certificate. This training can be followed by the *Fachschule*, a college giving advanced vocational training. The training and certificate qualifications are standardized throughout the country. This produces a well-trained national labor force with skills that are not company-specific.

What are the implications for MNCs? The extent of training will depend on what the MNC expects of its workers. If employers want to keep local

training and development refer to the efforts of the MNC to provide education and other programs to better equip their employees to do their job

workers out of headquarters' managerial ranks, there is more emphasis on respecting local training norms. However, if the MNC wants to source local talent for its worldwide operations, training practices should follow the corporate culture. The extent of localization of the training practices also depends on the nature of the industry. For instance, take the case of Linklaters, a law firm that operates in 30 countries. Linklaters has found that dividing the training into a legal aspect and "everything else" works well.[10] Selling legal services means that employees must be very knowledgeable about the law. However, other skills such as leadership and presentation skills can be provided through separate training. Linklaters has found that it needs to abide by cultural differences to ensure effective training. For instance, consider that it had to make training compulsory for its Japanese lawyers. In a society where leaving one's desk is not considered usual, the Japanese lawyers had to be convinced by their bosses that it was appropriate to leave their desks to undergo the training program. Making the training program compulsory is one way that the company can ensure that the Japanese lawyers won't feel guilty leaving their desks.

A large number of companies realize the importance of training in many of the emerging countries around the world. Consider the IB Strategic Insight below.

It should also be noted that the training elements will depend on who is being trained. For instance, in the case of expatriates and other managerial-level workers, important culture training may need to be offered. Such issues are discussed in depth in Chapter 7 on culture. Furthermore, for a multinational to

Training in China and India

IB STRATEGIC INSIGHT

Multinationals operating in China and India have slowly realized that training is an essential component of their ability to do well in these exploding economies. Why is training so important? Training is important to impart the necessary skills to develop the employees. However, many multinationals are finding that training is crucial if they want to be able to attract and retain talent. Consider that the demand for top talent in China is extremely high. It is not surprising for employees to receive phone calls from new employers with offers of double and even triple their current salary. However, companies in China also find that Chinese employees do not always place emphasis on compensation packages. Chinese nationals place very high value on training opportunities and those multinationals that provide such training to their employees are more likely to retain the talent.

John Deere has adapted its training programs to fit the Indian cultural reality. Because of the extreme competition for talent and the high turnover, John Deere needed to quickly train its Indian workers to learn the technologies used at John Deere while also training these employees to function in virtual teams with US employees. It has developed a ten-day rigorous program that provides technical, cultural and team-building training. Furthermore, by having a clear and effective learning path in place, John Deere ensures that it can retain these new hires.

Source: Based on D. Breitenstein, 2005, "Developing skills for success in an MNC," *China Staff*, 11(10), pp. 10–11; R. Davenport, 2006, "John Deere workforce," *T+D*, April, 60(4), pp. 40–3.

deploy a training program successfully, it needs to make sure that the training is consistent with local workplace customs and traditions. Consider Grace and Co.'s cultural gaffe when it was training employees in China. The Maryland-based specialty chemicals company had developed an "Eraser Man" concept to train its employees worldwide. The "Eraser Man" was used to emphasize the need to eradicate or "erase" costs.[11] However, Grace's trainers were surprised to see the Chinese trainees perplexed and even frustrated. After further investigation, they found that erasers in Chinese connote "invisible" rather than "erase." The Chinese trainees were not impressed with what was perceived as an "invisible" program. Furthermore, Grace's "Eraser Man" was pink and the Chinese did not want to be associated with what is perceived to be a feminine color. Grace and Co. had to adapt its training program to fit Chinese's local customs. Multinationals should generally strive to make such adjustments.

After the company has trained its employees, it also needs to assess its employees' performance. We discuss performance appraisal next.

Performance Appraisal

The process by which companies appraise their employees is known as **performance appraisal**. All companies must assess their employees' performance to identify people to reward, promote, demote, develop and improve, retain, or fire. Not everyone can move up the ladder of the organizational pyramid and the performance appraisal function serves as an important assessment tool.

performance appraisal
the process by which companies appraise their employees

The US performance appraisal system is highly rational, logical, and legally oriented. It represents cultural values that include individual rights, duties, and rewards, and respect of the legal system, thereby promoting equal opportunity. Ideally, US appraisal systems provide management with objective, honest, and fair data on employee performance. Consequently, human resource decisions, such as pay or promotion, can be based on these performance appraisal data. Although issues regarding seniority, experience, and security are not ignored, the US ideal is a meritocracy, where good performers get more rewards.

Similar to the other human resource management functions, performance appraisal is also dependent on the culture. One of the dimensions that seems to impact performance appraisal is the collectivist cultural dimension. Recall that in collectivist societies, the group takes precedence over individuals and harmonious relationships are emphasized. As such, in more collectivistic cultures, both employer and employee accept as correct and fair that human resource decisions should take into account personal background characteristics more than achievement. In such cases, the usefulness of a US-style performance appraisal system is less clear because who you are and how old you are may count more than how you perform. Furthermore, according to Hofstede, managers in collectivist societies often avoid direct performance appraisal feedback.[12] An open discussion of performance may clash with the society's norm of harmony, which takes precedence over other values. For example, during the first eight to ten years of their careers, Japanese managers may never encounter the appraisal system. All beginning managers get the same salary and promotions, based on age and seniority.

In other collectivist societies such as South Korea, there is preference for seniority-based promotions, rather than appraisal-based promotion.[13] This follows from the Confucian tradition that strives to preserve harmony (since it is unseemly for younger employees to supervise older ones). While job performance is important and most companies do have appraisal systems, seniority is most important for advancement. Because of the long-term orientation of Korean culture, Korean performance appraisal systems focus on sincerity, loyalty, and attitude on an equal footing with job performance.

As you can see, international performance appraisals can be very complex. Consider also that while the major objective of performance appraisal is to provide feedback, some societies may not engage in such practices. In many Asian countries, such as China and Japan, feedback is generally not given to save face.[14] Furthermore, to preserve harmony, appraisals may be done through group meetings rather than the more typical individual appraisals in individualistic societies.

As you saw with recruitment and selection, an MNC must often match its performance appraisal system to fit the local culture. Failure to do so may result in unnecessary conflict with local workers. Next, let's consider compensation.

Compensation

compensation

efforts of the multinational to distribute wages and salaries, incentives such as bonuses, and benefits such as retirement contributions

Compensation includes the efforts of the multinational to distribute wages and salaries, incentives such as bonuses, and benefits such as retirement contributions. Compensation is also a critical aspect of what human resource management policies companies use to motivate their employees. There are wide variations both among countries and among organizations within countries concerning how to compensate workers. Some differences stem from whether compensation should be based on achievement or performance. Other important differences include whether everyone in a team should be paid the same or whether compensation should be made based on individual performance. Below we consider the US compensation practices and consider compensation around the world.

The highly mobile US labor market requires that US companies design compensation systems that focus on external equity (i.e. Do we pay at or above market level?). The individualistic US culture views careers as private and personal, and mobility, advancement, and higher wages often require leaving a company. As such, most US companies develop formal and systematic policies to determine wages and salaries taking into consideration external and internal factors. External factors include local and national wage rates, government legislation, and collective bargaining. Internal factors include the importance of the job to the organization, the affluence of the organization or its ability to pay, and the employee's relative worth to the business (merit).

Most US companies also develop procedures to establish that people receive equitable pay for the types of jobs they perform. A variety of methods help establish a grading of jobs based on the worth to the company. Issues such as responsibility, skill requirements, and the importance of the job's tasks to the organization contribute to the worth of a particular job. Those who occupy the higher-ranked jobs are paid higher. Furthermore, although the worth of a job to the company largely determines the base pay assigned to a certain position, raises in pay are determined mostly by merit.

Compensation practices clearly vary around the world. Previous studies report that the cultural dimensions reported in the earlier chapter on culture can help MNCs design appropriate compensation systems. For instance, recall that uncertainty avoidance refers to the level of tolerance individuals living in a society have for uncertainty. It is therefore sensible to minimize uncertainty in high uncertainty avoidance countries by minimizing variable pay. As such, Latin American and Germanic countries (i.e. Austria, Germany) are more likely to favor fixed pay plans because multinationals want to minimize uncertainty.[15] However, despite the relatively low levels of uncertainty avoidance in the US, a recent survey of accountants' compensation shows that the US had the lowest level of variable pay where performance is linked to higher compensation. As you can see from Exhibit 14.3, many emerging markets are more likely to use variable pay. It is possible that such countries tend to rely on variable pay to motivate their employees to achieve their best.

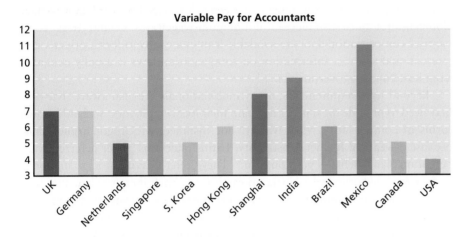

Variable Pay for Accountants

Exhibit 14.3 **Variable Pay Use Worldwide**

Source: Based on Towers Perrin, www.towersperrin.com

Another important cultural dimension that impacts compensation is the individualism–collectivism cultural dimension. Recall in the chapter on culture that in individualistic societies like the US, individuals are only loosely connected to each other. In contrast, in highly collectivistic societies, people tend to be more tightly connected to each other and there is focus on harmony. Given the above, it is advisable for multinationals to apply equity principles (compensate according to performance) in more individualistic societies. In contrast, equality or parity principles (compensate everyone equally) seem to be more sensible for collectivistic countries. In such countries, there is more emphasis on harmony and cohesion, and compensating all employees equally minimizes the risk of conflict.

Few studies have considered compensation practices around the world. The Best International Human Resource Management Practices Project represents one of the most extensive cross-national studies of compensation practices to date.[16] The researchers investigated cross-national variations in compensation practices in ten countries (Australia, Canada, China, Indonesia, Japan, Korea, Latin America, Mexico, Taiwan, and USA). Respondents were asked a number of questions pertaining to these compensation practices, both in terms of their assessment of the current state of practice and also the extent to which they felt that these practices should be used in the future.

The study showed, for instance, that pay incentives tend to be used relatively modestly in the selected countries. Only China, Japan and Taiwan had scores above the mean. Furthermore, only one country, South Korea, showed that pay incentives are a significant amount of pay. In most other societies, incentives are not as widely used. However, the results also showed some convergence. For instance, the results showed that all countries felt that benefits were an important aspect of any compensation package. Furthermore, all countries felt that compensation should be based more on job performance and other organizational outcomes than on seniority.

Given the above, how should a company approach compensation? An MNC with locations in several nations may need several different compensation systems, especially for host country nationals. For each host country, worker compensation levels must match wage levels in the local labor market. Compensation must also meet local minimum-wage rates. Country-level comparative compensation data are available from many government, private, and international sources. Information on compensation laws is usually available from host country governments.

Beyond legal requirements, many multinationals are also aware that they may need to provide local perks to retain their local employees. Such additional forms of compensation vary widely. For instance, McGregor argues that, because of years of financial instability, Latin Americans prefer deferred compensation plans such as a pension plan.[17] They prefer to avoid stocks and bonds as these have historically had little value with crashes. It therefore becomes very important for the multinational to carefully assess the local situation to provide perks that are deemed attractive. Global human resource consulting companies such as Hewitt Associates (www.hewittassociates.com) or Mercer (www.mercer.com) provide insights into locally relevant perks. To give you further insights into perks worldwide, Exhibit 14.4 provides information on local perks in ten different countries. The Exhibit also shows the expected salary for the head of sales and marketing and the number of days off most employees expect.

As seen in Exhibit 14.4, there are wide variations in terms of compensation and perks. The multinationals need to be aware of such differences and adapt their policies to conform with local requirements. However, although compensation practices vary widely, recent trends also suggest that the large MNCs are moving towards one compensation system for all of their subsidiaries. For instance, a recent survey of 275 companies worldwide showed that 56 percent of these companies were planning a more centralized compensation structure.[18]

Next, we consider labor relations.

Labor Relations

labor relations
provide an indication of the relationship between companies and their employees and the degree to which employees influence the company's operations

MNCs often have to take into consideration the labor relations in the various countries where they operate in order to effectively manage human assets. **Labor relations** provide an indication of the relationship between companies and their employees and the degree to which employees influence the company's operations. There are wide variations in the patterns of labor relations in different nations. These differences in patterns stem from cultural factors as well as historical factors. Historical factors, such as the state of technological development during early unionization and the time when governments recognized the legality

Exhibit 14.4 **Perks in Ten Countries**

Country	Salary (Head of Sales and Marketing, $)	Number of Days Off	Local Perks
India	56,171	31	Pay for health-care costs for parents of employees
China	92,402	23	Make contributions to housing funds to help employees buy a house
France	188,771	40	Offer use of company-owned chalets and beach houses for nominal fee
Hong Kong	149,905	26	Offer Chinese medicine coverage as part of overall health insurance
Mexico	163,591	23	Because of high pollution in Mexico City, companies offer all-expenses-paid "pollution escape trips" to the Pacific or Gulf coasts
Philippines	95,286	19	Offer rice or "rice allowances" that companies can convert into cash
Japan	148,899	35	Offer "family allowances" on top of pay
Brazil	208,691	40	Offer chauffeur-driven bulletproof cars to executives to avoid kidnapping
US	229,300	25	Offer free legal services or free financial planning to top executives
Russia	117,135	39	Offer company-sponsored mortgages to help employees get better credit rates

Source: Based on Jena McGregor, 2008, "The right perks," *BusinessWeek*, January 28, pp. 42–3.

of unions, influence current union structure and activities. Management's views of labor relations also differ from country to country.

In the US, most unions remain at the regional level. Most local unions associate with some craft, industry, or mixed national union. There are approximately 170 national unions in the United States. Local craft unions tend to represent workers in a local region, while local industrial unions tend to represent workers at the level of the plant. Although most collective bargaining takes place at the local level, in some instances, such as in the automobile industry, unions attempt to make company-wide or industry-wide agreements. However, the US has seen declining union membership. As trade globalizes, local unions are slowly losing their power on workers. Furthermore, management has typically had an upper hand on what unions can do.

In Germany, labor unions are more powerful and have an important influence in what companies do. At the company level, industrial democracy in Germany gives many workers equal representation on the board of directors with those elected by the shareholders. In fact, co-determination, or, in German, *Mitbestimmung*, means that management provides workers with a share of the control of the organization reserved traditionally for management and owners in the US. In Germany, co-determination exists at two levels. At the plant level, workers elect the works council. This group has certain prerogatives supported

South Korea

South Korea has had a long history of labor unrest and strikes. For a long time, the South Korean government has accepted that strikes are an acceptable ritual of the South Korean business environment. Workers typically strike during the summer and end up with significant raises. Furthermore, many companies have routinely paid the salary of union leaders and authorities have been reluctant to use police force to break strikes. Labor unions in Korea thus have significant political influence. Recent events show that South Korean workers are willing to continue to strike in order to get higher wages and better working conditions.

However, as trade globalizes and competition increases, South Korean companies are starting to find that they can no longer afford to pay higher wages. Frequent disruptions because of strikes have also taken a toll on companies. Consider the case of Hyundai Motors, which has had some form of labor disturbances every year for the past 12 years. In 2006, Hyundai Motors faced a month-long strike, resulting in work slowdown and losses amounting to $1.3 billion. Similarly, steelmaker Posco had to cave into its workers' demand of higher wages to end a nine-day strike.

For the Korean auto industry, such strikes have resulted in significant decreases in exports and losses.

To face the strong unions, many South Korean companies are slowly setting up operations in countries with lower wages and more favorable labor relations. For instance, Mando, a Korean car-parts company, now has a factory in Alabama. Mando also has operations in India, China and Russia. Both Posco and Hyundai either have planned or are planning major operations in India. Samsung also has many plants in China.

Will such movement to other countries lessen the influence of labor unions in South Korea? Many experts argue that continued strikes and wage increases are putting South Korean multinationals at a disadvantage. These experts believe that such changes are inevitable and necessary as such labor unrest continues to present the South Korean economy with a weak spot.

Source: Based on Choe Sang-Hun, 2006, "2 Hyundai companies deal far differently with labor," *New York Times*, July 27, p. C4; Henry Sender, 2006, "South Korea experiences growing pains as its workers strike for bigger slice of prosperity," *Wall Street Journal*, August 14, p. A2.

by law. Some decisions are shared with management, such as selection criteria. Some management decisions can be vetoed, such as reassignment. Finally, management must consult and inform the works council on other decisions, such as accident protection.

How can labor relations affect a multinational's operations? Consider the above Country/Regional Focus on South Korea.

How can a multinational manager assess the extent of labor influence? A strong factor that indicates the degree of labor influence is the **union membership density**. Union membership density refers to the proportion of workers who belong to unions in a country. Exhibit 14.5 shows the union density in selected countries.

As you can see, union membership levels vary around the world. In some societies, such as Thailand and the USA, union membership levels are relatively low, thereby suggesting minimal influence of labor unions on the multinational's operations. However, many former communist countries in Eastern and Central Europe have strong protection of worker rights. It is therefore not surprising to see high levels of union membership density for countries such as Hungary (shown in Exhibit 14.5) and Poland (38 percent), Slovakia (61.7 percent) and the Russian Federation (74.8 percent).[19] Although these countries have opened

union membership density refers to the proportion of workers who belong to unions in a country

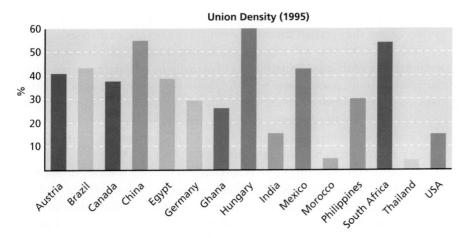

Exhibit 14.5 **Union Density for Selected Countries**

Source: Adapted from International Labor Organization, www.ilo.org.

themselves to foreign investment, labor still has important influences on company operations. Other countries such as Brazil and Mexico also show the significant influence labor has on company operations. It is interesting to note that in many European countries such as Austria (shown in Exhibit 14.5), Belgium (53.8 percent), Denmark (78.1 percent), and Norway (55.4 percent), the union density levels are high.

Despite the high union membership density in some societies, recent trends suggest that labor unions and their ability to negotiate higher wages are weakening.[20] As the world economy globalizes and there is declining local support for labor unions, more workers are being pressured to accept local wages. Furthermore, the increased emphasis on technological innovation and the willingness of multinationals to start operations in other locations are also decreasing union influence.

Although labor unions' influence is diminishing, MNCs have no choice but to adapt to local labor practices and traditions when they hire local workers. As a result, the impact of dealing with unions and related labor laws must be considered in any strategic decision regarding locating in another country.

In this section, you were exposed to the unique human resource management issues facing any MNC as it tries to hire local workers. However, the multinational also needs to deal with the human resource management issues of those managers who are sent abroad to manage foreign subsidiaries. We therefore consider the unique human resource management issues pertaining to expatriates next.

Expatriates

An MNC's human resource policies must take into account several types of employees in the multinational organization. In the previous section, you learned about human resource practices as an MNC hires workers. However, the MNC may also rely on **expatriate employees**, who may come from a different country from the one where they are working. Expatriates typically

expatriate employees
employees who come from a different country than where they are working

belong to the managerial and professional staff rather than to the lower-level workforce and thus present the multinational with unique challenges.

In this section, you will learn about human resource management issues pertaining to expatriates. Expatriates can actually be of different types. Some expatriate employees who come from the parent firm's home country are called **home country nationals**. Others who come from neither the host nor home countries are called **third country nationals**. Finally, local workers may also be hired in the host country where the unit (plant, sales unit, etc.) is located. These workers are known as **host country nationals**.

A basic dilemma facing the MNC pertains to whether it wants to hire host country or home country nationals. Each approach has advantages and disadvantages and is dependent on the multinational's strategy. Hiring host country managers can be advantageous because it offers the multinational the ability to hire someone who has a better understanding of the local cultural and institutional environment. Such knowledge can be valuable to the MNC as it tries to navigate a foreign environment. Furthermore, host country nationals are usually better able to develop a closer relationship with other local managers and workers and hence identify with the local subsidiary. However, the host country manager presents the MNC with a big challenge: How can a local person identify and personify with the company's headquarters corporate culture?

Because of many multinationals' desire to hire someone who is familiar with the headquarters corporate culture, many MNCs send home country nationals on expatriate assignments. As you will see in the next paragraphs, although this approach is popular it also presents significant challenges.

Cost of Expatriates

To entice employees to take international assignments as expatriates, the appropriate incentives have to be provided. Often, expatriates are middle- or upper-level management who have to be encouraged to take international assignments. They may be reluctant because they do not want to remove their children from school or may not want to sacrifice their partner's career.[21] As a result, the MNC has to provide significant incentives to encourage its workers to take such assignments and expatriates can be very costly. For instance, total compensation of expatriate managers can often be more than three to four times that of home-based salaries and benefits. An expatriate manager with a base salary of $100,000 and a family of four can cost as much as $360,000 in Tokyo, $275,000 in Hong Kong, $210,000 in Singapore and $250,000 in London. Furthermore, as you will see later, as more companies compete, compensation for expatriates is becoming an important source to retain such expatriates.

As you see, expatriates can be very costly in terms of compensation. However, expatriates also incur additional costs that can significantly add to the expatriate cost. For instance, some multinationals provide company cars with chauffeur, country club memberships, paid vacation airfare to the home country, and even a generous expense budget. Another critical cost aspect is the cost of living in a new city. For instance, sending someone to Moscow, Seoul or Tokyo may entail dramatically higher cost of living than sending someone to Toronto or Prague.

The compensation packages of expatriates are thus dependent on the cost of living in the particular country to which the expatriate is sent. Many multi-

home country nationals expatriate employees who come from the parent firm's home country

third country nationals expatriates who come from neither the host nor home countries

host country nationals local workers who are hired in the host country where the unit (plant, sales unit, etc.) is located

nationals use Mercer Human Resources Consulting's cost-of-living index to determine how much they will pay their expatriates. The index is a measure of the cost of living of American employees assigned to a foreign country. To compute the cost-of-living index, Mercer prices the cost of a two-bedroom unfurnished apartment, a cup of coffee, a fast-food meal and an international paper. For instance, in Moscow, an apartment will rent at $3,000 per month, a coffee costs $5.27, a burger and fries run for $3.87 while an international paper costs $3.40. To give you an idea of the costs of living in different cities, Exhibit 14.6 shows data on the cost-of-living index in the top ten and bottom ten cities in the Top 50 Cities list compiled by Mercer.

Exhibit 14.6 **Cost-of-living Indexes for Selected Cities**

Top ten		Bottom ten	
City	Index	City	Index
Moscow, Russia	123.9	Lusaka, Zambia	83.4
Seoul, South Korea	121.7	Amsterdam, Netherlands	83.4
Tokyo, Japan	119.1	White Plains, USA	83.2
Hong Kong	116.3	Shenzhen, China	82.9
London, UK	110.6	Abidjan, Ivory Coast	82.8
Osaka, Japan	108.3	Dakar, Senegal	82.8
Geneva, Switzerland	103	Toronto, Canada	82.6
Copenhagen, Denmark	101.1	Jakarta, Indonesia	82.4
Zurich, Switzerland	100.8	Bratislava, Slovak Republic	82.4
New York, USA	100	Prague, Czech Republic	82.1

Source: Based on Mercer Consulting, www.mercerhr.com.

Despite this high cost, expatriate failure remains high. Next, we consider some of the reasons for failure.

Expatriate Failure

Across industries, a very large portion of expatriates fail. **Expatriate failure** occurs when the expatriate decides to return to his or her home country before the international assignment is over, failing to meet the expectations of the MNC. Current research points that failure rates are very high, at around 16–70 percent expatriates actually failing, depending on the host country.[22]

Expatriate failure can be extremely costly for companies. Recent estimates suggest that each expatriate failure can cost a multinational around $1 million.[23] Collectively, expatriate failure costs US multinationals over $2 billion per year. Expatriate failure also results in indirect costs for companies. Such departure may result in loss of opportunities in and knowledge of the foreign markets. Other indirect costs can include loss of market share and damaged relationships with clients and local government officials.

expatriate failure
occurs when the expatriate decides to return to his or her home country before the international assignment is over

Given such a high failure rate, it is critical to understand why expatriates fail. Reasons for failure can include personal reasons such as inadequate adaptation to the new culture, lack of technical skills to perform the job, or lack of motivation for the new assignment. However, family reasons can also play a prominent role in failure. Sometimes, the family has difficulties adapting to the new culture, or maybe the partner or spouse fails to adapt. In addition, organizational reasons such as a lack of preparation for the international assignment or giving the expatriate an extremely difficult assignment may also account for failure.[24]

culture shock
refers to the anxiety or stress that is caused by being in a new and foreign environment

An important aspect of the failure to adapt is **culture shock,** which refers to the anxiety or stress that is caused by being in a new and foreign environment and the absence of the familiar signs and symbols of the home country. Culture shock can also cause failure because the expatriate may find the new environment too overwhelming. The added stress and anxiety caused by culture shock may result in poorer performance and less self-worth, thus lessening the expatriate's ability to adapt.

As you can see, because expatriates can be so costly, multinationals need to take every measure to minimize failure. In the next section, you will learn about what can be done to ensure expatriate success.

Ensuring Expatriate Success

What can MNCs do to ensure expatriate success? Recall some of the human resource management functions you read in the earlier parts of this chapter. The MNC needs to ensure that the various functions are applied to the unique situation presented by an expatriate. In this section, the emphasis is on selection and recruitment, which is arguably one of the most critical steps.

emotional intelligence
refers to the ability of being aware of oneself, understanding and relating to others and being empathetic and managing one's emotions

Because expatriate success is so dependent on choosing the right person for the position, the recruitment and selection process is extremely important.[25] While it is obviously critical for the expatriate to have the appropriate technical skills and knowledge to perform the task, possessing such technical skills may not be sufficient if the person does not have the right traits for the job. As such, it is important for the multinational to assess whether the person has the appropriate trait to adapt well in the new culture. Adaptability relates to an individual's ability to learn from experience and to use new experiences to improve. In addition to the ability to adapt, recent research suggests that expatriates need to have high emotional intelligence. **Emotional intelligence** refers to being aware of oneself, understanding and relating to others, and being empathetic and managing one's emotions. Emotional intelligence is seen as a critical factor in determining how an expatriate can adapt to the new environment. Expatriates who have high emotional intelligence are more likely to relate well with other local managers and can also use emotions to better deal with the situation. A summary of the relevant aspects of emotional intelligence is provided in Exhibit 14.7.

In addition to the qualities in Exhibit 14.7, it is crucial for the MNC to assess the family situation of the expatriate. Research shows that many expatriates fail because the needs of the accompanying family are not taken into consideration. In some cases, the spouse fails to adapt because he or she may feel lonely. While the expatriate has access to a social network through work, spouses are often left with chores such as finding schools for children and can

Exhibit 14.7 **Components of Emotional Intelligence**

- *Open-mindedness* The expatriate needs to be open-minded about issues and to be receptive to new ideas.
- *Tolerance for difference* The expatriate should have the ability to accept people who are different.
- *Curiosity* The expatriate should be continuously willing to explore.
- *Tolerance for ambiguity* The expatriate should be comfortable with uncertain and new situations.
- *Excellent social skills* The expatriate should be able to relate well to others.
- *Excellent communication skills* The expatriate should be able to communicate well and easily with others.
- *Flexibility* The expatriate should be able to explore new ways of doing things or change the way things are done.
- *Empathy* The expatriate should be able to put himself/herself in others' situations to identify with them.

Source: Based on B. Avril Alizee and Vincent P. Magnini, 2007, "A holistic approach to expatriate success," *International Journal of Contemporary Hospitality Management*, 19(1), pp. 53–64.

feel alienated. It is therefore important to include the spouse and other family members in the selection process.

While selection and recruitment are critical steps in ensuring expatriate success, training can also be a major contributor to success. Training should start even before the expatriate leaves. Many of the cross-cultural training methods you read earlier in Chapter 7 on culture should be followed. The expatriate needs to be provided with pre-departure training whereby important information necessary upon arrival is provided.[26] Expatriates can also be provided with skills to facilitate adaptation to the new culture.

Once the expatriate is in the host country, it is strongly advisable for the MNC to continue the cross-cultural training. Furthermore, training from locals or other mentors about operating in the host country can be very helpful. Many companies now have mentorship or buddy programs where new expatriates are paired with other expatriates in the host country. They can thus get access to new social networks and learn about potential difficulties relatively quickly. Finally, it is important to note that some training may also be necessary for the family. Offering cultural and other language-training programs may help the family better integrate into the new culture.

Another component of success is the provision of various forms of organizational support. For instance, by providing training programs, the MNC can show its commitment to help the expatriate succeed. It is also important for the MNC to keep communication gateways open. For instance, the expatriate should be given the opportunity to stay in touch with colleagues and others at home. Such open communication will show that the headquarters care about the foreign operations and how well the expatriate is doing.

Another crucial aspect of expatriate success is compensation. The MNC needs to provide the necessary incentives to motivate the expatriate to succeed. Components of the compensation plan can include premium allowances for accepting postings in international locations, hardship allowances for postings in dangerous locations, relocation and home allowances to provide for the cost implications of moving. Many MNCs are also providing other supplementary

Compensation for Expatriates in Emerging Markets

IB SMALL BUSINESS INSIGHT

As the emerging markets such as China and India continue their explosive growth, demand for senior talent remains significant. Both China's and India's schools cannot produce enough graduates to satisfy this demand. As a consequence, many smaller companies are finding that they need to send expatriates to manage their foreign locations. However, these multinationals are facing strong competition for talented expatriates from domestic firms. In fact, a recent survey showed that around 54 percent of companies in China have experienced increased turnover of professional staff.

What can small companies do to retain their expatriates? Many companies are finding that increased salaries seem to work. In fact, some global recruitment firms have seen salary increases of 200 percent in some of the emerging markets. For instance, in China many companies are offering additional benefits while senior managers at Pepsi are being offered stock options worth $500,000 if they stay for four years. While salary may not be everything, these examples show the importance of expatriate salary. Furthermore, as you saw earlier in Exhibit 14.4, multinationals are also finding creative ways to provide desirable perks to their employees.

Source: Based on *Employee Benefits*, 2007, "Cash emerges as king," January 16, p. 29.

benefits such as medical coverage and pensions. Taxes are also a key issue in compensation packages, as expatriates may sometimes face taxation in both the host and home countries. Recent trends suggest that cash and direct salary benefits remain crucial in some emerging markets. Consider the IB Small Business Insight above.

A final aspect of expatriate success is dealing with repatriation. Expatriates typically face the **repatriation problem,** representing the difficulties that managers face in coming back to their home countries and reconnecting with their old job. Furthermore, expatriates may also experience **reverse culture shock,** where on returning they experience significant challenges in reintegrating their domestic environment. For example, returning expatriates can experience significant stress related to their children facing new expectations at school. Furthermore, they may need to navigate a new social environment where they have to make new friends. Finally, the returning expatriate may also face significant challenges on encountering a new work environment.[27]

repatriation problem
the difficulties that managers face in coming back to their home countries and reconnecting with their old job

reverse culture shock
refers to the significant challenges returning expatriates experience as they return from their international assignment

These repatriation difficulties can be solved with proper preparation and planning by the expatriate and the company. For instance, the MNC can provide some training for the return. After being gone for a few years, things may have changed at home and it is crucial for the expatriate to be prepared to come back. Often, an important component of such training is to manage the returning expatriate's expectations. Returning expatriates generally expect to be rewarded with a promotion and an environment where their international skills can be utilized. A multinational would be well advised to provide an environment where such expectations can be met. If such expectations are not met, it is very likely that the expatriate may leave the organization upon return.

A survey of the practical literature suggests that there are programs to minimize reintegration challenges.[28] For instance, AT&T provides "Welcome

Electronic Human Resource Management

As multinationals rely on expatriates increasingly, the human resource management function can become very costly. Many multinationals are therefore developing electronic human resource management practices to become more sustainable and to save on costs. Consider, for instance, the case of IBM, discussed earlier. The in-house social networking site allows IBM employees to propose solutions to problems by contributing their expertise to virtual discussions. This software thus allows IBM to save on travel and other costs not incurred as employees cooperate online. Furthermore, an appropriately designed electronic human resource management system can also represent savings through the reduction of the use of paper-based forms. For instance, companies that have developed web-based travel reimbursement systems report significant savings over more traditional paper-based travel and expense applications.

Home" orientations for its expatriates and their families. This program includes components such as counseling to help the spouse find employment opportunities and counseling to help children reintegrate into the educational system. Other companies such as 3M provide mentors to help with both the expatriation and the repatriation process. The mentor can help the returning expatriate reconnect with the workplace and become more aware of the new job expectations and colleagues.

As you can see, multinationals can implement many programs to ensure a smooth experience for the expatriate. Consider the following IB Sustainability Practices above.

The Future: Women Expatriates?

Despite the increase in demand for expatriates, the number of females in expatriate positions has stayed at around 2–15 percent of all expatriate positions.[29] Such levels are surprising, given the scarcity of employees at the highest level. However, many MNCs tend to be reluctant to post women in expatriate positions. Some MCNs are simply not interested, while others assume that women will face prejudice once in the foreign country. Other reasons are simply seen as fiction. For instance, Adler[30] found that many companies simply assume that women are not interested in international assignments or that managers are reluctant to send women abroad. However, such assumptions are mere myths.

Although these myths may persist in some organizations, it is clear that the future will see a rapidly growing number of female expatriates. Such reasoning is logical given that women have some advantages compared to men. For instance, women are more likely to excel in relational skills, a major factor in expatriate success.[31] Women report that local male managers can be more open in communication with a woman than with a man. Local men, even from traditional cultures, can talk at ease with a woman about an array of subjects that include issues outside the domain of traditional "male only" conversations. In

Women Expatriates

A recent survey by Mercer Consulting suggests that more companies are increasingly using women for expatriate positions. For instance, European companies have relocated twice as many female expatriates than five years ago. Furthermore, women are also realizing that an international assignment can be an important career boost and are becoming much more likely to take such assignments to climb the corporate ladder.

The survey, which covered over 100 MNCs with around 17,000 expatriates, found that companies in the Asian-Pacific region sent 16 times more expatriates than they did five years ago. Furthermore, over half of the companies surveyed indicated that they expect female international assignments to grow steadily over the next five years.

Source: Based on John Duckers, 2006, "Women are going it alone," *Birmingham Post*, October 20, p. 27.

other cases, just in being unique, female expatriates tend to be more visible and thus more sought after. Furthermore, women may sometimes have cultural predispositions that are more compatible with local cultures. For instance, Varma, Toh and Budhwar[32] have shown that female expatriates are preferred in India, where collectivistic traits such as nurturance and collaboration are more valued. It is therefore likely that Indian home country workers prefer US female expatriates relative to male US expatriates, who may seem too aggressive.

What can MNCs do to encourage female expatriates? If necessary, the perception that women are not willing to take international assignments has to be changed. Managers need to provide equal opportunity for both genders to explore expatriate opportunities. Additionally, every effort should be made to provide potential female expatriates with mentors and networks of other female expatriates. This will provide potential candidates with an idea of expectations and potential challenges. Finally, MNCs are also strongly advised to address dual career issues.

The future is certainly likely to see more female expatriates. Consider the IB Strategic Insight above describing a recent survey of multinationals.

CHAPTER REVIEW

In this chapter, you read about international human resource management. As a multinational expands its operations, it has to manage its human assets to ensure that it keeps its ability to be competitive. Human resources are critical to enable a multinational to implement and realize its strategic objectives. International human resource management deals with managing the human resource functions at an international level. The chapter considers the unique circumstances pertaining to workers as well as more upper-level expatriates.

In the section pertaining to workers, you learned how the various human resource management functions of recruitment, selection, training, performance appraisal and compensation differ from country to country. Specifically, you read about how both cultural and institutional aspects affect these functions. Furthermore, the chapter also discusses some of the ways these differences can be addressed.

In the section on expatriates, you learned about the unique challenges facing MNCs as they send upper-level employees on international assignments. You read about the high costs of expatriates and also the high level of failure. The chapter also suggested some of the things companies do to ensure expatriate success. In the final section, you read about the situation facing women as they embark on international careers. However, you also learned about the scarcity of talented employees and how more women will fill such positions in the future.

As more companies go international and hire individuals from different countries, they will face important challenges with regards to the human resource management function. If these multinationals want to get the best out of their employees, they will need to deal with these employees appropriately. This chapter presented you with the many challenges and solutions to deal with such human resource management functions.

DISCUSSION QUESTIONS

1. Discuss the human resource management functions. How is international human resource management different from domestic human resource management?
2. What is recruitment and selection? How do US companies typically approach recruitment and selection? How are these functions different in other countries?
3. Compare and contrast US performance appraisals with performance appraisal practices in more collectivistic countries.
4. What is compensation? How is compensation around the world different from US compensation practices?
5. What are expatriates? Why are expatriates so costly for multinationals?
6. Discuss some of the important challenges facing multinationals as they send expatriates on international assignments. How can a multinational better prepare expatriates to succeed?
7. What are some of the important traits expatriates need to have to do well on their international assignments?
8. Discuss the current situation regarding female expatriates. What can companies do to encourage and support their women expatriates?

INTERNATIONAL BUSINESS SKILL BUILDER

Choosing a Plant Location

Step 1: Assume you are the owner of a small business or find a small business that has international operations.

Step 2: You are interested in opening a plant in a foreign location or in assisting the small business in making a plant location decision. You will need to hire employees to operate the plant.

Step 3: Consult the appropriate sources (Mercer Consulting, International Labor Organization, Towers Perrin) to provide the small business with the appropriate advice regarding hiring. Provide information regarding compensation, labor relations, performance appraisal, etc., in the selected countries.

Step 4: Considering four possible destinations for the new plant, provide comparative advice regarding each country. Justify the best alternative.

CHAPTER INTERNET ACTIVITY

Go to the World Bank "Doing Business" project website at **www.doingbusiness. org**. Examine the "Employing Workers" measure. What information does it provide to human resource managers? Discuss how the World Bank arrives at the measure. Select ten countries and compare their employing workers indexes. What do you learn?

KEY CONCEPTS

compensation

culture shock

emotional intelligence

expatriate employees

expatriate failure

home country nationals

host country nationals

international human resource
    management (IHRM)

labor relations

performance appraisal

recruitment

repatriation problem

reverse culture shock

selection

third country nationals

training and development

union membership density

INDIA: THE EMPLOYMENT BLACK HOLE?

CASE 14

page 1

After independence from Great Britain in 1947, India established a socialist-oriented government that discouraged foreign investment. Major industries were state-owned and government heavily regulated private businesses. Westerners viewed India as a very poor country with little to offer the international business community. In 1991, India experienced a currency crisis and was forced to fly its remaining stock of gold to London as collateral for an IMF loan. Faced with a very difficult situation, India then began to reform its economy. Since the early 1990s the Indian economy has transformed itself into a very competitive global competitor. With an abundance of workers and very low wage levels, India is attractive to international companies for low-end manufacturing and service delivery. Of special interest is the recent outsourcing of service jobs that can be performed over satellite and fiber-optics communication channels.

India produces over three million college graduates a year. With high unemployment, companies have no difficulty in finding young college graduates who are content to handle customer service for American and European companies, at a fraction of the cost of their American and European counterparts. Typical of this new approach is AOL which now employs 1,500 people in India to answer its calls for customer service. Even though AOL is not available in India, AOL customers in the US and elsewhere call an 800 number and may never realize that they are talking with someone halfway around the world. AOL reports much lower operating costs and lower turnover in its Indian call center than it experiences in the United States. Costs are lower, even though training costs are higher and the company must provide employees with transportation to and from work.

Like AOL, other well-known American companies have beaten a path to India to outsource their back-office services. Recently, Microsoft announced that it was moving some of its customer service jobs to India. Microsoft joins a long list of American companies already operating back-office operations in India, such as Oracle, IBM, Intel, and HP. Lloyds TSB, one of the UK's largest banks, has announced the closing of its call center in England and its movement to India. Lloyds TSB call center workers in the UK earn on average ten times the wages to be paid to their Indian substitutes. Even the World Bank has moved its accounting function from Washington to India. American businesses are realizing that almost any back-office or service job can be moved overseas.

While the call center and other lower-level service jobs which have moved to India are becoming commonplace, India is also embarking on a much more ambitious approach to job creation. India has attracted work from the United

. . .

States and Europe in software development, chip design, IT consulting, financial services, and drug research. An estimated 20,000 US tax returns were prepared in India last year, and the number is expected to skyrocket to 200,000 this year. The returns are prepared by Indian accountants familiar with the US tax code and are signed by CPAs in the United States. Indians now process mortgage applications, do legal and medical transcription, and book travel reservations. The management consulting firm McKinsey now outsources to India the design of its PowerPoint presentations that it shows its clients.

The skill level of jobs being outsourced is increasing. GE has established the Jack Welch Technology Center in India and employs 1,800 engineers, many with doctoral degrees, to conduct basic research. The relatively new center has already earned 95 patents in the United States. India has an abundance of well-trained engineers and scientists, and MNCs are beginning to realize the potential of this human capital. According to the managing director of the Welch Center, it isn't about saving money on labor costs. "The game here really isn't about saving costs but to speed innovation and generate growth for the company." Nevertheless, a top-of-the-line electrical engineer in India earns only about US\$ 10,000 a year, a fraction of the salary of an American or European with the same qualifications.

While GE may not be primarily concerned with cost savings, most companies moving to or establishing operations in India are doing so because of the labor rate differential. One UK travel agency has put a different spin on the outsourcing concept. Ebookings is moving both its work and workers to India. The London-based travel agency is not only moving the jobs of selling and booking travel, but also moving workers to India, and paying the prevailing Indian wage level. Ebookings is selling the idea of living in India as an adventure and a way to sell the world. The firm's employees in India, both European and Indian, will be paid about US\$ 6,000 a year, resulting in a significant cost saving to the company. While most companies that have moved their back-office operations to India are American or British, India is seeking additional jobs from other English-speaking countries such as Australia, and non-English-speaking countries in which customer service is conducted in English.

India has the advantage of having an educated workforce that can speak English and is willing to work for a fraction of the wage level of developed country workers. It does, however, have a number of disadvantages to consider when companies decide to outsource work. India has experienced very impressive economic growth in the years since economic liberalization; however, it is still very much a less developed country. An estimated one-third of the population is illiterate, and only the higher classes speak English well. The official language of India is not English but Hindi. And India still possesses a very poor infrastructure, with unreliable power sourcing and frequent flooding. Government bureaucracy is still very much a factor in business activity, and presently India's fiscal deficit is running at over 10 percent of GDP. While India has made great strides in eliminating excessive government, much improvement needs to be made. In addition to concerns over budget deficits, political tensions are also troublesome. India has an uneasy relationship with its neighbor,

. . .

Pakistan, and the tension between Muslims and Hindus produces violent conflict at times.

While educated Indians speak English, it is considered to be "the Queen's English" and has a different accent from American English. Although many Indians are enrolling in accent-reduction classes, some American customers have complained about the ability to communicate with Indian customer service personnel. Indians tend to speak rapidly, averaging 180 words a minute, compared to 120 for Americans and 90 for the British. Dell recently announced that it was moving its call center operations out of Bangalore, India, and back to Texas because it "had issues with differing Indian accents." GE, while investing heavily in research in India, nevertheless moved its appliance call center from India back to the United States. GE had discovered that many Indian employees could not relate well to the concerns of GE's customers because many did not own, or were not familiar with, the appliances they were discussing.

At the present time, India is the lead country in attracting service outsourcing, but other countries are now beginning to compete. Like India, the Philippines is an English-speaking country with a low wage level. Unlike India, the Philippines, a former colony of the United States, is closer to the US in language and culture. While the number of jobs outsourced to the Philippines is currently much lower, estimated to be around 30,000, the number is expected to grow rapidly. Currently, Filipinos work in the Philippines for American companies, doing medical and legal transcription, answering call centers, and providing technical support. In addition to the Philippines, a number of Eastern European countries may rival India for job outsourcing. One indication is the bidding process on a website for programmers called Rent-A-Coder. Companies, mostly small and medium-sized firms from the United States and Europe, post jobs for freelancing software developers. Indians still are able to solicit most of the programming jobs from the site, however, Romania is the second most popular country for this outsourcing. Under Soviet domination, Romania, like many Eastern European countries, emphasized science, math, and engineering instruction and now has an abundance of technically qualified people who are willing to work at low wage levels. Like Romania, the Czech Republic has an abundance of technically qualified workers who are available at a lower wage level. The Czech Republic also has the advantage of impending membership in the European Union. Recently, DHL announced a €500 million investment that will employ Czechs to track shipments, provide customer service, and perform billing operations. The Czech Republic has a strong telecommunication infrastructure, workers who are proficient in many languages, and a skilled and inexpensive labor force.

An additional factor which may slow the growth of outsourcing to India is the political backlash caused by job losses in the United States and Great Britain. In the United States, the state of Indiana recently cancelled a $15 million contract with the software arm of large Indian company, Tata Group, over fears of unemployment in the United States. Protection of domestic jobs is a very strong political motive and one that will likely be raised as more and more jobs are outsourced to India. Many will argue the costs and benefits of overseas

. . .

outsourcing. A study by the McKinsey Global Institute found that for every dollar invested in overseas outsourcing, $1.25 returned to the United States. Supporters of foreign outsourcing argue the benefits of free trade and comparative advantage, while critics argue that foreign workers are taking jobs and potentially destroying the country's technical competitive advantage.

CASE DISCUSSION POINTS

1. From the perspective of American and European companies, analyze the advantages and disadvantages of outsourcing work to India.
2. What would you recommend to Indian government officials to ensure continued job creation?
3. Is it fair to workers of developed countries when companies shift work to lower wage countries? Explain.

Sources: J. Slater, 2001, "Back-office bonanza," *Far Eastern Economic Review*, August 30; M. Andress, 2003, "You're speaking to Prague," *Financial Times*, November 19; J. Angwin, 2003, "AOL's tech center in India is money saver," *Wall Street Journal*, August 7; K. Delaney, 2003, "Outsourcing jobs and workers to India," *Wall Street Journal*, October 13; G. Vina and T. Mudd, 2003, "Call centers migrate to India, and North of England loses jobs," *Wall Street Journal*, November 5; L. Gomes, 2003, "Romanians become latest tech rivals for off-shore jobs," *Wall Street Journal*, November 17; M. Fox, 2003, "Where your job is going," *Fortune*, November 24; E. Luce and K. Merchant, 2003, "Dell cuts back Indian customer service center," *Financial Times*, November 26; B. Hagenbaugh, 2003, "Moving work abroad tough for some firms," *USA Today*, December 2; M. Kripalani and P. Engardio, 2003, "The rise of India," *BusinessWeek*, December 8; K. Merchant, 2003, "India's call centers drop fake accents," *Financial Times*, December 8; O. Teves, 2003, "A faraway wakeup call," *Miami Herald*, December 9.

Case prepared by Charles A. Rarick

15 E-commerce and the MNC

After reading this chapter you should be able to:

- Understand what e-commerce is and its importance in today's business environment.

- Define the forms of e-commerce and understand the importance of e-commerce.

- Appreciate global e-commerce and the key global e-commerce issues.

- Learn about how to build a successful e-commerce strategy.

- Understand cyber and e-commerce security.

The Preview IB Strategic Insight describes two situations where new business models emerged because of e-commerce. These and countless other examples provide evidence of the importance of e-commerce in today's business environment. The Internet economy is growing at a tremendous pace faster than any other business trend in history. No multinational is immune to its effects and companies ignoring e-commerce do so at their own risk. As you will see later, companies are being created solely on the Internet platform and are having significant influences on their respective industries almost immediately. E-commerce therefore presents tremendous opportunities as well as significant challenges for businesses. Successful companies are the ones that will be able to take advantage of e-commerce opportunities while tackling the challenges.

This chapter will provide you with an understanding of the dramatic influence of the Internet and e-commerce on business operations. You will first learn about the basic structure of the Internet economy and the many forms of Internet transactions. You will then read about how the Internet is shaping the globalization phenomenon. You will also read about the many ways e-commerce is being used by multinationals in their operations and the significant opportunities and challenges presented to multinationals as they use the Internet. You will also learn about the many unique challenges in implementing e-commerce cross-culturally. One of the key challenges facing multinationals with respect to the use of the Internet is cybersecurity. This chapter will also present to you the many challenges associated with building a secure online presence. Finally, you will also learn some of the key steps in building a successful global e-commerce strategy.

**PREVIEW IB
STRATEGIC INSIGHT**

New E-commerce Businesses

Christian Braun wanted to sell his digital camera on eBay. After spending three hours setting up the sale, he sold the camera for UK£ 40. The experience was very frustrating for him and he decided to start Auctioning4u. Auctioning4u works like eBay without the hassle of setting up the sale. Customers can drop their items at one of the Auctioning4u stores in many of England's major cities. The Auctioning4u staff inspect the item and do the posting on eBay. All customers have to do is wait for their check to arrive and Auctioning4u keeps one-third as commission. This business model has been very successful so far and even large corporations are interested in selling their old equipment and inventory through the company.

Business executives dread carrying their laptops with them on all trips. Sapotek, a company based in New York and Mexico, started providing virtual desktop software where users can access their personal files and applications from any location. Sapotek started by providing the service for free to 100,000 users in Mexico and Latin America. After testing and perfecting the product in that market, they are now selling English-language versions around the world. The company is already very successful, especially considering that it had spent only $2 million when it began operations in 2002.

Sources: Adapted from Robert Levine, 2006, "How to build a startup out of nothing," *Business 2.0*, August, p. 66; Jessie Hewitson, 2007, "Picking up where others leave off," *Director*, 60(9), pp. 64–6.

E-commerce: Definitions, Types, and Importance

e-commerce
use of the Internet to buy or sell products and services

E-commerce can be defined as the use of the Internet to buy or sell products and services. These goods or services include those delivered offline, such as FedEx shipping a book purchased through Amazon.com to a customer anywhere in the world. They also include goods and services delivered online, such as downloaded computer software. Furthermore, as you can see below, e-commerce can take place between individual buyers or corporations.

There are four main types of e-commerce. The first is the business-to-consumer transactions such as buying books from Amazon.com. The acronym **B2C** is commonly used to refer to these forms of purchases. The second type, known as **B2B**, or business-to-business transactions, represents selling among businesses. B2B transactions make up 70 to 85 percent of current e-commerce business. In addition to these e-commerce models, there exist two other forms of business transactions that take place over the Internet. For instance, eBay is a global player in the **C2C** (consumer-to-consumer) business of auctions. Anyone can sell something online and place bids. Finally, another form of business transactions through the Internet is consumer-to-business or **C2B**. Examples of these firms include price-comparison websites such as www.addall. com, which searches online bookstores throughout the world to provide price comparisons and shipping and delivery information.

B2C
business-to-consumer transactions

B2B
business-to-business online transactions

C2C
consumer-to-consumer business transactions

C2B
consumer-to-business online transactions

How important is e-commerce? Recent trends suggest that e-commerce is growing at an amazingly fast rate globally. Consider Exhibit 15.1 and Exhibit 15.2, showing the penetration and growth of the Internet around the world.

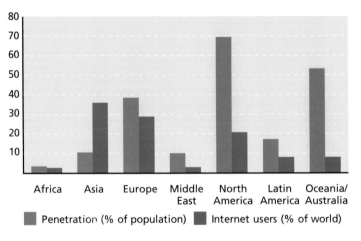

Exhibit 15.1   **Internet Penetration around the World**

Source: Based on www.Internetworldstats.com

Several important trends can be inferred from both Exhibits. First of all, as you can see from Exhibit 15.2, the growth of Internet usage between 2000 and 2007 has been tremendous. Although Africa only represents around 3 percent of the world's Internet users, growth of Internet usage in Africa has been around 638 percent between 2000 and 2007. However, most importantly, growth in Internet usage in other emerging areas in the world such as Asia, the Middle East and Latin America has ranged from 218 percent to 454 percent between 2000 and 2007. Furthermore, even in areas such as Europe and North America,

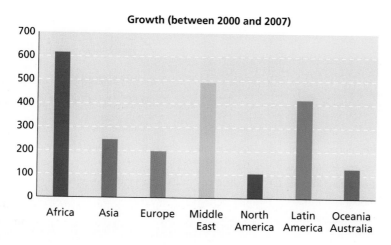

Exhibit 15.2   **Internet Growth around the World**

Source: Based on www.Internetworldstats.com

growth has been lower but steady. Such trends suggest that more individuals are getting access to the Internet, thus presenting tremendous opportunities to multinationals.

A second important trend is an assessment of the potential in these various geographic regions. Consider Exhibit 15.1, showing that while Internet usage in Asia has reached only around 10 percent of the population, this currently represents around 36 percent of the world's Internet users. On the basis of penetration alone, the Exhibit shows that the Internet still has the potential to reach a large number of new Internet users in Latin America and the Middle East. Such figures also point to the opportunities presented by the Internet globally.

While the growth of Internet usage provides evidence of the increased importance of e-commerce, MNCs will also have to pay attention to e-commerce because of its potential to help companies become more competitive. E-commerce allows companies not only to find new customers but also to find new ways to improve their operations. For instance, consider how you read in Chapter 14 about how the Internet and technology have helped many multinationals harmonize their human resource management practices around the world. In such cases, the Internet is allowing multinationals to harmonize their operations and reap significant cost savings.

The Internet and global e-commerce are also changing the way companies structure their operations. A recent study comparing Internet uses in companies shows that the top ten uses in 2000 are significantly different from the top ten uses in 1998.[1] While in 1998 companies were using the Internet mostly for data storage purposes (providing product information, advertising, newsletters, company policies, etc.), the 2000 top ten reveals more strategic uses of the Internet. For instance, the new list includes the Internet being used for purposes such as operational information and project coordination. Such changes show that companies are using the Internet for much more strategic reasons.

Global e-commerce can thus help companies reduce costs. For instance, e-commerce can reduce transaction costs associated with payments, ordering and invoicing by allowing more effective data storage and manipulation.[2] Such information can also be more effectively shared with employees, customers

IBM Software and Green Business

IB SUSTAINABILITY PRACTICES

Multinationals are currently confronting the perfect storm whereby it is becoming an economic necessity to become greener. For instance, consider that the European Union is mandating that 20 percent of energy should come from alternative sources. At the same time, oil prices continue to climb and energy usage can no longer be taken for granted. As multinationals deal with such challenges, IBM sees information technology and e-commerce as having significant potential to help companies solve such problems. They are actively developing software and hardware to help companies manage energy usage. IBM sees e-commerce and software as having the potential to help multinationals

- reduce international travel through online collaboration;
- reduce commuting through work-at-home programs;
- manage energy use and divert workloads to under-utilized servers;
- schedule workload during off-peak hours to reduce strain on electricity grid;
- reduce paper use through the development of secure online forms;
- reduce power use when workload decreases.

Source: Based on "IBM Software for a greener world," www.ibm.com

and retailers. Furthermore, B2B e-commerce has also helped retailers reduce inventory costs by letting wholesalers handle inventory and provide shipping services.

Finally, e-commerce can help companies build customer loyalty. A website can provide readily accessible information that is not possible with more traditional markets. Many companies such as Best Buy and Circuit City now provide online product demos. Such features provide additional information that can help customers make better purchase decisions.

E-commerce can also play an important role in furthering sustainability in a multinational. Consider the IB Sustainability Practices above.

As you can see, because of its many benefits to individuals and businesses, e-commerce will continue its tremendous growth in the future. Next, we consider the structure of the Internet and e-commerce.

Internet and E-commerce Structure

Before you read about the key e-commerce issues and how they affect MNCs, it is important to first understand the structure of an e-commerce website. According to Chu and colleagues, e-commerce websites have evolved from single buyer–seller interactions or repositories of information to more complex multiple exchanges between buyers and sellers.[3] It is therefore important to understand the many components of e-commerce websites.

At a basic level, e-commerce websites include participants. Participants can be registered or licensed to use the website. The management of the website also plays an important role. The website management decides the environment of the website ("boundary and its general business nature").[4] This defines whether the website is presented merely as a merchant site (i.e. seller of products) or as another form, such as a portal or broker. The website management also decides on the scope of the website—i.e. what relationships the website has with its host.

The website serves many functions. Chu et al. discuss four functions. At a simple level, the website can simply be a form of communication which allows, for instance, buyer and seller to establish a relationship. However, websites also fulfill the information presentation function. This function refers to the way the information is presented and the way its components (video, images, sound) are shown to participants. The storage and retrieval function refers to the process of recording or retrieving information. For instance, some companies rely on Oracle as a means of managing their information. Finally, the language function refers to the way data is manipulated to be converted into intelligent and useful information. For instance, a company can use C or C++ programming language to manipulate its data.[5]

A final crucial aspect of e-commerce is the core functions that e-commerce websites perform. According to Chu et al., e-commerce websites perform four key functions. These include **transaction incubation,** which refers to the process of setting up a relationship between the participant and the website. For instance, websites such as Facebook.com or MySpace.com require that participants register before their access can be validated. The **transaction negotiation** function refers to the facilitation of the purchase decision by the participant. For instance, one can review products on Amazon.com by browsing through the product offerings and then making a decision about which product to purchase. The **transaction formation** process pertains to the phase where the transaction is finalized. In such cases, participant payment is processed and approved and confirmation of purchase is sent to the buyer. Finally, in the **transaction management** phase, the company manages the various activities linked to transactions. In this phase, the company can integrate data collected at the various steps to facilitate e-business processes. For instance, in this stage, the purchase decision can be matched with inventory control for re-order decisions.

Now that you have read about the various important components of e-commerce websites, you will learn about the power of e-commerce to allow companies to go global. You will also read about the many important cross-cultural e-commerce issues.

transaction incubation
process of setting up a relationship between the participant and the website

transaction negotiation
facilitation of the purchase decision

transaction formation
process where purchase is finalized

transaction management
management of various activities linked to transactions

E-commerce and Globalization

The increases in information exchanges and efficiency through the Internet and e-commerce have made it possible for companies to reach customers worldwide and to become global companies. However, the Internet is also enabling the emergence of a new form of multinational called the **born-global firms.**[6] As you saw in earlier chapters, many companies tend to operate in the domestic market and gradually expand to foreign markets. However, born-global firms tend to adopt a global view of markets and develop competitive advantage to succeed in the various markets from the day they are started. Recent research suggests that born-global firms are increasingly appearing in large numbers in industrialized countries, with over 1,000 born-global firms estimated in the US.[7] Consider the following IB Strategic Insight.

born-global firms
companies that operate globally from the day they are founded

Vast.com

Vast.com is a search company (similar to Google) that was started in San Francisco. Vast.com was launched in 2005, and one year later it was employing 25 people working across five time zones. While all executives are based in San Francisco, Vast.com's main development team is located in Belgrade. Furthermore, the chief technology officer of the company is a Serbian national who lives in the Dominican Republic. He regularly chats with the development team in Belgrade through instant messaging. He can also check with his colleagues in Ireland through e-mail. Finally, he is in touch with the main office in San Francisco through Skype, a phone service available through the Internet.

Vast.com represents the new breed of born-global companies. Their personnel can be located anywhere in the world. Because of dramatic advances in communications technology, the employees can stay in touch with each other constantly. Furthermore, with globalization, MNCs now have easier access to the supply of talented engineers and programmers located around the world.

Source: Based on Michael V. Copeland, 2006, "The mighty micro-multinational," *Business 2.0*, July, pp. 107–14.

The Internet and e-commerce are not encouraging solely the creation of born-global firms. Many smaller and medium-sized companies are taking full advantage of e-commerce to expand their operations. Why is it easier to pursue e-commerce opportunities today? Many of the initial barriers to e-commerce are falling and e-commerce is becoming more cost-effective. According to Heilemann,[8] several important reasons account for the growth of e-commerce:

- *Extremely cheap hardware* Computers, servers and many other pieces of e-commerce hardware are commodities that can be acquired for very little. For instance, while a server used to cost as much as $60,000 over ten years ago, servers can now be purchased for $1,000.
- *Cheap software* Companies can now rely on open-source software to develop their service. Much free software, such as Linux, MySQL, now allows companies to develop their e-commerce presence without exorbitant costs.
- *Access to talent worldwide* Most companies can now access the vast pool of programmers available in India, Romania, and Russia. While such programmers were previously available only to larger multinationals, many smaller companies can now easily tap into these employees.
- *Cheaper Internet worldwide* Many countries are seeing increased availability and decreased price of the Internet. In fact, the OECD sees broadband development as a critical aspect of the Internet and e-commerce.[9] Broadband is a combination of digital technologies that allows rapid transmission of data and other digital services, often simultaneously. It is seen as a major reason for people adopting information and technology products and services, and as prices have come down more people are adopting broadband. See Exhibit 15.3 for growth of broadband penetration in selected OECD countries between 2004 and 2005.

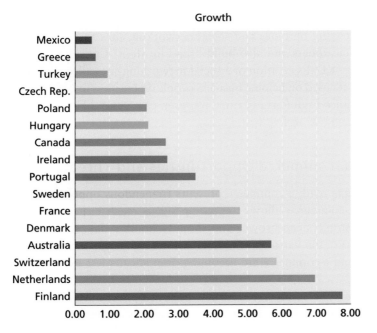

Exhibit 15.3 **Broadband Penetration**

Source: Adapted from OECD, 2005.

- *More targeted marketing* Search engines such as Google have made it easier and more efficient to target potential buyers. Companies do not need to spend large sums of money to reach potential customers effectively.
- *Easier and cheaper to stay in touch with employees worldwide* There are now a large number of tools available for companies to keep their worldwide employees in touch with each other. Consider the following IB Small Business Insight.

Communication Technologies for Small Firms

IB SMALL BUSINESS INSIGHT

You have a small business with employees located around the world. How difficult is it for you to keep in touch with all of your employees? Many communication technologies today make the process very efficient and easy. Consider the following:

- *Voice over Internet protocol (VOIP)* The VOIP technologies make it easy to speak with anyone around the world very cheaply. Programs such as Skype or Jajah allow people around the world with Internet access to talk to each other at a very low cost.
- *Instant messaging (IM)* IM also allows people to communicate with each other very easily and cheaply.

Popular programs include MSN Messenger and America Online Instant Messenger.

- *WIKIs* WIKIs allow companies to store data in a central repository available to all employees. PBWiki provides such services for free.
- *Online meeting services* While online meeting services are still somewhat expensive, new start-ups are slowly developing better and cheaper online meeting technologies. This segment is also predicted to grow.

Source: Based on Michael V. Copeland, 2006, "The mighty micro-multinational," *Business 2.0*, July, pp. 107–14.

- *Increased popularity of blogs and social networking* Many companies are now relying on blogs and social networking sites to better connect with their customers and also build brand loyalty.[10] Consider the case of Air France–KLM's creation of a social networking site called Club China. The site is focused on helping business people do business in China and provides assistance finding translators and even car rentals. This has allowed Air France–KLM to find better ways to serve its customers flying to China.

Global E-commerce Opportunities and Threats

As you have read, e-commerce presents tremendous opportunities for companies. E-commerce allows any company to reach customers on a global scale. Customers can browse and shop 24 hours a day, seven days a week. Furthermore, the various technologies you read about earlier show that the Internet and e-commerce are becoming dramatically less expensive and more effective.

However, e-commerce does not present opportunities only in terms of reaching new customers. E-commerce also allows a company to streamline its operations to become more profitable. Inventory can be managed more effectively and employees worldwide can communicate better. Furthermore, any multinational can coordinate more effectively with suppliers to get its supplies in a more timely fashion.

E-commerce is also spurring a number of new business models. For instance, many private tutoring businesses have flourished because anyone can use Skype for free. Instructors can simply call their students to provide more effective instruction. Consider also the case of Ecomiles. Ecomiles is a web portal that allows members to make charitable contributions to charitable groups and projects that need funding.[11] Ecomiles is linked to a large number of commercial websites, and when members purchase products they can also contribute Ecomiles dollars that can be awarded to charitable institutions.

Despite the significant opportunities, there remain significant challenges. For instance, it is expensive to maintain a website on a global level. There exist significant differences across cultures and languages, and the process can be very complicated. Furthermore, if a multinational is selling products, returns and shipping can also be very complex. Different countries have different regulations and tax systems in place, and multinationals may find it difficult to keep up with payment systems that conform to local regulations. Shipping worldwide can also be expensive. Consider that, recently, the US postal service announced that it was abandoning transportation of products through cargo ships for international customers.[12] Many online booksellers rely on this mode of transportation as it is much cheaper than air transport. They now have to find cost-effective alternatives or they will likely see sales drop internationally.

The previous paragraphs discussed some of the challenges facing any company taking e-commerce cross-culturally. In the next section, we consider some of the key cross-cultural e-commerce issues and the challenges they present. You will also read about solutions to these challenges.

Key Cross-cultural and Global E-commerce Issues

The use of the Internet and e-commerce at a global level presents companies with unique issues and challenges. In this section, you will read about many of these key issues. You will also learn about the ways many multinationals are dealing with these issues.

Cross-cultural E-commerce Adoption and Diffusion

An important component of any company's attempt to go global with e-commerce is e-commerce adoption. **E-commerce adoption** refers to the degree to which companies and individuals are willing to accept the new technologies inherent in performing e-commerce tasks. **E-commerce diffusion,** a related concept, refers to the degree to which e-commerce is spreading and being adopted in different societies. Because the focus for many MNCs is on selling products and services through the Internet in new countries (business-to-consumer, B2C), it becomes critical to understand the factors that encourage B2C in different societies.

At a basic level, research shows that e-commerce adoption and diffusion is dependent on the Internet infrastructure and the availability of Internet services at affordable prices.[13] Such findings are not altogether surprising. People are more likely to adopt the Internet if they can afford it. These findings suggest that multinationals may wish to locate their services in places where the Internet is readily available. The Exhibits discussed earlier provide some understanding of Internet penetration and the degree of use by the population, and can be used as the basis for market location decisions.

However, some research also shows that infrastructure and Internet cost alone don't completely explain the degree of e-commerce adoption and diffusion. Cultural factors and institutional factors also play an important role. To better understand e-commerce adoption, it is important to understand the Technology Adoption Model (TAM) developed by Davis.[14] The fundamental premise of the TAM is that acceptance of information technology or e-commerce is dependent on two important factors, namely the perceived usefulness and perceived ease of use of the technology. When applied to e-commerce, **perceived usefulness** refers to the degree to which an individual believes that using a B2C site will enhance his or her shopping experience[15] while **perceived ease of use** refers to the belief that the use of a B2C website is free of effort.

Research shows that the TAM model is dependent on the cultural and institutional aspects of a society. For instance, Parboteeah et al.[16] found that the cultural dimensions discussed in Chapter 7 on culture are linked to perceived usefulness of technology. This study found that uncertainty avoidance, which refers to the degree to which people are comfortable with uncertainty, discourages usefulness of technology. Furthermore, more masculine societies, emphasizing work and achievement, viewed technology as being more useful.

Additionally, consistent with Chapter 8 on institutions, the research also found that institutions affect how people see the usefulness of technology. Parboteeah et al. found that the higher level of development, the more useful people found technology.[17] To give you more insights on the matter, Exhibit 15.4 shows the average degree to which people perceived the usefulness

e-commerce adoption
degree to which companies and individuals are willing to accept new technologies inherent in e-commerce

e-commerce diffusion
degree to which e-commerce is spreading in different societies

perceived usefulness
perception that the use of a B2C site will enhance the shopping experience

perceived ease of use
belief that use of a B2C website is free of effort

433

Exhibit 15.4

Perceived Usefulness of Technology in Selected Countries

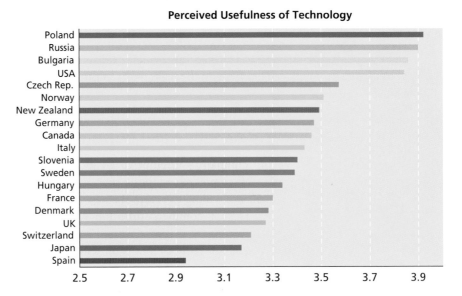

Perceived Usefulness of Technology

Source: International Social Survey Program, 2000, *International Social Survey Program: Work Orientations II* [computer file], Ann Arbor: Inter-university Consortium for Political and Social Research.

of technology in making their work more interesting across a large number of countries.

As you can see from Exhibit 15.4, clearly there are differences in terms of how different societies view technology, the Internet and e-commerce. Many industrialized nations such as Japan, the UK and Spain see technology as important. However, the most surprising finding is that many of the former socialist economies found in Russia, Poland, and Bulgaria view technologies as extremely important in terms of making work more interesting. Such findings are very important for MNCs. Many of the transitional economies have significant potential for e-commerce, and the fact that people view technology as important in these societies is very encouraging for MNCs wishing to expand their operations in these societies.

These differences also have important implications for which markets companies pick to have e-commerce presence. For instance, Shirky suggests that web entrepreneurs should target countries based on two factors.[18] First, attractive markets for e-commerce are those markets with inefficiencies, such as those found in many formerly state-controlled markets. In these markets, e-commerce shopping allows buyers to get better quality and cheaper prices because they are free from state control. Second, target markets should have attractive demographic characteristics. These include locations with an Internet population of at least 5 percent, a high literacy rate (to predict future growth of the Internet population), countries that participate in at least one free trade agreement, and a government with a viable legal system. It is also necessary to look at the general access of the population to the Internet. Exhibits 15.1 and 15.2 provided some information about the most attractive e-commerce markets.

As you read, understanding e-commerce diffusion and adoption is critical as MNCs decide which markets present the most potential. Next, we consider another crucial cross-culture e-commerce issue, e-commerce consumer trust.

Cross-cultural Consumer Trust in E-commerce

Consumer trust in e-commerce is seen as a critical factor in influencing consumer adoption of e-commerce.[19] Because the Internet involves significant uncertainty and ambiguity, trust is an important factor in reducing such uncertainty. **Consumer trust in e-commerce** thus refers to the willingness of an online consumer to depend on others, assuming that the other party will deliver as promised. In other words, Internet purchases involve some level of risk whereby purchase consequences have some level of uncertainty. The level of trust refers to the online purchaser's degree of comfort with this uncertainty. Because so many companies are now launching global e-commerce activities, understanding trust in a global environment is very crucial. By understanding what contributes to consumer trust, an MNC can design systems to build trust.

Research by Teo and Liu suggests that a company's reputation and size have positive effects on consumer trust.[20] In other words, the larger and more well-known a company is, the more likely people will trust the company. Such findings suggest that smaller and lesser known companies need to put forth extra effort to build trust. Later you will read about some of the ways companies can build trust in an online environment.

There is some evidence that consumer trust in e-commerce differs across cultures.[21] Using Hofstede's cultural dimensions as the basis (see Chapter 7), some have argued that more individualist societies are more likely to trust strangers than more collectivist societies. As you may recall from Chapter 7, people in collectivist societies tend to rely on in-group members (friends, family, colleagues) and are more likely to trust these people. As a consequence, one way for companies to build trust in more collectivist societies, such as China and South Korea, is by appealing to the in-group and the "familiar." In fact, it seems likely that local e-commerce companies do better than foreign ones. It therefore makes sense to engage in joint ventures locally if one wants to do well.

As you can see from the IB Strategic Insight below, consumer trust in e-commerce is clearly different across cultures. Consider also the cultural

consumer trust in e-commerce
willingness of an online consumer to depend on others

Jack Ma and Alibaba.com in China

IB STRATEGIC INSIGHT

Jack Ma is currently one of the biggest players in the e-commerce industry as he is the founder and CEO of Alibaba.com in China. Alibaba.com is seen as the Chinese answer to eBay. Why is Alibaba.com so successful? One can see that Ma appealed to the collectivistic nature of the Chinese in designing Alibaba.com. For instance, for his consumer-to-consumer e-commerce business, he offered instant messaging capabilities to consumers a long time before eBay bought Skype. By allowing buyers to contact sellers through instant messaging, Taobao.com offers buyers the ability to get to know the seller to build trust. Furthermore, the Chinese clearly prefer a local company for e-commerce purposes as many of the foreign e-commerce businesses have failed.

Source: Based on J. Heilemann, 2006, "Unlocking the middle kingdom," *Business 2.0*, August, pp. 44–6; K. Hafner and B. Stone, 2006, "eBay is expected to close its auction site in China," *New York Times*, December 19, p. C11.

dimension of uncertainty avoidance. As you recall from Chapter 7, uncertainty avoidance refers to the degree to which people in a society are comfortable with uncertainty and ambiguity. Clearly, the Internet presents uncertainty, and it is therefore not surprising that people are more wary and less trusting of the Internet in high uncertainty avoidance societies.

Given all of this, what can MNCs do to build trust? One key aspect that contributes to a trustworthy website is e-commerce and cyber security. You will read about what companies can do to make the Internet more secure later. Websites can also be designed appropriately to build trust. A new stream of research suggests that the presence of online characters can build loyalty.[22] An onscreen character can present a more human aspect of the website, allowing customers to interact and even discuss problems. Furthermore, onscreen characters can also be tailored to cultural preferences. In a worldwide survey, Luo et al. found that more human-like characters were more effective than cartoon-like characters in being likeable and trustworthy. However, female cartoon-like characters were more effective in terms of website interface.[23]

A final way that multinationals can build trust is by engaging in multi-channel integration.[24] In other words, a multinational can have both online websites and physical stores. By having both channels, an MNC offers customers the means to freely choose the purchase most comfortable for them. In fact, such multi-channel integration is becoming a source of competitive advantage. A key issue with multi-channel is the degree of integration between the online presence and the physical presence. Teo and Liu suggest that both channels should be fully integrated to get a unified view of customers and to also provide a consistent shopping experience.[25]

In this section, you read about cross-cultural consumer e-commerce trust. Another critical aspect of cross-cultural e-commerce is website design. You will therefore read about cross-cultural web design in the next section.

Cross-cultural Web Design

As multinationals increasingly use websites as a way to advertise and sell products globally, more of them are considering the extent to which web design should adapt to local preferences. MNCs need to determine whether they want a **standardized website,** where the company's website is fairly similar in layout and design around the world, or a **localized website,** where the values, appeals, and symbols in the communication content are adapted to the local culture.

The standardized website typically presents the same form of promotion messages translated for the local context. However, there are no other modifications of headings, illustrations or other sources of information. This form of website is based on the assumption that consumers anywhere around the world share the same needs and wants.[26] The amazing acceptance of the Internet has led to impressive growth, suggesting that standardized websites may be appropriate. For instance, Dell has very minimal website adaptation with websites in 50 countries using 21 different languages. It uses the same layout for the sites in all countries.

In contrast, the localized approach entails adapting the website and messages to local culture, available media and industry. Multinationals with localized websites assume that there are significant consumer differences because of cultural and other institutional differences. An MNC must then adapt its

standardized website
company's websites around the world are fairly similar in layout and design

localized website
website design and layout are adapted to fit local culture

website to suit local preferences. McDonald's is a company that localizes its website. A recent study by Wurtz shows that the highly individualistic Swiss and German McDonald's websites display images of individuals listening to music and relaxing (a very individual activity). In contrast, the collectivistic Indian McDonald's website shows a man running with a child in a shopping cart, emphasizing the family ties and group approach typical of more collectivistic societies.[27]

Should MNCs localize or standardize their websites? The answer is, of course, dependent on the nature of the product being sold, consumers and other factors. Some products, like PCs for instance, don't require much adaptation for the local cultures. However, food and clothing websites may need more adaptation.

If adaptation is needed, how should MNCs approach website adaptation? Recent research suggests that adaptation needs to go beyond mere machine-translated versions of websites.[28] Beyond language adaptation through translation, other issues such as the colors, icons, web page layout, date format, fonts and so on need to be adapted. Research on culture again provides some insights. For instance, consumers from more masculine societies where work and achievement is emphasized prefer more interactivity from their websites. People in more long-term orientation societies prefer more visual and other emotional appeals.[29]

Cross-cultural Website Challenges

IB SMALL BUSINESS INSIGHT

You have a small business and you have decided to set up international websites. What are some challenges you may face? The list below shows some of the unexpected issues facing any small business.

- *Website domain name* Most people in the US view websites ending with .com as the local and normal web address. However, individuals in other countries have preference for local websites (e.g. ending with .co.uk in England) and any small business has to acquire such domain names. Furthermore, registration and acquisition of domain names can be complicated and expensive in other countries. For instance, in France and Spain, one has to first establish a legal company before registering a website.
- *Preferred purchase methods* Consumers in the US are very comfortable using credit cards for online purchases. However, preferred payment methods are not the same in other countries. Consider, for instance, that in Japan people prefer to use a payment method that doesn't include credit cards. After making online purchases, Japanese consumers go to convenience stores, where a payment is made and the money transferred to their online accounts. In Germany, people have a strong cultural bias against debt and prefer to pay using local bank wires. A small company thus has to provide the culturally relevant method of payment if it wants to succeed.
- *Legal practices, taxes and other regulations* Countries have widely different policies regarding e-commerce. In some countries, value-added taxes on products shipped from a foreign country can actually double the price. It is therefore important for small businesses to navigate the legal and regulatory maze.
- *Security issues* Cyber security is a key issue that any small business has to be concerned about when operating in some markets, such as those found in emerging markets like Vietnam, China, etc. You will read more about cyber security later in the chapter.

Source: Based on Beckey Bright, 2005, "Planning to take your online business international? Beware; E-commerce can get lost in translation," *Wall Street Journal*, May 23, p. R11.

Further research reported by Wurtz shows that the website animation in high context culture (i.e. where communication is not direct but also includes implicit messages contained in body language and silence) is more centered on people, showing preference for complexity in communication. In contrast, low context culture websites (i.e. where communication occurs primarily through explicit statements through text and speech) are more static and use less animation. Furthermore, navigation on low context cultures tends to be more linear, while high context cultures have more new browser windows opening with less transparent guidance.[30]

Many organizations discover that developing local websites is extremely complex. Beyond cultural and language sensitivity, they also need to adapt their organizations to the information flow and customer demands created by web locations accessed from anywhere in the world. As such, many multinationals are finding that they are better off outsourcing these functions to specialized companies. One example of such a company is Digital River, which provides all activities (website development and hosting, order management, export and tax management, multi-language customer service, fraud prevention, etc.) needed to maintain localized e-commerce operations.[31]

What cultural challenges are faced by a small business interested in having an international website? Consider the IB Small Business Insight on the previous page.

In the next and final section, you will read about some of the key steps in building a successful global e-commerce strategy.

Building a Successful Global E-commerce Strategy

In the last section, you read about the important cross-cultural e-commerce issues. In this section, you will learn about some of the key steps in building a successful e-commerce strategy. You will also read about cyber security and the importance of building secure e-commerce operations.

Important Aspects of a Successful E-commerce Strategy

E-commerce strategizing is a new and evolving challenge and its application to the global arena adds more complexity. However, e-commerce has the potential to contribute to profits and competitive advantage for the multinational. It is therefore important for the multinational manager to build on sound, basic strategizing as a prelude to multinational operations. Below you will learn about some of these key aspects.

Experts agree that a successful e-commerce strategy starts with top management.[32] Successful e-commerce is only possible through dynamic and strong leadership coming from the top. At a minimum, the CEO and senior executives should strongly believe in the benefits of an e-commerce approach. As you realize, e-commerce involves strong resource and time commitment. Leaders should have expertise and vision to objectively assess the company's position on e-commerce in order to craft the most appropriate e-commerce strategy.

Beyond expertise, it is critical to assess some of the recent trends to determine the most appropriate strategy. Experts suggest some trends and potential solutions.[33] These include:

- *Speed* One of the most important trends is that customers now want to be able to perform any transaction with speed. Whether a multinational is considering a potential customer or a supplier for supply chain areas, that customer wants to be able to engage in the transaction as efficiently as possible. For the multinational, this suggests that all delays at any step of the process will drive away customers. For instance, if delays occur because of too many approval steps or inappropriate transaction processing, every effort has to be made to remove sources of such delays.

- *Self-service* Another important trend is the ability for a customer to be able to get self-service at any time. Most of the world is now living in a seven days a week, 24 hours a day, time frame. Everyone believes that they should have the ability to have access to real-time information to make purchases or solve other problems. As mentioned by Garrett and Parrott,[34] consider that Dell provides the ability for customers to order both software and hardware at any point in time. Furthermore, Dell also offers limited technical support without the assistance of a person. How can such services be provided? The website design and data management processes are very important. Websites should be user-friendly and fun. MNCs should also make adjustments to the website based on the popular means of getting Internet access. For instance, movies and other clips should be avoided where broadband is not available.

BlueNile.com

IB STRATEGIC INSIGHT

In 2002, at the age of 28, Mark Vodon, founder and CEO of Blue Nile, walked into a Tiffany store to buy an engagement ring. He left without buying any ring and was frustrated because of the lack of service. Because of his frustration with stores, he founded BlueNile.com. BlueNile.com is today one of the US's largest sellers of engagement and wedding rings, even surpassing Tiffany in that department.

How did he achieve such a feat in such a short period of time? Vodon says that to be successful and survive, an e-commerce operation has to find ways to provide superior customer service. For instance, he makes sure to listen to his customers' suggestions for improvement. He reviews customer complaints through as many ways as possible, such as listening to their phone messages, reviewing orders and talking to his executives. BlueNile.com then implements many of the customer suggestions.

BlueNile.com thus offers many unique customer service elements. Diamond purchase can be very intimidating,

and BlueNile.com has an important online section devoted to diamond education. Furthermore, phone calls to the company are typically answered promptly. Also, if a ring is to be given as a surprise gift, BlueNile.com provides helpful tips regarding ring size estimation. If necessary, BlueNile.com also allows customers to return their rings for resizing for free. BlueNile.com provides free overnight delivery for some diamond rings and also allows all customers to return their products within 30 days for full refunds.

These measures have allowed BlueNile.com to become successful in the very cluttered e-market. They now have international websites in Canada and the UK and hope to do well in these countries too.

Source: Based on J. Schlosser, 2007, "Engaging with the customer," *Fortune*, May 14, p. 28.

- *Customer service* An important trend noted by experts is the provision of superior customer service. Companies can no longer rely on their websites simply as a means of transmitting information. Multinationals are constantly looking for ways to use their e-commerce operations to provide better customer service. Furthermore, as more multinationals become intertwined with other businesses, there is a serious need to coordinate across organizations. Consider the IB Strategic Insight on the previous page.
- *Integration of various channels* Most MNCs are facing increased pressure to integrate the various channels through which they operate. For instance, retailers are under increased pressure to coordinate and integrate their online offerings with the store experience. Because of the national and international nature of the Internet, companies are finding that they need to have consistent policies between their online and offline operations. Research suggests that consumers are frustrated when they find that products offered online are not sold in stores, or that prices differ widely across the different channels.[35] Although this issue is not as critical with global websites, multinationals nevertheless need to ensure that a consistent message is being provided across countries.

In addition to the above trends, Epstein suggests that successful global e-commerce companies need to be willing to make significant financial investments if they want to succeed globally.[36] As you read earlier, having a global presence involves dedication of significant effort and resources. If a multinational is not willing to make such investments, its e-commerce operations will likely fail. Such investments need to include adequate financial resources for an IT department and appropriate resources for upgrading the multinational's information systems. Furthermore, some experts advise that the multinational should finance the e-commerce venture from the inside rather than seeking outside investors. By providing internal funding, the company's executives and personnel are more likely to believe in the potential of the e-commerce operation.

A final important aspect of any successful e-commerce operation is appropriate data management. The Internet and e-commerce provide incredible opportunities for data collection and manipulation. However, if the data are not properly collected and managed, a multinational will lose the ability to take full advantage of such data. Experts[37] suggest the following:

- *Track important data* Customer data can be very important given the potential insights that can be garnered from such data. The multinational must ensure that there are systems in place to collect the appropriate information from customer visits. Some companies prefer to focus on number of hits and visits a customer makes to a website. However, the experts argue that the type of interaction a customer has with a website is more critical, as it may reveal information regarding price sensitivity and general appeal of the website.
- *Enter accurate data* A multinational needs to take every step to ensure that the collected information is clean and accurate. For e-commerce operations, it is critical to emphasize to the customer the importance of accurate data. Furthermore, such data can then be compared with other outside sources of data. Additionally, it is important to make sure that the

data collected can be matched with visitors to the website. This will ensure a better understanding of previous purchases and future preferences.

- *Maintain data at the lowest level possible* Multinationals should ensure that data is collected at the lowest possible level. For instance, if an MNC is selling various types of products, it is imperative to keep the data at the customer level if possible. Data aggregation is always possible; however, breaking down the data is never possible. For instance, if the multinational combines all sales, it may not be able to analyze purchase patterns by products. Data mining thus becomes very difficult. Finally, it is also strongly advised that data is never destroyed. Data storing means are very inexpensive today and such storing can be done very easily.

In this section, you read about some of the key steps in ensuring successful e-commerce operations. In the next and final section, you will learn about one of the most crucial elements of e-commerce, cyber and e-commerce security.

Cyber and E-commerce Security

As e-commerce grows in importance, cyber security is becoming increasingly crucial for most MNCs. **Cyber security** refers to the challenges and other vulnerabilities the Internet faces as individuals try to exploit and attack weaknesses. While cyber security applies to the Internet, e-commerce security refers to the challenges customers face as they participate in e-commerce transactions. Specifically, **e-commerce security** refers to the degree to which customers feel that their private and personal information can be safeguarded in the hands of online companies collecting such information.

The growth of the Internet and e-commerce on a global basis has led to the creation of several associations to encourage global policy making. In that context, the Global Business Dialogue on Electronic Commerce (www.gbde.org) is an international government and private company partnership that is examining the key global e-commerce issues to be tackled. It identifies cyber security as one of the most important challenges that needs to be tackled. In fact, it argues that as the Internet and computer software is becoming more interconnected, exploitation of small security holes can lead to catastrophic damage. The Global Business Dialogue on Electronic Commerce identifies the following factors as the major reasons why cyber security is an important issue:

- *Rapid growth of viruses and worms* As more computers are now ever more connected, computer viruses and worms can rapidly copy themselves through e-mails and files, causing serious damage (computer malfunction, Internet slowdown, loss of data, etc.) to the Internet.
- *Hacking* More computers are now vulnerable to attacks from individuals from faraway locations. When hackers break into others' computers, they have the ability to manipulate important data and cause important damage to the data. The authentication and identification processes can become compromised.
- *Spam* The growth of spam or unsolicited mass mailings has become a major annoyance for Internet users. Spam not only reduces employee productivity

cyber security
challenges and other vulnerabilities of the Internet

e-commerce security
degree to which individuals feel that their private information is safe in the hands of companies collecting such information

as they search and delete such e-mails, but it is also slowing down network traffic because of the large amount of spam being sent.

- *Phishing* More Internet users are getting spam where they are requested to submit crucial information, such as credit card numbers and social security numbers, to a website disguised as a legitimate bank or credit card company website. The information collected is then used for fraudulent purposes.

- *Computer attacks and identity theft* Attacks on popular websites are increasing at a very rapid rate. Such attacks have resulted in theft of the credit card numbers of thousands of customers. As personal information gets stolen, the consequences can be very catastrophic, for the individuals involved (e.g. loss of privacy, loss of money, threats) and MNCs (e.g. loss of trade secrets, loss of business opportunities) alike.

An important but indirect challenge of the Internet and e-commerce operations today is e-waste. Consider the following Ethical Challenge.

E-waste in India

ETHICAL CHALLENGE

Although Bangalore has become one of the world's high technology capitals, it is facing a serious crisis with e-waste hazards. E-waste refers to the waste generated as old computers and other electronic appliances, such as large and small household appliances, are disposed of when they become old. Both India and China have become dumping grounds for old electronic equipment from other more developed countries. However, as poorly paid workers dismantle such equipment, they are facing significant health issues, and pollution to the environment is also very serious.

Why is e-waste such a critical problem? E-waste from computers, refrigerators, televisions and mobile phones may contain more than 1,000 toxic materials. Beryllium, cadmium, chromium and mercury are all chemicals contained in discarded equipment, posing significant health risks as well as environmental challenges. Because the workers are not properly equipped to deal with these discarded pieces of equipment, the health threat is obvious. Exhibit 15.5 shows some of the toxic waste associated with a typical desktop computer.

While the discarded electronic equipment from more developed countries poses important risks to India, India is also now facing a domestic battle. As income grows and the price of computers comes down, more Indians can

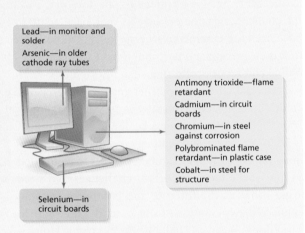

Exhibit 15.5

Toxic Chemical From Personal Computer

now afford computers. This is generating even more challenges as the greater turnover in computer technology is contributing to India's e-waste problems. Multinationals concerned about the future will find that they need to address the e-waste issue.

Source: Based on Habib Beary, 2005, "Bangalore faces e-waste hazards," http://news.bbc.co.uk; Ambika Behal, 2006, "Managing Indian e-waste," *Terra Daily*, www.terradaily.com/reports/Managing_Indian_E_Waste.html

What can multinationals do to minimize threats to e-commerce security? At a national level, many countries are taking steps to combat Internet threats. For instance, according to the Global Business Dialogue on e-commerce group, some countries such as the UK and Japan are setting up computer security incident response teams to provide guidance regarding how to handle potential Internet threats. Multinationals are being strongly encouraged to partner with such groups for their e-commerce security issues. Furthermore, countries such as Taiwan and South Korea have increased the punishments associated with cyber crimes such as phishing or hacking. Such punishment is assumed to act as a deterrent for potential cyber criminals. Both the US and Germany have also been active in addressing cyber security issues in a proactive manner.

In addition to the cooperation with governmental authorities described above, multinationals are being encouraged to take appropriate measures to beef up their Internet security. Specifically, most companies need to be concerned about a number of information security issues.[38] These include (1) confidentiality (making sure that private information is protected), (2) availability (ensuring that information is accessible to authorized users), (3) integrity (ensuring that the information collected is accurate and reliable), and (4) authentication (having systems in place to ensure that persons using the systems are legitimate). Companies are also under increased pressure to protect the privacy of individuals as more and more personal information is being collected, stored and shared by companies involved in industries such as health care, banking/finance, travel and the government.[39]

To ensure a multinational's Internet and cyber security is preserved, experts suggest using firewalls, intrusion detection software and antivirus shields, whereby systems are in place to keep outsiders from entering private networks.[40] Various companies are specialists in providing technologies to protect a company's network. As more instances of data theft emerge, it is becoming more critical for companies to adequately encrypt the data so that the latter is meaningless if it falls into the hands of criminals. Additionally, to prevent unauthorized access to information, more multinationals are now requiring two-phased authentication processes. Such systems require two forms of identity, namely a password and some identity token such as a key fob or other device. Finally, many multinationals are also using technology to monitor websites to detect any unusual page requests or other suspicious activity. This will provide some warning if a website is being attacked or is about to be attacked.

CHAPTER REVIEW

In this chapter, you read about the key e-commerce issues facing any MNC today. The chapter first defined e-commerce and described the many types of e-commerce. You also learned about e-commerce structure and the many aspects making e-commerce a critical aspect of any business today. Multinationals that ignore e-commerce do so at their own peril.

The chapter also discussed some of the key aspects of global e-commerce. You read about the many factors facilitating e-commerce for any company today. You also learned about the many opportunities and threats facing any company as it takes e-commerce globally. Key cross-cultural e-commerce issues such as e-commerce adoption, cross-cultural consumer trust in e-commerce and cross-cultural web design were also discussed.

In the final section, you read about the important aspects of any successful e-commerce strategy. You learned about the many important e-commerce trends and possible adaptation to such trends. An important section of the chapter was also devoted to cyber and e-commerce security. As more computers and networks get connected around the world, it is becoming imperative for companies to assure cyber and e-commerce security. This chapter discussed some possible steps to ensure cyber security.

As you realize, the Internet and e-commerce will continue to grow in importance in the future. As more people around the world gain access to the Internet, the opportunities presented by the Internet will remain crucial. This chapter hopefully provided you with an understanding of this importance and the many key issues as a multinational or small company takes e-commerce to the global level.

DISCUSSION QUESTIONS

1. What is e-commerce? What are the main types of e-commerce?
2. What are some of the ways e-commerce impacts a multinational's operations? Discuss how important e-commerce is for today's company.
3. What are some crucial functions of a website? Discuss the many core functions of a website as a commercial transaction is taking place.
4. What are some of the factors that make e-commerce more accessible to small companies today?
5. Discuss some of the key opportunities and threats of e-commerce.
6. What is e-commerce adoption? What are some of the factors determining e-commerce adoption across cultures?
7. What are some of the factors affecting consumer trust in e-commerce? Discuss some of the ways a multinational can build consumer trust in its global website.
8. How does culture affect cross-cultural website design? Discuss some of the advantages and disadvantages of having a standardized website and a localized website.
9. Discuss three key elements of a successful global e-commerce strategy.
10. What is cyber and e-commerce security? Why is cyber security such a crucial problem for any multinational? Discuss some of the key steps a multinational can implement to maximize e-commerce and cyber security.

INTERNATIONAL BUSINESS SKILL BUILDER

Designing an International Website

As the head of a website development firm, you have been contacted by a company producing dairy products, including cheese among others. The company has determined through market research that there is significant demand from large-scale resellers for its products. Furthermore, the company has also realized that a website in these countries would greatly enhance its market potential.

Step 1: You have been asked to design specific websites for the countries of Brazil, Russia, India and China (BRIC). Consult appropriate sources and websites in these countries. Provide extensive information regarding the key issues that will need to be considered in creating the websites. Assume that the websites will be used to place orders.

Step 2: Provide the company with information regarding the appropriate web design for each country. Be specific about the web design for each country (i.e. what elements will you use for each country? How will the products be featured?).

Step 3: Consult the US website of a similar company. Provide some information to the company regarding how each country's website will differ from the US website. Provide explanations for these differences.

CHAPTER INTERNET ACTIVITY

Step 1: You have been asked by a local small company to help them launch a website in a few selected countries. Pick a few countries that you are interested in.

Step 2: Research companies that already have websites in the selected countries. Inform the small company of the unique aspects of these websites.

Step 3: Provide a report to the company regarding web design and any other critical aspects you feel it is necessary to address.

KEY CONCEPTS

B2B	e-commerce security
B2C	localized website
born-global firms	perceived ease of use
C2B	perceived usefulness
C2C	standardized website
consumer trust in e-commerce	transaction formation
cyber security	transaction incubation
e-commerce	transaction management
e-commerce adoption	transaction negotiation
e-commerce diffusion	

CASE 15

page 1

BUSINESS > INTERNATIONAL

E-CASH: GLOBAL CURRENCY?

Prior to the creation of a medium of exchange, primitive commercial transactions were conducted using bartering. A cumbersome and inefficient method, the barter system gave way to the creation of money. Early forms of money included shells, stones, and precious metals. Over time, more sophisticated media were introduced, including paper as a unit of value. Paper money, issued by governments and banks, was later supplemented with checks and credit/debit cards.

. . .

During the 1990s a new medium of exchange emerged in conjunction with the increased popularity of the Internet. Electronic cash, or e-cash, was created by a number of companies to facilitate Internet transactions. Although each offering of e-cash was somewhat different, the basic idea included consumers depositing money by various means into an account, and when purchasing online they would use their "cyberdollars" to pay for their purchases. No checks or credit cards would be needed.

PayPal, which was started in 1998, is used by online auctions, including eBay (which owns PayPal), as a means of paying for transactions. Consumers in over 55 countries, including Australia, China, Germany, and South Korea, can bid on items and, if successful, use funds from their PayPal account to settle the transactions. Other companies such as BidPay, 99Bill, and AliPay offer similar services to global customers. In China, 99Bill sells prepaid payment cards that can be used for online payments, including fees to play video games on the Internet.

E-cash offers a number of advantages to both consumers and Internet merchants. It allows consumers without credit cards to easily make purchases, it can reduce transaction expenses for merchants, and it makes "micropayments" possible. Consumers who do not have credit cards can deposit money with an e-cash distributor and make their purchases without the time delay of sending a payment and waiting for their checks to clear. Merchants accepting e-cash payments are usually charged a lower processing fee than the fee charged by credit card companies. Perhaps one of the biggest advantages of e-cash is that this system makes micropurchases (0.1 cent to $1) more feasible. Such transactions are important for certain services offered on the Internet, such as purchasing information. As the Internet has become a truly global medium of communication and commerce, e-cash has the potential to facilitate transactions across national boundaries and differing currencies. While credit cards are still the most popular method of payment online, many consumers in less developed countries have not been able to acquire them, making Internet purchases difficult. While the concept of electronic cash offers many benefits to both consumers and merchants, many start-up e-cash companies have either gone bankrupt or shifted the focus of their business.

CASE DISCUSSION POINTS

1. Why hasn't e-cash become a more popular form of payment for Internet purchases?
2. How might e-cash help to develop entrepreneurial activities in less developed countries?
3. Do you think e-cash will ever become a universal currency? Explain.

Sources: *The Economist*, 2000, "E-cash 2.0," February 19; R. Buckman, 2005, "Online payment firms target China," *Wall Street Journal*, August 11; www.paypal.com.

Case prepared by Charles A. Rarick

Ethical Management

Ethical Management in the International Context

part five

16 Managing Ethical and Social Responsibility in an MNC

After reading this chapter you should be able to:

- Understand the definition of international ethics and corporate social responsibility and the reasons why multinationals are being criticized.

- Understand the three important global ethical issues, namely labor rights, environmental pollution, and corruption/bribery.

- Appreciate some of the key approaches to dealing with global ethics.

- Understand how multinational managers can build the socially responsible multinational.

As you can see from reading the Preview IB Strategic Insight, MNCs are facing increasing complexities as they strive to become better global citizens. On one hand, these MNCs need to understand the local conditions to determine the appropriate way to do business in all of the markets where they operate. On the other hand, they are facing increasing scrutiny of their business activities and practices. As a result, more MNCs are trying to find the balance between operating effectively locally to stay competitive while at the same time responding to the dramatic calls for better ethical practices.

In this chapter, you will read about global ethics issues. You will learn about the importance for MNCs to implement and enforce ethics programs. The chapter will discuss many of the core ethical issues facing any corporation involved in trade across borders. You will also learn about some of the tools and techniques available to multinationals to enable them to become more ethical citizens.

This chapter contains four major sections. In the first section, you will read about the basic definitions of international ethics and social responsibility. You will also learn about why multinationals are being criticized in the context of globalization. In the second section, you will learn about some of the key global ethics issues. This section of

---

International Ethics in China and Around the World

PREVIEW IB
STRATEGIC INSIGHT

As MNCs continue to expand business operations in China to take advantage of the tremendous opportunities the Chinese market has to offer, they are facing the challenges of tackling corruption in that market. Chinese officials argue that it will be difficult to eradicate corruption and bribery completely. These officials state that corruption is deeply ingrained in the Chinese environment, as people in higher office tend to view corruption as entitlement that goes with the official position. Attempts to investigate corruption charges often result in political battles between the Chinese government and the province officials.

Although some experts argue that corruption is an inevitable aspect of doing business in China, recent events suggest that China is very serious about eliminating bribery. For instance, the government has implemented new enforcement programs and procedures to reduce bribery. There is now clearer information detailing what constitutes bribery and the punishment accompanying such illegal activities. Furthermore, a number of officials have been punished in some form or other recently for corruption.

In addition to the complexities inherent in navigating the ethics waters in China, MNCs are also under pressure from their home countries to stop such practices. Consider, for instance, the media coverage of the companies recently fined in the US under the Foreign Corrupt Practices Act. Clearly, most multinationals are under increased pressure to behave more ethically while also facing the local reality that corruption may be an important part of the business culture. Furthermore, even when multinationals implement global ethics programs, they are finding that implementing global ethics policies is very difficult. Cultural differences often determine the extent to which local workers will take a global ethics program seriously.

Source: Based on Kris Maher, 2004, "Global companies face reality of instituting ethics programs," *Wall Street Journal*, November 9, p. B8; *China Law and Practice*, 2006, "Commercial bribery under fire in China," September, p. 1; Kenneth J. DeWoskin and Ian J. Stones, 2006, "Facing the China corruption challenge," *Far Eastern Economic Review*, 169(7), pp. 37–40.

the chapter will discuss three main issues, namely labor rights and issues, environmental issues, and finally corruption and bribery. In the third section, you will read about some of the approaches being used to build the global ethical corporation. Finally, in the fourth section, you will learn about the many steps and activities any multinational needs to engage in to become more ethical at a global level.

International Ethics and Social Responsibility

Before you read about international ethics, it is crucial to understand some of the ethical questions managers deal with. Multinational managers at all levels face ethical issues where they have to deal with questions such as: "If we can get cheap child labor overseas, and it is legal there, should we use it because our competitors do?" "Should we refuse to give a bribe to an underpaid government official, and lose the contract to our competitor's weaker product?" "Should we dump our waste in the river knowing well that it will pose pollution risks although it is acceptable in the country?" "Should we pay our female workers less than male workers because that's what all multinationals do?"

A multinational's approach to dealing with these questions represents its approach to ethics. As such, **ethics** pertains to behaviors or actions that affect people and their welfare. For instance, a decision by managers to knowingly sell a useful but dangerous product or to willingly bribe an official is an ethical decision. In both cases, the decision has important consequences for humans. In the first case, selling the dangerous product can end up hurting customers and perhaps the MNC in the long run. In the second case, provision of a bribe can prevent other companies from legitimately acquiring the business. In both cases, business ethics pertain to an assessment of whether the decision is right or wrong.

International business ethics refers to ethical problems faced by multinational managers as they do business with other countries. International business ethics is different from domestic business ethics on a few fronts. International ethics is more complex than domestic ethics because operations take place across borders. Differences in culture and institutions mean that people may not always agree on what is the right way of doing things. However, most importantly, the very large MNCs can have powers and assets that exceed those of some of the nations with which they deal. When using this power, managers in these large and powerful organizations often face challenging ethical dilemmas. How powerful are the largest corporations? Consider Exhibit 16.1.

Exhibit 16.1 shows a comparison of selected countries and the largest companies in the 2007 *Fortune* 500 list. The graph illustrates a comparison of countries based on GDP with some of the USA's largest multinationals based on revenues. As you can see, Wal-Mart's revenues are significantly larger than many countries' gross domestic product. Similarly, as you can see in the graph, both GE and Ford are larger than the economies of Israel, Pakistan, and Romania. While the graph only illustrates selected countries and multinationals, it does show that many of the world's largest corporations have significant financial assets to exert power on countries. This power and clout has led many to criticize MNCs.

What is the nature of criticisms against multinational corporations? Some argue that multinationals exploit the natural and human resources in the

ethics
pertains to behaviors or actions that affect people and their welfare

international business ethics
refers to ethical problems faced by multinational managers as they conduct business with other countries

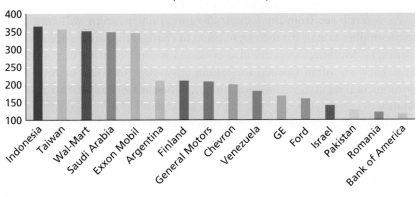

Gross Domestic Product/Revenues
(1000s of US dollars)

Exhibit 16.1 **Comparison of *Fortune* 500 and Country GDP**

Source: Based on *Fortune* 500, 2007, http://money.cnn.com; The World Bank, 2007, http://www.worldbank.org.

countries in which they operate. Companies such as Nike, Reebok and Gap have faced significant criticism because of their labor practices. Additionally, because of their size and financial assets, multinationals have been criticized for using this power to influence governments to get preferential treatment from the government. For instance, some countries give significant tax breaks to encourage investments. Such breaks generally mean the loss of revenue to support important local social programs.

Labor Rights in China

COUNTRY FOCUS

Despite significant economic growth, the average Chinese worker still earns very little and works in very poor conditions. Most workers lack the most basic rights. For instance, although a labor law was mandated in 1994 to give workers the right to a contract specifying salary and employment conditions, many workers do not have such contracts. As a consequence, most workers do not have access to basic rights.

To remedy the situation, the Chinese government is currently considering changing the current labor laws to give new rights to workers. The new law would require mandatory contracts between companies and workers, limits on probationary periods for new workers, provision of severance packages in case of lay-offs, and freedom to both change jobs and create trade unions.

Critics of multinationals, however, argue that many multinationals based in Europe and the US oppose the

new laws. Larger corporations such as GE and Procter & Gamble have voiced their opposition to these new labor laws. Furthermore, the European Union Chamber of Commerce in China, representing 860 members, is also actively lobbying against the new regulations. Associations such as the American Chamber of Commerce in Shanghai and the US–China Business Council representing many of the larger US multinationals have also opposed these new proposals. Will these multinationals and their representatives be able to influence the Chinese government in not adopting the new labor laws? Experts believe that even if the current law is not passed, workers will continue to find ways to demand basic rights.

Source: Based on Brendan Smith, Jeremy Brecher, and Tim Costello, 2006, "Multinationals to China: No new labor rights," *Multinational Monitor*, November/December, 27(6), pp. 34–7.

Multinationals can also influence the government in other ways. Consider the Country/Regional Focus on the previous page.

As you can see from the Country/Regional Focus, some will continue to criticize multinationals for their opposition to changes that are seen as favorable to workers. Multinationals are also criticized for exploitation of the environment. They are often blamed for taking advantage of weak or nonexistent environmental regulations and are thought to be a major cause of air and water pollution.

Are these criticisms justified? Some observers argue that multinationals have positive benefits. For instance, Meredith and Hoppough have argued that globalization and the multinationals have lifted around 200 million people out of poverty in China and India.[1] Many argue that as multinationals continue investing, the standard of living is raised and the proportion of the poor decreases. Many countries are seeing dramatic growth in average incomes, and in Asia alone the middle class is expected to be in the vicinity of one billion people within the next few years.

Given the earlier discussed criticisms, many MNCs are going beyond their legal responsibilities and adopting corporate social responsibility programs. **Corporate social responsibility** is defined as the responsibility multinationals have to society beyond making profits. That is, social responsibility means that a company must take into account the welfare of other constituents (e.g. customers, suppliers) in addition to stockholders. While you saw earlier in this section that business ethics usually concern the ethical dilemmas faced by managers as individuals, corporate social responsibility is usually concerned with the ethical consequences of policies and procedures of the company as an organization. Monitoring the working conditions of your suppliers, paying for the education of the children of workers, and donating money to the local community are examples of corporate social responsibility in action. Later in this chapter, you will read about the key components of an effective corporate social responsibility program.

In this section, you learned the basic definitions of ethics, international ethics and corporate social responsibility. You also read about why multinationals companies are criticized. In the next section, you will learn about some of these criticisms in more depth by reading about the key global ethics issues.

corporate social responsibility
refers to the notion that businesses have a responsibility to society beyond making profits

Key Global Ethics Issues

Multinationals face a multitude of ethical issues ranging from racial discrimination to air pollution to bribery. In this section, you will read about three of the most important global ethics issues multinational managers face. These are labor rights, environmental pollution and corruption/bribery.

Labor Rights

As you read earlier, labor rights represent one of the most crucial ethical issues multinationals are facing today. In the earlier Country/Regional Focus, you read about the very limited rights workers have in China. Workers generally don't have contracts and are not allowed to form unions. Additionally, workers are sometimes expected to work long hours without overtime pay. Finally, workers can be fired and hired at will and may not have any recourse to any form of severance pay.

One of the most important aspects of labor rights is the existence of sweat-shops. **Sweatshops** are typically plants where workers work very hard in very poor working environments, often for long hours. Global corporations such as Nike, Gap, Patagonia, and Reebok have all been hit with mainstream criticisms of using workers in sweatshops to produce their products. The media are now paying much more attention to allegations of use of sweatshops, even in cases where a multinational relies on another party to manufacture the product.

MNCs have also had to deal with allegations of the use of child labor. For instance, multinationals such as Nike and Adidas were in the spotlight for hiring child workers to stitch soccer balls in Pakistan. While local industrialists pros-pered as multinationals brought significant business to Pakistan, this prosperity did not necessarily trickle down to soccer-ball stitchers. Additionally, the use of female labor has also resulted in widespread condemnation of sexual dis-crimination. Women in less developed countries tend to be hired at much lower rates than men for similar occupations.

Surprisingly, views on sweatshops, child labor and women's labor have not always been negative. Bhukuth and Ballet, for instance, show that brick manufacturers in the Indian state of Tamil Nadu had no choice but to hire child labor to stay competitive.[2] Because the cost of raw materials tends to be fixed, employers have no alternatives but to reduce costs of labor. Furthermore, Khan argues that the media never took into consideration the social context in which children were stitching soccer balls in Pakistan.[3] While the media readily condemned multinationals for exploiting children and not affording them with the opportunity to go to school, the reality was that schooling was often absent or took place in very poor conditions. Children were often working at home with their parents, contributing to the household economy.

Multinationals cannot, however, rely on more accurate depictions of labor conditions to show their approach to ethics. Many multinationals have therefore been proactive and are taking many steps to ensure that they do not break labor rights laws. There haven't been as many sweatshops headlines lately, and Bernstein attributes the improved labor situation to multinationals taking better steps to respect labor rights.[4] Many large multinationals such as Nike and Gap are now working closely with labor rights organizations to ensure that working conditions in their and their subcontractors' facilities are acceptable.

In addition to self-monitoring efforts, MNCs can also rely on outside organizations for compliance with basic labor rights. Social Accountability International (SAI) and the Fair Labor Association are both examples of labor rights organizations that have defined labor standards and take care of enforcing these standards. These associations have developed codes of conduct addressing issues such as no child labor or no excessive overtime.[5] Furthermore, these groups also monitor plants and provide solutions to alleviate problems.

Despite these efforts, it is still necessary for more effort to be expended to reduce violations of labor rights. Many of the major multinationals have not yet cooperated with labor rights organizations to solve labor rights problems. Additionally, even those multinationals that work with labor rights groups still have some issues to resolve. Standards vary widely across the two associations mentioned above. Furthermore, there is still no agreement on the issue of wages (should a company pay a living wage?), disclosure (should companies freely

sweatshops
plants where workers work very hard in very poor working conditions

reveal the names of their factories?), factory inspections (should there be surprise visits?), etc.[6]

In this section, you read about an important global ethical issue, labor rights. Next, we consider environmental pollution. While, as you saw in Chapter 1, most multinationals are being pressured to become more sustainable, attempts to reduce environmental pollution are important elements of sustainability.

Environmental Pollution

Multinationals are frequently criticized for ignoring environmental regulations and for polluting the air and the environment. Well-publicized disasters such as the *Exxon Valdez* oil spill and the Union Carbide tragedy in Bhopal, India, have brought the spotlight on multinationals and their roles in less developed countries.[7] In fact, environmental degradation is seen as one of the most pressing and fastest growing problems facing societies, and multinationals are seen as having significant influences in minimizing such problems.

In developed countries, the media, environmental groups and the appropriate governmental bodies have tried to pressure multinationals to act responsibly. In such countries, governments have taken measures to enact laws to keep up with potential threats to the environment. As such, governments have systems in place to punish violators while rewarding those companies that act responsibly. Most developed nations have various laws and regulations whereby fines and other taxes are imposed when multinationals break environmental laws. At the same time, companies are also getting benefits by following "green" practices through subsidies and easier bureaucratic processes.

The situation is much more catastrophic in less developed nations. In these countries, multinationals have been more willing to break environmental rules and regulations. The reasons for these infractions are numerous. In less developed nations, the appropriate governments have not kept legislation to combat newer environmental problems. In many cases, the laws tend to be less rigorous and are rarely enforced. Furthermore, as you read earlier, multinationals often have assets that may exceed the country's gross domestic product. In some of these cases, the multinationals can simply compensate the relevant government for environmental damage.

Recent events suggest that most countries (developed, less developed, and emerging) are starting to strictly enforce environmental regulation. For instance, Chao and Oster discuss how studies by Chinese environmental organizations found that around 30 multinationals operating in China violated water pollution rules.[8] Because about a quarter of the Chinese population doesn't have access to clean water, the Chinese government is taking water pollution issues very seriously. Many companies have been cited for water pollution. However, in Brazil, non-governmental environmental organizations such as Greenpeace have forced companies to become more environmentally friendly. Gumbel discusses how a Brazilian judge ordered Cargill, the US agri-business multinational, to close its soy terminal in the Brazilian rainforest. Environmentalists argued that Cargill built the plant illegally while employing slave labor and destroying the rainforest rapidly. Cargill is currently appealing the ruling, stating that it observed the appropriate state regulations.[9]

Similar to the labor rights issues, multinationals are realizing that they need to be proactive to deal with the environment. The media is paying much closer

Corporate Social Responsibility in the Mining Industry

IB SUSTAINABILITY PRACTICES

The mining industry is seen as offering one of the most dangerous jobs while severely polluting the environment. Environmentalists see mining companies as major polluters and responsible for much environmental degradation. Additionally, recent accidents portray an industry where multinationals seem intent on extracting coal, iron ore and copper from the earth at the expense of a safe and healthy work environment. The mining industry is also seen as a major supplier of bribes in less developed nations in Africa and Southeast Asia.

Can such negative perceptions be changed? Rio Tinto, the world's third largest mining group, believes it can be done. Rio Tinto has implemented a corporate social responsibility program that attempts to minimize the negative impact of its activities on its many stakeholders such as employees, customers and even the local communities.

What are the elements of the program? First, Rio Tinto has implemented many safety programs for its various operations. Through such improvements, injuries and environmental accidents have decreased significantly. Rio Tinto also works closely with local communities to educate and inform people of the potential consequences of their activities. They ensure that appropriate stakeholders are consulted and potential measures discussed to determine how these issues will be managed. Furthermore, they avoid starting operations in communities who don't want them. Rio Tinto is also beautifying many of its old sites by filling up pits, creating lakes and even landscaping. Finally, Rio Tinto has implemented programs to eliminate all forms of bribery or "facility payments."

Rio Tinto hopes that these measures will show that it is possible for mining companies to be socially responsible.

Source: Based on Matthew Wall, 2006, "Mining cleans up its act," *Sunday Times*, May 7, p. 10.

---

attention to the actions of multinationals, and stories of environmental pollution and degradation are frequently publicized. As a consequence, many multinationals are implementing steps to minimize environmental degradation. Later you will read about how multinationals are implementing corporate social responsibility programs to address environmental matters. What form do such programs take? Consider the IB Sustainability Practices above.

In this section you learned about some of the key issues facing multinationals with regards to the environment. Next, you will read about one of the most critical ethical issues facing multinationals today. Specifically, you will learn about corruption and bribery and its prevalence around the world.

Corruption and Bribery

One of the most critical global ethical issues facing multinationals today is corruption and bribery. According to Transparency International (www.transparency.org), an organization dedicated to eradicating corruption, **corruption** is the "misuse of entrusted power for private gain." Corruption occurs when someone receives a bribe and does something that they are legally prohibited from doing. **Bribery** also refers to gifts or payments to someone to expedite a government action or to gain some business advantages.

corruption
process where entrusted power is used for private gain

bribery
gifts or payments to someone to expedite government action or to gain some business advantages

Levels of corruption and bribery vary significantly around the world. In that respect, the Transparency International Corruption Perceptions Index provides an understanding of the degree to which corruption exists among politicians and public officials. The organization collects data from various sources to compile an index that reflects the degree of corruption in society and the relative degree of corruption compared to other societies. Exhibit 16.2 shows the top seven and bottom seven countries based on the 2005 Corruption Index. The index ranks from a score of 10 (no corruption) to 0 (highly corrupt).

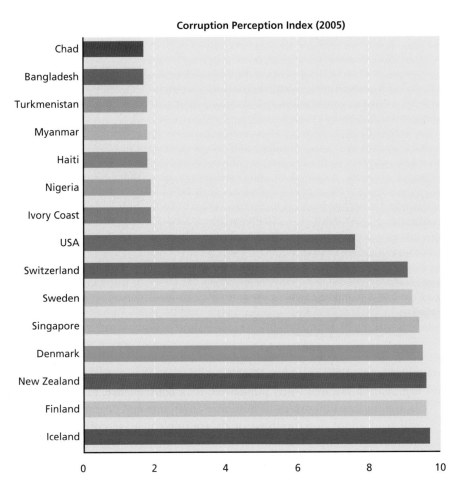

Exhibit 16.2

Top and Bottom Seven Countries (and USA) on the Corruption Perception Index

Source: Based on Transparency International, www.transparency.org

A look at Exhibit 16.2 readily reveals one important aspect of the nature of corruption. Corruption tends to be higher in poorer countries. In fact, countries such as Chad, Bangladesh, and Haiti are among the poorest in the world and score the lowest on the corruption index. Such findings are not altogether surprising. The trend, though, to be sure, is that more corrupt countries tend to channel funds into high-profile projects such as dams, power plants, etc., at the expense of schools or hospitals. Such corruption leads to the ineffective use of public funds, thereby leading to more poverty. However, Transparency

International notes that although wealthier countries tend to be less corrupt, these wealthy countries have not necessarily shown much progress in terms of the fight against corruption. The ultimate measure of effectiveness is movement towards less corruption, and wealthier countries have not necessarily shown such progress. Thus, while poorer countries have a lot to do to reduce corruption, Transparency International encourages wealthier countries to address corruption challenges.

Corruption and bribery are both attracting lots of attention because of the devastating effects on effective market functions. For instance, as mentioned earlier, corruption often results in waste of public funds, as only expensive and high-profile jobs get funded. Some also argue that companies typically make up for bribery by increasing the contract price by the amount of the bribe. As such, many developing countries suffer because they are charged higher prices. Many companies also routinely use poorer-quality products or materials to cover for the bribe, thus resulting in inferior products. Furthermore, corruption can result in collusion among firms, thereby resulting in even higher prices. As such, corruption and bribery usually result in higher public spending, lower-quality projects, undermined competition and inefficient allocation of resources.

In addition to the above negative effects on the market and quality of products, bribery can also have devastating effects on the effective political functioning and democratic nature of the society. According to Transparency International, corruption and bribery have the worst effects on the "social fabric" of a society. Because of the norms supporting corruption and bribes, most people tend to lose trust in the political system and in politicians. As a result, there is less participation in the democratic process. A weak democratic system supports the election of more corrupt politicians, thereby resulting in a vicious circle.

Given the real and damaging consequences of corruption and bribery, both countries and firms are taking steps to control and eradicate bribery. Several non-governmental organizations have taken steps to fight global corruption. For instance, the OECD has an anti-bribery convention which requires that participants make bribery of officials a crime. Participants are also required to demonstrate that adequate measures are taken to sanction those involved in bribery. This convention went into effect in February 1999 and has been ratified by all OECD members except Slovenia. Additionally, the United Nations Convention Against Corruption, which was adopted in 2003, includes legislation similar to the OECD convention. It requires members to criminalize bribery of government officials. Other regional groups are either implementing or have implemented measures to curb bribery. These include the African Union and the Convention on Preventing and Combating Corruption (July 2003), and the Pacific Basin Economic Council and their Statement on Standards of Transactions Between Business and Governments (November 1997).

The US government has also taken a very strong position on bribery. The **Foreign Corrupt Practices Act** (FCPA), which was passed in 1977, forbids US companies to make or offer payments or gifts to foreign government officials for the sake of gaining or retaining business. The Foreign Corrupt Practices Act is now being rigorously enforced by the appropriate authorities. For instance, three Vetco International subsidiaries agreed to pay $26 million in fines for violating FCPA provisions.[10] Baker-Hughes, a US-based oil service company also recently pleaded guilty to bribing officials and agreed to pay $44 million

Foreign Corrupt Practices Act legislation forbidding US companies from making bribes

Exhibit 16.3 **Critical Aspects of the Foreign Corrupt Practices Act**

Prohibited Foreign Trade Practices

It shall be unlawful for *any domestic concern* or for any officer, director, employee, or agent of such domestic concern or any stockholder thereof acting on behalf of such domestic concern, to make use of the mails or any means or instrumentality of interstate commerce corruptly in furtherance of an offer, payment, promise to pay, or authorization of the payment of any money, or offer, gift, promise to give, or authorization of the giving of anything of value to any foreign official for purposes of—

A. influencing any act or decision of such foreign official, political party, party official, or candidate in his or its official capacity, or

B. inducing such foreign official, political party, party official, or candidate to do or omit to do any act in violation of the lawful duty of such foreign official, political party, party official, or candidate, or

C. inducing such foreign official, political party, party official, or candidate to use his or its influence with a foreign government or instrumentality thereof to affect or influence any act or decision of such government or instrumentality, in order to assist such issuer in obtaining or retaining business for or with, or directing business to, any person.

Also prohibited is any offer, payment, promise to pay, or authorization of the payment of any money, or offer, gift, promise to give, or authorization of the giving of anything of value *when given to any person, while knowing* that all or a portion of such money or thing of value will be offered, given, or promised, directly or indirectly, to any foreign official, to any foreign political party or official thereof, or to any candidate for foreign political office, for purposes of A through C above.

Definitions

(1) The term *"domestic concern"* means any individual who is a citizen, national, or resident of the United States; and any corporation, partnership, association, joint-stock company, business trust, unincorporated organization, or sole proprietorship which has its principal place of business in the United States, or which is organized under the laws of a State of the United States or a territory, possession, or commonwealth of the United States.

(2) The term *"foreign official"* means any officer or employee of a foreign government or any department, agency, or instrumentality thereof, or any person acting in an official capacity for or on behalf of any such government or department, agency, or instrumentality.

(3) A person's state of mind is *"knowing"* with respect to conduct, a circumstance, or a result if—

(i)   such person is aware that such person is engaging in such conduct, that such circumstance exists, or that such result is substantially certain to occur; or

(ii) such person has a firm belief that such circumstance exists or that such result is substantially certain to occur.

(iv) Knowledge is established if a person is aware of a high probability of the existence of such circumstance, unless the person actually believes that such circumstance does not exist.

(4) The term *"routine government action"* means only an action which is ordinarily and commonly performed by a foreign official in such as obtaining permits, licenses, or other official documents to qualify a person to do business in a foreign country. The term *"routine governmental action"* does not include any decision by a foreign official whether, or on what terms, to award new business to or to continue business with a particular party, or any action taken by a foreign official involved in the decision-making process to encourage a decision to award new business to or continue business with a particular party.

(5) The term *"interstate commerce"* means trade, commerce, transportation, or communication among the several States, or between any foreign country and any State or between any State and any place or ship outside thereof.

Exceptions

A. Facilitating or expediting payment to a foreign official, political party, or party official the purpose of which is to expedite or to secure *the performance of a routine governmental action* by a foreign official, political party, or party official.

B. The payment, gift, offer, or promise of anything of value that was made, *was lawful under the written laws and regulations of the foreign official's, political party's, party official's, or candidate's country;* or

C. The payment, gift, offer, or promise of anything of value that was made, was a *reasonable and bona fide expenditure,* such as travel and lodging expenses, incurred by or on behalf of a foreign official, party, party official, or candidate and was directly related to the promotion, demonstration, or explanation of products or services; or the execution or performance of a contract with a foreign government or agency thereof.

Penalties

A. Any domestic concern that violates this section shall be fined not more than $2,000,000 and shall be subject to a civil penalty of not more than $10,000 imposed in an action brought by the Attorney General.

B. Any officer or director of a domestic concern, or stockholder acting on behalf of such domestic concern, who willfully violates this section shall be fined not more than $100,000, or imprisoned not more than 5 years, or both.

C. Any employee or agent of a domestic concern who is a United States citizen, national, or resident or is otherwise subject to the jurisdiction of the United States (other than an officer, director, or stockholder acting on behalf of such domestic concern), and who willfully violates this section, shall be fined not more than $100,000, or imprisoned not more than 5 years, or both.

D. Any officer, director, employee, or agent of a domestic concern, or stockholder acting on behalf of such domestic concern, who violates this section shall be subject to a civil penalty of not more than $10,000 imposed in an action brought by the Attorney General.

E. *Whenever a fine is imposed upon any officer, director, employee, agent, or stockholder of a domestic concern, such fine may not be paid, directly or indirectly, by such domestic concern.*

Source: *US Code,* Title 15—Commerce and Trade, Chapter 2B—Securities Exchanges.

in penalties. Both of these examples suggest that more multinationals will be scrutinized in the future. In fact, while the government pursued only about 60 cases for the first three decades of the FCPA's existence, recent events indicate that in one month alone the government investigated 43 corporate cases.[11]

Although the FCPA makes bribery illegal, it does make some exceptions. Payments made under duress to avoid injury or violence are acceptable. For example, in an unstable political environment, a company may pay local officials "bribes" to avoid harassment of its employees. Smaller payments that encourage officials to do their routine jobs and fulfill their duties are also legal. Payments made that are lawful in a country are also deemed acceptable by the FCPA. Rather than seeking illegal ends, these "grease" payments are acceptable as long as they just speed up or make possible normal business functions, such as necessary paperwork.

An important component of the FCPA for US companies is the law's reason-to-know provision. The reason-to-know provision means that a firm is liable for bribes or questionable payments made by agents hired by the firm. However, if the US firm has neither knowledge of the behavior of the agent nor any reason to expect illegal behavior from the agent, then the US firm has no liability under the FCPA. In contrast, a multinational management is considered "knowing" if: (1) he or she is aware of the high possibility that an illegal act will happen, (2) he or she actually knows an illegal bribe will be given, and (3) he or she perceives that the circumstances make it likely that an illegal bribe will be given.

Warin et al. argue that more companies will be prosecuted under the FCPA than in the past.[12] In fact, even shareholders are considering lawsuits for FCPA violations. As a consequence, companies will need to ensure that their practices respect the FCPA. To give you more insights into the FCPA, Exhibit 16.3, taken directly from the FCPA codes, shows critical aspects of the FCPA.

In the above section, you read about some of the most crucial global ethics issues. Next, you will learn about some of the key approaches to dealing with global ethical issues.

Dealing with Global Ethics

In this section, you will read about how the MNC and the individual manager can deal with global ethics. First, you will learn about the multinational's approach to global ethics. In the second part of this section, you will read about how individual managers can approach global ethics.

Multinational Approach to Global Ethics: Ethical Relativism vs Ethical Universalism

Multinationals deal with global ethical issues in two important ways. Some multinationals assume that all cultures are legitimate as a means for people to guide their lives—that is, what people consider right or wrong, pretty or ugly, good or bad, depends on their cultural norms and values. As such, these multinationals practice **ethical relativism**, whereby a multinational manager considers each society's view of ethics as legitimate and ethical. Thus, for example, if bribery is an accepted way of doing business in a country, then it is acceptable for the multinational to follow local examples, even if it would be illegal at

ethical relativism
consideration that each society's views of ethics are legitimate and ethical

home. Thus, for MNCs, ethical relativism means that, when doing business in a country, managers need only follow local ethical conventions.

In contrast, some multinationals practice **ethical universalism**. Ethical universalism holds that there are basic moral principles that transcend cultural and national boundaries. For the multinational manager, ethical relativism means that the same ethical standards are applied in all countries in which the multinational operates.

Both approaches present difficulties for multinational managers. Some argue, for instance, that when taken to the extreme, ethical relativism can become "**convenient relativism.**" Convenient relativism occurs when companies use ethical relativism to behave any way that they please, using the excuse of differences in cultures. For instance, a multinational can justify using child labor because it appears to be an acceptable practice in a country. Such logic can be applied to other activities with ethical consequences, such as bribery and pollution.

Extreme ethical universalism also has its problems. Assuming that one can identify universal ethics that all people should follow can lead to a type of cultural imperialism. In other words, multinational employees' managers who assume that they know the ethical ways of behaving can view the moral systems of foreign cultures as inferior or immoral. By assuming that there are universal ethical standards, a multinational may be imposing its own headquarters' culture in the host country.

Which way should multinationals go? Next we consider some of the pressures towards ethical universalism.

Pressures Supporting Ethical Universalism

Donaldson, an expert in international business ethics, argues that multinationals have a higher moral responsibility than ethical relativism.[13] As such, he suggests that multinationals should follow ethical universalism based on moral languages. **Moral languages** describe the basic ways that people use to think about ethical decisions and to explain their ethical choices. Donaldson further argues that three universal moral languages should provide important guidance to multinationals as they strive to become more ethical.

The three moral languages include avoiding harm (i.e. a multinational should avoid harming its stakeholders), rights/duties (i.e. a multinational has some duties that it needs to fulfill), and the social contract (i.e. the social agreement a multinational has with its employees). These should guide MNCs. He proposes **prescriptive ethics** for multinationals; that is, multinationals should engage in business practices that avoid negative consequences to stakeholders (e.g. employees, the local environment). While companies keep basic rights, such as profit motive, these rights also carry consequent duties, such as providing a fair wage to local employees. The multinational also has a social contract between itself and its stakeholders. This social contract defines the nature of the relationships. As an example, when a multinational enters a country, it accepts the social contract to follow local laws.

Donaldson believes that these moral languages are most appropriate for managing ethical behaviors among multinationals located in different nations. As such, regardless of their background, companies can agree with their stakeholders on the basic rules of moral behavior. However, for these ideas to work,

ethical universalism
there are basic moral principles that transcend cultural and national boundaries

convenient relativism
taking ethical relativism to the extreme

moral languages
basic ways people use to think about ethical decisions

prescriptive ethics
multinationals should engage in business practices that avoid negative consequences

there must be a code of conduct to guide the multinationals that is independent of national boundaries. Codes are one important component of the global ethical company. In the next and final section, you will read some of the key aspects of building a socially responsible global company and the importance of codes of conduct.

Building the Socially Responsible Company

As mentioned earlier in this chapter, corporate social responsibility refers to the idea that businesses have a responsibility to society beyond making profits. In other words, social responsibility means that a company must take into account the welfare of other constituents (e.g. customers, suppliers) in addition to stockholders. Obviously, a socially responsible company has to provide guidance to employees regarding how to deal with ethical dilemmas. The socially responsible company will go beyond merely reacting to ethical situations. Such companies will be proactive in devising systems to ensure that their actions do not affect others negatively.

In this section, you will learn about the many elements of a socially responsible multinational. The first step in building the socially responsible multinational is to understand the impact of one's actions on others. You will therefore read about stakeholder analysis.

Stakeholder Analysis

As you read earlier in this section, a socially responsible multinational is one that recognizes and addresses the impact of its actions on its constituents. In that context, any group or entity that is affected by a multinational's decisions or actions is known as a **stakeholder**. There are two main types of stakeholders. **Primary stakeholders** include those who are directly linked to a company's survival and have important influences on the multinational's strategy. Primary stakeholders include customers, suppliers, employees and shareholders. In contrast, **secondary stakeholders** tend to be less directly linked to the company's survival.[14] Secondary stakeholders include the media, trade associations, and other special interest groups.

To give you further insights into the impact of stakeholders on a multinational, consider Exhibit 16.4, which depicts the relationships between a multinational and its stakeholders, and potential questions the multinational has to deal with as it interacts with these various groups.

As you can see from Exhibit 16.4, a multinational has the potential to impact many groups through its actions. The socially responsible multinational is proactive in determining potential consequences of its activities and strategies on its stakeholders. However, to be proactive, the multinational needs to address stakeholder issues strategically. One approach is to regularly conduct **stakeholder analysis,** an approach whereby the influence and impact of stakeholders are assessed. Stakeholder analysis begins with an appropriate identification of stakeholders. This step can be facilitated by considering those groups that have the potential to affect or influence the company's survival.

It should also be noted that although it may seem that secondary stakeholders have less impact for multinationals, recent examples show that secondary

stakeholder
any group or entity affected by a multinational's decisions

primary stakeholders
those directly affected by a company's decisions

secondary stakeholders
those indirectly impacted by a multinational's actions

stakeholder analysis
influence and impact of stakeholders are assessed

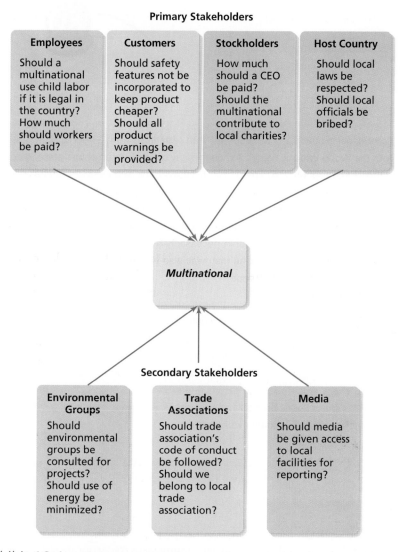

Primary Stakeholders

Employees

Should a multinational use child labor if it is legal in the country? How much should workers be paid?

Customers

Should safety features not be incorporated to keep product cheaper? Should all product warnings be provided?

Stockholders

How much should a CEO be paid? Should the multinational contribute to local charities?

Host Country

Should local laws be respected? Should local officials be bribed?

Multinational

Secondary Stakeholders

Environmental Groups

Should environmental groups be consulted for projects? Should use of energy be minimized?

Trade Associations

Should trade association's code of conduct be followed? Should we belong to local trade association?

Media

Should media be given access to local facilities for reporting?

Exhibit 16.4 **Stakeholder Analysis**

shareholders are as important as primary shareholders in terms of impact. Consider that Shell Oil has been forced to acknowledge its relationship with a corrupt government in Nigeria. Similarly, the agricultural giant Monsanto has been forced to deal with secondary stakeholders such as Greenpeace and Friends of the Earth as it tries to develop agricultural biotechnology products.[15]

One core component of stakeholder analysis is to understand the saliency of a stakeholder for the organization. This salience can be understood in terms of the power (how likely is the stakeholder to influence the multinational's strategy?), legitimacy (are the stakeholder's claims legitimate?) and urgency (how urgent are the stakeholder's claims?). A multinational manager can identify stakeholders and determine their salience for the multinational. Obviously, the more salient the stakeholder, the more necessary it is for the multinational to determine strategies to address these stakeholders' needs.

Stakeholder analysis thus serves some critical functions for the multinational. By showing its concerns for those it has the potential to affect, a

ABB and Corporate Social Responsibility in Africa

When Asea Brown Boveri (ABB), the global leader in power and automation energies, partnered with the World Wide Fund for Nature (WWF) to help in the rural electrification efforts in Africa, it met with some unanticipated reactions from its many shareholders. ABB had decided that it wanted to dedicate some of its funds to help with electrification in rural Africa because of the high proportion of people without access to electricity. WWF Tanzania chose the small village of Ngarambe because of the village's proximity to a nature reserve that is one of the world's most important living areas for elephants and rhinos.

The first unanticipated reaction came from WWF. ABB studied the many power options and decided that diesel made the most sense. However, WWF criticized the use of diesel because of its impact on the environment. After much discussion, WWF agreed with ABB's plans for diesel. ABB was in the middle of a financial crisis and WWF knew that if it did not go along with diesel, the project would stop. WWF nevertheless insisted on environmentally friendly forms of diesel.

ABB also met with resistance from a very unlikely stakeholder. Although many of ABB's international stakeholders (United Nations, World Bank, etc.) viewed rural electrification as extremely crucial, the village inhabitants were very skeptical of having electricity in their houses. Many of the villagers were not aware of the benefits of electricity and did not necessarily trust ABB. Furthermore, the local medicine man was also very reluctant to allow anyone in his house.

ABB nevertheless continued its efforts and the project was slowly implemented. However, other unexpected hurdles emerged from other stakeholder groups. For instance, when it had to choose individuals to be trained, it found that individuals were being recommended for tribal and family reasons rather than for technical competence. The financial maintenance is also a major hurdle that still needs to be overcome.

Source: Based on Niklas Egels, 2005, "CSR in electrification of rural Africa," *Journal of Corporate Citizenship*, 18, pp. 75–85.

multinational has the ability to show its commitment to corporate social responsibility. Furthermore, by identifying stakeholders, multinational managers are being proactive and can determine who has valid claims on the multinational. Finally, an understanding of stakeholders can help multinational managers determine the best approaches to achieve its multinational goals.

Stakeholder analysis is not always an easy or obvious process. The IB Strategic Insight above provides some understanding of some unforeseen stakeholder reactions.

As you can see from the IB Strategic Insight, conducting a stakeholder analysis is not always easy. However, conducting the stakeholder analysis is a critical step in terms of building the socially responsible multinational. Another critical aspect of a socially responsible multinational is the creation of a code of conduct. Next, you will learn about code of conduct.

Code of Conduct

codes of conduct
specification of appropriate employee behaviors and multinational responsibilities

According to Kaptein,[16] **codes of conduct** (also called codes of ethics) specify appropriate behaviors for employees while also defining the multinational's responsibilities and approaches in terms of its interactions with its stakeholders.

Codes of conduct emphasize the norms and values the multinational believes in while it is striving to achieve its business objectives.

Why are codes of conduct important? Codes of conduct announce to all of the stakeholders the ethical values of the multinational. By specifying the appropriate employee behaviors, the multinational also hopes that it can inform its employees of situations whereby unethical behavior may occur. By educating employees about such instances, the multinational hopes that incidences of unethical activities will be reduced. In addition to the above benefits, a properly implemented code of conduct can also help a multinational stay on the legal side and avoid prosecution. For instance, in the US, the appropriate legal rules (i.e. Federal Sentencing Guidelines) typically reduce fines for those companies that have properly enforced codes of conduct. Furthermore, recent regulations such as the Sarbanes–Oxley Act, enforcing appropriate accounting rules, require multinationals to have codes of conduct.

Which areas should a code of conduct address? The stakeholder analysis discussed earlier provides the basis for deciding which areas the code should address. More salient stakeholders suggest that these stakeholders have more influence on the corporation. It therefore becomes imperative for the multinational to develop codes of conduct to provide guidance as the multinational and its employees interact with these salient stakeholders. To give you more insights into the content of codes of conduct, Kaptein investigated the 200 largest corporations in the world. Of these 200 multinationals, only around 52 percent had a code of conduct.[17] Exhibit 16.5 shows the percentage of companies that had different areas mentioned in their codes of conduct.

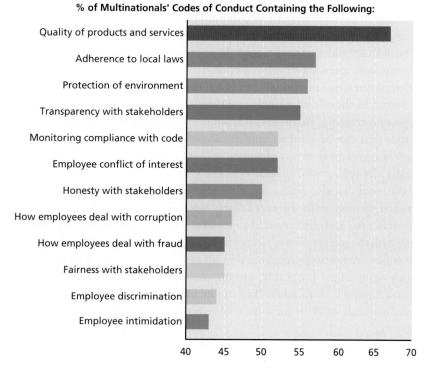

% of Multinationals' Codes of Conduct Containing the Following:

Exhibit 16.5 **Content of Codes of Conduct of World's Largest Corporations**

Source: Based on Kaptein, 2004, "Business codes of multinational firms: What do they say?" *Journal of Business Ethics*, 50, 13–31.

The study by Kaptein provides some important insights into the areas that most multinationals' codes of conduct cover. As you can see, an overwhelming majority of codes of conduct include elements pertaining to the quality of the product and services. This is not surprising given that the multinational's ability to survive depends on its ability to sell quality products and services to its customers. Providing quality products and services is crucial. However, beyond products and services, it is interesting to note that many of the world's largest multinationals' codes of conduct address other issues, such as dealing with stakeholders (transparency, fairness, etc.). These codes of conduct also provide important guidance to employees regarding how to deal with potentially unethical situations, such as use of company property, bribery, etc. Finally, most codes of conduct specify how the multinational will deal with its employees.

Which codes of conduct are perceived as being effective? A study of a number of large Canadian companies suggests that employees view more effective codes of conducts as having a number of characteristics.[18] Specifically, more effective codes of conduct were seen as containing real examples of ethical situations, were easier to read, were relevant, had senior management support, were communicated to employees through training, and had some reporting and enforcement component. While these characteristics may not apply to all multinationals, they provide some guidance as codes of conduct are developed.

Next, you will learn what multinationals can do to successfully implement a code of conduct.

Successful Implementation of Codes of Conduct

Once a code of conduct has been developed, the standards and rules contained in the code of conduct have to be communicated to employees. In that context, training becomes a crucial tool to inform employees of the appropriate way to deal with stakeholders. Some experts have argued that multinational employees are sometimes unaware of what's ethical and what's not ethical. By training their employees, multinationals can teach employees values and other qualities that matter to the multinationals and their stakeholders.

formal methods
using various means of control to ensure company is ethical

Beyond training, Adam and Rachman-Moore suggest that there are many methods that can be used to implement codes of conduct.[19] **Formal methods** include using various means of control to ensure that the multinational behaves ethically. In such cases, formal training plays a critical role. However, the multinational can also take a more strategic view of ethics and apply its ethics approach starting with the recruitment and selection process. Potential new employees are carefully screened to ensure that their personal values are consistent with the multinational's expectations. Furthermore, many multinationals have ethics orientation programs that all new employees have to go through. In such orientation programs, employees learn about the company values and how to apply them when they are facing potentially unethical situations. Formal methods work to socialize employees in understanding the appropriate behaviors.

informal methods
use of organizational culture to train employees to be more ethical

Multinationals can also rely on more **informal methods** to implement codes of conduct. In such cases, the organizational culture can play an important role in ensuring that employees behave consistently with the multinational's expectations. Employees can be pressured to conform to ethical norms by their supervisors or their peers in the multinational. Furthermore, if employees are behaving in ways that are not consistent with the multinationals' expectations, superiors or peers can disapprove or reject the employee to show their dissatisfaction with the employee's behavior.

Although formal and informal methods exist to implement codes of conduct, it is important to note that formal training remains the preferred method of informing employees of the correct and ethical behavior. Ethics training can serve many important functions.[20] Ethics training can educate companies about the multinational's expectations as well as the appropriate laws and regulations. Training can also be used to educate employees about the available resources at their disposal should they need advice regarding ethical situations.

Ethics training can take a variety of forms. Some training can be done in a passive format where employees can learn to respond to ethical dilemmas through self-study, lecture or reading. Such education can also take place in a regular classroom or in an online environment. However, passive ethics training has been criticized for being static and not being the most appropriate format where participants can learn about dealing with ethical situations. As such, more interactive forms of training where participants are exposed to actual ethical dilemmas and actively participate in such dilemmas are seen as more effective. Many experts argue that ethical decisions are complex decisions that involve focused cognitive reasoning that is only possible with active forms of training.

In this section, you read about the various ways a multinational can implement a code of conduct. In the next section, you will read about ethics monitoring.

Ethics Monitoring and Enforcement

A successful ethics program is not possible without some form of monitoring and enforcement. In other words, a program cannot be effective unless the multinational has some way of measuring performance and progress. Furthermore, some form of enforcement is necessary. Employees need to be rewarded if they are conforming to the multinational's codes and punished if they are violating these codes.

Veral argues that monitoring involves "the most detailed manifestation of specific performance criteria that the multinational has decided to attain."[21] Such monitoring provides valuable benchmarks to assess employee and company achievement of the elements of the code of conduct. For instance, if Nike has a mission of adequately compensating its employees and providing good working conditions, it can set measures that can be assessed. It can, for example, decide to set a goal whereby workers are allowed to work only eight hours per day. Through an audit, Nike can determine what percentage of workers are exceeding this goal. Similarly, any multinational can set a benchmark regarding bathroom breaks or living conditions whereby worker conditions can be assessed. In the IB Strategic Insight overleaf, you will read about how Johnson Controls, a multinational involved in automotive components and building efficiency systems among other products, has transformed into a socially responsible multinational.

As you can see from the IB Strategic Insight, it is important for a multinational to set goals to determine progress in terms of corporate social responsibility. In addition to such benchmarks, it is also important for any multinational to enforce appropriate ethical behavior through rewards and

Corporate Social Responsibility at Johnson Controls

IB STRATEGIC INSIGHT

Johnson Controls is a multinational that is involved in the automotive components sector, providing seat systems and electronic systems for cars. Johnson Controls is also the world leader in commercial building ventilation, heating and cooling systems, and provides such services to many hospitals, airports, government buildings, etc.

Over the past decade, Johnson Controls has decided to use corporate social responsibility and sustainability as the basis for competitive advantage. It sees sustainability as the "triple bottom line," namely achieving economic, social and environmental performance. To achieve sustainability, Johnson Controls has taken a very strategic approach to all stakeholders and set very specific goals for each of the three areas as they pertain to the various stakeholders. Performance is measured against these criteria to ensure that they are on the right track. Below are a few examples of how their performance is tracked.

Johnson Controls sees diversity as a very crucial element of its strategy. It has therefore set goals regarding purchases from minority and women-owned businesses. Johnson Controls is one of the few companies that has sales of more than $1 billion to minority and women-

owned businesses. Another critical element of Johnson Control's approach to social responsibility is how it treats its employees. It sees a safe environment as very crucial and constantly monitors injuries per 100 full-time workers. In 2006, Johnson Control's injury rate was only a third of the national average, showing a 14 percent improvement over 2005. As yet another example, Johnson Controls launched the "Blue Sky" initiative in 2006. The program funds employees' preferred charities in over 30 countries. Although this program is relatively new, more than 5,000 employees volunteered in various charities around the world, contributing more than 50,000 hours. As a final example, Johnson Controls is also very concerned about the impact of the material it uses on the environment. As such, Johnson Controls rigorously monitors the products it uses in production, the amount of waste it generates, the percentage of such waste that can be recycled. Johnson Controls also monitors the level of water use and water discharges, as well as its greenhouse gas emissions. It is continuously looking for ways to better use raw materials while having minimal impact on the environment.

Source: Based on www.johnsoncontrols.com

punishment. As Boudreaux and Steiner discuss, it is important to hold higher level executives to the same standards.[22] Specifically, it is useful to inform directors, officers and other top managers of the sanctions they face if they break ethical rules or laws. Infractions may result in disciplinary actions involving demotion or discharge. A multinational should also show its commitment to corporate social responsibility by rewarding ethical behavior. Annual meetings can be held to reward employees who have been ethical or who have contributed to making the multinational more ethical.

In the next and final section, you will read about some other key elements of a successful, socially responsible multinational.

Other Key Elements of the Successful Socially Responsible Multinational

While the earlier paragraphs discussed some of the major steps needed to build a socially responsible multinational, there are other important guidelines that need to be followed. In this section, you will read about these guidelines as recommended by experts:[23]

- *Setting the example at the top* For a multinational to truly demonstrate its commitment to ethics and ethical behavior, top managers and other top-level executives need to be upholding the same standards. By setting a good example, it is more likely that lower-level employees will behave ethically.
- *Making ethics part of the multinational's strategy* Successful, socially responsible multinationals are the ones whose ethical programs are made part of and integrated into their strategy and vision. All employees need to see how making ethical decisions on a daily basis is connected to the company's strategy and bottom line. Such efforts will ensure that the multinational is living and breathing ethics and is committed to being ethical.
- *Investing financial resources* A successful ethics program requires that a multinational devote the necessary financial resources to support such programs. For instance, new experts in ethics and compliance need to be hired. Business processes may need to be scrutinized and changed to comply with the new ethical direction. These and other efforts require commitment to support the programs through financial investments.
- *Involving all employees* Employees need to be able to voice their concerns and contribute to ethics efforts. By involving as many employees as possible, a multinational has a better chance to determine key ethical areas. Employees are also more likely to buy into such programs if they can participate in devising the ethics program.
- *Communicating* A corporate social responsibility program cannot succeed unless it is communicated regularly and thoroughly to all employees and stakeholders. Employees also need to be given the opportunity to communicate their views regarding the ethical efforts. Multinationals can thus provide communication tools such as 1-800 phone lines, whistle-blowing hotlines, notice boards and online forums. Managers need to regularly address ethical issues of great importance. Employees also need to feel that they can voice their ethics-related concerns when necessary.

CHAPTER REVIEW

In this chapter, you read about an area that is becoming increasingly important for multinationals. As more attention is paid to the actions of multinationals and the consequences of such actions, it is becoming more critical for these multinationals to become more socially responsible and ethical. In this chapter, you read about the key issues associated with international ethics and social responsibility. In the first section, you learned some basic definitions of international ethics and social responsibility. You also read about why multinationals are being criticized regularly.

The chapter also discussed three important ethical issues facing multinationals today. You read about labor rights and some of the most pressing issues pertaining to labor rights. You read about environmental pollution. Most importantly, you also learned about bribery and corruption and some of the efforts to lower incidences of corruption around the world.

In the third part of the chapter, you read about some of the approaches used by multinationals to deal with global ethics. You learned about ethical relativism and ethical universalism and the associated benefits and dangers of each approach.

In the final section of the chapter, we discussed the many different steps in building the ethical and socially responsible multinational. You read about codes of conduct and successful implementation of such codes. You also learned about the need to monitor and enforce ethics programs. Finally, you read about other key components of any ethics program.

 DISCUSSION QUESTIONS

1. What is international ethics? Why are multinationals increasingly being criticized? Are such criticisms always justified?
2. What is corporate social responsibility? How can a company implement a corporate social responsibility program?
3. Discuss two of the most important ethical issues facing multinationals today.
4. Compare and contrast ethical relativism and ethical universalism. Discuss some benefits and disadvantages of each approach.
5. What are some key elements of a successful ethics program?
6. Discuss some key components of a code of conduct.
7. What is stakeholder analysis? What are primary and secondary stakeholders? Give some examples.
8. Why do companies need to monitor and enforce ethics? Discuss possible ethical goals of a multinational.

INTERNATIONAL BUSINESS SKILL BUILDER

Determining Key Areas of Corporate Social Responsibility

Step 1: Go to the following companies' websites: Mattel Inc. (www. mattel.com), Nike (www.nike.com), and Freeport-McMoRan Mining (www.fcx.com).

Step 2: Locate the company's social responsibility statement or code of conduct.

Step 3: Compile a list of each company's key area of corporate social responsibility.

Step 4: Identify differences and similarities among these corporate social responsibility priority areas and approaches.

Step 5: Compile a general list of key areas of social responsibility for any multinational.

CHAPTER INTERNET ACTIVITY

Go to the Transparency International website (**http://transparency.org**). Identify the top ten and bottom ten countries of the latest corruption perception scores. Find out how the index is computed. Find out about some of the possible uses of the corruption perception index scores.

KEY CONCEPTS

bribery

codes of conduct

convenient relativism

corporate social responsibility

corruption

ethical relativism

ethical universalism

ethics

Foreign Corrupt Practices Act

formal methods

informal methods

international business ethics

moral languages

prescriptive ethics

primary stakeholders

secondary stakeholders

stakeholder

stakeholder analysis

sweatshops

MIGHTY-MART'S CONTRACT MANUFACTURING ISSUES

CASE 16

page 1

Mighty-Mart is a large retail chain that operates over 1,000 stores in the United States and Canada. The company has experienced phenomenal success over the years in terms of growth and return on shareholders' equity. The firm has gained market share over its competitors through a strategy of low-cost leadership and dedication to customer service. Mighty-Mart prides itself on its ability to reduce costs and to pass those savings on to customers. The company has been a model of efficiency among mass merchandisers, and its ability to control costs has given it a strong competitive advantage.

Mighty-Mart was founded in 1968 in a small town in eastern Kentucky by Jimmy John Whitlow. This now-deceased decorated war veteran left a legacy of uncompromising business principles, which included complete customer satisfaction, low-cost business operations, and a strong commitment to buy from American suppliers.

Anne-Marie Bradford is a well-known television personality who has developed a loyal following through her unwavering commitment to traditional American values. Most TV viewers see her as a kind-hearted and wholesome individual. Anne-Marie's early morning TV program promotes health, fitness, and family values. She also has a newspaper column, which provides advice on marriage, family, and wardrobe decisions. So it seemed logical for Mighty-Mart and Bradford to team up to market a line of women's apparel under the Anne-Marie name. Although Mighty-Mart did prefer to source its products domestically, increasingly it has begun to rely on foreign suppliers.

Under a contract manufacturing arrangement with China's Yellow Dragon Enterprises, Mighty-Mart and Anne-Marie developed the product line, which would be sold exclusively in Mighty-Mart stores. The cost of production in China was much lower than anywhere else, and Yellow Dragon had developed a reputation for quality. Under the manufacturing contract, Anne-Marie approved all product designs and Mighty-Mart handled the administration of the business relationship. Yellow Dragon Enterprises acted as an independent contractor; however, Mighty-Mart dictated what to produce, when to produce it, and, in many ways, how to produce the products. Day-to-day management of the operations was left to Yellow Dragon.

Although some Chinese manufacturers had been known to violate the human rights of their factory workers, Mighty-Mart was confident that it could force Yellow Dragon to follow Chinese labor laws and treat the employees well. Mighty-Mart had emphasized that it wanted nothing to do with any business that violated basic workplace rights. As a form of control, Mighty-Mart engaged one of the big

. . .

US accounting firms to audit Yellow Dragon employment practices over the term of the contract.

The US auditors visited Yellow Dragon factories from time to time and often found labor violations. None of the violations were considered to be of a serious nature and most involved the lack of payment for overtime. Yellow Dragon had been reluctant to pay overtime for Saturday work, which was mandated under Chinese law. A few safety violations were uncovered as well; however, Yellow Dragon always corrected the problems uncovered by the auditors and Mighty-Mart was unconcerned with the problems the auditors discovered.

Late one afternoon, Dexter Lewis, CEO of Mighty-Mart, received an urgent call from Carol Dempsey, director of external relations for the company. Dempsey explained that she had just received a call from an international labor watchdog group that was accusing Mighty-Mart of running a sweatshop in China. A representative from the International Organization for the Elimination of Sweatshops (IOES) had been told that an angry group of Yellow Dragon employees had stormed the local labor office in the Guangdong province of China, demanding that employment conditions at the company be improved. The workers accused the company of numerous unfair labor practices, including fines, beatings, and underpayment for hours worked. Lewis told Dempsey that she should look into the matter further, and he expressed concern that this incident could tarnish the company's image.

While Dempsey investigated the matter further, IOES alerted the media about the working conditions in "Mighty-Mart's Chinese sweatshops" and public criticism grew against the company and Anne-Marie Bradford. After a week of being attacked in the media, Anne-Marie went before her television audience and tearfully explained that she had no idea that her popular clothing line was being manufactured under sweatshop conditions. She assured the audience that she and Mighty-Mart would end their relationship with Yellow Dragon Enterprises and that her clothes would never again be made under such "horrible" working conditions.

An investigation by the IOES concluded that workers at Yellow Dragon had been working under sweatshop conditions. The IOES stated that the accusations against the company were true and that Mighty-Mart and Anne-Marie Bradford should be ashamed to have allowed these things to happen. According to the IOES, workers had routinely been beaten by company guards, denied overtime pay, forced to work 16-hour workdays, and exposed to unsafe conditions. Management fined workers who spoke out against the company and even refused to allow them to leave company property when they were not working. Yellow Dragon charged workers excessive prices for company housing and food, and sometimes had children as young as ten years old working in unsafe factory conditions. Many of the charges against the company violated Chinese labor laws.

It was learned that Yellow Dragon had deceived Mighty-Mart and the auditors, sometimes in elaborate fashion. For example, the company had created showcase factories for the auditors to inspect, when most of the clothes were being produced in other factories under less desirable conditions. The company warned

. . .

475

CASE 16

---

page 3

employees against speaking to the auditors unless they had good things to say about the company. Threats, beatings, and fines kept Yellow Dragon employees from informing the auditors about the real working conditions of the company.

Although Mighty-Mart had been duped by Yellow Dragon, a number of public interest groups began to speak out against the company. Mighty-Mart was accused of negligence in the control of its foreign manufacturing arrangements. Many in the press questioned the effectiveness of self-regulation of foreign manufacturing and they demanded more government regulation and social accountability.

CASE DISCUSSION POINTS

1. Is Mighty-Mart and/or Anne-Marie Bradford responsible for the working conditions at Yellow Dragon Enterprises? Explain.
2. Can a process of self-regulation ensure that labor rights will be upheld in foreign manufacturing operations? Explain.
3. What should Dexter Lewis do to solve this problem?

Note: This case is fictional; however, it is based on a similar situation as reported in D. Roberts and A. Bernstein, 2000, "A life of fines and beatings," *BusinessWeek*, October 2.

Case prepared by Charles A. Rarick

Notes

Part One

Chapter 1

1 WTO (World Trade Organization), 2002, *World Trade Organization: Trading into the Future*, Geneva: World Trade Organization; *The Economist*, 2003, "Heading east," www. economist.com, March 27; *The Economist*, 2003, "All aboard the Euro-train!" www.economist. com, April 3.

2 *The Economist*, 1996, "All free traders now?" December 7, pp. 23–5.

3 *The Economist*, 2002, "United we fall," www.economist. com, September 26; *The Economist*, 1996, "Spoiling world trade," December 7, pp. 15–16.

4 R.F.M. Lubbers, 1996, "Globalization: An exploration," *Nijenrode Management Review*, 1.

5 UNCTAD, 2007, *World Investment Report*, New York and Geneva: United Nations.

6 UNCTAD, 2000, *World Investment Report*, New York and Geneva: United Nations; UNCTAD, 2000, "World FDI flows exceed US$ 1.1 trillion in 2000," UNCTAD Press Release, December 7; UNCTAD, 2002, *World Investment Report*, New York and Geneva: United Nations.

7 UNCTAD, 2007, *World Investment Report*, New York and Geneva: United Nations.

8 UNCTAD, 2004, *World Investment Report*, New York and Geneva: United Nations.

9 UNCTAD, 2004, *World Investment Report*, New York and Geneva: United Nations.

10 UNCTAD, 2007, *World Investment Report*, New York and Geneva: United Nations; UNCTAD, 2008, *World Investment Report*, New York and Geneva: United Nations.

11 UNCTAD, 2007, *World Investment Report*, New York and Geneva: United Nations; UNCTAD, 2008, *World Investment Report*, New York and Geneva: United Nations.

12 Thomas Bradtke, Jim Hemerling, and David Young, 2005, *Navigating the Five Currents of Globalization*, Boston: Boston Consulting Group.

13 Thomas Bradtke, Jim Hemerling, and David Young, 2005, *Navigating the Five Currents of Globalization*, Boston: Boston Consulting Group.

14 http://money.cnn.com/magazines/fortune/global500/ 2008/countries/US.html

15 Boston Consulting Group, 2007, *The 2008 BCG 100 New Global Challengers*, Boston: Boston Consulting Group.

16 International Standards Organization, 2008, www.iso.ch

17 J. Levine, 1992, "Want EC business? You have two choices," *Business Week*, October 19, pp. 58–9.

18 G.C. Unruh, 2008, "The biosphere rules," *Harvard Business Review*, February, pp. 111–17.

19 CandaNewsWire, 2008, "Green movement offers significant market opportunities for the technology sector," February 13, p. 1.

Chapter 2

1 Sumatra Ghoshal, 1987, "Global strategy: An organizing framework," *Strategic Management Journal*, 8, pp. 424–40.

2 Michael E. Porter, 1986, "Changing patterns of international competition," *California Management Review*, 28, p. 2; Michael E. Porter, 1990, *Competitive Advantage of Nations*, New York: Free Press.

3 Michael E. Porter, 1985, *Competitive Advantage: Creating and Sustaining Superior Performance*, New York: Free Press.

4 C.A. Bartlett and S. Ghoshal, 1990, *Managing across Borders: The Transnational Solution*, Boston: Harvard Business School Press.

5 Michael E. Porter, 1985, *Competitive Advantage: Creating and Sustaining Superior Performance*, New York: Free Press.

6 Charles Hill, 2005, *International Business: Competing in the Global Marketplace*, Burr Ridge, IL: Irwin.

7 "Managing brands in global markets: One size doesn't fit all," http://knowledge.wharton.upenn.edu/article/1206. cfm, 2005.

8 Allen J. Morrison, David A. Ricks, and Kendall Roth, 1991, "Globalization versus regionalization: Which way for the multinational?" *Organizational Dynamics*, Winter, pp. 17–29.

9 George S. Yip, 2002, *Total Global Strategy II*, Englewood Cliffs, NJ: Prentice Hall.

10 George S. Yip, 2002, *Total Global Strategy II*, Englewood Cliffs, NJ: Prentice Hall.

11 George S. Yip, 2002, *Total Global Strategy II*, Englewood Cliffs, NJ: Prentice Hall.

12 www.tata.com

13 www.ustr.gov

14 OECD, 2003, "Foreign direct investment restrictions in OECD countries," *OECD Economic Outlook*, June.

Part Two

Chapter 3

1 www.explore-law.com/law/T/Tariff.html.

2 *The Economist*, 1996, "All free traders now?" December 7, pp. 23–5.

3 WTO, 2005, *Understanding the WTO*, Geneva: World Trade Organization; *The Economist*, 2003, "Heading east," www. economist.com, March 27.

4 WTO, 2005, *Understanding the WTO*, Geneva: World Trade Organization.

5 Jeffrey Sparshott, 2003, "Agricultural subsidies targeted," *Washington Times*, www.washtimes.com/business/20031207-114046-8545r.htm.

6 BBC News, 2005, "US limits Chinese imports," May 15, http://news.bbc.co.uk/2/hi/business/4546373.stm.

7 *The Economist*, 1996, "Spoiling world trade," December 7, pp. 15–16; *The Economist*, 2000, "Responsible regionalism," www.economist.com, December 2.

8 R.F.M. Lubbers, 1996, "Globalization: An exploration," *Nijenrode Management Review*, 1.

9 WTO, 2005, *Understanding the WTO*, Geneva: World Trade Organization.

10 WTO, 2005, *Understanding the WTO*, Geneva: World Trade Organization.

11 WTO, 2005, *Understanding the WTO*, Geneva: World Trade Organization.

12 WTO, 2005, *Understanding the WTO*, Geneva: World Trade Organization; *The Economist*, 1996, "All free traders now?" December 7, pp. 23–5.

13 *The Economist*, 2005, "With help from oil and friends," January 13.

14 Ram Upendra Das, 2004, "Rules of origin need proper perspective under trade pacts," *Financial Express*, May 10.

15 Peter B. Kenen and Ellen E. Meade, 2003, "EU accession and the Euro: Close together or far apart?" International Policy Briefs, Institute for International Economics, October.

16 *The Economist*, 2002, "Mega Europe," www.economist.com, November 18; *The Economist*, 2003, "Heading east," www.economist.com, March 27; *The Economist*, 2003, "All aboard the Euro-train!" www.economist.com, April 3.

17 http://europa.eu.int/abc/history/index_en.htm#top#top; European Commission, 2000, *Enlargement Strategy Paper*, Brussels: EC.

18 www.apec.org/apec.html.

19 www.apec.org/apec.html.

Chapter 4

1 David Hume, 1752 [1912], "Of money," *Essays*, Vol. 1, London: Green.

2 Adam Smith, 1776 [1937], *The Wealth of Nations*, New York: Modern Library.

3 David Ricardo, 1817 [1966], *The Principles of Political Economy and Taxation*, London: Cambridge University Press.

4 Eli Heckscher, 1919, "The effects of foreign trade on the distribution of income," *Economisk Tidskrift*, 21, pp. 497–512.

5 Bertil Ohlin, 1933, *Interregional and International Trade*, Cambridge, MA: Harvard University Press.

6 Wassily Leontief, 1954, "Domestic production and foreign trade: The American capital position re-examined," *Economia Internazionale*, February, pp. 3–32; Wassily Leontief, 1956, "Factor proportions and the structure of American trade: Further theoretical and empirical analysis," *Review of Economics and Statistics*, November, pp. 386–407.

7 Wenli Cheng, Jeffrey Sachs, and Xiaokai Yang, 2004, "An extended Heckscher–Ohlin model with transaction costs and technological comparative advantage," *Economic Theory*, 23, pp. 671–88.

8 Raymond Vernon, 1966, "International investment and international trade in the product life cycle," *Quarterly Journal of Economics*, 80, pp. 190–207.

9 Paul Krugman, 1983, "New theories of trade among industrial countries," *American Economic Review*, 73, pp. 343–7; Elhanan Helpman, 1999, "The structure of foreign trade," *Journal of Economic Perspectives*, 2, pp. 121–44.

10 Michael E. Porter, 1990, *The Competitive Advantage of Nations*, New York: Free Press, p. 1.

11 Gary S. Vasilash, 2005, "Bright strategies: Hella's independent approach," *Automotive Design and Production*, www.autofield guide.com, May.

12 Eleanor Beardsley, 2005, "When it comes to French business, the accent is on English," *The Christian Science Monitor*, www.csmonitor.com, August 11.

13 The Federal Reserve Board, 2005, *Testimony of Chairman Alan Greenspan, China*, Committee on Finance, US Senate, June 23.

14 Stephen Hymer, 1990 [1968], "The large multinational 'corporation'," in M. Casson (ed.) *Multinational Corporations*, Hants: Edward Elgar, pp. 6–31.

15 UNCTAD, 2003, *2002 World Investment Report: Transnational Corporations and Export Competitiveness*, New York: United Nations.

16 J.-F. Hennart, 2000, "Transaction costs theory and the multinational enterprise," in C. Pitelis and R. Sugden (eds) *The Nature of the Transnational Firm*, London: Routledge, pp. 72–118.

17 John H. Dunning, 1988, "The eclectic paradigm of international production: A restatement and some possible extensions," *Journal of International Business Studies*, 19, pp. 1–31.

Chapter 5

1 Joseph P. Daniels and David D. VanHoose, 2005, *International Monetary and Financial Economics*, Mason, OH: South-Western.

2 Robert J. Carbaugh, 2005, *International Economics*, Mason, OH: South-Western.

3 www.currencysystem.com/kb/3-138.html

4 Joseph P. Daniels and David D. VanHoose, 2005, *International Monetary and Financial Economics*, Mason, OH: South-Western.

5 Andy Mukherjee, 2005, "Commentary: Has the yuan just traded one peg for another?" *International Herald Tribune*, November 29.

Chapter 6

1 www.federalreserve.gov/monetarypolicy/reservereq.htm#fn3

2 Kirt Butler, 2004, *Multinational Finance* (3rd edn), Mason, OH: Thomson South-Western.

3 Kirt Butler, 2004, *Multinational Finance* (3rd edn), Mason, OH: Thomson South-Western.

4 Kirt Butler, 2004, *Multinational Finance* (3rd edn), Mason, OH: Thomson South-Western.

5 www.investopedia.com/university/advancedbond/advancedbond1.asp

6 Ryan Stever, Goetz von Peter, and Christian Upper, 2006, "Highlights of international banking and financial market activity," *BIS Quarterly Review*, December, pp. 15–26.

7 http://en.wikipedia.org/wiki/American_Depository_Receipt

8 Depository Receipt Division, Bank of New York, 2003, "The case for investing in depositary receipts." In *The Global Equity Investment Guide*, New York: Bank of New York; Anthony Moro, 2006, "Role of depositary receipts." In *A Guide for European Companies to Listing on the US Securities Markets*, New York: Bank of New York.

9 Gordon Platt, 2006, "The Russians are coming to London and Luxembourg to satisfy appetite for capital," *Global Finance*, 20(3), pp. 49–51.

10 Deepak Gopinath, 2007, "Strict IPO rules raise anxiety on Wall Street marketplace by Bloomberg," *International Herald Tribune*, February 21, p. 18.

11 Aissatou Sidime, 2007, "The good and bad of Sarbanes–Oxley," *Knight Ridder Tribune News*, February 16, p. 1.

Part Three

Chapter 7

1 G. Hofstede, 2001, *Culture's Consequences: Comparing Values, Behaviors, Institutions, and Organizations Across Nations* (2nd edn), Thousand Oaks: Sage.

2 Joseph Tarnowski, 2006, "Assimilate or perish," *Progressive Grocer*, 85(2), p. 92.

3 Cynthia Waller Vallario, 2006, "Creating an environment for global diversity," *Financial Executive*, 22(3), pp. 50–2.

4 Steve Hamm, 2008, "International isn't just IBM's first name," *Business Week*, January 28, pp. 36–40.

5 *The Economist*, 2008, "The challengers," January 12, pp. 62–4.

6 Bradley L. Kirkman, Kevin B. Lowe, and Cristina B. Gibson, 2006, "A quarter century of culture's consequences: A review of empirical research incorporating Hofstede's cultural values framework," *Journal of International Business Studies*, 37, pp. 285–320.

7 R.J. House, P.J. Hanges, M. Javidan, P.W. Dorfman, and V. Gupta (eds) 2004, *Culture, Leadership and Organizations: The GLOBE Study of 62 Societies*, Thousand Oaks: Sage.

8 G. Hofstede, 2001, *Culture's Consequences: Comparing Values, Behaviors, Institutions, and Organizations across Nations* (2nd edn), Thousand Oaks: Sage.

9 Bradley L. Kirkman, Kevin B. Lowe, and Cristina B. Gibson, 2006, "A quarter century of culture's consequences: A review of empirical research incorporating Hofstede's cultural values framework," *Journal of International Business Studies*, 37, pp. 285–320.

10 Wirefeed, 2007, "Bridging Indian–US business cultures: Will the twain meet?" *The Hindustan Times*, January 21.

11 Shannon Klie, 2006, "Cultural training a 'two-way street'," *Canadian HR Reporter*, 19(16), p. 9.

12 Brian J. Hurn, 2007, "The influence of culture on international business negotiations," *Industrial and Commercial Training*, 39(7), pp. 354–60.

13 Rhonda Singer, 2006, "Watch for cultural biases in assessing employees," *Canadian HR Reporter*, 19(12), pp. 15.

14 Jena McGregor, 2008, "The right perks," *Business Week*, January 28, pp. 42–3.

15 Bradley L. Kirkman, Kevin B. Lowe, and Cristina B. Gibson, 2006, "A quarter century of culture's consequences: A review of empirical research incorporating Hofstede's cultural values framework," *Journal of International Business Studies*, 37, pp. 285–320.

16 Bryan W. Husted, 2005, "Culture and ecology: A cross-national study of the determinants of environmental sustainability," *Management International Review*, 45(3), pp. 349–71.

17 R.J. House, P.J. Hanges, M. Javidan, P.W. Dorfman, and V. Gupta (eds) 2004, *Culture, Leadership and Organizations: The GLOBE Study of 62 Societies*, Thousand Oaks: Sage.

18 R.J. House, P.J. Hanges, M. Javidan, P.W. Dorfman, and V. Gupta (eds) 2004, *Culture, Leadership and Organizations: The GLOBE Study of 62 Societies*, Thousand Oaks: Sage.

19 Mansour Javidan, Peter W. Dorfman, Mary Sully de

Luque, and Robert J. House, 2006, "In the eye of the beholder: Cross-cultural lessons in leadership from project GLOBE," *The Academy of Management Perspectives*, February, pp. 67–90.

20 Jena McGregor, 2008, "To adapt, ITT lets go of unpopular ratings," *BusinessWeek*, January 28, p. 46.

21 Joyce S. Osland, Allan Bird, June Delano, and Matthew Jacob, 2000, "Beyond sophisticated stereotyping: Cultural sensemaking in context," *The Academy of Management Executive*, 14(1), pp. 65–79.

22 Joyce S. Osland, Allan Bird, June Delano, and Matthew Jacob, 2000, "Beyond sophisticated stereotyping: Cultural sensemaking in context," *The Academy of Management Executive*, 14(1), pp. 65–79.

23 William Maurice Baker and F. Douglas Roberts, 2006, "Managing the costs of expatriation," *Strategic Finance*, 87(11), pp. 35–41.

24 Lisa N. Littrell, Eduardo Salas, Kathleen P. Hess, Michael Paley, and Sharon Riedel, 2006, "Expatriate preparation: A critical analysis of 25 years of cross-cultural training research," *Human Resource Development Review*, 5(3), pp. 355–88.

25 Lisa N. Littrell and Eduardo Salas, 2005, "A review of cross-cultural training: Best practices, guidelines, and research needs," *Human Resource Development Review*, 4(3), pp. 305–34.

26 Leandra Celaya and Jonathan Swift, 2006, "Pre-departure cultural training: US managers in Mexico," *Cross Cultural Management: An International Journal*, 13(3), pp. 230–43.

27 Leandra Celaya and Jonathan Swift, 2006, "Pre-departure cultural training: US managers in Mexico," *Cross Cultural Management: An International Journal*, 13(3), pp. 230–43.

28 Lisa N. Littrell and Eduardo Salas, 2005, "A review of cross-cultural training: Best practices, guidelines, and research needs," *Human Resource Development Review*, 4(3), pp. 305–34.

Chapter 8

1 J.H. Turner, 1997, *The Institutional Order*, New York: Addison-Wesley Educational Publishers, p. 6.

2 Haradimos Tsoukas, 1994, "Socio-economic systems and organizational management: An institutional perspective on the socialist firm," *Organization Studies*, 15, pp. 21–45, p. 24.

3 Haradimos Tsoukas, 1994, "Socio-economic systems and organizational management: An institutional perspective on the socialist firm," *Organization Studies*, 15, pp. 21–45.

4 E. Heinrich, 2006, "Reality Czech," *Canadian Business*, March 26, pp. 29–30.

5 BBC Monitoring European, 2006, "Privatization of Serbia's only private mobile operator begins," May 16, p. 1.

6 J. Ewing, 2008, "Nokia's new home in Romania," *BusinessWeek*, January, pp. 41–2.

7 www.heritage.org

8 John H. Willes and John A. Willes, 2005, *International Business Law*, New York: McGraw-Hill–Irwin.

9 John H. Willes and John A. Willes, 2005, *International Business Law*, New York: McGraw-Hill–Irwin.

10 www.doingbusiness.org

11 Richard Schaffer, Beverly Earle, and Filberto Augusti, 2005, *International Law and its Environment* (6th edn), Mason, OH: Thomson South-Western.

12 John H. Willes and John A. Willes, 2005, *International Business Law*, New York: McGraw-Hill–Irwin.

13 Jared Wade, 2005, "Political risk in Eastern Europe," *Risk Management*, 52(3), pp. 24–9, p. 24.

14 Ian Bremmer, 2007, "How to calculate political risk," *Inc.*, 29(4), pp. 99–101.

15 Jared Wade, 2005, "Political risk in Eastern Europe," *Risk Management*, 52(3), pp. 24–9.

16 Rodney Stark and William S. Bainbridge, 1985, *The Future of Religion*, Berkeley, CA: University of California Press.

17 Laurence R. Iannaconne, 1998, "Introduction to the economics of religion," *Journal of Economic Literature*, 36, pp. 1465–96.

18 Mary Pat Fisher, 2005, *Living Religions* (6th edn), Upper Saddle River, NJ: Prentice Hall.

19 S. Nanayakkara, 1992, "Ethics of material progress: The Buddhist attitude," Colombo: The World Fellowship of Buddhist Activities Committee.

20 Mary Pat Fisher, 1999, *Living Religions* (4th edn), Upper Saddle River, NJ: Prentice Hall, p. 273.

21 Theodore M. Ludwig, 2001, *The Sacred Paths* (3rd edn), Upper Saddle River, NJ: Prentice Hall, p. 64.

22 S.G. Mozumder, 2007, "Indian employers discriminate against Dalit, Muslim candidates: US professors," *India Abroad*, November 30, pp. A43–4.

23 *The Economist*, 2007, "With reservations: Business and caste in India," October 6, p. 93.

24 *The Economist*, 2007, "With reservations: Business and caste in India," October 6, p. 93.

25 Richard Schaffer, Beverly Earle, and Filberto Augusti, 2005, *International Law and its Environment* (6th edn), Mason, OH: Thomson South-Western.

26 Theodore M. Ludwig, 2001, *The Sacred Paths* (3rd edn), Upper Saddle River, NJ: Prentice Hall.

27 Theodore M. Ludwig, 2001, *The Sacred Paths* (3rd edn), Upper Saddle River, NJ: Prentice Hall.

28 Mary Pat Fisher, 2005, *Living Religions* (6th edn), Upper Saddle River, NJ: Prentice Hall.

29 Mary Pat Fisher, 2005, *Living Religions* (6th edn), Upper Saddle River, NJ: Prentice Hall.

30 Loong Wong, 2005, "Chinese management as discourse: 'Chinese' as a technology of self and control?" *Asian Business and Management*, 4, pp. 431–53.

Part Four

Chapter 9

1 www.unzco.com/basicguide/c6.html

2 Jack S. Wolf, 1992, *Export Profits: A Guide for Small Business*, Dover, NH: Upstart Publishing.

3 Jack S. Wolf, 1992, *Export Profits: A Guide for Small Business*, Dover, NH: Upstart Publishing.

4 Franklin R. Root, 1998, *Entry Strategies for International Markets*, New York: Lexington Books; John B. Cullen, and K. Praveen Parboteeah, 2008, *Multinational Management*, Mason, OH: Thomson South-Western.

5 Franklin R. Root, 1998, *Entry Strategies for International Markets*, New York: Lexington Books.

6 Franklin R. Root, 1998, *Entry Strategies for International Markets*, New York: Lexington Books; Paul J. Beamish, Allen J. Morrison, Andrew Inkpen, and Philip M. Rosenzweig, 2003, *International Management*, New York: McGraw-Hill.

7 http://eng.baltika.ru/news/25

8 Paul J. Beamish, Allen J. Morrison, Andrew Inkpen, and Philip M. Rosenzweig, 2003, *International Management*, New York: McGraw-Hill.

9 Franklin R. Root, 1998, *Entry Strategies for International Markets*, New York: Lexington Books.

10 Mark Henricks, 2005, "Franchise your business," www.entrepreneur.com, December 1.

11 Ed Young, "Franchising in China: A dead duck," www.Brandchannel.com.

12 Paul J. Beamish, Allen J. Morrison, Andrew Inkpen, and Philip M. Rosenzweig, 2003, *International Management*, New York: McGraw-Hill.

13 http://about.puma.com/news.jsp?year=05&id=33&lang=eng

14 Paul J. Beamish, Allen J. Morrison, Andrew Inkpen, and Philip M. Rosenzweig, 2003, *International Management*, New York: McGraw-Hill.

15 www.answers.com

16 Paul J. Beamish, Allen J. Morrison, Andrew Inkpen, and Philip M. Rosenzweig, 2003, *International Management*, New York: McGraw-Hill.

17 UNCTAD, 2000, *World Investment Report: Cross-Border Mergers and Acquisitions and Development*, New York: United Nations; UNCTAD, 2005, *World Investment Report: Transnational Corporations and the Internationalization of R&D*, New York: United Nations.

18 UNCTAD, 2005, *World Investment Report: Transnational Corporations and the Internationalization of R&D*, New York: United Nations.

19 Franklin R. Root, 1998, *Entry Strategies for International Markets*, New York: Lexington Books.

20 Paul J. Beamish, Allen J. Morrison, Andrew Inkpen, and Philip M. Rosenzweig, 2003, *International Management*, New York: McGraw-Hill.

21 Franklin R. Root, 1998, *Entry Strategies for International Markets*, New York: Lexington Books.

Chapter 10

1 www.MyZeno.com/abouttyrell.htm

2 John B. Cullen and Praveen K. Parboteeah, 2004, *International Strategic Management*, Mason, OH: Thomson South-Western.

3 Mark Graham, 2005, "China's wine revolution," *The Wine Spectator*, November, pp. 60–74.

4 www.nokia.com

5 "The 1005 DS100: Consumer brands of the top 100 companies in the Muslim world," 2006, www.brandchannel.com, April 19.

6 "Going global: Risks and rewards," 2006, www.brandchannel.com, April 19.

7 Jean L. Johnson, Tomoaki Sakano, Joseph A. Cote, and Naoto Onzo, 1993, "The exercise of intercompany power and its repercussions in US–Japanese channel relationship," *Journal of Marketing*, 57(2), pp. 1–10.

8 Thomas L. Friedman, 2005, *The World is Flat*, New York: Farrar, Straus, and Giroux.

9 Masaaki Kotabe and Kristiaan Helsen, 2004, *Global Marketing Management* (3rd edn), Hoboken, NJ: Wiley.

10 Masaaki Kotabe and Kristiaan Helsen, 2004, *Global Marketing Management* (3rd edn), Hoboken, NJ: Wiley.

Chapter 11

1 www.prsgroup.com/ICRG.aspx

2 http://store.eiu.com/product/730000273-sample.html

3 www.aon.com/politicalrisk

4 This section relies heavily on Jeff Madura, 2003, *International Financial Management*, Mason, OH: South-Western.

5 John Graham and Campbell Harvey, 2001, "The theory and practice of corporate finance: Evidence from the field," *Journal of Financial Economics*, 60, pp. 187–243.

6 Franco T. Modigliani and Merton Miller, 1958, "The cost of capital, corporate finance, and the theory of investment," *American Economic Review*, 48, pp. 655–69; Franco T. Modigliani and Merton Miller, 1961, "Corporate income taxes and the cost of capital: A revision," *American Economic Review*, 53, pp. 433–42.

7 This section relies heavily on Jeff Madura, 2003, *International Financial Management*, Mason, OH: South-Western, pp. 513–17.

8 Claude Erb, Campbell Harvey, and Tadas Viskanta, 1995, "Country risk and global equity selection," *Journal of Portfolio Management*, 21, pp. 74–83.

9 Susan Chaplinsky and Latha Ramechand, 2000, "The impact of global equity offerings," *Journal of Finance*, 55, pp. 2767–89.

10 Claude Erb, Campbell Harvey, and Tadas Viskanta, 1996, "Political risk, financial risk and economic risk," *Financial Analysts' Journal*, 52, pp. 28–46.

11 This section relies heavily on Jeff Madura, 2003, *International Financial Management*, Mason, OH: South-Western, pp. 519–23. See also Raghuram G. Rajan and Luigi Zingales, 1995, "What do we know about capital structure? Some evidence from international data," *Journal of Finance*, 50, pp. 1421–60.

12 Mihir A. Desal, C. Fritz Foley, and James R. Hines Jr, 2004, "A multinational perspective on capital structure choice and internal capital markets," *Journal of Finance*, LIX, pp. 2451–87.

13 This section relies heavily on the US Department of Commerce, 2007, *Trade Finance Guide*, Washington, DC: US Department of Commerce.

Chapter 12

1 Hervé Stolowy, 1997, "The definition of international accounting through textbook contents," paper presented at the 8th World Congress of the International Association for Accounting Education and Research (IAAER), Paris, France, October 23–25.

2 This section draws heavily on the work of Shahrokh M. Saudagaran, 2004, *International Accounting: A User Perspective*, Mason, OH: South-Western.

3 S.J. Gray, 1988, "Towards a theory of cultural influence on the development of accounting systems internationally," *Abacus*, 24, pp. 1–15; Y. Yuan Ding, Thomas Jean, and Hervé Stolowy, 2005, "Why do national GAAP differ from IAS? The role of culture," *International Journal of Accounting*, 40, pp. 325–50.

4 H. Fechner and A. Kilgore, 1994, "The influence of cultural factors on accounting practice," *International Journal of Accounting*, 29, pp. 265–77; Chris Robinson and George Venieris, 1996, "Economics, culture, and accounting standards: A case study of Greece and Canada," *Revue Canadienne des Sciences de l'Administration*, June.

5 This section draws heavily on the work of Shahrokh M. Saudagaran, 2004, *International Accounting: A User Perspective*, Mason, OH: South-Western.

6 T.S. Doupnik and S.B. Salter, 1993, "An empirical test of a judgmental international classification of financial reporting practices," *Journal of International Business Studies* 24(1), pp. 41–60; G.G. Mueller, 1968, "Accounting principles generally accepted in the United States versus those generally accepted elsewhere," *International Journal of Accounting*, 3, pp. 91–103; C.W. Nobes, 1983, "A judgmental international classification of financial reporting practices," *Journal of Business Finance and Accounting*, Spring, pp. 1–19.

7 Quoted from www.iasb.org/About+Us/About+the+ Foundation/Constitution.htm.

8 http://ec.europa.eu/internal_market/accounting/ias_en. htm#070112

9 www.iasb.org/News/Announcements+and+Speeches/ Vice+Chairman+of+the+IASC+Foundation+addresses+ European+Parliament.htm, July 10, 2007.

10 M. Zafar Iqbal, 2002, *International Accounting: A Global Perspective*, Mason, OH: South-Western; Shahrokh M. Saudagaran, 2004, *International Accounting: A User Perspective*, Mason, OH: South-Western.

11 Financial Accounting Standards Board, 1981, *Statement of Financial Accounting Standards No. 52, Foreign Currency Translation*, Stamford, CN: FASB, December.

12 M. Saudagaran, 2004, *International Accounting: A User Perspective*, Mason, OH: South-Western.

13 M. Zafar Iqbal, 2002, *International Accounting: A Global Perspective*, Mason, OH: South-Western.

14 Nick Woodford and Christopher Schreiber, 2005, "Debt financing loses appeal as tax planning strategy," *International Tax Review*, April.

15 KPMG International, 2008, *KPMG International Survey of Corporate Responsibility Reporting 2008*, New York: KPMG, p. 14.

16 KPMG International, 2008, *KPMG International Survey of Corporate Responsibility Reporting 2008*, New York: KPMG.

17 Environmental and economic changes enable transfer prices to be adjusted to permit overall tax savings within a consolidated corporate group. The challenge is by how much, at what "cost" to whom, and whether the "cost" can be minimized among stakeholders.

18 Reproduced from www.sec.gov/investor/pubs/begfinstmt guide.htm.

Chapter 13

1 G. Bruce Friesen, 2005, "Organization design for the 21st century," *Consulting to Management*, 16(3), pp. 32–51.

2 G. Bruce Friesen, 2005, "Organization design for the 21st century," *Consulting to Management*, 16(3), pp. 32–51.

3 Gareth R. Jones, 2007, *Organizational Theory, Design and Change*, Upper Saddle River, NJ: Pearson Prentice Hall.

4 Gareth R. Jones, 2007, *Organizational Theory, Design and Change*, Upper Saddle River, NJ: Pearson Prentice Hall.

5 Gareth R. Jones, 2007, *Organizational Theory, Design and Change*, Upper Saddle River, NJ: Pearson Prentice Hall.

6 J.M. Stopford and L.T. Wells, Jr, 1972, *Managing the Multinational Enterprise*, New York: Basic Books.

7 Christopher Bartlett, Sumantra Ghoshal, and Paul Beamish, 2008, *Transnational Management* (5th edn), New York: McGraw-Hill.

8 Craig T. Williams and Juliet Rains, 2007, "Linking strategy to structure: The power of systematic organization

design," *Organization Development Journal*, 25(2), pp. 163–70.

9 Christopher A. Bartlett and Sumantra Ghoshal, 1989, *Managing across Borders: The Transnational Solution*, Boston: Harvard University Press.

10 David Cray, 1984, "Control and coordination in multi-national corporations," *Journal of International Business Studies*, Fall, pp. 85–98.

11 Roger Chen, and Mark V. Cannice, 2006, "Global integration and the performance of multinationals' subsidiaries in emerging markets," *Ivey Business Journal*, January/ February, pp. 1–9.

12 Gareth R. Jones, 2007, *Organizational Theory, Design and Change*, Upper Saddle River, NJ: Pearson Prentice Hall.

13 *Strategic Direction*, 2005, "The strategic message from IBM: Diversify or die," *Strategic Direction*, April, 21(4), pp. 13–15.

14 Gloria Barczak and Edward F. McDonough, 2003, "Leading global product development teams," *Research Technology Management*, November/December, 46(6), pp. 14–18.

15 Gloria Barczak, Edward F. McDonough, and Nicholas Athanassiou, 2006, "So you want to be a global project leader?" *Research Technology Management*, May/June, 49(3), pp. 28–35.

16 Janaki Mythily Kumar, 2006, "Working as a designer in a global team," *Interactions*, March/April, pp. 25–7.

17 Gloria Barczak, Edward F. McDonough, and Nicholas Athanassiou, 2006, "So you want to be a global project leader?" *Research Technology Management*, May/June, 49(3), pp. 28–35.

18 Terence Brake, 2006, "Leading global virtual teams," *Industrial and Commercial Training*, 38(3), pp. 116–21.

19 Pete Engardio, 2007, "A guide for multinationals. One of the greatest challenges for a multinational is learning how to build a productive global team," *BusinessWeek*, August 20, 4047, p. 48.

20 Terence Brake, 2006, "Leading global virtual teams," *Industrial and Commercial Training*, 38(3), pp. 116–21.

21 Susan K. Gerke, 2006, "If I cannot see them, how can I lead them?" *Industrial and Commercial Training*, 38(2), pp. 102–5.

22 Terence Brake, 2006, "Leading global virtual teams," *Industrial and Commercial Training*, 38(3), pp. 116–21; Susan K. Gerke, 2006, "If I cannot see them, how can I lead them?" *Industrial and Commercial Training*, 38(2), pp. 102–5.

23 Junxia Wang, Hans Peter Peters, and Jiancheng Guan, 2006, "Factors influencing knowledge productivity in German research groups: Lessons for developing countries," *Journal of Knowledge Management*, 10(4), pp. 113–26.

24 Sven C. Voelpel and Zheng Han, 2005, "Managing knowledge sharing in China: The case of Siemens ShareNet," *Journal of Knowledge Management*, 9(3), pp. 51–63.

25 J.G. Davis, E. Subramanian, and A.W. Westerberg, 2005, "The 'global' and 'local' in knowledge management," *Journal of Knowledge Management*, 9(1), pp. 101–12.

26 Stewart Johnston, and Angela Paladino, "Knowledge management and involvement in innovations in MNC subsidiaries," *Management International Review*, 47(2), pp. 281–302; C. Rivinus, 2007, "Demonstrating value at Parsons Brinckerhoff," *Knowledge Management Review*, January/February, 9(6), pp. 24–7.

27 Clyde W. Holsapple, 2005, "The inseparability of modern knowledge management and computer-based technology," *Journal of Knowledge Management*, 9(1), pp. 42–52.

28 Philip Weiss, 2007, "Looking through the portal," *Communication World*, May/June, 24(3), pp. 20–3.

29 Andreas Riege, 2005, "Three dozen knowledge-sharing barriers managers must consider," *Journal of Knowledge Management*, 9(3), pp. 18–35.

30 Jane McKenzie, 2005, "How to share knowledge between companies," *Knowledge Management Review*, November/December 8(5), pp. 16–19.

31 Mikael Schönström, 2005, "Creating knowledge networks: Lessons from practice," *Journal of Knowledge Management*, 9(6), pp. 17–29.

Chapter 14

1 Jena McGregor and Steve Hamm, 2008, "Managing the global workforce," *BusinessWeek*, January 28, p. 34.

2 G.W. Bohlander, S. Snell, and A.W. Sherman, 2001, *Managing Human Resources*, Cincinnati: South-Western.

3 International Social Survey Program (ISSP), 1999/2000, *International Social Survey Program: Work Orientations II, 1997* [computer file], Ann Arbor: Inter-university Consortium for Political and Social Science Research.

4 G. Hofstede, 1991, *Cultures and Organizations*, London: McGraw-Hill, pp. 99–100.

5 Z. Grainge, 2007, "Happy handover," *Personnel Today*, Spring, pp. 14–16.

6 David Stern, Yingquan Song, and Bridget O'Brien, 2004, "Company training in the United States 1970–2000: What have been the trends over time?" *International Journal of Training and Development*, 8(3), pp. 191–209.

7 M.E. Van Buren and S.B. King, 2000, "ASTD's annual accounting of worldwide patterns in employer-provided training," *Training and Development*, Alexandra, VA: ASTD, pp. 1–24.

8 David Stern, Yingquan Song, and Bridget O'Brien, 2004, "Company training in the United States 1970–2000: What have been the trends over time?" *International Journal of Training and Development*, 8(3), pp. 191–209.

9 Chris Brewster, Geoff Wood, Michael Brookes, and Jos Van Ommeren, 2006, "What determines the size of the HR

function? A cross-national analysis," *Human Resource Management*, Spring, 45(1), pp. 3–21.

10 Casper Van Vark, 2006, "Think global, act local," *Human Resources*, June, pp. 70–2.

11 Jonathan Katz, 2007, "Worlds of difference," *Industry Week*, December, pp. 39–41.

12 G. Hofstede, 1991, *Cultures and Organizations*, London: McGraw-Hill.

13 R.M. Steers, Y.K. Shin, and G.R. Ungson, 1989, *The Chaebol: Korea's New Industrial Might*, New York: Harper Business.

14 Jie Shen, 2005, "Effective international performance appraisals: Easily said, hard to do," *Compensation and Benefits Review*, 37(4), pp. 70–9.

15 Michael Segalla, Dominique Rouzies, Madeleine Besson, and Barton A. Weitz, 2006, "A cross-national investigation of incentive sales compensation," *International Journal of Research in Marketing*, 23, pp. 419–33.

16 J.M. Geringer, C.A. Frayne, and J.F. Milliman, 2002, "In search of 'best practices' in human resource management: Research design and methodology," *Human Resource Management*, 41, pp. 5–30.

17 Jena McGregor, 2008, "The right perks," *BusinessWeek*, January 28, pp. 42–3.

18 F. Hansen, 2006, "Current trends in compensation and benefits," *Compensation and Benefits Review*, November/December, 38, pp. 6–19.

19 Jelle Visser, 2000, "Trends in unionisation and collective bargaining," *International Labour Office*, September, pp. 1–18.

20 Jelle Visser, 2000, "Trends in unionisation and collective bargaining," *International Labour Office*, September, pp. 1–18.

21 *The Economist*, 2006, "Special report: Travelling more lightly—staffing globalization," 379, pp. 84, 83, 99.

22 R.H. Sims and M. Schraeder, 2005, "Expatriate compensation," *Career Development International*, 10(2), pp. 98–108.

23 R.H. Sims and M. Schraeder, 2005, "Expatriate compensation," *Career Development International*, 10(2), pp. 98–108.

24 Guilherme Pires, John Stanton, and Shane Ostenfeld, 2006, "Improving expatriate adjustment and effectiveness in ethnically diverse countries: marketing insights," *Cross-Cultural Management*, 13(2), pp. 156–70.

25 Alizee B. Avril and Vincent P. Magnini, 2007, "A holistic approach to expatriate success," *International Journal of Contemporary Hospitality Management*, 19(1), pp. 53–64.

26 Alizee B. Avril and Vincent P. Magnini, 2007, "A holistic approach to expatriate success," *International Journal of Contemporary Hospitality Management*, 19(1), pp. 53–64.

27 David C. Martin and John J. Anthony, 2006, "The repatriation and retention of employees: Factors leading to successful programs," *International Journal of Management*, 23(3), pp. 620–31.

28 David C. Martin and John J. Anthony, 2006, "The repatriation and retention of employees: Factors leading to successful programs," *International Journal of Management*, 23(3), pp. 620–31.

29 H. Harris, 2004, "Global careers: work–life issues and the adjustment of women international managers," *Journal of Management Development*, 23(9), pp. 818–32.

30 N. Adler, 1984, "Expecting international success: Female managers overseas," *Columbia Journal of World Business*, 19(3), pp. 79–85.

31 N. Adler, 1993, "Women managers in a global economy," *HRMagazine*, September, pp. 52–5.

32 Arup Varma, Soo Min Toh, and Pawan Budhwar, 2006, "A new perspective on the female expatriate experience: The role of host country national categorization," *Journal of World Business*, 41, pp. 112–20.

Chapter 15

1 Chang E. Koh and Kyungdoo "Ted" Nam, 2005, "Business use of the Internet: A longitudinal study from a value chain perspective," *Industrial Management and Data Systems*, 105(1), pp. 82–95.

2 Emin M. Dinlersoz and Pedro Pereira, 2007, "On the diffusion of electronic commerce," *International Journal of Industrial Organization*, 25, pp. 541–74.

3 Sung-Chi Chu, Lawrence C. Leung, Yer Van Hui, and Waiman Cheung, 2007, "Evolution of e-commerce web sites: A conceptual framework and a longitudinal study," *Information and Management*, 44, pp. 154–64.

4 Sung-Chi Chu, Lawrence C. Leung, Yer Van Hui, and Waiman Cheung, 2007, "Evolution of e-commerce web sites: A conceptual framework and a longitudinal study," *Information and Management*, 44, pp. 154–64.

5 Sung-Chi Chu, Lawrence C. Leung, Yer Van Hui, and Waiman Cheung, 2007, "Evolution of e-commerce web sites: A conceptual framework and a longitudinal study," *Information and Management*, 44, pp. 154–64.

6 G.A. Knight, and T. Cavusgil, 2005, "A taxonomy of born-global firms," *Management International Review*, 45, pp. 15–35.

7 G.A. Knight, and T. Cavusgil, 2005, "A taxonomy of born-global firms," *Management International Review*, 45, pp. 15–35.

8 John Heilemann, 2005, "Retooling the entrepreneur," *Business 2.0*, 6(10), pp. 42–5.

9 OECD, 2005, *Measuring the Internet Economy*, Paris, Organization for Economic Cooperation and Development.

10 Ellen Sheng, 2007, "Corporate connections: Companies find social networks can get people talking—about their products," *Wall Street Journal*, January, p. R8.

11 David Batstone, 2006, "One-stop shopping to save the world," *Business 2.0*, 7(6), p. 70.

12 Bob Tedeschi, 2007, "Online booksellers face higher costs for shipping abroad," *New York Times*, April, p. C6.

13 Alexander Yap, Jayoti Das, John Burbridge, and Kathryn Cort, 2006, "A composite-model for e-commerce diffusion: Integrating cultural and socio-economic dimensions to the dynamics of diffusion," *Journal of Global Information Management*, 14(3), pp. 17–38.

14 F.D. Davis, 1989, "Perceived usefulness, perceived ease of use, and user acceptance of information technology," *MIS Quarterly*, 13, pp. 319–40.

15 Zhang Pei, Zheng Zhenxiang, and Huang Chunping, 2007, "An extended TAM model for Chinese B2C websites design," *Journal of Global Information Technology Management*, 10(1), pp. 51–66.

16 D.V. Parboteeah, K.P. Parboteeah, J.B. Cullen, and C. Basu, 2005, "Perceived usefulness of technology: A cross-national model," *Journal of Global Information Technology Management*, 8(4), pp. 29–48.

17 D.V. Parboteeah, K.P. Parboteeah, J.B. Cullen, and C. Basu, 2005, "Perceived usefulness of technology: A cross-national model," *Journal of Global Information Technology Management*, 8(4), pp. 29–48.

18 C. Shirky, 2000, "Go global or bust," *Business 2.0*, March 1, pp. 145–6.

19 Thompson S.H. Teo and Jing Liu, 2007, "Consumer trust in E-commerce in the United States, Singapore and China," *Omega*, 35(1), pp. 22–38.

20 Thompson S.H. Teo and Jing Liu, 2007, "Consumer trust in E-commerce in the United States, Singapore and China," *Omega*, 35(1), pp. 22–38.

21 David Gefen and Tsipi Heart, 2006, "On the need to include national culture as a central issue in e-commerce trust beliefs," *Journal of Global Information Management*, 14(4), pp. 1–30.

22 E.g. J.T. Luo, Peter McGoldrick, Susan Beatty, and Kathleen A. Keeling, 2006, "On-screen characters: Their design and influence on consumer trust," *Journal of Services Marketing*, 20(2), pp. 112–24.

23 J.T. Luo, Peter McGoldrick, Susan Beatty, and Kathleen A. Keeling, 2006, "On-screen characters: Their design and influence on consumer trust," *Journal of Services Marketing*, 20(2), pp. 112–24.

24 Thompson S.H. Teo and Jing Liu, 2007, "Consumer trust in E-commerce in the United States, Singapore and China," *Omega*, 35(1), pp. 22–38.

25 Thompson S.H. Teo and Jing Liu, 2007, "Consumer trust in E-commerce in the United States, Singapore and China," *Omega*, 35(1), pp. 22–38.

26 Shintaro Okazaki, 2004, "Do multinationals standardise or localise? The cross-cultural dimensionality of product-based web sites," *Internet Research*, 14(1), pp. 81–94.

27 Elizabeth Wurtz, 2005, "A cross-cultural analysis of websites from high-context cultures and low-context cultures," *Journal of Computer-Mediated Communication*, 11(1), article 13.

28 Nitish Singh, Olivier Furrer, and Massimiliano Ostinelli, 2004, "To localize or to standardize on the Web: Empirical evidence from Italy, India, Netherlands, Spain, and Switzerland," *Multinational Business Review*, Spring, 12(1), pp. 69–87.

29 N. Tsikriktsis, 2002, "Does culture influence website quality expectations?" *Journal of Service Research*, 5(2), pp. 101–12.

30 Elizabeth Wurtz, 2005, "A cross-cultural analysis of websites from high-context cultures and low-context cultures," *Journal of Computer-Mediated Communication*, 11(1), article 13.

31 *Business Wire*, 2007, "Digital River expands global e-commerce platform with fully integrated physical fulfillment solution," *Business Wire*, March 27.

32 Marc J. Epstein, 2005, "Implementing successful e-commerce initiatives," *Strategic Finance*, 86(9), pp. 22–9.

33 Marc J. Epstein, 2005, "Implementing successful e-commerce initiatives," *Strategic Finance*, 86(9), pp. 22–9; Gregory A. Garrett and Gail A. Parrott, 2005, "E-business: Understanding key trends and applying best practices," *Contract Management*, 45(7), pp. 34–41; Julie Schlosser, 2007, "Engaging with the customer," *Fortune*, 155(9), p. 28.

34 Gregory A. Garrett and Gail A. Parrott, 2005, "E-business: Understanding key trends and applying best practices," *Contract Management*, 45(7), pp. 34–41.

35 Colin Beasty, 2006, "Retail's 2 worlds: Tips on integrating online and offline channels," *Customer Relationship Management*, 10(3), pp. 30–5.

36 Marc J. Epstein, 2005, "Implementing successful e-commerce initiatives," *Strategic Finance*, 86(9), pp. 22–9.

37 Hallie Mummert, 2003, "Best practices," *Target Marketing*, 26(9), p. 34; Marc J. Epstein, 2005, "Implementing successful e-commerce initiatives," *Strategic Finance*, 86(9), pp. 22–9; Gregory A. Garrett and Gail A. Parrott, 2005, "E-business: Understanding key trends and applying best practices," *Contract Management*, 45(7), pp. 34–41; Jim Wheaton, 2007, "The first five commandments of database content management," *Multichannel Merchant*, 3(2), p. 33.

38 L.A. Gordon and M.P. Loeb, 2006, *Managing Cybersecurity Resources: A Cost–Benefit Analysis*, New York: McGraw-Hill.

39 C. Karat, C. Brodie, and J. Karat, 2006, "Usable privacy and security for personal information management," *Communications of the ACM*, 49(1), pp. 56–7.

40 R. Grimes, 2006, "E-commerce in crisis: When SSL isn't safe," *InfoWorld*, 28(18), pp. 26–31.

Part Five

Chapter 16

1 Robyn Meredith and Suzanne Hoppough, 2007, "Why globalization is good," *Forbes*, 179(8), pp. 64–8.

2 Augendra Bhukuth and Jerome Ballet, 2006, "Is child labour a substitute for adult labour? A case study of brick kiln labourers in Tamil Nadu, India," *International Journal of Social Economics*, 33(8), pp. 593–600.

3 Farzad Rafi Khan, 2007, "Representational approaches matter," *Journal of Business Ethics*, 73, pp. 77–89.

4 Aaron Bernstein, 2005, "A major swipe at sweatshops," *BusinessWeek*, May 23, 3934, p. 98.

5 Aaron Bernstein, 2005, "A major swipe at sweatshops," *BusinessWeek*, May 23, 3934, p. 98.

6 Aaron Bernstein, 2005, "A major swipe at sweatshops," *BusinessWeek*, May 23, 3934, p. 98.

7 Gabriel Eweje, 2006, "Environmental costs and responsibilities resulting from oil exploitation in developing countries: The case of the Niger Delta in Nigeria," *Journal of Business Ethics*, 69, pp. 27–56.

8 Loretta Chao and Shai Oster, 2006, "Multinationals in China cited for pollution," *Wall Street Journal*, October 30, p. 12.

9 Andrew Gumbel, 2007, "Greens hail landmark victory in fight to save Amazon rainforests," *Independent*, March 26, p. 23.

10 Nick Snow and Eric Watkins, 2007, "DOJ fines Vetco record $26 million in FCPA case," *Oil and Gas Journal*, March 5, 105(9), pp. 31–3.

11 John Gibeaut, 2007, "Battling bribery abroad," *ABA Journal*, March, 93, pp. 48–84.

12 Joseph H. Warin, Robert C. Blume, Jeremy A. Bell, and J. Taylor McConkie, 2007, "The Foreign Corrupt Practices Act: Recent developments, trends and guidance," *Insight, the Corporate and Securities Law Advisor*, February 21(2), pp. 2–10.

13 T. Donaldson, 1992, "The language of international ethics," *Business Ethics Quarterly*, 2, pp. 271–81.

14 O.C. Ferrell, J. Fraedrich, and L. Ferrell, 2005, *Business Ethics: Ethical Decision Making and Cases*, Boston, MA: Houghton-Mifflin.

15 J. Hall and H. Vredenburg, 2005, "Managing stakeholder ambiguity," *MIT Sloan Management Review*, 47(1), pp. 11–13.

16 Muel Kaptein, 2004, "Business codes of multinational firms: What do they say?" *Journal of Business Ethics*, 50, pp. 13–31.

17 Muel Kaptein, 2004, "Business codes of multinational firms: What do they say?" *Journal of Business Ethics*, 50, pp. 13–31.

18 Mark S. Schwartz, 2004, "Effective corporate codes of ethics: Perceptions of code users," *Journal of Business Ethics*, 55, pp. 323–53.

19 Avshalom M. Adam and Dalia Rachman-Moore, 2004, "The methods used to implement an ethical code of conduct and employee attitudes," *Journal of Business Ethics*, 54, pp. 225–44.

20 O.C. Ferrell, J. Fraedrich, and L. Ferrell, 2005, *Business Ethics: Ethical Decision Making and Cases*, Boston, MA: Houghton-Mifflin.

21 Emre A. Veral, 2005, "Designing and monitoring corporate codes of conduct for multinational corporations," *Business Review*, Summer, 4(1), pp. 145–52, p. 147.

22 Greg Boudreaux and Tracey Steiner, 2005, "Developing a code of ethics," *Management Quarterly*, 46(1), pp. 2–19.

23 Diane Kubal, Michael Baker, and Kendra Coleman, 2006, "Doing the right thing: How today's leading companies are becoming more ethical," *Performance Improvement*, March, 45(3), pp. 5–8; Robin Zablow, 2006, "Creating and sustaining an ethical workplace," *Risk Management*, September, 53(9), pp. 26–30.

Photo credits

Index